MONASH
As Military Commander

Peter Pedersen

Copyright © Peter Pedersen

First published 2018

Copyright remains the property of Peter Pedersen and apart from any fair dealing for the purposes of private study, research, criticism or review, as permitted under the Copyright Act, no part may be reproduced by any process without written permission.

All inquiries should be made to the publishers.

Big Sky Publishing Pty Ltd
PO Box 303, Newport, NSW 2106, Australia
Phone: 1300 364 611
Fax: (61 2) 9918 2396
Email: info@bigskypublishing.com.au
Web: www.bigskypublishing.com.au

Cover design and typesetting: Think Productions
Printed in China by Hang Tai Printing Company Limited

For Cataloguing-in-Publication entry see National Library of Australia.

Author: Peter Pedersen

Title: Monash As Military Commander

ISBN: 978-1-925675-29-0

Cover image: Portrait of Lieutenant General Sir John Monash by John Longstaff (ART02986).

MONASH
As Military Commander

www.bigskypublishing.com.au

Peter Pedersen

THE AUSTRALIAN ARMY HISTORY COLLECTION

Madness and the Military
Michael Tyquin

*The Battle of Anzac Ridge
25 April 1915*
Peter D. Williams

Doves Over the Pacific
Reuben R.E. Bowd

The Lionheart
David Coombes

Battlefield Korea
Maurie Pears

Chemical Warfare in Australia
Geoff Plunkett

A Most Unusual Regiment
M.J. Ryan

Between Victor and Vanquished
Arthur Page

Country Victoria's Own
Neil Leckie

Surgeon and General
Ian Howie-Willis

Willingly into the Fray
Catherine McCullagh

Beyond Adversity
William Park

Crumps and Camouflets
Damien Finlayson

More than Bombs and Bandages
Kirsty Harris

The Last Knight
Robert Lowry

Forgotten Men
Michael Tyquin

Battle Scarred
Craig Deayton

Crossing the Wire
David Coombes

Do Unto Others
Alan H Smith

Fallen Sentinel
Peter Beale

Sir William Glasgow
Peter Edger

Training The Bodes
Terry Smith

Bully Beef and Balderdash
Graham Wilson

Fire Support Bases Vietnam
Bruce Picken

Toowoomba to Torokina
Bob Doneley

A Medical Emergency
Ian Howie-Willis

Dust, Donkeys and Delusions
Graham Wilson

The Backroom Boys
Graeme Sligo

Captains of the Soul
Michael Gladwin

Game to the Last
James Hurst

I Confess: A memoir of the siege of Tobruk
John Joseph Murray

Lethality in Combat
Tom Lewis

Letters From Timor
Graeme Ramsden

Beaten Down By Blood
Michele Bomford

Canister! On! Fire
Bruce Cameron

The Grand Deception
Tom Curran

Combat Colonels of the AIF in the Great War
David Clare Holloway

Snowy to the Somme
Timothy Cook

Pioneers of Australian Armour in the Great War
David A. Finlayson &
Michael K. Cecil

Stepping into a Minefield
Ian Mansfield

Anzac to Afghanistan
Glenn Wahlert

*Preserving Our Proud Heritage:
Customs and Traditions of the Australian Army*
L.I. Terrett & S.C. Taubert

Accommodating the King's Hard Bargain
Graham Wilson

*A Greater Sum of Sorrows:
The Battle of Bullecourt*
David Coombes

An Unending War
Ian Howie-Willis

Allenby's Gunners
Alan H. Smith

The Man Who Carried the Nations Grief
Carol Rosenhain

Lessons Learned in Tropical Medicine
Geoffrey Quail

Bully Beef and Balderdash II
Graham Wilson

The Lightning Keepers
Damien Finlayson

At Any Price
Craig Deayton

Contents

Foreword 1
Preface to 2018 Edition 2
Acknowledgements 8
Introduction 11
Chapter 1   A Wide Civilian Training 19
Chapter 2   My Long Cherished Hope for Military Advancement 30
Chapter 3   The Best Australian Brigade in Egypt 69
Chapter 4   Monash Valley 98
Chapter 5   I Thought I Could Command Men 147
Chapter 6   A Man of Very Considerable Ability 201
Chapter 7   The Theory of the Limited Objective 223
Chapter 8   Passchendaele: Things are Bloody, Very Bloody 276
Chapter 9   The Best Man to Command the Corps 337
Chapter 10 The Most Resolute Offensive 402
Chapter 11 Reputations 459
Appendix 1: The origin of the August Offensive, in particular the importance of Hill 971 474
Appendix 2: AIF Infantry Battalions 478
Endnotes 479
Acronyms and Abbreviations 484
References 487
A note on sources 515
Select Bibliography 517
Index 545

List of Maps

1. Gallipoli 92
2. The Anzac perimeter 102
3. The attack on Baby 700, 2 May 1915 121
4. The intended advance of the Left Assaulting Column, 6–7 August 1915 156
5. The actual and imagined position of the 4th Brigade, 7 August 1915 174
6. The attack on Hill 971, 8 August 1915 176
7. The Western Front in 1916, 1917, 1918 216
8. The attack on the Black Line, Messines, 6 June 1917 256
9. The retirement of the 37th Battalion, Messines, 6 June 1917 270
10. The Flanders Campaign 277
11. Flanders: attacks from 20 September to 12 October 1917 291
12. The attack on Broodseinde, 4 October 1917 301
13. The repulse before Passchendaele, 12 October 1917 313
14. The arrival of the 3rd Division on the Somme, 26–27 March 1918 324
15. The attack on Hamel, 4 July 1918 351
16. The attack by the Australian Corps, 8 August 1918 376
17. The advance astride the Somme after 8 August 1918 390
18. The final plan for the attack on Mont St Quentin and Péronne 414
19. The attack on the Hindenburg Outpost Line, 18 September 1918 431
20. The attack on the Hindenburg Line, 29 September 1918 446

MAP SYMBOLS

MILITARY

■	Australia and its Allies	⊢⊣	Limit of Attack
■	Enemy	▬	Front Line
▨	Area of Operation	×××	Offensive Start Line
⊠	Infantry	∿	Halt Line
⊡	Infantry Intended	▬	Objective (Red, Green, etc)
⊕	Machine Gun	—	Military Boundary
xxxxx	Army Group	➡	Unit Deployment
xxxx	Army	▪▪➤	Proposed Unit Deployment
xxx	Corps	⊼⊼⊼	Trenches
xx	Division	⊗	Unexploded Mine
x	Brigade	↑ N	North
III	Regiment		
II	Battalion		
I	Company		
••	Platoon		
•	Section		

GEOGRAPHIC

COUNTRY

DISTRICT/PROVINCE

Natural Features

★ Capital City

● City/Town

■ Village/Hamlet

▪ Structure

∿ RIVER

◯ LAKE

⊞ CANAL

Track

Road

┼┼┼ Railway line

)=(Bridge or viaduct

▨ Elevated ground

▦ Built-up Area

❀ Woods

⋇ Swamp

To Marylou

FOREWORD

In recent years an enlightened Army policy has allowed a few graduates of the Royal Military College, Duntroon, to undertake postgraduate studies in military history. Peter Pedersen is one of the most gifted of them.

When he began work on his doctoral thesis on General Sir John Monash, I was in the later stages of research for my biography of Monash. We quickly formed a very harmonious relationship – discussing, for example, the problems associated with what actually happened on Gallipoli early in August 1915, guiding each other to sources and exchanging our notes. It was Pedersen who drew my attention to the North Papers at King's College, London. We completed our work almost in the same month, without showing each other our drafts, and were eventually delighted to find how rarely we had disagreed.

As I am the most amateur of military historians, I was fortunate that the scale of my biography required only broad-brush treatment of Monash as a soldier; there was no space for any detailed treatment of battle or generalship. So Pedersen's is a far more authoritative study of Monash as a soldier than mine. He has worked on about three times the scale I did, has made much more comprehensive and detailed use of archival sources – and he is a professional soldier.

This is not only the first full-scale technical study of Australia's greatest soldier, but, surprisingly, the first of any of the AIF leaders on the Western Front in World War I.

Geoffrey Serle
Melbourne, 1984

PREFACE TO 2018 EDITION

The first edition of this book appeared in 1985. It was based on a considerably longer doctoral thesis on Monash's military development completed three years earlier. The study of Monash was an inchoate field back then. Geoffrey Serle was writing his magnificent biography, still perhaps the finest biography of a major Australian figure, but only one significant work on Monash the commander existed. As a hagiography done without access to Monash's papers and other primary sources, it relied heavily on Charles Bean's estimate in the *Official History*, though Bean would have winced at the description of Monash as having a computer in his head and petrol in his veins. The metaphors may have been mind-numbing, but at least they drew attention to Monash's formidable mind and his use of mechanical resources to increase combat power while conserving manpower.

Nowadays, Monash's papers and other relevant documentary collections are in the public domain and many books have been written about him. Going way beyond portraying Monash as an intellectual petrol head, their claims about him as a soldier have lifted the hagiographic bar to stratospheric heights. He was the king's general, he won a war, he moulded his nation – all in all, a pretty impressive record – but he has been largely forgotten all the same, a fate that adds the dollop of tragedy needed to make the record whole. There is nothing metaphorical about these claims. They are served up as fact, and, because they beat the nationalist drum, they are attractive. They also jar with the conclusions I reached about Monash the general in this book all those years ago, and by which I stand in this new edition.

Monash has not been the only recipient of increased scrutiny over the past few decades. Not before time, the Australian Imperial Force

PREFACE

(AIF) has itself become a fruitful subject of inquiry. Social studies have probed its composition, its outlook, its local interactions and its behaviour. Biographies of many of the AIF's senior commanders exist alongside numerous anecdotal accounts based on the diaries and letters of the rank and file. Most of its major battles have been examined – some many times over. The resulting publications – like those on Monash – range from the scholarly to the popular, but all serve a useful purpose by keeping the AIF's story and achievements alive. They also rely to varying extents on Bean's *Official History*. Drawn from a mass of primary records, official and private, often written from the standpoint of a witness and almost overburdened by detail, Bean's work has acquired an aura of infallibility, especially as regards what happened on the ground. The absence of rival studies for decades after its appearance ensured its stranglehold.

Bean's history was also my companion, but instead of rehashing it, I attempted an analytical tactical study of Monash and his battles at brigade, division and corps level. This required a grasp of tactics, an understanding of how formations and their commanders operate, and an appreciation of the tactical possibilities of ground from the perspectives of Monash and of his Turkish and German opponents. Plenty of walking and cycling across his battlefields were necessary, and I remember thinking how ironic it was that I should be doing something that Monash, who planned most of his battles from the map, very rarely did. For someone who was both a soldier and a historian to look at Monash was a new approach, and it sometimes led to conclusions different from Bean's. I questioned Bean's analysis of the planning for the Baby 700 attack at Anzac on 2/3 May 1915 and flatly disagreed with his criticism of Monash's handling of the 4th Brigade's night march on Sari Bair in August. Nor did Bean, I thought, properly consider what the ground offered the Germans at Hamel, or fully realise why Monash used the Americans in the costly first phase of the assault on the Hindenburg Line. I felt that the blow-by-blow account of the Australian capture of Mont St Quentin and Péronne in his final volume was so convoluted that it might as well have been written in Braille. In fairness, though, Bean had been

MONASH

writing the history non-stop for over twenty years by then. He was a very tired man.

Challenging Bean's work in those days, when it seemed etched in tablets of stone, was welcomed in some quarters, but regarded as tantamount to apostasy in others. One reviewer, an old colleague of Bean, publicly rebuked me for having the temerity to steer a different course from that of the master. Thankfully times have changed. Chris Roberts' brilliant and highly praised tactical study of the Anzac landing, the most important account to appear since Bean's almost a century earlier, brings out the flaws in his narrative and synopsis. Contrary to the belief held by some that the 'myth' of Gallipoli has finally crumpled, Roberts has shown that there is still plenty to say. Bob Stevenson's work on the 1st Australian Division and his history of Australian operations on the Western Front exude a level of sophistication that is to be envied. Both superb historians with a military background, Roberts and Stevenson are well equipped to reconsider the AIF from an operational standpoint unfettered by the legacy of Bean. But Bean is still the start and end point for most Australian publications on the war. Perhaps that is as it should be. It is a monumental work of scholarship and its weaknesses pale against its strengths. We are fortunate to have it.

Since *Monash as Military Commander* was written, one century has made way for another and a new millennium has been ushered in. The soldiers who fought in the First World War have all passed. Throughout the changing times, I visited the Western Front and Gallipoli on numerous occasions and was privileged to lead Australians and others on many tours of the battlefields. Each visit was an opportunity to study Monash's actions on the ground from a different vantage point or with another tactical consideration in mind. I was also able to bring a Staff College education to them, an asset I lacked when the first edition appeared. Despite this greater understanding, I have had little reason to modify my earlier military judgements on Monash, though there is of course always something new to learn.

As the passing years brought the mixed blessing of maturity, it was probably inevitable that I should have adjusted some of my views on

PREFACE

Monash's character. I can no longer look at him with the super-critical eyes of a twenty-something-year-old who has yet to make a mistake. Now that I am at an age where I can admit to one or two, and my eyes see things in mellower hues, I have become more forgiving. Yes, Monash had his faults – like all of us – but in this new edition I have moderated my previous view of them. It is worth reiterating here what I said in the earlier edition, and have repeated in this one: Monash never let his faults influence his actions in the field. I also wrote that his sometimes overly prescriptive approach to commanders and staff could not be justified in the second half of 1918, when the Australian Corps oozed experience at all levels. Now I have made greater allowance for this tendency. He was intellectually superior to his colleagues by a long way and knew their jobs as well as – and often better – than they did. And given that the buck stopped with him, it is perhaps surprising that he did not intervene more. I have also described how the war changed Monash for the better. Humbled by the simple nobility he saw in the soldiers he led, he grew to appreciate the common man as he never had before. I barely touched on this in the first book.

At that time, the historiography of the British Army and its generals in the First World War was largely mired in the 'lions led by donkeys' interpretation that had taken hold soon after the war ended. Thanks to a new wave of mainly British historians, the historiography now has a refreshing dynamism, resulting in a range of interpretations that provides rich food for thought. As Monash and the Australians, like the other soldiers of the British Empire, formed part of British armies and were subject to the British high command, I have considered them against the main arguments in these newer works. Again, what I originally said regarding Monash remains valid.

Command and control studies, for example, have revealed how command devolved as the war went on, enhancing the role of corps and divisional commanders. Monash's freedom as a corps commander in 1918, which struck me when I first wrote, attested to this devolution. Great attention has also been given to the evolutionary developments in materiel, technology and the British Expeditionary Force's (BEF) war-fighting efficiency, all encompassed by the term 'learning curve'. It wound and bumped upward rather than ascending in a smooth continuum, but the BEF ended the war far more capable in all respects than it had been at the beginning. The Australians were part of the progression. As a detailed study of Monash's development as a military commander, the original book traced his learning process. This edition places it more fully within the context of the general learning curve. In Monash's case, there were few bumps.

So long taken for granted, the superiority of dominion forces over British troops is now disputed. During the advance to victory in 1918, recent research has shown, dominion formations did not have a monopoly on winning. Even average British divisions were highly effective because the main determinant of success, it is said, was the preponderance of artillery that the BEF enjoyed in the second half of the war. This is true to a considerable extent, but to attribute every successful outcome to the guns is much like saying that wars can be won solely by airpower. In general, artillery, no matter how plentiful, can only neutralise an objective; when it lifts the infantry must still take the objective, which brings their tactical skill into play. Tanks and other forms of support can assist. Success therefore depends on the smooth working of a combined arms team and, as the first edition brought out, the Australian Corps under Monash functioned as one to an exceptional degree. It was also much larger than British corps and, unlike them, always comprised the same divisions. Monash's insistence on uniformity of thought, policy and tactical method took full advantage of its homogeneity. The quality of its soldiers was outstanding.

Judgements on how good those soldiers were are perhaps best left to those who fought with them, rather than to historians writing in comfortable offices a century later. One British officer who served alongside the Australians in 1918 and later became a general, reckoned that they were the best infantry of the war and perhaps of all time. Another British officer, who was a general, called them undoubtedly the finest troops in the world. Monash acknowledged that the quality

PREFACE

of his soldiers made military miracles possible. As the first book demonstrated, his skill as a general, which deeply impressed his British counterparts, was indispensable in making the corps greater than the sum of its parts. Like the Canadian Corps, and for similar reasons, the Australian Corps achieved consistent, rather than occasional, success. That lifted it above the ruck.

The story of Monash's rise from colonial Jewish militiaman to his nation's highest field command in its costliest war is as unlikely as it is inspiring. I felt this strongly when I first wrote; I feel it still. The story stands true on its own merits; it needs no embellishing by fanciful claims. Monash remains Australia's greatest general; some would say he is the greatest Australian.

I would like to acknowledge those who made this new edition of *Monash as Military Commander* possible. Dr Andrew Richardson of the Australian Army History Unit saw the need as the centenary of 1918 approached. Over a cup of coffee he persuaded me to undertake the project (I am easily bought), was indefatigable in obtaining photographs and spent hours converting an almost useless OCR scan of the first edition into a workable document. His dedication and belief were touching. Catherine McCulloch and Eric Olason drew the maps with the perfectionist's eye for accuracy and detail. Cathy McCullagh proofread the manuscript, a task made more demanding than usual by the plethora of spelling errors in the OCR scan (it read, for example, 'Blamey' as 'Blarney'). Knowing that I had heavy consulting commitments and was working on other books, Denny Neave of Big Sky Publishing compressed the production schedule to give me more time to complete this one. Peter Burness and Dr Robert Nichols, my two amigos from our Australian War Memorial days, offered advice and suggestions. Last and most importantly, a hurrah to my partner Marylou Pooley, whose patience and cheerful good humour are inexhaustible and make me wish I could be more like her. To one and all, my heartfelt thanks.

Peter Pedersen
Canberra, 2018

ACKNOWLEDGEMENTS

This book could not have been attempted without the wonderful support of my parents. Because of their devotion, I had nothing on which to concentrate but my writing. That my mother passed away without seeing the finished work will remain the greatest regret of my life.

I remember with affection the generous assistance offered by colleagues and friends. Dr Geoffrey Serle allowed me access to Monash's personal papers, patiently discussed many aspects of Monash's career and commented on the drafts. I was honoured by his offer to write the foreword. Alec Hill gave me valuable advice, derived from his own considerable military experience, at every stage of the project. His detailed reading of the manuscript drew attention to my frequent breaches of the rules of English usage. A special thanks to Alec's wife, Patsy, who had to endure for four years our interminable prattle on Monash. Dr John McCarthy, Gerry Walsh and Professor Alan Gilbert gave me encouragement at a time when I needed it more than they knew. Warren Perry was a bottomless mine of knowledge on Monash's pre-war career, a difficult area in which I was also helped by Professor Theodore Ropp and Dr Roger Thompson. I thrashed out many ideas with Denis Winter, an eminent British historian of the Western Front. Robert Rhodes James, MP, John Terraine, A.J. Smithers, C.E. Carrington and, above all, Major General E.K.G. Sixsmith gave generously of their time and hospitality while I was in England. They were also among many correspondents who included Dr R.J. O'Neill, Brian Bond, Professor A.M.J. Hyatt, Lieutenant Colonel A.A. Argent, Captain B.H. Perry, Hon. J. Montgomery-Massingberd, Martin Middlebrook and Captain Eric Bush. All have saved me from numerous errors and for those that remain I alone am responsible.

My research was made enjoyable by Michael Piggott, Bill Fogarty and Peter Holmes who guided me through the magnificent collections at the Australian War Memorial. Their enthusiasm was inspiring.

ACKNOWLEDGEMENTS

The Trustees of the Memorial awarded me a grant for overseas study, without which this work would have been barren indeed. No request was too great for Jan Blank and the staff of the Bridges Memorial Library, Duntroon, nor for the staff of the Australian Archives at Middle Brighton, Melbourne. David Smurthwaite of the National Army Museum made many enquiries which assisted my endeavours at other institutions in London and Edinburgh. The Royal Marines Museum sent me copies of the 'Jerram Journal' and the 'Diary of the Royal Marine Brigade' at very short notice.

Howard Vinning of the National Headquarters of the Returned Services League placed my advertisements for information in the League's *Bulletin* and directed me to the Gallipoli Legion of Anzacs. Through the latter I met F.R. Hocking, F. Berrisford and H. Clive Newman, all veterans of the First AIF, with whom I had several memorable discussions. Howard also introduced me to the Commonwealth War Graves Commission. S.T. O'Grady, Director, France Area, sent Les Reid and John Harris, supervisors of the Somme and Villers-Bretonneux areas respectively, to guide me over Monash's 1918 battlefields. The Ypres office assisted my visit to the salient. Tony Malpass drove me across the Gallipoli Peninsula and arranged my accommodation among the Turkish gardeners at Anzac during my stay there. The dedication of these men to the work of the Commission will ensure that the memory of the fallen of the 'Great War' lasts forever.

Rhonda Buckley retyped the manuscript promptly, deciphering my frequent corrections without complaint. Her constant cheerfulness throughout the ordeal was an unending source of amazement to me.

The first two maps, 'Gallipoli' and 'the Anzac perimeter' were taken from Geoffrey Serle's *Monash: A Biography* (Melbourne, 1982) and I thank him and the publisher, Melbourne University Press. The map of the Flanders Campaign was taken from J.E. Edmonds' *Military Operations: France and Belgium 1917*, vol. 2 (London, 1948). Jill Gregs spent many nights and weekends drafting the other maps and the results bear eloquent testimony to her diligence.

I wish to thank Colonel E.J. O'Donnell for his confidence in my ability to undertake the postgraduate study on which this book is based, and the Australian Army for granting me three years in which to do so.

Finally, for allowing me to reproduce the photographs and quote from material over which they hold copyright, I thank the Trustees of the Australian War Memorial; Mrs C.E.W. Bean (for the Bean correspondence in the Australian War Memorial); the Trustees of the Imperial War Museum; the Trustees of the Liddell Hart Centre for Military Archives, King's College, University of London; the Council of the Mitchell Library, New South Wales; the Trustees of the National Army Museum, London; the Council of the National Library of Australia; the Controller of H. M. Stationery Office for Crown copyright records in the Public Record Office, and particularly Lord Haig. He was unaware of how my treatment of his father would evolve. A lesser man might have denied me permission to use his copyright material when confronted by such uncertainty.

Peter Pedersen
Sydney, 1984

Conversions
Currency:
1d (penny)   0.47 cents
1s (shilling) $5.69
£1 $114.00
(Reserve Bank of Australia calculator, 2018)
Distances:
1 inch   2.54 centimetres
1 foot   0.30 metres
1 yard   0.91 metres
1 mile   1.60 kilometres

INTRODUCTION

Few aspects of military history have aroused as much controversy as the performance of British commanders on the Western Front in World War I. Postwar revulsion from the enormous casualty lists led to portrayals of them as a group of incompetent fumblers, rarely leaving the comfort of their well-appointed châteaux as they presided over the destruction of a generation in the mud of the Somme and Passchendaele. The particular target of this odium was the Commander-in-Chief (C-in-C), Field Marshal Sir Douglas Haig. His army commanders, particularly Generals Sir Hubert Gough and Sir Henry Rawlinson, also shared in it. While their reputations have been rehabilitated to some extent by more modern scholarship, Haig and his generals remain controversial figures.

By contrast, the star of Lieutenant General Sir John Monash has always shone brightly. Yet Monash served in the comparatively junior appointment of commander of the Australian Corps, and then only in the last six months of the war. In 1919 he reputedly took one month to write his own account of his leadership of the Corps, entitled *The Australian Victories in France in 1918,* while supervising the demobilization and repatriation of the AIF. It stands up well overall, despite the inevitable factual errors resulting from such haste and the occasional tendency of Monash, who had no way of knowing what was happening at higher levels of command, to claim credit for himself and the Corps that rightly belonged elsewhere. His formation always operated as part of the British Fourth Army and, with one notable exception during the advance astride the Somme at the end of August 1918, he was strictly bound by the orders of its commander. Therefore, Monash's decision-making was limited, and it is safe to say that the outcome of the war was not decisively influenced by him.

C.E.W. Bean discussed the crucial offensive operations of 1918 in his *Official History,* but he was concerned more with the achievements of the Australian soldier than with those of his commander. Though Bean refuted some of Monash's claims, he let others pass, possibly because the material against which they could be checked was not available. Much of the considerable literature on Monash that has appeared in recent years has relied heavily on these two sources. The result has been the constant repetition of the same time-worn clichés and conclusions, accepted almost invariably without question. Emphasis on his prewar civil career, rather than his militia service as a factor in explaining his wartime success, is one notable example. The statement 'Monash got better as he went along. He was a better divisional than a brigade commander and a better corps than a divisional commander' is another.

As opposed to the amount of ink that has been spilt in either condemnation or praise of Haig and his colleagues, no detailed professional study of Monash the commander exists, though a spate of popular works on him has appeared. His battlefields on Gallipoli and the Western Front have rarely been traversed (except by Bean), to assess the advantages the terrain offered to him as a general or to his opponent. Similarly, the question of how much his service as a brigade and a divisional commander assisted him at corps level has almost never been asked, let alone answered. He is often presented as a general who willingly delegated responsibility and did not interfere with subordinates once he had done so. This apparently contradicts the meticulous attention to detail that was another of his well-known qualities. No explanation of the paradox can be found. Alluding to the absence of worthwhile knowledge of this commander who occupies such an important place in its historiography, John Terraine once remarked: 'Monash has collected a mythology as has so much else of World War One'.

The qualities that Field Marshal Lord Wavell thought the successful general must possess form a useful starting-point for an assessment of Monash. Wavell placed robustness, 'the ability to stand the shocks of war', at the top of his list. These shocks did not merely embrace the unexpected turn of events, such as an unforeseen enemy action or a

INTRODUCTION

change in the weather, for such is the rule rather than the exception in war. Wavell was also referring to the strain imposed upon a general by his responsibility for the lives of those he commands, in Monash's case the 150 000 men of the Australian Corps.

Moral courage is obviously an important element in the discharge of that responsibility. The other form of courage, physical bravery, is not as essential 'as it was in the old days of close range fighting, but it still is of very considerable importance today in determining the degree of risk a commander will take to see for himself what is going on'. Monash's failure in this respect was the most frequent charge made against him. While he utilized successfully other abilities to plan and conduct operations without seeing the battlefield, there were several instances where a plan might have been improved or casualties reduced had he done so. The same criticism is often levelled at Haig.

While an understanding of strategy and tactics is important, according to Wavell 'the real foundations of military knowledge' are topography, movement and supply. Monash's excellence in all three areas distinguished him from his contemporaries, as did his view, a given nowadays, that the administrative functions of command, embodied in movement and supply, were just as important as the operational function. As a brigadier on Gallipoli, he was as much concerned with the retrieval of his men's personal kits from Reserve Gully, the position they had just left, as with the consolidation of the line gained after the advance of 6-7 August. Good administration generates a soldier's confidence in his leaders. He knows that no effort will be spared to ensure that he is well fed, rested and looked after when wounded or sick. For a general who cares for his men's welfare, the reward is their willing response to demands that other commanders might hesitate to make.

But the strain of operations ultimately tells on even the best troops, irrespective of the tactical skill or the administrative ability of those commanding them. The good general knows when this limit has been reached. With good reason, Monash kept the Australian Corps in the line despite its exhaustion. The Germans were even more tired, but the constant pressure applied against them prevented any chance of their recovery on his front. At a time when the war was in its decisive phase, Monash displayed great determination, another quality required of a general. The example of Haig in 1916 and 1917 suggests, however, that determination can be dangerous, unless it is tempered by tactical insight or flair. Wavell went further: 'no general can be lucky unless he is bold. The general who allows himself to be bound and hampered by regulations is unlikely to win a battle'. Boldness and good fortune were important elements of Monash's success.

In one respect the works of Wavell and other writers on generalship, such as Sir Basil Liddell Hart and J.F.C. (John) Fuller, are not really appropriate to the study of Monash's military development: they apply mainly to the C-in-C. Major General E.K.G. (Eric) Sixsmith asserts that the degree to which the various qualities should be emphasized depends on the level of command under consideration. As a brigadier, Monash's responsibility was usually confined to four battalions. The concentration of guns and ammunition, the administration of labour in rear areas, the employment of aircraft and corps or divisional troops, were not his concern. They came within the purview of a divisional or a corps commander. At these levels, Monash had to know the capabilities of the arms and services at his disposal and how they should be employed. Problems of co-ordination between them increased. There were experts on his staff who could assist him, but he had to assess their advice on the basis of his own knowledge.

Monash's age was less important on the Western Front than it had been on Gallipoli. Youth was an asset for an infantry brigadier on the Peninsula, but Monash was almost fifty when he landed there. While he withstood the campaign's rigours better than many of his contemporaries, there was at least one occasion, on 8 August 1915, as his brigade attacked Hill 971 in the Sari Bair range, when his years told against him.

Conversely, as a brigade commander, Monash was far removed from political pressures. While commanding the Australian Corps, he was directly answerable to W.M. Hughes, the Prime Minister. Twice, in 1918, he disagreed strongly with Hughes's proposals. At this level, then, political considerations added to his burdens as a commander. As Field Marshal Montgomery has written: 'The soldier and politician have got to learn to understand each other; this is essential for the conduct of modern war'.

Unlike the senior British commanders, Monash was not a regular soldier. To what extent did his prewar civil training and experience as a brilliant engineer benefit him as a higher commander? Liddell Hart concluded in 1936:

> Since technical proficiency and executive habit count for more in the lower grades, it is to be inferred that a non-professional soldier who proved himself barely the equal of many regulars as a battalion or brigade commander might prove outstanding when and if he reached a higher command. That inference was confirmed by actual experience in the Dominion Forces, notably in the case of General Monash.

Morris Janowitz has argued that the same problems of administration, research and development and the maintenance of initiative and morale are shared by both the civilian and military establishments. Consequently, the professional officer must 'develop more and more of the skills and orientations common to civilian administration and civilian leaders'. Reinforcing Liddell Hart's contention, he suggested that a routine military career diminishes the effectiveness of the military leader; most of the great American commanders 'have complied with conventional career forms; but in addition, they have frequently had specialised and innovating experience which have increased their usefulness to the military profession'. In his controversial study of high command, Norman Dixon claimed that in principle, Monash was no different:

> We can only assume that he, like Janowitz's great Americans, was lucky to have escaped the mind blunting, routinized career of a large mercenary military organization, where the real skills demanded by the complex task of generalship are gradually expunged by orthodox militarism.

Dixon's use of the word 'militarism' is inappropriate, but the point is made, nevertheless. It contains a contemporary lesson for those who wish to find one.

Owing to its stultifying effect, the military experience of many British generals made them singularly unfitted to command on the Western Front. Field Marshal Lord Carver, one of the most literate of modern military writers, was not surprised that its conditions overwhelmed them:

> The means of transport available, and the short distance between base and front line, permitted the deployment of hordes of men and mountains of material. Not only was the latter available in large quantities (although never enough to satisfy the consumers), but it included entirely novel developments: the motor car and all its variants up to and including the tank; the aeroplane; radio-telephony; … all in use for the first time in Europe. The machine gun, the mine, gas, greatly improved explosives: all these added complications not only to the direction of operations, but also to their logistic support and to the problems of industrial production and the labour required for it.

Clearly, service on the Indian Frontier or against the Boers in South Africa was no preparation for the breaching of a trench system, scientifically sited and skilfully defended, which stretched from the Swiss border to the North Sea. As Marshal Ferdinand Foch, the Allied Generalissimo in 1918, remarked: 'I have only one merit. I have forgotten what I taught and what I learned'.

The size of the battlefield and the vast numbers of troops involved prevented commanders directing operations from vantage points as in ages past. They had to remain at communication centres in headquarters well to the rear, waiting for information – that was scanty, unreliable and, owing to fire, frequently delayed – in order to form a mental picture of the battle. Success was often measured by the commander's ability, in spite of these limitations, to visualize the positions of his own forces and those of the enemy on terrain the shape of which he could deduce from the map. Field Marshal Baron von der Goltz, a famous German military writer, described this

INTRODUCTION

quality of creative imagination as 'most essential to a commander', and cited the example of Napoleon to demonstrate it:

> The positions of his corps, divisions and brigades at any given time were always present to his mind. He therefore forgot nothing, and he never failed to notice chance means for the attainment of the end in view; he thought of things which everyone else would have forgotten.

Perhaps more important is the quality of creative originality in the planning of an operation, for a sound plan is the foundation of success in battle. Faulty plans rarely result in victory. The general has to appreciate the strengths of his opponent and formulate his plan to minimize their effect. None of the principles he employs is new. Flexibility, good communications and administration, economy of force, surprise and secrecy, mobility, concentration, concealment and originality have existed as fundamental tenets ever since war began. Thus surprise may be obtained by launching a feint elsewhere, making all preparations for the battle at night, when the enemy cannot observe them, or by doing the unexpected, such as attacking on a flank instead of frontally. The method of achieving it is the manifestation of creative originality. The principle itself remains constant. Usually the qualities of creative imagination and creative originality are indistinguishable. Commanders have to visualise or 'imagine' their plan unfolding almost at the same time as they prepare it before the battle or are forced by circumstances to change it during the battle.

Although he believed that the mind of a commander could only be examined through the medium of historical examples, Liddell Hart added:

> But such study of military history should be directed mainly to discover the commander's thoughts and impressions and the decisions which sprang from them … For it matters little what the situation actually was at any particular point or moment; all that matters is what the commander thought it was.

Whenever possible in this work, Monash has been allowed to explain in his own words his decisions and the reasons for them and also his feelings and attitudes on questions of personal importance to him.

MONASH

Often a curious mixture of contradiction emerges: humour, bravery, ruthlessness, stupidity and vanity, as opposed to tragedy, timidity, humanity, brilliance and humility. These elements are inevitably revealed by the study of how one man prepared himself successfully to overcome the various challenges war set for him. They are also inevitable in war itself.

Chapter 1
A Wide Civilian Training

John Monash was born to Jewish parents in West Melbourne on 27 June 1865. His father, Louis Monash, was the fourth of ten children and emigrated from his birthplace in Krotoschin, Prussian Poland, to Australia in 1853, intending to seek his fortune on the Victorian goldfields. Once in Melbourne, however, he soon appreciated the tremendous commercial opportunities generated by the heady expansion of the colony and joined a firm of soft goods importers as its junior partner. It was a secure occupation, though less glamorous than the brawling, romantic transience of the gold rushes. Towards the end of 1862, Louis Monash returned to Poland to buy stock for the company and visit his relations in Prussia. The journey was significant in a personal sense, too, for in Stettin he met and married Bertha Manasse, ten years younger than himself and the sister of his brother's wife. The couple arrived in Melbourne on 5 June 1864. John was their first child and only son.

John Monash's education began at St Stephen's Church of England School in Richmond, where he was described by his headmaster as a 'boy of much present intelligence'. In 1874 the family moved to the remote New South Wales (NSW) town of Jerilderie, where Louis Monash opened a general store. John was exposed to the ways of the bush and the character of its earthy inhabitants as he joined their children in the classroom of William Elliott, Jerilderie's only schoolteacher. Elliott tried to cater for the sharpness of his new pupil's intellect by teaching him much that was outside the school curriculum, including higher mathematics. He also employed the ten-year-old Monash as a pupil-teacher to instruct the more backward children. Within three years, however, it was obvious that Monash's developing mind was being stifled by the isolation and absence of challenge in Jerilderie. Elliott strongly urged his parents to send him back to the city. At the end of 1877 Bertha Monash returned to Melbourne with her three children, leaving her husband in Jerilderie, and later in Narrandera, to provide for the family. Louis did not rejoin them until 1883. Jerilderie had been a source of fascination for Monash. He spent much of his time among the Aborigines or just rambling through the bush, chasing kangaroos and watching the bullock teams that brought provisions to the town. He also saw the tragedy of country life as drought gripped the land. His love of bushwalking probably had its origins there.[1]

In October 1877 Monash entered Scotch College, and Elliott's expectations were more than fulfilled. He left in December 1881 as equal dux of the school, dux in mathematics and modern languages, and winner of the Matriculation Exhibition in mathematics.[2] In addition, he had won the English prize almost every year. One of his contemporaries at Scotch described Monash as a quiet, studious boy who took no part in games. If drawn into a quarrel, he totally disarmed his opponent with obloquy and argument; his command of English was not confined to the written word alone. Although the college's emphasis on academic excellence rather than sporting prowess contributed to his development, the greatest single influence on Monash in these early years was his mother. A matriarchal figure, she was convinced of her son's destiny as a great man. Under her guidance he became an accomplished classical pianist and acquired a love of literature that included Dickens, Scott, Lytton, Eliot and many of the finest French and German works in their original languages.

Monash's own literary aspirations began when he was thirteen with a report on a concert, and later included occasional pieces for country newspapers and university journals. In 1878 he saw *Struck Oil*, and so captivated was he by the play that for a long time afterwards he acted scenes from it with his sister Mathilde (Mat), coaching her in her lines. As he grew older, she noticed his organising ability in the direction of games at his sisters' parties and the staging of memorable fireworks displays in the backyard of their home. At Christmas 1882 Monash went on a walking holiday with his friend

CHAPTER 1

George Farlow, who was impressed by his careful calculation of the number of miles to be walked each day in order to make certain towns by nightfall. Monash planned to carry no food and very little clothing. The adventure unfolded exactly as he intended. His charm and manners always obtained food and drink and, on one occasion, his ability at the piano secured them accommodation.

In March 1882 Monash enrolled in the Faculty of Arts at the University of Melbourne, hoping ultimately to become a civil engineer. He was soon disenchanted by the soporific and repetitious lectures of professors whom he censured frequently in later years for their inability to keep abreast of modern thought and research. Abandoning formal instruction, he spent hours at the university and Melbourne public libraries, reading literature and history. He did not absorb knowledge uncritically: a lecture by a Mr Beavis on 14 July 1882 was straight plagiarism, while the reading of Macaulay's *Life, Letters and Diary* 'will probably have the effect of altering the style of my diary'. Monash became a strong debater, took painting lessons, occasionally attended Parliament or the Law Courts and, as a sign of things to come, travelled all over Melbourne to watch the operation of dredges and any form of engineering construction. These activities left him little time for lectures. Not surprisingly, Monash failed his first year and had to sit supplementary examinations. A more deliberate approach to study produced nothing better than third class honours for 1883. Deliverance from despair came through his deep involvement in student politics. He was instrumental in the foundation of the students' union and championed student grievances in the university paper with his fluent pen. But his academic results for 1884 were again mediocre. Troubled by the fatal illness of his mother, he ignored study altogether in 1885 and, short of money, sought full-time employment in engineering.

Joining the firm responsible for the Princes Bridge over the Yarra, Monash displayed almost a natural aptitude for field engineering work. His approach was one of constant enquiry: 'He was most enthusiastic and embarrassingly curious. He always wanted to know the reason for things.' Over the next two years Monash was engaged in design and construction planning, opened a quarry ten miles away from the bridge site and ran a supply yard. In 1888 he switched to the company constructing the Melbourne Outer Circle suburban railway and was soon in charge of the entire works.

Monash's situation resembled that of the platoon commander. Supervising a group of men working on difficult tasks in arduous conditions, he was responsible for their welfare, and to his employer for the completion of the project as efficiently as possible consistent with the standards required. If the comparison is taken further, the disadvantages under which Monash laboured become apparent. Unlike the platoon commander, he could not fall back on a hierarchical system of discipline to manage the labourers under him, who 'were not, as a rule, persons of refinement'. At an early age then, Monash began to develop the art of managing men, relying on his powers of leadership and expression alone to persuade them to work for him.

Monash's reasonable hopes that the work on the railway might lead to more profitable employment were dashed by the onset of an economic recession before the project was completed. His marriage to Hannah Victoria Moss (known as Vic) in April 1891 and the birth of their only child, Bertha, two years later, made this financial hardship even more difficult to bear. Emotionally, the relationship was a disastrous one, marked by unending quarrels that flowed from the couple's basic incompatibility. They separated in September 1894 and, although the marriage slowly improved after Vic's sudden return the following July, Monash recalled that his daughter 'had a most unhappy time until she was eighteen or so.' She was his deepest pride: 'there has never been a cloud between us and never anything but perfect confidence and trust.' Ironically, Monash now scored the academic success that had eluded him during several years of comparative serenity. Just before his wedding, he had finished his engineering degree, winning the *Argus* scholarship as top student. By the end of 1893 he had gained his master's degree in engineering, finally completed his Bachelor of Arts and equipped himself with a Bachelor of Laws.

CHAPTER 1

Monash was next employed by the Melbourne Harbour Trust as Assistant Engineer and Chief Draftsman, designing the swing bridge over the Maribyrnong River, the first in Victoria, transit sheds for the Yarra wharves, and roads and drainage schemes. He detested the monotony, inertia and absence of challenge typical of government service, while the security it offered was temporary, for the depression forced his retrenchment in April 1894. Almost immediately he joined an old friend, J.T. Noble Anderson, in partnership as a patent agent and a civil, mining and mechanical engineer. Desperate measures were often taken as the pair sought to establish their company, Monash & Anderson. Their fees were the lowest permitted by the London Institute of Civil Engineers, they approached shires to engage them as consultants rather than employing a shire engineer and, hoping to win future lucrative contracts, accepted many jobs for expenses only. In January 1896 Monash camped in a bark hut for three weeks while engaged on the design of an aerial railway carrying quartz from a mine in Gippsland. The complexity of the work, delays in the arrival of materials and mounting debts prevented completion by the agreed date. Although Monash and Anderson won the court case when the mining company cancelled the contract, they earned nothing from the project but experience.

While the company struggled, Monash's work in legal engineering as an advocate and expert witness increased, justifying his earlier foresight in studying law. The work took him to other colonies for long periods. His penetrating lucidity was always apparent, future prime minister R.G. Menzies regarding him as the greatest advocate he had heard. Meanwhile Anderson had secured an agreement making Monash & Anderson Victorian agents for Carter & Gummow, a firm holding the Australian patent rights for Monier reinforced concrete construction. The Anderson Street bridge across the Yarra was the largest work yet attempted in Australia with the new technique and demonstrated its efficiency. Monash had little to do with the project, although rarely refuting claims attributing it to him. He soon mastered the process, which used iron rods or grids to bear tensile strains while the concrete moulded around them took the compressive strains.

MONASH

Construction of the Anderson Street bridge over the Yarra River, Melbourne, 1899 (Monash University Archives).

Monier work seemed a profitable alternative when a slump overtook conventional engineering activity. But the company was so straitened financially that work on several bridges in Bendigo and a gold mine in Maryborough could begin only after the institution of further severe economies and the forbearance of creditors. Impecunious shires defaulted on payments, necessitating legal proceedings that were often costly and protracted. Monash's health suffered and he occasionally surrendered to fits of depression:

> For years he was to be humiliated by his indebtedness, suffering scores of demands for payment and solicitors' letters. He was often months behind with his rent and life assurance payments ... he did not send a cable to his sister Lou on her wedding day ... he had to let his associateship of the Institution of Civil Engineers lapse ...

Salvation came from the Monier Pipe Company, formed in 1901 to capitalise on the suitability of reinforced concrete for pipe manufacture. Dame Nellie Melba's father, David Mitchell, provided the working capital and held a 40 per cent share, the same as Monash & Anderson. Monash divided his time between the two concerns and threw himself into studies of the wider uses of reinforced concrete. His fluency in German gave him a distinct edge because most of the relevant journals were written in the language. By 1905 the partnership with

CHAPTER 1

Anderson had been dissolved, and a new company – The Reinforced Concrete and Monier Pipe Construction Company – was established with Monash as superintending engineer, Mitchell as its chairman of directors and John Gibson its managing director. As many as a dozen different jobs proceeded concurrently. Erected in 1911, the Janvale bridge boasted the largest spans in Australia for a structure of its class. Extensions were added to the Melbourne Town Hall and hospital. A South Australian branch, founded by Monash in June 1906, was equally successful. At the end of 1913 he estimated his worth at over £30 000, the present-day equivalent of almost $3.5 million.

Monash and his wife (left) with workmen on site at the Fyansford bridge, which spanned the Moorabool River near Geelong, 1899 (Norman Photo IN202, Monash University Archives).

Monash was at the zenith of his pre-war fortunes. He purchased Iona, a house in the prestigious Melbourne suburb of Toorak, and the beautification of its gardens became a pleasure to be recalled wistfully during the war years. In 1909 he assumed the presidency of the University Club and subsequently was elected to the University Council, 'a body of twenty who have the entire government of the University.' Another triumph was his unopposed election as President of the Victorian Institute of Engineers in 1912. Two years earlier, Monash had taken his family on a world tour. He was struck by the 'extraordinary development of means of transit, chiefly underground, in the great European cities' and by the application of engineering to the 'daily conveniences of life', such as 'mechanical ventilation' and 'cooking by electricity at the breakfast table'. By comparison, Australia seemed 'a little provincial place', while its engineers, Monash told the Victorian Institute, could not 'think big' and saw no reason to remedy their ignorance of advances elsewhere. He urged communication between engineers in order to create a community of knowledge and experience.

Monash's expression of his strong beliefs in such forthright terms took considerable moral courage, an indispensable asset for command at a high level, where political as well as military pressure sometimes result in suppression of contrary or 'uncomfortable' views. He was also showing other qualities essential in a military commander. Monash insisted on punctuality and tidiness. He planned each day methodically, crossing off agenda items with horizontal and vertical lines. Gaps in the latter signified uncompleted tasks, and these would head the agenda for the following day. This simple method ensured that nothing was overlooked and illustrated the extreme thoroughness that characterised his every action. In later life he was reputed to sleep with a dictaphone by his bed in case he was struck by a good idea during the night. Monash was also a man of patience. As chairman of the Inventions Board in 1909–10 he encouraged inventors, even if their ideas seemed chimerical. Though expressing little interest in sport, he exercised by taking long walks with the Wallaby Club in Melbourne.

Considerable weight attaches to Monash's engineering and business background when explaining his wartime performance. Bean maintained that Monash prepared operations with the same infinite care and using largely the same administrative methods that he employed in the construction of a bridge. Later generations of military historians have agreed with the analogy. Major General Hubert Essame, a British military historian who fought in both world wars, claimed that Monash's experience in the planning and execution of large-scale engineering projects was based on qualities

CHAPTER 1

equally applicable to the command of a corps: foresight, flexibility, cooperation, economy, delegation of authority and awareness of time. Nor was Monash reticent on the subject, writing on the day after the Armistice in 1918:

> ... engineering work has played an important role in this war. Not only are the whole of our battle operations based upon scientific technique of a high order, but every commander of a Corps is constantly confronted with vast problems of engineering and construction, in the form of roads, railways, bridges, water supply and sanitation, and all these on a scale of magnitude larger than is easy to convey.

However, the qualities enunciated by Essame are fundamental characteristics of any competent commander or business leader. They are certainly not the exclusive province of the engineer. The important distinction lies in the definition of engineering as 'literally a mode of looking at things', its practitioner 'the man with the genius first to recognise the real conditions of the technical problems before him and then by skilful effort to discover an adequate solution.' As his pioneering of reinforced concrete shows, Monash possessed these attributes in high degree. In addition, his powerful mind, itself an important factor contributing to the development of a commander, greatly exceeded those of his contemporaries. Finally, his vast knowledge endowed Monash with tremendous versatility, allowing him to grapple with the essentials of most matters. When these qualities of intellect were ordered by the rigours of the engineering mode of thought, the result was formidable, as his wartime chief of staff, the future Field Marshal Sir Thomas Blamey, recalled:

> ... the most highly trained mind that I had to deal with in the war. He brought to bear on any problem a most intense concentration of thought which produced a clarity in details of plan not often met with.

Of the five divisional commanders who served under Monash in the Australian Corps, only one, Major General Ewen Sinclair-MacLagan, was a regular officer in 1914. Like Monash, the remainder were citizen soldiers, whose livelihood remained their civil profession. Thomas

Glasgow was a grazier, Charles Rosenthal and Talbot Hobbs were architects, while John Gellibrand was an orchardist, although he had served in the British Army and graduated from its staff college at Camberley. Monash felt that such civil experience conferred positive advantages on the 'amateur' generals of Australia and Canada who rose to high rank during the war:

> This advantage rested upon a wide civilian training as engineers or architects or as captains of industry – a training far more useful for general applications to new problems than the comparatively narrower training of the professional soldier.

There is a less abstruse reason for stressing the importance of Monash's pre-war civil career. From the outset he was confronted with adversity: his parents' penury, completion of his education by part-time study, the fragility of his marriage, the struggle to support a young family with limited means, and the demands made on his time by military and university activities. In the immediate pre-war years his life was a constant struggle in the business world, where profit was the sole criterion of success. Monash's output of work was staggering. Though 1910 and 1911 were relatively easy years, he resumed the principal burden in 1913 when his partner, Gibson, went overseas. Spanning thirty years, such an environment could not be conquered by intellect alone. Equally important were the capacity to translate thought into action and the ability to persist with great driving power in the face of difficulties.[3] By requiring the quality that Wavell called 'robustness', Monash's circumstances provided admirable training for the 'frictions' experienced at every level of command in war. As his prosperity increased, so too did Monash's confidence in his own judgement, another essential ingredient of successful command.

The vicissitudes of civil life did not distinguish between those with technical backgrounds and those without. Monash's great contemporary, Lieutenant General Sir Arthur Currie, the commander of the Canadian Corps, experienced troubles that matched his own. After some years as a schoolteacher and insurance salesman, Currie turned to real estate, capitalising on the boom conditions then prevailing in British Columbia. But, unlike Monash, he failed to

CHAPTER 1

preserve a proper balance between his business and outside interests. His attention to the former became 'more perfunctory' as he concentrated on service in the militia. When the crash came in 1913–14, Currie was almost ruined, and his debts remained a millstone around his neck throughout the war. Nonetheless, he commanded his corps with conspicuous success, demonstrating abilities that rivalled Monash's. The example of Currie shows that the value of civil experience does not derive only from the technical professions.

Lieutenant General Sir Arthur Currie. Like Monash, Currie was a pre-war militiaman who stood for sound planning, technical expertise and innovative tactics. He ranks with Monash as one of the most able commanders in the BEF (AWM H06979).

Monash's powerful mind, his comprehensive education, his professional experience and the challenges he faced were the outstanding themes of his pre-war civil career. Others possessed some of these attributes or surmounted similar obstacles, but none combined them to the degree that Monash did. His pre-war army career was also important for the training in military organisation, tactics and administration it offered. Together with Monash's personal qualities, the union of soldier and civilian was a preparation for high command at least equal to that of Haig and army commanders such as Henry Rawlinson, Hubert Gough or Edmund Allenby, and, in terms of potential results in a war such as that which began in August 1914, far greater.

Chapter 2
My Long Cherished Hope for Military Advancement

With the departure of British garrison troops in 1870, the Victorian government assumed responsibility for the defence of that colony. A small permanent force was augmented by about 4000 volunteers, organised into cavalry, infantry, artillery, engineers, torpedo (sea mine) and signal units. Each volunteer corps was largely self-contained and heavily dependent for its effectiveness on the personality and drive of the commanding officer, usually the man who raised it. This excessive concentration of authority was only one of the several serious faults of the volunteer system. Its very nature precluded a high standard of uniform training and officer education at a time when ominous portents pointed to the need for capable defence forces. The growing armaments race in Europe, the Anglo-Russian crisis of 1878, the fear of Asian immigration, which accompanied the rise of Japan, and anxiety over French intentions in the New Hebrides combined to stimulate the colonies into action. Victoria established a Department of Defence, becoming the only Australian colony to maintain a state department, headed by a minister, concerned solely with defence matters. The Volunteer Force was progressively disbanded and, under the Discipline Act of 1883, replaced by a corps of paid militia. Serving officers of the British Army, who were engaged to fill the senior command positions in the Victorian Military Forces, supervised the reorganisation and, subsequently, the new training programs. Among the militia units formed were the four infantry battalions of the Victorian Rifles. 'D' Company of the 4th Battalion was furnished by Melbourne University, and one of its members was John Monash, who had enlisted as a private in July 1884.

CHAPTER 2

Colour Sergeant Monash (left) University (D) Company, Victorian Rifles, 1885 (Norman Photo IN1409, Monash University Archives).

Monash's reasons for joining the University Company remain obscure. The increased defence consciousness may have stimulated his interest. Many of his friends – for example J.W. Parnell and George Farlow – had enlisted, possibly placing peer pressure on him to do the same. In October 1884 he was promoted and soon acquired the nickname 'Corporal Potash'. He became sergeant in 1885 and was awarded a certificate of proficiency for flag signalling. In the following year he was promoted to colour sergeant, the senior sergeant in his company and responsible to his captain for its efficient administration and the preparation of ration returns and duty rosters. On parade he was to 'call the roll, fix bayonets, open the ranks and then report to the officer commanding the company.' Participation by the University Company in the annual contest for the Sir William Clarke prize afforded limited opportunities to develop minor tactical skills. As was to be expected in these early days, however, the standard attained by militia units was generally low. Constant training was the only remedy, but the University Company was hampered by its members' inability to attend regular parades. For this reason it was disbanded on

23 July 1886. As Monash's first military experience, it was too short and its activities too disjointed and rudimentary to be of any lasting and practical benefit. But it was an important awakening:

> He had recognised his natural talent in this calling. Military theory had begun to excite him, he enjoyed the control of men in a hierarchical disciplined structure, and military precision appealed to a man who detested untidiness and disorder.

The University Company had also come to represent a means by which his burning ambition might be realised. Shortly after the unit was disbanded, he confided to his diary:

> The matter which is now uppermost in my mind is the prospect of a near fulfilment of my long cherished hope for military advancement. I can scarcely understand why this wish is so intense within me, for I have been fully warned against expecting any ultimate advancement from the holding of a commission. Nevertheless the gorgeous uniform and all the pomp of officership bear for me sufficient attraction to make this attainment a matter of fierce desire.

His hunger for promotion, combined with childish delight in a dazzling uniform and the status inevitably bestowed on its wearer, suggest that Monash did not take too seriously those who told him there would be no long-term advantages. He had long forgotten this diary entry when he reflected on his life from the vantage point of a knighthood thirty-two years later. Handicapped by humble beginnings, Monash could only provide 'the utmost that life can give' for his family through 'wealth and position'. They were equally important: 'That is why, while working hard for so many years to get the most out of my profession in the way of monetary results, I devoted so much of my labours, also, to non-productive effort in both military and university spheres.' He regarded politics as an avenue that was closed to him, probably because of his religion, and hence either the military or the university constituted 'the only other road by which I could secure an unchallengeable position for ourselves.'

Monash heard that several vacancies existed in the Garrison Artillery units, particularly the North Melbourne Battery, which

CHAPTER 2

several members of the defunct University Company, including Farlow, had joined or were about to join. In August 1886 he told his friend Joe Miller, senior subaltern of the battery, that he would be 'only too glad' to be one of them. He asked Miller to give the battery commander, Major Jacob Goldstein, a character reference before meeting him. Though 'feverishly awaiting' the outcome of Goldstein's decision, Monash was not formally attached to the battery until 3 March 1887. He was commissioned on 5 April, which enabled him to attend the Easter camp of the Militia Garrison Artillery at Port Phillip Heads.

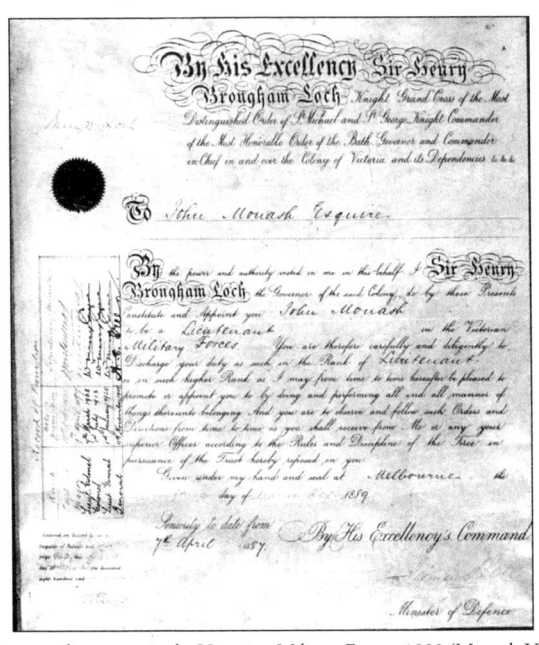

Monash's commission as a lieutenant in the Victorian Military Forces, 1889 (Monash University Archives).

The two brigades of the Victorian Garrison Artillery (VGA) defended Port Phillip Bay and several smaller harbours. Monash's battery was one of the four that formed the 1st Brigade. At the six-day Easter camp, batteries manned the forts they would occupy at Port Phillip Heads in time of war – in the case of the North Melbourne Battery, the fort at Point Nepean. The tactical working of coastal artillery was based on the division of guns into groups of two to four, commanded by a group officer. Two or three groups were then placed under a sub-commander, usually a captain, who was accountable to the fort commander. As a group officer, Monash planned the fire of his guns and was responsible for their efficient operation, duties requiring a thorough knowledge of both the equipment and the men who manned it. He had obtained his commission after demonstrating a detailed grasp of all the subjects taught on the annual gunnery course, comprising gun drills, construction and maintenance of guns and the use of sighting scales. By September 1896 Monash had risen to command the North Melbourne Battery, promotion to major following six months later, after he passed exams that rigorously tested his knowledge of all three arms. He was exercised practically in the formation and movement of a battalion and a cavalry squadron and examined theoretically in this work at brigade level. The cooperation of infantry, cavalry and artillery was emphasised, Monash being assessed as commander of a combined force in the four phases of operations: attack, defence, advance and withdrawal. There is no doubt that Monash's military horizons were broadened by the study necessary for promotion. He was introduced to arms other than his own, the tactical and administrative difficulties they faced and the concept of all-arms cooperation.

Captain Monash (front row, fifth from left) with other officers of the Garrison Artillery, 1895 (Norman Photo IN1417, Monash University Archives).

CHAPTER 2

Unlike the infantry or cavalry, where physical endurance and the ability to cope with the unexpected were at a premium, the Garrison Artillery was a precision arm, demanding exact calculation to score direct hits on moving targets. It was an environment to which Monash's technical training was particularly suited and soon applied. In common with its sister units, the North Melbourne Battery enjoyed only limited opportunities to train on modern breech-loading weapons. Having grappled with the problem for some time, Monash and Captain John Stanley planned to erect in each militia battery orderly room a full-scale working model of a 5-inch breech-loading gun. The design was Monash's. Every part of the mechanism and mounting was reproduced, affording 'a means of preliminary instruction quite as valuable and much less cumbersome than would be obtained from the gun itself.' Undeterred when the Defence Department refused the £100 needed to build it, Monash and Stanley produced the first model at their own expense in November 1889. It worked successfully and soon proved indispensable. Ministerial approval was finally given for the purchase of the Stanley-Monash gun for the Harbour Trust, Port Fairy, Portland and Warrnambool batteries.

Monash was fascinated by the intimate relationship between technology and the development of modern weapons. As he said in an address to the University Science Club in August 1892: 'no better instance of the enormous expansion of the field of applied science can be quoted.' Monash discussed his subject in great technical detail, explaining various explosions in chemical terms and the trajectory of projectiles according to physical formulae. Of special interest were the advantages of breech-loading weapons and advances in small arms. He simplified this address for presentation to the United Services Institution of Victoria on 4 October 1894. Still a lieutenant, Monash spoke to an audience that included the Victorian Commandant, Major General Sir Alexander Tulloch, and several colonels and majors. Monash gave many other lectures on the science of artillery. His study did not occur within a contextual vacuum, for he understood fully *how* technology had changed the nature of warfare. 'Fighting Machinery' had replaced physical force and brute courage, Monash maintained, while 'success in a great war of modern days will only be achieved by the perfect unity and accord between the forces on land and those at sea, acting together as a machine.'

As with all junior officers, many of Monash's responsibilities were routine: conducting courses and examinations at home training parades, drafting instructional schemes and investigating cases of loss and damage. But already there were the first glimpses of a style of command as distinctive as it was practical. Commanding the North Melbourne Battery as a lieutenant at the Easter camp at Queenscliff in 1893, he stressed the importance of projecting a good image to the public. Singing was forbidden on railway stations and on arrival in camp; there was to be no skylarking; men were to retire quickly and quietly. He instructed his officers: 'Settle all trivial complaints without referring to me, yet I want to know all that goes on.' Monash demanded adherence to the chain of command. Although not so aloof as to be ignorant of the state and feelings of his battery, he did not want to be bothered by problems subordinates were competent to solve.

Monash's ideas on training were also starting to emerge. His insistence on the constant exercise of their responsibilities was a method of instructing young officers and non-commissioned officers (NCOs). Soldiers should not merely learn drill by rote; they should understand 'the nature of all machinery appliances used and the reasons for every operation.' Within two months of being appointed to command it in 1896, he had reorganised the North Melbourne Battery, dividing it into two half batteries, each under a subaltern, for instructional and disciplinary purposes. These were then split into three subdivisions, each commanded by a sergeant, to allow monitoring of training and ensuring a more equitable distribution of responsibility. It was 'absolutely essential that all instruction should be thorough and effective', an aim frequently achieved by posting the officers as instructors. They had to be fully conversant not only with their own duties, but with the personnel and training of their sub-units, so as to be able to cope with any unforeseen contingency.

CHAPTER 2

Backward soldiers received special attention, while the training of all ranks concentrated on familiarising them with those functions in which they were least proficient.

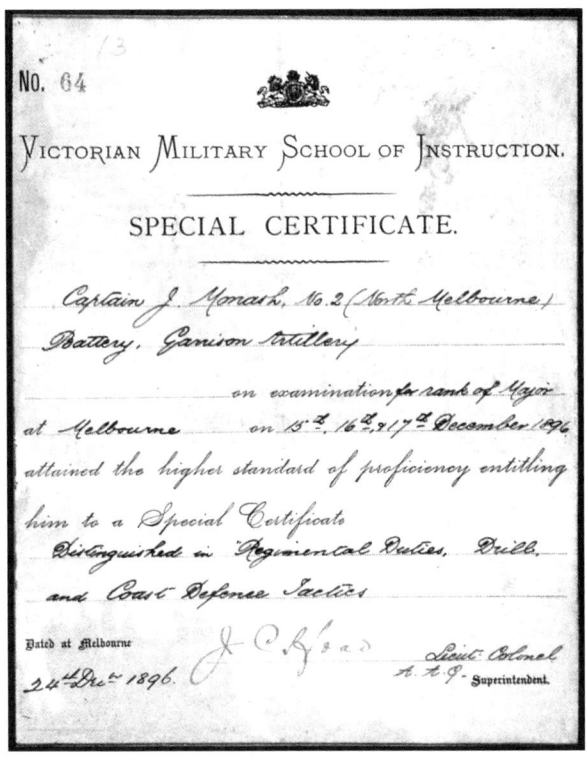

Captain Monash excels in the examinations for promotion to major, 1896 (Monash University Archives).

A unique picture of Monash as commander and trainer of the North Melbourne Battery was left by Colonel George Farlow:

> His orders were models of conciseness and at the same time completeness. Nothing was overlooked and at our camps if the slightest inconvenience to the men seemed inevitable, Monash would certainly hear of it and send his orderly for Captain This or Lieutenant That and it would be found that such a possibility was foreseen and provided for in the orders. He never buzzed about the tents of his men to see if they were properly provided for but what he did do was to think out all things and detail officers to work out the details and report to him as to their satisfactory development.

He supported his officers by asking each one as if casually to let him know later on how that particular officer was arranging his part of the scheme. I have often heard such a conference in which Monash would quite approve the officer's scheme and then make what appeared to be a casual suggestion. To one experienced this little suggestion would enable the officer to achieve his project fully to the CO's satisfaction and the officer was probably unaware that the smooth working came about 1/10 from him and 9/10 from the casual suggestion.

What Farlow did not make clear was the extent to which Monash, who was promoted to major in 1897, trespassed on the responsibilities of his subordinates when he 'thought out all things'. Also missing is any mention of the critical relationship between commander and soldier. Monash's service in the Garrison Artillery was his only experience of command at a level in which he was directly involved with the soldiers under him. When he felt they had been wronged, he defended them vigorously, as in July 1905, when seven men were recommended for dismissal for alleged fraudulent use of railway coupons. Protesting that there had been no formal trial and that his advice not been sought, Monash regretted that the action he consequently felt compelled to take might be construed as disloyalty to his commanding officer. He possessed the common touch, a quality all too often lacking in senior commanders of that period. No more eloquent testimony to Monash's power of leadership exists than the touching words of one of his senior NCOs, Staff Sergeant A. Hollingsworth, a man who had joined the British Army twenty-five years before, in 1883: '... during the whole of that period, I have never had a better Officer and Gentleman to deal with. Nor have I had to deal with a better Artillery Officer, either Permanent or Militia.'

Monash's success as commander of the North Melbourne Battery was achieved in a climate of great frustration, for the economic slump that had caused his retrenchment from the Harbour Trust also made deep inroads into the Victorian forces. As defence expenditure was slashed, units were disbanded, pay reduced and recruiting for the Permanent Forces stopped. The effects were especially severe in the

CHAPTER 2

Garrison Artillery. Many trained gunners resigned, leaving the corps with a large number of recruits. The Commandant commented soberly in his report of 1896 that 'every effort is being made to drill and train these men – but it must be remembered that the artillery militiaman requires considerable training before being fit to take his place in the ranks.' The problem was still evident in 1900, compounded by a lack of practice drill guns, which the government refused to provide.

The minor irritants were constant. Annual ammunition allotments were paltry. In 1892 a total of only 557 rounds was fired by the Garrison Artillery as a whole. Purchase of the latest weapons gradually resulted in a multiplicity of different types of guns, creating problems of training and supply. Monash criticised the deplorable condition of the minor equipment on which efficient functioning of the guns depended: no proper range-finders, primitive communications and the fighting positions in some forts badly chosen. Militia officers had frequently reported these matters, but nothing was done, a typical reaction of the permanent cadre, who studiously ignored their militia counterparts and allowed things 'to go sailing on in a beautiful laissez-faire way'. Monash detested the permanent officers: he laughed at Tulloch's installation of an obsolete gun at Point Nepean as a waste of money, and commented acidly on Colonel Dean-Pitt's attempt in 1894 to fight all the forts as a single fortress system: 'It was an egregious failure, clumsily planned, without previous instructions and the few hours which the work lasted were spent in abusive messages to the various [militia] Fort Commanders.' Monash's dislike of permanent officers was rooted in what he perceived as their inability to grasp the importance to their profession of military science:

> None of the present VA [Victorian Artillery] officers have the necessary largeness of intelligence, skill of administration, or general scientific knowledge to grapple with the large and critical questions on which our success depends.
>
> Their little minds are devoted to gun drill and petty routine, and such questions as the working out and teaching of a fighting

scheme, the tactical study of the locality etc, etc, etc, never in the knowledge of militia officers seem to have been touched.

Monash served in the VGA for twenty-one years. It was the longest and most misunderstood period of his military career. Necessity dictated his choice of arm. He joined the VGA as the easiest avenue to commissioned rank, not because it epitomised the vital nexus between science and warfare. Monash's awareness of that connection came gradually and probably accounted for the appeal of the corps – the number of training activities he attended at a time of personal and financial difficulty attested to his enthusiasm. The conviviality arising from membership of the United Services Institution of Victoria and the Naval and Military Club was an added source of pleasure. Despite the short-sighted cutbacks and the galling incompetence of its so-called 'expert' permanent officers, the Garrison Artillery was a useful training ground. It gave Monash lengthy experience of regimental command. The stereotype of the plodding 'concrete gunner' simply does not fit.

The distant rumbles of the Boer War were consigned to oblivion by Monash, who did not serve in South Africa for several cogent reasons. Personally and professionally, he could not afford a long absence from Victoria. Furthermore, the British War Office had requested infantry first and then cavalry. No artillery, least of all garrison artillery, was wanted. The second major event of the period was less remote. On 1 January 1901 the colonies federated into the Commonwealth of Australia and, exactly two months later, the Commonwealth Government assumed control of the various defence forces. The Defence Act, as formally proclaimed on 1 March 1904, provided for an army of Permanent and Citizen Forces, whose members could serve overseas only if they volunteered to do so. Viscount Esher's recommendation for the British Army was also adopted through the replacement of the General Officer Commanding (GOC) appointment, then held in Australia by Major General Sir Edward Hutton, by a Military Board responsible for administration and an Inspectorate-General for discipline. After almost three years as GOC, Hutton departed on 15 November 1904. The effects of the Hutton

CHAPTER 2

era would not have escaped Monash, whose battery was now known as No. 3 Victorian Company, Australian Garrison Artillery. The GOC had been a tireless worker, travelling constantly to watch training, inspect troops and offer advice as part of his policy of tight central control over the state forces to assist their rapid integration into a national army. He had also inspired a group of younger officers that included Henry ('Harry') Chauvel, Cyril Brudenell White and, most important of all, Colonel William Bridges, the Chief of Intelligence and a member of the Military Board.

Major General William Bridges. After joining the NSW permanent forces in 1885 as an artillery officer, he held mainly staff postings, through which he helped shape the pre-war Australian Army. The AIC, in which Monash served, was Bridges' creation. But he had almost no command experience. As a field commander on Gallipoli, Bridges was a dud (AWM A02867).

Bridges was also concerned with training and general staff duties, creating a workload beyond the capacity of his understaffed department. In February 1907 he resurrected a suggestion that it should be split into two branches, training and intelligence, under directors answerable to a Chief of the General Staff (CGS). When the Defence Minister, Thomas Ewing, was unsympathetic, Bridges adopted a different approach, advocating the creation of an Intelligence Corps, which would ensure that the Army had men trained in intelligence duties and in the collection of information on Australia and her potential enemies. Embarrassed by press reports of the appalling state of intelligence, Ewing approved, and on 6 December 1907 the Australian Intelligence Corps (AIC) was formed. Initially, it consisted of about sixty militia officers organised into state sections, with Bridges directing the work through its commanding officer, Colonel James McCay. A former Defence Minister, then in command of the 8th Infantry Regiment, McCay's intellectual power and political experience were overshadowed by his volatile temperament. But he wasted no time in asking his old friend Monash to command the Victorian section of the AIC. Monash accepted and was promoted to lieutenant colonel on 28 March 1908.

Major General James McCay. A colleague of Monash from their school days together, McCay was highly intelligent and personally courageous, but his harsh leadership style and scathing tongue bred dislike and even loathing. The 5th Division was shattered under his command at Fromelles in July 1916 (Public Records Office Victoria VPRS 8933-P18).

CHAPTER 2

Inspired by Monash, progress in Victoria outstripped that in other states, and by August the section was only two short of its establishment of fifteen.[4] Except for staff clerks and draughtsmen, the AIC was composed exclusively of officers possessing 'by virtue of their civil training or occupations, special qualifications for service in the Corps.' Eleven in Monash's section were professional men of some standing.[5] Seven had previous military experience, ranging from four to twenty-six years, in which they had gained high qualifications in corps as varied as infantry, transport and engineers. Of the six civilians who applied for commissions, all but one had served in the militia or cadets. By Monash's own admission, all were excellent officers, industrious, diligent and enthusiastic, and six months after their transfer to the AIC he was recommending the first promotions. Monash allocated to each of them responsibilities related to their civil occupations or military training. Lieutenant Reid, a stationmaster, was in charge of rail transport; Lieutenant Walters, a survey draughtsman, planned the preparation of maps, while Major James Semmens, his second-in-command and a secretary for the Ports and Harbours Department, handled contacts with the Navy among his many duties. Similar criteria governed Monash's selection of officers throughout the tenure of his command. They were all generally qualified with civil skills of unique relevance to the corps. The final characteristic of the Victorian section was that its members were all almost as old as Monash, then forty-three. Clearly, it was no command in the conventional sense, as was the North Melbourne Battery. Monash was not leading young regimental officers and men whose military work bore little resemblance to their civil occupation. The reverse was true. These were older men of wide knowledge, skill and experience, both civilian and military. His role was more that of the business manager, directing diverse talents in the execution of a variety of tasks – in other words, the relationship between a commander and his staff.

The demands his new command made on Monash far exceeded those of the North Melbourne Battery. As many as six evenings per month were devoted to supervision of the four sections, which 'were responsible, firstly, for the collection and collation of information on the transport, supply and manpower resources of the Commonwealth; secondly, for foreign information; thirdly for topography, including the preparation of maps; and finally, for a library, holding records, indexes and producing corps publications.' Officers were allocated technical and service periodicals, from which articles of interest were noted, enabling them to keep abreast of developments in Europe and America more readily than their colleagues in the other combatant arms. As the only German speaker in the section, Monash examined the journals *Kavalleristiche Monatschäfte, Militär Wochenblatt* and *Deutsche Kolonial Zeitung*. He undertook to compile two chapters for the 'Victorian Military Handbook' and, when this project was cancelled, to prepare the chapter on harbours and landing places for the proposed *Military Handbook of Australia*.

Monash was also responsible for the training of his section, which involved lectures and attendance and instruction at various intelligence courses, the first of which he organised at the end of 1908. It was designed to prepare his officers for more advanced work at the AIC Instructional Course in Melbourne in January 1909. At this first meeting of the AIC as a corps, McCay spoke on mobilisation, logistics and the development and organisation of the Australian Army. It was appropriate that Bridges should deliver the keynote address, during which he made two points of critical importance. In his efforts to form the corps, he had battled to convince the authorities that more was required from it than the collection of intelligence in peace. He regarded its most vital function as the preparation of intelligence in war. Secondly, Bridges hoped that the AIC would provide staff officers for brigade and division headquarters should such formations ever be brought up to war establishment. These men would need knowledge beyond mere intelligence work, for they would be responsible for the full range of general staff duties.

The immediate tasks of the Victorian section, though, were very much those of a peacetime intelligence corps. In July 1908 it reported on the suitability of lighthouses as signal stations for an exercise designed to test Australia's warning system. Information on numbers, types and the suitability of civilian vehicles for military use was hastily acquired for use in defence schemes. Compilation began of the 'Intelligence Diary', listing references to items of even the remotest military significance on Victoria, Australia and New Zealand, the Pacific and Indian oceans and general subjects. Information was also collected on consular representatives in Victoria and their staffs. Of all AIC functions, none was so important as map-making, which included reports on suitable defensive positions, communications and water supply. The urgent demands for maps were undiminished, probably spurred on by pressure from a government facing bitter criticism for the scarcity of topographical information on Australia. Monash's experience of surveying and railway construction gave him unusual qualifications for this work, and he assumed control, specifying that the officer commanding the section normally responsible would remain 'in subordinate charge'.

Monash's understanding of the technical aspects of cartography was readily acknowledged by fellow officers skilled in the field. In March 1914 Lieutenant Walters protested to the CGS that the system of topographical survey about to be introduced in Australia was a retrograde step, suggesting instead a continuation of that 'inaugurated by Colonel Monash, whose professional qualifications are beyond question'.[6] By the end of 1912, maps had been completed for the Seymour-Avenel, Kilmore, Broadford, Glenaroua and Burrumbeet areas, and the map of the Melbourne region was well advanced. But overall progress was slow, as the information was usually gathered on weekends by teams of two men on bicycles, another example of the dedication of Monash's officers. Despite his strenuous efforts to overcome the problem, which included a forthright letter to shire engineers appealing to their 'patriotic spirit' for assistance, it remained insoluble. At Monash's suggestion, McCay approached Colonel C.F. Close, Chief of the Geographical Section of the Imperial General Staff, who recommended the transfer of mapping to the permanent staff. Monash's practical knowledge of map-making was crucial to his style of command for it endowed him with the ability to visualise ground instantly by studying the map on which it was depicted. He was not concerned with maps as a means of accurate position finding; rather, map accuracy was only that which gave a true conception of the *general* form of ground and the *general* relation of levels.

The distinction between 'pure' intelligence functions and what would now be called operational staff duties was soon blurred, as at least some of Bridges' hopes for the corps were realised. In October 1908 Monash's section began preparing plans for the mobilisation of each unit in Victoria, and in the following year for the trans-shipment of troops at Albury-Wodonga, a result of the absurd difference in railway gauge from NSW. Monash's scheme was an ideal staff solution, a masterly example of logical and precise thinking. Train destinations were immaterial. Each state was to inform the other of the easiest procedure for loading and despatching units, and then modifications would be made according to the railway means available, with a view to rationalising train loads. When compromise had been reached, officers met at Albury and Wodonga to inspect fully one another's facilities and to decide exactly the location of each waiting body of troops and the stopping places for trains. Monash also sat on the Victorian Defence Committee and contributed to its defence scheme. At a much lower level, he set simple staff problems involving an infantry brigade; his officers had to calculate the road space occupied and the amount of supplies needed and prepare the march orders.

Monash's writings and lectures reveal a profound appreciation of the importance of staff work in both its operational and administrative forms. Though nowadays administration is considered in the same breath as operations, it had little status in this period and was one of the least respected, as well as one of the least understood, functions of command. Monash was appalled. He embraced administration within his own broad definition of 'operations', which meant 'a great deal more than actual fighting operations such as pitched battles or putting out outposts'; instead, 'marches, movements by rail and water, laying down lines of communication or supply, selecting and occupying a bivouac, billeting in a town – are all *operations* of war.' It was useless to confine training only to fighting techniques, because 'The best tactics, best rifle shooting or gunnery and best leadership cannot compensate for failure in organisation.' The crack battalion could be crippled by a breakdown in ammunition supply, while a small error in calculating time and space could ruin an attempted concentration. Its ammunition, food, forage and water and its animals and vehicles – all were integral components of a force. His views were held with conviction and were identical to those of a commander of a later generation, Bernard Montgomery:

> I believe that the task of bringing the force to the fighting point, properly equipped and well-formed in all that it needs is *at least* as important as the capable leading of the force in the fight itself. In fact it is indispensable and the combat between hostile forces is more in the preparation than the fight.

The parallels with a construction project were striking. Comparing a bridge or railway to a battle, the actual building was the final link and depended on the design, the acquisition of material, its transport to the site and the proper division of labour.

Monash held strong views on what constituted the ideal staff officer: 'unfailing patience under the most trying conditions, unquenchable zeal under rebuffs and tireless energy'. As well as familiarity with tactical principles in the use of all arms, the staff officer had to understand fully the situation and how his commander intended to react. It was essential that the staff officer gained and kept the commander's confidence by tact and using suggestion devoid of forcefulness. He had to be able to speak and write fluently, telling the commander precisely what he needed to know and nothing else. Monash was especially critical of his own officers in this regard. When giving verbal reports, they stammered, hesitated and became confused, using incorrect names and words. He instructed them to anticipate what they were going to say, 'then say it crisply, without hesitation, correctly and fluently', while in written reports, the object was 'to convey pithily only the essentials'. Here was an outstanding reflection of his practice in civil life.

Ambiguity in any form was intolerable. Asked to comment on a draft exam paper for promotion to lieutenant colonel, Monash objected to the words 'The heights East of Frimley', because the map showed no definite heights there. Confusion would be avoided by saying 'about half a mile East of Frimley or simply 'at Frimley'. The thoroughness and attention to detail that struck Farlow at the North Melbourne Battery were even more noticeable in the AIC. When his officers were attached to brigades for the 1911 Easter camp, Monash directed them to learn 'every minute detail of their brigade, personnel, horses, guns, waggons, etc, etc.' Commanding officers had to be known by sight and principal officers by name, because 'This knowledge will assist you in understanding the Brigade and Regimental Orders as on mention in orders of Colonel XYZ your mind instantly reminds you of the man's appearance and of the Regiment or Brigade to which he belongs.' Following the teaching of the *General Staff Manual*, Monash insisted on uniformity of thought, and dismissed the faddist, a principle that guided his command of the Victorian section: 'It is essential that every tendency for the work to be carried on in "watertight compartments" shall be discouraged. On the contrary, the utmost co-operation between officers must be practised.'

The AIC exercised Monash's knowledge of tactics up to infantry brigade level. He drafted schemes for the camp at Seymour in January 1910 and prepared the narrative for the manoeuvres at Kilmore at Easter 1911 of infantry and light horse, singly and combined, and a strategic reconnaissance exercise. After the annual training camps of 1909, 1910 and 1911, Monash compiled the tactical portion of the Annual Report of the Commandant, 3rd Military District (Victoria), which he described as involving 'the observation, analysis and draft criticism of the tactical handling of four composite brigades.' He was usually employed as a senior umpire, judging the performance of his fellow militia officers and seeing in practice those things of which he had only a theoretical knowledge. His comments were diverse, from criticism of the way a commander handled his brigade to matters of the smallest

CHAPTER 2

administrative detail. He accompanied the Field Force on its manoeuvres at Langwarrin in 1908 and studied 'the design and working of the transport, supply and signalling and medical arrangements and the dispositions for protection and security.' During the advance phase of the exercise, he observed that flanks were completely unguarded while lamentable reconnaissance resulted in the force deploying in full view of the enemy position. Monash continued:

> A point which impressed me seriously was that operation orders did not appear to have been promulgated at all effectively. I found even several senior officers who had neither maps, nor any notion of the scope, purpose and meaning of the strategical or tactical operations in which they were taking part. If only for instruction purposes, the effective promulgation and explanation of orders right down to subordinate commanders seems to me indispensable to proper training.

He was very critical of the junior leadership. Finding tents improperly pitched and poor cleanliness and sanitation, Monash did not blame the soldiers. It resulted from the chain of responsibility being ignored by regimental commanders at one extreme and NCOs at the other. Company commanders, in particular, seemed to 'grope about rather aimlessly' before determining their obligation in these matters. Subalterns had little knowledge of the organisation of their own units – strengths, establishments, equipment and supplies – information 'which they ought to have at their fingertips.'

The most important camp attended by Monash was held at Seymour between 10 and 16 January 1910. It was one of several inspected by Lord Kitchener, C-in-C in India and the Empire's most prestigious soldier, during his visit to Australia to report on the state and efficiency of the defences and advise on the soundness of the proposed Universal Training Scheme. Monash was attached to the staff of the District Commandant as, for the first time in Victoria, complete brigades with part of their transport attached were exercised in combined operations, confronting all ranks with problems and situations beyond their previous experience.

The manoeuvres were progressive, beginning with simple march operations and culminating in a divisional attack. From the level of its headquarters, Monash actually saw a division in the field, the area it occupied and the immense logistic support it required. His report on the tactical aspects was replete with many of the recommendations he had made in the past. Promulgation of orders was again 'not only slow but ineffective'. One of the greatest defects was the failure to instruct junior ranks in the object and nature of the exercises as well as the roles of the units participating. There was no excuse for such neglect, because commanders had many opportunities to explain the situation to their subordinates: 'Such a procedure would raise the spirit and enterprise of the troops, and enhance that individual initiative which is the foundation of modern tactics.' The divisional commander ignored his brigadiers and tried to control their brigades directly, while some officers were unaware of the direction of an attack they were supposed to lead. Only once did a brigade act on a prepared appreciation, which, incidentally, neither gave the reason for the course adopted, nor foreshadowed the situation that actually arose. Press coverage of the manoeuvres was universally unfavourable. Drawing attention to the incompetence of commanders, the *Australasian* stated that a staff must be trained and 'Above all, the military necessity of the moment is to educate officers.'

Complementing what he learnt at these camps was the instruction Monash received as a student at two War Courses, each of a fortnight's duration, conducted by Colonel Hubert Foster, the Director of the Department of Military Science at Sydney University, in October 1909 and 1911. Their object was to teach the duties of a commander and staff in various tactical and administrative situations. Both permanent and militia officers attended. Tactical schemes at brigade level were practised without troops, the students taking turns to fill the various positions on the brigade staff. There were exercises in repelling landings and the advance and withdrawal phases of war, staff problems in billeting and marching and lectures on the military use of railways, based on principles and techniques used by

CHAPTER 2

the Germans in the Franco-Prussian War. Monash's solutions were generally praised and showed his understanding of the essentials of any problem. His plan for a brigade attack on a position covering an enemy embarkation at La Perouse was based not on capturing the position at the outset, but on seizing ground from which his entire artillery could fire on the embarking troops. Only then would the enemy position be assaulted. He was keenly interested in the orders given to various arms: infantry, artillery, engineers, cavalry and the ambulances.

Lieutenant Colonel Monash (seated second from left) and other AIC officers on Colonel Foster's War Course, Sydney, 1909.

Monash recognised that: 'Staff work in war is exactly on the same lines as here in this room. Troops are just as non-existent as they are at exercise.' In the same way as he could visualise ground by studying a map, Monash developed the art of imagining the position of his own troops, the location of the enemy, and how both were affected by orders he issued. Liddell Hart asserted that this ability to grasp immediately the picture of the ground and the situation and relate each to the other is 'a vital faculty of generalship ... It is that flair which makes the great executant.' Monash was deeply impressed by Foster and entertained no doubts as to the lasting value of his courses. Just before leaving for the Western Front in command of the 3rd Australian Division, he wrote to his old mentor:

> In common with many others who have in the past enjoyed the privilege of instruction under you, I recognise every day the great value to myself which has accrued from the various skeleton exercises and the systematic lectures which I was privileged to attend under your guidance. Although much of the technique of modern warfare, so far as concerns the individual soldier is new, it is wonderful how little the fundamental principles of strategy and tactics can be safely trespassed upon and how the principles of organisation and staff work which you inculcated, have stood the test of war.

He expressed similar views as commander of the Australian Corps.

The problems set by Foster were, nonetheless, abstract exercises in which mythical forces were brought together in imaginary circumstances. An essential supplement – and then, as now, the only means of learning about command under the strain of real battle – was the study of military history, which Monash undertook at three levels. Firstly, there was a growing recognition of the importance of the subject throughout the Army. Orders and instructions issued by commanders on actual operations and observers' reports on recent battles were distributed and lessons drawn from them. Secondly, McCay set exercises on reading prescribed for AIC officers. In 1911 the course of the Russo-Japanese War, from the battles of the Yalu to Liaoyang, was studied. It had been preceded in 1909 by questions based on Lieutenant Colonel George Henderson's *Life of Stonewall Jackson*. The third and most important level was Monash's personal study of military history. He was no armchair strategist. Just as he examined critically his university lectures, Monash visualised the situation and ground described in, for example, Henderson, and then applied to them the principles of command, staff work and logistics. Then he would read the account in full, noting where these principles were violated. It was also necessary to go out into the

CHAPTER 2

bush to cultivate an eye for country, a sense of direction and what he called 'mental photographs' of terrain. For Monash, a campaign was a living thing, its manoeuvres not sterile, but the expressions of fallible commanders acting under intense strain amid the fog of war. In this context, his comment on the problem of deducing an enemy's strength and intentions was noteworthy:

> ... it should be remembered that on service it is never possible to collect sufficient information to reach definite unimpeachable conclusions; that the conclusions arrived at can seldom be more than shrewd guesses at the truth.[7]

In 1912 Monash won the inaugural Gold Medal Essay Competition on the subject 'The Lessons of the Wilderness Campaign –1864', from which tactical, administrative and organisational principles applicable to the defence of Australia were to be drawn. Although open to all officers in the Commonwealth, only seven entries were received, Monash submitting his under the pseudonym 'Patriotism'. His mastery of language was readily apparent, prompting one of the judges, Colonel James Legge, to remark that it was 'by far the best in style'.[8] Another judge, Chauvel, felt that Monash had exposed many salient points: the similarity between the Australian and the American soldier, both men without previous military training or tradition; that tactical victories, while dependent on accurate appreciations, rapid decision, energetic execution and choice of ground, were influenced above all by the personal qualities of the commander and the morale of his army, 'by far the most pregnant lesson of the campaign'. Monash argued forcefully that commanders must be free from political interference imposed by ill-informed public opinion, a basic weakness of democracies and a temptation to which Australian governments might yield. At a lower level, subordinate commanders required initiative and should not be hampered by masses of orders. Finally, he remarked yet again that the fundamental principles of tactics were as valid in 1912 as they were in 1864.

For its period, Monash's 'Wilderness Essay' was a good piece of work. Some new sources had been consulted, particularly *The Photographic History of the War*, which he had read as soon as it appeared, something that few people had done. But there were several weaknesses as well. Monash ascribed the power of a defending force solely to the strength of well-constructed field fortifications, omitting the vital fact that the rifle had also made this possible. Infantry formations were inadequately discussed. Insufficient importance was attached to the wooded terrain of the Wilderness battles, which limited the effectiveness of artillery with no method of indirect fire. Perhaps his familiarity with recent advances in artillery and ammunition made him overlook the limitations of this arm in 1864, although he did insist that it should remain under the direct control of the divisional commander if prompt and effective support was to be provided for the infantry. Conceding the merit of Monash's essay, Roger C. Thompson comments:

> ... it lacks a thorough historical sense in a total view of the Civil War and appreciation of the difficulties confronting the armies. The strategic appreciation of the role of cavalry, the importance of railways and economic destruction is weak.

Monash's training and leadership of the Victorian section were based on the techniques and principles evolved at the North Melbourne Battery, although the contrasting nature of the commands necessitated their practice in a different form. He wanted even theoretical training to be as realistic as possible, remarking that a force mentioned in an exam question should be allotted a supply column because 'This will impress upon candidates the definite obligation of considering the trains in their dispositions.' He was director or assistant director of intelligence staff tours in Melbourne in 1908 and Sydney and Kilmore in 1912. In each of them, logistics as well as tactical problems were prominent: railway movements, transport required to move a force, and its food, forage and ammunition needs. If subordinates failed him, it was a slur on the corps rather than a personal blow. He won the respect and loyalty of all his officers and enjoyed good relations with his superior, McCay. At the same time, his treatment of soldiers had not changed. He refused to be distracted by the comment of Lieutenant Colonel Victor Sellheim, the Assistant Adjutant-General (AAG), in

CHAPTER 2

July 1909, that his new clerk, Military Staff Clerk Newlands, was 'slippery as an eel'. Monash gave Newlands a fair chance to prove himself and found him extremely industrious and enthusiastic. He wrote to Sellheim subsequently that Newlands was performing in 'a highly satisfactory manner' and made several representations on his behalf as to pay and conditions.

The Victorian section was probably the most efficient in the AIC. At the end of 1909 McCay expressed formally his appreciation of 'the great amount of work being done', and in 1911 the Victorian Commandant remarked on its keen spirit, which he felt was largely attributable to the energy and drive of Monash. It was a fair judgement. Monash was dedicated to furthering the prestige and capacity of the corps. He espoused the use of photo-topographic methods; urged the completion on time of manoeuvre maps, which would 'go a long way towards establishing our position permanently as an integral portion of the military machine', and suggested the creation of volunteer AIC detachments to assist with map-making in remote areas. But the AIC never realised its initial promise. Monash's command was wracked by a series of demoralising blows, for which he was neither responsible nor able to take remedial action. He was disgusted by lack of progress towards the adoption of distinctive mess dress for the AIC more than one year after his officers had expressed their desire for it. Consequently, some officers had to attend the Lord Mayor's Dinner in civilian clothes, and to remain seated when their uniformed counterparts in other arms responded to the Army toast. Inability to appear socially on an even footing with them 'encroaches upon the amour propre of the man himself, and impairs the influence of the Corps upon other branches of the service.' There was the animosity towards it, engendered by McCay. Early in 1909 McCay decreed that the AIC Section Commander in each district had the right of direct access to the District Commandant, bypassing the latter's staff. The furore was settled only by a Military Board decision that some matters might be referred to the Commandant direct, but others to the appropriate senior staff officer.

Bridges' early hope that the corps would provide staff officers for formation headquarters was never properly fulfilled. Appearances invariably belied reality. Before the Kitchener camp, Monash hoped that though his officers were under the orders of their respective brigadiers: 'During the actual manoeuvres, Brigadiers will doubtless permit the General Staff Officer to employ the junior Intelligence Officer also on General Staff Duties.' He was to be disappointed, for only one of his officers worked continuously at such duties. Most performed no useful task at all, 'or were merely tolerated as assistants to *officers who apparently knew little about staff duties* ... the Brigadier or the officer acting for him had no understanding of the organisation of a Brigade staff, or the scope of staff work for which Intelligence Officers are being trained.' The Kilmore camp of the following year was a pathetic waste of time for the same reason. His bitter comments to McCay revealed the depth of Monash's despondency:

> Except for a keen desire on the part of myself and my officers to live down, by hard and laborious service to the forces, the attitude of either passive indifference or active suspicion which is manifested towards us, our status is very unsatisfactory. Speaking broadly, there is no role, except such as each officer seeks for himself, and the performance of duty such as narrative work seems to get on the nerves of Brigade Staff, who, in many cases, make the narrative officer feel that he is very much in the way.

By 1912 the future of the AIC was gloomy. Its estimates had been slashed for 1910–11 and again for the following year. The Inspector-General, Major General George Kirkpatrick, felt that its establishment increases since 1908 were not reflected in the results obtained, concluding: 'The General Staff is gradually developing and it seems to me that the time has arrived for the AIC to become an integral part of that organisation.' From 13 August 1912 McCay took leave for an overseas trip until the expiry of his five-year term as Head of Corps in December. He had no objection to proposals to abolish the position when it fell vacant, but in the meantime urged his replacement by Monash 'as being absolutely essential to AIC matters being put in order before the command ceases to exist.' Monash duly succeeded McCay, and shortly afterwards the

Military Board informed him that the appointment of Head of Corps was to be terminated from 5 December 1912. On 6 December the AIC underwent its final reorganisation. Its headquarters was absorbed into the Victorian Military District Command, and the six sections became an integral part of the Australian section of the Imperial General Staff. Accordingly, its work was directed by the CGS through the Director of Military Operations, Major Brudenell White, and General Staff Officers in each district.

Monash was angered by the disrespect shown him throughout the reorganisation. It was the unhappiest period of his pre-war military career. In one of his few emotive letters to a person outside his immediate family, he confided to McCay: 'I have been subjected to a considerable amount of annoyance, procrastination and neglect.' When Monash finally saw him, Brigadier General Joseph Gordon, the CGS, began an inaccurate discourse as a prelude to reasons 'neither substantial nor convincing', for abolishing the Corps Headquarters. Monash flatly refused Gordon's suggestion that he command the corps without a staff, in addition to his duties as commander of the Victorian section, because the workload would be impossible. Gordon instructed White to ensure that Semmens was appointed to command the Victorian section, but this promise was forgotten. The Military Board told Monash he was to have the dual command, whereupon he protested in even stronger terms. The matter was not resolved to Monash's satisfaction until mid-October. When he discussed the planned organisation with White, Monash formed the impression that White had little idea of the scope and character of past work done by the corps and was even hazier as to its future. Monash's attempt to draw White was curtly rebuffed:

'It seems to me Major, that, under the proposed organisation, you are not going to have any suitable place or duty for a senior Lieutenant Colonel like myself' ... and the man had the hardihood to look me straight in the face and say, quite coolly, 'No, I don't suppose we will.'

Monash lamented, 'I shall have to face the prospect of going out of active duty or looking for some soft place to fall on.'

Brigadier General Cyril Brudenell White in his dugout at Anzac during the Gallipoli campaign. Courteous, restrained, cerebral, he was the staff officer *par excellence*. Monash later described him as 'far and away the ablest soldier Australia has ever turned out.' The pair had the greatest mutual respect (AWM C01815).

In the meantime, Monash sought one of the new infantry brigade commands. Among the permanent officers who supported his quest were his friend Lieutenant Colonel Julius Bruche, who urged that Monash was a genius and should be given a brigade, and White. The District Commandant agreed with them, and accompanying his recommendation was a confidential report that described Monash as 'One of the best militia officers in this District, of very high professional attainments, keen and loyal, who has done excellent service in the organisation of the AIC in this command.' On 21 June 1913 he was appointed to command the 13th Infantry Brigade. Militarily at least, Monash had taken on a new lease of life at a time when he was facing the very real possibility of retirement – a fascinating thought in view of his achievements five years later. It was incidental that the means of his salvation was an infantry command; necessity had dictated his choice of arms as it had the Garrison Artillery twenty-six years before. Monash hoped his inexperience would be offset by his recent training in 'command and staff work', adding that senior officers, such

CHAPTER 2

as Bridges, Stanley, Foster and McCay, would attest to his 'theoretical and practical knowledge of the duties and responsibilities of Brigade Command.' But these higher authorities adopted a cautious policy on his promotion, stating that his performance at the annual camp would be considered first. Always inclined to bluster when he did not get his own way, Monash pointed out that his appointment was unconditional and submitted his past record 'as justifying the expectation that my work in a new sphere is likely to be satisfactory.' On 12 August he was informed of his promotion to colonel, backdated to 1 July 1913. The ambition he had harboured since 1887 seemed satisfied at last.

There was another reason for Monash's ire at the proposed probation. His brigade was recently formed, with several inexperienced battalion commanders and a large percentage of untrained officers and soldiers. The opportunities for training in the nine months to the next camp were too few for him to create an efficient command. It was a problem faced by commanders of all formations raised under the Universal Training Scheme, which had been established by the Defence Act of 1909 in response to widespread dissatisfaction with the militia system. The scheme was not introduced, however, until 1 January 1911, after a review of Kitchener's report on Australia's military needs. It called for a trained citizen army of 80 000 men, conscripted for part-time service between the ages of eighteen and twenty-five. Monash had been elected by his colleagues as the Victorian Military District representative to a conference of militia officers convened to discuss its implementation in October 1912.

The 13th Infantry Brigade comprised the 49th, 51st and 52nd battalions, with two more, the 46th and 48th, attached for the 1913–14 training year. Monash was now removed from the rank and file, and he exercised authority through his battalion commanders. Hence the Garrison Artillery remained the foundation for his judgement of men, while the AIC years gave him the staff experience essential for successful command in the field. Thus the 13th Brigade was the fusion of Monash's pre-war career in two disparate arms. He stated his views on his own role at his first conference with the battalion commanders on 12 August 1913, called because he sought closer personal touch, thereby engendering mutual confidence. Monash enjoined them to achieve a harmonious whole: 'welded together, healthy rivalry, yet mutual sympathy. No washing of dirty linen outside.' He interpreted his training responsibilities widely, candidly admitting the possibility of trespassing in areas that were normally the preserve of subordinates. His insistence on high standards, which had characterised his previous commands, was again evident. When Major J.A.R. Kruse, commanding the 48th Battalion, departed from the regular form of an operation order, Monash commented bluntly: 'it is just as easy to do the thing correctly as incorrectly.' He was regarded with the same mixture of affection and respect by his subordinates. Before leaving for Egypt in command of the 5th Battalion AIF, Lieutenant Colonel David Wanliss, who had led the 52nd Battalion in the 13th Brigade, wrote:

> I don't think you realise the great effect your leadership has had upon us all and I would like to take the opportunity of thanking you, before we go, for the assistance you have been to us. I think all the commanding officers of the 13th Brigade realised it.

Monash's fears regarding the difficulties of training this raw formation were well founded. Problems were inevitable in the early stages of a scheme under which the Army would not reach its full strength until 1919. The first recruit intake, on 1 July 1912, swamped the small number of qualified instructors and caused urgent organisational and administrative needs in the new units. Though the recruits' enthusiasm, intelligence and adaptability were praised, training in 1912 did not, therefore, proceed beyond elementary levels. Equipment shortages exacerbated matters. Monash's 48th Battalion was formed without rifles to equip it. The machine-gun section in three of the battalions had only one gun, and although the inexperienced machine-gun officers were keen, live firing was badly needed. Drawing attention to these issues at a conference on Universal Training in October 1913, Monash urged that permanent cadres be detached less frequently from their militia units and warned that unless shortages were rectified quickly, the success of the scheme was imperilled. The intention of training in 1913–1914 was the promotion of the intelligent initiative

CHAPTER 2

of the rank and file as a major condition for success in war. But the reality was different. Units continued to attend camp with insufficient basic knowledge, leading to proposals to train recruits separately and hence more thoroughly. The war intervened.

Amid these obstacles, the training of the 13th Brigade began. Ten half-day and twelve night parades were prescribed in addition to an eight-day camp. Great emphasis was attached to improving home training, which the battalions conducted in their Melbourne drill halls, covering such subjects as musketry, unit formations and that favourite of most armies, drill. Monash's main concern was officer training. In October he lectured his company commanders on the duties and responsibilities of officers. In December he directed a Tactical Exercise Without Troops at Lilydale. The District Commandant envisaged these exercises as a means of evolving the best methods for the training of battalions and companies on the ground selected for the annual camp. Monash went further, planning a rehearsal for the work to be examined by Sir Ian Hamilton, Inspector-General, Overseas Forces. It was a novel approach, enabling the battalion commanders to see how well their theoretical solutions worked in practice and, given the limitations, how well they themselves coped with the frictions that could not be foreseen. As usual, Monash included logistical problems: the quantity of auxiliary transport required to keep the brigade supplied from its railhead and the number of trains needed to bring it from Melbourne. He completed his own preparation by reading those parts of *Infantry Training 1911–Infantry in Battle* that dealt with fire, battle formations, use of cover and principles of attack and defence.[9]

Monash's command of an infantry brigade in the field made the Lilydale camp, held from 7 to 14 February 1914, the most important single event in his pre-war military career. Its short duration necessitated the judicious use of training time, and so Monash directed that pauses between activities were to be used for musketry instruction. Realism was stressed. He sought medical advice on the planning of the longest possible marches consistent with the physical capability of his men, writing, 'This is really a medical question.' Monash watched closely those things affecting the soldiery. During inspections he was critical if tents were not aired or if punctuality was ignored. 'The Development of a Soldierly Spirit', a note he made in January 1914, lists the following ten points: obedience, respect for authority, unselfishness, self-sacrifice, mutual help and cooperation, self-respect, personal tidiness and cleanliness, courage, determination, making the best of things – optimism. Finally, he began each day with 'a half-hour's sharp burst of brigade drill'. With all five battalions on parade, 'the effect was wonderful in stiffening everybody up and in emphasising the brigade ideal.'

General Sir Ian Hamilton. Urbane, tall, beanpole-thin, and a published poet and author, he had seen more action than any senior serving British officer. He was impressed with Monash while touring Australia as Inspector-General in 1914 and the pair renewed their acquaintance on Gallipoli (AWM A03549).

CHAPTER 2

The Lilydale camp culminated in two days of brigade manoeuvres, before which Monash emphasised to his officers and senior NCOs the need 'to let all ranks know what is going on'. Lieutenant (later Air Marshal Sir) Richard Williams was astonished to learn that Monash had written the battalion commanders' orders for them. Acting as the enemy, the 52nd Battalion withdrew to a strongly held position on Mount Mary as the rest of the brigade advanced. Monash attacked frontally with two battalions, while two more pressed home a flank assault after a concealed march of four miles. The machine-gun sections swept the creek beds on the approaches. A brigade withdrawal to Lilydale concluded the exercise. Afterwards, Monash mixed criticism with praise. Attacking formations were good and well covered by fire, but the field ambulance was late and the enemy did not harass the beginning of the retreat. After 'quite a hard day with 13 Brigade', General Sir Ian Hamilton reported: 'I was well pleased with the technical parts of the work and very well pleased with the go and keenness of the officers and men.' He had expected Monash's criticisms to be tempered by extreme politeness. Instead, he 'hit out straight from the shoulder', prompting Hamilton to recommend to the Defence Department that 'if war broke out, General Monash would be a man who would do them well.'[10]

Moreover, the Lilydale camp was the first in which responsibility for every aspect rested with the brigade commander, whereas before the District Commandant had lived in the camp, running it with his staff. Monash was very satisfied with the results and looked forward to 'a successful term of command as my prestige is now well established.' He was not blind to the faults, either, but most were beyond his control. Transport and equipment were chronically inadequate, food supply, preparation and distribution needed improvement if future disciplinary problems were to be averted, and, as Monash himself noted, training without artillery and light horse was very unreal. One incident saddled him with temporary notoriety. The *Age* alleged that he worked his troops to exhaustion, ignoring Hamilton's suggestions that they had done enough. Vivid descriptions of soldiers collapsing with tongues swollen from thirst coloured the story. The article was the signal for a torrent of abuse and innuendo, which even extended to Parliament, where the opinion was ventured that, being on horseback, the fifteen or sixteen-stone Colonel Monash was unaware of his troops' suffering. The *Leeton Call* published a derogatory poem about him after remarking: 'If anything is calculated to kill compulsory training it is people like Monash, who, being temporarily elevated to small leaderships, imagine themselves Napoleon-Wellington-Roberts all rolled into one.' Monash vigorously denied the charges after canvassing his battalion commanders and medical officers. Their reports showed that the *Age* had greatly exaggerated the affair. Publicly, Monash blustered, demanding ministerial authority to deny the allegations, a course he deemed essential 'for the proper maintenance of my prestige and authority within the command.' Privately, he wrote to Bruche: 'I shall adhere to my policy of training for war and not for picnics and shall always strive to set tasks which will compel everybody to put forth his best energies.'

The 13th Brigade was Monash's last pre-war command, the pinnacle of a military career that, so far, had spanned thirty years. He was proud of his position and infuriated by the persistent attempts of permanent officers to diminish its status. When a junior staff officer said publicly that brigadiers should be 'encouraged to accept responsibility', Monash was quick to respond. He fought for the right of militia officers to wear full dress uniform, another example of discrimination against them. Reflecting in 1913 on his long years of hard work in so many areas, Monash yearned for a more peaceful existence, intending to withdraw gradually from public affairs. The Army and the university would be the last to go, indicative of the very important part these institutions had come to occupy in his life. After another world tour in 1915, he planned to liquidate his affairs and invest the resulting capital, which, with a few 'easy' directorships, 'would have kept us going in luxury for the rest of our lives.'

Monash's pre-war military service cannot be considered apart from his civil education and experience. Each complemented the others. Where, then, did he stand in comparison with the Camberley

CHAPTER 2

graduates of the mid-1890s, the men who would command the BEF during the First World War, and alongside whom he would serve? His theoretical knowledge was derived from the same sources as theirs, because the Australian Army subscribed generally to British military teaching. Training in the second year at Camberley included appreciations, operation orders for a small mixed force and outdoor exercises in minor tactics. The level of this work was similar to Monash's as a student on numerous courses and as a student and director on many staff rides. His time in command of a brigade was extremely brief, and it cannot be argued that profound and far-reaching effects resulted. Haig held the two divisional Aldershot Command for two years, while Gough and Allenby both commanded cavalry brigades for long periods. But the infrequency and inadequacy of field training imposed much the same limitations on them as on Monash. The day's training ended with an assault that was always successful; partial success or failure was rarely considered. Reorganisation and exploitation after an assault were textbook subjects and went largely unpractised. The Lilydale camp – and indeed almost every major tactical manoeuvre exercise in Australia between 1908 and 1914 – could be described in the same terms. In other respects too, Monash and the British generals were similarly disadvantaged. Their respective armies were far too small to permit practice in the handling of large bodies of troops, as was common in the much bigger French and German armies. As Fuller contended, manoeuvres at this level are essential, for they constitute the sole means by which a general can practise his art.

Nor was Monash's staff training grossly inferior to that of his British counterparts. He did not baulk at the administrative and logistic sides of warfare; on the contrary, he understood the mechanics of these subjects and stressed their importance. Defence schemes, railway transportation problems, planning for annual camps and the many other responsibilities of a corps, which was itself a surrogate general staff, exercised Monash constantly between 1908 and 1913. His civil profession was superimposed on the work. The planning and assembly of resources for an engineering project, its labour requirements, and the importance of remaining within time and cost estimates involved considerations similar to those of staff problems. This wide range of experience contrasted with the rigorously confined staff training in the British Army. Though more relevant courses were gradually developed, particularly after the Boer War, little importance was attached to factors such as morale, while 'individuality and imagination [were] suppressed and cleverness deemed suspect.' At Camberley, the dour approach of the Commandant between 1910 and 1913, the future Field Marshal Sir William Robertson, curbed enquiry as Wavell found to his cost when he left the bounds of minor tactics to consider the influence of politics on conflicts and the irrelevance of Britain's small wars to modern conditions.

If it is contended that against his Camberley contemporaries Monash would not have been handicapped educationally, what was it that lifted him above the ruck and with what advantage? Firstly, none of these men was Monash's intellectual equal, and, as Henderson said, 'In all ages the power of intellect has asserted itself in war.' The second distinction seems so simple as to be absurd: Monash was a citizen soldier, the others were professional. But Monash had definite thoughts on the Army as a career. Long before Liddell Hart or Dixon expressed their ideas on the subject, he advised a young militia lieutenant who was thinking of joining the permanent forces:

> I do not regard and never have regarded permanent soldiering as an attractive proposition for any man who has some other profession at his command. In plain language, if a man could command an income no larger in private practice than he could in military employment, I would recommend him to stick to private practice every time. There is something about permanent military occupation which seems to confine a man's scope and limit his opportunities, and after he has a few years under the circumscribed conditions of official routine, he generally finds himself wholly out of touch with civil occupation.

The majority of regular soldiers were no different to those government engineers whose mental sterility Monash attributed to

CHAPTER 2

the absence of the stimuli offered by private employment. Most of their service was in peacetime, when soldiering was – and is – a sheltered occupation, with the exacting test of competition absent. But Monash and Currie had to survive in a fiercely competitive environment, gaining 'constant practice at conflict and unceasing experience of its psychological conditions.' Though he worked hard as Director of Military Training and then Director of Staff Duties, Haig never faced, nor surmounted, the tremendous obstacles that confronted Monash in his civil career. Haig's routine at Aldershot in the two years before 1914 contrasted markedly with Monash's in the same period:

> The days passed evenly. The early hours of the morning he spent on horseback, supervising the training of the units under his command; when the inspection was over he would indulge in a sharp gallop across country … At eleven o'clock he reached his office at Army Headquarters and worked there until lunch time. From lunch to tea was play time – either golf or tennis … or sometimes he preferred the role of onlooker and watched the games of some section of his command. After tea two hours were devoted to reading and this brought the day to a close.

The alliance of a powerful intellect unfettered by convention and the hardening effect of civil experience was among the most important of the many factors in the development of Monash as a commander. It governed his approach to the military problems he faced, and conferred on him the greatest advantage over his contemporaries, who had difficulty adapting to the conditions of modern, high intensity warfare. Even after extensive analysis of the humiliation of the Boer War, they missed the main tactical lesson: 'the smokeless, long range, high velocity small bore magazine bullet from rifle or machine gun – plus the trench – had decisively tilted the balance against the attack and in favour of defence.' From this time on, battles could no longer be won merely by massing superior numbers at the right place. When war came, the real test of commanders would be how quickly they divested themselves of pre-war doctrine or modified it according to the situation faced.

As for Monash's pre-war military career, it was an excellent foundation for, and more than a useful contribution towards, his execution of higher command in 1918. But it could not prepare him adequately for the tactical situations demanding instant action that he faced as a brigade commander on Gallipoli. It is also true that Monash lacked extensive practical experience in the handling of infantry. These were limitations imposed by the inevitable deficiencies of a training scheme in its infancy and shared by all his Australian colleagues: 'few had handled even a brigade for more than a day or two at annual camps and this was just as true of regulars like Chauvel as it was of militiamen like Monash.' Even by this standard, his command of the 13th Brigade and his continuous assessment at camps of brigade commanders over five years in the AIC gave Monash a better start than most.

Chapter 3
The Best Australian Brigade in Egypt

When the assassin's shots rang out at Sarajevo, Monash was forty-nine. His short stature – he was only 5 feet 8¾ inches tall – drew attention to his weight, about fifteen stone, giving him a decidedly corpulent, almost ponderous and certainly unsoldierly appearance. His face suggested 'both strength and sensitivity. He had a prominent Jewish nose and his limpid brown eyes, watchful and intelligent, were his most unforgettable physical feature.' His hands were highly expressive, adding another dimension to a voice usually quiet and contained. When in conversation, or just listening, he had a peculiar way of standing with his chin thrust forward and his head hunched.

Monash's wartime career began inauspiciously, with his appointment on 17 August 1914 to succeed McCay as Deputy Chief Censor in the Department of the CGS. He was now responsible for the organisation and administration of the cable and newspaper censorship services of the six states and cipher communications with the War Office. Although censorship orders had been prepared by Bridges six years previously, Monash was soon confronted by a host of difficulties unforeseen before the outbreak of war. There was the unpleasant task of interning a number of German academics whom he had invited to Australia as guests of the Association for the Advancement of Science. War Office insistence on the rigid application of censorship procedures had to be balanced against the clamour of a population resentful at the lack of authentic news. Among the principal factors contributing to public frustration was the absence of uniformity in the judgements of the various censorship stations as items suppressed in one district appeared in a newspaper in another. Monash drafted regulations to ensure consistency, but they did not solve the problem: 'even if already published, objectionable matter should not be repeated.' As in McCay's case, Monash's term as Deputy Chief Censor was brief. On 15 September 1914 he was named to command the 4th Infantry Brigade, AIF.

Monash did not initially volunteer for active service. His business and public interests figured prominently as he stated his position to the Director of Military Operations, Major Edgar Reynolds, on 10 September:

> These large interests would be so much affected by my withdrawal that I do not feel justified in gratifying my personal impulse to volunteer for service; or to urge my claims for selection in competition with other men equally suitable.
>
> At the same time my services are at the unreserved disposal of the Government; and if in the light of what I have stated above, the authorities consider me qualified for so great a responsibility and that it is in the best interests of the community that I should take up this task, I am entirely ready to do so without any qualification.

In response to a request by Legge, now CGS, the District Commandants had already submitted their recommendations for the command of the 4th Brigade and the unit to be raised with it, the 2nd Light Horse Brigade. Because Monash's position was unclear, the Victorian Commandant proposed Colonel Richard Linton, then commanding the 18th Infantry Brigade. Reynolds' opinion was unfavourable. He sent Legge a copy of Monash's note, but cautioned the CGS: 'You may possibly think it inadvisable to send him at this juncture.' Legge finally recommended either Monash or the less preferable Colonel G.R. Campbell for the command of the 4th Brigade. At fifty-six, Campbell was even older than Monash, and his nomination by Legge represented one of the serious problems faced by the AIF in the first year of the war: the appointment to brigades of men who were simply too old for the rigours of command at that level. In one of his last acts before relinquishing his portfolio to George Foster Pearce, the Defence Minister, Edward Millen, approved Monash's appointment.

CHAPTER 3

Major General James Gordon Legge. He had just taken over as CGS in Australia when war came. Though Legge recommended Monash to command the 4th Brigade, Monash soon crossed swords with him over officer appointments. Intelligent but argumentative, Legge performed indifferently as commander of the 2nd Division at Pozières in 1916 (AWM A03754).

A sordid whispering campaign against Monash began, alleging that, because of his Prussian-Polish parentage, his sympathies lay with Germany. Pearce declared himself quite satisfied with Monash's loyalty, whereupon anonymous letters condemning the Defence Minister appeared in the press. Only when he challenged these muckrakers to reveal themselves did the campaign subside. Pearce commented later: 'If I had listened to gossip and slander as I was urged to do, Monash would never have gone to the War.' Monash's own belief in the Allied cause was uncompromising, as he wrote to his American cousin:

> It may cause you and your people surprise that I should take up arms in this quarrel, but then, you must not fail to remember that I am Australian born, as is my wife and daughter, that my whole interests and sympathies are British, and that Australia is very vitally and very effectually concerned in this horrible war and that every man who can, and is able to do so, must do his best for his country.

The recipient of this letter, Gustav Monasch, had retained the Germanic spelling of the family name, and while understanding fully the reasons for Monash's decision, regretted that their views were so divergent: 'our sympathies are naturally with Germany in the struggle.' Congratulating Monash on his later achievements, Gustav's brother, Leo, explained further that their loyalties 'as developed from our early associations and upbringing, and from all the facts and logic of the German cause itself, are strongly pro-German.'

As Australia's Defence Act restricted the Army to home defence, a new force, the AIF, had to be raised for overseas service when war came. Beginning with Bean, historians have waxed lyrical at the brisk efficiency surrounding the formation of its first contingent. Comprising the 1st Division and the 1st Light Horse Brigade, it was largely the child of Bridges and White, who overcame every obstacle by a combination of initiative and sheer driving energy.[11] Bridges was appointed to command the division, choosing White as his chief of staff and Colonels Henry MacLaurin, McCay and Sinclair-MacLagan to command the 1st, 2nd and 3rd infantry brigades, respectively. For his own staff, Bridges 'picked the eyes of Australia ruthlessly'. Five were graduates of Camberley or Quetta, and before the end of the war eleven of its original members were generals. The formations were recruited on a territorial basis, a system retained until the Armistice and the strongest factor making for *esprit de corps* in the AIF. Enlistment was voluntary and began on 10 August. Within six weeks 20 000 men were clothed, equipped and partially trained. By any standard it was a remarkable achievement.

CHAPTER 3

However, the attention concentrated on Bridges' force has obscured the difficulties that befell the second contingent. As the commander of its largest formation, Monash was at a disadvantage from the start. Militia service, no matter how long or distinguished, could never generate the weighty influence wielded by Bridges to get his way on most important issues. Moreover, Bridges was often unable to see beyond the needs of his own force, even though it seems he was one of the few who realised that it represented only the first instalment of the formations likely to be sent. If that is true, his action of stripping the Australian Army of its most capable officers bordered on the irresponsible. It deprived units raised subsequently of experienced cadre and necessitated the recall of officers already retired for health and other reasons. Bridges allowed commanders at every level to select their own subordinates, but after allegations that they were chosen by 'a coterie of the Australian Club in Sydney', the job was transferred to selection committees, each comprising the District Commandant and three senior officers. The formation of the 4th Brigade was seriously handicapped by this arrangement.

Monash described the raising of the 4th as 'an enormous and soul-racking undertaking'. Throughout the war it was the only infantry brigade recruited from all six states, but in September 1914 Monash rued the problems posed by its diverse origins. Having already experienced with the 13th Brigade the difficulties of creating solidarity in scattered units concentrated for the first time, he recommended to Legge the assembly of the formation in Melbourne for collective training before departure. Secondly, he sought the appointment of a permanent officer as brigade major and, in each battalion, as second-in-command or adjutant, to assist commanding officers in the organisation of their units and in the instruction of subordinate leaders. Because the 4th Brigade was likely to contain a smaller percentage of experienced officers and NCOs than its predecessors, the burden on these men would be intolerable unless additional staff were provided. So Monash also asked for sixteen permanent NCOs to fill certain specialist positions in each battalion. The total permanent staff requested, twenty-one, was insignificant in a brigade of 4 100 and certainly represented far less in proportion than the number taken by Bridges.[12]

The results were mixed. By 1 October ministerial approval had been given for the concentration of the brigade in Melbourne for three weeks' training before embarkation. Monash received a nasty shock three days later when Bruche informed him that Legge had arranged otherwise, but fortunately the rumour proved untrue. Monash and Bruche, the AAG of the Queensland Military District, perceived Legge as a highly strung obstructionist, creating repeated difficulties where none should exist. Alluding to the CGS, Monash wrote: 'People who live in [the] big stone building on St Kilda Road seem to spend their time in spragging other people's wheels.' Conversely, Monash and Bruche admired each other. Long before the war, Bruche had said Monash was the only militia brigadier under whom he would serve. Now he acted as Monash's confidante, reassuring him when he was assailed by doubt and offering sensible advice to ease his difficulties.

Monash's second recommendation, the inclusion of permanent staff, was only one aspect of the wider issue of officer selection, which quickly gave rise to needless annoyance. Again the culprit was Legge. The CGS seemed to think 'an invasion of Australia is imminent, and that therefore, no man who is any good at all should be allowed to leave Australia. He is even talking of filling my ranks of officers by promotion from the ranks.' Legge's attitude prevented Bruche's appointment as Monash's brigade major, leaving him as the only commander in either contingent whose chief staff officer was a citizen soldier – Lieutenant Colonel John McGlinn. He came strongly recommended and Monash had formed a high opinion of his capacity and enthusiasm within a few days of their meeting. Perhaps because they were both militia officers and engineers, Monash and McGlinn became close friends and constituted what was probably the outstanding brigadier-brigade major combination in the AIF until its reorganisation in 1916. For his staff captain, Monash secured a permanent officer, Captain Carl Jess, whose ability had impressed him before the war. Anxious to remove any doubts on Jess's part, Monash spoke to him in a frank and personal manner despite their

CHAPTER 3

substantial difference in rank: 'Now I hope for your sake as well as my own, that you will be glad to come with me ... I think we know each other sufficiently that I may say that we are certain to work well together.' Monash was now circumventing Legge by taking advantage of Pearce's decision to allow one permanent officer and four NCOs in each battalion, provided no qualified militia personnel were available. He wanted every opportunity to be taken to 'persuade' the responsible authorities that suitable militiamen simply could not be found. By the end of October permanent officers had been named as adjutants of the 13th, 15th and 16th battalions.

Soon after his own appointment, Monash began the selection of his battalion commanders. They would then nominate their own subordinates. Monash's instructions were explicit. Officers should be allocated to those duties for which they were best fitted by reason of knowledge, temperament or previous training. Specialists in excess of establishment were to be recommended as company officers. In this way, if one battalion could not provide a machine-gun officer, for example, its deficiency could be met by transfer from another. The most important requirement was left until last:

> More will depend upon the judicious selection of officers than upon any other factor. Therefore, while not an unnecessary moment is to be lost, sufficient time is to be taken over this task to ensure that recommendations shall be the very best under the circumstances.

The work was well advanced when Monash was told on 20 September that, henceforth, the District Selection Committees would be responsible for all commissioned appointments in the AIF. His nominations were now subject to their approval. As McGlinn bitterly remarked, he was being penalised for 'the questionable judgement displayed by others'. Monash protested angrily to the Secretary of Defence, Samuel Pethebridge, that it was a humiliating insult that he, the officer 'most vitally concerned, and directly responsible to the Government for the honour and lives of the men of the brigade', was not to be consulted, while a board of officers, all junior to himself, should be vested with powers of selection for which they would not have to answer subsequently. He was eventually informed that the Committee's recommendations would be referred to him for veto or approval. Similarly, his battalion commanders could reject nominees they regarded as unsatisfactory, Monash readily endorsing their decisions because he was determined that no unwanted man should be forced upon them. Nevertheless, the board system imposed delay and Monash watched its work with bemused resignation:

> It is the slowest job I have ever struck in my life. If they had left it to me, with the action I took the day after my appointment, and with the help of men like yourself [i.e. Bruche] ... I would have had a satisfactory selection of officers made throughout the Commonwealth inside of a week. However, I am now just sitting back and waiting for things to happen, being assured that the logic of events will make most things work out the way I want.

Although the battle over officer selection showed Monash at his best, he lacked at first the self-assurance expected in a man who had enjoyed a brief but successful term as a militia brigade commander. His doubts were only temporary:

> I started this job very much overwhelmed with the sense of responsibility, but, now that I have got well into the work and done a lot of thinking ahead, and have moreover had repeated opportunities of observing how not to do things [in McCay's brigade at Broadmeadows], I am rapidly gaining not merely confidence, but a considerable measure of enthusiasm and pleasure in the anticipation of a good measure of success.

Elementary training began, mainly bayonet fighting and muscle-toughening exercises, semaphore, field work, drill and musketry. On 20 October the 14th Battalion was cheered by large crowds as it marched through Melbourne on a twenty-mile endurance test. The 15th Battalion, 85 per cent of which had had no previous military training, completed a similar march in a temperature of 92° F (33° C) at Enoggera in Brisbane with very few men falling out. The stamp of Monash's authority was everywhere. He devised a scheme using flags to denote the effects of defensive fire during exercises, and asked the 14th Battalion to test a method of company attack training suggested in a recent military journal, so that he could assess its potential for employment throughout the brigade. Units were to move to and from training areas in formations based on a definite tactical picture and appropriate to the terrain. On 6 November Monash inspected the 13th Battalion in Sydney and was 'well pleased with the personnel enlisted there and their state of training.' However, he had noticed in both the 13th and 14th battalions unshaven and long-haired men parading in badly soiled jackets. Commanding officers were to ensure that such lapses did not recur. Monash was intolerant of slovenliness, insisting on strict attention to dress and bearing as a means of inculcating the discipline essential in a fighting unit.

At the end of November, the 4th Brigade was concentrated at Broadmeadows camp, some ten miles from Melbourne. The units from other states were depressed at the conditions they found. Private Rupert Nixon wrote: 'this is the dirtiest place I have ever seen as there is not a blade of grass here and when it rains it is a perfect pigsty and the mud is up to the knees.' No tents had been erected, nor latrines or showers provided. On 1 December troops returned after a long march to find no water available for washing or cooking. Cases of lice infestation were starting to appear. After the failure of repeated representations on these matters to the Camp Commandant, Monash approached District Headquarters directly. Until the situation was rectified, he declined to accept responsibility for the health of his men or any outbreaks of discontent. The only compensations were the accessibility of Melbourne for those with leave and the Sunday visiting days when the public inundated the camp. Training was guided by White's syllabus for the first contingent. The elementary work done before concentration was repeated with greater emphasis on infantry skills such as field fortification, musketry, formations under fire and night operations. Officers and NCOs received additional instruction in map-reading and staff duties. Basic collective training at company and battalion level was introduced by demonstrating each exercise and then repeating it with troops.

A comparison of Monash's training of the 13th and 4th brigades yields common principles reflected in identical methods. The notes for his conference with battalion commanders on 28 November had a familiar ring. Officers were to have 'an absolute hold' on their men, making stern examples of those who misbehaved publicly. He would not 'adopt the rule of explaining orders. Hence unquestioned obedience once orders given.' These thoughts were among those expressed in his pamphlet *100 Hints for Company Officers*, originally prepared for the 13th Brigade and now issued to all officers and sergeants in the 4th 'to create a uniform spirit, and to ensure a satisfactory morale.' As A.J. Smithers says, it contained no revolutionary aphorisms. But it was a codification of every aspect of the philosophy Monash had developed in his military career so far. One point was of particular relevance to himself as commander of the 4th Brigade on Gallipoli or of the Australian Corps in France. No doubt recalling his remarks to his officers in the AIC, Monash wrote:

> The power of imagination is a most valuable faculty for an officer ... It means the capacity of rapidly constructing a definite mental picture of an event, situation or locality, the description of which is being heard or read.

The officer's duty to his men was stressed. He must put their needs for rest, food and hygiene before his own, and his constant thought must be 'the preservation of the soldiers' fighting spirit and physical condition.' Inefficiency usually resulted from lax supervision or poor instructions by a commander. However:

> Never interfere with the performance of any duty for which a subordinate is responsible, unless his performance of it is incorrect. If you do the responsibility becomes yours and you are checking the initiative of the subordinate, and his desire to bear responsibility.

Commanders must always be optimistic, even in the worst situations: 'A regiment is doomed when the men hear the officers complaining.' On that most vexed question concerning Australian soldiers in the First World War:

> Discipline which is obtained by punishment cannot be compared with that of a force animated by the honour of the regiment, confidence in their officers and comrades, and the knowledge

CHAPTER 3

that in their spirit, equipment and training, they are equal, if not superior, to any force they may meet in battle.

Recoiling from the immature attitudes held by his contemporaries, Monash was emphatic that 'Courage is not synonymous with reckless exposure to danger.' Several episodes on Gallipoli soon proved him correct. But the truth of the corollary was repeatedly demonstrated throughout the war:

> ... on service, in action, in trenches, or in stress, the presence of the officers is a great factor in keeping up the men's spirits, when they see that their officers are no better off than themselves, but are still cheerful, energetic and sanguine of success.

In each of his commands, Monash's men rarely saw him under these conditions. This departure from his own creed would become the most telling and enduring criticism of his performance at all levels.

At the end of its three weeks' training in Australia, the efficiency of the 4th Brigade was about the same as that of the 13th Brigade after Lilydale. The only brigade exercise was held on 15 December, when the 14th and 15th battalions opposed the advance on Melbourne of the 13th and 16th. Monash strove for realism, supplementing each force with a half squadron of light horse and allocating half the ammunition to the regimental transport so that resupply could be practised. His criticisms were identical with those he made on similar exercises before the war: continual stoppages by the leading unit, indifferent reconnaissance, prolixity in messages and poor communications. On the first occasion that a brigade, with all its first line transport, marched through an Australian city, Monash led the 4th in a farewell march through Melbourne on 17 December 1914. It was also an important training exercise, as he tested the endurance and march discipline of his men. In his planning notes, Monash calculated the length of the brigade as 2¼ miles, and that it would take 40 minutes to pass a single point on the 22¼-mile route. On 22 December the battalions passed through the gates of Broadmeadows for the last time. Heavy rain during the previous night had reduced the camp to a quagmire and many men's uniforms still bore traces of the 'singularly tenacious' Broadmeadows mud as far away as Egypt and Anzac. After watching them embark, the Governor-General, Sir Ronald Munro Ferguson, informed Sir Ian Hamilton: 'they looked more like veterans, being older men, than new levies ... Colonel Monash of this last Brigade is an able Jew, and was press censor.'

By this time the first contingent had begun its final training in desert camps in Egypt, forming with the New Zealand contingent the Australian and New Zealand Army Corps (ANZAC) under the command of a cavalry officer from the Indian Army, Lieutenant General Sir William Birdwood. According to the organisation he proposed, the ANZAC would consist of a mounted division and two infantry divisions, the 1st Australian Division and the '2nd'or New Zealand Division, the latter comprising the New Zealand Infantry Brigade and the 4th Australian Infantry Brigade and a further brigade if available. As this was by no means assured, the 1st Australian Light Horse Brigade and the New Zealand Mounted Rifles Brigade, originally intended to form half of the mounted division, took the place of the third infantry brigade in the newly named New Zealand and Australian (NZ and A) Division. It was led by the unpopular commander of the New Zealand Expeditionary Force, Major General Alexander Godley, a British mounted infantry officer, and staffed by officers he had brought from New Zealand. Monash, who would be associated more with Godley than any senior officer during the war, was then beginning the voyage that was the start of a five-year absence from Australia.

Appointed Senior Military Officer of the Second Australian Convoy, Monash sailed in the flagship *Ulysses*, one of the sixteen vessels that transported the 10 500 troops of the second contingent. They were joined by three more transports, bringing 2000 troops from New Zealand, at Albany, the port of assembly. There Monash complained bitterly to Legge and Lieutenant Colonel Thomas Dodds, the Adjutant-General, about the lamentable arrangements for the voyage and, in consequence, the grave difficulties he was struggling to overcome. The Military Board orders for the convoy arrived half an hour before sailing. No agreement had been reached with the Navy on inter-ship communication and, once at sea, signals were restricted

CHAPTER 3

to urgent naval matters, so that 'though the ships are all in sight, we are as much cut off from them as if we are a thousand miles apart.' At Albany, rough waters impeded despatch boats, which required a whole day merely to distribute the orders received by Monash in Melbourne. The convoy's second senior officer, Colonel Granville Ryrie, commander of the 2nd Light Horse Brigade, interfered with his arrangements for the use of the boats and joined several others who went ashore without leave. 'Their example', Monash wrote bluntly, 'distinctly added to my difficulties and contributed to the chaos.' The convoy's arrival had brought a flood of complaints from every ship, and these revealed just how widespread this chaos was. Some vessels had leaking pipes or toilets that did not flush. Essential medical stores were either inadequate or missing altogether. Many men were allocated to the wrong ships, their whereabouts unknown to their commanders, as a result of the secrecy with which staff officers had approached the embarkation.

A big man. Monash flanked by his wife and daughter on the wharf before leaving Australia in December 1914. The other officer is Captain Carl Jess, Monash's staff captain. In May 1915, Jess was promoted major and went to the 2nd Brigade as its brigade major (AWM PB1076).

MONASH

After leaving Albany at the end of December 1914, the 4th Brigade settled into a routine that continued for the remainder of the voyage. Training of the rank and file concentrated on musketry and theoretical work in minor tactics. NCOs received more advanced instruction during evening lectures. Monash concentrated on the training of officers, ordering the establishment of schools on each transport, 'to be regularly attended by all officers of the brigade.' He gave two lectures on reconnaissance, of which Captain William Forsythe, a company commander in the 13th Battalion wrote: 'I have never in my twenty years experience met an officer who could lecture as effectively as he. It was a distinct pleasure to listen to him.' He also chaired evening discussions on topics as diverse as the use of mounted troops with flank guards to the signing of a charge sheet. Monash was well satisfied with these schools for 'the keenest interest has been manifested which cannot but have a very beneficial result.' His remaining time was fully occupied. On 5 January he had begun a 'systematic perusal of textbooks', which included the first reports by British officers of fighting on the Western Front. Dressed in deck shoes, KD slacks and a 'comfy' lightweight shirt, he observed the numerous activities aboard *Ulysses* and was particularly interested in the wrestling and blindfold boxing bouts organised to relieve the tedium of shipboard life for the men. Unable to see, each pugilist relied on instructions from a mate. During one contest, Monash was standing very close to the proceedings when a mischievous wag yelled, 'One yard front. Low!', and the commander of the 4th Brigade was ignominiously felled by a punch to the stomach.[13] But the most curious aspect of the voyage was Monash's obsession with his health. Each vaccination and its effects were carefully noted and he developed a nervous fear of falling overboard – 'probably due to slight gastric trouble'.

When the convoy reached Colombo on 13 January 1915, all leave was prohibited. Next morning 210 men slipped ashore by climbing down the anchor chains to a large number of native boats. Ashore himself, Monash signalled *Ulysses* for a strong guard, and by daybreak on the 15th all but twenty men had been apprehended. The incident was magnified out of all proportion by the fantastic allegations of

CHAPTER 3

the GOC Colombo, Brigadier General Henry Malcolm, whose report described lurid scenes of drunkenness, wild brawling and violence towards officers. Monash vigorously denied Malcolm's accusations. The troublemakers represented only 1½ per cent of the total number of troops in the convoy and came mainly from the two ships carrying reinforcements for Bridges' force. They had embarked in Melbourne with a grossly inadequate proportion of officers and NCOs, and hence were much more difficult to control during a long voyage. Monash recommended the staffing of future reinforcements according to the normal organisation of platoons and companies. Once again, the consequences of oversights in the preparation of the first contingent had befallen the commander of the second.

Monash (right) and Lieutenant Colonel Granville Burnage, commander of the 13th Battalion, aboard HMT *Ulysses* in January 1915. At 56, Burnage was the oldest of Monash's battalion commanders, but proved a vigorous leader. He was invalided home after being wounded at Anzac in May (AWM A01224).

On 29 January 1915 the convoy entered the Suez Canal amid scenes that Monash described as 'a revelation of Empire': the British and French navies guarding the approaches and a 'continuous storm of cheers' from the Gurkha, French, Indian and British soldiers defending its shores. On the 31st *Ulysses* docked at Alexandria, and next day the first units of the 4th Brigade arrived in Cairo, from which, led by the bands of the New Zealand Infantry Brigade, they marched five miles to Aerodrome camp on the outskirts of Heliopolis. Whereas expanses of bare desert greeted most of the first contingent, Aerodrome had already been established by the New Zealanders, one of the measures taken by Godley to ensure that his combined division began well. The 1st Division was at Mena Camp, twelve miles away. Two days later the Turks began an attack on the canal, which was easily defeated. Their magnificent feat of crossing the Sinai by a route never before attempted was totally ignored in the derisory dismissal of their fighting qualities that followed. A.J. Smithers remarks: 'This splendid euphoria was paid for at a very heavy price before the year was out.'

On his first night in Cairo Monash dined with Birdwood: 'a fine dapper little chap, with whom I shall get on very well.' Godley was delighted that 'such a fine brigade of Australians, as I hear they are, should be placed under my command.' But Monash was depressed. He had been 'horribly homesick' in the last days of the voyage, as the realisation set in of 'what a rooting up of everything in which I have any interest this business has been.' From news gathered in Colombo, he guessed that the Australians would be used to garrison Egypt and might possibly remain there until the end of the war, a heartbreaking prospect, especially as 'we have not even the consolation of knowing whether the sacrifice we are making is going to end in the right way.' Nor was Monash's discomfort relieved by Egypt itself: 'Everything is dirty, squalid, smelly and repugnant to any refined sense ... no theatres, no opera, no gaiety ... Only a sullen, scowling French and Egyptian tradesman population', and the climate was 'horrible'.

While the novelties of Egypt – the Pyramids, the mosques and the museums – had quickly worn off for most Australians, the dubious attractions of Cairo seemed irresistible to them. Descending on the city night after night, they did not let behavioural norms interfere with a good time. Much of their unruliness could be attributed to high spirits, but by the end of 1914 the preservation of discipline in the AIF was seriously threatened. Birdwood asked Bridges to appeal to all not to disgrace Australia. Humiliated by the rebuke,

CHAPTER 3

Bridges immediately instituted a series of strong measures, the most drastic of which was the return home in disgrace of a large number of disciplinary and venereal cases. By 1 February, the combined effect of these measures and an exhausting training program had restored peace to Cairo.[14] As if he expected a resurgence, Godley told Monash: 'It would be a great feather in the cap of your brigade if their advent made no difference to the orderliness which now reigns ...' Much of the blame for the trouble devolved onto Bridges, who had next to no experience of command, having spent his career mainly in staff and instructional appointments. The remoteness he had shown on the voyage was even more marked in Egypt, as he ignored the need for recreational outlets for troops isolated in a desert camp without a single amusement. The more experienced Godley did not make the same mistake and the problem in the NZ and A Division was nowhere near as great, although it was blessed by better training areas.

Lieutenant General Sir William Birdwood aboard HMS *Cornwallis*. His indifference to danger and informality made him popular with the Australians, whose affection he reciprocated. But Birdwood was no tactician and often failed to grasp the big picture (AWM H10400).

MONASH

The 4th Brigade's lines at Heliopolis in early 1915 (AWM C02600).

Monash's diary records few meetings with Bridges, which was probably just as well, for basic differences quickly rose between them. Monash felt that his brigade was not subject to Bridges' authority. Where Bridges had been nominated by an Order-in-Council to 'raise, organise, equip and command' the first contingent without reference to the Military Board, that body discharged all of these functions with respect to the 4th Brigade except that of command, which was, of course, entrusted to Monash himself. In no sense whatsoever did he come under Bridges:

> I was indeed frequently told by Legge, Dodds and other members of the Board that I must take no notice of the orders of the GOC Division, or his decisions, and that my only source of authority was the Board through its Military Orders.

Just before embarkation in Australia, such an order placed the second contingent at the disposal of the War Office and subject to the authority of a GOC Imperial Force. On arrival in Egypt, Monash insisted: 'the GOC of the Division to which Imperial Authority has allotted us should be the only source of inspiration, authority and control in every department.' That was not Bridges, but Godley.

CHAPTER 3

Bridges was infuriated. Both men were partially correct. Bridges had no jurisdiction over Australian units in Godley's division in command issues, although he was ultimately responsible for their administration under the powers granted him as GOC AIF in September 1914. But Bridges was determined to shed the administrative burden, fearing that he might become enmeshed in its work at the expense of command. Thus he attempted to foist promotions outside his division onto Birdwood and dismissed the importance of the administrative centre, the Australian Intermediate Base, ignoring its problems and lumbering it with officers he thought unsatisfactory.

The 4th Brigade began the final phase of its training on 2 February 1915. Monash's ambitions for his formation depended largely on the creation and maintenance of a strong identity within it. From the outset he preached the doctrine: 'my best weapon was not the powers of discipline which I could wield, but the healthy public spirit of the men themselves, who would not allow a slacker to live among them.' Concerned that the 4th Brigade should not suffer in any comparison with the first contingent, which had been in Egypt for some weeks, he appealed to all ranks to strive harder to compensate for their late arrival, thereby furthering 'the efficiency and prestige of the brigade'. The competitive aspect was a recurring theme throughout the training, Monash frequently writing that the brigade had done 'splendidly', or that he, personally, had made a creditable showing. After a divisional advance on Cairo on 15 February, Godley told Monash that he and Birdwood had been watching the 4th for the past ten days and 'we have quite made up our minds that it is the best Australian brigade in Egypt.'

Though his opinion would soon change, Monash was initially impressed with Godley and pleased to be in his division. He was 'tall, elegant, graceful, genial and expansive. His strength lies rather in his magnetic and stimulating personality than in high technical ability but he has the habit of carrying everybody with him.' Godley watched closely every aspect of the training of the 4th Brigade, fulfilling his assurance to Pearce to do all he could for it. He wanted to know why battalions were not played to and from training by their bands;

on another occasion Monash promised him that 'nails in boots will receive immediate attention'. Monash accepted his suggestion that each battalion form its instructors into a company to be trained in what they themselves would later teach others. Godley insisted that routine administration should take second place to field training, once chiding Monash whom he felt had failed to understand the priority. Monash demurred: 'it really seems a counsel of perfection because one is confronted with difficulties all along the line.' On the day in question, divisional duties alone required ninety-six men from a single battalion. It was the first instance of a concern Monash expressed repeatedly throughout the war.

Lieutenant General Sir Alexander Godley. Having the regimental background that Bridges lacked, he was better able to maintain discipline in Egypt. As a field commander, he bungled operations on Gallipoli and relied on Monash and Russell, both able subordinates, to get by on the Western Front in 1917 (AWM P03717.003).

CHAPTER 3

A daily ritual. The 4th Brigade marches out of Heliopolis to train in the desert (AWM C02608).

Unlike Bridges' division, which never reached the stage of full-scale divisional training, the NZ and A Division began work at that level immediately after Monash's arrival. Just what did these advanced exercises comprise? On 19 February the division, with the 4th Brigade in the centre, attacked and turned the flank of a position occupied by the notional Turkish Third Army, which was 'advancing' on Cairo along the Suez Road. The scheme was intended to practise moving to a starting point from scattered billets, protection on the march and march discipline, reconnaissance, deployment on contact, the attack and the pursuit. These aims were largely the same as those set for the manoeuvres Monash had attended as an umpire in the AIC. Though his brigade performed well, mistakes were inevitable, some of them made by Monash himself. Instead of galloping ahead to a suitable position to prepare an appreciation and orders at the same time as it was marching forward to meet him, Monash halted his brigade while he did these things, and a large gap arose in the advancing column. Communications were 'indifferent': Monash received few messages from his commanding officers, and no attempt was made to run out the five miles of cable carried by the mules. He also learned the need for flexibility if maps were inaccurate. The maps did not show that the ground on his right flank was open and 'as flat as a billiard table', but his attacking formation remained unchanged even after the error was discovered. Occasionally, Monash expressed irritation if a plan went wrong or a stupid error was made. During night operations on 17/18 March, he rushed up to a company commander who had positioned his men on a skyline and abused him harshly: 'Are you a stark, raving, staring lunatic Captain – ?' Of this early stage of Monash's AIF career, Bean remarked: 'those who looked on noticed the methodical extreme thoroughness with which he worked out every detail of the activities of his brigade, and the extreme lucidity with which he could explain to his officers any plan of operations.'

In Egypt Monash was building on the foundations acquired during his pre-war militia career. His 'Draft Standing Orders' for the 4th Brigade reaffirmed Godley's emphasis on communications and efficient battle procedure, including the direction that while commanders prepared and issued orders: 'Movement of units in the direction of places of assembly or places of employment must not thereby be arrested or retarded.' He was gratified by the spirit of his command, writing after the divisional manoeuvres of 3 March: 'The punctuality, steadiness and co-operation of all ranks reflected credit upon the brigade and cannot fail to enhance its fighting value.' His staff had proved its ability, leaving him 'practically nothing to do except give orders and sit back, with the certainty that my wishes will be carried out to the letter.' Monash had grown very close to McGlinn, whose precision and capacity for work had impressed him on the voyage. The sight of these two overweight men, almost bursting out of their small open car, prompted their being named Tweedledum and Tweedledee. But Godley was pleased with Tweedledum:

> I find him a very energetic and capable commander, and believe that he will do well in the field. He is always very ready to act upon all my suggestions and orders, and is evidently keen to make the most of and do justice to, his brigade.

Birdwood was less impressed. While considering Monash 'an exceptionally able man on paper, observant – and with knowledge', he doubted whether Monash would do well as field commander as he did not cut a good figure on horseback.

CHAPTER 3

Although Monash was delighted by the rapid progress of the NZ and A Division compared to the slower, methodical approach of Bridges, he worried about the inadequate sub-unit training, which resulted from Godley's policy. Conceding 'the great education in the exercise of command' it afforded him, he did not know 'whether it is recognised to what extent the training of the junior personnel is thereby retarded and that a very rapid improvement in any shortcomings observable on manoeuvres can hardly be expected.'[15] Serious shortages further hampered individual training. The 4th Brigade had arrived in Egypt neither fully organised nor fully equipped, and its inefficient transport defied all attempts at remedy. Ammunition was strictly limited to a paltry seventy-five rounds per rifle.

For Monash personally, the most serious consequence of the period in Egypt had only the remotest relevance to matters of training. Attached to the 1st Division Headquarters at Mena was Charles Bean, the Official Australian Correspondent, who associated constantly with White, Bridges, Gellibrand, Blamey, Glasfurd and others from that formation. He was infatuated by White, who was 'the ideal staff officer. He never forgets anything ... White is a soldier above everything ... He is the only man I know to whom there is never any necessity to mention a thing twice.' Conversely, Bean's contact with the 4th Brigade was minimal. Only once did he watch the brigade training and then after difficulties in finding it that were hardly calculated to improve his mood. Hence his opinions were not coloured by friendship, as in the case of White, and, unlike White, Monash did not fit Bean's romantic notion of what a senior officer should be. Monash would inevitably suffer in any comparison of the two. Belonging to a society that was mildly anti-Semitic, Bean also counted Monash's religion against him. When Bean met the second contingent, 'Monash and McGlynn [sic] were exceedingly kind and made us stay to dinner with them.' Whether caused by that meal or not, Bean became ill. It was an omen of the strained relations that were to exist between the two men throughout the war.

MONASH

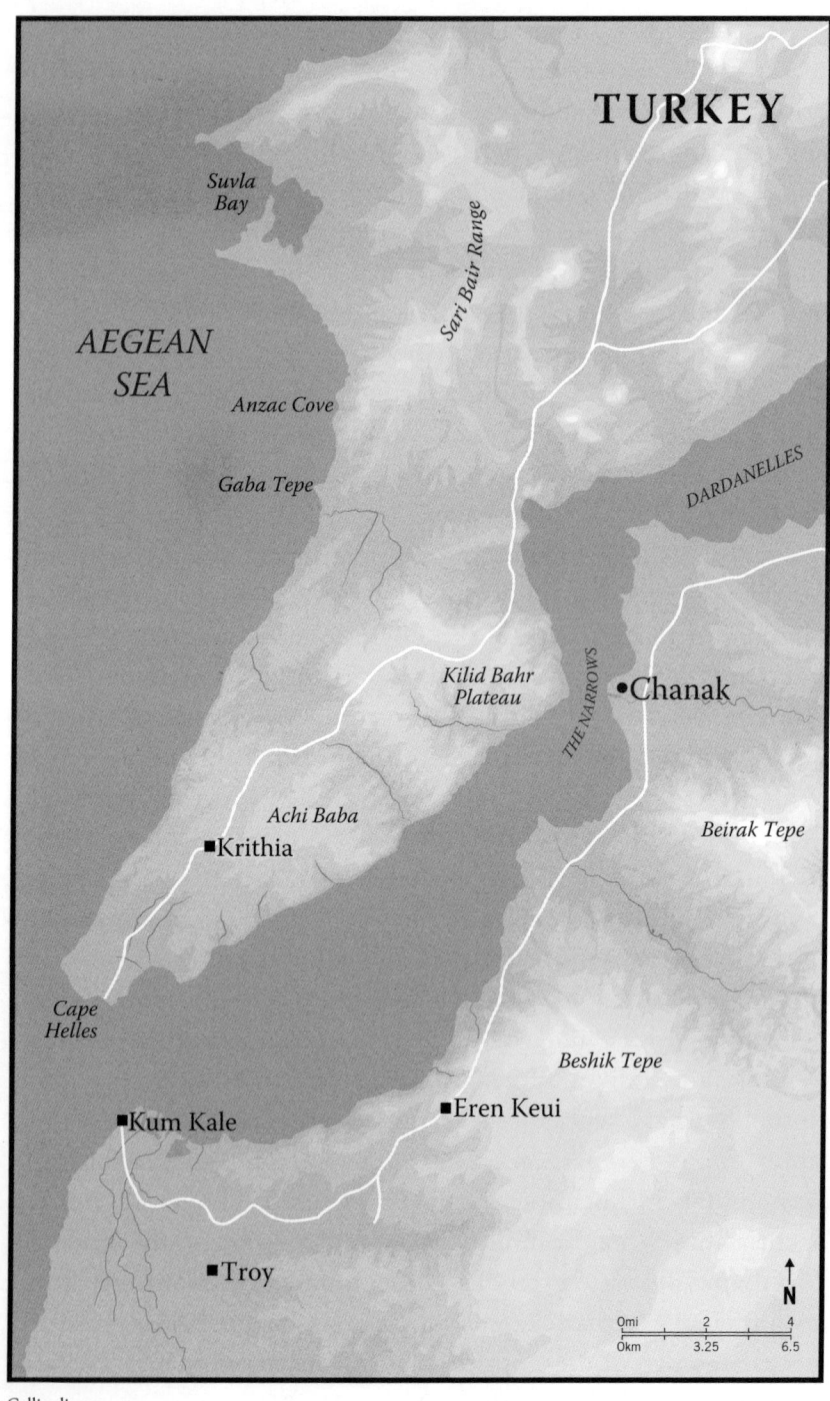

Gallipoli

CHAPTER 3

Charles Bean in a communication trench at Anzac in July 1915. Tall, gangly and bespectacled, he was nicknamed 'Captain Carrot' on account of his red hair. As Australian Official Correspondent during the war, he had an uneasy relationship with Monash; as Australian Official Historian after it, he was sparing in his praise of Monash (AWM PS1580).

Bean described the training in Egypt as 'one of the finest achievements of the AIF.' But training is not an end in itself. It has to fit the conditions expected in battle. The training of both divisions was based on British experience in South Africa and differed little, except in scale and level of skill, to the manoeuvres on pre-war camps of continuous training in Australia. There was certainly no proper preparation for undertaking operations in the intended theatre, the Western Front, which Bridges was extremely anxious to reach even after the true destination of the ANZAC was revealed. As the notes received by Monash before embarkation and during the voyage show, it is fallacious to argue that no advice came from that theatre. In Egypt more comprehensive information was available on artillery/infantry cooperation and the growing importance of artillery itself, a sure sign of the direction taken by operations in France and Belgium. None of this was reflected in the training programs in Egypt. Only one substantial exercise in constructing field fortifications was carried out by the 4th Brigade, each company building a trench system capable of accommodating a hundred men. But no thought was given to living in and fighting from those trenches.

The baptism of fire of the ANZAC was not to be on the Western Front, but on the Gallipoli Peninsula, after the failure of attempts to force the Dardanelles Straits by sea power alone. With a French corps and the British 29th and Royal Naval divisions, it formed part of the Mediterranean Expeditionary Force (MEF). Commanded by Sir Ian Hamilton, the MEF would reduce the Turkish defences commanding the Straits, allowing the fleet unimpeded passage to Constantinople and, hopefully, resulting in Turkey's surrender. After landing on the toe of the peninsula at Cape Helles, Major General Sir Aylmer Hunter-Weston's 29th Division was to advance five miles inland to seize the Achi Baba Ridge by nightfall on the first day. Supporting the main operation, the ANZAC would capture the high backbone of the peninsula, directly opposite The Narrows, to cut the Turkish lines of communication to Helles thirteen miles further south. Feints were planned for the French at Kum Kale and the Royal Naval Division at Bulair. There were no reserves to speak of as Hamilton was committing virtually his entire force in the hope of fooling the Turks as to where the main blow would fall. From his departure from London on 13 March to the first landings was forty-three days. The planning of the Normandy invasion took over a year.

Birdwood's corps was to land between the Gaba Tepe promontory and a point about three miles to its north, known as the Fisherman's Hut. Immediately behind Gaba Tepe was a flat saddle, which continued to The Narrows four miles away. It was bounded to the south and north respectively by the heavily fortified Kilid Bahr plateau and by the Sari Bair range, whose three summits – Chunuk Bair, Q and the highest, Koja Chemen Tepe, or Hill 971 – crowned the most rugged terrain on the peninsula. Birdwood was instructed to seize the inland spur of Hill 971, especially Mal Tepe, the cone-

CHAPTER 3

shaped feature at its end. The Maidos–Gallipoli road, running over the foot of Mal Tepe and vital to the Turkish forces at Helles and on Kilid Bahr, would then be severed. Hamilton suggested that a covering force of one brigade should first capture the main ridge about Chunuk Bair. Birdwood agreed, and the 3rd Brigade was given the task, largely because of Bridges' faith in Sinclair-MacLagan, its commander.[16] McCay's brigade would then extend the left flank past Chunuk Bair to Hill 971, with the 1st Brigade remaining in reserve. Coming ashore after Bridges' division, the NZ and A Division was – if all went well – to push inland through it to Mal Tepe. Colonel Francis Johnston's New Zealand Infantry Brigade would disembark first, followed by the 4th Brigade.

Major General Ewen Sinclair-MacLagan. A British officer and a natural pessimist, he gave way to his fears as a brigade commander at the landing and wrecked any chance of the ANZAC reaching its objectives. As a divisional commander on the Western Front, he was solid rather than brilliant (AWM A03064).

Yet the training of the corps was as unsuited to its task on the peninsula as it was to operations on the Western Front. The seizure and holding of the Sari Bair range and Mal Tepe entailed the establishment of strong fortifications and the conduct of defensive operations that could be prolonged. Moreover, the intricate terrain made any defensive battle in the area a more daunting prospect than on the Western Front. In sum, then, the ANZAC was trained for the very antithesis of the type of warfare that would prevail. Excessive concentration on the Anzac myth, based on the spirit and dash of the Australian soldier from the landing onwards, has tended to obscure this vital fact. Though there were some misgivings at the time, they were engulfed by the 'romantic sense of adventure' that pervaded the entire MEF.

From mid-March onwards, Monash was aware that departure from Egypt was imminent: 'Everything points to a direct move to the place where we shall be most wanted, and appearances indicate that that place will not be far away.' Godley's confirmatory orders arrived on 3 April. With the exception of its mounted units, the NZ and A Division was to be ready to leave Egypt at 'short notice, sailing in a convoy of fourteen vessels, six of which were allocated to the 4th Brigade.' Monash had already written a glowing report to the Governor-General on the state of his formation and its good behaviour in Egypt. The physique, endurance and morale of the men were 'beyond all praise', while their officers had learned to handle them with 'judgement and decision'. On 13 April the 4th Brigade left Alexandria for the island of Lemnos. Monash delivered a stirring exhortation:

> Now lads, you are shortly going on active service ... I told the general on your behalf you are ready to go anywhere and do anything. You may be faced with privation and hardship, sometimes hungry, often tired and miserable. That is what soldiering amounts to ... I call on you with confidence to do your level best for the sake of your manhood, for the sake of Australia and for the sake of the British Empire.

Monash arrived in Mudros Harbour, Lemnos, aboard *Seeangchoon* on 15 April. For the next week, landings from ships' boats were practised, hindered by the poor weather and lack of small craft. Rather than

CHAPTER 3

rehearsals for the coming operation, they were 'simply disembarkation practices undertaken at battalion level, generally followed by route marches.' After witnessing one of these exercises on 20 April, Monash was concerned. Some boats were sent ashore with no officers or NCOs in charge, while the move inland could be followed by the quantity of ammunition dropped by soldiers; unless checked: 'result disastrous'. The experience of the 1st Brigade during its rehearsals showed that these shortcomings were not confined to Monash's formation alone. Bean realised, possibly for the first time: 'This landing is clearly going to be a tremendously difficult thing.'

At 7.00 pm on 22 April Monash issued his first real operation order of the war. The intention: 'To land between Kaba Tepe [sic] and Fisherman's Hut immediately after the New Zealand Brigade and to concentrate brigade.' Next day he was informed that the landing would take place on 25 April. An 'irritable and cross' Godley held a final conference to discuss kit and landing arrangements on the 24th. In spite of the flurry of activity and last-minute problems demanding his attention, these few days were an intensely personal period for Monash. He was overjoyed to receive 'belated letters from Bert – these I read many times.'[17] In turn, he wrote two brief replies whose emotional impact remains undiminished more than a century later. Freely admitting the possibility of death, his one regret was the grief it would bring to his family. He himself regarded the prospect with equanimity. He had lived a 'full and active life' and at best had 'only a few years of vigour left. Then would come decay and the chill of old age and perhaps lingering illness.'

At 9.30 am on 25 April *Seeangchoon* left Lemnos for Anzac. By that time the 3rd Infantry Brigade was ashore, landed at the wrong location and engaged in confused fighting with the Turks at a place that would become known as Anzac. For Monash, the most controversial period of his wartime career was about to begin. For the rest, Hamilton's grim prophecy would come to pass:

> Death! He is fed up with the old and sick – only the flower of the flock will serve him now, for God has started a celestial spring cleaning, and our star is to be scrubbed bright with the blood of our bravest and our best.

Chapter 4
Monash Valley

The main operations at Helles failed largely because of General Hunter-Weston's concentration on the beaches where resistance was fiercest at the expense of those landings that were almost unopposed. Failure at Anzac was due to an entirely different cause. The 3rd Brigade should have landed about one mile north of Gaba Tepe, where the southern foothills of the Sari Bair range were easily negotiable, but it went ashore 1.5 miles further north instead and was confronted by precipitous scrub-covered cliffs. As Brigadier Chris Roberts has convincingly shown, it was still in reasonable shape to carry out its covering force task once it had reorganised. But Sinclair-MacLagan, its commander, feared a counter-attack. Shortly after the reorganisation, he halted his brigade on Second Ridge, which left the range at Baby 700 and ran 1.5 miles south to the heart-shaped 400 Plateau. Expecting the counter-attack to come from Gaba Tepe, he then diverted the 2nd Brigade rightwards to the 400 Plateau to guard against it. McCay's brigade should have gone leftwards to the Sari Bair heights, which had to be held for the landing to fulfil its aim. As Roberts says, 'Sinclair-MacLagan had supplanted his divisional commander and ... abort[ed] the 1st Division's mission without any battlefield information justifying such a decision.' Over 8000 Australians were ashore, stationary, largely undisturbed by firing, and with fewer than 500 Turks directly facing them when Bridges landed at 7.20 am. Yet he did nothing to get the plan back on track. By nightfall Baby 700 had been lost for the last time, while McCay reported that many men were leaving his line, their nerve shaken by the intense shrapnel bombardment of the 400 Plateau. Doubt that a massive Turkish counter-attack could be withstood was the final factor leading to consideration of whether the ANZAC should be evacuated before morning.

CHAPTER 4

Godley and Bridges were extremely pessimistic, advocating immediate re-embarkation without consulting Hamilton or the Navy. Birdwood's fiery chief of staff, Brigadier General Harold Walker, who was temporarily commanding the New Zealand Infantry Brigade, opposed them, rightly charging Bridges with making inadequate attempts to ascertain the situation. Consequently, Bridges 'had trouble making up his mind what to do.' Birdwood was summoned ashore and passed the buck to Hamilton, who told him that the worst was over, and 'now you have only to dig, dig, dig until you are safe.' Shielded by darkness, the men in the line were already following that advice, as Walker had realised. Extremely disappointed with Birdwood, Hamilton wrote of the courage needed to face 'the various alarmist and despondent tendencies of some of my commanders which were more frightening than the Turks.'[18] The events of the first day and night are vital to an assessment of Monash's performance on Gallipoli, for once the Anzac plan was abandoned, so too was the intended task of the 4th Brigade. In this tense situation, Sinclair-MacLagan's performance and the contrasting attitudes of Walker, Bridges and Godley offer a useful yardstick against which Monash should be judged, the only difference being that he endured such strain for five weeks.

The short voyage from Lemnos was as fascinating for Monash as the passage of the canal. Brigade Headquarters was accompanied by his fellow Victorians of the 14th Battalion, now known as 'Monash's Bodyguard'. As Cape Helles was passed at 2.00 pm, he watched the 'furious bombardment' of Achi Baba and felt a 'keen expectation, the thought of the world stirring drama in which we are taking part overshadowing every other feeling.' About two hours later, *Seeangchoon* anchored off Anzac Cove, and Monash, one of the few Anzac commanders who had not been on a reconnaissance of the peninsula, studied the shore for the first time.[19] The rattle of musketry was clearly audible, but the beach was shrouded by a thick pall of blue smoke punctuated by the flash of guns. Above the haze towered the ridges with the white puffs of bursting shrapnel shells overhead.

Monash was equally struck by the apparent nonchalance of the men. As the officers crowded the bridge to await orders, he pointed to the many groups of soldiers playing cards on the deck with a mug of tea alongside and remarked: 'What did they care if the greatest naval bombardment in history was going on; when their job came, there would be time enough for them to sit up and take notice.' Had these men known that they were urgently needed to relieve a desperate situation ashore, their indifference would have been short-lived. The 16th Battalion left *Haidar Pascha* at 6.00 pm, and when 1½ companies had landed, Lieutenant Colonel Harold Pope, joined by one company each from the 15th Battalion and the Auckland Battalion, was ordered by Godley to reinforce Sinclair-MacLagan. Two more companies from the 15th filled the 300-yard gap between the 2nd and 3rd brigades on MacLaurin's Hill. Bean expressed the feelings of the sorely tried men ashore: 'never was one more glad to see any body of troops'.

By now Monash's expectations were probably less than keen, for he was fully aware that the operation had gone awry. His brigade was landing in driblets later than planned and further north than originally intended. The disorganisation on the crowded beach and the time lost while re-embarkation was considered imposed further delay. Thus the landing of the 13th Battalion, begun at 9.30 pm, was not completed until six hours later. The possibility of withdrawal made the clearance of wounded an urgent priority and at 7.00 pm the first boatload was brought aboard *Seeangchoon*, which soon resembled a hospital ship. As the 14th Battalion watched the grim spectacle, the opinion was freely expressed that their only task would be that of a burial party. Wild rumours spread. One company of the 15th was reported to have lost 150 men while going ashore. For Monash it was 'a dreadful night ... with very little sleep.' Shortly after 8.00 am on 26 April, he landed with his 'bodyguard' under shrapnel fire, and both were sent to a bivouac on the beach, where the 14th Battalion stayed in reserve until next day.[20]

The much-feared Turkish counter-stroke did not eventuate, and such attacks as were delivered on the 26th were 'either accidental collisions or attempts by the local commander to gain some particular

CHAPTER 4

vantage point.' With no more reserves immediately available, the Turks were as exhausted as their opponents and had lost grievously, the two regiments that bore the brunt of the fighting suffering almost as many casualties on 25 April as the entire 1st Australian Division. It was also clear that no blow could be struck against the Turks until the hopelessly mixed Australian and New Zealand units were thoroughly reorganised. Though its location in some places was still obscure, Bridges was responsible for two-thirds of the Anzac line, while the northern third, the vital area around Baby 700, came under Godley. His headquarters was now functioning and had assumed control of both the New Zealand and the 4th Infantry brigades. Determined to begin the reorganisation at once, he sent Monash to Sinclair-MacLagan's headquarters on MacLaurin's Hill during the afternoon to arrange for the collection of the 4th Brigade, 'which had been distributed piecemeal all over the line.'

The sight of Monash and McGlinn panting and heaving their way inland caused some to marvel at how two such corpulent men were able to negotiate the daunting ground. From the southern end of the beach, Monash turned left up Shrapnel Gully, immediately coming under 'a hail of shrapnel and a chaos of whistling and cracking bullets.' He souvenired a spent shrapnel pellet that had hit him. The debris of battle was everywhere, and dead mules lay scattered in helpless attitudes, while the wounded streaming back were a grisly reminder of the fight going on ahead. Vicious thornbushes, their spikes an inch long, combined with prickly dwarf oak to ensure his personal discomfort. Then there was the atmosphere of outright hostility projected by the place, its barren, baked yellow heights standing in stark outline against the azure sky, watching in impassive – almost mocking – indifference, the epic struggle.

On Monash's left, in the area held by the Otago, Auckland and Wellington battalions from the New Zealand Infantry Brigade, MacLagan's Ridge rose gradually to Plugge's Plateau, which then plummetted to a spoon-shaped hollow called Rest Gully. Monash knew from his brief stay on the beach that the razorback enclosing Rest Gully fell away on the other side to Reserve Gully and, towering above it, the Sphinx, a sheer gravel-faced cliff, some 400 feet high. Further north again was Walker's Ridge, overlooking the Fisherman's Hut, where the Australians had sustained heavy casualties the previous morning. Walker's and the Sphinx were the seaward spurs of Russell's Top, the commanding plateau whose southern finger climbed out of Shrapnel Gully, and, as Monash skirted around it, he entered a narrow cleft that ran for about half a mile to the north-east. Its rocky sides rose, sometimes almost vertically, from the valley floor, creating a claustrophobic oppression not felt elsewhere at Anzac. This sinister re-entrant would soon be known as Monash Valley.

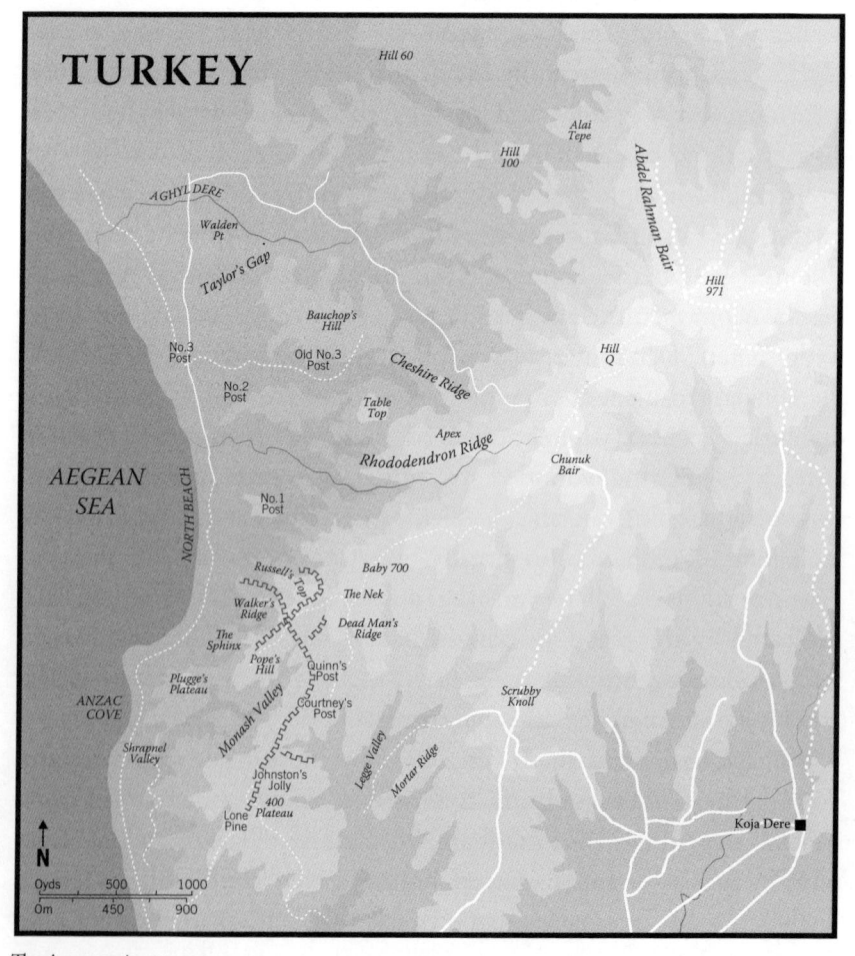

The Anzac perimeter

CHAPTER 4

Monash Valley from Russell's Top. Courtney's Post is on the ridge to the left of the streak (actually spoil from the trenches), with the shoulder of Quinn's to its left. The shelters are at the foot of Pope's Hill, which is out of picture on the left of Quinn's. MacLaurin, whose needless death Monash criticised, was sniped on the right skyline (AWM G01071).

Bounded by Russell's Top on its western side, the valley ended in a fork, whose left branch climbed steeply to The Nek, a saddle barely 100 yards wide that linked the Top to the main range at the imperceptible rise of Baby 700. The right branch petered out at The Bloody Angle and between the two branches was 'a long razor-backed hill, fitting into the jaws of the valley as a stopper fits into a bottle.' Covered in goat tracks, this was Pope's Hill, named after the commanding officer of the 16th Battalion; to its right was the eastern wall of Monash Valley, which began at Baby 700 and ran southward for 1000 yards along the line of the Second Ridge. The steep slope was corrugated by four 'shallow gullies, or landslides, like the flutings of a column.' The Bloody Angle was the first, followed by Quinn's, Courtney's and Steele's posts: together they formed the apex of the triangular-shaped line that the Anzacs, as the Australians and New Zealanders were called, tenuously held. It was 1.5 miles long and 1000 yards from the sea to Quinn's, the furthest point inland. The Turks beheld it as would 'a man looking down from the top of a cliff at his adversary clinging to a precarious ledge below him.' But it would remain unchanged for the next three months, corresponding exactly with what Major General Walter Braithwaite, his chief of staff, had previously pointed out to Hamilton as 'the irreducible minimum which must at all costs be made good.'

Bridges was present when Monash finally met Sinclair-MacLagan and the three settled the reconstitution of the 4th Brigade before Monash returned to the beach, relieved to spend another secure night with the 14th Battalion, which was still in reserve. Already, he could feel encouraged by his brigade's effort and rewarded by his insistence on thoroughness in the selection of every officer. When Lieutenant Colonel Granville Burnage, at 56 the oldest of the battalion commanders, had led the 13th Battalion out of Monash Valley and onto Pope's Hill that morning, the line faltered as men came under fire for the first time. In stentorian tones Burnage roared: 'Forward men! Damn it, what are you stopping for? Forward and use your rifles!' The leading waves charged the Turks vigorously. Burnage had earned the admiration of his battalion and, continually in the front trenches thereafter, was respectfully nicknamed 'the game old Colonel'. Two companies reinforced Pope's and were joined by a third under Major Sydney Herring, which had been forced from Russell's Top under heavy fire. Vaguely aware that the remnants of the original garrison were nearby, the remaining company under Captain Forsythe occupied the northern half of Quinn's and began to dig trenches immediately.

The disorganisation was worst in the 15th Battalion. Commanded by Lieutenant Colonel James Cannan, it had been scattered throughout the 1st Division. The two companies sent to MacLaurin's Hill had arrived 'with little but their own judgement to guide them', and then, 'in handfuls [sic], taken by one officer here and another there, and sometimes not directed at all ... reached in the empty scrub the line which it was intended to occupy.' There was scarcely time to dig more than a series of shallow pits before dawn broke and the shrapnel fire resumed. Another company entered the line between Steele's and Courtney's and, hampered by a lack of tools, dug furiously in the intervals between bayonet charges to repel encroaching Turks. The fourth had halted in Monash Valley, while its commander, Captain Hugh Quinn, reported to Cannan. On his return, Quinn found that

CHAPTER 4

Brudenell White had peremptorily detached two platoons 'up to the high country', leaving him to press on to the 400 Plateau with only half his original number.[21]

Misfortune also befell Pope's party. It had been sent to the head of Monash Valley, which lay open to the Turks. Guided slowly up Shrapnel Gully in the failing light on 25 April by Major Charles Villiers-Stuart of the corps staff, the column was split in two when the mules of the 26th Indian Mountain Battery crossed its path. Villiers-Stuart took the rear half to Courtney's, while Pope led the remainder to reinforce the 50 to 100 men from various units he found on the feature that subsequently bore his name. Narrowly avoiding capture when a party of Turks was mistaken for Indian troops, Pope ordered the entrenchment of the summit. Lack of information was Pope's greatest concern. Shortly before midnight he had advised the 1st Division: 'In great confusion. No one knows our general plan or position of neighbouring troops.' Trying to reorganise its own divisional line next morning, the NZ and A Division's headquarters was still unsure of Pope's precise location and whether he was under MacLaurin's or Sinclair-MacLagan's command.

During 26 April the fire from the Turks, who could be seen stealing onto Russell's Top, almost rendered Pope's untenable and casualties among the supports, lying in the open on the back of the hill, were heavy. Pope moved all his men into the safer forward trenches, which had reached a depth of four feet overnight, and engaged the Turks with his two machine-guns, ensuring the position was held and the Top kept relatively clear. His action had important consequences, for any strong incursion onto the undefended inland slopes of Russell's Top would avoid the Australian line on the crest, thereby giving the Turks access to Monash Valley and Shrapnel Gully and thence the beach, as well as exposing the unprotected rear slopes of the Second Ridge to a withering fire. Fighting continued throughout the day as the defences were improved. An order was issued warning all ranks against Turkish ruses. The irony that the Turks, universally regarded before the landing as dull, incompetent bunglers, should now be attributed 'an almost superhuman cunning' was probably lost on most.

MONASH

Monash's satisfaction with the performance of his brigade in its first engagement augured well for the campaign ahead, but the lesson he had just learned remained with him to the end of the war: after any operation, immediate reorganisation was fundamental. Addressing his commanding officers while training the 3rd Division in England eighteen months later, he used the post-landing period to illustrate the consequences if this simple maxim was ignored: 'If you get disorganised, you cease to exist. You cease to have a command. There is no use issuing orders if you do not know where to find your men.' The solution rested with the proper discipline and training of subordinates, who had to be drilled that 'after an offensive has caused dislocation and disorganisation, both in point of personnel and geographical distribution, it is above everything a commander's first business to get in touch with a superior near him, and say what he is doing and how many men he has and so on.' Monash insisted that if this had been stressed to all ranks before the landing, the dispersion of units and consequent losses would have been greatly reduced.

However, firm guidelines for the reorganisation were not issued by ANZAC Headquarters until early on 27 April, and those for Monash were imprecise. He was to assume command of the line from the 15th Battalion's present position, even though this was unclear, 'and with 14th Battalion and other units of 4th Brigade, extend to the north along the line now in occupation, relieving such units as he finds there, on a front to be decided by himself.' An essential for the establishment of any defence, the exact definition of the boundaries enclosing the front to be held, had therefore been omitted for the most vital sector of the Anzac area. Although his brief visit to Sinclair-MacLagan was the only occasion he had seen his part of the line, Monash does not appear to have queried the order, for at about 8.15 am, he accompanied the 14th Battalion as it moved inland. The blunder was obviously recognised elsewhere. When halfway along Shrapnel Gully, Monash was recalled to attend a conference at 10.30 am with Birdwood, Godley and Walker on Plugge's Plateau, from which they could view the entire front line and then allocate formations to the various sectors.

CHAPTER 4

The NZ and A Division was made responsible for the left and left centre, the New Zealand Infantry Brigade (still commanded by Walker) holding from Walker's Ridge to Russell's Top, and Monash's brigade from the Top to Courtney's. The line immediately south of Monash was allotted to a mixed group from the 1st and 3rd brigades under MacLaurin, with McCay's brigade on the extreme right. Monash was also to return men from other units then in his sector to their own brigades as soon as they could be spared, leaving him his 13th, 16th and, after some discussion, 14th battalions, while the 15th remained temporarily with MacLaurin. With sufficient foresight by the corps staff, these measures could have been included in the guidelines issued earlier, especially as they more or less confirmed the arrangements made between Bridges and Godley the previous day. Monash's annoyance was manifest as he wrote of rejoining the 14th Battalion 'after an unnecessary delay of two hours'. Meanwhile, the second major Turkish counter-attack had begun. Poor communications, the terrain and demoralisation among tired troops already in the line caused it to degenerate into a number of weak and disjointed assaults that were easily broken. Much more serious for Monash was the debacle that accompanied the arrival of the 14th alongside the other battalions of the brigade.

While digging in after reinforcing Quinn's Post at midday, two of the 14th's companies suffered heavy losses when a machine-gun fired at short range from the direction of Courtney's. Allegations that the carnage was mistakenly caused by the 15th Battalion gained currency and seemed credible because one of its companies was defending the sector from whence the fusillade came. Although the truth will never be known, it seems likely the incident was the cause of an animosity between the two battalions that persisted until after the evacuation and gravely affected the 4th Brigade's performance at least once.[22]

Without naming them, Bean linked the episode to 'a certain feebleness' of the 14th's senior officers. Evidence from Monash suggests that one may have been the commanding officer, Lieutenant Colonel Richard Courtney. Monash had known him from pre-war militia days and readily acknowledged his great contribution both to the raising of the 4th Brigade and to the organisation and training of 'a very fine battalion'. But he soon considered Courtney unequal to the strain at Anzac: 'the sight of blood, the heavy losses, the noise and clamour and the stress of war completely overwhelmed [him] ... and his work was done for him by his very loyal subordinate officers.' Monash traduced him mercilessly in private letters, ridiculing Courtney's claim that he was afflicted with heart trouble. Whatever Monash's personal feelings, the normal functioning of the brigade was hampered. The 14th Battalion required closer supervision than the others, which restricted its employment. It alone did not participate in any of the offensive operations launched during May, causing an inequitable distribution of tasks and disproportionate casualties in the other battalions. The 16th disparaged it as 'the Yellow Streak' battalion.

Digging support trenches behind Courtney's Post in May 1915. Crowded and resembling an anthill, Courtney's was typical of the posts above Monash Valley and on the ridges at Anzac. The lack of defence stores is evident (AWM A01210).

Monash, too, finally reached his brigade area about midday on 27 April. After establishing his headquarters at the foot of Courtney's Post, he fixed with MacLaurin the precise location of the boundary between

CHAPTER 4

their respective sectors. Walker and Sinclair-MacLagan were also present, the latter evidently handing over to MacLaurin and 'very done up'. Then Bridges arrived, informing Monash that the 15th Battalion would be returned to him that afternoon. Shortly after Monash left the conference, MacLaurin and his brigade major, Francis Irvine, were killed by snipers. Standing on Steele's Post in full view of the Turks, Irvine attracted repeated pleas of 'Down Sir – you'll be sniped for certain', to which he replied, 'It's my business to be sniped at.' These needless deaths conformed to Bridges' rashness at the landing, except that now men were no longer so shaken as to need the inspirational example of their leaders' casual indifference to danger. Monash fully endorsed the views of those whose warnings Irvine had foolishly ignored: 'it was undoubtedly avoidable and such unnecessary exposure does no possible good, but seriously impairs morale.' He insisted on the exercise of reasonable caution by all ranks. Men were not to remain stationary in dangerous places and were to observe and reconnoitre only from covered positions. Despite the deaths of MacLaurin and Irvine, the wasteful recklessness of Australian commanders continued, culminating in Bridges' death two weeks later.

Returning to his own headquarters, Monash issued his first orders since coming ashore. The 11th and 12th battalions would be released from his sector as soon as possible, consistent with leaving no gaps in the line, followed by the 3rd and 10th as more troops became available. Any similarity to the instructions received from Birdwood that morning ended there, for Monash's orders were based on the prevailing confusion as the dominant consideration. His only reserve was a single platoon from the 14th Battalion, and he had no communications with Walker on his left except for the telephone line from both sectors to Godley's headquarters on the beach. He wrote of his own area: 'The 4th Brigade section is presently held by parts of the 3rd, 10th, 11th, 12th, 13th, 14th and 16th Battalions and it is also reported that portions of two companies of 15th Battalion are somewhere in this section.' For the present, all that could be accomplished was the gradual collection and distribution throughout the sector of the scattered units of the brigade. Wisely, Monash did not attempt any internal reorganisation, for the time was inopportune. His own dictum stressed reorganisation immediately *after* an operation, but that condition certainly did not pertain in the last days of April, when the 4th Brigade was heavily engaged and threatened by further Turkish counter-attacks. In such circumstances, the inevitable disruption as companies returned to their parent battalions could not be countenanced.

Monash divided his line, after discussions with his commanding officers, into sectors proportionate to the strengths of units then in their charge. Each was to form his own reserve because no reinforcements were expected until the planned arrival of the 29th Indian Brigade next day.[23] Godley left Monash in no doubt as to the importance of his position: 'You *must* ensure that the *head* of your ravine is held and strongly entrenched.' Monash's attention was also directed to the numerous stragglers congregating behind the line. Straggling was still rife in all units, and at a time when reinforcements were needed everywhere the continued absence of strong measures to check the rearward flow was inexcusable. Monash was by no means blameless. Two days after instructing him to remedy it, Godley intercepted a large number of 4th Brigade stragglers on their way to the beach and brought them back with him. Only then did Monash take the necessary steps to curb such irregularities.

During 27 April, the fighting at the head of Monash Valley was as confused as it was heavy. At the height of the Turkish attack, the 3rd Brigade was ordered to retire to the beach, although the 14th Battalion had not yet arrived on Quinn's and Monash was still in conference with Birdwood. The sight of the 14th stationary in Shrapnel Gully while awaiting Monash, and the numerous stragglers both there and in Monash Valley, brought repeated appeals for reinforcements from the hard-pressed units on the heights. Pope wanted to use them to drive the Turks from the high ground north of his position, probably meaning Baby 700, but decided against the operation because he doubted whether he could hold the trenches gained. Efforts to establish and maintain contact with flanking formations, emphasised by Godley, were constantly frustrated. The Otago Battalion's advance over Russell's Top to link with Pope was

CHAPTER 4

checked by fire from the 16th Battalion, which had mistaken the New Zealanders for Turks. On the right flank, contact was lost with the 3rd Battalion under Lieutenant Colonel Robert Owen, whose near-hysterical pleas for reinforcement as 'A matter of life and death' suggested he would soon be broken by the same strain that had cracked Sinclair-MacLagan. Monash, who was to command under such conditions until the end of May, could spare only one platoon and offer enfilade fire support. The men in the line endured cold and wet nights without blankets or greatcoats, when sleep was impossible, due as much to the groans of the wounded lying in the open as to the action of the Turks. As Private Albert Jacka of the 14th Battalion tersely recorded: 'Having hard time in trenches.'

The lull that descended over the battlefield for the next two days was quickly noticed in the 4th Brigade. Pope was still worried by his tenuous link with the New Zealanders across the 250-yard gully separating his position from Russell's Top. Each time contact was broken, his left flank was exposed, and infiltration of the gap by Turkish snipers recommenced. Proposals that the Otago Battalion and the 16th Battalion should cooperate to clear them were rejected by Walker. Bereft of further ideas, Monash told Pope that he 'could do nothing except to order holding on and suggest digging.' Considering the grave problem facing Pope, such advice was hardly calculated to inspire confidence in the man who offered it. Moreover, neither Monash nor any of his brigade staff, it seems, had yet gone to Pope's Hill, and for some time it was believed at 4th Brigade Headquarters that the adjacent ridge, Dead Man's, was occupied by friendly troops.[24]

The excuse that Monash remained at his headquarters to control his brigade during battle was inadequate, for there were sufficient pauses to enable him to visit Pope and see for himself the nature of his exposed flank, the persistent Turkish threat there, and the difficulties of communication with Walker. After all, these matters had been the subject of numerous exchanges with Godley. Though he was learning fast, Monash's *naïveté* in elementary infantry tactics was obvious. It contrasted with Walker's long experience, which was shown in his stand on Monash's counter-sniper proposal. Walker opposed it on the perfectly sensible grounds that the two parties might become mixed and fire on each other in the ensuing confusion. Eventually it was agreed that the New Zealanders would sap across the gully to Pope's Hill, thereby securing its left and rear. In the meantime, Pope could be supported by enfilade fire from Russell's Top. No wonder a relieved Pope wrote at dusk on the 28th: 'Things have worked out all right up to now.'

There was a strong element of unwitting irony in that comment, for Pope, like all the commanders at Anzac and Hamilton himself, was unaware that the landing there had drawn and held for two days almost the whole Turkish reserve in the south of the peninsula. Hamilton did know that the Turks were far weaker in the Helles area and was anxious to reach Achi Baba while such a favourable situation prevailed. Consequently, the 29th Division and the French attacked on 28 April, but this, the First Battle of Krithia, was a costly failure, leaving the 29th Division 'badly bent' and the line still three miles short of Achi Baba. No further advance could be made without substantial reinforcement. Anzac would assist by continuing to attract as many Turks as possible. But the weariness at Anzac matched that at Helles, which Hamilton recognised by sending Birdwood four battalions from the Royal Naval Division. The Chatham, Portsmouth and Deal battalions of Brigadier General Charles Trotman's Royal Marine Light Infantry Brigade and the Nelson Battalion from Brigadier General David Mercer's Naval Brigade landed on 28 and 29 April. When the Australians and New Zealanders saw their pale, slender physiques, the immense relief at being reinforced by a prestigious formation of British regulars, of whom they had heard much, rapidly wilted. For the men of the 4th Brigade, 'the only real advantage we gained, was that they brought several machine guns with them.'

Nonetheless, the arrival of the Marines enabled the exhausted brigades of the 1st Division to be relieved and the various parties of the 4th Brigade scattered among them to return to the head of Monash Valley. However, the strain on the 4th began to approach

CHAPTER 4

that in Bridges' division before its relief. The condition of the 16th Battalion was particularly serious, Pope pointing out to Monash on 30 April that he had been holding Pope's Hill for the previous 4½ days under continuous fire, during which:

> ... the limit of physical and mental endurance has very nearly been reached. No matter how willing men are to endure, the strain will shortly be too great to risk holding such an important section of the line with men at the limit of their powers.

Monash had no choice but to leave Pope's Hill to the 13th and 15th battalions, while the 16th withdrew to a 'rest camp' in Monash Valley. Sniping from Dead Man's Ridge, which inflicted fifty casualties, precluded rest; in any case the 16th was ordered to relieve the 13th on 2 May after the defeat of the last Turkish counter-attack the day before. Despite this final obstacle, the reorganisation of the 4th Brigade was largely complete, its companies again under their original commanders. Unlike his contemporaries in the 1st Division, whose units reorganised in the comparative peace of the beach area, Monash had accomplished the task while still directly threatened by the Turks. So ended the first five days, a period during which 'We had nothing but what we stood up in ... then gradually came water, food and boxes to sit on ...'

The continued existence of the tenuous foothold at Anzac depended entirely on the successful defence by the 4th Brigade of its positions at the head of Monash Valley. Pope's, Quinn's and Courtney's comprised a sector that was 'necessarily the most difficult in the line'. The Turks on Baby 700, The Chessboard, The Nek and Dead Man's Ridge could fire into the back of each and, indeed, commanded the length of Monash Valley, the only avenue of communications to the beach. Except for Pope's, the head of the valley, from Quinn's to and including the northern half of Russell's Top, lay open to them. The slopes behind each post rose precipitously from Monash Valley to heights of 50 to 100 feet, and could be climbed only with the aid of ropes dangled from the summit. The effort required to carry ammunition, food, water and rations to these positions by night defies comprehension.[25] There were gaps between them, and for

MONASH

some time men on the flanks of one post reported the activities of their comrades on the next as those of the enemy. Though Quinn's was later linked to Courtney's by a tunnel, Pope's remained separated from Quinn's by The Bloody Angle and Dead Man's Ridge. At best, the Australians' grip on Monash Valley was fragile, their forward trenches mostly below the crests, with the supports, crowded 'like martins, in ledges and holes' on the exposed slopes in rear, firing over the front line or charging to expel the Turks from it if the need arose. Initially, noise was the greatest trial, Monash himself noting that ten seconds was the longest period of silence in the first three weeks. Then came the awful stench of decaying bodies: 'you can almost fancy you are chewing it every time one breathes, it is so thick.' From the corpses crawled swarms of maggots to infest the trenches, which had to be swept out regularly.

The view down Monash Valley from the Turkish trenches on the left of Quinn's. This image explains why the head of Monash Valley had to be held. The valley floor leads directly to Shrapnel Valley and the sea, which can be seen beyond the cut between Johnston's Jolly and MacLagan's Ridge at far left and right respectively (AWM G01765).

CHAPTER 4

The head of Monash Valley: the three ridges, from top to bottom, are Russell's Top, Pope's Hill and Dead Man's. In the foreground is the extreme north of Quinn's. A bombstop separates the Australian trench on the left from the Turkish one on the right (AWM G01925).

No position was more precarious within this line than Quinn's Post, which became the centre of fighting at Anzac for the next month. Domination by German Officers' Trench and The Chessboard precluded occupation of the crest, while fire from Dead Man's Ridge, 100 yards to its left rear, so commanded the reverse slope of Quinn's that the post could be approached only by night. Methodical erection of wire obstacles was impossible; they were simply thrown out in front of the trenches. A South African veteran remarked that one night on Quinn's was as bad as the whole Boer War. The interminable cacophony of bursting bombs and cracking bullets, nights spent in packed trenches staring at the crest a few yards ahead, and stories of fire so intense that rifles jammed and bayonets twisted with heat as furious Turkish attacks were repelled – these caused each man in Monash Valley to glance up at Quinn's 'as a man looks at a haunted house'. The indefatigable Quinn commanded with 'the air of a proprietor', and warned reinforcements: 'Don't talk too loud or they'll hear what you say. They know my name all right now and they call out, "Come on, you kangaroo shooting bastards!"' But Quinn's had to be held. The Turks, then only 30 yards away, were constantly sapping closer and needed only to force the garrison back 5 yards to hurl it into Monash Valley below, thus threatening the entire Anzac line. Their failure to do so was largely due to Monash's organisation of the defence of his sector, which impressed Bean as 'an object lesson in covering fire'. Machine-guns on Pope's and Courtney's interlocked in front of Quinn's, while its guns could enfilade those two positions. Arrangements were also made with adjacent sectors to protect the front of the 4th Brigade by placing machine-guns on Russell's Top and Steele's.

Thus did the 4th Brigade defend Monash Valley, regarded by the Turks as a direct threat to Chunuk Bair and Hill 971, which they knew were the objectives of the Anzac landing. The danger was reduced by their retention of Baby 700, and it was on this feature that the gaze of their opponents rested. Like Sinclair-MacLagan, Monash had recognised the importance of Baby 700 from the day of his arrival and repeatedly urged its capture. Birdwood and Godley were equally aware of the need, while the artillery were enthusiastic because of the excellent observation it offered. Early on 30 April Godley hinted at an imminent forward move to Monash, but his brigade was in no condition to participate. He informed Godley bluntly that, apart from Courtney, none of his commanding officers had more than half their battalions with them, the total number under his command not exceeding 2000 men. As regards a further advance, the 4th Brigade was 'by no means an organised command, capable of co-ordinated action.'

In view of Godley's keenness for the attack, there was little likelihood that Monash's fears would be communicated to Birdwood, whose operation order appeared that evening. It prescribed a general advance by the ANZAC to capture not merely the summit of Baby 700 and the Turkish positions overlooking Monash Valley, but also Mortar Ridge and the whole of the 400 Plateau as well. Only in a few places did the length of the assault exceed 500 yards, but the axes were divergent, the NZ and A Division, reinforced by naval troops,

CHAPTER 4

moving north-east towards Baby 700 and linking at the southern end of Mortar Ridge with the 1st Division, which would move due east. Hence the scheme was fraught with difficulty because the ever-widening gap between the formations would have to be filled progressively as the attack developed. Yet the advance was to begin at 5.00 pm next day, 1 May, allowing less than twenty-four hours for preparation. Several more hours passed before Godley explained the plan at a conference attended by Monash, who immediately voiced concern about the gap already existing between the left of his brigade and Russell's Top. Before he could press the point, he was urgently recalled to his headquarters by a report that the Turks had breached the Marine trenches he had earlier sent a party from the 14th Battalion to reinforce. Godley's parting reassurance that the gap would be considered was not apparent in his divisional orders. The 4th Brigade's role was a microcosm of the corps plan, for its right was to maintain 'close touch' with the 1st Division, while the left, moving north-east, joined the New Zealand Infantry Brigade on the summit of Baby 700.

Given the main responsibility for solving the problem posed by the separate axes, Monash responded with a plan which reflected 'all that scrupulous care which was to mark his operations throughout the war.' Conforming to the advance of Bridges' division, the 14th Battalion would move over Courtney's, extending as far northwards as its strength permitted. The 15th would fight its way along Pope's Hill to Baby 700, leading the 13th, which 'will prolong to the right and face in an easterly direction endeavouring to get touch with the left of 14th.'[26] Monash recognised that the measures for coordinating the inner flanks of these two battalions were imprecise, but any clearer definition was precluded by the uncertainty as his front expanded. He intended to rectify the weakness by using Pope's battalion, in reserve, to fill any gaps occurring during the advance or remaining on its completion. Equal importance was attached to the logistical aspects, as Monash arranged to have his brigade fed just before the operation began and for the construction of roads for its resupply by mule afterwards.

These complex orders defied the criterion of simplicity as a principle of war. A sharp change of direction, ordinarily the most difficult of manoeuvres for an assaulting formation, would have to be executed under heavy fire if the inevitable gap in the brigade frontage was not to remain open. Monash knew that resistance would be fierce, urgently requesting 200 000 rounds of ammunition before 1.00 pm on the day of the attack. Yet it is hard to see how else he could have overcome obstacles not of his own making, but inherent in a scheme conceived by Birdwood, it appears from a map, and merely passed on by Godley. The inadequate time they had allowed subordinate commanders was reduced even further by the Turkish counter-attack then in progress. Intending to confer with his commanding officers at 11.00 am, Monash was unable to do so before 1.00 pm and his orders were dictated to battalion adjutants by his staff captain at noon. The attack was to begin five hours later.

Even more forcible than Monash's objections were those of Walker, MacLaurin's successor as commander of the 1st Infantry Brigade, which would advance on the right of the 4th across the 400 Plateau. As far as Walker was concerned, the operation was 'hopeless'. After the heavy losses they had sustained, he thought the units involved would be too weak to bridge the expanding gap between them, particularly over the rugged ground, with which he was personally familiar. On the morning before the attack, he impressed these arguments on Bridges, whom he had asked to see for himself the junction point of his own brigade and the 4th Brigade. Monash joined them at noon. It may be assumed that he reaffirmed Walker's emphatic views, for Bridges telephoned Birdwood soon after and then told both men: 'I take it on myself; the First Division will not attack. You [addressing General Monash] may tell General Godley so from me.'

As his vacillation on the evening of the landing showed, Bridges was hesitant in tactical matters and deferred readily to his highly experienced subordinate. But Monash did not have the same clout with Godley, who, when informed of Bridges' decision, replied that the NZ and A Division would attack alone. In what may have been

CHAPTER 4

a heated exchange, Monash finally persuaded Godley to send one of his staff to view the ground in question. Major William Pinwill accompanied Monash, Bridges, Walker and Jess to Courtney's Post and, looking out over Mule Valley, agreed that the risks involved in the divergent advance were unacceptable. At 3.00 pm on 1 May Monash was informed that the operation would be postponed for twenty-four hours rather than abandoned. Birdwood was limiting it to what had essentially been the NZ and A Division's role in the original plan. The attack would now be directed wholly against Baby 700, the 4th Brigade swinging the line forward to it from Quinn's. There was to be no advance to Mortar Ridge and, most important of all, Bridges' division would take no part.

The revised plan was also circulated at 3.00 pm, but Monash was not apprised of the alterations in detail until 2.15 pm next day, even though his line, from Quinn's to Baby 700, was that from which the attack would be launched that evening. His changes to the 4th Brigade plan were necessarily rushed. The 16th Battalion, supposedly fresh after its so-called 'rest', was to climb out of Monash Valley at The Bloody Angle and seize its crest. Simultaneously, the Otago Battalion would emerge from the western branch of Monash Valley, between Pope's Hill and The Nek, and capture the seaward slope of Baby 700. Linking both battalions was the 13th, which would follow the 16th but wheel left across The Chessboard and extend to the Otagos. Responsibility for ensuring this junction, whose importance was stressed 'above all', rested solely with Monash, but the lateness of Godley's order left him little time to discuss his arrangements with the New Zealanders. Any gap between the two brigades would be filled by a company from the 15th Battalion following the Otagos. There was little else Monash could do. For the first time at Anzac, a combined naval and artillery bombardment would precede the operation, the fire concentrating on Baby 700 at 7.00 pm and then lifting to Battleship Hill and Chunuk Bair when the infantry attacked fifteen minutes later.

Many of the weaknesses in the original scheme had been repeated in this new plan, which Bean foolishly described as 'simple'. There were the same directional changes after the assault had started, the same vagueness about boundaries between units when it was completed. Although it was known the attack would begin after dark, brigades were not notified exactly when until 4.00 pm. At that time, the New Zealanders were still awaiting their brigade operation order. When it finally appeared at 4.20 pm, Lieutenant Colonel Athelstan Moore, the British regular commanding the Otago Battalion, must have been more than confused, for there was no mention of the route the Otagos should take to reach the head of Monash Valley. Monash, who had already issued his orders and discussed them with his battalion commanders, merely warned units to be ready at 6.00 pm.

After 'a week's irksome defensive', the prospect of finally attacking the Turks in earnest was enthusiastically welcomed. Men's spirits were also lifted by the sound of the bombardment, the heaviest yet, although Monash was unimpressed as several shells landed short, bursting uncomfortably near his headquarters. As often happened, the effect of the artillery on the enemy's defences was exaggerated. Yelling its password 'Yarragabbah', the 16th Battalion attacked when the bombardment lifted, but its leading companies immediately came under heavy fire from The Nek and The Chessboard as they tried to extend their line to Quinn's Post. Monash heard the cheers as well as the sound of the supports just below the crest singing 'Tipperary' and 'Australia Will Be There'. However, the foothold gained by the 16th across The Bloody Angle from Quinn's was extremely fragile: its left flank was open, and its defenders, after repulsing a quick Turkish counter-attack, struggled to entrench under fire so intense that, by morning, communication with them was virtually impossible. Behind the 16th came the 13th, led from the front by Burnage, not just to inspire his men but also because he wished to grasp instantly the course of the fighting on this strange ground. It was a wise decision, enabling him to direct the capture of a known Turkish trench when his column reached The Chessboard. There it was exposed to the same fire as the 16th, whose rifle flashes were visible across the head of The Bloody Angle. The gap remained between them although the 13th Battalion managed to dig a shallow trench on The Chessboard and a linking communication trench to supports 50 yards in rear.

CHAPTER 4

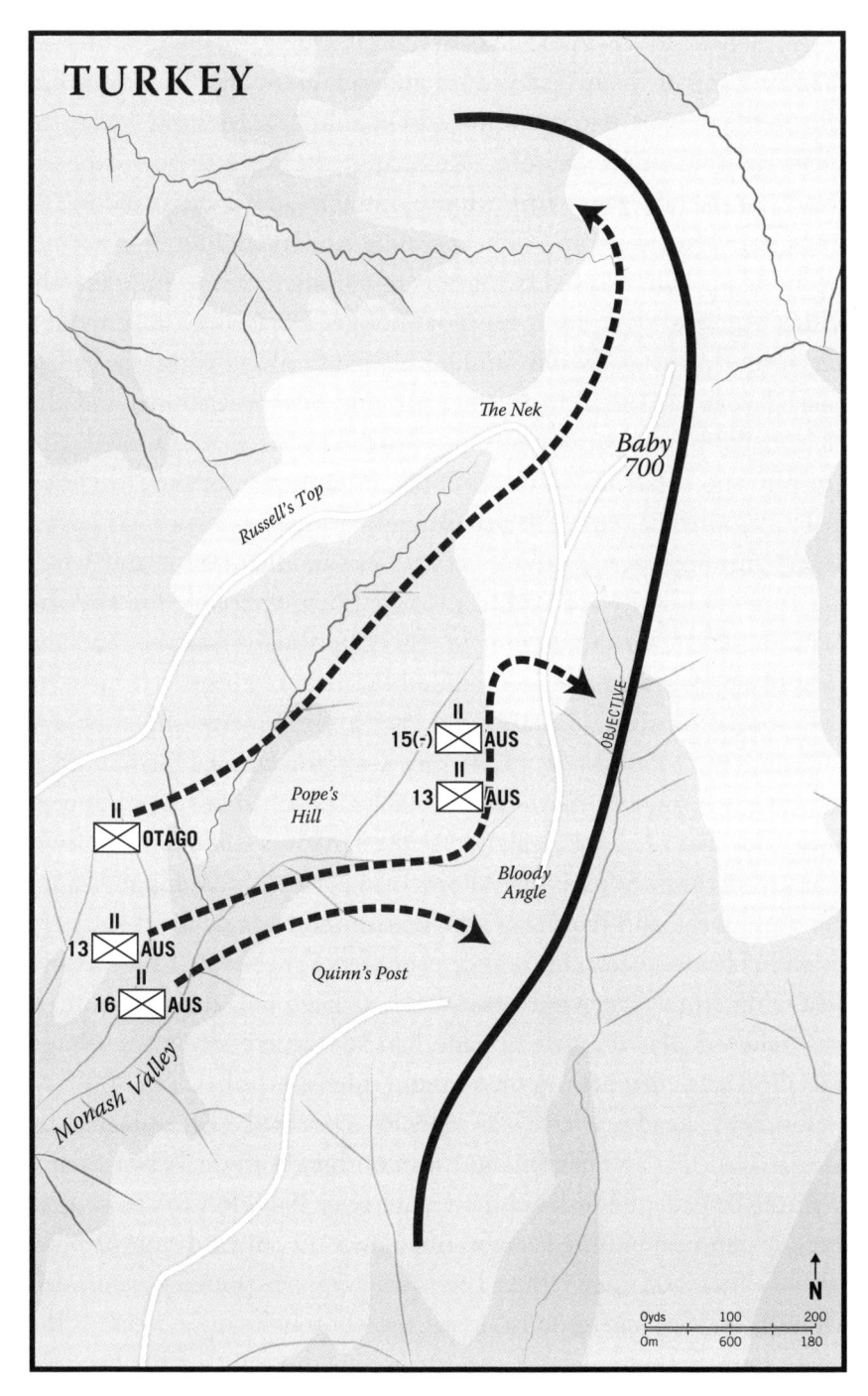

The attack on Baby 700, 2 May 1915

MONASH

All depended on the Otago Battalion, but it was hamstrung by the fumbling of the brigade commander, Colonel Francis Johnston, and Godley, who left the choice of a route to Monash Valley to Lieutenant Colonel Moore. Rejecting the direct but exposed approach over Russell's Top, Moore opted to move along the beach from his position near Walker's Ridge and then follow Shrapnel Gully inland. He allowed two hours to complete the 1½ mile march, which began at 5.15 pm. It was not enough. Delayed by the crowded beach and picking its way under sniper fire along Monash Valley, packed with wounded from the 13th and 16th battalions, and the Nelson Battalion, which had not cleared the track, the Otagos did not pass their starting point on Pope's Hill until 8.45 pm. Intended to be concurrent with the 4th Brigade assault, their attack began ninety minutes later, without an artillery bombardment and when the Turks were fully aroused. It dissolved before terrible fire and the survivors sheltered at the foot of The Chessboard, just beyond the crest of Pope's. His battalion a shambles, Moore blundered into the 13th Battalion line, lost and 'wild with excitement'. By now the situation was critical. At 11.30 pm, Captain James Durrant from the 13th informed Monash that Moore's attack had failed, adding an hour later that the New Zealanders' left flank was still open and their shaky junction with his battalion, bridged by the company from the 15th, weak and requiring support. In the New Zealand Infantry Brigade Headquarters, ignorance prevailed, for the line to Johnston, observing from a forward position, had been cut at 10.30 pm. It was believed that the 4th Brigade had succeeded, while the Otago Battalion was entrenching on a 'useful' line short of Baby 700.

Godley's headquarters was equally confused. Encouraged by Monash's success and hearing nothing contrary from the New Zealand Infantry Brigade, he ordered the Canterbury Battalion to attack over The Nek and extend the Otagos' line down the seaward spur of Baby 700. Failure was inevitable. Then, at 1.35 am, Godley reminded Monash that he was responsible for the 'thorough connection' of the entire line, from the left of the Otagos to the right of his brigade. The Portsmouth and Chatham battalions would be sent to assist

CHAPTER 4

with entrenching and to act as his reserve. Monash intended them to occupy a support line behind the newly won positions, but they did not reach his headquarters until dawn. By then the scene on the heights was incredible:

> ... men from the firing line driven back, reinforcements coming up from the gully, stragglers looking for their units, perhaps a Turk or two caught up in the confusion of the night battle, officers looking for orders, or for men to obey them.

Stressing the need for urgency, Monash allotted the Portsmouth Battalion to Pope, who sent his senior major, Les Tilney, to guide the greater part of it to the left of his firing line. Just then five shrapnel shells from one of the batteries on the beach burst over and in the 16th Battalion trenches, destroying them completely for 80 yards. Part of the 16th broke, carrying the Marines with them. As it grew lighter, Turkish machine-guns prevented any reinforcement of the position, and by 1.00 pm it was finally abandoned. Dawn also forced the retirement of the Otagos, leaving the 13th Battalion holding out alone below The Chessboard, temporarily supported by half the Nelson Battalion, which apparently strayed into its line by mistake. Communication was impossible and losses very heavy. At 3.00 pm Burnage went back to Brigade Headquarters, where it was decided that the 13th would withdraw. The 13th left The Chessboard after dark, Burnage again leading the way. The first attempt at a major forward move had ended in disastrous failure. It was 'a ghastly dream', remembered Lieutenant Basil Fletcher from the 13th Battalion, while Private George McLintock, also of the 13th wrote: 'I did not want any more like Sunday May 3 [sic]. It was just hell pure and simple with the gates open wide at that.' Private Henry Lewis of the Otagos called Godley 'a bloody mongrel of a general'.

Monash did not remain unruffled by the fiasco, as Smithers asserts. Visiting the 4th Brigade Headquarters with Blamey on the afternoon of 3 May, Bean was struck by his appearance and the bitterness of his remarks:

> Monash seemed to me a little shaken. He was talking of 'disaster' and said our men would certainly have to retire from the part

of the new ground which they still held. The Turks would get a machine gun to the head of the valley and make the gully untenable. I'm sure I can't see why they should. The reason may be that our men have been there ... seven days without relief ... 'They've tried to put the work of an Army Corps onto me,' [Monash] said yesterday.

Bean's account was corroborated by Major Charles Jerram of the Marines, whom Monash had sent to hasten the laborious move of the Marine battalions during the attack. He described Monash as 'a beaten and tired man. I don't suppose that anyone at that time thought he could ever become the Corps Commander.'[27]

Jerram's comment was hardly fair to Monash. He had left Godley in no doubt of the barely organised state of the 4th Brigade before the attack and pointed out fundamental weaknesses in the plan. When his concerns were ignored, he continued to urge Godley to abandon or at least alter the scheme. Expression of these contrary views to the imperious Godley demanded great moral courage. Monash's own plan was complex, but dictated by the role his brigade was allotted. Refuting a frequent criticism, on this occasion he had seen the ground over which the attack was to be made, unlike Birdwood, who did not visit the head of Monash Valley and view the area beyond it until 4 May. In contrast to Birdwood, Godley and Johnston, Monash made sure his subordinates received their orders in time to prepare their own plans, although that time was necessarily limited. The constant flow of information to his headquarters, enabling him to follow the progress of the attack, resulted from his insistence in Egypt on an uninterrupted stream of reports once an operation had begun. By remaining at his headquarters, he was able to exert some slight control over the battle, judging the time to commit the company from the 15th Battalion and urging haste on the Marines. Conversely, Johnston, isolated in a forward position, had left his brigade leaderless.

As Chris Pugsley points out, 'Monash's brigade did everything demanded of it.' But for the accidental shelling of the 16th Battalion and the failure to hold the Marines in readiness the night before,

CHAPTER 4

Monash himself contended that it could have held its line on The Chessboard. He was mistaken. As long as Baby 700 and The Nek were in Turkish hands, the positions captured were untenable. Curiously, Monash did not mention the strength of the Turkish defences as a factor in the failure, although he believed, as did many of his men, that the attack should have been launched in the first few days, when the Turks were weaker.[28] Nevertheless, Monash's views on the operation were clear cut: 'it would not, in my opinion, have been possible with the troops available, to carry out the original plan to seize and hold Knoll 700 and the line there to Quinn's.' Despite this rather direct criticism of both Birdwood and himself, Godley appeared satisfied with his detractor: 'Colonel Monash had a very heavy responsibility, and a most anxious time – without sleep or rest of any kind for about a week, and has done most admirably.' After the reinforcement of the 4th Brigade sector by the Marines, its command passed to the more senior Trotman, allowing an exhausted Monash 'a short rest to recover fatigues of action [sic]'. The next week was quiet, and on at least one occasion he swam off the beach, emulating his corps commander, who would 'rather be knocked out clean than live dirty.'

Monash was now engaged in fighting of a different kind. His brigade was spent and, with only 1800 men, weaker than any of Bridges' brigades on their withdrawal from the line. Relief was urgently necessary, as Godley recognised when he informed Birdwood that the 4th was ineffective. At one stage its replacement by the Marines was considered, but they had suffered heavily as well. Hence Godley's congratulatory message to the 4th Brigade on the afternoon following the attack enjoined the men 'to stick it and maintain their present position. There is no immediate prospect of either support or relief.' His confidence that they would make 'a special effort to overcome their fatigue' was not shared by Monash, who not only repeated the casualty figures, but also pointed to their effect on the efficiency of his formation. Some battalions had no staffs or machine-gun sections, while several companies were entirely without officers or senior NCOs. He concluded: 'It is obvious that both for administrative reasons and as a fighting machine, it is imperative that this Brigade should be withdrawn for reorganisation and the appointment of new staffs and leaders.' Godley did not reply until next morning, when he trusted that Monash, his staff and his men were 'somewhat rested'. Monash thanked him for his 'kind enquiries'. He was quickly becoming disillusioned with Godley, who had impressed him so favourably in Egypt a few months before.

In fairness to Birdwood and Godley, the relief of the 4th Brigade was beyond their control, determined instead by Hamilton's decision to renew the offensive against Achi Baba on the arrival of the reinforcements he had requested. Early on 3 May he met Birdwood, who told him that the Anzac line was reasonably secure for the present. A great anxiety removed, Hamilton directed Birdwood to desist from any major offensive action and send what troops he could spare to Helles. Birdwood despatched his two strongest brigades, the 2nd Australian and the New Zealand Infantry, leaving Anzac no reserve. Therefore the 4th Brigade had to remain in what was now known as No. 3 Section of the Anzac defences, although Birdwood confessed himself 'a little anxious' at having to rely on what was 'undoubtedly my least efficient brigade'. He was struck by its morale, which was higher than expected, but when Monash reported that he had only 1750 men, his reply was far more original than Godley's had been: 'I have informed [Monash] that I cannot accept this and that he must produce more.'[29] Evidently Birdwood thought Monash was blessed with supernatural abilities.

The command of No. 3 Section rested with Trotman, but Monash was the dominating figure, reorganising its defence by a depleted garrison of which his brigade still formed the core. Pope's was held permanently by the 13th and Courtney's by the 14th, one company from the supports in each relieving daily one in the firing line. Every forty-eight hours the 15th and 16th alternated on Quinn's, a system adopted by Monash to minimise the strain of holding the post. 'I daresay he's right', wrote Bean of Monash's arrangements, because, in this 'most awkward corner to deal with', half his men in both lines were always fresh. However, Monash had rekindled the animosity

CHAPTER 4

towards the 14th Battalion, whose casualties were the lightest of the four because it had not been involved in the Baby 700 attack. Consequently its allocation to the easiest point in his line, directly above his headquarters, provoked allegations of favouritism. The 100 Marines on each of Pope's and Quinn's and the rest in support were 'quite useless', as Trotman admitted to him. In one incident they burst out of Quinn's screaming that an attack was imminent after a bomb exploded nearby. Godley, present on the rearward slope, began to 'shout and wave his stick' and ordered the supports to the summit, where several were quickly shot. Gellibrand noted laconically that 'the 4 Bde lads [were] not too pleased with him.' The Marines were called 'Royal Malingerers' or, from their initials, 'Run My Lads, Imshi.' Monash wrote: 'our boys, capably led, can give the British regiments points and a beating at *any* part of the game.'

Godley's visits to No. 3 Section seemed a prescription for disaster, either while he was present or after he left. Early on 9 May, he met with Monash and his four battalion commanders to discuss unconfirmed reports of Turkish mining on Quinn's. Cannan thought the line opposite weakly held, as the Turks were using all available men to contain the attack at Helles. But he joined the others in opposing Godley's insistence on 'some offensive enterprise', and it was finally decided to determine the strength and nature of the Turkish defences by patrols. A forward move at Quinn's that night would depend on the information gained. Reports obtained from other positions should have settled the issue. A party from Pope's was decimated, while the experience of a Marines' patrol further to the left suggested that 'there are still a considerable number of men in the trenches who sleep most of the day keeping a few on lookout.' It was inconceivable that the Turkish grip on Quinn's should be any weaker than on these lesser sections of the line, and this was realised by the NZ and A Divisional Headquarters, whose report on the period noted that the Turks were 'alert and occupying their fire trenches in considerable force, even during the day.' Nevertheless, during the afternoon Godley telephoned Monash, ordering an operation that night to ascertain the Turkish strength and dispositions before

Quinn's and whether they were indeed mining, and, if possible, to secure an advanced line of trenches.

Godley's ineptly expressed orders ran counter to the fundamental military tenet that an operational plan has only one aim. Nonetheless, Monash clearly understood the main object. As Jess later remarked: 'The orders were definite ... We were instructed to capture and hold the trenches ... there was no idea of other than assaulting and capturing the Turkish trenches.' Those instructions formed the basis of the plan explained to his officers by Cannan, whose 15th Battalion was entrusted with the operation and welcomed it as an opportunity to relieve their situation on Quinn's. One hundred men in three assault groups would seize the Turkish trenches and, if the fields of fire from them were poor, push on to more advanced positions. But the confusion created by Godley's twin aims still lingered. Cannan replied that the object was reconnaissance, in answer to a criticism that Turkish machine-guns on both flanks would force a withdrawal from any positions gained once daylight came.

A long burst of machine-gun fire from Pope's heralded the start of the assault at 10.45 pm. The Turkish trenches were seized and communication trenches to them started while the 16th Battalion stood to on the rearward slope of Quinn's in support. Until about 3.30 am it appeared the positions won could be held, but the Turks had penetrated the gaps between the parties, showering the men on either side with bombs. A charge by the 16th failed to remove them. Heavy counter-attacks followed and, as dawn broke, the machine-guns mentioned in Cannan's conference the night before raked the captured trenches from the front, both flanks and right and left rear. At 5.00 am Cannan ordered the remnants to withdraw. Most of the 207 casualties came from his shattered battalion. The survivors were deeply affected by the memory of the terrible fire daylight had brought. Bean remarked later that they no longer displayed that 'careless readiness to "take a chance" that was so valuable an attribute of the Australian soldier.'

The blame for the debacle rested squarely with Godley. He persisted with the scheme even after reconnaissance had warned of the likely

CHAPTER 4

outcome. His emphasis on holding the captured trenches necessitated the constant commitment of reserves, resulting in casualties that greatly exceeded the number of men Cannan had originally allotted to the assault. Next morning Godley had the temerity to tell Monash that he knew 'all along the Turks were still present in large numbers.' Monash limited himself to the rather trivial conclusion that the operation was worthwhile because useful knowledge was gained, both of the Turkish line on Quinn's and its method of reinforcement. The one was already known, the other deducible from a map. Further ensuring that the losses counted for nothing, the confirmation of Turkish mining 'did not at the time deeply impress the staff.' Monash's tendency to bridle at criticism, even when the critic was far better placed than himself to comment, also became evident in the aftermath. Visiting the 15th Battalion on 11 May, Birdwood asked Staff Sergeant Major Corbett about machine-gun support and was told that it was 'rather inadequate'. Giving him a stern look, Monash contradicted the NCO. After they had passed on, Corbett murmured to his mates that Monash was 'a bloody liar'.

Even before Cannan's withdrawal was complete, Monash asked Godley to relieve the 15th and 16th battalions on Quinn's with the Marines, who had taken no part in the fighting. Godley refused. As the post was vitally important, it must be held by 'sufficient Australian troops under a specially selected officer', but, subject to that condition, Monash could reorganise his brigade as he chose. With three battalions crippled after bearing the brunt of all serious fighting at Anzac for the past eight days, Monash must have thought Godley's advice rather hollow. His commanders, too, were showing signs of exhaustion. Cannan was deeply upset, while Pope mused on 'The difficulty of deciding in one's own mind whether one has done the best possible with the fewest possible casualties.' A measure of relief was imminent nonetheless, because on 12 May Colonel Chauvel's 1st Australian Light Horse Brigade arrived at Anzac and replaced Trotman's Marines in Monash Valley.[30] Next day, its 1st and 2nd regiments relieved the 13th and 15th battalions on Pope's and Quinn's respectively. After Monash had taken him round the line, Chauvel assumed command of No. 3 Section. He was quickly impressed with his colleague:

> I am living cheek by jowl with Monash here and find he really is a very fine soldier. He has been of great assistance to me the last few days, and very willing indeed, considering I have ousted him out of the command of the section.

Birdwood (hatless), Godley (in helmet) and Chauvel hold a conference alfresco, probably in Monash Valley, in May 1915 (AWM H15753).

Monash was also gratified because he was able to rest for a whole night, 'which is exceptional'. Relations between the two were always harmonious, but Monash regarded Chauvel as he had Trotman, writing on 17 May:

> Chauvel rather annoys me by undue interference with internal administrative matters, but I can easily hold my own if I take the trouble. He is always grateful for my help when he gets into a tangle.
>
> ... Chauvel is very fidgetty and frequently calls to consult me during the night.

CHAPTER 4

Despite Monash's condescension, Chauvel's anxiety was understandable. With no briefing whatsoever, he had been thrown into the most difficult sector of the Anzac line, to be confronted by fighting whose nature was unlike anything in his previous experience as a regular soldier. After the first day at Anzac, siege conditions set in, but with the difference that the attackers were themselves besieged. In the trench warfare that ensued, Chauvel's ignorance was shared by each of his colleagues, from regulars like Birdwood and White to militia officers like Monash. The soldier in the ranks was disadvantaged even further. He had landed with little more of substance than his training in Egypt, whose nature was determined by the vision of warfare held by his commanders. With both needing about two months to complete their education, tactical superiority in the defensive fighting throughout that period rested with the Turks. Though all units felt the effect of this learning process, none endured it more than the 4th Infantry Brigade and its commander at the head of Monash Valley.

The art of entrenchment had to be learned. On 12 May McGlinn pointed to the inadequacy of many of the trenches in the 4th Brigade. They were either too deep or too shallow, and lacking loopholes, while some had no means of exit for attacking troops. The criterion established in the NZ and A Division was that trenches must be 'deep enough for Godley to walk upright in and wide enough for McGlinn to walk in without touching the sides.' Manning of trench systems was imperfect. Monash's supports were too far behind his front line and in dugouts too widely separated to permit close control. Godley told him that the men must bivouac and sleep close behind the forward trenches. The Turks' skill in the use of machine-guns was especially noticeable. Admitting their fire superiority all along the line, Godley told his commanders: 'We have ourselves seen what an important part [they] are taking against us. No sooner do we capture an enemy trench than we find ourselves under the enfilade fire of one or more of their machine guns.' He was only too well aware of the unnecessary casualties caused by disregard of concealment: 'The excellence of the discipline of the enemy in this matter is a standing reproof to us.' Bombs, the most important weapon for close-in trench fighting, were possessed in abundance by the Turks, who were trained in their use at the insistence of their German commander, Marshal Otto Liman von Sanders. The Anzacs had never heard of these devices, and although manufacture of an improvised bomb began on the beach, it was notoriously unreliable and, at this stage, available only in small quantities.

Owing to its proximity to the Turks and the ceaseless fighting that went on there, the defenders of Quinn's were handicapped most by unfamiliarity with trench warfare. This was not appreciated by Bean:

> The fire trench is shallow; the parapet is very low – and they look very thin – and the tunnels through which you grope your way from one trench to another are simply a rabbit burrow – you can scarcely get through some of them.

Bean made these comments after his *initial* visit to Quinn's on 24 May, a full month after the landing and three weeks since he had last been to the 4th Brigade area. As Bean rarely left Bridges' sector, whatever understanding he had before his visit to Quinn's of the reasons for the state of its defences came from the very few men from Godley's division he encountered, hardly sufficient foundation for the opinion he was now airily imparting. The depth of the trenches on Quinn's was prescribed not by Monash but by Birdwood, who insisted that they must remain shallow so that the garrison could man the parapet quickly in the event of a Turkish rush. At first, sandbags were the only defence stores provided. Corrugated iron for overhead cover and wood for revetting, both in scant supply, were used for headquarters on the beach, and it was from that source that they were eventually obtained at dead of night by a party whose leader renewed a pre-war friendship with the stores officer. Only then was the construction of vitally needed bombproofs on Quinn's commenced. Trench periscopes were initially unavailable and the newly invented periscope rifle, 'The most important single factor in the salvation of Quinn's', was not tried there until 25 May.[31] Building materials and equipment did not arrive in quantity until after Lieutenant Colonel William Malone's Wellington Battalion

CHAPTER 4

took over Quinn's in June, and Malone's much praised building of iron-roofed terraces for the supports behind Quinn's must be seen in that context. The New Zealanders knew the reason for the primitive trenches they found, acknowledging that the retention of Quinn's by their predecessors 'had been perhaps the most magnificent of the many great achievements of the Australians up to that date.'

The rear of Quinn's, probably towards the end of May, when small quantities of defence stores started to become available. The fire trenches and the roofs of bombproofs can be seen towards the summit in the centre (AWM A02009).

According to Bean, there were bitter complaints against Monash because he was seldom seen at Quinn's. Gellibrand, for one, was critical of Monash – and McGlinn – in this regard. Lieutenant Colonel Claude Liardet, a British officer, went further, telling Liddell Hart that Monash remained in his dugout and did not go near the front line, a serious charge in view of Monash's derision of Courtney. Conversely, Albert Jacka, shortly to win Australia's first Victoria Cross (VC) of the war, always spoke highly of Monash. As one of his friends recalled: 'Jacka, who had no love of the "top brass", would have criticised Monash if there was any need to.' So would Regimental Sergeant Major (RSM) Goldstein of the 16th Battalion, who was unaware at first that the 'fatherly and considerate' man speaking to him in Monash Valley was his brigade commander: 'Since that day I found I was only one of many that you "bucked up" when things seemed rather thin.' Perhaps Monash considered that accompanying Birdwood and Godley during their frequent visits to the line – Birdwood being hit at Quinn's on 14 May – was sufficient. Certainly the fighting efficiency of his brigade was in no way impaired. He relied heavily on reports from his battalion commanders and from staff officers such as Jess. In this way, Liardet admitted, Monash became so acquainted with his position 'that he could discuss it as if he knew every inch of it by sight.'

From the soldier's viewpoint, such an approach encourages a belief that his commander is not only unfamiliar with his situation but also unwilling to share it. At Anzac, commanders were very conscious of the need to set an example to those under them. Still, the effect was exaggerated. Bridges took risks that Monash would have thought foolish, and many soldiers regarded his disdain of cover during his visits to the line as sheer stupidity because it attracted Turkish fire onto their positions. Birdwood toured the trenches regularly as a means of boosting morale, but he was never able to bridge the gulf between himself and his men. Though they regarded him as 'a decent enough bloke', 'Birdie's Bull' was the subject of increasing ridicule among them. Moreover, it was not as if Monash enjoyed comparative safety for, as Birdwood told the Dardanelles Commission, brigade commanders were 'very close to the front line'. Monash's headquarters looked up at the rear of his sector and was a stone's throw from each of the positions in it. Careless exposure was likely to result in death from sniping or shells, as the twelve casualties among the headquarters personnel by mid-May proved. When Aubrey Herbert visited Monash for the first time, the shelling overheard was 'terrific', the noise making it impossible for him to speak on the telephone. Monash looked at Herbert and said: 'We laugh at this shrapnel.' As if to emphasise the danger to commanders, Bridges was mortally wounded by a sniper on 15 May while on his way to No. 3 Section. Monash annotated the signal warning him of the visit: 'M-G Bridges was hit 20 yards from me, just as I was walking down to meet him at the head of Monash Valley.'

CHAPTER 4

The arrival of the Light Horse did not fundamentally alter the defence of No. 3 Section. Its relief on Pope's allowed the 13th Battalion to become the section reserve, but the 14th still held Courtney's and of necessity the 15th and 16th continued to alternate on Quinn's. At Godley's suggestion, the 13th joined them on 20 May, since that position was more trying than any other and experience during Cannan's attack had shown that it could not be entrusted to raw troops. When a Turkish counter-attack was imminent, some of Cannan's newly arrived reinforcements from Australia had begun to waver, and a distressed Cannan passed the order: 'Threaten to shoot the first man that shows any sign of panic.' The mounted troops resembled these newcomers and were bombed heavily by the Turks as soon as they entered the line at Quinn's. Their commander, Lieutenant Colonel Robert Stodart, began to show signs of 'fidgetyness' (sic), prompting Birdwood and Godley, who visited Quinn's next day, to relieve all but one squadron of Light Horse with the 15th Battalion. To ensure continuity in trench improvement, Chauvel appointed permanent commanders to each post. Monash may have disagreed, for his complaint about Chauvel's 'interference with internal administrative matters' was made at this time.

At midnight on 18 May, Courtney's and Quinn's were subjected to 'the hottest [fire] we have known yet' and many men were partially deafened for some days afterwards. At 3.00 am the gleam of bayonets was discerned, and the whole line erupted as the final Turkish attempt to drive the Anzacs into the sea began. It stood no chance. By 5.00 am the assault had collapsed, though it was renewed sporadically until midday, by which time 10 000 Turkish casualties littered no man's land in the greatest disaster to befall the Turks in the entire Gallipoli campaign. The attack fell heaviest on Courtney's, which alone was briefly penetrated; most of the enemy before the position 'melted like soft mud'.[32] Two companies from the 16th Battalion moved into support behind Quinn's, but not one Turk succeeded in crossing no man's land there. Artillery made a significant contribution, but by far the most important factors in the defence of Quinn's were the enfilading machine-guns on Courtney's and Steele's. Monash noted after the fight: 'Everybody exhausted with want of sleep and heavy mental strain.' He had not found the battle too demanding: 'The firing line at one point was not more than 100 yards from the HQ, and I kept on reading my letters in the intervals between the long streams of inward and outward despatches, orderlies and messengers.'

Albert Jacka. Having become the first Australian VC of the war at Anzac for ejecting the Turks from Courtney's, Jacka was awarded the MC and Bar in France for actions that many thought also deserved the VC. He returned home as Australia's most famous fighting soldier, and always spoke highly of Monash (AWM A02868).

A still heavier assault was expected on the afternoon of 19 May, but already the sanitary problems caused by the thousands of Turkish dead near the Australian line were a source of serious concern. Besides the stench, the spread of disease was inevitable and could be averted only if an armistice were quickly arranged to bury the dead.

CHAPTER 4

The initial approach was made by the Turks in front of the 1st Brigade on 20 May, and then at sunset on 22 May they raised white flags opposite Quinn's. In response, two medical officers stood on the Australian parapet. One, Captain Roy McGregor, the 16th Battalion Regimental Medical Officer (RMO), met the Turks, who asked for a truce as the troops on either side exchanged greetings and cigarettes. Monash claimed he sent McGregor forward when the Turks cried out 'Docteur, Docteur,' and then spoke in French to 'a young Turkish officer, smartly dressed.' As he had no power to treat, Monash told him his commander must 'send an accredited parlementaire along the beach from Gaba Tepe to meet our parlementaire halfway'. He strongly disapproved of his soldiers' fraternisation with their opponents:

This [incident], and such interchange of good feelings at Xmas time, as the English and Germans in France, destroys the will to kill. And we must discourage, and rightly put down, everything in the way of attempting to fraternise with the enemy. Never encourage it. Suppress it. Give the men to understand they are dealing with some human vermin they are going to eradicate.

Birdwood had already informed the Turks that if they wanted an armistice they would formally have to ask for one. They did and it was fixed for 24 May. Scottish novelist and Marine lieutenant Compton Mackenzie wrote after leaving Quinn's Post during the armistice: 'I cannot recall a single incident on the way back down to the valley. I only know that nothing could cleanse the smell of death from the nostrils for a fortnight afterward.' Monash felt the Turks obeyed the rules punctiliously. When he directed a Turkish officer's attention to a soldier repairing a loophole, the man received 'a sound belting with a stick'. Nevertheless, commanders on each side surveyed the front of the other. Birdwood, Godley and Monash walked the length of the trenches in front of Courtney's, Quinn's and Pope's, meeting Bean and White, whom Birdwood asked to reconnoitre the 400 Plateau. Monash enthusiastically explained to Birdwood a scheme to take Baby 700, but he was more subdued that evening when his dugout collapsed, 'causing much discomfort'.

MONASH

Anzacs and Turks mingle in no man's land while burying the dead during the armistice that followed the massed Turkish attacks on 19 May. Like many senior officers on both sides, Monash took the opportunity to reconnoitre the opposing line (AWM A05614).

The Turkish repulse was followed by a lull that continued for the next week. Monash was able to spend one day repairing his own dugout and another used as a mess room. On 26 May, he enjoyed his first real rest since coming ashore. Handing over command of the 4th Brigade to Pope, he joined Hamilton aboard *Arcadian* as part of the C-in-C's policy of inviting one officer from each division to be his guest for forty-eight hours. The visit began inauspiciously when Monash, still overweight, was asked to climb a ship's ladder, provoking the angry reply: 'I have come for a rest and not to do gymnastics.' A gangway was duly lowered and a mollified Monash embarked. He welcomed the respite: 'After 9 hours sleep in a comfortable bed, amid perfect quiet, a hot bath and a clean up, I feel very much refreshed and almost keen to go back to resume work at Anzac.'

CHAPTER 4

Monash was very impressed with Hamilton, who remembered him from Lilydale: 'he was as usual most gracious and charming and considerate.' These comments resemble those made after his initial meeting with Birdwood and Godley and, in fact, all senior officers he met during the war. His diary entries recounting the visit are lengthy, much more so than, say, those for 2/3 May or 10 May, when his brigade was involved in heavy fighting. Conscious of his background and driven by ambition, Monash enjoyed the company of generals, displaying a childish delight whenever they complimented him or sought his advice. He returned to Monash Valley at 7.00 pm on 28 May, noting in his diary, 'Evening quiet.' Eight hours later the Turks exploded a mine under Quinn's, immediately followed by 'Grenades like a shower of peas, and the noise and the flashes and confusion in the darkness, together with thick curtains of acrid smoke, made this portion of the line a terrible Hades.'

Although Cannan's attack on 9 May had confirmed Turkish mining on Quinn's, no precaution was taken beyond maintaining the listening posts already dug. On 17 May, the sound of picking was definitely audible, but again the information was ignored. Finally, on 25 May, Monash and Chauvel arranged to fire one of the listening posts as a camouflet to destroy the Turkish tunnel. It was judged successful, and counter-mines were begun. But picking on the Turkish side continued, and at 6.00 pm on 28 May the Australian miners warned that an explosion was imminent. The mine was fired at 3.20 am on the 29th, but the assault that followed was quickly contained, the Turks being unable to advance beyond the bombproofs into which they had been forced and cut off from their own line by the machine-guns on Pope's Hill. Two companies from each of the 15th and 16th battalions and a reserve from the 13th assembled on the slope behind Quinn's, now under Pope, who arrived at 4.10 am after being ordered by Monash to replace the wounded Burnage. Fearing that the change in command at the height of the battle might cause confusion, Chauvel followed Pope, and at 5.00 am took personal control of Quinn's, where he remained for several hours. Monash was left to command the troops in the valley.

Major Hugh Quinn, accountant, auditor and North Queensland light-heavyweight boxing champion. The post named after him, and for which he died – perhaps unnecessarily – remains the most precarious position ever held by Australian troops (AWM H17420).

From the beach, Godley urged the recapture of the lost trenches 'at all costs'. That need was obvious, but the question was how to fulfil it. A worried Monash sent messages constantly: 'Have you charged? You must charge and drive the Turks out.' Lieutenant Terence McSharry, the post adjutant, who knew Quinn's thoroughly and virtually controlled the action even after the arrival of Pope and Chauvel, realised that a charge over the crest was dangerous and unnecessary. The same object could be achieved by filtering through the trenches on both sides of the Turks, the method used by Captain John Hill, who led the second company of supports onto the post shortly after the explosion. But, like McSharry, Hill found that 'The senior officers present were not as

CHAPTER 4

intimately acquainted with the conditions as we were.' Each of them – Burnage, then Pope, and finally Chauvel – was convinced of the necessity to charge over the maze of trenches towards the crest, even after it was certain that only a few Turks remained in the post. When Chauvel ordered a charge to clear them, Hill tried to prevent it, urging on him: 'how disastrous [it] would be: that the trenches were no longer trenches and that although we were not actually in them [i.e. the front trenches] yet we held them and clearing was only a matter of time. He seemed convinced.'

Supports from the 15th Battalion in a recess on the rear slope of Quinn's waiting to charge Turks trapped in a bombproof near the skyline early on 29 May. The left wall of the recess was sheltered, the right wall exposed. Bean took this photograph about the time of Quinn's death (AWM G01011).

However, the decision stood. Herring's company from the 13th Battalion and Quinn's from the 15th were ordered to make the attempt. Understandably, 'Quinn seemed very nervous about the whole business and kept asking for another minute or two.' Further postponement was refused. Quinn went forward to reconnoitre and was killed. Incredibly, the charge regained the front line with few casualties, because the Turks attacked at the same time and had to cease firing on Quinn's for fear of hitting their own men. It did not fully clear them, though, for a handful still held out in the bombproof until their surrender at 8.00 am. Monash was struck by the magnanimity shown by the Australians, who gave the seventeen prisoners water, biscuits and cigarettes as their own wounded were carried past. Less impressed was one of his officers, 'of sallow complexion, wearing a Wolsely knitted head covering', whom Monash counted as one of the Turks.

As he had remained at his headquarters through the action, Monash's contribution to success was small. Unable to see Quinn's in the darkness, he relied on the fragmented and conflicting reports sent by junior commanders, themselves trying to ascertain the situation. In these circumstances, when the Turks seemed about to pour down the communication trenches into Monash Valley, his orders to charge were logical, a decisive response when quick action was needed.

Chauvel merits closer attention. There is no doubt that his coolness set a fine example to those around him; Durrant recalled that throughout the fight there was 'no soldier whose demeanour was cooler than General Chauvel's.' Before he reached Quinn's, however, any danger of a breakthrough had passed, and it remained only to mop up the seventeen Turks in the bombproof. Once there, Chauvel rejected the advice of officers whose experience on the position and knowledge of the ongoing fight greatly exceeded his own. The charge he ordered had no effect on the battle and was saved from annihilation only by sheer chance. Even his admirer, Durrant, called it 'a forlorn hope'. Chauvel's conduct was typical of a commander in his first major action. There was also the inevitable frustration associated with the waste of his mounted brigade in positional warfare. 'From the time of his arrival here, he has always struck me as taking the gloomiest view of everything connected with the Expedition and he never seems to put life into things as he might', wrote Birdwood. When Chauvel gave Hamilton a very pessimistic view of conditions at the head of Monash Valley, Birdwood suggested to Godley that he should be relieved of his command there. Birdwood knew that the C-in-C had spoken to the more optimistic Monash, who 'I trust ... did not give you anything like the same idea as Chauvel has done.' In fairness to Chauvel, he did improve and, as the campaign progressed, Birdwood gave him temporary command of both the 1st and the NZ and A divisions in preference to Monash.

After the engagement at Quinn's on 29 May, and perhaps to some

CHAPTER 4

extent because of it, the 4th Brigade was finally relieved by the New Zealand Infantry Brigade and withdrawn into divisional reserve. The 13th Battalion was typical of the rest. Its men had grown beards and left the line looking like 'dreadful scarecrows'. On the afternoon of 2 June Godley addressed the brigade in Reserve Gully, the natural amphitheatre formed by Walker's Ridge and the Sphinx:

> Yours is a fine record, and one of which you yourselves and the whole of Australia have the fullest reason to be proud. You have made and are making the military history of Australia – a military history equal to that of any other Brigade or body of troops in the Empire or in the world – and you have performed deeds and achieved successes of which the Commonwealth has the fullest reason to be proud.[33]

With the Sphinx towering above, Godley addresses the 4th Brigade in Reserve Gully in early June. Reserve Gully would be its home until the breakout in August. Monash spoke to all the leaders there on the eve of the breakout. The overcrowding helps explain why the 4th Brigade was anxious to escape its confines (AWM G01016).

Although self and mutual congratulation flowed in torrents on Gallipoli, Godley's praise was not exaggerated. Writing with the benefit of hindsight and most of the facts at his disposal, Bean described the 4th Brigade's defence of Monash Valley in the *Official History* as one of the four finest feats of the AIF during the war. For now, he was moved by this 'rather remarkable sight' and, unconsciously illustrating the legacy of Bridges' imperious style in the 1st Division, called the 4th 'a fine brigade – rather easier and freer with their officers and not so neat or rigid as our division but fine free chaps with some good officers.' Monash, too, praised their qualities: 'it is not too easy to write temperately when alluding to their courage and endurance, their enterprise and initiative and their unflagging cheerfulness and spirit.' But the brigade was now less than half its original strength, and 'much shaken both in numbers and nerves.'

A different casualty was Monash's passing acquaintance with Bean, whom he accused of misrepresenting the 4th Brigade's role at the landing. When Bean's article about the Turkish attack on Quinn's claimed that it was held by the second contingent, 'who with the exception of the first few days of the Landing, had been subject probably to the severest strain of any portion of the force', Monash was incensed. He described his brigade's action on 25 April in detail, presumably for the benefit of Bean, who 'has on several occasions, gone out of his way to emphasise that the troops of the 4th Brigade did *not* take part in the first landing.' Thus began Monash's campaign for publicity for himself and those he commanded, which continued throughout the war. His letters were no longer likely to be censored in Australia, and there was no reason why its populace should not be told of events at Anzac and the honours won there. The public would never hear anything of the 4th Brigade otherwise, because 'Charley Bean seldom comes our way, nor is he allowed to write anything of a personal bearing.' Monash hoped that Charles Smith, the *Argus* journalist who had accompanied him on the voyage, would publicise the 4th Brigade in his newspaper. He urged Vic to give Smith his letter enclosing Godley's address 'without delay, *personally*,' and urge its publication in full. Similarly, he sent another copy to his brother-in-law in London. Monash's reasons were simple:

> One ought not to hide one's bright light under a bushel, nor fail to have an eye to the future and any little discreet publicity may weigh heavily in the scale when later on it becomes a question for those in authority to decide on a recommendation for the War Honours list.

CHAPTER 4

Soon his letters were appearing in Australian newspapers, as though in competition with Bean's despatches, which did nothing to improve relations between them.

What of Monash's military performance since the landing? Birdwood and Godley were satisfied, Godley informing Pearce in July 1915: 'Monash is very well, and continues to command his brigade excellently.' Monash's appreciation of the prevailing conditions had been consistently more realistic than the views held at Corps and Divisional Headquarters, whose delusion encouraged contrary attitudes on the part of subordinate commanders. Like Walker, Monash did not lack the moral courage to press them. They were based on his ability to foresee the unfolding of a plan on the ground and hence the weaknesses it contained. His operation orders were unambiguous and the arrangements for coordination in them – the area where many schemes founder – as detailed as the situation permitted. Monash's grasp of the importance of the machine-gun was fundamental to his defensive planning, while his pre-war emphasis on administration was reflected in his concern for the construction of roads behind his sector. Throughout his command in Monash Valley, heavy fighting and the scarcity of defence stores limited improvement of the positions he held. Perhaps his most striking feat was the reorganisation of his brigade, by far the most difficult to accomplish of any of the Australian or New Zealand formations.

Monash was always aware of the exhaustion of his battalions and repeatedly urged their relief. When it was refused, he organised the defence to minimise the strain on those holding the worst parts of the line. The discipline in the 4th Brigade might have been more relaxed than in the 1st Division, but Monash still insisted on the outward trappings and high standards essential to the preservation of *esprit de corps*. Men who had removed their shoulder patches were to be 'dealt with firmly by commanding officers'. Cleanliness of the area was always stressed, as much to discourage the slovenly as to prevent disease. Monash may not have been conspicuous by his presence in the forward trenches, but it is far from certain that his brigade thought poorly of him as a result. Conversely, Monash did not share the indifference to danger of Bridges or McCay. Like many soldiers in the ranks, he thought their reckless exposure foolish and unnecessary. He did not have to make the crucial decisions of Sinclair-MacLagan, but he did command the most important position at Anzac for five weeks when others broke down after a few days. Monash was distraught after the Baby 700 attack, but this does not mean he lacked robustness. His outburst was the natural reaction of a commander of a brigade shattered in an operation whose futility he had predicted. Unlike Chauvel, his optimism never waned, surely a more important factor in any assessment. Admittedly, Monash was helped by three excellent commanding officers out of four and, within their units, by superb junior officers and men. He had been largely responsible for their training in Egypt. Now, on Gallipoli, there was never a doubt that he was anything but the captain of the team.

Chapter 5
I Thought I Could Command Men

A daily swim and frequent evening concerts partially relieved the inevitable boredom as the men of the 4th Brigade lived under a burning sun in Reserve Gully, an area about the size of Sydney's Martin Place. The unreliability of the mail was particularly galling, and Monash lamented the lack of news, which made it 'impossible for us here to form any sort of opinion on the probable duration and outcome of the war.' Men's spirits were also lowered by the monotony of the diet, which consisted of bully beef, bacon, salt cheese, hard biscuits and apricot jam. Monash, who fought for canteen stores for them, ate sparingly and drank only boiled water. Then there were the flies, which bred rapidly in the heat and unsanitary conditions until they were regarded as a worse enemy than the Turks. Monash was exasperated by this plague: 'they crawl over every inch of exposed surface of face and hands ... I have never experienced such savage flies. They fight for your food and make for the eyes, nostrils, ears and mouth ...'

What little chance of recuperation remained for the 4th Brigade was extinguished by the use of its troops on arduous labouring tasks. Lieutenant Fletcher's sarcasm made the point clearly: 'we have been resting for over a week – constructing inner defence trenches.' The 4th Brigade began this work as soon as it arrived in Reserve Gully, when Monash sent parties to improve the defences in No. 4 Section. By mid-July the daily requirement from his formation for labour, beach parties, guards and pickets was 1706 men.

The combination of depressing conditions, tiring work under shellfire, food men would rather throw away than eat and, above all, the flies, made the onset of intestinal disease certain. At the end of July the 13th Battalion, with sixty hospital cases per week, was typical of the ANZAC as a whole, which was losing 10 per cent of its numbers weekly through sickness. As evacuations matched the arrival of reinforcements, the rebuilding of the 4th Brigade, a formation already grossly under strength, became impossible. Moreover, these figures give a false impression, because dysentery was out of control, afflicting most men in varying degrees, and therefore lowering the vitality of those still on duty.[34] Gellibrand's comment was appropriate: 'Most of us have forgotten what solid motion means and when it happens I guess we'll think we are in the family way.' Monash was one of the few spared the disease, catching the preferable alternative of a heavy cold, which made him 'sniffy and thick headed'.

Monash outside his dugout in Reserve Gully. The flimsy shelter provided little protection against a chance shell and explains why no part of Anzac was safe (AWM A02026).

CHAPTER 5

The humanitarian aspects of the problem did not overly concern Monash, for he was interested in sickness only as a threat to the efficiency of his formation. He vented his anger at the hopelessness of the medical arrangements on Godley. It was inexcusable that once wounded or sick were evacuated, they 'disappeared', commanding officers having no idea when or whether they would return. In some cases units did not even know if a man had left Anzac. When his efforts evoked sympathy rather than action, Monash asked his battalion commanders for details of instances in which men evacuated should already have returned to their units. The results that he sent to Godley were astounding. In one battalion, 120 men were evacuated for trivial reasons, but only twenty had returned; in another, some were actually told they 'might as well take another week or two off', while several sergeants from a third battalion were fully recovered but employed as instructors in Egypt. Monash urged the despatch of an officer to Egypt to expedite the return of these badly needed men, but his suggestion was ignored, and the maladministration of its responsibilities by the Base continued, a crippling legacy of Bridges' original neglect.

The heavy losses of experienced officers and NCOs during the first five weeks was another matter about which Monash harried his divisional commander persistently. Within four days of arriving in Reserve Gully he submitted to Godley statistics showing that of the 132 original officers only thirty-seven remained, to which had been added eighteen partly trained reinforcements, leaving a deficiency of seventy-seven, including two battalion and twelve company commanders. The figures for NCOs were even more alarming: eighty-three originals and fifty-eight reinforcements to replace losses of 377. The structure of competent officers and NCOs central to the effectiveness of any formation was non-existent in the 4th Brigade, and Monash recognised that the selection and training of some 400 new leaders was his most urgent task. He recommended Tilney, the most senior major in the brigade and the one 'with the most force of character, judgement and military experience', to replace Burnage in command of the 13th Battalion. When Tilney's promotion was jeopardised by Legge's proposal that all appointments above the rank of major should be based on selection from the force as a whole, Monash objected strongly. It would result in battalion commanders new to the brigade, 'to the policies, doctrines and ideals under which [the brigade] has been formed and trained', as well as threatening the territorial distinction between its battalions. Godley agreed fully and Monash got his way. For the rest it was a slow process. After five weeks in Reserve Gully Monash was still short of over half his majors and captains, the senior officers in his battalions. Nevertheless, he would not rush matters, preferring to be sure in his judgement rather than make an error in haste that could have serious consequences later.

Conditions in Reserve Gully were hardly conducive to training the new officers and NCOs required, and so 'reliance must be placed on the experience they would gain with the lapse of time.' Unfortunately, the experience gained in Reserve Gully was negligible, and the lament of a senior officer in the 14th Battalion was echoed throughout the brigade: 'those promoted have not had opportunities of exercising their commands. This is most important if the operations of the battalion are to work successfully.' Furthermore, the originals among the rank and file tended to be slack in discipline, while the returning wounded were nervous and lacked their previous daring. These men had undergone what Bean called 'an internal revolution', which began after Cannan's attack at Quinn's on 9/10 May. They had abandoned their dream of returning home as they realised the future held only battle after battle, the only escape being by wounds, sickness or death.

The lack of experienced junior leadership and the less-than-satisfactory leavening provided by the veterans doubly disadvantaged the reinforcements trickling into Reserve Gully. Comprising about half of the brigade, they desperately needed the assistance that might have been expected from both sources, for their training was abysmal. They had done no field work and only occasional range or field firing practices in Egypt. Some men arrived at Anzac unable to load their rifles properly, placing one round at a time in the chamber of their Lee Enfields, instead of ten rounds in the magazine. Intensive efforts were made to remedy their deficiencies, even to the extent of conducting route marches and sub-unit attack exercises during the

CHAPTER 5

brief 'rests' enjoyed by the 14th and 16th battalions on Imbros in July. But time was too short and, like the reinforcements who complained to Brudenell White before the attack on Lone Pine, they realised that they would go into battle with little chance of survival.

Reserve Gully was an ordeal that offered every discouragement to a commander, but Monash was unrelenting in his insistence that standards remain high. When the 16th Battalion failed to supply a fatigue party, he rejected Pope's explanation in exceptionally severe terms:

> ... you will please state in detail the steps which were taken to ensure compliance with Brigade orders ... when orders have been promulgated in your battalion what is the internal procedure, which officers and NCOs see the order, what officers and NCOs take the necessary action, and upon whose orders ...

Widespread foul language and a recurrence of badgeless jackets were signs of a reluctance of those with rank to exercise their authority. Monash did not hesitate to address the whole of the 13th Battalion on Tilney's appointment, aware of possible resentment at what some regarded as the supersession of Durrant and Herring.

With Walker, Pope, Cannan and some New Zealand officers, Monash visited Helles on 19 June, going ashore at Lancashire Landing under a heavy bombardment from the Asiatic side and meeting Hunter-Weston to end 'a most thrilling day'. On his return to Anzac, Godley told him 'to start to think things out' for the next advance, in which the 4th Brigade was expected to take 'a leading part'. More hints were given at a conference one month later, when among the points Godley raised for consideration were: 'advances over rough country by night, small columns – should they stop to fire; use of compasses; train connecting files – specially select men.' At the end of July, the landing of vast quantities of ammunition, the terracing of the gullies for use as accommodation by incoming formations and the arrival of several hospital ships offshore confirmed the imminence of a new offensive. Few men were as well informed as Monash's wife, to whom he wrote on 18 July of the 'careful and complete preparations on lines which just can't go wrong ... [for] "the Day" which is coming very soon.'

'The Day' was 6 August, and it marked the transfer of the main Allied effort on the peninsula from Helles to Anzac, according to a plan that was largely Birdwood's.[35] Lieutenant General Sir Fred Stopford's IX Corps would land at Suvla to seize guns troubling Anzac and protect Birdwood's flank as his force carried out the main operation, a breakout to the north of Anzac to capture the crests of the Sari Bair range. It was thought that heavy guns and searchlights installed on them would prevent Turkish use of the Straits and render their positions across the peninsula untenable. The Anzac offensive was to begin with a major feint on the southern flank at Lone Pine. Command of the enveloping advance to the north was entrusted to Godley, who would have at his disposal the NZ and A Division, the 29th Indian Brigade and battalions from the New Army divisions London had recently sent to Gallipoli, 20 000 men in all. At 9.30 pm the New Zealand Mounted Rifles (NZMR) Brigade, known as the Right Covering Force, would seize Old No. 3 Post, Bauchop's Hill and Table Top to allow the advance of the Right Assaulting Column, Brigadier General Johnston's New Zealand Infantry Brigade, along Rhododendron Ridge to Chunuk Bair. The Left Covering Force, comprising two New Army battalions, had to seize the Damakjelik Bair by 10.30 pm, thereby protecting the advance of the Left Assaulting Column along the Aghyl Dere. Commanded by Brigadier General Vaughn Cox, this column consisted of his 29th Indian Brigade and Monash's 4th Brigade; they were to seize Hills Q and 971 respectively. At dawn on 7 August part of Johnston's brigade would advance towards Battleship Hill, meeting the 3rd Light Horse Brigade, which was to debouch across The Nek at 4.30 am to seize Baby 700. Each attacking column would be guided by Major Percy Overton's scouts from the NZMR. They had explored the intricate ravines north of Anzac in the first fortnight of July, although detailed reconnaissance of the actual routes was impossible for fear of alerting the Turks.

For the first time, an outflanking movement would be replacing a clumsy frontal assault. Though breathtaking in its boldness and imagination, it was hardly simple. The many elements of the plan had to go smoothly and be properly coordinated for it to work. As Les

CHAPTER 5

Carlyon wryly remarks: 'It was like an exotic bet on a series of horse races. If the first leg got up, the second leg was alive; if the third leg didn't get up, the whole bet was lost.'

An unavoidable flaw in the plan affected only Monash's brigade, and is invariably overlooked by historians, who examine the scheme in its component parts rather than as a whole. Turks retreating from the right covering and assaulting columns would likely head north-east, either inland before swinging around to Anzac, or towards Suvla. They would therefore collide with the right flank of the 4th Brigade as it moved along the Aghyl Dere and, with the collision occurring in darkness, create confusion out of all proportion to their numbers. Moreover, the approaches to Monash's objective, Hill 971, along the Aghyl Dere and Abdel Rahman Bair verged on the impossible as General Cox stated before the Dardanelles Royal Commission:

> It was an extraordinarily difficult bit of country and confused country. There does not seem to be any reason why the hills should go where they do … It is mad looking country and very difficult.

Winding inland, the Aghyl Dere scatters into five branches, intersected by at least thirty precipitous gullies and ravines that tumble crazily into the creek bed. Abdel Rahman Bair is also a major obstacle, with slopes whose steepness exceeds those of Chunuk Bair. Lieutenant Hedley Howe, who walked over it with Bean in 1919, described the spur as 'without exception, the most forbidding ridge on the Peninsula.'

Cox did not mention before the Royal Commission that he had wanted to skirt the worst of this terrain. He proposed to march along the beach road to Damakjelik Bair and then turn 'sharp right' to follow that spur to Abdel Rahman, 'thus also avoiding most of the rough ground with the exception of the crossing of the Asma Dere.' But when Cox issued his final orders to Monash on the evening of 4 August, after a conference with Godley and Overton, the principal resemblance of the route in them to his first suggestion was that both terminated at Hill 971. The 4th Brigade would advance south-east along the bed of the Aghyl Dere to its most inland confluence before turning north-east to climb a difficult spur to Abdel Rahman Bair. What had happened? Overton, who had reconnoitred a short distance along it, strongly opposed the use of the Aghyl Dere, advocating instead a route that differed from Cox's original route only by an easterly march across the Suvla Plain at the foot of Damakjelik instead of along the feature. Hence it is likely that Godley ignored Cox and overruled Overton, resulting in the use of a route unwanted by both, which still crossed the Asma Dere and with a length of five miles, not much shorter than the routes they recommended. There is no record of any protest by Monash. Only by retracing this route can one appreciate the problems created for him by Godley's decision.[36]

The view from Hill 971 over the country through which the 4th Brigade attempted to reach this height on 6 and 8 August 1915. Abdel Rahman Bair is the long ridge in the foreground, and the Suvla Plain and Salt Lake are in the background. The difficulties of navigation and movement in this terrain, particularly by night, are obvious (AWM G01845A – left).

Opportunities for 4th Brigade officers to examine the terrain were limited. The week 15–22 July was spent in reconnaissance at the New Zealand outposts, from which the Aghyl Dere and Abdel Rahman were invisible, and at Walker's Ridge, where the view was too distant to be of value. Monash, Cannan, Pope and Tilney were shown the left flank from a destroyer on 13 July, while Monash accompanied Godley, Cox, Johnston and Brigadier General Andrew Russell of

CHAPTER 5

the NZMR to see it on 2 August. Neither the ruggedness of the terrain nor the intricate navigation it demanded was obvious from the sea. Accurate navigation was difficult even in daylight. By night, when Monash would advance, it verged on the impossible, for no prominent landmarks were visible from the tangled bed of the Aghyl Dere. The New Zealanders had no such problem. Their route was half as long as Monash's and the mass of Rhododendron Ridge was always on their right, a beacon to Chunuk Bair. Contrasting the two operations, Bean concluded:

> The task of reaching Chunuk Bair was child's play compared to the extraordinary difficulty of making those right and left hand turns into gully after gully across the foothills before Abdel Rahman was reached.

The Official Historian doubted whether Birdwood and his chief of staff, Lieutenant Colonel Andrew Skeen, realised the immense difficulty of the task they had set the 4th Brigade and blamed their inexperience: 'In France ... we should have considered about half this task practicable and would never have dreamed of setting more with any hope of success.' Godley said as much years later and reflected that the 4th Brigade should have been used against Chunuk Bair and the Nek. He was right – in hindsight.

However, the May fighting and the 'rest' in Reserve Gully had rendered the 4th Brigade less able to participate in a major operation than when it left Egypt four months previously. No better description exists of Monash's formation on the eve of the attack than Cannan's:

> Our physical condition was very poor, and we had heavy loads to carry. We had not our original highly trained unit, but too many untrained reinforcements who, though keen and willing, had not the unit esprit de corps ...
>
> Most of our men were very weak and I doubt if they could have marched the distance required in the time – given daylight, proper guides and no opposition.

In 1931 Monash made particular reference to the physical condition of his brigade when he described the plan as impossible. That concern was not readily evident at a conference with his RMOs at the end of

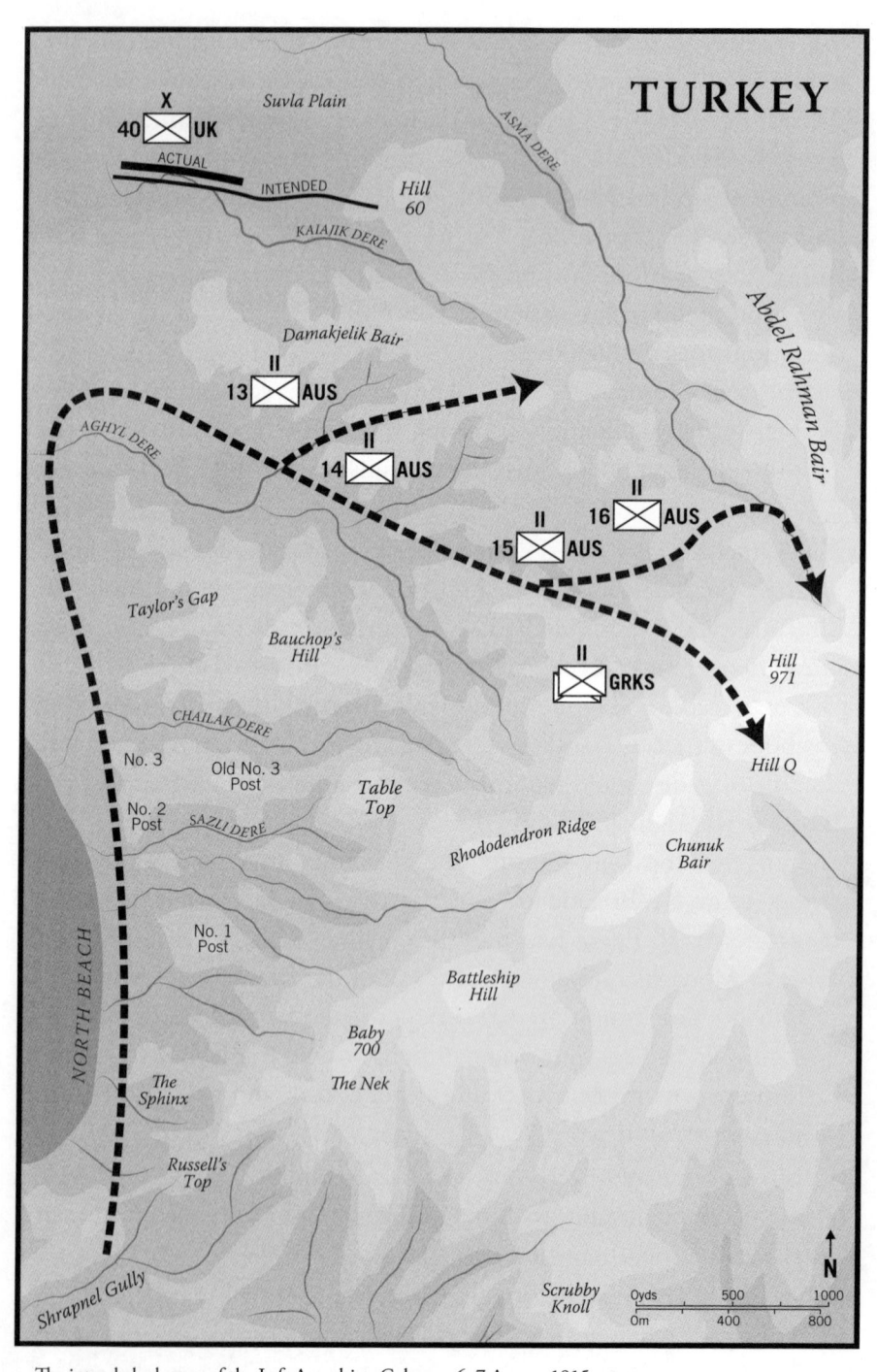

The intended advance of the Left Assaulting Column, 6–7 August 1915

CHAPTER 5

July 1915. Three of them thought the men unfit, but Monash, whose medical knowledge was considerable, agreed with the contention of the fourth that while they were in poor health, 'any change from the present conditions would be welcome, and that the stimulus of active operations would call out their reserve powers.' He did not regard the position as serious, leading to the charge often made against him that he was not fully aware of his brigade's debility. The *Official Medical History* supported his estimate. Furthermore, Monash asked for as much relief as possible, a request which, with his heavy correspondence with Godley on this matter, hardly indicates ignorance on his part.

Except for its route, the planning of the advance of the Left Assaulting Column was left largely to Cox, who had just recovered from a breakdown caused by his brigade's long tour at Helles.[37] The 4th Brigade would lead the column, halting three-quarters of a mile along the Aghyl Dere to allow the first two battalions to seize a dominant spur nearby. This was an interim measure to save time, as it afforded immediate protection of the northern flank. Once the feature was secure, the advance would resume and these two battalions were to move to far stronger outpost positions further north, meeting the Left Covering Force about the Kaiajik Dere and extending east to Abdel Rahman. When the column reached the Aghyl Dere confluence, it would split, Monash's remaining two battalions leaving to cross the Asma Dere to Abdel Rahman and assembling there before moving along that ridge to attack Hill 971. Behind Monash, two Gurkha battalions from Cox's brigade would march due east, climbing the Chamchik Punar to Hill Q. The column was to leave Reserve Gully at 9.35 pm, with Overton and some Greek guides at its head.

Monash respected Cox, though he was bemused by his habits and appearance: 'he is one of those crotchety, peppery, livery old Indian officers, whom the climate has dried and shrivelled up into a bag of nerves. But he is very able and knows his job thoroughly.' He was not so complimentary as regards the forthcoming advance. 'Cox hampered me greatly, as I had constantly to refer to him and defer to his views.' Monash had apparently forgotten that Cox, as the column commander, was entitled to have his views deferred to and that, as the selection of route showed, Cox was also constrained by higher authority because his column, like the Right Assaulting Column, would be advancing within a corps setting.

Still, there was some substance to Monash's charge. He was ordered by Cox to remain with his headquarters in the centre of the 4th Brigade; that is, after the two leading battalions. An elementary principle of the advance is that its commander moves closely behind the head of his column where he can exercise quick and effective control should the need arise. With every indication of early contact with the Turks, Cox's order was inexplicable. Even more so was the instruction that orders for the final assault on Hill 971 would not be issued until the 4th Brigade had reached Abdel Rahman. At brigade level this is ordinarily a lengthy process, for leaders must be assembled and time allowed for the dissemination of the orders down to platoons and sections. Cox may have thought there would be sufficient time available, for he expected to arrive on Abdel Rahman by 2.00 am. But that was a hopelessly optimistic forecast, making no allowance for delays imposed by the terrain, the Turks and other causes. It was a jarring note in a plan that stressed speed at every turn.

Except in one important respect, Monash's preparations were characteristically thorough. He drew a scaled and contoured longitudinal section of the ground between Abdel Rahman and the coast, illustrating the gradients to be negotiated. Bean observed: 'it was typical ... that he had drawn up a provisional time table of the march, showing the hour at which various points should be reached.'[38] Surprisingly, the timetable seems not to have taken into account the time the 4th Brigade would take to pass a given point. Had he done this calculation, Monash would have realised that it would have been complete on Abdel Rahman almost too late to attack Hill 971, especially since orders were to be given there before the attack. He chose the 13th Battalion to lead the march, followed by the 14th because they could then form the picketing outposts, a relatively easy task for their new commanders, Tilney and Lieutenant Colonel Robert Rankine. In view of their inexperience, Monash prescribed in detail the action to be followed in case of contact with the Turks. Each

CHAPTER 5

had only to decide how much of his battalion to commit. The more difficult assault of 971 was entrusted to Pope, who would command the brigade if Monash became a casualty, and to Cannan. Discussion at a long conference with the battalion commanders on 5 August extended to the smallest details of the operation.

Although Monash included every control measure suggested by Cox, his position in the column made him entirely dependent for their implementation on junior leaders – section, platoon and company commanders – most of whom lacked the experience to prevent the night march crumbling into chaos. So that they might 'get that confidence by which, with great determination, all instructions will be carried out and success assured', he addressed all leaders in the brigade down to lance corporal. As lack of space prevented him speaking to the whole brigade as he would have liked, this assemblage of 300 leaders was to impress on the men 'everything regarding the warnings and instructions I am about to give.' Perched high on the slopes of Reserve Gully, they heard Monash outline the entire offensive before describing the 4th Brigade's role, their responsibilities and the problems likely to arise. Finally, and rather ironically in view of what was to happen:

> The most important thing in night operations is perhaps the moral attitude of men. Keep cool. It is mighty hard to keep cool when there is a din like that we may experience in a few hours. But every man must make up his mind now, no matter how much clatter there is, to keep calm. If all leaders are cool and collected there will be no difficulty in carrying out the most difficult part of the attack. An attitude of this kind has a visible effect on all men, who, many of them, at any rate, would otherwise be confused and carried away with orders being repeated and bandied about by excited individuals. A leader who is cool himself will inspire confidence and maintain throughout a grip of his men, who in turn will respond to orders in a workmanlike manner, and not as spinning tops.

Speaking under 'a perfect tornado of artillery fire', which wounded a man near him, Monash was the embodiment of this truth, although he did admit that it required 'some effort to keep one's voice steady and an uninterrupted thread to one's remarks.' As he listened to the plan unfold, Sergeant Albert Compton concluded that it would be 'hell all right – some of the boys are not too game – I think they are too ill to be fighting.' The rush to complete the planning meant that Monash's address was the only worthwhile briefing that many of these men received. He left the explanation of minor details to battalion staffs, but they were 'very vague' as Company Sergeant Major (CSM) Les Bain recalled and, 'summed up, the position was that we knew just what the Brigadier had told us.'

Members of the 4th Brigade at a church service conducted by Chaplain Andrew Gillison, the 14th Battalion's padre, in Reserve Gully before the night march on Sari Bair. Loved by the 14th Battalion because he shared the dangers, Gillison was mortally wounded while rescuing wounded men on Hill 60 (AWM A03808).

The men were generally enthusiastic, despite their wretched condition. As Monash predicted at the medical conference on 29 July, their spirits soared at the prospect of leaving 'the latrine riddled soil of Reserve Gully, its stinks, its sun, its shrapnel and its flies – for clean country', and inflicting a defeat on the Turks that would assuredly end the war. The evening before the attack was strangely quiet, and

CHAPTER 5

the gully echoed to the sound of music rather than the crash of shells. With the whole brigade joining in the singing of the appropriately titled hymn 'Lead Kindly Light', 'one could sense that thoughts were for the moment swept right back to the shelter of hearts and prayers in a far off land.' At 4.30 pm on 6 August, the slow bombardment of Lone Pine reached a crescendo and one hour later tremendous firing and shouting erupted as the 1st Brigade attacked it from a newly opened underground line and the old trenches in rear. The 4th listened 'with great interest' and at 6.00 pm heard that the assault had succeeded. Two and a half hours later, Russell's regiments left their bivouacs behind the northern outposts, and by 1.10 am Bauchop's Hill, the last of their objectives, had fallen. By 1.30 am the British 40th Brigade had occupied the Damakjelik Bair and the way was open for Cox's column to begin its advance.

Actually starting at all was a feat. The 13th Battalion left punctually at 9.35 pm, but the remainder had waited in their bivouacs to allow the passage of the 40th Brigade, which prevented an ordered assembly. Each group made its way to the beach as best it could and, to regain time lost, rushed off along the road without waiting for those behind. Seeing no-one in front, the next party would hurry to catch up and so the process was repeated, turning the march into 'a concertina affair'. The 15th Battalion found that to maintain contact 'an even pace amounting at times to a steady double was necessary.' Consequently, the 4th Brigade moved off as a series of disjointed detachments rather than a continuous column. Shells were bursting on the road ahead. Though there were few casualties, Monash described the feeling as 'like walking out of a warm house into a thunder storm'. At No. 3 Outpost the 13th Battalion collided with the rear of the 40th Brigade, which had become mixed with Russell's column while crossing the Chailak Dere. A delay of half an hour ensued, enabling men to regain their breath. Monash, who had jogged all the way from Reserve Gully, probably needed it more than most.

At 11.00 pm the march resumed, briskly at first then quickly degenerating into 'a shuffle, slower than a funeral, with innumerable halts.' Men threw themselves into the scrub, imitating those in front, without knowing the cause of the alarm. The bewilderment and delays increased along the length of the column, hampering the unfortunate Indian units bringing up the rear most of all. Major Cecil Allanson needed almost two hours to assemble his 6th Gurkhas, and instead of leaving behind the 4th Brigade at 10.30 pm as planned, they eventually caught up with it at 12.50 am. At 2.30 am Major Pinwill told Godley that the Indian Brigade was only just beginning to file past the NZ and A Division Headquarters at No. 2 Outpost. Expecting that both brigades had drawn clear, Godley was 'rattled', and asked Pinwill if the Gurkhas were supposed to be behind Monash. Bean's comment was restrained: 'It seemed to me rather an elementary part of the attack for the general to have forgotten.' Another example of Godley's customary panic in a crisis, the episode portended the rotten command he would exercise throughout these operations. Bean was about to leave No. 2 Post to seek news of the 4th Brigade, and Godley asked him to tell Monash to push on immediately. The war correspondent was hit before reaching him. Unknown to Godley, Monash had already issued an identical order after acting decisively to revive an advance that had stalled for reasons beyond his control.

The trouble occurred at the head of the column where Overton marched with an interpreter and a Greek miller alleged to know the area well. From the start they tended to wander away from him, and on several occasions were nearly shot by the ten scouts of the guiding party. As the column approached Walden Point, it swung northeast towards Taylor's Gap, a narrow defile separating Walden's from Bauchop's Hill, instead of continuing along the beach road past the point and then turning into the Aghyl Dere, the route intended, and that reconnoitred by Overton. There was a halt, and an argument followed as the guide tried to convince him that Taylor's Gap was always used by his people as a much shorter track to the Aghyl Dere. Eventually, Overton deferred to the local man's knowledge. Understating the result, an officer from the NZ and A Division staff said that the alteration 'muddled things', for shortly afterwards came the first encounter with the Turks, firing from the eastern slope of Taylor's, which should have been cleared by the New Zealanders.

CHAPTER 5

There was no time to consult Tilney as Overton deployed the leading company to engage them.

Although successful, capturing several Turks, the majority of this company lost touch with the 13th Battalion and did not rejoin it until the following afternoon. The fight continuing above, Overton led the column further along Taylor's Gap, but within 100 yards movement slowed to a crawl as the gully narrowed and its bed filled with dense, prickly scrub. Even in single file its passage was difficult and the 13th Battalion Pioneers were called forward to cut a path to the Aghyl Dere. Once through, a second company attacked about thirty Turks, who maintained a steady fire from the right bank of the dere, and attempted to capture a field gun that had been firing at the New Zealanders from the left bank. Contact with this company, too, was lost, and as the rest of the battalion had fallen behind in the struggle through Taylor's Gap, its headquarters found itself isolated with Overton 'at the head of [the gap], looking into a dark ravine in front with only a few heavily laden signallers as guard.'

At the centre of the column, Monash had no idea of the cause of the delays and was powerless to intervene. Tilney despatched at least two messengers but neither reached him, while the staff officers Monash sent forward did not reappear. Among them was McGlinn, who impaled himself on a bayonet. After gaining Cox's permission, Monash finally went to the head of the column, along the way struggling laboriously through Taylor's Gap 'as it was choked with troops and the medical officers were giving field dressings.' At the Aghyl Dere,

> I found that the column was halted because one (or two) platoons of the 13th had been sent forward ... and had not yet reported back!! I found Overton, Eastwood [Staff Captain] and Tilney conferring and arguing, and apparently unable to decide what to do. I vividly remember saying, 'What damned nonsense! Get a move on, quick.'

Temporarily establishing his headquarters at the head of Taylor's Gap, Monash led the first two platoons across the Aghyl Dere under persistent fire from a Turkish bivouac nearby. A third company of the 13th and some of the 14th were despatched to deal with this nuisance.

The reorganisation of the remainder, personally supervised by Monash in an open cornfield at the foot of a wide valley, later known as Australia Valley, took half an hour. It was now 2.30 am, almost one hour after the 4th Brigade should have reached Abdel Rahman. As there was no time to find the companies of Tilney's battalion scattered on both sides of the Aghyl Dere, Monash ordered him to leave them behind and lead his single company and the 14th Battalion north along Australia Valley to its outpost positions. Although both assumed that this was the point where Tilney's force should leave the Aghyl Dere, it was 700 yards short. Overton was unable to correct them. After the Taylor's Gap fiasco, Monash adjured him to keep to the original route, but Overton was clearly lost, unsure how far along the Aghyl Dere its junction with the gap was. Henceforth he was of little value.

Hastily returning to Taylor's Gap, Monash 'found Cannan and his battalion again stuck there uncertain what to do.' Monash 'bustled' him eastwards along the flat beside the Aghyl Dere, and the 16th Battalion followed. Two positions in the re-entrants leading into the dere were rushed and a telephone wire cut; these were signs of stiffening Turkish resistance. When the last company of the 15th Battalion fell behind, Monash led it forward again. At 3.00 am Cannan thought he was approaching the confluence marking the change of direction north-east for the advance on Abdel Rahman. He asked Overton, who questioned the Greek guides closely before pointing out Cannan's objective, which he said was a quarter of an hour distant. His task completed, Overton moved back along the column to lead the Gurkhas to Hill Q, passing Monash, who remained with his headquarters about 500 yards east of Taylor's Gap. Meanwhile Cannan had struck the heaviest opposition so far:

> Our line of advance now took us over rough, broken, stony ridges, densely covered with low prickly undergrowth in which the Turks had taken cover and were obstinately disputing every yard of our advance; control was hard to maintain, officers and NCOs had to take exceptional risks in collecting their commands and keeping them in hand so as to get the assault vigorously pushed on and to keep the enemy in retreat.

CHAPTER 5

Here was the practical result of the weakness in the offensive plan, for these Turks were the remnants of the garrison of Bauchop's Hill, retreating across Monash's advance after being dislodged by the NZMR in the Right Covering Force. Monash responded by disregarding Cannan's request for the 16th Battalion to close up behind him, and deployed it on Cannan's right instead, thereby protecting the inland flank of the 15th, where the firing seemed heaviest. When dawn broke, Cannan ascertained that Tilney's force was on his left, while Pope had seized a knoll on the same ridge to his right and he filled the gap between them. Convinced that they could go no further, Cannan and Pope ordered their battalions to dig in. Across the front of the brigade a series of spurs corrugating the side of a deep ravine were assumed to be offshoots of Abdel Rahman Bair.

Monash was in touch with his commanding officers by runner soon after dawn but it was not until telephone contact was established at about 5.00 am that he was fully conversant with the situation. The news was not encouraging: 'All battalion commanders reported that their men were absolutely done and were lying panting instead of digging.' In the latter stages of the advance they had fallen asleep at every halt, and it was difficult to rouse them for the next move. Pope noticed the 'marked difference between the old battalion and the new', and Bean wrote later that the veterans fought more keenly than the newly arrived reinforcements. As their men tired, the burden on the experienced leaders at all levels increased. Pope posted himself at the head of the 16th Battalion and personally led three rushes, while Cannan, exposed to similar danger, had his water bottle shot through. Above all, the momentary stimulus engendered by the offensive had passed and the lethargy induced by sickness reasserted itself:

> The sudden burst of physical effort necessary for the night march, heavily laden, against unknown enemy localities, could not be expected to last. Excitement and a rum issue bucked them up, but a reaction, an anti-climax must have set in. The spirit was willing but the flesh was very weak.

The resistance had been persistent rather than heavy and at 300, mainly in the 15th Battalion, casualties were relatively light.

Monash thought the line established by his brigade was about as extended as it could hold. Just after speaking to his commanding officers, he informed Cox that its right flank, occupied by Pope's battalion, lay on a spur of Abdel Rahman Bair. Cox ordered him to leave half a battalion on his present line and, reinforced by the 14th Sikhs, attack Hill 971 at 11.00 am. But there was controversy about the position actually reached. Visiting Pope, Monash found the battalion commander was in error and persuaded him that the deep ravine across his front was the Asma Dere, with the nearest point of Abdel Rahman still 500 yards away. Also evident was the exhaustion and, worse, the disorganisation in the 16th Battalion and the 15th alongside it. They were the two battalions that would assault Hill 971. Convinced that Cox's order could not be carried out, Monash returned to his headquarters, now set up in the Aghyl Dere at Australia Valley, finding there, at about 7.00 am, Allanson, whose 6th Gurkhas had also been sent forward to support him.[39] Then followed an exchange with Allanson that, at the hands of Robert Rhodes James, achieved notoriety:

> ... what upset me most was that Monash seemed to have temporarily lost his head, he was running about saying 'I thought I could command men, I thought I could command men'; those were his exact words ...
>
> I went up and told him that my battalion had been placed in reserve at his disposal, but he said to me 'what a hopeless mess has been made of this, you are no use to me at all.'
>
> I said nothing more, but got back to my battalion as soon as I could, wrote a message to General Cox to say that Monash had come up against a dead end, did not require my battalion, and that I thought the best thing that I could do was to start up the hill on my own.
>
> I was in reality anxious to get away from Monash as quickly as I could, as I felt thoroughly upset by what I had seen.

Allanson was also keen to leave Monash because his headquarters in the Aghyl Dere was so exposed. Stung by Allanson's report, Cox arrived 'with one armed Gurkha as escort. He had been slightly wounded

CHAPTER 5

and was bleeding.' After a heated argument, he reluctantly allowed Monash to entrench on his present line. Meanwhile the Chamchik Punar proving impassable, Allanson advanced along the re-entrant immediately to its south and was within 500 yards of the crest of Hill Q with few casualties by 7.30 am. But, for some unknown reason, he was recalled. On Rhododendron Ridge the New Zealanders were within 500 yards of Chunuk Bair and eating breakfast while Johnston dithered about whether the summit should be attacked. When the assault was finally launched at 10.30 am, the Turks had occupied the hitherto undefended crest and unleashed a hail of fire that made its capture impossible. Six hours earlier, 650 Light Horsemen, almost half the number engaged, were lost in attacks on The Nek, Pope's and Quinn's, which were intended to assist Johnston's assault. At Lone Pine, savage fighting continued, drawing upon itself the whole of the available Turkish reserve.

Establishing the 4th Brigade's headquarters at the Aghyl Dere/Australia Valley confluence on 7 August. Monash captured two Turks near the dugout, whose previous occupant had reputedly been a German officer, and found the stretcher inside conducive to sound sleep. It is now in the Australian War Memorial (AWM A02018).

Although there was no basis for comparison, the inevitable contrast between the heavy sacrifices at The Nek and Lone Pine and what seemed an inability to advance against light opposition in the Aghyl Dere created ill-feeling towards the 4th Brigade and caused aspersions to be cast on its commander. Cox condemned Monash, and there were comments that his brigade 'lacked some of the dash and energy which might have been expected from such men.' In a famous letter to the Australian Prime Minister, the journalist Keith Murdoch wrote of 'a disposition to blame Monash for not pushing further in', but added a qualification overlooked by most of Monash's contemporary detractors: 'I have been over the country, through the gullies and over the hills, and I cannot see how even as much as he did could have been expected.'[40] Recalling the advance in 1934, Godley ventured the comment that Monash 'was hardly a Napoleon and a Caesar rolled into one.' Unfortunately, much of what happened on the night of 6/7 August will never be known; but one fact is apparent. Emotion and the deplorable tendency to denigrate those who do not conform to a conventional image, in this case Bean's developing ideas on the qualities required in a successful commander, have ridden roughshod over sound judgement of the evidence. It is also clear that Monash's habit of exaggerating his own achievements contributed to the misconceptions that prevail.

Doubtless Monash was a shaken man on the morning of 7 August. CSM Bain had noticed him at 2.30 am 'looking rather worried' as he directed the 13th and 14th battalions across the Aghyl Dere, while the state of his brigade, obvious during the visit to Pope, would have undone whatever composure Monash may have regained in the intervening hours. Hence Allanson's account of *what Monash said* during their meeting is plausible. With his plan wrecked, control lost and close to exhaustion after the exertion of the night march, Monash's mood resembled that following the 2/3 May attack, when he complained to Bean, or his interview with White over future employment after the Intelligence Corps had been disbanded in 1912. They produced similar outbursts, and seen in this context his remarks in the Aghyl Dere were nothing unusual. What is troubling

CHAPTER 5

is Allanson's picture of a man in despair and unable to control himself – let alone others.

At the end of August, Bean had two lengthy discussions with Allanson about what they both saw as the incompetence of certain older commanders on Gallipoli: 'poor old things, they are doing their best; it is really rather pathetic.' There was no mention of Monash breaking down, which suggests that Allanson thought so little of his outburst that he did not consider their meeting worthy of mention. If he had mentioned it, Bean, whose dislike of Monash was manifest, would hardly have failed to record it. Instead, Bean's conclusion was a grudging compliment: 'Sleepy old John Monash – cautious if ever a man was – is one of the worst sort of men for such a move but he's probably brilliant compared with some others.' The reason for Allanson's reticence was simple: he was unable to support the 4th Brigade as Cox had ordered, because he found the Australians 'hopelessly stopped by a big precipice in front.' Hence he swung to the right, admitting before the Dardanelles Royal Commission his 'tremendous luck in striking good country … The reason we got forward much better than anybody else was largely due to the fortune of the route we chose.'

Allanson told the Commission that the Australians '*meant to co-operate*', but they were 'tied up in impossible country'.[41] This statement so contradicts the account of his abrupt dismissal by Monash that Allanson's evidence – or memory – must be questioned. Godley, Birdwood and Cox all thought Allanson an 'excitable and unreliable witness', although their collusion to ensure uniformity in their accounts before they were called before the Commission reduces the value of such comments. But the future Field Marshal Lord Slim, who knew Allanson well, told Robert Rhodes James: 'Allanson, although a fine soldier, is not a reliable witness; he tended to "embroider" badly in later years.'

Yet the account used so dramatically by Rhodes James was written several years *after the war*! Allanson 'never liked the Australians very much' and revealed the incident only when he read in Monash's published *War Letters* that 'the Indian Brigade came up on our right, but did not do nearly so well.' Although Monash intended these letters for home consumption, his patronising treatment of what John North rightly calls 'one of the miracles of the war' was bound to incense Allanson, and his reaction was natural. Rhodes James's bias may be explained by the fact that his uncle was a subaltern in Allanson's battalion.[42]

There is one other aspect of Monash's 'breakdown'. If true, A.J. Smithers asserts that it could not have escaped notice by others. Conversely, A.J. Hill contends that, as a brigade commander is normally sheltered by his staff from all except the most important matters, only a few officers would have witnessed the incident, and their loyalty, often mentioned by Monash, inclined them to suppress it. But Hedley Howe knew all of his staff very well, indeed, many were old school friends. They never mentioned it to him. Furthermore, Monash's agitation was not the sudden result of meeting Allanson, but had been evident long before as Bain's account suggests. Most AIF soldiers hardly knew their battalion or brigade commanders, but on this occasion Monash was a familiar figure, if only for his address to all his officers and NCOs the previous day. He was recognised during the night advance by Captain Henry Loughran, Chaplain Frederick Wray and Bain, to name only three. Their comrades in the 16th Battalion would have seen him trudging to and from Pope's headquarters next morning, and had his behaviour been as erratic as Allanson suggests, it could not have escaped notice. In that case, comment throughout the brigade was inevitable; as one veteran said, 'Monash would have gained a reputation.'

The most virulent critic was Bean, whose first account, written on 8 August 1915, charged Monash with wrecking the whole scheme of operations north of Anzac. Beginning with the deduction that its low casualties meant that the 4th Brigade had met trifling opposition, Bean attacked Monash for not 'pushing on in spite of fatigue till he was actually stopped by the enemy; he stopped short of his objective without being stopped.' It was 'a decision which many weak commanders would make but utterly unjustifiable.' His conclusions were based on what he heard from others, anger at the

CHAPTER 5

casualties of his brother's battalion at Lone Pine, which exceeded those of the entire 4th Brigade, and a dislike of Monash that was not entirely Bean's fault. Monash's growing frustration at Bean's reporting of his brigade's role at the landing had now come into the open. About the end of June, 'I gave [Bean] a good talking to about it and perhaps he will mend his ways.' Bean did not obtain Monash's own account of the night march until 20 August, on the eve of the first battle for Hill 60, hardly an appropriate occasion, as Monash wrote: 'Bean to tea and he lengthily and wearily cross-examines me on operations of August 6/7.' Although the tone of the *Official History* was more moderate, the criticism of Monash remained: 'he was not a fighting commander of the type of Walker, McCay or Chauvel, and the enterprise in which he was now engaged was one calling for still more – the touch of a Stonewall Jackson, and the recklessness of a J.E.B. Stuart.'

Had he accompanied Monash, Bean would have realised how inappropriate this comment was. The 4th Brigade could not be pushed further, irrespective of who commanded it. Bean had no idea of the extent of its disorganisation. The 13th and 14th battalions had finally collected all their missing personnel by 5.10 pm on 7 August. The 15th and 16th battalions were still incomplete at that time, their men scattered throughout the brigade area. These were the two battalions that were to have assaulted Hill 971 at 11.00 am that morning! Clearly Monash could not go on, and his decision to halt was correct, as was his rejection of the 6th Gurkhas. In the circumstances he could not have used them. Although they were mountain troops, this single battalion was still only half the force originally considered necessary to attack a feature the strength of whose defences was unknown. There was also no reason to believe that the Gurkhas would not be weakened by increasing Turkish opposition before reaching Hill 971 in the same way as the 15th and 16th battalions were. Finally, the men's fatigue was emphasised to Monash by his battalion commanders, who were uncompromising in their belief that the 4th Brigade was unable to continue.

MONASH

With one exception, Monash's performance in his first essay at independent command cannot be faulted. He sought to overcome weaknesses in his brigade for which he was not responsible before the advance and his preparations for it, overall, were thorough. When stuck hopelessly in Taylor's Gap after the advance began, it was 'General Monash [who] was personally responsible for getting the column moving again.' His vigorous action there was typical of the 'younger fighting general of Walker's capacity', whom Bean and Rhodes James felt should have been in command. But Monash should have gone forward much earlier instead of sending 'staff officer after staff officer'. Overton would have been told to avoid Taylor's Gap and the disastrous consequences resulting from its passage averted. Even when it was obvious that he must take control, Monash asked permission from Cox to go to the head of the column, evidence of how strong was Cox's insistence that he remain in the middle. Walker would certainly have ignored Cox's order. Perhaps Monash's reluctance indicates his lack of infantry experience. His brief command of the 13th Brigade and the sedentary weeks at Anzac in no way equipped him for a night advance through unknown country. But he learned quickly. Much closer to the front when the march resumed, he corrected another breakdown when the companies of the 15th Battalion became separated. As resistance increased after daybreak, he deployed Pope's battalion to give Cannan the best chance of reaching Abdel Rahman. When that proved impossible, he went forward to assess for himself the accuracy of his brigade's position and the reports of exhaustion by his commanders. His decision on meeting Allanson was correct, but his fatigue and agitation were greatly exaggerated by the Gurkha commander. Monash's contribution did not stop there. He also captured two Turks hiding near his headquarters in Australia Valley. More practical was a Turkish officer's folding bedstead, which he found 'comfy' and used for the rest of the campaign. In a much more complimentary account, which appeared shortly after Monash's death, Bean said that he was 'always very proud of his participation in that night's fighting.' Monash had every reason to be.

CHAPTER 5

The 4th Brigade's headquarters, now firmly ensconced. Monash looks up from the centre of the table between Lieutenant Colonel McGlinn, the brigade major (on his right), and Lieutenant Locke, the staff captain (left) (AWM G01187).

Apart from desultory sniping, the early morning of 7 August was quiet. Lieutenant Douglas Marks of the 13th Battalion reconnoitred 1½ miles north to a farm on the Suvla Plain. He and a few others filled their water bottles from some wells, picked blackberries and robbed beehives of their honey. The promise of rest quickly faded. Dazed by exhaustion, men tried to dig, but the Turkish fire increased from the ridge opposite, which terminated in an imperceptible rise known as Hill 60. Lying on the ground to avoid the sniping, they scratched holes and then rolled into them, remaining there for the rest of the day without water under the scorching sun. 'It was a horrible plight and one would wish to be back – even at Anzac Cove again.' At nightfall, officers were finally able to move about freely and to continue the reorganisation of their units. As orders were given and preparations made for another assault on Hill 971, Monash received a message from Godley that reflected his dissatisfaction with the performance of the 4th Brigade on 6 August:

> I feel confident that after today's rest and starting comparatively fresh, your brigade will make a determined effort to capture the key of the position tomorrow morning. In selecting it for this task I had the original brigade in mind and I hope you will ask

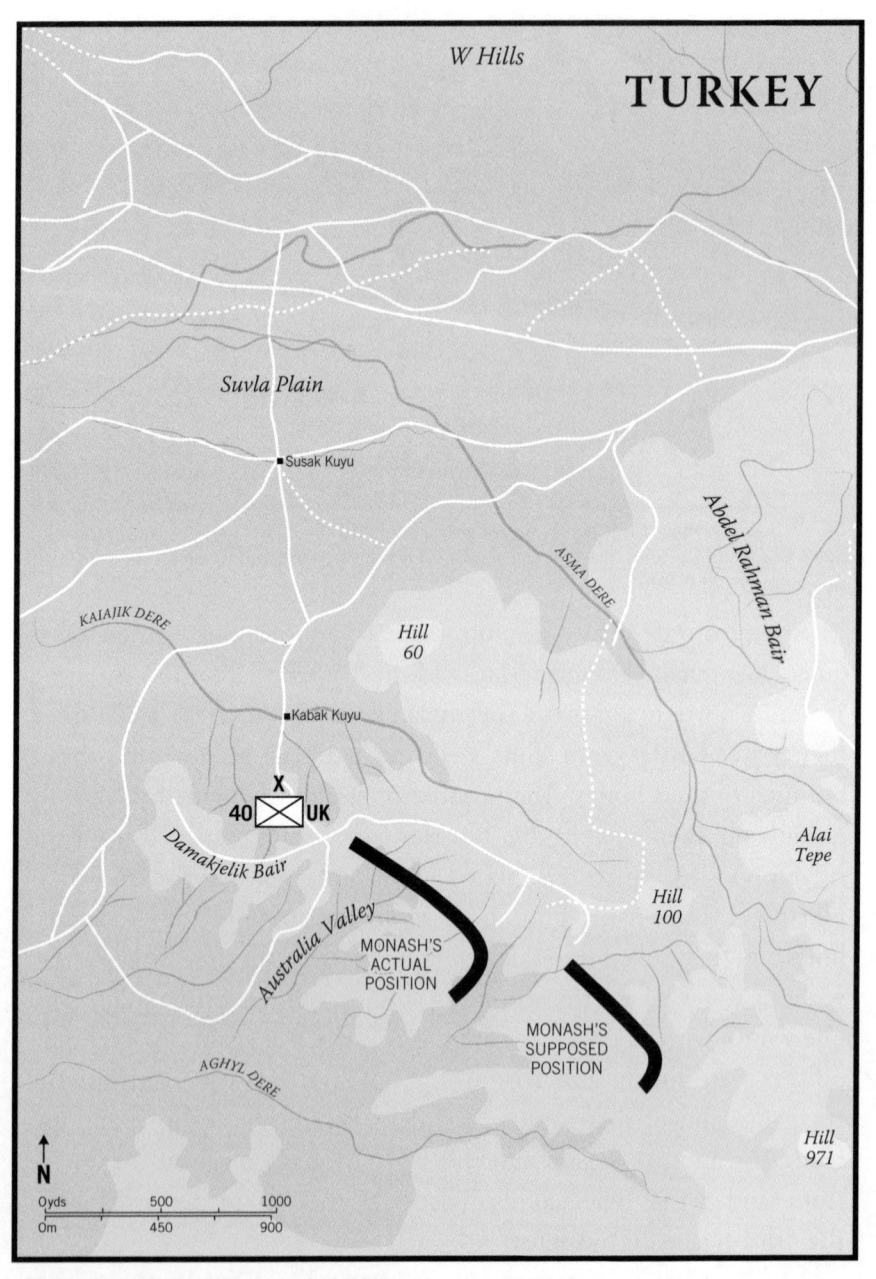

The actual and imagined position of the 4th Brigade, 7 August 1915

CHAPTER 5

your excellent COs to let the men know from me that we all expect the reconstituted brigade to live up to the traditions of the original.

According to Monash, the plan outlined to him by Cox at 5.30 pm on 7 August was for 'an attack with such troops as I could get up Abdel Rahman Spur, so as to draw the enemy down the spur from attacks the other way.' It was clear that the emphasis of the operation had shifted to the southern crests, Q and Chunuk Bair, which would be assaulted respectively by Cox's and Johnston's reinforced brigades. Monash told Cox that his weary formation was too weak for the task if it was expected to continue responsibility for its present positions as well. Cox agreed and reinforced him with a New Army unit, the 6th King's Own Royal Lancasters, which would hold the line with Tilney's battalion, releasing the 14th, 15th and 16th for the attack. The men were ordered to cease digging and rest as Monash issued his orders at about 7.30 pm. Cannan's battalion, guided by William Locke, Monash's staff captain, would lead the 14th and 16th across the Asma Dere to Abdel Rahman and move south along it towards Hill 971. Monash would be commanding a mobile operation at the tactical level. As the night march had shown, he had to be well forward in this setting. But in an amazing decision, Monash put Pope in command of the attack, proposing to remain in telephone contact with him from a signal station established above the Aghyl Dere. Yet he did not give Pope the necessary staff and communications for the task, even though Pope was expected to command his own battalion as well. This arrangement, and Pope's failure to discuss the operation with the other commanding officers, gravely reduced the chances of success even before it began.

Although Locke had reconnoitred in front of the brigade during the afternoon and Monash also examined the ground for some time, the plan was based on Overton's navigational error, which had gone undetected. The 4th Brigade was not where its commanders believed it to be, but 700 yards to the west, the same distance that separated Tilney's actual and intended departure points from the Aghyl Dere the previous night. When Monash told Pope he was on the Asma

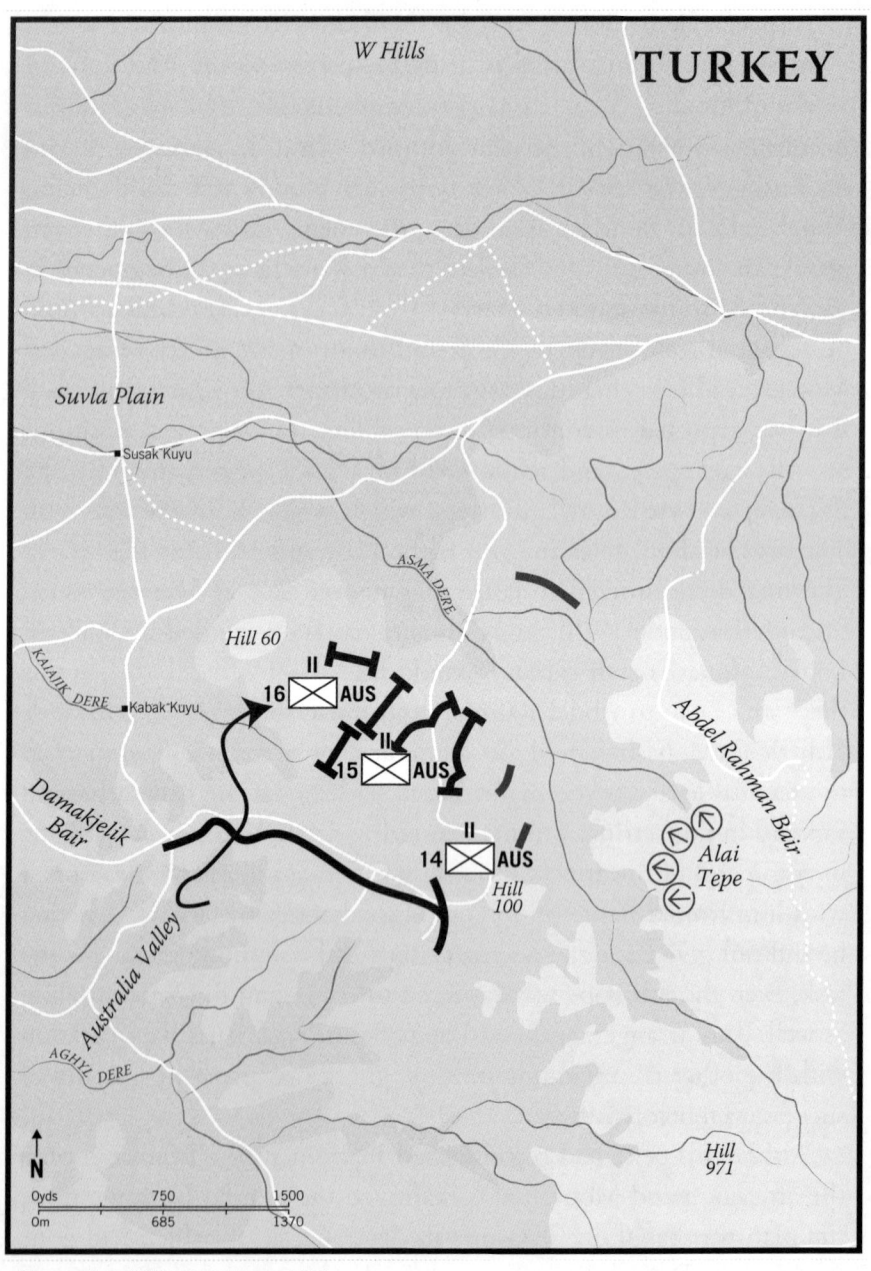

The attack on Hill 971, 8 August 1915

CHAPTER 5

Dere, his battalion was in fact overlooking the Kaiajik Dere, the next westerly re-entrant. Any advance to 971 had to cross both these deres before climbing the spurs of Abdel Rahman. That distance could not be covered in the time between 3.00 am, when the operation began, and 4.15 am, when the supporting bombardment lifted from the Sari Bair range. Confusion also surrounded the medical arrangements. The 4th Field Ambulance had not rejoined the brigade after losing it at Taylor's Gap, and during 7 August all clearance of wounded was done by the 3rd Light Horse Field Ambulance, which had established a collecting station in the Aghyl Dere. That unit was not informed of the attack about to be made.

Tiredness and the rugged terrain, which forced the column into single file, retarded the advance. At 4.15 am on 8 August the last elements of the 16th Battalion had not yet left the line occupied the previous morning, while the 14th was just crossing the Kaiajik Dere. The sun had risen and the bombardment had ceased as the head of the 15th Battalion climbed out of the Kaiajik Dere onto what Cannan thought was a spur of Abdel Rahman, entering an oat field whose crop had been gathered and stooked. After a few Turkish scouts were driven off, 'there was opened upon it a fire of machine guns, which rapidly increased to tornado-like intensity.' They were sited perfectly, on the very spur on which Cannan imagined he was advancing, and looked down on the oat field whose stubbled slope inclined towards them, 600 yards away, across the Asma Dere, so that its whole surface was grazed by bullets. For the 14th Battalion following, the carnage presented a grisly sight. 'The 15th Battalion seemed to wilt away from in front of us and their casualties lay thickly along our line of advance.' Already unnerved, Rankine fainted in the Kaiajik Dere and 'was quite useless for the remainder of the day.' Major Charles Dare assumed command of the 14th and led it past the 15th to Hill 100, which Dare thought he could hold if supported on his left. But the Turks were already attacking the 15th Battalion and Cannan's desperate attempts to stem them with some platoons from the 14th represented 'the last controlled movement in that part of the field.' The remnants of the 15th, isolated and leaderless on the northern end of the spur, broke in face of the Turkish onslaught, which was prevented from enveloping the rear of the column only by half of the 16th Battalion, still strung out across the Kaiajik Dere.

Monash must have guessed from the volume of fire and the absence of movement on Hill 971 that his brigade had been stopped by heavy opposition a long way from the summit. But he was powerless to influence the battle, because the telephone line run out to Pope had been cut by shellfire. Pope sent a runner back at 6.20 am, but the wire was repaired before he reached Brigade Headquarters. At 7.05 am Pope recommended withdrawal to Monash, after informing him that Turkish strength and the heavy casualties precluded the capture of 971. This was one of the three options Monash offered Cox. Did Cox want him to dig in where he was, advance further (in which case Monash wanted two more battalions) or withdraw, as Pope suggested? Cox ordered him to withdraw, but an orderly retirement was impossible for the 'organisation of the battalions had been utterly broken.' Cannan had joined Pope, but the two were in contact only with those nearest them: 'There seemed no defined system of attack or defence; even the officers were scattered about and apparently were in complete ignorance of what was taking place.'

As the right flank of the 14th Battalion had linked up with the 14th Sikhs, Dare refused to withdraw, again asking for support on his left, but complied when told the 15th and 16th battalions were pulling out. Though the 4th Brigade's machine-gun sections shattered Turkish attempts to impede it, the retirement was marred by the simmering hostility between the 14th and 15th battalions, neither of which wished to cooperate with the other. When Captain Loughran, the 14th Battalion RMO, passed on to his counterpart in the 15th, Captain John Luther, a message from Pope that the wounded must be evacuated as quickly as possible, Luther demanded to know its source and then sneered: 'Oh! It's only a bloody rumour invented by the 14th. They always want to withdraw ... I refuse to take any notice of you.' Throughout the morning, the survivors trickled across the Kaiajik Dere to their old line, 'a mournful procession played out,

CHAPTER 5

carrying and helping along the wounded.' The plight of the latter was pitiful. As the 3rd Light Horse Field Ambulance did not know of the attack, no provision had been made to relieve the stretcher-bearers of the 4th Brigade, who thus had to carry their loads all the way to the beach. Once there, exchange of stretchers was forbidden, forcing them to return empty-handed and so most of the wounded had to be evacuated on the backs of their comrades. Some still remained in the 4th Brigade area at 4.35 pm that afternoon. Others who would normally have been picked up were left behind. The spirit of the 4th Brigade was deeply affected by this fight. Pope described his men as 'very worn and depressed' and had to address them to 'buck them up'.

The undue focus on Monash's actions on the night march on 6 August and the unjust contumely heaped on him for them since, both instigated by Bean, have allowed what was a staggering lapse in command by Monash in this attack to slip by unnoticed. According to his dubious public account, he was against the operation, and he did seek reinforcements when his protests were overruled. But the failure to inform the responsible medical staff was an omission whose consequences were no less disastrous than the mistake made by Overton, even allowing for the haste with which orders were usually issued at all levels. The oversight may have resulted from the absence of his own ambulance, but that would be contrary to Monash's thorough attention to detail. Whatever the reason, soldiers' morale rests on the knowledge that they will be treated promptly and efficiently if they are wounded. The agonising scenes during the retreat, with the uncharacteristic abandonment by Australian soldiers of their dead and wounded comrades, were a potent reminder of the extent of the demoralisation in the 4th Brigade after the attack. The night advance had demonstrated the need for personal control, yet Monash entrusted the operation, involving three of his four battalions, to Pope – admittedly nominated by him as his successor, but not carrying the same authority. Although most of the disorganisation resulted from Turkish fire, it may be doubted whether Dare's refusal to retire or the bickering between the 14th and 15th battalions would have been tolerated by Monash. When the battle reached its zenith, he did not go forward, even after the telephone cable to Pope, a tenuous link at best as Monash well knew, was broken.

No records survive – certainly none of Monash's – that might shed light on his inexplicable action; nor does any inquiry appear to have been held afterwards. Could it be that he foresaw a 'bloody holocaust' as evidenced by his protest to Cox, and, when his objection was dismissed, offloaded the operation onto other shoulders? The carelessness that reeks from every aspect of its preparation was atypical of Monash, and certainly makes such a theory plausible. His involvement ceased with his own orders. He did not even insist on a further conference between Pope and the battalion commanders, a fundamental error. The inevitable confusion that followed, as commanders were unsure of who was responsible for what, may well have caused the medical fiasco. However unpalatable the conclusion, it almost appears that Monash 'funked' command. He slept for nine hours after the attack, indicative of fatigue that was a legacy of the night march. But his brigade was as tired, if not more so, and they depended on him as its commander to avoid the errors he made. It is ironic that in 1918 one of Monash's greatest successes would be won on the anniversary of his worst performance of the war.

The successes won elsewhere were temporary. The New Zealanders gained a tenuous foothold on Chunuk Bair, which gave a glimmer of hope because the feature dominated the Turkish line at Anzac. But the two New Army battalions that relieved the New Zealanders were driven off it by a massive Turkish counter-attack on 10 August. Allanson's brief occupation of Hill Q on 9 August ended when six shells from Anzac landed among his Gurkhas. At Suvla IX Corps was opposed for two days by a mere four battalions, but Stopford did not grasp the astonishing opportunity. The Turks' successful assault on IX Corps ensured that they retained the dominating heights inland of Suvla. The August offensive had ended in abject failure. Monash blamed the reverse largely on the New Army troops and he lashed them unmercifully:

The real cause of our failure is the poor quality of British troops ... I have had numbers of them under my personal command at

CHAPTER 5

various times ... and although some are better than others, they can't soldier for sour apples. They have no grit, no gumption, and they muddle along and allow themselves to be shot down because they don't know how to take cover.

It will be a sorry lookout for the Empire if this is the class of soldier they are going to rely on in Flanders.

Even more important as a cause of failure was the mismanagement by Birdwood and Godley. From the start the command arrangements for such a complex and ambitious operation were woefully inadequate. Godley's responsibilities, which included the Light Horse attacks at Anzac and the two divisions allotted to him for attacks on Sari Bair, effectively made him a corps commander, yet neither he nor Birdwood thought to augment his divisional staff to obtain the necessary control. The only assistance Godley could render was 'simply to throw additional troops at the brigade commanders', but they in turn did not have the staff to handle them. Thus Cox found himself in the absurd situation on 8 August of trying to control the operations of thirteen battalions advancing over different routes to attack widely spaced objectives, with only his brigade signals section, manned by Gurkhas who could not speak English. Birdwood and Godley were as ignorant of events as their oft-criticised counterparts at Suvla. Godley rarely ventured from his headquarters at No. 2 Post, and neither attended nor sent a representative to the most crucial conference of the campaign, at which the final attacks on Hill Q and Chunuk Bair early on 9 August were planned. On the afternoon of the 9th, he and Birdwood, still unaware that the attacks had failed, were confidently predicting to Hamilton that they would have the key to The Narrows next day!

The historian is hard put to explain how Birdwood occupied himself during the offensive. With Godley the answer is easy. He made a point of watching the mounted despatch riders from Suvla try to reach his headquarters, much as a race caller follows the progress of a race. On one occasion, Arthur Temperley, brigade major of the New Zealand Infantry Brigade, who had just left the carnage of Chunuk Bair, was treated to the spectacle as Godley angrily rejected his claim that the New Zealanders had lost two-thirds of their men:

> Don't talk like a bloody fool. By God ... I believe this fellow *will* get away with it after all!
>
> A man who's been in action always comes out with some cock-and-bull story about the thousands of casualties – Christ, did you see him duck that time. By God, look – look! – they've got him at last, by God, they have! That *was* a bloody fine shot! When's the next one due to come along? And where's that fool ...

A lull in the fighting followed the loss of Chunuk Bair. Birdwood had suffered 12 000 casualties, and with no more reserves his formations were incapable of further effort. The ground won by the offensive was divided into two sections, the first extending from No. 1 Outpost along Rhododendron Ridge to the Aghyl Dere, and the second, commanded by Cox and including the 4th Brigade, from the dere to Damakjelik Bair. Monash's position overlooking the Kaiajik Dere was largely the same as the line he had occupied on 7 August. Cox described it on the 17th as 'generally a strong one', and added, 'A great deal of good work has been done in the time.' On 19 August 'Numerous reconnaissances' finally revealed the error in the location Monash had been reporting since the first morning.

The preparation of the new line for defence prevented the rest so urgently needed. Observing his platoon in the 13th Battalion, Lieutenant Tom Crooks wrote: 'The boys are properly worn out with fatigue.' Scarcity of water, so serious in 'New Anzac' that Birdwood and Godley sometimes doubted whether it could be held, and the perennial dietary deficiencies, contributed as heavily to the weak state of Monash's formation as they did in June and July. Cases of bronchitis appeared, caused by men sleeping without their blankets, which had been left in Reserve Gully. Monash finally succeeded in having personal kits and bedding brought forward on 18 August, nearly two weeks after the offensive began. He also appealed to Godley to use his personal influence to ensure the return of such detachments as the 150 to 200 men still employed on the beach *ten weeks* after the landing and another 100 sent to help 'somewhere on the right'. Monash described

CHAPTER 5

himself as 'doing all possible to calm people down.' Pope raised his men's spirits by talking to them in small groups and managing the engagement of Turks seen moving inland as he would a shooting gallery. But the commanders could do little to revive men who had already drawn on their last reserves of endurance. Nevertheless, the 4th Brigade was to participate in the forthcoming attack on Hill 60, which, if taken, would secure the fragile junction between the Anzac and Suvla forces.

Bean took this image in 1919 and used it in the *Official History* to illustrate the 4th Brigade's role in the attacks on Hill 60. Assaulting across the Kaiajik Dere on the right flank in the direction of Bean's arrow, it was enfiladed by Turkish fire sweeping down the valley and few men reached Hill 60, which Bean had to outline to make visible (AWM G02074).

Flat-topped and covered in scrub too low to afford cover, Hill 60 is so imperceptible from the surrounding plain that in photographs of it in the *Official History* it is outlined in ink. The feature was undefended on 7 August, when men from the 4th Brigade had wandered over it to collect water and honey. Monash realised its tactical importance even then, and vainly urged the 40th Brigade next to him to push forward and occupy the knoll. On 14 August he discussed with Cox a plan to cooperate with an advance by IX Corps in which his brigade's role 'would, of course, take the form of operating down the Kaiajik Dere.' After another conference with Cox and Russell on 19 August, the plan was settled for the attack two days later. Russell would command an assault across the Kaiajik Dere with his two NZMR regiments, barely 400 men, and a detachment of 500 from the 4th Brigade, while assaults by the 29th and 29th Indian brigades on his left prolonged the line to IX Corps. Monash's detachment had the most difficult task. Attacking on the extreme right flank, it would be enfiladed by the Turks on Hill 100, who looked straight along the Kaiajik Dere. Godley and Cox hoped to lessen the danger by extending the bombardment beyond the line to be attacked to encompass Hill 100 and positions nearby. It would commence at 2.15 pm, three-quarters of an hour before the assault.

Monash's orders, issued on 20 August, were as detailed as those for the Sari Bair march, even though the march was a far more complex operation. Commanded by Major Herring, 250 men from each of the 13th and 14th battalions would debouch on a frontage of 150 yards from the 13th Battalion line, which Monash called the pivot. 'Every facility' was to be given them to enter, move along and leave the trenches. To the right of the pivot, 'an energetic and sustained covering fire' would be directed at the Turkish front opposite, which battalion commanders were to divide between themselves according to the fields of fire they enjoyed from their posts. In this way no portion of the Turkish trenches was missed and, by controlling the fire carefully, Monash hoped that their occupants would be forced to remain under cover throughout the attack. As quick reorganisation was vital to prevent the Turks on Hill 100 isolating Herring once they had recovered from the bombardment, the 15th Battalion would leave its trenches when the assault had crossed the Kaiajik Dere and begin the construction of a sunken way connecting the old and new lines. At the same time fifty men from the 13th were to move along the dere, clearing it of snipers who might interfere with the work of the 15th.

Like its Sari Bair predecessor, Monash's plan promised to overcome the weaknesses in Cox's scheme, but the state of the brigade, as in the Sari Bair march, did not augur well for success. In the 14th Battalion the RMO had great difficulty finding 250 men fit to participate,

CHAPTER 5

while the 13th was functioning 'by sheer force of will.' No signals officers were available, forcing Monash to make the communications arrangements himself. The issue of orders at lower levels was confused. Lieutenant Hubert Ford of the 13th Battalion, who would lead the first wave, was told only that he would attack 'a certain part of the Hill with 150 men' and not until afterwards did he ascertain the extent of the assault. At the last moment the timetable for the bombardment was 'somewhat curtailed'. Godley had agreed to support the concurrent attack by IX Corps, because his guns enfiladed its southern flank. His generosity meant that unless the Anzac attack was postponed, it would have to be made without artillery preparation. At 1.15 pm Monash was informed that the assault would begin at 3.25 pm, the artillery commencing its bombardment at 3.00 pm after switching from the targets in front of IX Corps.

Watching the attack with Bean from the 13th Battalion trenches, Monash saw the first wave take only two minutes to reach the far bank. But they were met with torrential machine-gun fire and only sixty-six of the 150 men remained. The second wave under Major Dare suffered similarly before joining the first on the slope of a small indentation, about 70 yards from their objective, which offered some shelter from the fire sweeping down the Kaiajik Dere. On the left, the New Zealanders had rushed the first Turkish trenches, and at 4.00 pm Russell instructed both Monash and the Indians to push forward to support them. Burdened with picks and shovels for the reorganisation of the position, the third wave could not advance beyond a gutter in the bed of the dere, and the 10th Hampshires, trying to reinforce Dare, broke when a heavy shell exploded among them. It set fire to the scrub, and those wounded not incinerated were shot by the Turks as they tried to escape the flames. At 5.00 pm Monash told Russell that his men could go no further and were digging in. When darkness fell, the 15th Battalion began the trench across the Kaiajik Dere. Of the detachment of 500 men, 173 were casualties.

The attack showed that commanders were still learning the methods of trench warfare and making the same mistakes as their contemporaries on the Western Front. Monash's detachment had no chance of success unless the enfilade fire against it could be subdued, for which reliance was placed on the artillery. But the guns had failed in similar circumstances on 2/3 May when the Turks – like the Germans in France – simply sat out the bombardment before emerging from their shelters to pour fire into the assault. Another lesson learned from that attack was ignored, because the bombardment lifted to its second-phase targets as soon as the attack began, instead of when the infantry were an appropriate distance across the Kaiajik Dere. As a result, it was 'just sufficient to put the Turks on the alert', and they could be seen standing waist high behind their parapets, shooting at the attackers, who were still climbing over theirs. Smoke could have been used to blind the Turks, particularly on Monash's flank, but 'such devices were then unthought of at Gallipoli.' The covering fire from the 4th Brigade could not hope to compensate for the absence of these and other forms of support.

Monash himself learned an important lesson from the conduct of this operation. He recalled the attack a year later in another lecture to the officers of the 3rd Division, which demonstrates once again just how important a preparation was his Gallipoli experience for the higher command that came after:

> ... orders had to be altered only because at the last moment the Artillery authorities decided that certain batteries would not be available ... Consequently commanders did not know what was going to happen and the whole operation was more or less, though not entirely, a failure. And simply because a change of orders had been made when everybody was thoroughly settled on a certain plan of campaign which had to be altered in a hurry ... everybody got rattled, everybody waited, it was altogether a miscalculated, and misdirected operation. The result was considerable loss of life and little gain.

Monash insisted that once orders were issued, they should not be modified unless 'absolutely necessary for the safe conduct of the operation and men, then as little as is consistent with that safety'; hence his adoption of Napoleon's aphorism: 'Order, Counter Order, Disorder.'

CHAPTER 5

As the 4th Brigade's effective strength was now under 1450, Monash asked for a reduction in the length of his front and the relief of the 'survivors' of Herring's detachment across the Kaiajik Dere. Godley was furious at the use of the word 'survivors', which he thought might provoke alarm and despondency. Monash also inferred that he was dissatisfied with the performance of the brigade. He defended his men, saying their work was 'exceptionally good', and that, while he intended no reflection on Godley, 'survivors' was an appropriate term in view of the casualties sustained. Godley apologised. Bean was less understanding, and blamed the failure to reach the Hill 60 trenches squarely on Monash who, on this as on two or three other occasions, 'certainly knows less of the situation than any other Brigadier I have seen.' The charge was true in the case of the attack on 8 August, but as Bean stood beside Monash to watch the Hill 60 assault, it is hard to understand how the two men could have had anything less than equal knowledge of the situation. His long discourse on the reasons for Herring's wave 'running away' when hit by shellfire – naturally attributed to Monash's ineffectual leadership – showed in fact that Bean was rather poorly informed, because these men were not from the 4th Brigade at all, but from the 10th Hampshires.

The *Official Medical History* describes the condition of the 4th Brigade at this time as 'deplorable'. Russell was so shocked at the state of the 300 men who replaced Herring's detachment that he asked if they, too, could be relieved. In reply, Monash pointed out that they were 'the fittest and best left in the brigade ... to find 300 men to take [their] place is quite impossible.' The measures taken were not palliative but draconian. Colonel John Beeston, Assistant Director Medical Services (ADMS) of the NZ and A Division, told the RMOs from the 4th Brigade that while he did not wish to reflect on their competence, there were too many evacuations. After rebuking Captain Loughran for his retort: 'Yes, nearly everybody has diarrhoea', Beeston urged them not to send away men fit enough to stand in a trench and hold a rifle. Monash was on his side, asking him on 26 August to prevent any 'avoidable evacuations' from a party sent to the Field Ambulance by Captain Stanley McGregor, RMO of the 16th Battalion, among whom, said McGregor: 'several ... were scarcely able to walk ... others had collapsed while at work ... and others had definite complaints requiring treatment.' But Monash was not merely fulfilling instructions from Godley; he knew that his brigade was about to take part in another attack on Hill 60.

Godley, Cox and Russell prepared the plan at a conference at 4th Brigade Headquarters on 25 August. The sickness and heavy losses dictated that small detachments of fit men from each formation comprise the 1000-strong attacking force. Russell, who had graduated from the Sandhurst Military Academy with the Sword of Honour and served in India before returning to civil life in New Zealand, would again command it. The objective of the 250 men from the 4th Brigade was the same as in the previous attack. As the Turks, unknown to Russell, had reoriented and improved their defences, his scheme was based on inaccurate information. Another disadvantage was the time of the attack. After the experience of 21 August, Monash and Russell urged a night assault, but Cox overruled them, misguidedly relying on the bombardment to crush the opposition. It would last one hour before the attack began at 5.00 pm on 27 August. Afterwards, Cox remarked that it 'proved a much more difficult and complicated job than I expected.'

Monash's orders hardly differed from those of the previous attack. Lieutenant Colonel John Adams of the 14th Battalion would lead 100 men from each of the 13th and 14th battalions and fifty from the 15th, while the remainder of the brigade provided covering fire, during as well as after the bombardment, to catch any Turks disturbed by it. But Russell's instructions were skimpy, merely repeating the orders already issued by Cox. Details such as routes to and coordination arrangements in the forming-up place, attacking formations and covering fire, were omitted from orders that barely filled two pages of a field notebook. Adams's orders took even less space – twenty-six lines – because he proposed to explain the plan to his men 'on the ground' just before the attack. After four months of

CHAPTER 5

heavy fighting, the continuing ignorance of commanders at all levels of the importance of staff procedures is striking.

A message received by McGlinn at 7.30 pm told the story of the attack: more stretcher-bearers were required to cope with the number of incoming wounded. As before, the bombardment of the trenches opposite the 4th Brigade was 'just a stand to arms signal for the Turks.' Only two small calibre shells hit them, enabling the Turks to 'cut up 4 Bde as soon as it moved.' Lieutenant Alan Brierley, who led the 13th Battalion party, had never experienced such a concentration of fire as fell upon his wave, some of whom leaned forward 'as if bracing oneself against a strong headwind.' Some 230 casualties were suffered by the 350 men from the 4th Brigade and the newly arrived 17th Battalion from the 2nd Australian Division for a gain of a few yards on the extreme left flank, where their sector joined the New Zealanders. Watching the attack with Cox and Russell, Monash expressed his disgust in his strongest diary entry of the war: 'The whole was a rotten, badly organised show – and those who planned it are responsible for heavy loss to this brigade.' The attack as a whole took what turned out to be a false crest; Hill 60's summit remained in Turkish hands.

The aftermath was an unpleasant time for Monash. Cox was 'naturally very disappointed that your men failed to make more ground', ascribing the absence of corrective action when the advance strayed across the front of its objective to poor leadership. Monash did not mince words on the cause of the trouble: the detachments 'were under Russell's orders and not mine and I do not know what orders Russell gave them.' Monash tolerated the harassment until 3 September, when he had 'a straight talk to Godley about Cox and his bullying.' Godley explained that this was just Cox's gruff manner. The battalion commanders were nearing the end of their tether. Depressed at the outcome of an attack whose futility he had predicted, Adams begged Monash to relieve him as he was 'broken up and unfit'. Dare succeeded Adams, who had only just replaced Rankine, in command of the 14th Battalion. Tilney also had collapsed and was replaced by Durrant. Pope was in 'a low state' and asked for seven days' leave. Recommending the request to Godley, Monash confirmed that his 'mainstay' was 'not far from a breakdown'. As the loss of officers continued, 'the work of keeping up efficiency gets harder and harder.' Now, for the first time in the campaign, Monash was unwell. For the next two weeks he alternated between attacks of acute dysentery and lumbago.

'The absolutely rotten condition of the Brigade' was a source of 'extreme worry'. The 14th Battalion's strength of 158 all ranks was the lowest in its history, but it was still an important contribution to the total number left in the brigade, about 890. According to the establishment figures of the time, therefore, Monash was commanding a brigade of battalion strength. On 31 August it began to move to a quieter sector, holding the line from Cheshire Ridge across the Aghyl Dere to Bauchop's Hill. Prospects for rest were dimmed by Godley's and Cox's decision that 350 'effectives' must remain in the trenches in the Kaiajik Dere and Hill 60 to bolster the 'young and untried troops' of Brigadier General Daniel's relieving 161st Brigade. Monash told Cannan, the commander of the detachment, that he should 'make every effort to induce the GOC 161 Bde to withdraw all 4 Bde at the earliest possible moment.' He had already protested to Godley, sending him a careful analysis of his brigade's strength to show that, with the numbers available, it was virtually impossible to defend his new line and assist the 161st Brigade as well. As usual, Godley was sympathetic, but did not alter the arrangement. He suggested that Monash use his Brigade Headquarters to hold the line if he was so short of men.

The episode demonstrated Monash's disdain for Godley. When the detachment was still unrelieved on 4 September, he told Cannan to 'work on General Daniel', because 'If he waits for General Godley to *ask* for them to be returned, I am afraid you will still be over the Kaiajik next Christmas.' Piqued, Cannan replied that as Monash had 'evidently lost interest in our welfare', he was quite prepared to remain with the 161st Brigade until Christmas, when 'there won't be many of us left ... so we will be still less trouble.' Monash rejected the imputation, blaming Godley, who had snubbed his efforts to

CHAPTER 5

have Cannan released, and the selfish attitude of General Daniel, a British officer whom he regarded as typical: 'They "take" freely enough – but they never "give". I have suffered nothing but annoyance in my dealings with them.' His jibes against Godley and Daniel may have been justified, but to repeat them to Cannan to avoid any blame himself was a poor example from a commander who had enjoined his own officers not to complain in front of their subordinates. But the 4th Brigade's first real rest was imminent. After touring his new line on 6 September, Birdwood foreshadowed a move to Lemnos, and one week later embarkation for Sarpi camp on Lemnos began. So ended a period whose fighting Monash described as the 'toughest and fiercest and most sustained of any we have ever had (not excluding our first landing).' Albert Jacka expressed the view of the rank and file: 'Lost count of everything but the heavy fighting of Aug 8, 19 [sic], 27. Worst month we ever had. Practically whole battalion wiped out in these stunts.'

The 16th Battalion resting on Lemnos in October. It numbers well under 200 men. As the 16th had landed 959 strong in April and received eight reinforcement drafts since, the image shows not just the cost of the August offensive but the cost of the campaign (AWM C00499).

Sailing only by night, the fifty-mile journey to Lemnos took forty-eight hours, allowing Monash 'a decent sleep, some beer and a hot bath', before he arrived to find the camp 'badly pitched and totally inadequate for our numbers.' On 23 September he became Commandant of Sarpi and experienced his first real contact with the mismanagement and inefficiency of the General Headquarters (GHQ) Lines of Communication staff. A typical example was the tent shortage. There were ample stocks in store, but Ordnance would not release them without the endorsement of the Commandant of Mudros West, which Monash had been trying to obtain for four days. Inevitably, heavy thunderstorms flooded the campsite, making life miserable for the 2000 men of the 4th Brigade and other units still without shelter. He reserved special sarcasm for the staff aboard the *Aragon*:

> They told us that they were going to do, oh, such a lot to make us thoroughly comfortable! They gave us some travelling kitchens. They came a few days after and took them away at very short notice, and told us to requisition for dixies ...

Monash, who had always emphasised the importance of administration and aspired to the same standard of efficiency in military matters as in his civil career, found the efforts of GHQ deplorable. It was the inevitable result of sending the best men to the fighting front, leaving the service and rear areas in the hands of the mediocre and inefficient.

Still, there were many enjoyable moments on Lemnos. Basking in the sun, Monash found it difficult to believe 'there was a war on somewhere' as he contemplated 'the rolling meadows and hills topped with windmills, their sails turning around lazily in the breeze, with flocks of ridiculous little black and white sheep about the size of poodles and caravans of picturesque Greek peasants in their national dress on lines of little donkeys.' He explored the island on horseback, took a hot sulphur bath in the thermal springs and enjoyed the fresh fruit and other luxuries obtainable in the Greek villages. In this peaceful but invigorating environment and the three weeks' leave in Egypt that followed, his dysentery and lumbago gradually abated.

CHAPTER 5

Monash in Cairo. He took leave in Egypt in October and returned to Anzac in early November, just after his brigade (AWM A01241).

The rest was just as therapeutic for the men. No parades were held for the first four days, and then light work began, gradually increasing in intensity to return the 4th Brigade to the level of fitness and training it had reached before the landing. In recognition of the nature of warfare at Anzac, officers and NCOs were instructed in the tactical handling of men in trench fighting, while the new drafts were taught bomb-throwing and the use of the periscope rifle. The condition of the brigade improved steadily, Godley remarking on its return to Anzac that it looked 'so much restored in health and appearance.' But Monash was dissatisfied with the trickle of reinforcements, only forty-nine of whom had joined his formation by 30 September, nearly three weeks after its arrival at Sarpi. Even after convalescents were collected from Egypt, the 4th Brigade numbered only 2171 when it left Sarpi, half its original strength. Meanwhile the remainder of the 2nd Australian Division had disembarked at Anzac, but it was woefully untrained, Birdwood remarking on the 'painfully apparent inexperience of leaders at all levels.'

With many of the veteran units depleted, the new formations capable only of holding the trenches and the Turks in similar straits, the period after August saw no serious fighting. Monash realised that the situation had reached stalemate and feared the wet and stormy weather of the approaching winter as 'a far worse enemy than the Turks.' The construction of shelter against it became the first priority throughout the ANZAC and received added impetus from reports that German heavy guns were being sent to the peninsula. Monash emphasised to his battalion commanders that the work must be carried out 'with the utmost possible speed' and increased shifts from four to eight hours daily. Though the demands on them were heavy, he harked back to his old adage that the men would respond cheerfully 'if they are made to understand that it is in their own vital interests.' Underground barrack rooms with fireplaces were dug in Cheshire Ridge, as well as tunnels to link them to kitchens, dining areas and the firing line, which were improved every day. The quietness produced a laxity in both personal and trench discipline: rifles left uncleaned, equipment lying about 'promiscuously', sentries playing cards and 'men keeping their pipes in their mouths or failing to come to attention ... when addressing or being addressed by superiors.' Monash responded as he usually did by stressing to his commanding officers their responsibility to maintain a high standard and the need to exert unremitting pressure on their subordinates to combat faults 'because unless this is done a condition of dry rot will set in.'

CHAPTER 5

In October Hamilton was replaced by General Sir Charles Monro, and Birdwood took charge of the Dardanelles Army, which with the Salonika Force now comprised the MEF. Godley succeeded him at Anzac, and Russell assumed command of the NZ and A Division. On 13 November, ten senior officers gathered on the Anzac pier to meet Kitchener. The Field Marshal told Monash, who happened to be the first Australian in the group, that the King admired what had been accomplished. Monash was unaware that the visit presaged the end of the campaign. One month later, 'Like a thunderbolt from a clear blue sky has come the stupendous and paralysing news that the best and wisest course to be taken is to evacuate the Peninsula and secret orders to carry out that operation have just reached here.'

Men and stores were sent to Imbros on the pretext of reducing the garrisons for winter, when no offensive operations could be mounted. The worsening weather and the discomfort caused by a blizzard on 27 November gave credence to the order. The 15th Battalion and elements of the 14th Battalion left on 13–14 December. Before the final evacuation on the nights of the 18th and 19th, the Anzac garrison had been reduced to 20 000 men.

Monash had nothing to do with the planning, which was brilliantly done by White, the ANZAC chief of staff since Skeen had left the peninsula with enteric on 9 September. It was based on 'a gradual reduction from our present fire trenches – time of withdrawal being determined by time at which troops will be required to embark and distances from places of embarkation.' Monash, who was also acting as second-in-command of the NZ and A Division, remained until the last night, leaving with the second of the three parties to be withdrawn that evening. By 10.00 pm the entire eight-mile front of Anzac was held by 1500 men, 170 of whom defended the 4th Brigade line under Major Herring. Monash had cards prepared for each man, setting out his duties, the time he should leave for the beach and the route to be followed: 'All this means *organisation* and makes all the difference between success and failure.' Dare wrote a skit on the orders for their move to the beach. 'Disputes to be fought with judges at competitors' own risk … Batman will act as a spy and proceed to 971 and endeavour to penetrate Turkish lines and keep them busily engaged ... General Monash and Colonel McGlynn [sic] will act as stretcher-bearers to the patrol.' Monash's batman had another task, running back to the Brigade Headquarters dugout to retrieve the leather portfolio his commander had forgotten.

Reflecting on the campaign in 1920, Monash felt that it could not be described as a failure. Above all, it had created the Anzac tradition, which was to sustain the AIF throughout the war. It had also delayed Bulgaria's entry into the conflict and destroyed the cream of the Turkish Army. But the Turks had not been Monash's only concern between April and December 1915. He arranged the transfer from the 2nd Brigade to the 14th Battalion of his nephew, Lieutenant Eric Simonson, intending to use him as his aide-de-camp (ADC), and advised a second nephew, Aubrey Moss, to accept a commission as officer in charge of the bomb factory. Until then, Moss had worked well as an intelligence draughtsman at ANZAC Headquarters, giving Monash access to information he would not normally have. When Godley assumed command at Anzac, Moss opined: 'he is very unpopular with all here, his manner is so different from General Birdwood's.'

Monash's quest for recognition intensified and manifested itself in numerous ways. Towards the end of the campaign he was annoyed by the omission from recent maps of the name of Monash Valley and asked Moss to ensure that it was included whenever possible. He was gratified at being made a Companion of the Order of the Bath (CB) in October because 'Having gained this *during* the campaign, the chances of my getting something *after* the campaign are much improved.' Even a lowly Mentioned in Despatches was welcomed as 'It ought to shut up some of my enemies for good.' At the same time, he could not understand the reason for Russell's award of the Knight Commander of the Order of St Michael and St George (KCMG): he was only a brigadier, considerably junior to Monash, had not arrived until the end of May and 'in comparison ... had done nothing conspicuous.' The publication of extracts from Monash's letters was pleasing, but publication of McCay's letters was 'atrocious self-advertisement which will do him no good at all.'

CHAPTER 5

Although at times the fight for promotion among AIF officers seemed as bitter as the struggle against the Turks, Monash was a more willing and versatile combatant than most. The immediate cause of the discord was the appointment of Bridges' successor. Initially considering the former Inspector-General, George Kirkpatrick, now in India, as a replacement, Birdwood gave the 1st Division to Walker, who had already proved an outstanding success as commander of the 1st Brigade. Unknown to Birdwood or Hamilton, however, Pearce had sent Legge, whom he had marked for advancement before the war, to succeed Bridges in both his capacities as GOC 1st Division and GOC AIF. The result was a seething resentment among the Australian brigadiers on the peninsula, who protested their supersession by an officer their junior and without experience of the front. McCay could 'hardly stand the idea of being under [Legge]' and told Bean he would leave when Legge arrived. Monash regarded the appointment of his old opponent as 'an awful piece of logrolling ... and it is a severe blow to the ambitions of McCay, Chauvel and myself.' He asked McGlinn to ascertain from Blamey their relative seniority and questioned in a letter to Chauvel the Australian Government's right to make appointments in a force it had put at the disposal and under the control of the War Office: 'It has no more right to *appoint* a Commander of a British or Colonial Division than it has to appoint a Battalion Commander or Corporal.' Chauvel agreed, and approached Birdwood, who 'would not take any stand in the matter at all.' Birdwood quelled their talk of resignation, pointing out that this was unthinkable in war, and if Legge was as weak as they had said, he would need their loyal support. The storm passed quickly. When McCay, who had been appointed to the 2nd Australian Division, broke his leg in July, Birdwood sent Legge to Egypt to command it, and Walker resumed charge of the 1st Division. Legge's transfer made easier the assumption by Birdwood of the powers of GOC AIF, which he held in the interval after Bridges' death and which Legge had appeared reluctant to exercise.

In issues affecting his own seniority, Monash did not hesitate to approach the man whose appointment he had opposed. Like the other Australian brigade commanders, he was rightly peeved at holding the rank of colonel, which automatically made him junior to his counterparts in the British or New Zealand forces who were brigadier generals. Legge could say little because the matter was under consideration, but, possibly reminded of his treatment at the hands of Monash and others, he pointed out that 'seniority means experience, but this without capacity is a negative asset.' When the Australian Government approved the promotion of its officers to brigadier general in July, Monash found himself junior to McCay, as he had been in militia days, but senior by three months to Chauvel. In September and October, Chauvel commanded the NZ and A Division for short periods in Godley's absence, and on 6 November replaced Hobbs, then temporarily in charge of the 1st Division. 'Much perturbed', Monash began an 'energetic correspondence' with Godley, Major Tom Griffiths, the Military Secretary, and Birdwood. It was Monash's 'unvarying rule throughout my 31 years' service, [not] to place myself in competition with any other officer for military advancement', yet he felt a duty to protest 'in order to safeguard the inherent rights of seniority.' Godley's view – that *Commonwealth Military Regulations* prescribed the rank of brigadier general as 'temporary and local' – was invalid, Monash thought, because the Military Board specified the promotions as substantive. As he feared that Godley might induce Birdwood to approach Pearce, Monash pre-empted his corps commander, writing himself to McCay and Pearce. Claiming that the 'Army Clique' felt threatened as to their 'future possibilities' by these substantive promotions, Monash had no qualms about adducing the very arguments he had used against Legge:

> The Australian Government is entirely within its rights in assigning whatever status and rank it chooses to its own officers, in its own Imperial Force; and it seems unbecoming of anyone to question, as has been done, the propriety of such action.[43]

The most interesting aspect of Birdwood's stance on the issue was not his subsequent rebuke of Monash, but his thoughts on him as a brigade commander:

> Monash has, I think, certainly done well. He looks after his Brigade thoroughly well – knows all details concerning it, and is an excellent

CHAPTER 5

organiser. At the same time, I cannot look upon him as a leader in war, and I consider the others more suitable than he.

There the matter rested. Was Birdwood's assessment objective? Firstly, like Bean at this time, he was mildly antagonistic towards Jews. Secondly, his conception of a leader in war differed fundamentally from that of Monash, whom he contemptuously called after the war 'the Dug Out King'. Finally, his own performance on Gallipoli was hardly perfect. Inspecting Anzac in its last days, the one thing he noticed was the signal wire, which he wanted reeled up. White remarked: 'Heavens – What does he think we are doing here – why I would gladly have left all the guns behind if we could only get the men off safely.' Some of the other Anzac commanders might well have acted as Birdwood did. Their inexperience was evident in every aspect of warfare, from operational staff work to administration, to which were added the peculiar problems of trench fighting and the sickness of the men they commanded. All of them were feeling their way; predictably, all made mistakes. It is in this context that Monash must be judged and not according to a standard of perfection that was absent from Gallipoli.

This is not to say that Monash's performance was unblemished – far from it. On the other hand, he left his superiors in no doubt of his thoughts on operations and strove to overcome weaknesses in their schemes as they affected his brigade. Except for 8 August, his planning revealed a depth of detail and coordination missing from the efforts of his contemporaries. As experienced leaders became casualties, he gave the easiest tasks to the new men and took great care to prescribe the manner of their execution. Enough has been said of the night march on 6 August to make further comment unnecessary. He maintained a strict control of manpower, questioning to the end the reasons why men were evacuated. In each of these areas were parallels with his engineering background: the same need for order, detail, method and economy. He appreciated fully and informed his superiors of the state of his men, but ruthlessly balanced operational requirements against it:

> If one stops to count the cost, or worry over the loss of friends or the grief and sorrow of the people at home, one simply could not

carry on for an hour. The moment a man becomes a casualty, pick your man to take his place, and go right ahead with the work in hand ... There is absolutely no other way ... it is the whole secret of successful leadership in war. The objective is everything – the means do not count.

At the final reckoning, the ledger entry on Monash's performance on Gallipoli can be entered in black. He was a very competent brigadier. As it was said at the time that he would make an even better divisional and corps commander, the future was promising indeed.

Chapter 6

A Man of Very Considerable Ability

The ANZAC returned to Egypt. Monash thought the Turkish threat to it – and hence to the Suez Canal – 'all bluff'. Kitchener thought differently. The forces released by the Allied evacuation of the peninsula would enable the Turks to concentrate an army of 250 000 against Egypt and there was also the German promise to encourage native uprisings. Birdwood expected a strong attack within six weeks, but a more immediate threat loomed. Reports received on 19 January 1916 indicated that the Turks were reinforcing their 13 000 troops at Beersheba, 120 miles away across the Sinai, for an advance on the canal, and it was likely to begin in a fortnight. Both Australian divisions left their camps at Tel-el-Kebir to occupy the No. 2, or Central Section, of the canal defences, which stretched twenty miles from Ferry Post in the north to Serapeum in the south. The NZ and A Division remained at Moascar, one mile from Ismailia and directly across the canal from Ferry Post. The 4th Brigade joined it there on 21 January 1916.

Monash warmed to Ismailia, 'a beautiful little town – with lovely gardens, avenues and plantations', and dined and bathed at its French Club regularly. These comforts were his main solace at a time of intense worry and depression. On 18 January he received a telegram from Gibson: 'Your wife seriously ill, immediate major operation necessary.' As there had been no hint of sickness in letters from his wife or daughter, Monash was naturally overwhelmed. He became more hopeful as succeeding days brought increasingly optimistic messages, culminating on 1 February in 'Danger Past'. Initially unaware of the nature of the illness, Monash had shown all correspondence to his medical officers, whose hardening opinion was confirmed when he finally received the diagnosis by Vic's doctor: uterine cancer. He had wanted to 'rush home', but informal conversations with Birdwood and Godley convinced him that if he left Egypt, his honour would be impugned. How anomalous it was that because he was healthy, leave must be denied him, but if he had broken down or yielded to many temptations to go sick, he could have returned to Australia with his reputation intact. This was not the first time that Monash contemplated returning home, for the previous July he had confessed:

> Most certainly if the war goes on till next winter, one could be forgiven for feeling that one had made a sufficient sacrifice in giving up over twelve months of one's life and there may be a chance of getting one's discharge with honour and credit.

The reaffirmation of this sentiment on the occasion of his wife's grave illness was more than the natural concern of a man whom circumstances had rendered impotent to assist. Monash's resigned cynicism reflected a growing disenchantment with the war, his commanders and his own prospects, which the crisis brought to a head. It was iniquitous that brigadiers still received the salaries and allowances of colonels, particularly in the case of a wealthy man like himself, who had made a heavy financial sacrifice to serve in the AIF. He was peeved at 'all the absurd slobber' over McCay on his return to Australia after barely five weeks' actual service in the line at Anzac because 'When *we* get home, everybody will have forgotten all about the war.'[44] But McCay's great influence with Pearce might counteract the 'Army Clique', chief among whom was Godley:

> [He] has a violent temper which he tries very hard to control – often not very successfully. He is also very pernickety. He is also very selfish. While in a formal way, he is very dignified, a fine speaker and a strong administrator, he has not that urbanity and tact which makes a man really liked by his Staff and Commanders.

Godley was detested by the New Zealanders, whose letters home brought calls from incensed parents for his replacement. But he was unconcerned: 'Heaven help us when and if I ever become popular.' He felt that Birdwood's style, with its constant visits to the line, bred

CHAPTER 6

familiarity and a consequent breakdown of discipline. While Monash admitted that he had been treated fairly, he sensed that Godley held him in contempt as a militia officer, '*a mere Amateur*', whose interests would always be subordinated to 'any Australian *permanent* officer knocking about like Legge or Chauvel or Irving or Sinclair-MacLagan. They will have a better chance for a Division than I or Holmes would have.' On the other hand, Monash had no reservations about Russell, whom Godley had left in command of the NZ and A Division. He was 'a splendid fellow and a close friend of mine ... urbanity itself, without weakness.' As for his own command:

> I am getting busy with the entertaining occupation of refitting and recruiting and knocking discipline and a semblance of fighting capacity into a few thousand more Australians who have recently materialised, so that in a month or two they may, with all due circumstance, get blown into little pieces or get holes drilled into themselves, for the honour of Australia and for the good of posterity.

Major General Sir Andrew Russell. A Sandhurst graduate who returned to the land in New Zealand, Russell led the NZMR on Gallipoli and the New Zealand Division in France. Like his colleague, Monash, he proved to be outstanding as a divisional commander. Haig wanted to give him a British corps in 1918, but Russell preferred to stay with his New Zealanders (AWM E04712).

At their first meeting after the evacuation, Monash told his commanding officers that the coming period was 'an opportunity to pull things together', which would demand 'special activity and special energy'. He threw himself into the work, setting an example for them to emulate. There would be no relaxation of the established standards of personal discipline and turnout, which were fundamental to *esprit de corps*, a point demonstrated by his dissatisfaction with the brigade guard. Its members were often 'unshaven or with long hair or clothing and equipment put on carelessly' and had little knowledge of their duties. Unless there was an improvement, the guard would not be allowed to mount and its commander would be punished. Platoon and company commanders were to devote ten minutes daily to systematic instruction in the paying of compliments and disciplining men who failed to salute. Monash harped on officer responsibility, the theme of his first lecture to the new arrivals. He mentioned the importance of psychology in leadership as well as the traditional criteria: 'justice, firmness, fairness and strictness'. Discipline was equated with 'the power of securing co-ordinated action'. He sought variety in training and confidence, based on knowledge, in instructors. They should not hesitate to correct faults and make their presence felt. There must be 'no [public] washing of dirty linen'. Monash concluded with an emotional appeal to preserve the reputation of the brigade: 'We owe it to ourselves; we owe it to our dead.' He had outlined the same principles at his first meeting with the battalion commanders of the 13th Brigade on 12 August 1913.

Training followed a program prepared by Godley and White for all formations in the corps. In the 4th Brigade, musketry, bayonet fighting and marching with gradually heavier loads figured prominently. Monash's additions reflected matters that his own experience had taught him were important. Signals training was stressed, while every sub-unit was to be instructed by its commander, thus developing teamwork and mutual confidence. He lectured his officers on navigation and the importance of precise staff work. During brigade manoeuvres, Monash simulated as closely as possible the physical demands of operations by ensuring that his men wore field marching

CHAPTER 6

order and carried all their equipment, including machine-guns and ammunition packs. An exercise on 31 January was identical to the scheme at Lilydale, a frontal attack by part of his brigade while the remainder enveloped the position from a flank. Explanations at every stage helped to illustrate the lessons Monash aimed to teach: coordinated action, the use of ground and – his favourite – the passing of information within the battalions and within the brigade. Russell watched the exercise, and Monash described it as 'very successful'.

The opposite was true of divisional schemes. On 8 February, Monash felt 'very tired and depressed' after Russell attempted 'to move the whole division as one body, with rather ludicrous results.' This was a rehearsal for an advance north of Ismailia on 10 and 11 February, of which Monash wrote: 'very stupid and elementary work.' Field exercises against the NZMR on 17 February were nothing but 'a most delightful muddle and confusion of orders.' Monash blamed Russell. He regarded him highly as a man, but held a low opinion of his ability as a commander, confiding to McCay:

> The proceedings on Divisional Manoeuvres here would make you scream! They put at defiance every fundamental principle of command and staff work and of ordinary common sense. Those years we spent at War Courses, Staff Exercises etc. were so much labour wasted.

Monash predicted these results to Russell, just as he had warned Godley in similar circumstances the previous year. Each day was an obvious reminder of the poor standard of elementary work and how much training both the men and their instructors needed. Monash questioned the wisdom of brigade and divisional manoeuvres with such weaknesses still evident, and suggested the extension of company and battalion work by at least two weeks. Watching his friend lurch from one blunder to another was further convincing proof to Monash of a truth that had often been demonstrated to him since the war began: the great relevance of his own civil experience to many of the functions of higher command:

> [Russell] has given me an insight into the awful confusion, cross purposes, constant changes of plan and policy which characterise

the higher command and get worse the higher you go. Here are professional soldiers trying to be railway traffic managers, wholesale providers and similar things without knowledge or expertise.

Monash suffered from Russell's apparent nonchalance towards administration, for Russell usually delegated administrative matters to his staff and did not bother himself further. When Monash calculated the exact number of tents required for his brigade at war strength, Russell approved the indent, but they still did not arrive. The establishment of Moascar camp was delayed by this 'characteristic example of how a commander can be let down by his staff.' Their incompetence and Russell's inexperience at this level contributed directly to Monash's dissatisfaction with 'the set-up, appearance and bearing' of his brigade after six weeks' training. Birdwood thought its discipline was about the poorest in the corps until Russell pointed out that the New Zealand units were worse.

After the decision was taken to evacuate the peninsula, reinforcements and convalescents who would normally have been sent to Anzac remained in Egypt. Their numbers had reached 45 000 at the end of the campaign. Still commanding the ANZAC, Godley proposed to absorb them into two new Australian divisions, making a total of four. On the arrival of another 50 000, promised by Hughes, a third new division might be constituted with an adequate reinforcement reservoir for all divisions. Reinforcements and another infantry brigade from New Zealand would enable the creation of the New Zealand Division. The new divisions would be grouped with the existing ones into two Anzac corps. General Sir Archibald Murray, Monro's successor as commander of the MEF, approved Godley's scheme when Birdwood, arriving in Egypt on 19 January after the breaking up of the Dardanelles Army, urged that an Australian and New Zealand Army might be created, because the two corps would be as strong as the original BEF. This was rejected by the War Office, but its proposal that the third division should be raised in Australia was accepted by the Commonwealth on Birdwood's recommendation. He would command 1st ANZAC and Godley

CHAPTER 6

2nd ANZAC, while Cox supervised the organisation and training of the new 4th and 5th divisions at Tel-el-Kebir. Birdwood nominated Cox and a British cavalry officer, Major General Herbert Lawrence, to command them, and suggested McCay for the 3rd Division. He continued to exercise administrative command of the AIF, much to the chagrin of Murray, whom the Chief of the Imperial General Staff (CIGS), Sir William Robertson, had suggested should assume control. Murray warned Robertson that 'a distinct eye to his future', underlay Birdwood's 'preposterous views on his Australian charter.'

Birdwood appointed Australians to command the battalions and brigades created by the expansion. But his contention that few Australian brigadiers were capable of leading a division was a great disappointment to Pearce, who had been encouraged by his praise of their performance at Anzac. The Australian Government considered Monash, Chauvel, White and Brigadier General William Holmes fit for divisional command, but Birdwood's nominee, Lawrence, 'did not seem to be an officer of high attainment.' Birdwood demurred. Holmes, commanding the 5th Brigade in the 2nd Division, was inexperienced and did not enjoy Godley's confidence. Chauvel, who now impressed Birdwood as decisive and resourceful, would command the new Mounted Division, and White, though 'undoubtedly fitted to command a division and would ... do it admirably', was indispensable as his chief of staff. Birdwood's assessment of Monash was unchanged:

> Monash I regard as a man of very considerable ability and with good administrative powers, and I think he would do capitally commanding a division in peace time. It was owing to the fact that I was not, however, at all sure of his ability to do this, and to do full justice to the troops serving under him that I felt I could not conscientiously recommend him as suitable in all respects to command a division in the field, when actually fighting the enemy. He has not shown that resolution which I believe is really essential, while as you probably know, there is, I believe, among a considerable number of the force a great feeling against him on account of what they consider his German extraction.

Monash had not been allowed to forget his German origins ever since the whispering campaign against his appointment to the 4th Brigade in August 1914. Before the landing, Bridges showed Gellibrand a bundle of letters referring to his alleged German proclivities. At Anzac it was said that he was a German spy, which evoked a sympathetic comment from Bean that the perpetrator of the rumour should have been cashiered. In Australia his cousins the Behrends had recently begun using his name in a manner that drew attention to his family background. Monash demanded that they cease 'this unwarrantable impertinence' before it was grasped by his 'many enemies who are only too glad to seize upon anything that may injure me.'

Birdwood ignored the prejudice, but its prevalence meant that he could recommend Monash for advancement only if he was acceptable in all other respects, and this 'I do not consider to be the case.' Mindful of the protest aroused by his peremptory imposition on Birdwood of Legge as Bridges' successor, Pearce reluctantly agreed with the corps commander, but he insisted that McCay should command one of the new divisions in Egypt. Birdwood gave him the 5th and Cox took charge of the 4th. As the 3rd Division would not arrive for some time, he proposed to leave its command vacant, although he inclined to transfer Chauvel from the Mounted Division, which was 'not ... nearly such an important command as an Infantry Division.'

Monash professed indifference. The 'thoroughly successful command' of the 4th Brigade and satisfactory performance of every task were his ambitions. He knew what Cox, Godley, Birdwood and Murray thought of him, and 'if they want me to command a division they know where to find me.' Blissfully ignorant of their real opinions, Monash remained detached:

> At any rate, I have fairly resolved not to intrigue or canvass for promotion in any way, and if Australia chooses to let her forces be exploited to find jobs for unemployed senior British officers, that is not my affair.

Therein lies a hint of Monash's real attitude, because his disinterest was feigned. Godley had told him of his plan for an 'Australian Army

CHAPTER 6

Corps' on 22 January. Next day Aubrey Moss apprised Monash of a telegram just received from Australia, asking for the names of potential divisional commanders. As McCay's name was mentioned, Moss assumed he had been chosen already. On 4 February he sent Monash extracts from a telegram to the New Zealand Defence Ministry, which confirmed Australian agreement to the formation of two divisions in Egypt with the inclusion of the 4th Brigade in one of them. When rumours of Cox's appointment reached Monash about 11 February, he drafted a strong letter to McCay. Surely Australia would not tolerate this 'crowning infamy'? As he was the only Australian brigadier to serve continuously throughout the campaign without a single day's absence from wounds or sickness, securing 'three mentions', Monash had a 'very live interest' in the matter:

> ... there will be at least two, if not three commands of Australian Divisions vacant very shortly and it is surely not an unreasonable aspiration that in the light of my training and service, I should be selected for one of them ...
>
> I am hoping that, as one of those who has borne the heat and burden of the day and who have made enormous sacrifices for Australia, I will not be overlooked.[45]

Meanwhile his self-advertisement continued. Objecting to the 'piffle' that constantly appeared in the Australian press, he asked Vic once again to approach her many journalistic friends: 'What counts most is the snappy personal or news paragraph ... in the daily papers, or failing them in *Punch* and *Bulletin* ... a campaign of quiet insinuating publicity every now and then can do no harm.' She was not to confine her attention to the press. 'Do all you can to cultivate Hughes. He is one of the Wallabies and I like him very much. It may help me for you to be charming with Mrs P.M.' For the moment Monash's efforts were unavailing. He still remained in command of his brigade when it was allotted to Cox's division in Godley's corps at Tel-el-Kebir.

The formation of the new divisions followed an important principle laid down by Birdwood. As the 8th Brigade had recently arrived from Australia, sixteen new battalions altogether would be required. To create them, the sixteen original battalions would be split and reinforcements used to bring both halves to full strength. Fearing the shock to the pride and tradition of the older units, White and commanders at all levels in them urged the transfer of selected officers and NCOs only, but Birdwood stood fast. His resolve 'gave a veteran character and a feeling of brotherhood to the whole force.' Every aspect of the reorganisation was directed by White. Smoothly executed, it was an outstanding administrative achievement and, following so soon after his planning of the withdrawal from Anzac, formed the second of 'the two most brilliant and successful operations ... hitherto carried out by an Australian soldier.' Monash's praise of White was sincere: 'He is far and away the ablest soldier Australia has ever turned out ... He is also a charming good fellow.'

Monash (right) judging the 4th Brigade's close order drill competition at Tel-el-Kebir. Standing next to him is Lieutenant Lofty Williamson, 14th Battalion, whose platoon came second. Williamson was killed at Bullecourt in France in April 1917 (AWM A01194).

The implementation of the split in Monash's brigade on 1–2 March was typical of the force as a whole. Sixteen hundred men from the 4th Brigade, comprising its 'second wing', formed the nucleus of its 'twin', the 12th Brigade, commanded by Brigadier General Duncan Glasfurd, formerly of the 1st Division's staff. They were divided among the 45th, 46th, 47th and 48th battalions, the 'daughters' of the 13th, 14th, 15th and 16th, respectively. Some bitterness was inevitable. The 14th was 'a seething mass of discontent' for a few days as platoons and companies were broken up. Monash dwelt on the

CHAPTER 6

psychological aspects of the reorganisation, suggesting to White that the new battalions should wear vertically on their sleeves the same colour patches worn horizontally by their parent units. In this way *esprit de corps* would be preserved and the hostile complaints of men leaving their old battalions minimised.[46] He was also struck by the immensity of the new army compared to its pre-war strength in Australia, where 'we never ... had anywhere more troops collected together at any one spot or camp or review than would make a single *Brigade.*' The 4th was now 'a very different body, both as regards its personnel, and a very much larger and more complex command.' In addition to the infantry battalions, there were machine-gun, pioneer and field engineer companies, a company from the Divisional Train and a signal section. The ranks quickly filled; by 10 March the brigade strength was 4402, only 160 below establishment. At the end of May Monash wrote: 'The 4th Brigade has never been in better form and fettle than it is today.'

Field Marshal Sir Douglas Haig, C-in-C BEF 1916–18. He thought highly of Monash and the pair got on well from the time they met. The same could not be said of Haig's relations with Birdwood and White (AWM A03713).

MONASH

Monash surmised well before the reorganisation that the Dominion Forces in Egypt were destined for the Western Front. He was correct. The appointments of Haig as C-in-C of the BEF and Robertson as CIGS brought to positions of supreme authority commanders who believed that the war could be won only on the Western Front and, therefore, that all forces should be sent to France except the absolute minimum required for defence elsewhere. In fulfilment of this policy, Murray intended to commence the transfer of divisions to Europe as the Turkish threat subsided with the drying up of the winter rains in March. The urgent need to relieve the French after the German onslaught against Verdun began on 21 February altered his plan. When Robertson cabled that three Australian divisions now would be worth six later, Murray promised to send them immediately, first setting down his poor opinion of them as a fighting force for communication to Haig. Robertson replied with perverse glee: 'It will be a good thing for the Australians to get to France. It is an excellent training school and the Germans will soon put them in order.' As for Birdwood acting as GOC AIF: 'I can have no personal nonsense of the kind ... [he] must go to France to command his corps and leave it at that, for the time being at any rate.' The 1st, 2nd and New Zealand divisions of Birdwood's 1st ANZAC began to leave for the Western Front on 13 March 1916. They and their commander would soon prove Robertson wrong on both counts.

The rolling stock that 1st ANZAC's embarkation move required left very little for the 4th and 5th divisions of 2nd ANZAC, which were taking over the canal line. Apart from the 16th Battalion and the 8th Brigade, which went by train, the two divisions had to deploy to the canal on foot, and it was decided to make the march a test, with the men carrying full kit, packs and ammunition. Commanders realised that the three-day trek over forty miles to Serapeum would be demanding for new troops. Monash forecast that it would be 'very severe as it was very hot and not much water could be carried.' His plan to start in the cool of daybreak was thwarted by the men's inability to load in darkness the camel trains that had to precede the column and clear its bivouacs before the march commenced.

CHAPTER 6

The other preparations worked well. Accompanied by two mounted officers from each battalion, Durrant scouted miles ahead, seeking a track over hard sand, which he indicated by posting his officers along it. The lead was changed regularly, and there were frequent halts, with a three-hour break at the hottest time of the day. Hardly any straggling occurred on the first leg, but on the second 132 fell out as Moascar was reached. Durrant described these men, who were helped in by the New Zealanders there, as 'boozers mostly – drunk too often to stand fatigue.' A combination of dust, clouds of biting insects, soft sand and the heat caused about 460 stragglers in the last three miles before Serapeum, Monash admitting that the march discipline was very bad. He felt that they had relaxed their efforts and told them their sisters could have done as well. Lieutenant Edgar Rule of the 14th Battalion remembered this as the only time he heard men curse him.

Monash believed that the heat and distance had little to do with the straggling, which he felt was due mostly to blisters and chafing caused by poorly fitting boots and trousers. He also noted that much remained to be learned in the proper carriage of packs, lending weight to Bean's comment that 'if staff and troops had been more experienced, greater success might have been achieved even by leaders as careful as Monash and Glasfurd.' But, according to the 13th Battalion's history: 'The 4th Brigade came through better than any other ... owing to the well thought out plans of Monash ... and Durrant.' In contrast, the 14th Brigade had staggered into Moascar 'practically out of hand and without any attempt at formation, like the remnant of a broken army.' The men demonstrated against its commander, Brigadier General Godfrey Irving, when the Prince of Wales reviewed them next day. Against the strong arguments of Monash, who did not want to lose him, Pope replaced Irving. Their parting was emotional. Pope was struck by the slackness he found in his new command, writing to Monash:

> ... we have not yet by any means got the mature and clockwork organisation of the 4th Brigade. Indeed it was not until I came over here that I properly realised the excellence of your organisation.

MONASH

Frequent sports meetings and invitations to the messes of other brigades were a pleasant diversion for Monash, as was the visit on 29 April of Murray, Godley and the Prince of Wales, whose staff consisted of 'kids like himself – Marquis and Earls – and old Dad the Colonel who does Daddy to him.' They had also witnessed the moving commemoration of the first Anzac Day. Those who had served on Gallipoli wore a blue ribbon, and if present at the landing a red one as well. On 'this famous day – *Our Day*', Monash noted sadly, 'how few of us are left who were entitled to wear both.'

Monash was nonetheless depressed by Serapeum. The intense heat prevented work between 10.00 am and 5.00 pm, and on one occasion a *khamsin* raged for 'twenty mortal hours', leaving him 'gasping, choking, eyeballs inflamed, bent low with coughing, with severe headaches and symptoms of catarrh . . . and generally down and out.' Savage insects and the barrenness of the desert topped off the dismal conditions, which Monash found 'really more trying than those at Anzac in the height of the summer.' Watching a demonstration of the Stokes mortar on 8 May, he was struck by a mortar bomb fragment. He now believed that a Turkish attack on the canal was 'by no means a mere chimera', and preparations to meet it continued. When Cox fell ill, Monash temporarily commanded the 4th Division: 'It has meant a good deal of rushing about, and hard riding ... Apart from dispositions for local defence I have organised a mobile column for counter offensive. Of course the big difficulties are water and transport and for these I am using the Camel Corps exclusively.' Real or imagined, the Turkish threat necessitated skill in open warfare. But training in trench warfare did not proceed beyond sub-unit level. There was no simulation of trench routine by battalions, nor practice assaults on fortified positions by brigades. With the certainty in early April that Godley's corps would follow Birdwood's to the Western Front, the neglect of training for the conditions there is difficult to understand.

The instruction of officers was pursued much more vigorously. To help overcome their inexperience, notes containing suggestions for training were prepared for platoon and company commanders. In the

CHAPTER 6

4th Brigade *100 Hints* was reprinted for issue to every officer and senior NCO. A brief perusal by Cox was 'eno' to 'wish that every company officer in the division had a copy.' On 29 April he addressed all officers of the 4th Division, and then invited Monash to speak. Monash remarked afterwards: 'I make a great impression', and sent a copy of his talk to the *Argus* for publication. He directed his comments to platoon commanders, the officers closest to the rank and file and hence the means by which they were reached:

> ... the Platoon is, for all purposes, the unit for whose perfection we strive. Because, a perfect Platoon means a perfect Battalion and Brigade or Division; and, the efficiency of any army corps is to be measured by that of its Platoons.

The greatest failing he had observed in his own officers was their failure to correct mistakes 'promptly, efficiently and on the spot.' The wrong way then became a habit, which had to be eliminated before the correct techniques could be taught. Training, said Monash, 'consists largely in the patient, energetic and thorough elimination of all that is wrong.' An officer had to be loyal to his superiors, whose responsibilities were greater than his. Monash was not referring to fair-weather allegiance:

> Anybody can yield *that* kind of loyalty. But it is not so easy to render loyal service to a man when you think he is wrong ... Nevertheless, [that] is the only kind of loyalty that is worth a hang, the only kind that counts in the stress of war.

Monash also impressed Cox with his ideas on discipline. As the 4th Division's departure for France approached, Cox drafted a personal message, to be pinned in each man's paybook, asking him to uphold the high reputation of the British Army there by his general behaviour, especially towards French women, and by his courage against the Germans. Monash did not entirely agree, suggesting that Cox adopt his method of creating and then employing 'a sound and healthy public opinion in each unit. If the great majority of men are stirred up to range themselves *actively* on the side of authority, and good order, the slacker will soon have to mend his ways.' He made such an appeal after the first of his battalion inspections on 21 May: 'If one man

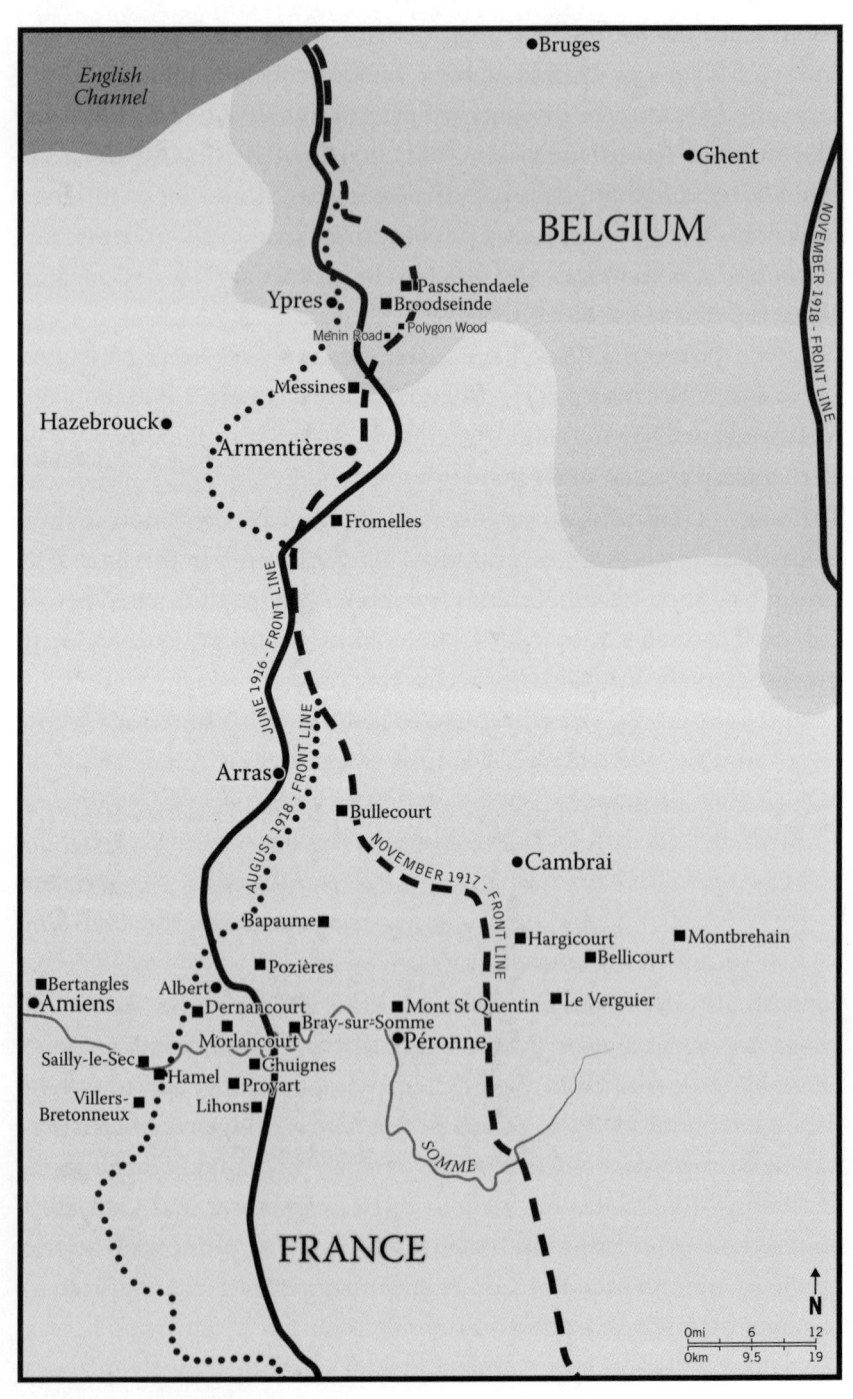

The Western Front in 1916, 1917, 1918.

CHAPTER 6

shirks his work, another must do it for him as well as his own; if one man disgraces the battalion, every man has to share in it.'

Monash could not level the same complaints at Cox as he had against Russell. The energy, enthusiasm and experience of the new divisional commander were often demonstrated, as Cox spent part of every day visiting the camps and canal posts, driving his subordinates hard and demanding the reason for any faults. Monash's relations with him were now extremely harmonious, with no trace whatsoever of the animosity of the previous August. He described Cox as 'very gracious and amiable' and himself as 'entirely in General Cox's confidence.' It was an accurate assessment, for Cox was highly impressed with Monash's training of the 4th Brigade and with his performance as acting divisional commander on two occasions. He never missed an opportunity to attend Monash's conferences with his battalion commanders, 'simply for the educational value and pleasure of hearing him speak.' On 3 May he wrote to Birdwood about the command of the 3rd Division, which was still unresolved:

> If it is desirable to put in a local product, I should like to say that I am prepared to recommend that Monash be given a trial. He is a very able man and now has long experience of training and of war. He is very tactful and his judgement is reliable.
>
> Any little weaknesses which appeared when he was in command of a brigade at Anzac would not count so much in a Divisional command. He seems to me to have 'come on' very much. This is, of course, entirely off my own bat. He has never said a word about it.

Godley agreed too, after careful consideration, that Monash 'would command 3 Div all right', although he did not depart from his views on 'amateurs': 'one cannot pretend that he is as well qualified to command a division as a trained regular officer, but he is a capable, sensible and reliable man and has now had 18 months of troops in the field and has done it well.' He concurred with Birdwood on Chauvel's claims, but pointed out that if he were selected, the Mounted Division would remain vacant, because Monash was quite unsuited to command it. Conversely, Monash's appointment to the 3rd Division would mean Australian officers commanding both divisions, an arrangement that he strongly favoured. Birdwood finally agreed and recommended the appointment of Monash: 'I hear that he has carried on excellently with what to all intents and purposes has been a new brigade ... and I felt therefore it is only right that he should be given the chance.'

Monash left Egypt as he had come, as GOC troops aboard a transport, the *Transylvania*. To a tumultuous welcome, it docked in Marseilles on 7 June 1916. The train journey north was the most delightful experience in the 4th Brigade's history. After the glare of the desert, the lush greenness of the countryside, with its orchards, vineyards and wooded châteaux, was like water to the lips of a thirsty man. Travelling by night express, Monash missed the sights, but the two days he spent in Paris while his brigade assembled was more than adequate compensation, until he learned with some alarm that Cox was en route for Calais. Monash arrived there on 10 June, meeting the divisional commander, who, much to his relief: 'is very pleased and makes no comment at catching us up.' From Merris, the headquarters of the 4th Division, which was now attached to 1st ANZAC in General Sir Herbert Plumer's Second Army, Monash reached his Brigade Headquarters at Bailleul, where command was infinitely more enjoyable than at Anzac or in Egypt: 'Imagine the change from sweltering, dusty, fly infested desert, to a two storey mansion, the best in the old Spanish town in beautiful surroundings.'

Recalling the pre-war instruction he had received in Foster's war courses, Monash planned the billeting of his brigade in the area, some sixty miles square, allotted to him. No sooner did he complete the work than he was ordered to Erquinghem, near Armentières. 1st ANZAC would shortly move to the Somme, where a great British offensive was about to begin, and Birdwood wanted the 4th Division to relieve his formations in the line as soon as possible. On 17 June Monash's brigade began to replace the 7th Brigade as the reserve brigade of the 2nd Division, and as a preparatory step to relieving the 5th Brigade in the line at Bois Grenier, four miles south of Armentières. Battalion commanders were shown personally over the trenches of the 5th Brigade, while company commanders and small parties of signallers and NCOs spent one day in them. Platoons were rotated through instructional tours lasting seventy-two hours. On 30 June Monash assumed responsibility for the Bois Grenier sector from Holmes. During the previous night, the 14th Battalion captured the division's first prisoner. Cox offered his congratulations after an inspection of the trenches in which he found 'all ranks very keen and cheerful'.

From Monash's standpoint, the 4th Brigade's entry into the line was not the smooth operation that appearances suggested. Within three days of moving to Erquinghem, he told Cox's chief of staff, Lieutenant Colonel Denis Bernard: 'People in this part of the world change their minds pretty often, and a lot of valuable time has been lost.' Monash was trying to resolve three separate problems: the training of his brigade, especially officers and specialists; its relief of the 5th Brigade; and its task as divisional reserve, providing all work parties for field defences. Meeting all of these needs would have been difficult enough under normal circumstances, but the constant dispersion of his officers throughout the division made it impossible. Matters came to a head when an order requiring the appointment of understudies to staff captains in brigade headquarters was promulgated. Dare threatened to resign when Monash asked for an experienced officer to fill the position and offered a recently promoted man instead. Monash accepted, but disagreed strongly 'with the view that a commanding officer should allow himself to think (much less say), he would sooner be relieved than agree to something distasteful to him.' But he sympathised with Dare as he put the case before Bernard in forthright terms:

> Since I arrived in France I have not met anyone who seems to care a jot about safeguarding the fighting efficiency of the Unit. It is 'grab, grab' all the time; and what with schools of all kinds, and ultra specialisation in all directions, we shall soon have no organised fighting efficiency left.

Higher headquarters seemed unconcerned about the functioning of companies and platoons. His own brigade of comparatively raw troops was about to enter the line, yet in some companies the second-in-command was engaged in liaison work with another brigade and all platoon commanders and half the NCOs were absent at schools.

As was the case at Anzac, no Australian commander attacked the inefficient use of manpower more than Monash, whose civil career had been vitally concerned with economy and foresight in that regard. The problem was much more acute on the Western Front; but, as at Anzac, it was never overcome.

The quiet Australian sector was known as a 'nursery', where new troops were acclimatised before employment in more active theatres. As such, it was atypical of the main centres of fighting, and Monash's initial estimate of the Western Front persisted: 'It hasn't taken us many hours to tumble into the regular routine of trench life – but oh dear! compared to Anzac, the people here don't know what war is.' However, the issue of gas respirators and steel helmets, the constant presence of aeroplanes and the proficiency of the Germans, who brought down a heavy and accurate bombardment at the slightest movement and fought stubbornly for control of no man's land, were signs that this theatre would really be far tougher. On 5 May, a German raid on the 20th Battalion in the Bridoux salient inflicted over 100 casualties and captured two of the still secret Stokes mortars in an incident that embarrassed the AIF for a long time. Legge remarked: 'At present along the whole front of our Army, the enemy has possession of the initiative and is so far as he can [be] without actually attacking, somewhat superior in the offensive.'

The 4th Brigade's first engagement on the Western Front was also a raid, one of a number launched by 1st ANZAC to coincide with the Somme offensive, in accordance with Haig's directive to his armies to deceive the Germans about the front of the attack and wear down their reinforcing divisions. In early 1916, these raids 'were organised more like night raids on dormitories in a public school than serious exercises of war', but considerable experience had been gained since the Australians' first raid on 5 June. The use of that experience was the main feature of Monash's planning for his raid on 2 July, which would be launched by eighty-nine men from the 14th Battalion. He chose La Houssoie on the right of the 14th's line as the objective, because the 6th Brigade would attack a little further north on 29 June, and it was unlikely that the Germans, inactive in the area, would expect

CHAPTER 6

another raid so soon. Monash asked Russell for the loan of orders for 'minor enterprises' already carried out by the New Zealand Division, which Russell now commanded. A replica of the German trenches was constructed at La Rolanderie Farm, where the raiders trained for the operation after spending four days in their own line to familiarise themselves with no man's land. The value of authentic rehearsals had been demonstrated in the first Australian raid, as had diversionary bombardments either side of the point of entry. This, too, was adopted by Monash. Covered by a box barrage to seal off the penetration, the raiding party would spend ten minutes in the German trenches, gaining information and inflicting as many casualties and as much destruction as possible. In previous raids the signal to retire had sometimes been missed in the heat of the moment. Monash's method eliminated this possibility. Runners would be sent to both flanks to call 'Out! Out!' which would be taken up by all within hearing. Three green Very lights were to be fired as an extra precaution.

As the New Zealanders had found, the importance of 'orders and arrangements elaborated to the minutest detail' could not be emphasised too strongly. Monash spent several days on the planning, but despite his efforts the recent arrival of the 4th Brigade in the line necessitated the preparation of several aspects of the raid by the staff of the 2nd Division. It did not fail for that reason. The trench mortar barrage left intact four belts of barbed wire, each about 16 yards deep. They were crossed with extreme difficulty. The trenches were almost empty, the Germans relying on machine-guns and shrapnel directed onto the position and along the wire to cut the raiders off from their own line. Three dugouts were destroyed at a cost of thirty-eight casualties to the raiding party. The Germans apparently expected the attack, and it may be that the 6th Brigade's raid alerted instead of lulling them, as Monash had hoped. But ten raids between 25 June and 2 July had roused them along the whole Anzac line. As Bean says: 'the "nursery" ... in this week, from being one of the quietest sectors on the front ... became one of marked tension.'

This action was destined to be Monash's last as a brigade commander. On 24 June 1916 he had heard that 'my appointment to 3rd Division has been unofficially approved and that the rumour is quite reliable.' Birdwood told him that he would leave for England in the first week of July, and the congratulations of Cox and Godley followed. Monash thought that authority 'sufficiently unimpeachable' to allow relatives and friends to be informed, though he began to worry when he was still in France on 8 July. But five days later he accompanied his successor, Brigadier General Charles Brand, to Bailleul, where the journey to England began. Monash told Vic that now his next award, a KCMG or KCB, should not be long delayed. He reflected on his achievement with pride:

> Coming now to look at it, I recognise the disadvantages I had to labour under to get to where I now stand. I suppose McCay and I are the only citizen officers in the whole Empire to have attained this grade, and then there is the question of religion and parentage, and it is very gratifying, in spite of these solid handicaps, and without any intrigue whatever on my part, to have got the honour and status of my present rank. I am wondering what my enemies at home will be saying.

Chapter 7

The Theory of the Limited Objective

With Monash's appointment to divisional command, there began a run of luck that continued virtually unbroken to the Armistice, and which cannot be lightly dismissed when assessing his military reputation. He was the only Australian commander who could bring personal knowledge of the Western Front to the training of his formation, while the instructional facilities at his disposal in England were far more attuned to warfare on the Western Front than those available in Egypt. Though spared the trials of the Somme, its costly lessons were available to him. The 'creeping' barrage, a curtain of shells that lifted steadily ahead of the infantry assault, suppressing the defences as it went, and the launching of attacks just before dawn broke, instead of in daylight, were becoming standard. Consequently, the 3rd Division arrived in France after 'a training such as not even the original 1st Division at Mena had experienced.' It did not enter the line on the Somme, where the bitter winter endured by 1st ANZAC was probably the Australians' hardest period of the war, but at Armentières, where conditions were less severe. Monash knew the area as the scene of the 4th Brigade's first raid. His heavy reliance on recently proven methods in the planning of that raid is an important factor in explaining Monash's performance on the Western Front. Two conclusions follow. Firstly, his success rested, to some extent, on imitation rather than innovation. Secondly, the existence of techniques to imitate showed that commanders were grappling with the problems of trench warfare and starting to overcome them. But progress was uneven; operational practice did not always reflect lessons already learned.

Showing what could be done, the 18th (British) Division took the hitherto impregnable fortress of Thiepval as part of a wider attack by Gough's Reserve Army on the Somme on 26 September 1916. Major General Ivor Maxse, the 18th Division's commander, and his planning of the Thiepval assault are relevant to the study of Monash as a commander. Monash's and Maxse's names could be interchanged with regard to every aspect of the operation. Maxse stated in his after-action report:

> The secret of successful attacks in modern trench warfare may be summed up in two words: PREVIOUS PREPARATION. Without it the bravest troops fail and their heroism is wasted. With sufficient time to prepare an assault on a definite and limited objective, I believe a well-trained division can capture almost any 'impregnable' stronghold ...

It could well have been Monash speaking. Before the attack, Maxse covered every conceivable detail in a conference whose agenda listed twenty-two main headings and numerous sub-headings. The corps chief of staff addressed all brigade and battalion commanders at Maxse's request; several told him later that 'it put life and intelligence into their preparations. They felt they were being trusted ...' As soon as he received it, Maxse passed on information to his subordinates, so that the operation order 'became merely the final form taken by previous instructions, conferences, messages etc.'[47] Frequent rehearsals perfected the formations he had evolved after studying earlier attacks on the Somme. Maxse's thoroughness was rewarded by the result. The infantry advanced 'as if glued to the barrage', while the effect of casualties among leaders was reduced because every soldier knew his task and how he should carry it out. But the success was dimmed by Haig's failure to ensure that his entire command profited by it.

The omission was an instance of the C-in-C's neglect of one of his most important responsibilities. His Director of Intelligence, Brigadier General John Charteris, claimed that Haig 'enforced the issue' from GHQ of a series of memoranda to guide every aspect of the fighting. They were an important means of addressing the

CHAPTER 7

inexperience at all levels in a BEF that had expanded from four divisions on arrival in France in 1914 to fifty in 1916. Some were of questionable value; many more were not. Notwithstanding his injunction that 'close supervision' by commanders was not 'interference', but 'legitimate and necessary' due to the BEF's inexperience, Haig did little to make certain that the guidance was studied or its suggestions implemented. McCay ignored GHQ advice on consolidation when the untried 5th Division attacked at Fromelles on 19 July 1916 to prevent the transfer of German reserves from the area to the Somme. The last Australian division to arrive in France, but the first to attack, it was all but destroyed when the Germans got behind the line gained. Before the Somme offensive began, formations were warned against wasting reserves 'in impossible frontal assaults against strong places. They should rather be thrown in ... where our advance is progressing.' This principle was frequently disregarded, not least by Rawlinson, whose Fourth Army had the main role in the offensive. Illustrating the poor example they set, Garry Sheffield raises 'the inability of Haig and Rawlinson consistently to apply the lessons of successful attacks ... especially the importance of careful preparation and massed artillery.' Similarly, the efficacy of 'bite and hold' tactics, which meant taking a limited objective that could be easily defended and repeating the process from it, had been proven. But objectives were all too often expanded. Far from being a smooth parabolic arc, the BEF's so-called 'learning curve' resembled instead the track made by a home-bound barfly – 'a winding and bumpy continuum', as Robert Stevenson remarks of the 1st Australian Division's experience.

Monash found that the attitude of senior commanders towards material innovations was sometimes just as casual. Though they were not so unresponsive as some historians have suggested, the narrowness inevitable in a long military career, he said, had moulded 'the type of mind which would [not] permit of their adapting themselves very readily to the use of new ideas.' An example of what could result from all these failings was the situation that Brigadier General George Jackson, formerly Monash's General Staff Officer Grade 1 (GSO1), found after leaving the 3rd Division to command the 87th Brigade in the 29th (British) Division:

> No continuity of policy between the divisions and the inherent waste of labour. The tactical knowledge and general grasp displayed by the corps is a negative quantity ... I am thoroughly disappointed with the British Army. It is brave but unorganised and unbusinesslike and I have seen quite enough to account for the failures you and I used to wonder about and marvel at.

John Terraine made much of the British generals' tactical inexperience at this stage of the war. Monash was similarly disadvantaged; but he studied every document on tactical methods that he received, becoming thoroughly conversant with the successful techniques practised in his own army and with German and French doctrine as well. In other words, he seized on the innovations of others, which stood him in good stead as a divisional commander, but which benefited him enormously when he enjoyed the wider scope of a corps commander. It was not a demeaning approach; after all, what were the lessons for, if not to be heeded?

The gulf between divisional and brigade command was considerable. In comparison to the 4th Brigade's four battalions of infantry, the 3rd Division had all the auxiliary and fighting arms and services needed to make it a self-contained fighting formation. Monash's infantry comprised the 9th, 10th and 11th brigades, which were supported by three artillery brigades, each with its own ammunition column, three companies of engineers, a pioneer battalion and bridging train and a divisional signals company. Including medical and supply services, the whole command, he told Vic, amounted to 'over 20,000 troops, 7,000 horses, 64 guns, 18 motor cars, 82 motor lorries and 1,100 other vehicles, so that you will see that it is some army.' Moreover, the most effective level of battle control on the Western Front was divisional: 'this was the nearest point to the front where co-ordination of all arms took place, where reserves could be committed, held back or redirected, where plans could be significantly modified. It was also the key point for the collection and transmission of information to corps, army, GHQ.'

CHAPTER 7

The 3rd Division Headquarters, November 1916. Monash is seated centre, with Lieutenant Colonels Jackson (GSO1) on his right and Farmar (Assistant Adjutant and Quartermaster General) on his left. Both were British officers (AWM H00465).

Thanks to the great care taken by Birdwood in the selection of its senior members, Monash's divisional staff was 'a very fine one ... mostly English and Indian officers.' Monash's chief staff officer, Jackson, had formerly held that appointment in the 2nd Division, earning the esteem of Legge. His transfer to the 3rd Division dealt a body blow to Legge and his staff, neither of whom performed well at Pozières on the Somme after his departure. Monash praised Jackson's contribution to the training of the 3rd Division as 'of exceptional merit and value'. His performance in the field was equally notable, Rosenthal, later commander of the 9th Brigade, describing him as 'a very able officer indeed.' The Commander Royal Artillery (CRA), Brigadier General Harold Grimwade, had commanded an artillery brigade in the 2nd Division. After Grimwade's guns had supported the 4th Brigade at Bois Grenier, Monash agreed with Birdwood that he was 'really an excellent officer'. His two aides, Simonson and Lieutenant Arthur Colman, and the Deputy Assistant Quartermaster General, Captain Clarence Pyke, belonged to 'the chosen people', which was 'Quite a record ... probably quite unique.'[48] When ill health forced Colman's return to Australia, Monash arranged for his replacement by Aubrey Moss, then in the 2nd Division, so that the 'record' remained intact. Interestingly, Brudenell White's nephew was also in Monash's division, and in response to a request from White, Monash was 'pleased to do anything for him.' His reply disarms the oft-made but baseless criticism that Monash only looked after the interests of his own.

Of the three infantry brigade commanders, only Brigadier General Walter McNicoll of the 10th had fought at Anzac, where he was badly wounded in the 2nd Brigade's charge at Krithia. Brigadier General Alexander Jobson, commanding the 9th Brigade, compensated for his inexperience with 'an active mind and a great industry. He is ... learning every day, is easy to manage and influence.' The commander of the 11th Brigade proved unsuitable, as much due to his general ineptitude as to his intemperance. Birdwood approved Monash's recommendation to replace him with one of his former battalion commanders from the 4th Brigade, Lieutenant Colonel Cannan. The anxiety that Monash felt most, his influence and authority over the senior commanders, soon vanished: 'I have nothing but praise for the splendid loyalty they are showing to my policies and methods. My orders, no matter how distasteful, are always implicitly obeyed without murmur.' Characteristically, Monash enjoyed the attention lavished on him as a divisional commander: 'quite a tremendous person', who could not 'travel anywhere by rail except in a reserved compartment.' As McGlinn said, it was 'such an effective slap in the face to those miserable curs who tried to injure [Monash] at the start.'

The arrival of the 3rd Division in England at the rate of 3000 men per week in July and August permitted the concentration for the first time of battalions into brigades and companies into battalions. They were virtually untrained, despite McCay's introduction of a more up-to-date training program in Australia and the inclusion of many permanent soldiers hitherto kept there. An acute shortage of weapons and equipment had handicapped McCay's scheme, while the primitive conditions in some of the Australian camps, particularly

CHAPTER 7

at Casula, where a riot had erupted in February, were inimical to discipline. Whether men from the 9th (NSW) Brigade were involved in the Casula fracas is unknown, but the incident caused McCay to warn Monash that discipline in his division would be indifferent. Monash was unconcerned for he had 'very definite views about the best methods of handling Australian troops and they have not failed ... in the past.' A second reason for his confidence was the exceptional quality of the men:

> I am bound to say ... that the raw material of this Division is far and away better than any of the raw material we have previously had to handle in the 4th Brigade, not even forgetting the original personnel. There is a certain air about the men which was absent on previous occasions. There are very few young men, most of them averaging about 25 years of age and they all have a mature, independent, hard and active look, the outstanding characteristic being intelligence.

The behaviour of the men was exemplary. Their quiet determination, characteristic of the 3rd Division, was 'encouraged by the nature and methods of its commander ... [whose] Jewish blood gave him an outstanding capacity for tirelessly careful organisation.' Monash had to call on that talent as he commenced at Lark Hill the training of a raw formation for the third time since his military career had begun. The knowledge and experience he had acquired during twenty months of war comprised the third reason for his confident prediction of success: 'we are going to have some Division – far and away better than Bridges took away with him ... – because ... there will not be a minute wasted in teaching things the men will afterwards have to unlearn.'

At Monash's first conference with his brigadiers, he enunciated principles that were now second nature: '1. Discipline–loyalty–esprit–obedience of orders–no dodging. 2. Cohesion of units–helpful spirit ... 5. Making the best of all situations.' The divisional training policy was not new either, as Monash practised on a larger scale methods on which he had relied at Serapeum. Each brigade built its own bombing course and each battalion its own bayonet course.

All of the artillery and the engineers, and much of the infantry, were sent at once to British Army schools. The infantry detachments were trained at the schools to be instructors in musketry, machine-gunnery, and trench and gas warfare at the same time as divisional schools were established in these subjects by the few men already qualified. It was a wise move, which overcame the scarcity of efficient instructors and allowed training to begin well before the division had been fully equipped. When the various detachments returned: 'Instead of an isolated instructor in modern bayonet fighting, we have one per battalion, similarly as regards bombs, sharp shooting ... and all other specialist work.' Monash aimed to prepare his division for war 'in simultaneous progressive stages; the idea being that there would be no advantage ... in having some units much further advanced in their training than others.' All units down to platoons were rotated through the same exercises, ensuring tactical uniformity as well. The Inspector of Infantry, Major General Sir Francis Howard, was impressed: 'This Division is going to come on well ... Everything I saw was being run on sound and sensible lines. Keenness and anxiety to learn are evident throughout and from eight to ten hours put in daily.' The artillery, whose training was more technical, took longer to reach the necessary standard. This had also been the case in the divisions created in Egypt.

Battalion and brigade work began when Monash judged that companies and platoons were sufficiently advanced to benefit from training as part of the larger formations. He had learned from the mistakes made by Godley and Russell in Egypt. His determination to introduce elements of static warfare whenever possible was very evident at these higher levels of training. An 'engineer platoon', comprising mainly miners, was formed in each battalion for the rapid digging of trenches. Numerous trench assaults taught inexperienced commanders the importance of thorough preparation and orders. In one instance an 'attack' by the 9th Brigade failed because the need for exit gaps in its wire had been forgotten, trapping the attackers within an obstacle of their own making. At the Bustard, six miles from Lark Hill, a brigade trench system was dug, 'replete in every detail

CHAPTER 7

with bomb stores, observer stations, sniper's positions [and] complete wiring.' It was occupied by each brigade for five days at a time, during which the two battalions in the front line were relieved by the two in support according to the *Trench Standing Orders* Monash had used at Bois Grenier. Patrols reconnoitred the 'enemy' trenches, which were then raided by each battalion, while the 10th Brigade blew a mine to practise the capture and consolidation of craters.

A constant stream of information from Birdwood and Headquarters Southern Command in England kept Monash apprised of the latest tactical developments in the Somme fighting. Birdwood advised him that 'you cannot have too many men trained in the use of the Lewis Gun.' Brand confirmed the necessity in notes accounting for his brigade's success at Pozières, which, to Monash's satisfaction, also stressed the need for uniformity at all levels of training. Monash acknowledged the increasing importance of aircraft with 'some elaborate exercises in which a number of Infantry Units are co-operating with Aeroplanes and Artillery in offensive and defensive operations.'

The climax of the 3rd Division's training was an exercise at the Bustard on 6 November 1916, involving 2000 men from five battalions, four batteries of artillery, signallers and engineers and four aircraft. A large mine was exploded under the 'enemy' trenches, the infantry rushing the crater as the artillery laid down a protective box barrage around it. Men blocked the communications trenches as Lewis gun teams cooperated with bombers on either flank to cover the wiring parties consolidating the position. The exercise was a personal triumph for Monash, watched by over 120 senior officers representing GHQ, the War Office and all commands in England, for crater fighting was a much-discussed subject at this time. He explained the means and principles employed, the reasons for them and, significantly, the faults he thought had occurred. One of the audience asked Bruche, who was also attending, about Monash's background and, on being told, remarked: 'I don't know any British officer who could stand up there for a quarter of an hour and give an idea of the operation and criticise it in such a lucid and clear way.' His reaction typified the response of many senior British officers who met Monash during the training of the 3rd Division. There was no patronising on their part: 'in fact these big men all asked how long he had been a professional soldier and could not agree that he had not devoted his whole career to it.' Birdwood heard nothing but praise for Monash's efforts, calling him 'a tremendous Napoleon ... [who] lays down some excellent maxims for his men.'

The predictable attention given to officer training was especially deserving of Birdwood's comment. Monash brought *100 Hints* up to date and arranged the printing of 2000 copies for the division. In the meantime, his Serapeum address to platoon commanders was reissued. After the first divisional march on 13 November, most of the seventy-two points listed by Monash dwelt on the reluctance of junior officers to assert their authority. Many men required haircuts, the transport of several battalions was very dirty, and control during the march was sometimes lost: 'It is high time officers knew their duties in this connection.' He visited the ranges daily, watching company commanders conduct practices and impressing on them 'the necessity for good organisation and quiet, orderly, well-regulated and deliberate shooting.'

The instruction of brigade and battalion commanders and their staffs was closely supervised. Monash's lectures to them, which have been quoted a number of times already, drew on the whole range of his civil and military experience to illustrate his philosophy. The remarks on tactics, battle procedure and command resembled many of the principles espoused by Maxse, though Monash had derived them independently of his British colleague:

On the promulgation of orders:

The one element of success is to allow plenty of time for orders to percolate, and detailed action to be taken for all things ... You will ... at the earliest possible moment prepare preliminary orders [so that] understanding and final reading and actual execution of orders should really take very little time ... the order should permeate right down to every man in the ranks ... Take all pains to see that everybody understands.

CHAPTER 7

On the understanding of orders:

... if you are not perfectly clear about orders, do not hesitate to ask questions ... Unless an officer worries unduly or unnecessarily, I will take care he is not snubbed for asking questions in this Division.

On welfare:

The fitness of the fighting soldier depends upon food, and rest, and upon his being made as comfortable as possible ... on all occasions. We do not look after him the way we do or try to do, because we think it is humane and he is our fellow man ... but because we want to keep him going as a fighting machine.

On optimism:

It is the first duty of every officer, no matter how he may feel, to keep himself and his men cheerful, and no matter how bad the situation. We are going to face winter conditions ... But we are going to have the greatest time of our lives.

On the importance of information:

... 9/10 of the operations which come to grief are due to the absence of accurate and proper information ... Subordinate leaders, whether ... Platoon or Brigade Commanders, must be made to regard it as a duty of prime importance to keep the next superior informed of what is going on and what is *not* going on ... I want to drum that in again and again that it is a paramount duty ...

On casualties:

You must get yourself into a callous state of mind. A commander who worries is not worth a damn, is not a bit of good ... Hypnotise yourself into a state of complete indifference over losses ... It will not be tolerated because a man says, 'I have a certain percentage of losses and cannot carry on'... A unit can fight with reduced numbers, even if 50% of losses have been suffered.

Monash began these lectures with his usual appeal to his officers' pride and moral sense. He concluded them by reaffirming his trinity: 'unity of purpose, unity of principle and unity of policy'. Monash also addressed members of a court martial on their judicial functions, since they tended to be overawed by their responsibilities, leading to 'a curious paralysis of [their] reasoning faculties.' They should be fair rather than lenient and not hesitate to allow an accused man to incriminate himself.

Salisbury Plain was not only more suitable for training, but it also did not have the sordid temptations that had so bedevilled the camps in Egypt. Monash arranged for the provision of sporting facilities to lessen the chance of boredom in the few spare hours his men enjoyed. He himself took frequent walks, losing the weight that had plagued him on Gallipoli. But he still enjoyed his food, smoked heavily and continued to drink the red wine forbidden by his doctors because they said it aggravated his rheumatism. Other habits were unusual to say the least. After Monash had eaten fish, Jackson watched him 'take the backbone ... fold it over, crunch it up and swallow it.' Brudenell White felt that his long period on Salisbury Plain gave Monash just the opportunity he needed to fit himself for divisional command. It also gave him an easier war on the whole than many of the other higher commanders, White thought.

Monash was keen to show off his division whenever an opportunity arose. He suggested that a composite battalion of a thousand men, 'specially selected for physique and appearance to make a thoroughly good show', should participate in the Lord Mayor of London's Procession. Field Marshal Sir John French, C-in-C, Home Forces, rejected the offer. But Monash's chance came with the Royal Review at Bulford Field on 27 September 1916, in which he benefited from his experience in preparing the farewell march of the 4th Brigade through Melbourne two years earlier. His orders were so detailed as to be pedantic, even stating that *all* officers were to salute with their right hand. There were 26 700 troops on parade, forming a line 2200 yards long that took nearly two hours to march past. Monash's lengthy account dwelt on his conversation with George V, who urged him to 'get the very best of woollen clothing ... It really is very cold in France in winter.' The impression made by this parade was important for Monash personally. Among those who enjoyed a favoured position with George V was Sir Douglas Haig. They had known each other long before he ascended the throne, and Haig's wife had been a Maid of Honour to

CHAPTER 7

Queen Alexandra. There is no direct evidence, but it is likely that the C-in-C became aware of Monash in the course of correspondence or conversation with the King after the very spectacular Bulford Review. It is too much of a stretch though, to suggest, as one historian has done, that Monash was 'the King's general' from now on.

Fortune smiled on Monash, but he had earned her favour by overcoming obstacles compared to which the training of his division was a straightforward task. There were vexing equipment shortages following the great expansion of the British Army after the introduction of conscription in January 1916. Monash's division simply had to wait its turn for equipment: 'They tell us that they "Have not yet begun to think about the 3rd Australian Division" as there are some British Divisions on which they are concentrating their attention.' Not until 9 October did its 'turn' arrive. Another War Office decision caused Monash's worst setback. The casualties of the four Australian divisions at Fromelles and on the Somme were so great as to exceed the replacement capacity of their training depots. With the Somme offensive still underway, another call on these formations was probable, making their depleted ranks a cause of great anxiety. On 11 August Monash was 'much perturbed' at the 'inner meaning' of an apparently innocuous query from the War Office on the level of training reached at Lark Hill: 'It might foreshadow the breaking up of the Division.' He was not far wrong. Next day, Haig told Birdwood that the provision of reinforcements from the 3rd Division was under consideration, and on 15 August this course was adopted by the War Office. Monash had to send 2800 men to the Tidworth Training Centre. Birdwood wrote: 'Poor Monash is naturally very much upset at the idea of his division being emasculated to provide reinforcements for the divisions out here.'

Monash's frustration was understandable. Had the training battalions despatched drafts more frequently, the gulf between the casualty and reinforcement rates would not have been so wide as to necessitate the drastic action just taken. But Army Regulations, which did not distinguish between British and Australian troops, specified that *all* troops *must* receive fourteen weeks' training before posting to France. Monash recalled the reorganisation under much harsher conditions in Egypt, which produced soldiers ready for active service in eight weeks, to emphasise his disgust. With the crying need for reinforcements on the Western Front, it was 'little short of a scandal that the Administration should sit down tight upon the basis of the fourteen week training period ... a counsel of perfection unnecessary for the average Australian.' His attempt to prove the point by having his division fit for service in October would have been realised but for its slow equipment. After the 2800 had been withdrawn, Monash was informed that if shortages persisted beyond September, another 5000 might be required. Birdwood tried to enlist the support of Haig, who merely remarked: 'no-one except the Germans wished to see [Monash's] arrival in France delayed.'

At Birdwood's suggestion, Monash ascertained the exact number of reinforcements in England, France and en route from Australia, which proved conclusively that all needs could be filled without further demands on the 3rd Division. Going further, Monash also examined the convalescent policy, with results as depressing as those he had shown to Godley after a similar enquiry in Reserve Gully in June 1915. Irrespective of his previous experience in the trenches, every convalescent was to receive five weeks' compulsory instruction according to a standard syllabus before returning to France. Hence specialist snipers or bombers, for example, were uselessly retained in England until they became proficient in skills they might never use. Monash's principle was that as soon as a man was declared fit he should be returned to his unit immediately. White was familiar with similar delays imposed by the Base in France, but he was unaware of the situation in England, apologising to Monash for his ignorance.

The 3rd Division was not milked merely to bolster the others in France. White confided to Monash: 'the 3rd Division and apparent lack of reinforcements are being used to aid in forging conscription in Australia.' The AIF voted for conscription in the referendum of October 1916, but not by a large majority. Before the referendum Murdoch had warned Hughes of the possibility of a 'No' vote, which would imperil the chance of a favourable result in Australia,

CHAPTER 7

whereupon the Prime Minister asked a reluctant Birdwood to use his influence with the troops to induce them to carry the issue. Birdwood issued an appeal to 'The Boys' and postponed the poll for several days to allow its distribution. Eighty per cent of the 3rd Division had voted when news of the postponement arrived. A message to stop the voting was ignored by Monash, and it proceeded to completion. He advised strongly against a second vote, fearing the consequences if the anti-conscriptionists in the AIF informed their colleagues in Australia that a legal and fairly conducted vote had been declared void. Monash personally favoured conscription but, perhaps shocked at Birdwood's action, he agreed with many of the views of those who did not, 'although it would be inconvenient for me to be quoted during the war, as having said so.' When the 'No' vote in Australia precluded the provision of a special reinforcement of 20 000 men and the increased monthly reinforcements promised by Hughes, the Prime Minister suggested instead that the 3rd Division remain in England to replenish the others. Fortunately for Monash the War Office disagreed: 'As already arranged the 3rd Division must proceed to France on the 21st November.'[49]

The move to France was praised by all the British officers involved in it, a reflection of the success Monash had achieved on Salisbury Plain. Echoing his initial comments on the 3rd Division, he said later that he had 'the right kind of human material [for] creating a formidable fighting unit.' Though true, this underestimates the effect of Monash's contribution. His decision to send as many men as possible to schools overcame the shortage of instructors and mitigated the consequences of the shortage of equipment. He involved himself at every level and set the example in thoroughness that he demanded from others. No detail was overlooked in making instruction as realistic and as relevant as possible. When the very existence of the division was threatened, Monash tried valiantly to preserve it. The effort told on him despite White's comment about 'an easy war'. Walter Rosenhain, with whom Monash spent his last weekend in England, wrote:

> ... the training and organisation of this Division has been an extremely severe strain on John ... he looked very tired indeed –

and admitted that he felt it. I think he looks forward to France as distinctly a rest from the arduous work of Salisbury Plain.

The 3rd Division joined Second Army as part of Godley's 2nd ANZAC immediately south of the Lys in French Flanders. Birdwood was relieved that it had left England. He had been unable to dispel the grievance of the other divisions – expressed in such derisive nicknames as the Neutrals, the Lark Hill Lancers and the Eggs-a-Cook – who felt that it was enjoying the good life there while they were fighting hard. The 3rd was acutely conscious of this animosity, particularly the taunts of the others that they had been 'down on the Somme'. Its desire to be accepted as one of the five was not fulfilled for some time, partly because of Monash's attempts to increase its *esprit de corps* by distinguishing his division from them. He tried to make the attached medical officers wear its oval colour patches. Rejecting Monash's flimsy plea that his prestige would be shaken, Surgeon General Neville Howse rightly insisted that they wear the patch of the medical service. Monash also ordered that hat brims would be worn not looped up but down, which he claimed looked neater, gave greater protection from the weather and prevented the easily recognisable 3rd Division being blamed for the misbehaviour of others. The order was finally revoked at Birdwood's insistence when the 3rd Division joined the Australian Corps in November 1917. The practicality of Monash's policy notwithstanding, the 37th Battalion had begun unofficially to wear hat brims looped up on reaching France. It was a curious policy for a commander who professed to understand the psychology of his men.

On balance, however, that claim was justified. Monash published in orders any laudatory press references to his division's achievements. He adopted Cox's policy of sending congratulatory cards to soldiers who were decorated or had performed well. When Cannan had submitted no recommendations for awards after almost two months in France, Monash impressed upon him the desirability of bringing under notice every instance of good work, 'because ... the granting of a few awards ... has a most stimulating effect and bucks everybody up.' His disciplinary policy was as it had been in the 4th Brigade, to create

CHAPTER 7

a community spirit that was intolerant of misbehaviour and to extend privileges, the abuse of which would be punished severely. He refused to invoke strong police control and to establish large pickets in the town of Nieppe during Christmas 1916, trusting his division would not repeat the earlier excesses of the New Zealanders there. The 3rd Division enjoyed the lowest crime rate of all the Australian divisions and, Monash thought, the lowest of any division in France. In other matters, such as his advocacy of the death penalty as a deterrent to desertion, he shared the views of his contemporaries.

On his return to France, Monash found that little had changed with regard to the detachment of officers from fighting units: 'Scarcely a day passes but that some fresh order or direction comes along requiring the withdrawal from their units of still more officers.' Monash's response was predictable – he asked his brigadiers for a census of all officers on strength on a single day, 22 January 1917. The result was predictable too. Of the 192 platoons in the 3rd Division, 104 were being commanded temporarily by NCOs instead of officers. Monash was more sarcastic than he had been at Bois Grenier: 'To put it plainly, when we fulminate against the misdeeds or the neglect of the platoon commanders as a body, we are in the majority of cases going for a man who does not in fact exist.'

Planned largely by White, the policy for training replacement leaders aggravated the problem. Monash sympathised with White's desire to impart adequate knowledge, but the time required reduced the supply at a stage when the need was desperate. Up to eight officer candidates were to attend the 3rd Division's school each month, after which two would be commissioned immediately and the remainder sent to England for a more advanced course. Monash urged White to waive this rule for three months so that he could send as many men as he required to the divisional school and then commission them without further training. White agreed, but tried to absolve himself of any blame for the trouble. He realised conditions would be difficult for the 3rd Division and had every intention of modifying the policy, 'but not before impressing the new system on all those concerned.' Why this was admitted only after Monash's appeal, he did not say.

A similar situation threatened with the other ranks, 1757 of whom were detached within three months of the 3rd Division's arrival. Fortunately, it was overcome by a long overdue instruction from Haig on the organisation of infantry battalions, which directed the reduction of extra-regimental duties whenever possible to ensure the strength of a platoon did not fall below twenty-eight men. Monash reinforced it with measures of his own, curbing the zeal of junior commanders for guards and pickets by abolishing all non-essential duties. He sought permission to withhold all shell-shock victims from the casualty clearing stations until he was personally satisfied that the cases were genuine. Brigadiers were to approach their RMOs about what Monash considered was their excessive leniency in the evacuation of trench foot casualties. It was giving the division 'a very bad record'. Birdwood described Monash at this time as 'undoubtedly doing extraordinarily well in command of his division.' It was praise well earned.

There was another reason for Birdwood's satisfaction. Earlier, he had complained that brigade and divisional commanders treated their training battalions in England contemptuously, lumbering them with the staff they wished to jettison from their formations in France. Monash was an exception, as he explained to McCay, now commanding the training depots in England: 'I think that I have been from the earliest days more sympathetic than most other commanders to the principle of the closest possible liaison between the fighting units and their training commanders.'

When Lieutenant Colonel Malcolm Lamb took command of the 3rd Divisional Training Group, comprising the division's three training battalions, Monash encouraged him to write frequently on his needs and troubles. He treated the Training Group as a fourth brigade, staffing it with officers in need of rest, but well qualified to train. Monash felt that service with these battalions must be as attractive as possible and joined McCay in urging that the promotional chances of those sent to them should not be diminished. He converted his field commanders to the view that an instructional posting in England was not a punishment but 'a reward for good service at the front'. Officers

CHAPTER 7

of the 3rd Division on leave would spend a few hours at the camps to update instructors on the latest techniques. Major Francis O'Donnell of the Divisional Base Depot at Étaples was not neglected either. At Monash's request he visited the division several times to discuss his problems with its commanders, another example of Monash's policy of attaching 'considerable importance to the personal factor'.

A soldier from the 39th Battalion in the line at Houplines, near Armentières, shortly after the 3rd Division's arrival in France in December 1916. The winter was the coldest in 40 years (AWM E00084).

Though it was still quiet, Monash found that the Armentières sector had changed since his brief stint there with the 4th Brigade. Intelligence indicated that the Germans thought offensive action south of the Lys impracticable for both sides, and Haig ordered a reduction in the number of divisions defending it. At first, Monash's front was nearly five miles long, but by April it had increased to eight miles, more than half the length of line initially established by the BEF in 1914. There were no trenches because the clay soil was perpetually waterlogged, so elaborate breastworks had been constructed above the frozen ground. At night the temperature dropped to -15° C. In two months, evacuations through illness exceeded 2200, almost four times the number of battle casualties. But for Monash's efforts, the figure would have been much higher. He garrisoned his sector with only four battalions, holding the remainder in reserve in Armentières, 'under cover in comfortable billets with two blankets per man.' The front and support trenches were always manned as thinly as possible, Monash directing his brigadiers' attention to the plentiful dugout accommodation in the reserve line, 600 yards in rear. Many commanders equated quiet periods with a lack of tension and therefore assumed that their front-line garrisons were always fresh. Monash disagreed. The forward trenches were tense under any circumstances, and meaningful rest was impossible in them. He instituted a strict rotation system by which men in the front trench were given at least eight hours' rest daily in either the support or the reserve line.

Monash's personal crusade against any form of laxity was unremitting as usual. Assured by Cannan that some of his men were not wearing hat badges and shoulder flashes because they were unobtainable, Monash saw the divisional ordnance staff, who assured him that stocks were ample. Their records for the preceding five weeks revealed that no demands whatsoever had been made by Cannan's brigade. He admonished Cannan:

> ... I attach no particular importance 'per se' to the absence of a badge ... but if it is evidence of laxity on the part of the platoon officer or NCOs, it assumes a totally different aspect. If a man is allowed to go about for weeks with[out] ... a badge, one wonders whether he is allowed also to go about with a rusty rifle or without a gas mask – or some other essential deficient.

Monash found divisional command, even in a quiet sector, very demanding. He spent at least half the day in his office coping with 'the mountains of administrative work', and it is not without significance that a long letter to Vic, written after seven weeks in the line, dealt largely with the difficulties of supply, keeping warm and maintenance of the area, rather than with actual fighting. But for all his complaints, Monash admitted that 'life on the whole is fairly pleasant for me ... and we live comfortably and eat well.'

CHAPTER 7

On 22 December 1916 Monash finally met the C-in-C during his inspection of the 3rd Division as part of a tour of 2nd ANZAC. 'Douglas Haig looked grey and old. On parting he put his arm around my shoulder (as I rode beside him) and with much feeling and warmth he said – "You have a very fine division. I wish you all sorts of luck old man."' This meeting warrants comment, and not merely because of the obvious emotion of the man described by Birdwood shortly before as not having 'any great human sympathies, and … inclined to regard men more as part of a machine than human beings.' After inspecting divisions as C-in-C for almost a year, Haig had lost some of his aloofness. Apart from White, the Australian senior officers had failed to impress him during the Somme, and he had long disliked Birdwood as an Indian Army officer. Conversely, his first encounter with Monash occurred in circumstances in which the latter's ability was 'never more brilliantly displayed'. Of course, Monash was unproven in a major battle, but Haig's response was indicative of a lasting impression and it never changed. As Terraine says: 'His admiration for Monash was noted after every meeting, perhaps the greatest volume of unmitigated approval for any one man in the whole of his diary.' (Those on parade thought differently. Heavy rain had fallen before Haig's arrival, but they were forbidden to don greatcoats because Monash thought that the coats prevented good marching. The remarks of the sodden infantry were unprintable.)

Haig's encouragement offered Monash incentive, the comfort of his headquarters at Steenwerck and the entertainment of Baroness La Grange at Château La Motte offered him relaxation. But neither could alleviate the 'considerable amount of distress, anxiety and mental trouble' caused by Vic's flightiness. Monash's questions on the company and their finances went unanswered, an omission compounded by Gibson's failure to send Monash a single letter during the preceding six months. Vic had lost confidence in Gibson, confiding to her husband her fear that business had declined because of his mismanagement and that he was trying to 'worm' Monash out. Monash tried to reassure Vic, alluding to Gibson's honesty and the way he had cared for her during her illness. Nevertheless, 'I am constantly beset with the fear that our business interests will break down.' They did not; compared to Currie's financial woes, Monash's problems were trifling. But to Monash they were real enough, and had he surrendered to them his command of his division must have suffered. To dispel any idea that he had intentionally left the whole burden to Gibson while continuing to earn glory abroad, Monash expressed his revulsion of war to him:

> ... I am heartily sick of the whole business. I have been from the first. It is not a business in which one can take any pride or pleasure or even pretend to. Its horror, its ghastly inefficiency, its unspeakable cruelty and misery has always appalled me, but there is nothing to do but to set one's teeth and stick it out as long as one can.

Haig's policy during the winter of 1916–17 was to allow the Germans no respite from the battering they had taken on the Somme. Monash saw in it an opportunity to establish the reputation of his division and spoke in terms of 'gaining credit'. Except to support the infantry, artillery would rarely be used because bombardments invited retaliation, which complicated the maintenance of the defences. Detracting from that common-sense approach was his comment that 'Artillery ... will not bring the same credit to the Division as *infantry* offensives.' His ambition was realised by raiding, and the Official Historian remarked that in this activity the 3rd Division soon became the most experienced of the Australian divisions. It launched its first two 'minor enterprises' on 23–24 and 24–25 December 1916, but the German line was found to be almost deserted, just as it had been in six previous raids by units from other formations. The muddy ditches and waterlogged shell holes had retarded the raiders' approach, so that the time allowed for crossing no man's land was insufficient. Artillery covered the withdrawal, but did not 'box in' the Germans, allowing the few that were seen to escape. These were valuable lessons for Monash, who regarded the raids 'as stepping stones to more extended and aggressive enterprises.'

On 27 February 1917 the 10th Brigade launched a raid at Houplines that was 'the most important ever undertaken by Australians.' Some 824 men penetrated to the third German line and occupied it for

CHAPTER 7

thirty-five minutes on a frontage of 800 yards.[50] The 37th Battalion historian commented: 'if good staff work could ensure success, success was undoubted.' Monash's performance was outstanding. He did not treat the raid as a brigade operation, which would have left its planning largely to McNicoll, but as a divisional operation carried out by a brigade, for whose preparation he would therefore be largely responsible. It began six weeks earlier with a long appreciation that provided for every foreseeable contingency. The objective would be a German salient behind which the communication trenches were widely spread. This would allow maximum concentration of the artillery, prevent the Germans interfering with the flanks and make quick reinforcement by them impossible. Besides two weeks' general training, the raiders were to spend ten days rehearsing the operation on a replica of the enemy trenches. At the suggestion of one of his staff, Monash introduced 'flavoured smoke', possibly for the first time in the BEF. In the three days before the raid, the artillery fired smoke *and* gas, inveigling the Germans into wearing gas masks whenever they saw smoke. The final bombardment was of smoke and high explosive only, enabling the raiders to attack without gas masks and catching the Germans in theirs. Monash was delighted with the result, which he asked White to pass on to Birdwood:

> The whole system of enemy works was thoroughly demolished, a minimum of over 200 dead have been counted, 17 prisoners were brought back; as also a very large quantity of valuable material, including several quite new types of Minenwerfer Fuzes, a complete portable electric searchlight plant, several medical panniers, a miscellaneous collection of rifles, helmets and equipment, and a large mass of papers, maps and documents.

Raids accounted for three-quarters of the 2500 casualties suffered by the 3rd Division in its first six months in France. Monash was a staunch advocate of GHQ's policy on them. They were 'invaluable in keeping up the fighting spirit ... Each such success acted as a powerful stimulant to all ranks ... and prevented the lethargy engendered by weary months of trench warfare from being chronic.' But for every successful raid there was at least one failure, and they were generally detested by the men. The truth of the counter-argument was openly admitted by the Kirke Committee, appointed in 1932 to examine GHQ's tactical handling of the war. Its report criticised the wastage of the best leaders and men: 'As a morale raiser [raids] may be definitely ruled out, at any rate as conducted on the Western Front.'

Less controversial was Monash's use of liaison officers at brigades' headquarters during every operation. They acted as a personal link, allowing Monash to ask questions, modify plans and inform the brigadier of the situation elsewhere without requiring him to come to the phone. The arrangement applied at divisional level what Monash had practised on Gallipoli. It was a powerful tool because of that characteristic of Monash's that impressed all those who worked with him, in this case Jackson, who was struck by his amazing aptitude for seeing through other men's eyes. As at Anzac, Monash relied exclusively on his creative imagination to make visits to the line unnecessary, at least in his eyes, which revives the question of his courage. Like Cannan, Jackson thought he showed marked moral courage, but his physical courage was not outstanding. Still, there was a faint hint of approval in Jackson's observation:

> ... no Divisional Commander in France knew his line better and yet he never visited it, so far as I know. He may have gone to Brigade Headquarters occasionally but I never got him nearer than the third line and he did not seem to enjoy even that. He studied aircraft photographs minutely and discussed details of the front line with me and other staff officers and acquired the most astounding grasp of local conditions. This 'seeing through other men's eyes' is to my mind not sufficiently practised in our Army.

Irrespective of the moral effect on troops who never saw their commander in the line, Monash's method depended for its success on a correct view prevailing at brigades' headquarters. In the inevitable confusion of battle, accuracy was contingent on the ability of brigade and battalion commanders to judge the appropriate time to undertake a personal reconnaissance, knowing they might be absent from their headquarters, with its communications, for two or three hours. Unless they did so, Monash's power of creative imagination would be

CHAPTER 7

undermined by wrong information. A notable failure occurred during the 3rd Division's first major battle, the attack by Plumer's Second Army on Messines Ridge.

Both Monash and his division were singularly fortunate to have served under Plumer from the time of their arrival on the Western Front. In appearance Plumer might well have been the inspiration for Low's Colonel Blimp, but he employed at army level the methods used by Maxse and Monash at corps and divisional levels, reinforcing the conclusion that principles did exist which, if followed, often resulted in success. Plumer's partnership with Major General Charles Harington, his chief of staff, was exceptionally close and symbolic of the cooperative spirit that marked the relations of Second Army's staff with the fighting troops. Monash agreed wholeheartedly: 'Harington's doctrine that all staffs exist to *help* units and not to make difficulties for them is the only one that can possibly lead to success, and I am constantly preaching that doctrine myself.' Moreover, Plumer had led Australians – and New Zealanders – during the Boer War and understood them better than any other senior British commander. The mutual affection they had shared then was again evident.

Plumer introduced important innovations such as the 'Army Centre', which assembled information from all sources during a battle and provided commanders at all levels with an accurate and up-to-date picture of events. Like Monash, he emphasised the training of regimental officers, because the tactical onus rested on them, and insisted on meticulous planning and preparation and the 'issuing of orders right down … to the private soldier'. But any similarity between the two ended with their respective relationships with Haig. Harington recalled: 'I think the only real enemy he had was Douglas who was jealous of him.' The C-in-C tended to avoid him, an attitude probably formed at Staff College when Plumer, an outside examiner, gave Haig low marks. It was the sort of slight Haig never forgot.

The defence of the Ypres salient had been Plumer's responsibility since May 1915. Asked what was 'the greatest strategical and tactical objective on the Second Army Front' by Sir John French in June, Plumer pointed to the Messines-Wytschaete Ridge, 264 feet at its highest point. It bulged westwards through Messines and Wytschaete to create another salient before meeting the ridge that curved through Gheluvelt, Passchendaele and Staden to form the southern side of the Ypres salient. As the Messines Ridge commanded the communications into the Ypres salient, mining operations were begun with a view to capturing it in spring 1916, but by then Haig had succeeded French. In January 1916 he asked Plumer to consider the operation as one of three possible attacks to divert attention from the Somme and by mid-June, even thought of transferring the main British offensive to the Ypres salient if the Somme stroke was checked. That plan never eventuated, but it was never far from Haig's mind. Following disappointments elsewhere, Haig announced on 7 May 1917 that he was shifting the BEF's weight to Ypres. Monash had been informed several months earlier that Second Army must be prepared to assault the ridge at one month's notice. The date now set was 7 June.

The two years since the first hint of the attack allowed Plumer to make preparations on a scale unique in the BEF, but necessary in view of the tactics employed, namely, 'bringing up to date and vastly expanding the methods of siege warfare as practised by Marlborough.' The most devastating feature was 21 mines, packed with over 500 tons of ammonal, under the German line; some of them had been ready since June 1916.[51] Some 2266 guns, 756 of them heavy, were assembled, representing one gun to every seven yards of front, the highest concentration yet in the British Army. To feed them, 144 000 tons of shells had been dumped. The bombardment lasted seventeen days, entering its final phase on 31 May with wire-cutting, counter-bombardment and the engagement of German supply routes. Plumer conceived the barrage from the viewpoint of the attacking infantry. Half the field guns provided the creeping barrage, while the remainder, with many of the heavier guns, struck positions up to 700 yards in rear. This would silence machine-guns firing from them at long range, a favourite German tactic since the Somme. As each objective was taken, the barrage would advance 1000 yards to engage any counter-attacks. Containers of gas and boiling oil, lobbed into the German trenches, increased the demoralisation of the occupants, while the

CHAPTER 7

Royal Flying Corps (RFC), recovered from its mauling of 'Bloody April', roamed freely above the battlefield.[52] Seventy-six of the new Mark IV tanks would also be used.

Messines village under bombardment. Although this photograph was taken on 8 June 1917, the view is as it would have been during the bombardment before the battle. The Douve, where crossed by the 3rd Division, is in the middle distance and the trees on the crest to the right mark Huns' Walk (AWM H12264).

Nevertheless, attacks on salients presented difficulties that did not arise in assaults against linear objectives, and Messines was no exception. The attack frontage followed a curve, ten miles long, which skirted the western foot of the ridge between St Yves in the south and Mount Sorrel in the north. Along the crest ran the German second line, forming an inner curve, while across the base of the salient were two chord positions, the Oosttaverne Line on the flats two and a half miles to the east, and, another mile away and parallel to it, the Warneton Line. The central sector was extremely well fortified and the length of the assault was naturally greatest there. As the depth of the attack from the outer parts of the curve was shorter, precise coordination would be necessary if the chord were to be attacked simultaneously along its length. A disciple of 'bite and hold', Plumer proposed to assault over several days, first from north and south and then 'pinching out' the centre at Wytschaete. Haig rightly rejected his plan as over-cautious and on 3 April ordered a bigger bite – the capture of the entire ridge in one day. X Corps and 2nd ANZAC, on the northern and southern flanks respectively, were to advance direct to the final objective on the crest, known as the Black Line. Encompassing the German second line, it would be reached two hours later by IX Corps in the centre. At the beginning of May, Haig extended the operation further, to the Oosttaverne or Green Line, to capture as many guns as possible. However, the Black Line remained the main objective, Plumer drawing attention several times to the 'supreme' importance of its 'immediate and effective consolidation' and its retention 'at all costs'. The exploitation to the Green Line was 'just as far as, and no further than, the point where German numbness began to wear off.'

By describing the gestation of the Messines attack in terms of the contribution of the higher commanders and the interchanges between them, the part played by Monash as a divisional commander becomes clear. Though he disagreed with some of them, he had no say in any of the principal decisions reached: the method of dealing with chord and arc, the setting of the objective lines and the pauses between them. Godley disclosed the corps plan to him on 23 March. The 3rd Division would form the right flank of the entire assault, with Russell's New Zealand Division next to it capturing Messines itself. The 25th (British) Division was to extend 2nd ANZAC's frontage on the left to IX Corps. Monash's reconnaissance immediately afterwards revealed that the task allotted was 'a fairly heavy and responsible one for a staff and troops that had never before engaged in a major operation.'

Under shellfire, Monash left Hyde Park Corner at the western end of Ploegsteert Wood and climbed to the observation post in the ruined Château de la Hutte on the crest of Hill 63. Its south-eastern slope formed the left flank of his attack frontage, which extended 2000 yards to the right across the northern end of Ploegsteert Wood. On the skyline was the southern end of the Messines Ridge, the village easily discerned by the shell of its church, which was the subject of several watercolours by the future nemesis of his people, Corporal Adolf Hitler. On the eastern slope of the ridge he could see the

CHAPTER 7

dense copses of Steignast Farm midway between the wire belts of the Oosttaverne and Warneton lines. Monash's eye rested on La Potterie Farm, a major strongpoint in the Oosttaverne Line, and as his gaze returned westwards he could easily spot the fortified ruins that littered the German first and second lines as they crossed the valley floor: Bethleem, Grey, Schnitzel and La Douve farms. The last lay on the south bank of the Douve, a small stream that trickled past the foot of the ridge into German territory. On its northern bank was La Petite Douve Farm, through which ran Monash's boundary with the New Zealanders. Three things over which he had no control were clear. The fate of his own attack depended on the New Zealanders' capture of Messines and its facing slope, for the Uhlan and Ulcer trench systems located there enfiladed the length of the 3rd Division's attack. Secondly, its position on the extreme right of the arc meant that the depth of the advance to the chord varied: 'the right hand man of the 3rd ... had to stand still while the left hand man had some three thousand yards to go.' Finally, his division's approach routes behind Hill 63 and Ploegsteert Wood would be shelled with gas and high explosive for they were an obvious concentration area for 2nd ANZAC's artillery.[53]

An Australian transport wagon dodges German shelling of the Anzac gun lines behind Hill 63 on 5 June. The Germans drenched this area with gas when the 3rd Division moved through it for the Messines assault two days later. Monash had earlier viewed the battlefield from the top of Hill 63 (AWM E00650).

Returning to Steenwerck, Monash drafted his preliminary notes for Magnum Opus, the name given to the operation to preserve secrecy. At this stage he dwelt mainly on the administrative and tactical preparations necessary *before* the attack, such as the provision of forward supply and ammunition depots for the artillery and infantry. Once surveyed, the infantry's assembly trenches were to be 'renovated and made anew – to permit of definite allotment in frontage and depth down to platoons.' By using them, brigades could enjoy a protected rest while still in their attack formations, avoiding the discomfort and vulnerability inherent in the usual method of awaiting zero hour on jumping-off tapes laid in no man's land. Monash was adamant that on no account were his troops to wait in the open. Assaulting in two bounds on right and left respectively, the 9th and 10th brigades would take the German front and support lines in the first bound and the Black Line in the second. Monash said no more about the actual conduct of the attack, but asked his brigadiers to submit plans after listing for their consideration both general points and those matters pertinent to the front of each. His first divisional plan appeared on 10 April and again described the operation in general terms, the rear four battalions leapfrogging through the leading four to establish the Black Line and a chain of protective posts beyond it.

Monash was probably still engaged with his Assistant Adjutant and Quartermaster General (AA&QMG), Lieutenant Colonel Harold Farmar, on the administrative scheme, which was now far more advanced than the tactical. Traffic control, on which the speedy forwarding of stores depended, was stressed. Small dumps and aid posts were to be sited in or near the front line to minimise the distance carrying parties and stretcher-bearers had to travel under shellfire. Mindful of Plumer's emphasis on thorough consolidation of the Black Line, Monash detached 200 infantry to the field engineering companies, one of which he allotted to each attacking brigade. Not until 15 April was the tactical and barrage plan issued in a remarkable document in which he

> ... purposely did not aim at the condensed phraseology of official instructions, but rather at a colloquial discussion of the problems

CHAPTER 7

and difficulties which will confront Brigade and Battalion Commanders, to the end of starting their thinking about the general plan and crystallising their own views as to the details of their tasks.

It was much more than this. The plans submitted by McNicoll and Jobson, in particular, were by no means weak and, with one important exception, Monash approved their proposals for employing their battalions. But the breadth of Monash's exposition made their plans look ordinary. Written mainly at company level, Jobson's scheme rarely mentioned platoons; McNicoll's did not at all. Monash considered them frequently, denoting each battalion's frontage by the number of platoons needed to occupy it. Where necessary, he outlined platoon tasks, explained the criteria for consolidation and prescribed the length of new trenches to be dug and the number of tools needed. As soon as the 33rd Battalion, on the extreme right flank, had taken its objective:

> ... bombing blocks must be established and garrisoned ... in all the trafficable trenches leading southwards from the captured territory. The total length of trench to be captured by each wave does not exceed 550 yards. This task can be adequately dealt with by six platoons in each wave ... The distance being short, comparatively small carrying parties should fully serve the needs of this battalion. The total length of the new trench to be dug and consolidated is about 1,500 yards. This would require the continuous labour of 300 men for 48 hours. Thus 250 shovels and 100 picks should be available for this battalion.

Doubtlessly recalling his experience at Baby 700, Monash was much more aware than his brigadiers of the directional changes, necessitated by the shape of the German line opposite, after the attack had begun. His explanation of how the most affected battalion, the 33rd, could be assisted was much more precise than Jobson's, who, it seems, barely considered the problem. McNicoll attached no great significance to Schnitzel Farm, but for Monash it was 'of the *very highest importance* as it will form the Southern pivot upon which the subsequent defence of Messines Hill will depend.'

Maintaining momentum. One of the footbridges thrown across the Douve by the 40th Battalion at the start of the Messines attack (AWM E01286).

The outstanding feature was Monash's audacious plan for crossing the Douve, which he prudently assumed was unfordable and which patrols established was heavily wired. The German defences overlooking it on the northern side formed a crude triangle, the front line approaching the stream at right angles from La Petite Douve Farm and then swinging parallel to its northern bank to meet the support line about 300 yards further back. The parallel section, or base of the triangle along the stream was thus an effective switch line, able to resist any attack on the support long after the front line had fallen. Monash suggested that one company of the 40th Battalion should attack in four platoon waves from the New Zealand area north of the stream, the first going straight to the support line, which the Germans would never expect, while the second attacked the front trenches. Soon after, the third platoon would attack from within the triangle to take the base in rear, meeting a party from the 39th Battalion assaulting the same trench from the east. The fourth platoon was to seize a switch running off the support line, as two more companies from the 40th Battalion placed at least six footbridges across the stream. By allotting each trench as a separate objective, Monash nullified the depth and mutual

CHAPTER 7

support that were the strengths of the triangle and which would likely have defeated the simple frontal assault by two companies proposed by McNicoll. Every commander in the division was to be familiar with the plan of his colleagues on either flank and to front and rear, because once his objectives were taken, he had to assist them to achieve theirs. This unity of action was the principle on which Monash's planning was founded.

On 9 May Godley announced the impending arrival of the 4th Australian Division as 2nd ANZAC reserve and intimated that the Black Line 'may be slightly altered in definition'. Specific details emerged two days later. Haig's decision to attack the Oosttaverne (Green) Line necessitated the advancement of the Black, which, on McNicoll's front, was swung forward to Bethleem Farm, increasing the length of his assault by 500 yards. It was lengthened a further 800 yards by Godley's 'tentative ruling', confirmed on 16 May, that the 3rd Division was to capture a 300-yard stretch of Uncanny Trench in the Green Line. Changes had to be made to the divisional plan. Jackson suggested employing the 11th Brigade, a course that Monash would adopt only as a last resort. Neither brigade or battalion headquarters nor the signals network between them had been prepared for the 11th, whose use would also disrupt the carefully planned assembly arrangements and deprive Monash of a divisional reserve. The only recourse was to alter the tasks of the attacking battalions of the 9th and 10th brigades.

In the existing scheme no single battalion was allotted as brigade reserve. Some battalions had reserve companies, which McNicoll or Jobson could form into a larger force to continue the attack if heavy resistance were encountered. With eight battalions assaulting, the sectors allotted to each were small, minimising the loss of time in the assembly of the reserve companies should they be required. The enlargement of the operation increased the importance of strong reserves that could be deployed rapidly, and to obtain them Monash expanded the role of some battalions to release others. The 9th Brigade would keep the 36th Battalion in reserve, attacking initially with the 33rd and 35th, to be joined by the 34th as the Black Line was reached.

McNicoll was to secure the Douve crossing with the 40th Battalion, as before, and attack on the northern and southern side of the stream with the 38th and 39th respectively. The 39th's assault would overlap the 34th's, and it would hand over to the 34th its section of the Black Line, making the 9th Brigade responsible for the entire area south of the Douve. Monash's adjustment of the inter-brigade boundary *after* the capture of the Black Line was a wise move. It permitted the use in the first stages of the attack of the same boundary and associated control measures prescribed in the original plan. The 39th Battalion would be released to become McNicoll's reserve, leaving him to defend the Black Line north of the Douve on a single battalion frontage with the 37th still available for the assault on the Green Line. The 44th Battalion from Cannan's brigade would be trained in the 37th's task while the 43rd Battalion was to be fully acquainted with the plan of the 9th Brigade.

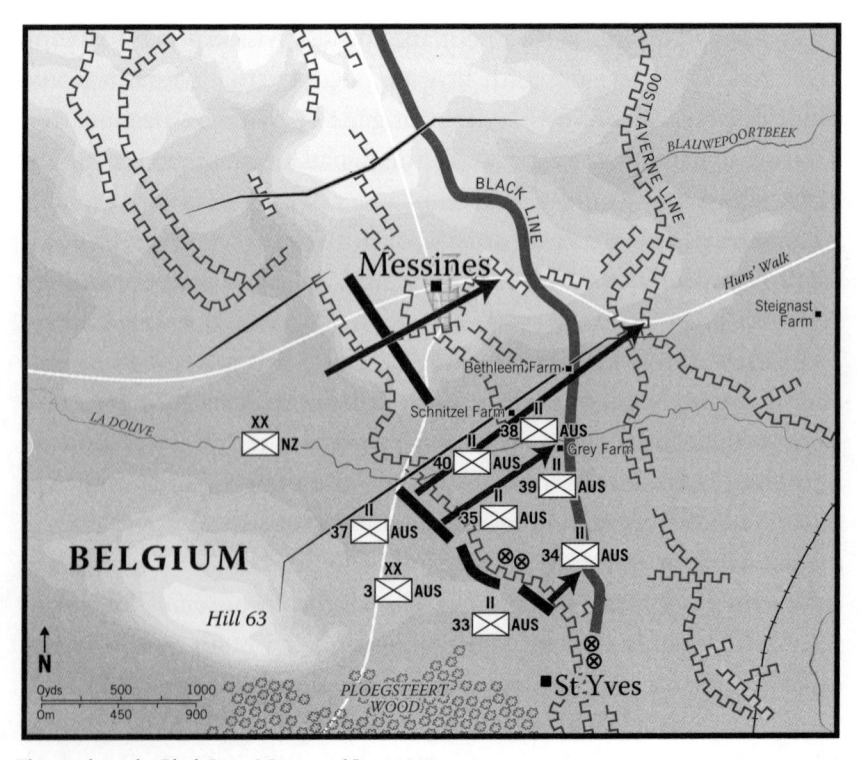

The attack on the Black Line, Messines, 6 June 1917

CHAPTER 7

Monash had gone a long way towards usurping the role of his brigadiers. He virtually stated how they must employ their battalions, instead of allowing them to prepare brigade plans within the framework of a divisional scheme that did not descend beyond brigade level. McNicoll and Jobson were so circumscribed that their plans were nothing more than a regurgitation of what Monash had already laid down. As Jobson said after receiving Monash's suggestion on the assembly for the attack: 'the plan set out by you is the best possible and should work satisfactorily.'

Precisely how and when the Green Line was to be taken remained unclear. Godley's plan of 16 May stated that the operation would be ordered 'at any time ... by commanders "on the spot"' within one hour of the seizure of the Black Line. It was not to be a 'formal operation', but an advance by 'bounds', for which there would be no creeping barrage, the artillery searching the area between the two lines instead. Coordination arrangements between the artillery and infantry and between Monash and the New Zealanders were not mentioned, which restricted the planning of the 37th Battalion's attack in matters such as the location of assembly areas and timings for the move forward. Despite Godley's personal request on 21 May, Monash would not submit a final scheme for the operation until proper guidelines were provided. As usual, Monash's foresight and deliberation prevailed against Godley's urgency. Because of the excessive length of the IX Corps assault in the centre, Plumer, on 18 May, permitted the use of its reserve division for the attack on the Green Line, which was now to be undertaken by all corps simultaneously ten hours after zero. Monash was informed by 2nd ANZAC on 20 May, discussed proposed amendments to the artillery barrage with Godley on 23 May, and next day issued the plan agreed on with Russell for the continuation of the advance to the Green Line. It answered the questions previously raised by Godley. Incredibly, more alterations followed, for Godley was vacillating over the employment of the 4th Division. On 24 May he ordered it to prepare plans for counter-attacks on any of the three divisional fronts, but on 27 May he conformed to the arrangement in IX and X Corps, giving the 4th Division, held in reserve during the attack on the Black Line, the task of attacking the Green Line in place of the New Zealanders. 'I have reason to think that matters have at last reached finality', wrote an exasperated Monash as he explained the revision to McNicoll.

The disruption within the 3rd Division was reduced by its staff procedures. Modifications announced at corps conferences were passed on by Monash at a divisional conference, not more than one day later, and incorporated in Magnum Opus circulars. The first of thirty-six appeared on 15 April, and each was to be 'treated as if it formed part of the Operation Order, unless subsequently cancelled or revised', thus avoiding the issue of a lengthy operation order before the attack. They covered in detail every aspect of the operation, the instruction on machine-guns, for example, comprising seven parts. The theory of Monash's Lark Hill lectures was given practical substance, and the efficacy of his method demonstrated by the appearance of the 3rd Division's operation order on 27 May, the day on which Godley made his last alteration and two days before the 2nd ANZAC order materialised. After the war, Harington remembered that on 4 June Monash presented him with all the divisional orders and instructions pertinent to the battle, compiled in a single document six inches thick: 'I never saw such a document – wonderful detail but not his job. He would tell you which duckboard needed repairing but never in his life went near a front line trench.'

Harington's disparagement of Monash's grasp of operational staff work to score cheap points on the subject of his physical courage was surprising for a staff officer of his reputation. Jackson, however, praised Monash's attention to detail, which he felt resulted from his engineering career and distinguished him from many British generals. Jackson was right: that characteristic was the most striking feature of Monash's planning. He himself wrote: 'Everything is being done with the perfection of a civil engineering construction so far as regards planning and execution ...' In practical terms this meant that Monash thoroughly examined seemingly unimportant details, for he realised that even the smallest oversight could be paid for in lives.

CHAPTER 7

Monash plotted the exact location of the trenches in his sector from the latest aerial photographs, which revealed that the secret maps issued by 2nd ANZAC were incorrect. Supplementing 2nd ANZAC's terrain model of the battlefield, the 3rd Division built one at Brune Gaye for its own assault, again using aerial photos instead of maps. Two feet separated the highest point from the lowest, and an encircling platform enabled each company in turn 'to get quite a comprehensive picture of their line of advance and of their final objective.' The effect of probable German shelling of Ploegsteert Wood would be reduced by preparing four separate approach routes, each to be shared by two battalions. All NCOs and officers were to reconnoitre the route to be taken by their companies and practise assembling them in the dark. At Monash's insistence, a direct telephone line was laid from his office to Russell's headquarters. Documents on the recent operational experience of other formations were studied for techniques that might prove useful.

Australians from the 13th Brigade study one of the large terrain models of the Messines battlefield on 6 June. They would participate in the 4th Division's assault on the Oosttaverne (Green) Line the next day (AWM E00632).

MONASH

Plumer visited Monash at least eight times between Monash's return from leave on 23 March and 7 June, Monash 'talking him through' the 3rd Division's attack. Like Plumer, Monash learned from the Canadian capture of Vimy Ridge, which had opened the British Arras offensive in April. He saw it at first hand and admired it as 'a truly astonishing feat'. Accompanied by Jackson, he visited the Canadians there on 8 May. Monash noted that they had suffered unnecessarily because their assembly was rushed and that the ground was so disturbed by the bombardment that German dugouts were only visible as holes in the sides of craters. The former demonstrated the importance of his own assembly procedures, while each of his brigades promulgated instructions on the need for careful mopping up to counter the threat posed by the latter.

As an example of the thoroughness of the 3rd Division's staff, Bean cited its preliminary bombardment program, which listed in seven appendices 446 targets to be shelled before 7 June. The Official Historian missed the more important point – that in his use of artillery and indeed, other arms, Monash was already inclining towards the theory that he elaborated at some length after the war:

> ... the true role of the Infantry was not to expend itself upon heroic physical effort ... (I am thinking of Pozières, and Stormy Trench and other bloody fields) – but on the contrary, to advance under the maximum possible protection of the maximum possible array of mechanical resources, in the form of guns, machine-guns, tanks, mortars and aeroplanes ... to be relieved as far as possible of the obligation to *fight* their way forward ...

Like the French general, Philippe Pétain, Monash always sought a preponderance of artillery. He complained to Godley on 21 May that guns should be distributed according to the length of front divisions held *after* the attack. With an allotment of only one-third of the field artillery in the corps, it was preposterous that the 3rd Division should be expected to occupy half of 2nd ANZAC's Black Line. But the distribution was not altered, while Monash's request for a number of Stokes mortars for gas bombardment brought the curt reply: 'the work can easily be done with fewer guns than you propose.' He pestered

CHAPTER 7

Godley about clearing troops from the locations he had selected for his artillery brigades' headquarters and, within his division, ordered the closest liaison between artillery and infantry commanders, particularly in regard to the wire-cutting program.

Monash was thinking of more than just artillery to ease the task of his infantry. Twenty tanks were allotted to 2nd ANZAC, but Godley informed Monash that his division would probably receive none. Monash was convinced they would prove useful, pointing out that works near Septième Barn were a suitable objective. He raised the matter again when aerial photos showed that the Germans had improved the works, and even outlined how two tanks could cooperate with infantry to take them. Monash's specialist engineering knowledge was advantageous on many occasions, beginning with the design of a strongpoint that could be constructed rapidly at Bethleem Farm. He rejected the abandonment of the most northerly of three mines on his division's front when only a fortnight's digging was required to complete it. But the drive should be deflected slightly westward, for then the explosion would better assist the Douve crossing. Deception was important. At zero hour, the two battalions of the 57th Division under his command beyond the right flank were to raise their bayonets above the parapet and engage the German trenches with heavy machine-gun and rifle fire to convey the impression that they, too, were attacking.

Conscious that Messines was his division's first major battle, Monash took great care that commanders at all levels knew what was expected of them. Rather than just familiarise himself with the instructions for the 3rd New Zealand Brigade on his left, McNicoll was directed to study the New Zealand Division's operation order, which 'will help you better to grasp the underlying policy of the New Zealand attack, which may possibly not be sufficiently clearly disclosed by the 3rd Rifle Brigade's order.' To ensure that orders had been properly passed on by the brigadiers, Monash questioned each battalion commander on fifty-three separate points related to his task. The brigadiers followed his advice to question company commanders and, in the 9th Brigade, platoon commanders were specifically directed to '"organise" [their] unit so that all men in each section know what the section's task is.' No finer example exists of the policy on 'percolation of orders', which he outlined at Salisbury Plain. But Monash's supervision of his commanders did not mean the neglect of his senior staff. As they occurred to him, he jotted down his thoughts on numerous matters and gave them to Jackson and other members of the staff to follow up. Whether similar points would have been raised as a matter of course by the staff of a less thorough divisional commander is a question that is difficult to answer. Durrant provided a clue:

> I have seen [Monash] ask an officer for a list of points to be attended to; and when it was submitted to him he would say, 'Have a look at this one', and that astonished officer would be handed a list containing about twice as many items as he had produced.

An essential element in Monash's exercise of command, the divisional conference, brought commanders and staffs together as a group. He had explained to Grimwade before one of the first divisional meetings in December 1916: 'I want to leave nothing to chance ... so we are going to talk these matters out to a finish and will not separate until we have a perfect mutual understanding among all concerned.' Conducted according to this principle, the lengthy conferences before Messines were very tiring. On 19 April, Monash chaired 'a heavy conference ... lasting from 2.30 to 7 with an adjournment for tea.' He described the attack from start to finish and then turned to administrative matters. Agreement was reached on questions asked by him and of him, usually as they arose, to save overloading formal orders.

Attending these conferences were the infantry and artillery brigadiers and their staffs, senior members of the operational and administrative staffs, the heads of branches of all arms and services and, frequently, battalion commanders. Showing that he had learned since Gallipoli, Monash laid down that 'The ADMS was not only permitted but required to attend staff conferences in any matter that concerned his department.' All were asked to give their ideas on items listed on an agenda circulated several days before. Monash listened to and often sought the opinions of those who would normally remain silent. Major Geoffrey Drake-Brockman was surprised when

CHAPTER 7

he asked the commanders of the field engineering companies for their views: 'This was a new experience for me; on other similar occasions the engineer opinion always came from the CRE [Commander Royal Engineers].' Monash would then outline the policy, after displaying powers of analytical assessment that invariably impressed those present. On 24 May, Haig came under Monash's spell. The C-in-C's eyes were fixed on him as he expounded the activities of each arm. Afterwards, Haig wrote:

> [Monash] is in my opinion a clear-headed, determined commander. Every detail had been thought of. His brigadiers were equally thorough. I was most struck with their whole arrangements. Every suggestion I made was carefully noted for consideration.[54]

According to Smithers, Monash saw himself 'not so much as the chief handing down tablets of stone but as the man in overall charge of a great engineering project consulting with his most important subcontractors.' The meetings were a vehicle for his commanders to express their own ideas, and he would adopt them unhesitatingly if they improved on his own. This alone was sufficient reason for holding them, but the interchange also served to balance Monash's intrusion into responsibilities that would normally be considered theirs. Although Monash was its most renowned practitioner, the conference method was a prominent weapon in the command armoury of the best British generals, a fact that tends to be overlooked. Currie attributed the Vimy success 'largely ... to the way in which everything had been carefully explained to those concerned.' Plumer's army was famous for its careful briefings, as were Maxse, Cavan and Jacob at corps level and Feilding and Babington at divisional. It is prudent to assume that they extracted as much from their conferences as Monash did from his.

Important as careful planning and thorough preparations were, success depended ultimately on the quality and training of the assaulting infantry. Messines would be the first attack by Australian troops using the revised platoon doctrine issued by GHQ after its study of the Somme and the French Chemin des Dames offensives. Derived largely by the Canadians, it was considered to have worked well at Arras.[55] Monash had trained his division according to many of its principles even before the policy became official; and the first rehearsal for the Messines attack, at Quelmes in April, drew praise from Godley and the training staff: 'The work of Companies and Platoons in the new organisation appears to be very good and on sound lines. The Platoon Commanders seem to have a very good grasp of what is required.' As the blowing of mines made practical instruction in the consolidating of craters essential, Monash designed an appropriate exercise that each platoon was to carry out. In the days immediately before the attack, junior commanders spoke to their men during any pause in training on such matters as the importance of 'sending a stream of information to the nearest superior'. Godley's notes on the need for determination in the attack were issued by Monash as a personal appeal to be 'used on every suitable occasion that offered'. A more extreme measure was his circulation of an account of 'the brutal treatment meted out to defenceless Australian soldiers' taken prisoner at Bullecourt in April; Messines would provide an opportunity of 'striking a heavy blow at a cruel, inhumane enemy, to avenge [them].'[56]

The 3rd Division took over its attack frontage on 27 April. During the next month, brigades rotated through the training area at Quelmes. Detecting the frequent changes of units holding the line, the Germans raided on 17 and 18 May, but were unsuccessful. Five raids had also been repelled in March and April, prompting Bean's comment that in defence, the 3rd was 'to say the least, fully up to the standard of the older divisions.' As the attack approached, it launched its own series of raids to obtain prisoners and to ascertain the effect of the bombardment on the German wire and defences. To reduce losses caused by the much lighter German counter-bombardment and any retaliatory raids, the 3rd Division's entire line was held by the 41st Battalion after 31 May. The 9th and 10th brigades were resting in their concentration areas between Pont de Nieppe and Romarin, which they began to leave shortly after 11.00 pm on 6 June. One hour later Monash retired, but he could not sleep because of the noise, his excitement and a swarm of mosquitoes. By then the eight assaulting battalions were undergoing a terrible ordeal in Ploegsteert Wood.

CHAPTER 7

A German pillbox upended by the explosion of one of the mines on Messines Ridge and flung onto the lip of the crater. Such was the destruction caused by the mines and the bombardment that the initial advance encountered only sporadic resistance (AWM E01320).

On 3 June the Germans had begun nightly gas bombardments of the wood, and on the 6th the shelling commenced just as the 3rd Division started to move through it. The approach march of each battalion was seriously hindered as the gas dispersed slowly in the stagnant air. Prolonged wearing of gas masks on this sultry night distressed all ranks, while leaders were frequently overcome when they lowered their masks to direct the men. Desultory high explosive shelling added to the confusion, and the march began to resemble that of 6 August 1915. At 2.00 am, when the assembly should have been almost completed, the four columns had just cleared the wood and suffered about a thousand casualties. But the organisation for the attack remained, which Bean ascribed to the 3rd Division's training and spirit: 'Throughout the night the moving factor was the determination of the men themselves to reach the "jumping off" position in time.' Bean disregarded the effect of Monash's foresight on this initial phase of the attack. The congestion and hence the delays would have been much greater had Monash used fewer than four approach routes. Even then it was bad enough. He was rewarded for his decision not to assemble in the open as the dazed infantry flung themselves into their assembly trenches. Many fell asleep after drinking the water especially stored there. Then it was 3.10 am:

> ... Zero hour arrives like the switching on of a distant line of blinking lights, and while all noises mingle, one distinguishes that the mines have gone by the dull, red mass of flame, with, later a rising cloud of smoke which settles for a moment above the ridge – and now everything is awake – a tornado of noise, myriads of wicked stabs of light and the hundred and one kinds of flare which the Boche immediately puts up.

Mines and barrage combined to shatter German resistance and the attack 'proceeded with machine like precision'. Monash could follow its progress closely, because every five minutes contact aircraft dropped at his headquarters reports of the latest positions reached. At 5.02 am he informed Godley: 'Left brigade holds Schnitzel Farm and Ulster Reserve. Left of right brigade going to program. Right of right brigade reached Black Line.' Shortly after 5.15 am the Black Line had been captured on the entire 2nd ANZAC frontage and its consolidation began, carried out in the 3rd 'with the particular care that was to become a recognised characteristic of [that] ... Division', wrote Bean. Lieutenant Colonel Leslie Morshead of the 33rd Battalion saw his men digging in the midst of a German bombardment 'as if at the Bustard'.

The shelling increased markedly after an enemy aircraft penetrated the British aerial scout screen; but through it moved the 37th Battalion for the attack on the Oosttaverne Line, due to be launched at 1.10 pm. The commanding officer, Lieutenant Colonel Walter Smith, felt that the bombardment was too heavy, and did not accompany his battalion, leaving it in the hands of a company commander, Major Charles Story. When the 37th reached the Black Line at midday, it had lost 10 per cent of its strength; worse still, news was received that the attack had been postponed to 3.10 pm. With the 45th and 47th battalions from the 4th Division alongside, the 37th had to endure the bombardment in the meantime. The delay allowed the Germans to reinforce the Oosttaverne Line. In contrast to the morning's operation, reports on the progress of the Australian assault on it were 'extremely fragmentary and vague'.

CHAPTER 7

A German dugout captured by the 39th Battalion near La Douve Farm. The Messines Ridge rises in the background (AWM E01285).

Monash had experienced the same trouble within his division during an abortive German counter-attack at 2.30 pm. Urgent messages from divisional headquarters were being answered very slowly by brigade headquarters because the officer manning the telephone was not conversant with the situation. Monash's peremptory order to his brigadiers to rectify the problem may have had great ramifications. The 37th and the company from the 40th supporting it had stopped slightly short of the Green Line between Huns' Walk and the Douve. Severe casualties, particularly among the leaders, were caused by pillboxes, which the Australians were encountering for the first time. Only by establishing a series of outposts could the 230 survivors of the 37th garrison their 1200 yards of trench. At about 5.30 pm the isolated groups from the 37th and the neighbouring 47th Battalion on Huns' Walk, already under heavy fire from Steignast Farm, were counter-attacked, but they did not fire flares for overflying contact aircraft for fear of showing their position to the Germans. The supporting artillery, unsure of their location, fired a barrage that fell on their trenches instead of the German ones. The 47th retired to the Black Line, but the 37th remained, swinging back its left flank to avoid the shelling. It was now shortly after 7.30 pm.

MONASH

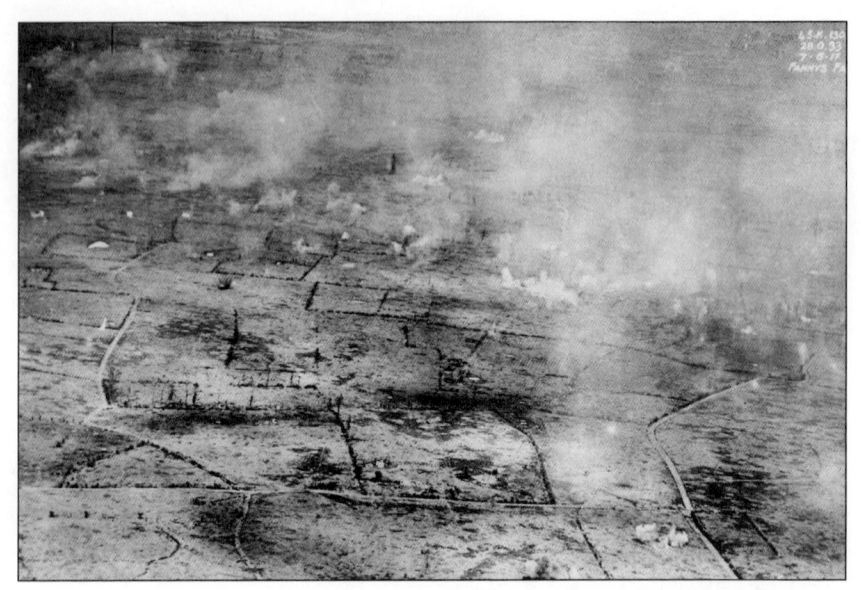

An aerial shot, looking eastwards from above Messines, of the British barrage falling on the Oosttaverne Line at about 6.00 pm on 7 June. Arising from a confused situation, it caused the Australians who had reached the Oosttaverne Line to withdraw, leaving much of it open (AWM J00272).

Monash's actions during this crisis can best be described as decisive but unfortunate. One of the commanders in the New Zealand Division on his left believed that the 37th Battalion, as well as the 47th, had pulled out and so the New Zealand barrage was shortened, bringing it back to the Black Line. Part of the 37th was forced to withdraw, whereupon Story, hearing of the retirement of the 47th, ordered the remainder of the 37th to retire. Still smarting from Monash's afternoon rebuke over slow reporting, the brigade commander, McNicoll, passed this to divisional headquarters immediately. Monash responded by shortening his barrage, which fell on those groups of the 37th Battalion whom Story had not yet reached. They completed their withdrawal at 9.00 pm. At the core of the muddle was Plumer's extreme caution. As the Black Line was the critical objective, the artillery was organised for its defence, even though counter-attacks would naturally strike the Green Line first. The 4th Division occupying the Green Line was thus dependent on guns whose priority was the support of the New Zealanders behind them. Bean says: 'this system was bound to break down',

CHAPTER 7

notwithstanding the close relationships between the two staffs. As the 37th Battalion was inextricably mixed with the 47th, it too would suffer. Nevertheless, Monash's pride was deeply dented and, rather unfairly, he accused Smith of commanding the only battalion in the division that failed to take its objective.[57]

Amid the confusion prevailing at Godley's headquarters, there arrived at 9.12 pm detailed information from Monash on which trenches were held on his front. The report was the most accurate Godley received that night, and his order, issued at 10.45 pm, to recapture the lost ground was largely based on it. Anticipating this second attack, Monash warned McNicoll at 9.20 pm to get ready and reinforced him with Lieutenant Colonel William Mansbridge's 44th Battalion from the 11th Brigade. Monash explained to McNicoll how he should execute it, the 44th Battalion forming 'a sort of mobile left flank', and told Charles Gwynn, the Brigadier General, General Staff (BGGS) 2nd ANZAC, not to interfere with his barrage. Then a runner interrupted with a startling message that the 3rd Division was steadily re-establishing itself on the Green Line. Reaching the limit of his patience, Monash sought clarification from McNicoll: 'I want to take this opportunity of asking whether this is thoroughly clear or not – whether you are *in partial* or *in full* control of the country already? We do not know – do you know?'

This time there would be no withdrawal: 'If 4 Div fall back tomorrow, Mansbridge must hold his ground ... even if he has to form a salient.' Monash and Holmes, now commanding the 4th Division, agreed to attack at 3.00 am on 8 June. It was the beginning of a controversial day.

Late receipt of information delayed the 44th Battalion until 3.20 am, and the 48th Battalion from the 4th Division on its left even longer. As a result, Mansbridge had to bend his left flank back towards the Black Line when he reached the Green Line at 3.45 am, forming the salient that Monash expected. Bean says the 44th's position was 'promptly and accurately reported', but this is hardly corroborated by Monash's message to 2nd ANZAC, at 4.20 am, that McNicoll knew nothing of the progress of Mansbridge's assault. Both Godley and Monash were uncertain of his junction with the 48th Battalion on Huns' Walk long after the 48th had begun its advance. Not until 1.00 pm were the two linked by Mansbridge's patrols. Because the 48th could find no trace of the 44th in the meantime, it reported that the 44th was not in its correct position, dumbfounding Monash who believed that it was. At the last corps conference before the battle, Godley had emphasised: 'Divisional Staff Officers including Administrative Staff Officers to go right forward to ascertain the situation.'

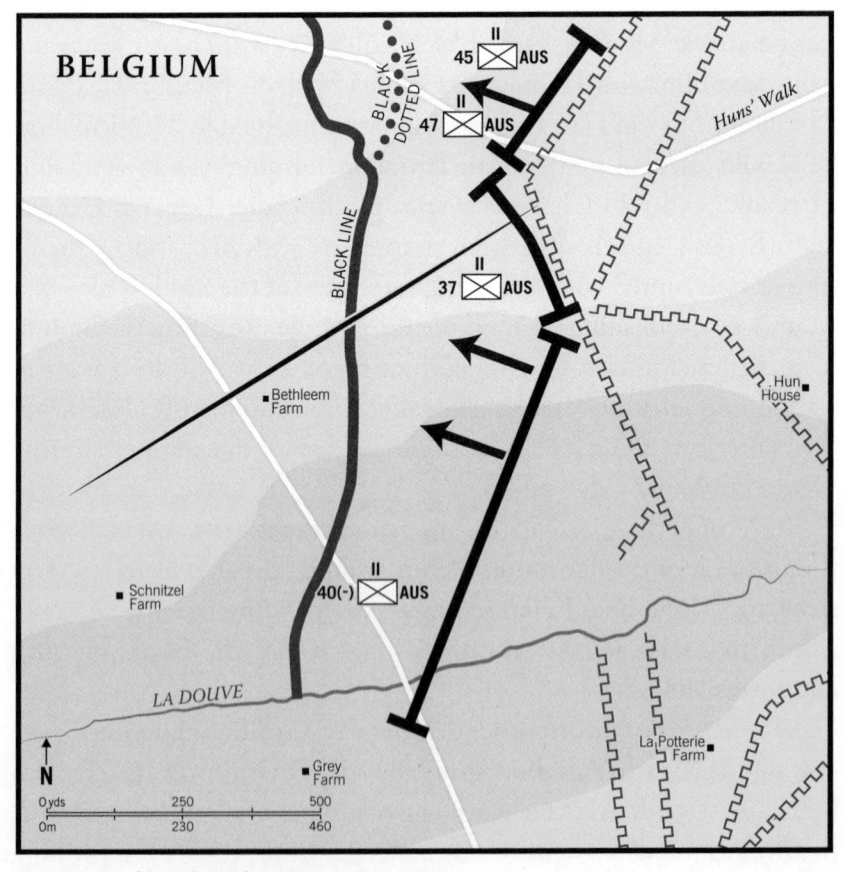

The retirement of the 37th Battalion, Messines, 6 June 1917

Monash sent his GSO2, Lieutenant Colonel John Peck, as a terrific German bombardment erupted. At 3.10 pm a message arrived, ostensibly from Mansbridge: 'We are driven out of trenches. Wires

CHAPTER 7

all cut', and the 44th Battalion's SOS rocket was seen. Monash immediately told McNicoll 'to take the situation in hand and restore it. Must not give an inch of ground.' Subsequent messages indicated that Mansbridge had not been attacked, and Peck confirmed them. Despite being subjected to a continuing heavy bombardment, Monash's front was intact.

The twenty-four hours that had elapsed since the start of the Green Line attack were the most strenuous of the battle for Monash, and an assessment of his performance must be based on this period. Bean remarked that in comparison to the other Australian divisions, the 3rd

> ... lacked as yet their general high standard of personal supervision in battle by commanding officers. Well trained though its leaders were, many of them (as those whose practice was different often complained) were content to acquiesce in the theory, with which General Monash possibly agreed, that the commander's duty in time of battle was to remain strictly at his headquarters. Thus, in too high a proportion of units, reconnaissances at critical times, or even during the pauses in an action, tended to be left to intelligence or other staff officers, who did not carry with them the power of decision and of spurring to effort, which officers in command would have possessed.

The Official Historian had struck the classic problem confronting World War I generals. Field Marshal Lord Carver comments: 'If there is one characteristic which stands out in the battles of 1914–18, it is the almost total lack of control once the battle had started. Very few commanders at any level had the faintest idea of what had happened or what was happening on their own side, let alone on the other side of the hill.' Monash's belief that his place was at divisional headquarters *was* unwavering and with one exception during this action, it *was* proven correct. On the night of 7 June his was virtually the only headquarters able to give Godley accurate, up-to-date information. Long before Godley issued orders for the recapture of the Green Line, Monash had begun preparations for the 44th Battalion's part in it. The presence of Cannan and McNicoll at their headquarters at this time was of tremendous assistance, because Monash could talk to them directly, dealing with problems as they arose. The same verdict applies to the afternoon of the 8th. Monash knew that the message from the 44th was mistaken forty-six minutes after receiving it and, once more, allayed Godley's fears.

During the early morning of 8 June, however, McNicoll had done nothing to restore a situation that demanded his personal intervention. Mindful of Monash's ire at the running of the brigades' headquarters the previous afternoon and the firm order it produced, he did not move from his headquarters at all on the 8th, despite the confusion surrounding Mansbridge. Cannan later criticised McNicoll severely for his failure on this score. Nor was Monash blameless, for the breakdown in the 10th Brigade could not be restored by an officer with Peck's limited authority, particularly in this case, as McNicoll was the least manageable of the three brigadiers. It required Monash's personal presence. Holmes had visited his *battalions* at 3.50 am that morning, taking his brigadiers with him when they could not say why the 4th Division had not advanced. He recognised that this was no task for staff officers, and he did not use them. Unlike many of his opinions on Monash, Bean's judgement on this occasion was at least partly justified.

On 7 June Monash had submitted to Godley a plan for an attack on a frontage of about 2000 yards to establish a new line between the Douve and Factory Farm. It included the important trench system at La Potterie and relied heavily on surprise. He suggested attacking one hour before the end of twilight on 10 June, 'so that the line may come to rest before darkness sets in, and consolidation can be done under cover of darkness.' The southern flank would be screened by smoke as an extra precaution. Though sound, Monash's scheme was already obsolete, for Godley was planning a much larger attack on both sides of the Douve with two divisions about 14 June. As a preliminary, the 3rd Division was to establish a chain of posts ahead of the existing line. Monash's instructions to his brigadiers were as detailed as ever. Jobson 'ought to provide strong mopping up parties to follow the line of posts in order to deal with cellars or dugouts ... You would want ... about 150 men on the posts and at least 150 on the mopping up job.' After sharp fighting on the nights of 9 and 10 June, the Oosttaverne

CHAPTER 7

Line was dotted with posts as far south as and including La Potterie. Two nights later the 3rd Division was withdrawn into corps reserve. Since midday on 7 June it had suffered 4122 casualties.

Assessments of the Messines attack often place too much emphasis on the time spent in its preparation, leading to comments such as A.J.P. Taylor's: 'Two years of preparation and a million pounds of explosive had advanced the British front at most two miles. How long would it take at this rate to get to Berlin?' The mines for which the operation is remembered, and which were its most time-consuming element, lie at the heart of this view. Haig had them in mind when he said that 'but for pressure from home, the Navy and the French', he would have fought the war using siege methods. But the attack would probably have succeeded without the mines, as it had at Vimy Ridge, where none were used. Plumer did not mention them among the reasons for success, which he attributed to good staff arrangements, efficient counter-battery fire, thorough training and rehearsal by the assault divisions. The mines constitute only one of seven factors listed by Harington and by German prisoners.

The key to the victory in tactical terms was the setting of limited objectives – the essence of the principle of bite and hold. Supported by a slowly advancing barrage, the infantry could reach them in sufficient strength to consolidate, having deliberately stopped long before resistance hardened. Quick counter-attacks, which the Germans were so adept at launching, invariably failed against the heavy standing barrage in front of the newly captured line. This was a pointer to the critical role played by the artillery, whose effectiveness had been vastly increased by technological development and a quantitative superiority. Mines apart, Messines had convincingly shown that as long as the objectives lay within artillery range, attacks were no longer 'foredoomed to failure and massive human loss'. That said, the toll, 26 000 casualties, was hardly trifling, though it compared favourably with previous attacks on this scale. On the German side, General Erich Ludendorff, the army's de facto commander, remarked gloomily of Messines that it 'cost us dear … the drain on our resources was very heavy. Here, too, it was many days before the front was again secure.'[58]

If not gloomy, Monash had been uncertain before the battle: 'The attack always has everything against it, the defence always everything in its favour.' Thinking that the imbalance might now have been redressed, he was more optimistic after it:

> I am the greatest possible believer in the theory of the limited objective. So long as we hold and retain the initiative we can in this way inflict the maximum of losses when and where we like. It restores to the offensive the advantages which are natural to the defensive in an unlimited objective.

The 3rd Division had performed well in its first battle, capturing 314 prisoners, 11 field guns and holding its line under heavy shelling until relieved. Haig and Godley both congratulated Monash on its efforts, while Birdwood was pleased because the animosity of the other Australian divisions towards it might now abate. Returning to the line on 23 June, the 3rd Division held the trenches between the Douve and the Blauwepoortbeek, which Monash described as a liquid sector: 'that is, with no clearly defined alignment, my forward patrols and posts being mixed up with those of the enemy.' His first year as a divisional commander drawing to a close, he left for London on 29 June.

Birdwood's faith in Monash's ability had been rewarded. Despite the advantages he enjoyed, his training of the 3rd Division was a considerable feat, less glamorous than, but the equal of, any battlefield success. With the exception of Bridges, said Arthur Bazley, Bean's assistant during and after the war, 'no commander left his stamp so clearly marked on any Australian division.' The leading principle in Monash's exercise of command was the welfare of the men, and one obvious result was that, in April 1917, the 3rd had half the average sick rate of any division in Second Army. He expected administration to be perfect within and outside his division because 'any lack of perfection [and] ... the men in the ranks ... get it "in the neck" every time.' On the evening of 7 June those in the forward trenches at Messines received hot meals, while wounded were evacuated expeditiously throughout the day. 'Fatigue parties' were not to be called by that name in the 3rd Division, and those in them were always to be told why their work was significant.

CHAPTER 7

Tactically, the year was dominated by Messines. Enough has been said of Monash's meticulous planning for and largely competent handling of his division in that battle to make further comment superfluous on all but three points. Firstly, he was always concerned for coordination within his formation, with those on his flanks and with the barrage, much more so than Godley. Secondly, his involvement in planning descended to levels that properly belonged to his subordinates. Though he listened to them and changed his views if necessary, their freedom of action was frequently limited to the execution of a scheme made by Monash rather than themselves. Finally, his brigadiers may have felt bullied, for Monash's conduct of the battle was decisive, even ruthless; but it was marred by his failure to rise to the one occasion when the authority imposed by his presence was essential. Remaining at his headquarters was the correct decision many times, but the uncertainty surrounding Mansbridge on the morning of 8 June, with the fog of war at its densest, was not one of them.

Monash's appetite for recognition was undiminished. His transfer from the 4th Brigade to command the 3rd Division and his lengthy stay in England disqualified him from any mention in honours lists before the battle. Both Birdwood and White agreed that his exclusion was unjust. Calling himself 'nobody's child', Monash felt personally slighted. Asking Godley to give Pearce his impression of the 3rd Division since it had been in 2nd ANZAC, Monash added:

> If at the same time, you should feel justified in adding a few words about myself, it might help to counteract the bad impression which has doubtless been created in Australia, owing to the pointed omission of my name from the last two despatches.

Godley gave Monash the scorching reply he deserved, pointing out that he had not been mentioned either, 'but it doesn't worry me, especially as we have now really done something [i.e. Messines], worth being mentioned about!' Monash returned to his headquarters, now at Ravelsberg, on 10 July. The Third Battle of Ypres, better known as Passchendaele, began exactly three weeks later.

Chapter 8
Passchendaele: Things are Bloody, Very Bloody

Haig's enthusiasm for a major offensive in Flanders dated from August 1914, when he advocated moving the BEF by sea to Ostend to strike at the German lines of communication. Since then the BEF had twice saved the Flemish town of Ypres and held the salient around it. They now meant as much to the British as Verdun did to the French. Once the BEF assumed the main burden on the Western Front after the collapse of the Chemin des Dames offensive launched by Haig's French counterpart, General Robert Nivelle, in April 1917 provoked mutiny in the French Army, 'there was no doubt as to where his efforts would lie.' When the loss of the Messines Ridge deprived the Germans of a position from which they had commanded the Ypres Salient in enfilade, Haig could launch his main stroke from the Salient 'with the eventual object of securing the Belgian coast and connecting with the Dutch frontier.' Fifth Army would open the attack by clearing the Passchendaele-Staden-Clercken Ridge and the intervening low ground to Dixmude before advancing on the Ypres–Roulers railway to take the German coastal defences in rear.

It was assumed that Haig would conduct the offensive according to the agreement reached at the Anglo-French conference of 4 May: 'wearing down and exhausting the enemy's resistance ... by relentlessly attacking with limited objectives, while making the fullest use of our artillery.' In fact, he did not have the accepted concept of a limited offensive comprising a series of bite and hold operations in mind at all; as Fuller so aptly remarked: 'Actually a limited offensive was not what Haig cherished.' According to Gough, Haig 'very definitely' viewed the battle as 'an attempt to breakthrough', a conclusion supported by the ambitious objectives he set. Attacking on 31 July 1917, Haig

CHAPTER 8

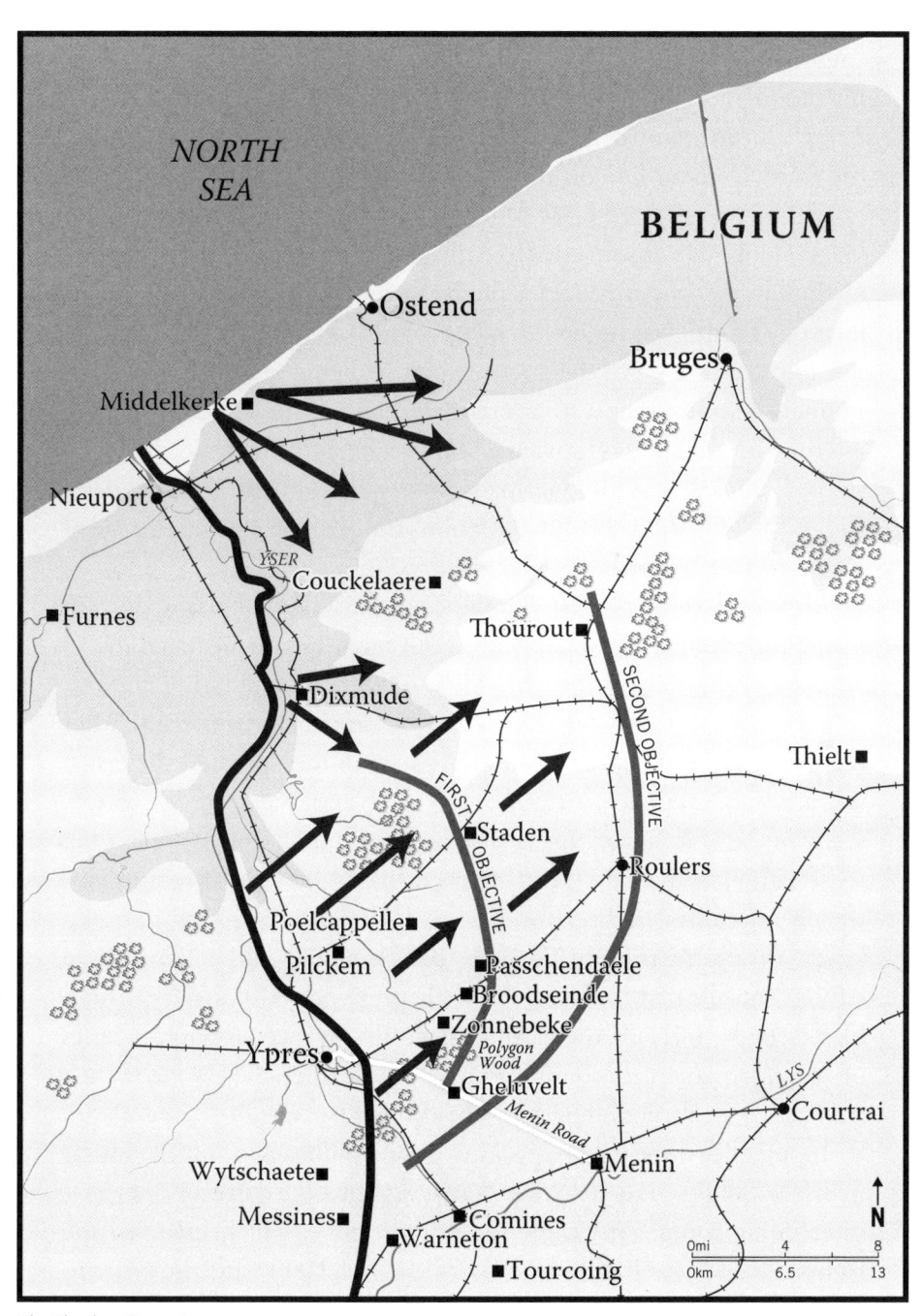

The Flanders Campaign

hoped to clear the ridge, parts of which were eight miles distant, by 8 August in order to catch the high tides necessary for an amphibious operation in conjunction with an attack along the coast by Fourth Army. In turn, Gough planned an advance of 4500 yards to capture the third German line on the ridge on the first day, going further if resistance was slight. Haig's Director of Military Operations, Major General John Davidson, criticised the plan as contrary to the principles of the limited offensive and Gough, who privately confessed that at least one month was needed to take the ridge, eventually agreed. In an inexplicable reversal of the doctrine that had guided him at Messines, Plumer demurred and the original scheme stood. The surprise essential for the success of what was thus a breakthrough aim had long since disappeared as the Germans observed from the Passchendaele Ridge 'the long drawn-out preparations for this, the greatest "battle of material" ever fought.'

Also threatening success was the German system of elastic defence in depth. More so than GHQ, the German command encouraged regimental officers to express their views on tactical matters; Ludendorff, in particular, lost no opportunity to question them personally. After evaluating the results, the Operations Section incorporated them in a uniform tactical policy, introduced in the Flanders case after a careful study of the Somme and Arras. The massive bombardments preceding these battles had made linear defences based on several continuous trench lines obsolete because they could be discerned with ease and systematically destroyed. Now the British would not be faced by a strong front line, through which their more powerful artillery could blast a path. Instead, they would have to advance through a series of defensive zones, becoming weaker the further they went. When sufficiently weakened, they could be thrown back.

In practice this meant packing more pillboxes – ultimately as many as 2000 – and machine-gun posts into the existing lines and intervening zones. First came the outpost zone, which included the front line and was lightly held to a depth of 1000 yards in order to minimise casualties during the bombardment. Extending just over a mile eastwards from it to the second (Albrecht) line, which ran across

CHAPTER 8

the start of the 200-feet-high Gheluvelt Plateau, was the forward zone. More strongly held, it consisted of machine-guns and infantry scattered in shell holes, pillboxes and farm ruins. Similarly organised, the battle zone stretched another mile east to the third (Wilhelm) line, which crossed the Gheluvelt Plateau near Polygon Wood. Rapid counter-attacks by designated units would spring from it when the attacker, 'organising the defence of a strange system of trenches', was most vulnerable. If they failed, more formal counter-attacks would be launched by specially trained divisions from the rear zone, which rolled up to three miles back to the Flandern 1 Line. Skirting Poelcappelle, Flandern 1 passed behind Zonnebeke and Polygon Wood. Flandern 2 branched off Flandern 1 near Passchendaele and paralleled it southwards, while Flandern 3 tracked behind Passchendaele to Menin. The key to the doctrine was the concept of a fluid battle that:

> ... will not take place for or in a rigid defensive line but on a battleground of considerable depth, extending ... far into our own position, where the enemy, at every step of his advance will be faced by more and more numerous and unexpected difficulties. The defender is, therefore, not tied down to one position ... he is entitled to fight a mobile action ... and consequently, to advance or retire as necessary.

Thus organised, the Germans confidently awaited the attack.

These tactics should have come as no surprise. Before Messines, Haig had warned Plumer: 'the enemy now fights not in but for his first position. He uses considerable force for counter-attack.' Yet GHQ sought the opinions of army commanders, who in turn asked corps and divisional commanders, on the best methods of defeating an elastic defence one week *after* the Ypres offensive began. The answer, of course, was the step-by-step attack, which Haig had spurned.

Among those who realised this was Monash, whose views, expressed in a paper seven pages long, indicate that he had thought carefully about the problem. Many moppers-up, organised into small groups and using Lewis guns and Stokes mortars, would be needed to reduce pillboxes while the leading assault waves kept close to the barrage. The depth of the attack was still governed by the range of the supporting artillery; its frontage, surprisingly, by the infantry's ability to resist counter-attack. The Germans relied heavily for the success of their counter-attacks on the fatigue of the opposing infantry, which was due less to the demands of the assault, argued Monash, than to the length of time they had to remain exposed under arduous conditions after it. By attacking on a frontage that required only half the strength of a formation, the other half could relieve the assaulting troops, preferably on the first night following the attack and certainly no later than the second. But the most effective means of defeating counter-attacks, a protective barrage by machine-guns and artillery, was often hampered by uncertainty as to the position of the infantry. Monash insisted that 'the utmost extent of their advance' must be limited 'strictly and very definitely' by orders:

> While we cannot be certain that they have reached their objective, we ought ... to be certain that they have not passed beyond their objective. We can, therefore, predetermine the protective barrage line, and ensure that all our forward troops know where that barrage will come down, *before even, they move out to the assault.*

Finally, orders for any attack were incomplete unless they included 'minute and detailed' arrangements for meeting a counter-attack that were thoroughly understood by all. Provided these measures were taken, Monash was confident that an assault would succeed. By identifying and eliminating the factors that favoured the Germans, he had applied the same scientific approach to the attacking problem as they had to the defensive.

Monash was unable to test his theory against the strongest sector of the German line until October. For the present 2nd ANZAC's divisional commanders were to prepare minor operations on their respective fronts, which, it was hoped, would lead the Germans to conclude that an attack on Warneton, accompanied by a passage of the Lys, was intended. These operations were Godley's contribution to Plumer's larger feint towards Lille, itself designed to divert attention from Gough's main thrust further north and to spread the fire of the German artillery. For Monash it was the start of a busy,

CHAPTER 8

but frustrating period during which he commanded 2nd ANZAC for three weeks while a sick Godley took leave.

Action on Monash's front was complicated by its confused or 'liquid' state. When his division took charge of the Messines sector on 23 June, it found that the outgoing 25th Division had mistakenly sited the centre of the line too far back at Steignast Farm, forming a salient that protruded well behind the positions on either flank. Monash ordered the digging of a new front system across the chord of the salient, which was accomplished by Cannan's brigade in a difficult period known thereafter as 'the eighteen days'. The Germans responded by reinforcing their advanced posts, the strongest of which were located on Windmill Ridge, a low spur overlooking Monash's line and preventing observation from it of the Warneton Line. After the failure of attacks by small patrols on 3 July, Cannan proposed a larger operation to clear the ridge. Suggesting it as a diversion, Jackson forwarded the plan to 2nd ANZAC on the 4th, one day *before* Godley's instruction on diversionary attacks appeared. The existence of Cannan's scheme did not deter Monash, on his return from leave on 10 July, from making his own appreciation, which yielded a wider and deeper assault as a second course. It would end the Germans' domination of no man's land by confining them to the Warneton Line; more important, it was 'the better scheme from a tactical point of view in forming a line to hold throughout the winter.' But Monash adhered to Cannan's less ambitious alternative because it permitted a heavier concentration of the men and guns available. He had deliberately rejected an attack with more tempting objectives in favour of a smaller operation with greater prospects of success.

To convince the Germans that a serious attack was imminent, Monash suggested the commencement of wire cutting on the Warneton Line well before the start of the Third Ypres offensive on 31 July and the mopping-up on that date of the outposts in their sectors by the 37th and New Zealand divisions on his flanks. The impression would be reinforced by assaulting when Fifth Army's attack at Ypres opened at 3.50 am and not four hours afterwards, as suggested by the 37th. There was a sound tactical reason for Monash's rejection of the later time. It entailed a long wait in daylight in packed assembly trenches, exposing the occupants to the German counter-barrages that would follow Gough's attack. Monash's use of smoke to screen the operation relied heavily on smoke bombs developed for the Stokes mortar by a subaltern in the 3rd Division, Lieutenant Ambrose Varley. His willingness to employ the device before it had been proven on a large scale reflected Monash's 'engineering way of looking at things', an attitude that welcomed rather than suspected technical change.[59] This attack, his raids and the screening of the exposed flank in the operation he proposed at Messines on 7 June, showed that Monash was already a firm believer in lavish quantities of smoke to conceal movement from and to confuse the Germans. One of the AIF's most capable senior officers, Brigadier General Harold 'Pompey' Elliott, considered that Monash's employment of smoke and the exact synchronisation of effort that characterised his operations were his main contributions to warfare.

On 11 July the 9th Brigade entered the line to allow the 11th Brigade to commence training for the attack. Monash discussed the plan thoroughly with Cannan, critiqued his rehearsals and held a 'long and important conference ... of all concerned' on 24 July. The ground was a quagmire, and the approach marches of the 42nd and 43rd battalions on 31 July took five and seven hours respectively, after buses dropped them at the old Messines front line. By 4.05 am the first wave had reached the wire of the Warneton Line to protect the second and third waves while they established outposts in rear.

The smokescreen on both flanks was effective. It seemed as if the Germans believed that a heavier attack was about to follow, for they began to withdraw their guns, resulting in little shelling until 2.00 pm. Realising by then that the advance had ceased, they bombarded the new line heavily as steady rain fell. One post was temporarily lost during the night; when a second counter-attack struck at dawn it was broken by the artillery and the machine-gun barrage, which the *Divisional Account* described as excellent. Monash was observing his own principles when he relieved both assaulting battalions shortly

CHAPTER 8

after daybreak and when he explained the operation and its lessons to the commander of his training brigade in England.

As the Germans knew that Gough's was the main offensive, the diversionary aspect was a failure. On the 3rd Division's front, though, they believed for some time that the Warneton Line was to be attacked. Monash's skilful planning of the artillery and machine-gun barrages contributed in no small way to the retention of the ground gained. In some other sectors, no preparations were made to meet the counter-attacks, which might have been considered certain, and several positions had to be abandoned. The contact aircraft, the role of which was also emphasised in Monash's orders, 'did some particularly good work'.

Now at his peak as a divisional commander, Monash's confidence was unlimited. When heavy shelling on the north of Second Army's line on 15 July was not mentioned in corps or army situation reports next day, he was adamant that the 'very good' bombardment discipline 'into which I have tried to drill the 3rd Division needs extension Inter Division and Inter Corps.' He treated the 2nd ANZAC staff, which was almost entirely British, with weary resignation. Never bothering to acquaint itself with AIF procedures and regulations, it caused 'acrimony and unnecessary work' by repromulgating army instructions that conflicted with policies laid down by Birdwood as GOC AIF. On 9 August 1917 Monash handed over his sector to Sinclair-MacLagan, who had assumed command of the 4th Division when Holmes was killed shortly after Messines.

Six weeks' rest followed the 3rd Division's move into Second Army Reserve at Lumbres and Bléquin, and it was sorely needed as the exhaustion during the march to the rear showed. Monash restored the verve of his formation by allowing ample time for relaxation despite the demands of training. When McNicoll planned strenuous activities on two Sundays, he suggested limiting the work to the mornings only. Monash also took the opportunity to regain the high standard of administration and discipline that tended to be relaxed in the line because the necessary close supervision was impossible. Commanders were to ensure that their men were always clean shaven and well dressed, while the turnout of officers was to be exemplary. He rejected the notion of certificates stating that a battalion commander had carried out an inspection of each company because their issue would inevitably become mechanical, thus creating a false security. The brigadiers were to assemble their commanding officers regularly instead, satisfying themselves by 'close and personal inquiry' that they were attending to the matters mentioned in the proposed certificates. He set the example himself by frequent visits to his arms and services units, training schools and reinforcement depots. The results were evident when Haig reviewed the division near Drionville on 22 September in a parade whose pomp resembled that at Salisbury Plain one year earlier: 'A very fine body of men ... Every detail had been carefully thought out beforehand, hence the parade was so successful. I think Monash has a good head and commands his division well.'

Haig invited Monash to dine at Blendecques that evening, where they were joined by the BEF's chief of staff, Lieutenant General Sir Launcelot Kiggell, and his deputy, Major General Richard Butler. Presumably contributing to the discussion of 'some very important and confidential matters', Monash basked in the 'charming ... affability and camaraderie of these three great soldiers, upon whom rests the whole burden of the British Army on the Western Front.' Even though he was their intellectual superior, Monash regarded them with awe, and his description was written in the same deferential tone as the narrative of his stay with Hamilton aboard *Arcadian* at Gallipoli. He was the only Australian treated in this manner by Haig. John Terraine agrees that the C-in-C's unguarded expression of his inner thoughts to a divisional commander was startlingly uncharacteristic and confirmed that Monash now occupied the central place in his views on the Australian leadership. By this time Haig was well satisfied that his ability was not confined to the parade ground, for he had commented after Messines that Monash, '(evidently of Jewish descent) and by trade head of a Ferro-Concrete firm ... is a most practical commander and has done well.' Monash knew he was highly regarded, for Birdwood had told him that Haig 'had gone out of his way to express himself in terms of praise of my work. Birdwood added that it was rare for the

CHAPTER 8

Chief to do this.' According to Plumer, Haig intervened to return the 3rd Division to strength as soon as possible. His influence enabled Monash to circumvent the ironclad rules of the Base authorities in France when they agreed, following 'much trouble and argument', to release reinforcements after a course lasting a few days instead of the normal program.

The delicate nature of another personnel matter demanded sensitivity and tact from Monash. In February, he had suggested that one of Jobson's battalions lacked an offensive spirit. Bean observed that Jobson's brigade as a whole could not compare with Cannan's, 'the happiest in the AIF', or McNicoll's: 'The 10th and 11th are remarkably healthy … they are great families. The battalions in them stick together, are enthusiastic about one another and don't crab one another as some of our battalions do.'

Later, Bean blamed the difference squarely on Jobson's shaky leadership. Jackson had warned Monash of Jobson's indecision when Jobson temporarily commanded the division in March: 'he fusses himself and can't make his mind up and if I attempt to do it for him everything is well for 24 hours and then he may go back on it.' Jobson's praiseworthy performance at Messines seemed to justify Monash's inaction then, but Jobson began to lose his grip soon after the battle. Requests from battalion commanders for a heavy artillery barrage were not coordinated, leading to the failure of the 34th Battalion's raid on Windmill Ridge on 16 July. At a conference eight days later, Jobson made the 'worst possible impression' on Monash and a number of junior officers when, 'in a thoroughly unnerved state', he claimed: 'We can't stand anymore after the 26th … we shan't be able to carry on.' It did not matter that the ADMS had already warned Monash that the 9th Brigade had the highest sick rate in the division and was fit only for 'a short effort, if necessary'. By openly expressing his pessimism and magnifying instead of minimising his difficulties, Jobson had violated one of Monash's fundamental principles of command:

You must realise that in the case of a higher commander, one looks for the very reverse of such a frame of mind; and, backed as he always is by the full weight of higher authority, he should be the last man of his whole command to become disorganised, or to let others plainly perceive that he has.

Monash offered Jobson the chance to resign gracefully in order to avoid any official action that might later reflect poorly on him. On 29 August Jobson returned to Australia. Although he might have acted sooner, Monash had preserved the reputation of a man who had served him loyally for twelve months. The two parted 'the very best of friends'.

Major General Charles Rosenthal. An architect and militia gunner, Rosenthal was also one of Sydney's leading oratorio singers. Physically huge, he made his reputation at Anzac by siting his guns almost in the front line. Rosenthal re-invigorated the 9th Brigade on taking over when its commander broke down after Messines. He served Monash with great loyalty (AWM H19207).

CHAPTER 8

Jobson's successor was the ebullient Brigadier General Charles Rosenthal, the CRA of the 4th Division, whom Birdwood had already decided to appoint to the command of the next vacant division once he had gained sufficient experience as an infantry brigadier. On Gallipoli Rosenthal had emplaced his guns in the trenches, ignoring Bridges' fear that they might be lost; and now, as the commander of the 9th Brigade, he could be found directing a wiring party in no man's land at night. Though the antithesis of Monash's, this style of leadership was for the 9th 'like a fresh draught to a man thirsty for natural stimulant.' Still, as an architect and militia gunner, Rosenthal had much in common with Monash, whom he had often met before the war. He wrote of their first meeting in the 3rd Division: 'Mutual confidence was quickly established between us, and ever afterwards I enjoyed to the full this mutual understanding.'

Monash did not possess the 'knockabout' attitude and belligerent air that endeared Rosenthal to his command, but his attachment to those he led was just as strong. He designed portable baths, enabling brigades some distance from regular bathing facilities to enjoy a proper weekly wash. 'A Corner of Blighty in Paris', a free club founded by a Miss Butler to keep Australian soldiers from unsavoury parts of the city, earned his enthusiastic support. He even asked Vic to form a committee to raise funds for its development. Although his ardent belief in the connection between welfare and efficiency may have motivated Monash in these matters, his response in others was based solely on a sense of fairness and compassion. When Lieutenant Goldstein, the former RSM of the 16th Battalion on Gallipoli, complained that a man his junior was to be promoted to captain in France while he recovered from wounds in England, Monash secured a promise from Dodds, now Birdwood's Deputy Adjutant-General (DAG), that the case would be reviewed. After another 4th Brigade NCO, Sergeant Herbert Upjohn, had been serving as a temporary staff sergeant for some time, it was decided he was no longer entitled to the rank and must refund all the extra pay received. The injustice was rectified when Monash brought it to the attention of Upjohn's superiors.

From his study of captured German documents and GHQ instructions, Monash identified tactical problems encountered in the ongoing Ypres offensive and devised practical solutions to them. He advocated 'protective patrols' in front of final objectives to see off the remnants of counter-attacks that had penetrated the protective barrage and to cover dead ground. Two lines 200 yards apart should be consolidated, forcing the Germans, who could not shell both simultaneously with the same guns, to guess which one it was intended to hold. Resurrecting a question he had first considered after Gallipoli, Monash sought extra telephones to link the infantry and the divisional machine-gun officer and his batteries with each other. The resulting flexibility would permit the full potential of massed machine-guns to be realised, unlike 'present conditions [where] we are compelled to have a fixed timetable program with fixed and predetermined dispositions and programs for action in expected eventualities.' These limitations were not even mentioned at a demonstration of massed machine-guns held concurrently at Camiers and attended by Haig and army, corps and divisional commanders, including himself.

Besides arresting the decline in fighting efficiency caused by the long rest and the infusion of reinforcements, Monash's training program ensured that his division would be ready for the German tactics of elastic defence on its return to the line. Troops practised assembling on tapes by night instead of by day and were accustomed to a realistic protective barrage, which lasted much longer than the one-hour maximum suggested by Godley. The 2nd ANZAC's preparation of a sandbox exercise for platoon commanders prompted Monash to reintroduce the Tactical Exercises Without Troops that he had instituted for them before Messines: 'I personally attach almost more importance to the mental than to the technical training such exercises afford, i.e. they teach the platoon leader what to think about and "what to do next".' Even before instructions were issued by corps or army, Monash had acted to remedy the lack of initiative shown by junior officers. Directing his brigadiers to study the problem, he complained: 'all the drive still comes from above. Junior commanders to catch hold

CHAPTER 8

of the show more ... rather than let things run themselves.' Collective training proceeded concurrently:

> Concerted attack and defence of strong points, in semi-open warfare, were sedulously rehearsed by platoons and companies, principles being applied that seemed likely to be useful in fighting round the pill boxes of Flanders. In brigade movement, the necessity for 'mopping up' the ground won ... was stressed again and again. In 'attacks' on limited objectives, one battalion would move through, or 'leapfrog' another, as had been done in the Battle of Messines, but on a narrow front and against more limited objectives.

These exercises were carried out under the widest variety of conditions. Every battalion rehearsed night attacks and spent one day on each of the following: capturing an area rather than a line, repelling counter-attacks, and practising approach marches while wearing respirators, a legacy of Messines. Whenever time permitted, Monash watched and critiqued, while Jackson and other staff officers lectured on German tactics. On 5 September, Monash was informed that the 3rd Division would join the Ypres offensive within four weeks.

Haig's grandiose scheme had degenerated into a repetition of the unimaginative and costly 'battering ram' attacks that had proved so fruitless on the Somme. The fault lay largely with the C-in-C, whose conduct of the offensive was as flawed as his planning of it. At the outset, he suggested to Gough the seizure in a separate operation of the high ground on his right, the Gheluvelt Plateau, which straddled the Passchendaele Ridge. Until this flank was secured, the advance in the low ground to the north would be enfiladed. Gough demurred, wanting to make the attack 'part and parcel of the main operation, as a partial attack, even if successful, would only draw the troops employed into a very pronounced salient.' Terraine says that Haig's climb down 'is extremely difficult to understand', adding that he 'should have taken steps to make sure that his intentions were being implemented.' Haig's failure to do so, remarks Nick Lloyd, was 'one of the fatal moments prior to the attack.'

When the offensive opened on 31 July, the German second line (Albrecht) on the flats and the Pilckem Ridge overlooking it were taken and the third line (Wilhelm) briefly reached, but the advance on the right could not penetrate beyond the first line. The high ground, beginning with the Gheluvelt Plateau, now assumed central importance, but attacks on 10 and 16 August and six days of continuous assaults on narrow fronts after 22 August still left Gough with only part of the Albrecht Line on the edge of an objective that should have been taken on the first day. He had already urged Haig to abandon the offensive and now observed that 'the heart had gone out of the Fifth Army.' Conditions were dreadful: 'The battlefield became a bog; in every depression the flooded waters lay brim to brim like the footprints of monstrous animals in the slimy margin of some primeval waterhole.' On 15 July, 3091 guns, allowing a greater concentration per yard of front than before Messines, had begun the bombardment. The weight of shell smashed the intricate drainage system of dikes and culverts, and the country reverted to the vast swampland from whence it had been reclaimed. Warnings to this effect from Tank Corps Headquarters were ignored by GHQ, which also banned the swamp maps prepared by Lieutenant Colonel J.F.C. Fuller. Haig could not have foreseen that the August of 1917 would be the wettest for thirty years, but he did know that the records of the past eighty years foreshadowed no more than three weeks of fine weather.

On 25 August Haig transferred responsibility for the attack on the Passchendaele Ridge to Plumer. Having carefully analysed the operations conducted so far, Plumer prescribed the bite and hold approach with strictly limited objectives that he had apparently shied away from in the debate over Gough's operational concept in June. He demanded and got three weeks to prepare his first attack, for which 1259 guns would support an advance of 1500 yards on a frontage of 4000 yards, the densest British artillery concentration of the war. After a halt of six days to allow the artillery to be brought forward, a second attack, identical to its predecessor, would be launched. Four such operations, it was calculated, should result in the capture of the ridge. Monash wrote: 'If all goes well, it should be the most decisive offensive of the whole war.' The first results seemed to substantiate that claim. In the battles of Menin Road and Polygon Wood on 20

CHAPTER 8

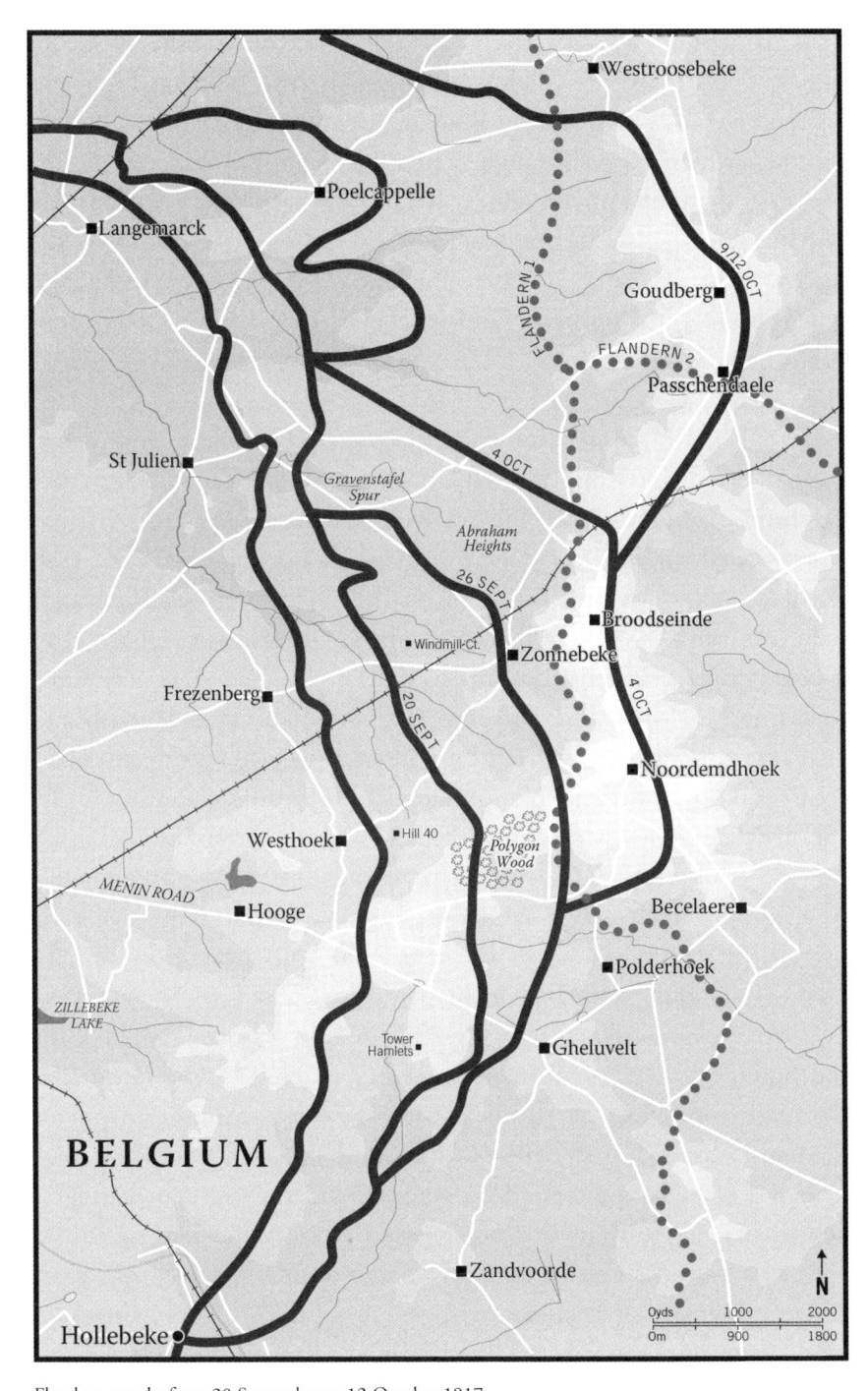

Flanders: attacks from 20 September to 12 October 1917

and 26 September respectively, 1st ANZAC formed the centre of attacks that carried the Gheluvelt Plateau and the Wilhelm Line, and reached as far as Zonnebeke. Both operations were favoured by fine weather, which lasted through September. October was 'on average the wettest month of the year ... It rains on average every other day and in some years on three out of four.' Accordingly, the third step, the attack on Broodseinde, was brought forward two days to 4 October, and because Birdwood and White believed that 1st ANZAC would be too weak to participate, Godley was informed that 2nd ANZAC might have to assume the main role.

At a lengthy conference on 18 September Monash announced that the 3rd Division was to attack south of Zonnebeke from positions captured in the Polygon Wood assault by the 5th Division, commanded since December 1916 by Talbot Hobbs. The 10th Brigade on the left and the 11th on the right would each advance on a frontage of 400 to 600 yards, with the 9th in reserve. Even after a corps conference next day it was still 'not yet possible accurately to define the tasks of the brigades as a whole', because Monash had challenged Godley on two critical points. The corps commander had set the objective at the maximum depth, 1500 yards, requiring for its capture the employment in the attack of all four battalions from each brigade. Monash urged a lesser penetration, 1150 yards, which could be accomplished by three battalions, leaving a battalion in reserve for use against counter-attacks. The divisional boundary with Russell's New Zealanders, attacking on his left, also caused argument. As it satisfied the principle that easily recognisable features should form the boundary between formations, Godley's choice was automatic: the road from Molenaarelsthoek to the Keiberg, a southern spur of the main ridge. Monash realised what Godley seemingly did not, that it would soon be obliterated by his own and the German barrages. Moreover, the road ran in a north-easterly direction, slanting to the left away from the lines of assembly, barrage and objective, instead of meeting them at right angles. The assaulting troops would therefore tend to gravitate towards the left, leading to congestion on that flank at the expense of the right. An added difficulty was that the road bent

CHAPTER 8

sharply, forcing a rapid extension of Monash's frontage as the attack proceeded.

As Messines had proved that the direction of an assault could be maintained without relying on fixed features, Monash proposed for the boundary an imaginary line running due east between the heads of two prominent gullies. Anticipating Godley's approval, he advised his brigadiers:

> Each front line platoon should have one man with nothing else to do but keep the direction, given to him by the platoon commander, by magnetic bearing, at the outset of the advance ... every platoon and company commander of the leading wave of every battalion should carry a luminous prismatic compass for this purpose.

This instruction showed that Monash was continuing the close supervision he had practised at Messines. It was reasonable then because Messines was his division's first major battle, and perhaps on this occasion because almost his entire staff had changed apart from Jackson, one brigade had a new commander and another an inexperienced brigade major. On the other hand, this *was* how Monash commanded his division irrespective of any justificatory circumstances. He tended to disregard his enjoinder in *100 Hints* not to trespass on a subordinate's responsibilities, which made his complaints that too much direction came from above rather hollow.

Godley's reaction to Monash's advice is unknown; a major change in Second Army's plan made it unimportant in any case. The 1st and 2nd divisions from 1st ANZAC had emerged so fresh from the Menin Road attack that it was decided they should join 2nd ANZAC for the attack on Broodseinde, as originally planned by Plumer and Harington. Side-slipping slightly northward to bring its axis of advance directly onto the ridge, Birdwood's corps was to remain in the centre, between the British IX and X Corps on the right and, after its relief of V Corps, 2nd ANZAC on the left, while Gough's army debouched across the low ground further north. Godley retained his original dispositions – the New Zealanders attacking on the left and Monash's division on the right, separated from Major General Nevill Smyth's 2nd Division from 1st ANZAC by the Ypres–Roulers railway a few hundred yards north of Zonnebeke. Spirits soared with the realisation that four Anzac divisions would be attacking shoulder to shoulder for the first time. The feeling was particularly noticeable in the 3rd Division, as Bean observed after passing the 11th Brigade on 28 September: 'The 3rd beside the 2nd and 1st will make a splendid combination – all keen to win and keep their reputations and their place in the force. It will bring the 3rd Division among their fellows at one step.'

The Ypres Ramparts, headquarters of the 3rd Division during the battles of Broodseinde and Passchendaele. They were damp and rat infested. Note the intricate maze of telephone cables. This image was taken the day before the 3rd Division's relief by the Canadians (AWM E01183).

Corps commanders were warned of the revision on 21 September, but Monash was not informed until the 23rd. Three days later he submitted his first plan for the attack. On 1 October his battle headquarters was established in the Ypres Ramparts near the Menin Gate. The cluster of narrow dugouts allotted to him was 'cold and dark and overrun by rats and mice and altogether smelly and disagreeable.' Although the weather was fine, the view from the

CHAPTER 8

ramparts told him nothing. A shattered road crossed a slight rise, the Frezenberg, before climbing through Zonnebeke to the Broodseinde crossroads. From where Monash stood, five miles away, this part of the ridge was obscured by atmospheric haze and the Frezenberg masked the re-entrant immediately to its north, across which the 3rd Division would attack.

Its right resting on the railway, Monash's front stretched 1000 yards to Dochy Farm behind the Windmill Cabaret Spur, which ran north-west off the Passchendaele Ridge from Broodseinde. The 3rd (British) Division had been unable to seize its crest on 26 September. The spur descended gently into the Hanebeek Valley, defended on its western side by a chain of pillboxes, Israel, Judah, Alma and Springfield. Overlooking the eastern bank of the Hanebeek were Bordeaux and Seine, two strongpoints on the slopes of another spur, the Gravenstafel, whose crest left the Passchendaele Ridge 1900 yards from the Windmill Cabaret. It was crossed by the Flandern 1 Line. The strength of these defences was increased many times over by the natural advantages the Germans enjoyed. Swinging diagonally across Monash's right, the railway formed an effective switch line, and the entire Hanebeek Valley could be commanded from several of its cuttings and embankments. Like the Windmill Cabaret, the Gravenstafel curved to the north-west and from its highest point, the Abraham Heights, lay in the New Zealand sector on Monash's left. The 2nd Division was to advance along the crest of the Passchendaele Ridge, which commanded his right. Unless both formations carried their objectives, every yard of the 3rd Division's advance would be contested by enfilade fire from both flanks. Just as it had at Messines, the success of Monash's attack depended on the efforts of others.[60]

The plan Monash gave Godley on 26 September seemed capable of significantly reducing the danger from both flanks as well as from the defences wholly within his sector. It prescribed two halts before the final objective. The first, 800 yards past the Windmill Cabaret, would last half an hour, permitting a leapfrog of two fresh battalions through the leading units, which might have lost heavily in the fight for the Springfield blockhouses. In the meantime, the barrage could switch to the potentially troublesome Desmond Trench, protected by an impassable moat of mud on his right flank. After the advance had proceeded another 300 yards, it would halt for forty-five minutes, allowing the attacking line to swing parallel to the final line of consolidation, which lay on a small spur 100 yards beyond. The protective barrage would fall on the Gravenstafel, 300 yards further east across the head of a sharp re-entrant.

This scheme resembled the plan prepared by Monash when it seemed that 2nd ANZAC was to attack south of Zonnebeke. At most, three battalions from each brigade would be required. The long halts afforded time for the consolidation of the line just captured, allowed a bombardment to be brought down on positions on the flanks likely to threaten the next stage of the attack and accommodated any delays arising from a check in the advance of either flanking division. By choosing a final objective short of the junction of the Passchendaele Ridge with the Gravenstafel, Monash avoided the widest part of the ridge and, for the Germans, the easiest part to counter-attack.

On 28 September Monash advised McNicoll that the depth of the attack might be increased substantially, requiring 'in all probability' the employment of all four battalions from his brigade and Cannan's. Next day Monash ascertained that his final objective, the Blue Line, was to lie on the very feature he had shunned, the Gravenstafel Spur. Some 900 yards short of it was the first objective, the Red Line. Both had been accepted by Second Army on the recommendation of Birdwood and White. After their success at Menin Road, Plumer let them assume the major role in the planning of subsequent operations. Once the participation of 1st ANZAC was decided on 21 September, provisional objective lines, boundaries and barrage programs should have been set immediately and confirmed or adjusted according to the results of the Polygon Wood attack. But planning does not appear to have begun until after Polygon Wood, necessitating the revision of schemes already prepared within Godley's corps. Arrangements for the barrage were not completed until 1 October, although the program was essentially the same as for the Polygon Wood attack, comprising five belts of fire to a depth of 1000 yards. The assembly positions and the Blue Line had to be shifted again. Most blame attached to Second Army, the headquarters that directed the planning of the attack overall. Given its excellent reputation, the lack of foresight, one of the most important principles of staff work, was surprising. Commanders at Monash's level were most affected. 'Very busy and harassing day', he confided to his diary on 3 October. It was a typical entry for this period.

Birdwood's proposals combined an advance which, for the 3rd Division, was the longest of any division in the attack, with a reduction in the number of halts to a single one-hour pause on the Red Line. An alarmed Monash adopted a compromise that retained most of the strengths of his own scheme. Instead of one halt, there would be three. As before, the first was just short of Springfield, though now lasting only twelve minutes. This was still time enough for two battalions to leapfrog as well as keeping the 3rd Division's left flank aligned with the New Zealanders, who would be crossing the boggy Hanebeek further north. After another leapfrog during the halt on the Red Line, there was to be a third pause of twelve minutes on the small spur that Monash had originally proposed as his final objective, but which would now form his support line. The Gravenstafel would be attacked following a third leapfrog. Small parties detailed to maintain touch with the flanking divisions were to keep Monash informed of their position throughout the advance, while an 'ample supply of Runners' had to be available because 'Signal communications are not likely to be as good as during the Messines Battle.' A smoke barrage would blind the machine-guns on the high ground at Daring and Dash crossings.

Monash's plan reflected the principles established since 31 July. It divided the attack into a series of progressively shorter advances, for each of which fresh infantry would be available. While he disliked committing all four battalions from the assault brigades, the heavy casualties that the flanking positions were likely to inflict along the length of the advance made the prompt relief of the leading battalions essential, especially after the extension to the Gravenstafel. The battalions carrying out the final phase would then be strong enough to resist the counter-attacks that seemed certain on that spur. An extra artillery observer was allotted to one of them, the 40th Battalion, and three strongpoints were to be built there afterwards for additional protection.

The plan also showed Monash's mastery of the tactical importance of ground, from his anxiety about the Gravenstafel and Passchendaele ridges to less obvious concerns, such as the fields of fire enjoyed by the Germans from the two railway crossings. Its most remarkable feature, however, stemmed from the fact that he made no apparent effort to reconnoitre the sector, even though aerial photographs were not available at least until 26 September. Monash prepared his plan entirely from the map, relying on a mental picture of the terrain and the defences supplemented by reports from liaison officers. Here was another aspect of creative imagination, in this case developed by his pre-war experience in map-making and the use of maps to plan railways and bridges. But it is a foolish engineer who does not first inspect the site on which such structures are to be built. In the second phase of the battle the analogy was applicable to Monash the soldier.

Monash used liaison officers to assist his division in another way. On 16 September Hobbs allowed the attachment to his headquarters of an officer from the 3rd Division, who was to report to Monash on the preparation for and the conduct of the Polygon Wood attack, the enemy and the ground. A second liaison officer was sent to the 1st Division, still commanded by Walker. Their reports were promptly disseminated in the 3rd Division, so that commanders at every level knew what the difficulties would be and how they could be avoided or overcome. None benefited more than Monash himself. The liaison officer with the 1st Division reported that it had assembled in no man's land, occupying as small a depth as possible until the attack passed beyond the German barrage, when the various waves shook out to their proper distance. Sent forward by Monash, Jackson was averse to the idea because it necessitated the crowding of each brigade into a space about 300 yards square, thereby running the risk of appalling casualties if it were caught by the barrage. Because of the narrowness of his assembly area at the head of the Zonnebeke swamp, Monash

CHAPTER 8

agreed with Jackson and adopted the method used by the 2nd Division. The two battalions destined for the first objectives assembled near the front line with the others well to the rear, 'taking advantage of gaps and periods when the [barrage] has thinned down, in order to move forward to their respective objectives.' Jackson informed Monash that 1st ANZAC had praised the use of smoke to indicate halts in the barrage and the allocation of 100 infantry to each of the field engineer companies. Monash included both in his plan.

Efficient staff work could moderate but not eliminate the effect on preparations of the short time available. Cable burying was completed between divisional and brigade headquarters, but wire to the battalions had to be left largely above ground. Pioneers laid two duckboard tracks from the assembly areas to the starting line, but roads and foot tracks further back were left unfinished. Rain fell on 2–3 October and on the night before the attack, making the area behind Monash's jumping-off tape marshy, but he had foreseen the possibility and ordered the construction of seven crossing points.

For 1st ANZAC the preparations were comparatively easy. Its roads for the third stage had been made before the second, 'its systems of supply and control were in working order' and 'operation orders and instructions largely consisted of references to those for the previous steps.' A problem shared by each corps was to move its assault formations into so small an attacking frontage at the same time as the troops holding the line were withdrawn to make room for them. White, the first to grapple with it before Menin Road, claimed that it was his hardest task of the war. The solution was the same in both Anzac corps. In the 3rd Division over 4500 troops from the 10th Brigade on the left and the 11th on the right would attack on a frontage of 1000 yards. On the night of 2 October half this number would move from their positions in rear to the fields and old front-line trenches east of Ypres, remaining there under cover next day. Monash explained:

> The Battalions to move ... will be the battalions allotted for the first two objectives. These Battalions may suffer from lack of sleep, but it is better that [they] ... thus suffer than the Battalions who have to go right through and hold the ultimate objective.

MONASH

The battalions attacking that objective would march direct to their assembly areas during the night before the attack. On the choice of zero hour Monash differed from his colleagues. He agreed with Second Army's suggestion that the attack should be launched at about 4.00 am to escape the barrage that the Germans had recently begun to put down at dawn. It also appealed to Monash because of 'the probability of gaining complete surprise', and for the reason he had advanced before Warneton: 'the aptitude of Colonial troops for night fighting'. He did not get his way. In 2nd ANZAC, Russell favoured 6.00 am, the time nominated by a majority of the divisional commanders.

Although Monash had no way of knowing, the earlier time would have prevented disruption of the attack by tactics Ludendorff had reluctantly approved to counter the step-by-step method. Following Ludendorff's decision, General Sixt von Armin, the commander of the German *Fourth Army* holding the Flanders front, ordered on 30 September a partial return to the old method of holding the forward positions in strength with additional machine-guns and the launching from them of deliberate counter-attacks: 'The losses incurred ... [will be] no heavier than those incurred when lying inactive under enemy fire, the enemy must hold his forward zone in great strength and thus provides a better target for our artillery.' Some units had employed these tactics well before the appearance of von Armin's order. Second Army's suspicion of their use during the Menin Road attack was confirmed on 22 September, and on 1 October Plumer's headquarters forecast a counter-attack launched from Broodseinde within the next two days to retake some of the ground lost in the Polygon Wood stroke. It had still not occurred when Monash advised his brigadiers on 3 October of the action they were to take if the Germans attacked next morning shortly before zero hour. A defensive barrage would be brought down immediately while the infantry, 'sitting tight' on their start line, engaged those Germans who penetrated it. When the attack barrage opened at 6.00 am, the assault had to commence as planned: 'whatever happens, the advance both of the infantry and the artillery must begin precisely at ZERO.'

CHAPTER 8

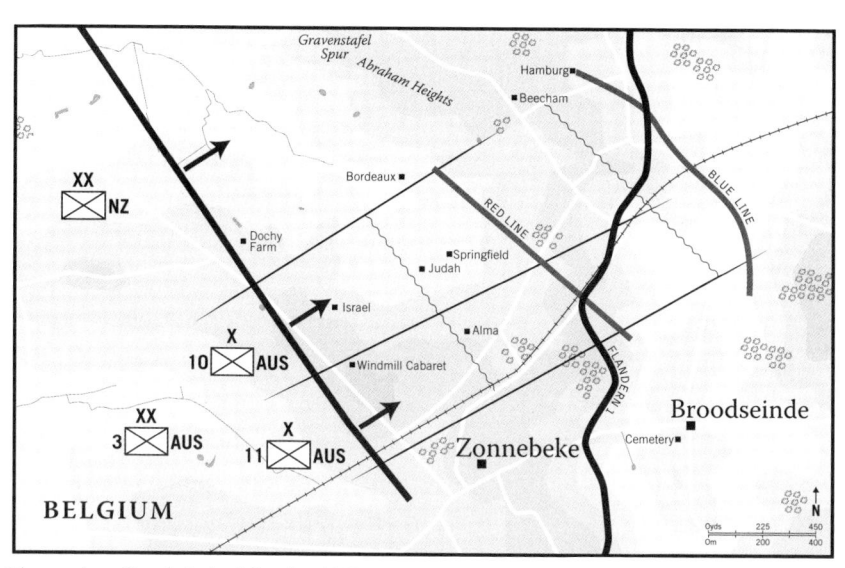

The attack on Broodseinde, 4 October 1917

Looking like a surreal moonscape, this photograph shows the level crossing in the area of the Windmill Cabaret at Zonnebeke before the Broodseinde attack on 4 October 1917. The 3rd Division's right flank advanced along the axis of the railway, which is more prominent than the road. Dochy Farm was on the road out of picture to the left (AWM J00189).

The German attack came, but the 3rd Division did not have to respond as Monash had ordered. Its approach march was without incident, but the assembly arrangements that Monash adopted from the 2nd Division were discarded immediately on the initiative of the brigadiers. The area allotted to the 41st Battalion was the

Bremen Redoubt, 1200 yards behind the start line and captured in the Menin Road attack. When Cannan found that it was frequently shelled, he sent the 41st to join the forward battalions at Zonnebeke marsh. The assembly area was now rather cramped, but there is no doubt that large casualties were avoided. McNicoll moved the 40th for the same reason. At 5.30 am a German barrage fell. It fell heaviest on 1st ANZAC, and losses were severe. The cause of the barrage became apparent at zero hour, when a line of troops emerged from the German positions opposite. Directed mainly at 1st ANZAC, the assault expected since 2 October had begun.

It was a stroke of fortune for Monash's attack. The rear waves of the 3rd Division crowded against the leading battalions, which had moved forward to escape the barrage. Thus the 37th Battalion had crept to within 30 yards of the posts on the Windmill Cabaret, and at 6.00 am was on the Germans 'before they realised what had happened'. Monash's setting of the first intermediate line to permit a leapfrog between Judah-Israel and Springfield-Bordeaux was justified by the heavy resistance encountered in the vicinity of each. A temporary halt caused by machine-guns on the Abraham Heights illustrated the danger from the left flank until the position was taken by the New Zealanders. Similarly, the decimation of a company from the 40th Battalion in front of the Blue Line explained Monash's concern to limit the advance to the subsidiary spur before it. The fighting for the high ground on which the Blue Line rested was 'very severe' and the main counter-attack at 3.00 pm developed across the junction between the Gravenstafel and Passchendaele ridges. It was shattered by Stokes mortars carried forward by the 11th Brigade, an experiment that proved they could be used very successfully in the mobile role. In reaching the Blue Line, the 3rd Division had taken the stretch of Flandern 1 on its front. At the end of the attack, 'the 3rd quickly dug ... perhaps the most complete and accurately sited front and support lines ever made by Australians in battle.' The division's war diary stated: '[The attack] was carried out successfully, exactly as laid down in orders. Our arrangements worked well.' The description was apt for most of Second Army's front. But one aspect disturbed Monash

CHAPTER 8

as he reported to Godley at 10.40 am: 'Everything going well. My information is about an hour late. Have every reason to believe on Blue Line.'

Most First World War commanders would have welcomed information that was an hour late, but Monash complained that the delay was caused by 'an absolute choking up of the signal traffic.' His irritation was not unwarranted. As a commander who remained at his headquarters, his control of the battle was threatened by even the briefest breakdown in communications. Fortunately, there was no repetition of the chaos on the Green Line at Messines, and he directed his brigadiers firmly at every stage of the battle. McNicoll was the recipient of a terse message at 11.08 am:

> Artillery observers have seen some of our men in the Cemetery East of the Blue Line. That is just exactly where our barrage will come down at 12.26 ... You have an hour and a quarter to take some steps about it.
>
> We may expect counterattack in the next 2-3 hours ... Now is our time to prepare. You are perfectly satisfied 40 Bn have got a good supply of SOS rockets? Are you in touch with Lord (CO)? Has he told you where he is on the Blue Line?
>
> Well, McNicoll, I will trust you to do your best.

Monash's deference to senior officers vanished in the urgency of action. Godley was left in no doubt of Monash's annoyance that the operations staff of the relieving division had not appeared at his headquarters at 10.40 am. 'I think it is high time that the Division following me should send up their G Staff to begin to take hold. Will you kindly arrange that?'

Certain that a major success had been won, Godley was urging Plumer to allow 2nd ANZAC to exploit to the Bellevue Spur, which joined the Passchendaele Ridge at the village. Asked for his opinion, Monash pointed out that the leading battalions had suffered heavily, but nonetheless: 'It all depends on the time to get the orders through. I have the worst possible communications.' He agreed that an improved line might be secured for the next attack if he swung his right forward to Augustus Wood and, in the same conversation, explained the arrangements for the move to Godley. By 1.30 pm his brigadiers had been briefed, but, possibly because he conceded that the delay in signal traffic made the accuracy of his information uncertain, Monash asked them to 'Think it over.' The episode revealed Monash's ability instantly to imagine a situation and elaborate the steps it demanded, almost as though he could visualise his plan unfolding. Jackson recalled a less dramatic example:

> ... one day when a quick change had to be carried out I sat down and wrote the orders and when they were finished I asked him if he would like to read them, he said, 'No, but listen to this and tell me what you think of it.' He ... read out to me a carefully thought out change of policy with regard to work, reliefs etc., in the line necessitated by the orders about to be issued.

Godley's proposal was abandoned by Plumer, who had found Birdwood implacably opposed to it.

With little time for preparation, Monash's performance at Broodseinde was perhaps his most capable as a divisional commander. He had given his division the most relevant training possible. His original and revised plans were based entirely on the principles of limited objective attacks and conformed to the tactical demands of the ground. His use of smoke and mobile trench mortars contributed to the success. He was a driving force throughout the battle and, towards its end, coolly handled a rapidly changing situation. Afterwards he asked battalion commanders twelve questions on how techniques could be bettered.

The only criticism that can be made is a just one. Rain fell heavily on 4 October shortly after midday. Coming on top of the rain of the previous two nights, it returned the battlefield to the swamps of August. Those parts of Monash's sector over which there had been no time to prepare duckboard tracks became a terrible obstacle for his stretcher-bearers. The evacuation arrangements duly collapsed, although the *Medical History* states that the 3rd Division 'seems to have been in no way responsible'. But Monash's headquarters in the Ypres Ramparts was ill-equipped to cope with the crisis. Insufficient accommodation had prompted him to leave his administrative staff,

CHAPTER 8

the medical staff officers among them, at Brandhoek, several miles away. Bean conceded that his decision was inevitable. The badly wounded soldiers left lying overnight under rain and shellfire would not have thought so. Monash could have put the medical staff under canvas or, alternatively, brought them forward on the night of the 3rd, allowing them to follow the battle next day. Given the stakes – and his stress on administration – a little congestion was tolerable for twenty-four hours.

When the battle is considered overall, though, Harington's assessment stands: 'the way in which the Division made its plans at short notice, and carried the operation through is beyond all praise.' On its effect, Monash surmised:

> Great happenings are possible in the very near future, as the enemy is terribly disorganised and it is doubtful if his railway facilities are good enough to enable him to re-establish himself before our next two blows, which will be very severe.

In his attempt to vindicate Haig's subsequent policy, Terraine remarks that Monash's comment showed that he 'entirely shared the GHQ view of Third Ypres possibilities, at a level of much closer practical concern.' But Monash's opinion was more restrained than GHQ's, where Charteris cried exuberantly: 'Now we have them, get up the Cavalry, now we have them on the run – Push on, push on etc.' It was also based solely on the crushing result of 4 October, omitting the effect of the rain, which began that afternoon and became torrential a few days later. The battlefield degenerated into a stinking morass on which it was impossible to find stable positions for the guns and to keep them supplied with the massive quantities of ammunition needed by the bite and hold method: 'Barrages were, in consequence, feeble and wild, no protection to the infantry after the first round … The Air Force could give no help whatever.'

According to the British Official Historian, Brigadier General Sir James Edmonds, Gough and Plumer jointly proposed ending the campaign at a conference with Haig on 7 October, but Haig disagreed. Not only does the contemporary record raise grave doubts about whether this conference actually took place, but Gough and Plumer appear to have endorsed Haig's inclination to continue. Yet many of the reasons originally advanced for the offensive no longer held. It had been intended to bolster the flagging Russians and mutinous French, but the Russians had already collapsed and a successful attack at Verdun in August was clear evidence of a French recovery. By this stage, too, Haig's stated desire to secure a good winter line needed to be balanced against the exhaustion of his own army. But he did not want to let the operation tempo slacken, especially as he thought the strongest German defences had been reduced. It was the most controversial decision of his career. Haig's optimism seemed to infect Second Army, which had the principal role in the next attack, on 9 October. Harington proclaimed the evening before that the crest of the Passchendaele Ridge was 'as dry as a bone'. Bean, who was present, commented: 'I suspect that they are making a great bloody experiment – a huge gamble and no more than that; a deliberate attempt to see how it works.' As Bean predicted, the attack, known as the Battle of Poelcappelle, failed, and even Charteris now told Haig that there was no hope of success in 1917. But Passchendaele was now an obsession, and 'it would take the impact of a travelling planet to shift him.'

Passchendaele village and church. The shattered road runs north-east along the summit of the ridge from Broodseinde. The 3rd Division attacked in the general direction of the road on 12 October 1917. Note the intact Belgian countryside behind the German lines (AWM J00285).

CHAPTER 8

The day after its relief on 6 October, Godley warned Monash that if 2nd ANZAC's two British divisions, the 49th and 66th, failed on the 9th, the 3rd Division 'would have to do it on the 12th.' Monash immediately told his brigadiers: 'Things now rushed. No time to prepare, refer to orders as we go along.' The casualty of this haste was the material preparation for the battle: 'matters were very incompletely attended to ... or had to be almost totally neglected.' There was no time to lay duckboard tracks across the mud nor bridge the many rivulets, and cable was not buried beyond brigades' headquarters. Once the results of the Poelcappelle attack were known, it was clear that this would be a larger operation for the 3rd Division than Broodseinde had been. Starting from the line assumed to be held by the 66th Division, the 3rd Division was to advance almost 2000 yards on a frontage of 1600 yards. As 1st ANZAC was too exhausted to assume a major role, its action would be limited to covering Monash's right flank. The New Zealand Division attacked on the left.

Taking the comparison further, the positions Monash was about to attack were far stronger than the ones at Broodseinde. From the line reached on the Gravenstafel, the ground dipped gently into the valley of the Ravebeek, which was overlooked on the other side by three stretches of high ground, as in the letter E. The southernmost was the main ridge, extending from Broodseinde to Passchendaele. To the north of Passchendaele and curving around from it was the Bellevue-Meetcheele Spur, crossed by Flandern 1 and paralleling the main ridge. Between and parallel to both was the smaller, middle arm of the E, the Crest Farm Spur, across which the Blue Line ran. Until this feature was taken, any attack must break against it like a wave against an outlying rock. Each feature could bring devastating enfilade fire onto the others, while the frontal field of fire for the German machine-gunners was as extensive as that enjoyed by their Turkish counterparts on the Alai Tepe on 8 August 1915. Moreover, the German division defending this sector seems not to have reverted to the defence-in-depth system reinstituted by Ludendorff after the Broodseinde reverse on 4 October, and it was equipped with double the normal number of machine-guns. Most would emerge unscathed from the weak barrage to engage the 3rd Division floundering over the flooded Ravebeek below them, described by Second Army on 7 October as 'Quite impassable. Should be avoided by troops at all times.'

The area of the Alma and Springfield strongpoints, captured by the 3rd Division in the Broodseinde attack on 4 October. Drenched by heavy rain afterwards, it reverted to a quagmire. The 3rd Division's assault on Passchendaele on 12 October had to cover ground worse than this (AWM E01047).

Time was not the only factor restricting Monash's planning. The attack would be made over the same ground and with largely the same objectives as were laid down for Poelcappelle on 9 October. Monash intended two leapfrogs, the first on the Red Line corresponding to the second objective of that attack and the second on the Blue just short of

CHAPTER 8

Passchendaele, before the assault on the Green Line 400 yards beyond the village. His anxiety about Passchendaele, which 'was believed to be strongly held', explained why there was one less leapfrog despite a longer advance than at Broodseinde. McNicoll, whose brigade was to take it, would have a battalion in reserve if difficulties arose. The measures for its capture were the most elaborate in the divisional plan. If the 38th Battalion, strengthened by an additional company for the task, and then McNicoll's reserve were repulsed, the units that had assaulted the Red and Blue lines would assist. Rosenthal, whose brigade was attacking on the right, was to detach his reserve battalion to meet the New Zealanders beyond Passchendaele, preventing its reinforcement by the Germans while units from the 10th Brigade completed the mopping up. Each assaulting brigade would have six mortars and eight machine-guns ready to move forward. Great efforts were made to avoid a repetition of the medical breakdown: 224 infantry were attached to the medical units as extra stretcher-bearers, while further to the rear:

> I [Monash] have introduced the system of working the motor ambulances on the cab rank principle, i.e. each car as it returns from its last job goes into the rank like a taxicab, and as they are wanted, the cars are taken in turn from the head of the rank and the next moves up …

Perhaps because he considered the effort of the 4th Division on his right too limited to support adequately the 9th Brigade's assault against the strongpoints on the southern slopes of the Passchendaele Ridge, Monash's chief fear was Rosenthal's flank. Perhaps, too, because he thought the New Zealanders would repeat their Gravenstafel success on the Bellevue-Meetcheele Spur, he was not concerned about the left. Whatever the reason, there is no mention in his own or the 3rd Division's records either of the importance of the spur or of any special measures to deal with the defences on it. Yet it was known by the evening of 9 October that the 66th Division had been halted by enfilade fire from that spur.

The precise line reached by that formation was obscure and, according to Bean, Monash did not ascertain until 11 October that 'the line was practically the same as before the last attack [i.e. Poelcappelle].' By then it was too late to change the barrage orders, which were based on the assumption that the 66th had been stopped near its first objective. Yet Rosenthal had gone to the 66th's area at 1.00 pm on 9 October to look for a suitable headquarters for his own attack. Failure was obvious, and he wrote next day: 'Appears from this morning's information that the British retired to the old front line handed over to them several days ago.' At 4.40 pm on 10 October McNicoll told Monash that troops in his forward positions stated that 'there was no-one in front of them as far as they knew.' Finally, Jackson spent the whole of the 10th in the forward area. There seems no doubt that on *10 October* Monash was fully cognisant of the dangerous situation, which would lengthen the 3rd Division's assault by 500 yards. This helps explain why he 'personally used every endeavour to secure ... a twenty four hour postponement. The chief decided that every hour's postponement gave the enemy breathing time ...'

No amount of seeing through other men's eyes – Rosenthal's, McNicoll's or Jackson's – could have the same impact as a personal reconnaissance. Besides urging a postponement, if Monash had seen for himself, he might not have consented to the corrective action taken: the commencement of the 3rd Division's barrage 300 yards further back, but an increase in its rate of advance so that it caught the general line of the barrage within 500 yards. This required the infantry to cover those 500 yards in twenty minutes instead of the forty allowed at the normal rate. Bean commented:

> If Generals Monash and Godley had had experience on the Somme, it is unlikely that they would have agreed to this arrangement ... how could [Godley] have hoped for success with deeper objectives than any since July 31st, shorter preparation and with the infantry asked to advance at a pace unattempted in the dry weather of September?

Bean's suggestion is to some extent misleading, for Monash had based the 3rd Division's training in England on his study of material received from the Somme. It illustrates instead the consequences of his habit of remaining at his headquarters, where the revision of the

CHAPTER 8

plan might have appeared reasonable. This may have been the cause of Birdwood's subsequent criticism to Haig of Monash's leadership during the operation, which the C-in-C lightly dismissed. Haig was touched to hear on 10 October that the 38th Battalion had promised to raise a specially woven flag above Passchendaele and told Monash that as soon as it was planted the news would be cabled to Australia. He did not go as far as Godley, who told Monash that it was his 'sacred duty' to fly the flag from the ruins of the village. Haig also reassured himself about the length of the advance: 'The enemy is now much weakened in *moral*[e] and lacks the desire to fight.'

As Glyn Harper says, 'the attack of 12 October should never have gone ahead.' The depressing story of the fight was encapsulated in a few lines scribbled by Lieutenant Colonel Morshead before noon:

> Things are bloody, very bloody. We have got past the blue line and I've just got word that the 9th and 10th Brigades have withdrawn to Augustus Wood. The New Zealanders and 1 Anzac have suffered very heavily and so have we.

The approach march had been carried out under gas shelling and rain, exhausting the troops before the start line was reached. When the barrage opened at 5.25 am, 'it seemed as if a few pebbles were being tossed into the mud.' On the Bellevue-Meetcheele Spur, where the dense wire was uncut and the pillboxes were intact – though mud-splattered – 'The massing of machine guns and the intensity of fire was pronounced.' The New Zealanders fell in droves and the Germans turned on the 10th Brigade struggling below them through 'gluey mud, generally knee deep, and in some places, waist deep' towards the Red Line. By 2.30 pm the 10th had retired to the start line. On the right, the 9th, like the 10th, had quickly fallen behind the barrage, but resistance was weaker and the Blue Line was reached. The Germans responded with an artillery and machine-gun barrage, which all agreed was the heaviest they had yet experienced. At the end of the attack the 3rd Division held a line slightly more advanced than the original. The situation was still obscure next day. Bean thought several groups still occupied positions near the Blue Line 'although the SOS line had been brought back by General Monash in superabundant caution the previous evening and a practice barrage put through.' This criticism was unfair. Monash had done the same at Messines to protect the Black Line after it seemed that the outposts on the Green Line had been lost.

Dead and wounded Australians and Germans in the Ypres–Roulers railway cutting east of Broodseinde after the attack on 12 October. Private Austin Henderson of the 38th Battalion faces the camera at far right (AWM E03864).

Poor communications hampered Monash's control of the battle. Initial reports suggested that the serious resistance and difficult ground on the left had been overcome and at 9.32 am Monash informed Godley that both brigades had begun their advance to the Blue Line. The first intimation that the 10th Brigade was in serious trouble arrived at 9.55 am, but the picture was confused by persistent reports, received up to an hour later, that advanced groups had reached Crest Farm. Not until 10.50 am was Monash aware that the New Zealand Division had stalled well before its Red Line. He asked them to bring their barrage back to the Red Line and ordered McNicoll to use his reserve battalion to secure the ground already won, replacing it with

CHAPTER 8

the 41st from Cannan's brigade. By 12.24 pm the situation was clear. McNicoll confirmed that his brigade had definitely not taken the Red Line, while a report from the 36th Battalion, *sent at 10.05 am*, stated that the 9th Brigade was too weak to go beyond the Blue Line. Monash abandoned any hope of reaching Passchendaele village, but he was concerned about the 9th's left flank, which had been exposed when the 10th Brigade stalled. At the same time, the 9th had seized a significant slice of the crest, and every effort should be made to retain it. Monash instructed the 9th Brigade to secure its gains by pushing towards Crest Farm from the south, for he realised that a frontal attack was impossible, in conjunction with a renewal of the New Zealanders' attack at 3.00 pm. All arrangements were completed by 1.15 pm, when Godley cancelled the New Zealand attack, forcing Monash to do the same. Comparing casualties to the ground won, Messines had cost the 3rd 3.23 men per yard, Broodseinde .93. The corresponding figure for Passchendaele was 35.54.

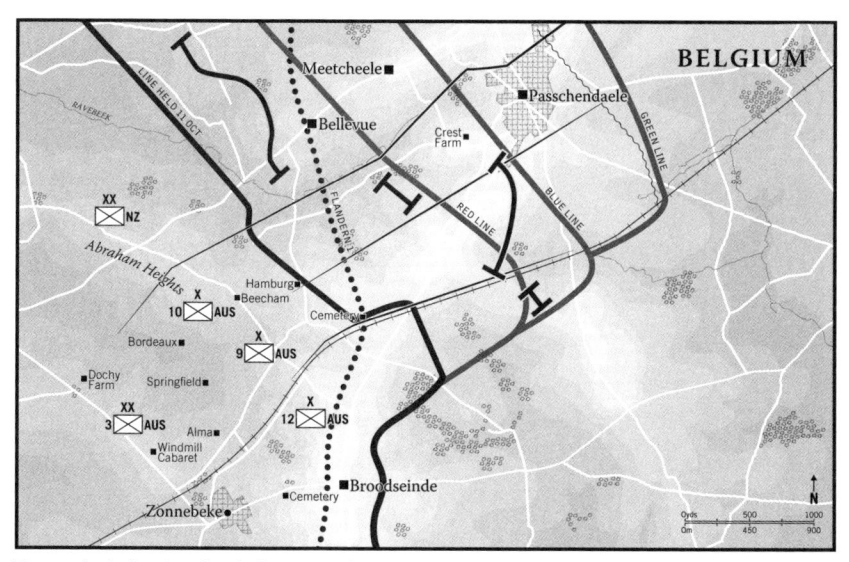

The repulse before Passchendaele, 12 October 1917

Major General Eric Sixsmith asserts that this fight refutes the contention that Monash was never tested in adversity. He had no opportunity before the battle to prepare a plan that would influence its course. The administrative and tactical lessons of 4 October were nullified by the dreadful conditions – Monash argued later that all the trouble flowed from the state of the ground. Yet he did not go near the front line, unlike Currie, 'who was almost continuously forward' during the Canadians Corps' preparation for its successful assault on Passchendaele in November. Nevertheless, Monash's performance during the battle was able. His deployment of reserves was prompt, but when success seemed unlikely, he did not hesitate to forbid a further advance in favour of holding the vital ground on the Passchendaele crest. As evidence of their thorough training, Monash praised his battalions for the speed with which they took over the advance from units in front that were checked. Yet his criticism that 'senior officers must go forward when the situation was ugly' was somewhat hypocritical in view of his own failure before the battle. Monash's belief that the plan would have worked in fine weather was not unreasonable, because the barrage, the critical factor in past successes, would not have been so ineffectual as it was on 12 October. But to proceed in spite of the weather was criminal: 'Our men are being put into the hottest fighting and are being sacrificed in hare-brained schemes like Bullecourt and Passchendaele, and there is no one in the War Cabinet to lift a voice in protest.'

The Flanders offensive, in which four months were needed to advance 5½ miles at a cost of 250 000 casualties, had important consequences. There were no infantry reserves left to exploit the brilliant initial success at Cambrai on 20 November, when an attack led by 381 tanks penetrated five miles in one day for a loss of 4000 men. To prevent a recurrence of another attritional offensive in 1918, the British Prime Minister, David Lloyd George, withheld men, forcing a reduction in the number of battalions per division from twelve to nine. But 1918 began with the Germans launching a colossal offensive of their own. As Robin Prior and Trevor Wilson point out, the ten or more British divisions represented by the losses in the Flanders campaign 'formed the missing reserve that might have halted the German advance a great deal sooner and at less cost.' Comparing the two armies in that year, Lieutenant General Sir Beauvoir de Lisle, an able British commander, judged

CHAPTER 8

that the average German division was as good as the best British division. Henceforth, the Dominion troops, particularly the AIF and the Canadians, would be the spearhead of the BEF. But the 38 000 Australian casualties suffered at Third Ypres created an acute reinforcement problem for the AIF that was insoluble. Each of Monash's battalions, for example, was on average 400 men under strength.

The solution recommended by Birdwood and approved by Haig ended a frustration felt by the Australians since June 1916, when the C-in-C refused a proposal for an Australian Army. Agitation continued in 1917, and in October the Australian government made its strongest request that the five divisions should be grouped under Birdwood. Haig believed that this was too large a command for one man to handle and the system of reliefs in it too complex. In his view a corps of four divisions was ideal. Not only was it a more manageable command, but it also avoided the relief problem, because two divisions could be in the line with the other two ready to relieve them. He hinted that the Australians might be formed into two corps, presumably with British divisions making up the balance in each, but this was hardly an advance on the existing arrangements. When the manpower crisis intervened, Birdwood suggested that the 4th Division, which was the most battle worn, should become temporarily a depot division to supply reinforcements for the others.[61] Besides averting the 4th Division's break-up, this would result in a corps of the magical four divisions. Haig agreed, and on 1 November 1917 the Australian Corps came into being, with Birdwood as its commander and White its chief of staff. The 3rd Division transferred officially on 15 November. Bean wrote: 'Old Monash will be pleased to be within the fold again with his 3rd Division.' It was an inadequate expression of Monash's feelings:

> So at last I have parted from Godley. I have not much to be grateful to him for. I served him loyally and faithfully for nearly three years and he has done nothing for me that he could help doing. However, towards the end he was very nice and amicable and gave me quite a splendid farewell banquet.

The reorganisation came at the end of a three-week rest in the familiar Bléquin area. Monash found it hard to believe that the war continued as he spent many hours walking in the peaceful countryside. There was no trace of the well-upholstered figure he had cut in 1916: 'my health is better than ever it was, my weight is stationary at 12.8 and I have lost all appearance of corpulence about the waist and neck.' He had allowed Eric Simonson to join the Australian Flying Corps (AFC), replacing him with his brother Paul. In January 1918, Jackson left to command the 87th Brigade, and Jess, Monash's staff captain on Gallipoli, became the new GSO1.

Another change was Monash's own title, for he had been created Knight Commander of the Bath (KCB) in the New Year's Honours List. He was certain that he had 'more than earned a knighthood already', and that it resulted wholly from Birdwood's pressure on Godley. In what he admitted was 'a monstrously egotistical letter', he painted the future for Vic:

> The University is pretty sure to claim my services in a still higher capacity ... possibly soon as Vice-Chancellor and later on perhaps as Chancellor. That they will desire to confer on me a high honorary degree is quite probable – possibly a 'DCL' or 'LLD'. (It might be well to keep this in mind when talking to any members of the Council ...) ... the difficulty will be what to choose and what to leave alone ... There is still another possibility ... I merely write of it because I am in a frank humour – and that is a Governorship.

On 14 November 1917 Monash assumed control of the Ploegsteert sector, which extended 7000 yards from the Lys to the Windmill position captured by the 11th Brigade on 31 July. As the steady transfer of German divisions from Russia made a massive spring offensive certain, urgent emphasis was placed on the improvement of the defences, which, in this area, were in a shocking state of repair. Haig had now ordered a layered system of defence in depth that resembled the method used by the Germans at Third Ypres. The present forward line was to become part of a lightly held outpost zone, breaking up attacks and compelling the Germans to use as large an assaulting force as possible. A mile or two behind the outpost zone, a battle zone

CHAPTER 8

extended up to 3000 yards, and it was there that the attack would be defeated. Both the outpost and battle zones were based on well-wired redoubts that were mutually supporting. Depending on the labour available, a rearward zone some miles further back was prepared as a precautionary measure.

Monash implemented the GHQ directive according to the policy he had used on his division's arrival in France: 'safe defence, minimum work, maximum comfort.' Labour was not to be wasted on positions of questionable value; better sited trenches were to be dug instead. Private soldiers competent to act as foremen were placed in charge of working parties. Brigadiers were not free to determine how their battalions should occupy the line, as Monash directed that each of the first two positions in the outpost zone would be held by two lines of two platoons, with two companies holding the third position. This system allowed frequent relief of the occupants of the waterlogged foremost line, where conditions during the winter were miserable.

Much more difficult was the instruction of new leaders to replace those who had become casualties at Passchendaele. Monash called this 'the pressing outstanding question' and urged commanders at all levels to waste no opportunity 'through lectures, classes and practice handling of bodies of troops to give them the necessary confidence.' He used the address he had given at Serapeum in 1916 as the basis for a 'short heart to heart talk' to the junior officers of each brigade on their responsibilities. Monash was particularly anxious to achieve uniformity of thought and policy in his division; this approach had been used by the Germans since the earliest days of their military organisation and was, he felt, the key to their success. He did not wish to cramp initiative, but he did not want violent heresy either:

> … which is the more desirable? … for each man to try and adopt the best that he can irrespective of its total disagreement with what his predecessors have done and neighbours are doing; or is it better to adopt a reasonably good plan and a good policy and have everybody in the whole command thinking in the same way and acting in the same way.

The British Army had yet fully to resolve this issue. Monash also pleaded 'most strongly' for the 'careful study' of all educative material issued by higher authority, particularly translations of captured German documents: 'Whenever I am able to do so, I try to secure an issue of these pamphlets in adequate numbers to enable quite junior officers to get them into their hands.'

Besides the impetus he provided, an important factor in the 3rd Division's revival was Monash's use of psychology. His men were imbued with the need to excel in all things, not merely to prove themselves to the older Australian formations now serving alongside them. He reminded all of their obligation to avert the 4th Division's fate: 'we must be and remain the *best* Australian Division. I call upon all to work in harmony, with the utmost industry and judgement and to apply our accumulated experience.' Monash had created an excellent incentive by a deliberate distortion. He knew that the 4th Division was made a depot division because of its weariness after being the most used of the Australian divisions in 1917. Sinclair-MacLagan's opinion that it was no longer fit for the line may have saved the 3rd, for its strength had been the lowest in November. After the failure of the second conscription referendum in Australia in December, the manpower crisis continued, despite the temporary reprieve granted by the quiet winter months, when the infantry strength of the 4th Division rose to 12 000 and the remainder to over 13 000.

Under the defensive policy, domination of no man's land was to be achieved by patrolling. Except in special circumstances, raids were forbidden. Only five major blows were struck by the Australians during winter, of which the 3rd Division was responsible for four. Monash immersed himself in the preparations for them, using new methods to ensure surprise and inflict casualties. On the night of 30 November, a raid by the 39th Battalion was followed by another on the same objective seven hours later, 'the time that it would probably take the enemy to restore his situation and garrison.' Next evening the German line was shelled for three minutes, Monash presuming that the Germans would try to run clear in anticipation of another raid. The barrage range would then be lengthened 'and therefore our

CHAPTER 8

guns ought to get "some sort of a bag".' On 10–11 February 1918, twenty silhouette figures were raised and lowered in no man's land by wires from an outpost to divert the German barrage from the real objective 400 yards away. The feint completely deceived them: 'They saw the dummy figures start up and drop down again ... and so riddled them ... that they were not afterwards recovered.' On 3–4 March, the 9th Brigade attacked with 300 men in twenty separate storming parties, repeating the operation against the same objective the next night. Monash submitted a plan for a divisional attack on Warneton with the twin aims of diverting German strength from another part of the front and of 'securing the moral effect likely to follow the seizure by us of a locality which has figured largely in official communiques.' The 3rd Division went into corps reserve before the scheme could be carried out.

The formation of the Australian Corps brought Monash closer to White, and differences of opinion on tactical matters soon emerged. After a brief course at the Machine-Gun School at Camiers in February confirmed views on this weapon he had long held, Monash wrote a pamphlet for his officers on the principles of its use. It began: 'The machine gun is to be regarded more as an offensive than as a defensive weapon. Next to artillery it is the most effective weapon we possess.' Its defensive role was not neglected; on the contrary, Monash stated that it should be used to deny a feature to the Germans by sweeping its approaches and thus breaking lateral communications, instead of defending a trench line. Monash considered the latter role wasteful and obsolete; in any case it could be performed by Lewis guns. His experience with machine-gun barrages to support the attack and the sending forward of machine-guns behind the assaulting waves to assist consolidation proved the efficacy of Monash's ideas. White's opinions remained conservative: 'I think we must guard against any ideas which make the weapon more an offensive than a defensive one.'

Monash thought the artillery policy ludicrous. Most of the guns were sited some 3500 yards from the German line, so that they could support a major offensive to gain ground. This arrangement was hardly appropriate in the present circumstances, when a devastating

German offensive was expected. After consulting Grimwade, Monash proposed a redeployment of the artillery in depth to conform to the infantry dispositions. When Monash had raised this question over two months previously, White replied that he was 'going to be slightly inconsistent': guns were to be disposed for defence, but 'for all that we want to use them offensively and deny the initiative to the Germans.' His offer to explain this cryptic answer to Monash later was evidently forgotten. 'I score heavily', Monash wrote after a long conference with White on 10 January. It was a comment that applied on any number of occasions.

Operation Michael, the most spectacular offensive of the war, began on 21 March 1918, when 47 German divisions fell on the British Third and Fifth armies on the fifty-mile front between Croisilles, near Arras, and La Fère on the Oise. The right of Third Army was pushed back, but Gough's front, on the left of the French, crumbled. On 22 March he ordered a retirement to the line of the Somme ten miles in rear. Next day he was fighting behind the river. The Germans had opened a breach forty miles wide 'across which was loosely strewn the exhausted wreckage of Gough's command.' Albert was lost on the 26th, and the fall of the vital railway junction at Amiens seemed inevitable. Within a few days the Germans had taken more territory than all the Allied advances of the past three years. There were many reasons for the debacle, not least the tactics used by the Germans, which represented another triumph for their Operations Section. Storm troops penetrated the line at its weakest points, ignoring their flanks and bypassing centres of resistance, which were dealt with by succeeding waves. Due to the speed of the assault, many of the redoubts on which the British defence was based were either quickly overrun or isolated, fates presaged by the scepticism in which they had been held. As a seasoned NCO grumbled: 'The British Army fights in line and won't do any good in these bird cages.' Though weaker in infantry than a British division, a German division was much stronger in mortars and heavy machine-guns, coinciding with Monash's views on the importance of material assistance to the infantry.[62] The artillery was ranged with sound-

CHAPTER 8

location and flash-spotting equipment, as the British had done at Cambrai, instead of firing several rounds to register and forfeiting surprise. Beginning five hours before the attack, the bombardment was 'the most terrible and accurate concentration of fire of the whole war.'

Notwithstanding the novelty of the German offensive method and the shortage of manpower, GHQ and Haig were not blameless. There was ample warning of where and when the offensive would fall, and indeed Haig's only fear, as he explained to both the Cabinet and the King, was that 'the German would find our front so strong that he will hesitate to commit his Army to the attack with the almost certainty of losing very heavily.' His dispositions, based on the need to retain the Channel Ports, had left the divisional frontages in Gough's sector, which was furthest from them, the longest in his five armies. Privately, Haig expected that Fifth Army would probably yield ground, but that it could do so in some safety as it was not holding a vital area. He also reckoned on a gradual German advance, allowing time to bring up reinforcements. Gough's warnings before the storm about the danger facing him were therefore ignored, and he had difficulty convincing GHQ of the gravity of the situation when it broke. Initially, David Stevenson says, 'there seems to have been a confidence at GHQ that the Germans were driving into a trap that had been snared for them.' Gerard de Groot sets out the ramifications: 'This confidence explains why it took ... three days before the seriousness of the crisis dawned upon Haig, and why he expressed incredulity at the extent of the damage.' He did not visit the army commanders until 23 March, an inordinately long time after the offensive had begun, even allowing that he was in telephone contact with them.

Haig's optimism was hardly supported by the tempo evident in the tactics employed by the Germans at Riga, on the Eastern Front, and at Cambrai in 1917, and now in Michael. GHQ was fully aware of them and circulated captured orders for the Riga attack. At a conference with his battalion commanders at his headquarters at Ravelsberg on 26 February 1918, Monash urged them to study Riga and to put themselves in the place of the Russian defenders. He continued: 'I want you therefore ... *to educate* our men, educate their morale, to fortify them against panic due to the surprise action of the enemy in adopting some new means which may look very terrible, but one not really so at all.' Maxse went further, describing in detail the counter-tactics to be employed: defence in depth and rehearsed counter-attacks. But the defensive policy was changed just before the German onslaught. As Birdwood told his divisional commanders: 'Strengthen our forward dispositions.' This reinforcement of the forward zone at the expense of the battle zone deprived the defence of its depth, the most effective counter to the German doctrine.

Haig's demand that the French should assist in the defence of Amiens, thus keeping the two armies united, and the concern of Nivelle's replacement as French C-in-C, General Pétain, to cover Paris, even if the British right had to be abandoned, caused a crisis in the Allied command. It was resolved by the Doullens Conference, which appointed Foch, the French military representative on the Allied Supreme War Council, as Allied Generalissimo. Haig's famous description of Pétain at this meeting as 'much upset, almost unbalanced and most anxious' diverts attention from his own 'somewhat haggard' appearance. The cause may have gone beyond the exhaustion suffered by all senior commanders in the crisis. After the disproportionate losses of Third Ypres and the sharp loss of the initial gains at Cambrai, Haig could well have been shaken by the success of an offensive he had confidently expected to contain.

When the Germans struck, the 3rd Division was resting at Nielles-les-Bléquin, with its commander on leave on the Riviera. Monash was recalled on 24 March, and next day received advice from Jess and his GSO2, Major George Wieck, that the 3rd was to move south to Blaringhem, entraining there for Doullens and Mondicourt, where it would join the 4th and 5th Australian and two British divisions in X Corps. This formation was in GHQ reserve, but Wieck could obtain no worthwhile information when he visited its headquarters at Frévent. Monash was also frustrated by a lack of news when he went on to Doullens, so he returned to Blaringhem that evening to find his division entraining at three stations, with its artillery and

CHAPTER 8

ammunition columns already marching south. Later he praised his staff who 'responded capably to the heavy demands made upon them ... all this preparatory work was efficiently done.'

On 26 March, X Corps could only tell Monash to concentrate his division east of Doullens. From his arrival, fortune smiled on him. The first troops of the 9th Brigade were detraining, and Monash instructed Rosenthal to establish a strong outpost line east of the town to protect the rest of the 9th and the 11th Brigade following. He issued similar instructions to McNicoll at Mondicourt and then, learning that Sinclair-MacLagan was at Basseux, further north, left to coordinate the defensive arrangements with him. At 7.25 pm an order was received from Third Army, allotting Monash's division to VII Corps, commanded by Lieutenant General Sir Walter Congreve VC. The move by bus to Franvillers commenced once the division was complete. About three hours later, Monash was summoned to Congreve's headquarters, newly arrived at Montigny. Congreve, whose corps held the southern flank of Third Army, had interpreted an instruction to retire only 'if the tactical situation imperatively demands it' as an order to fall back regardless. By early afternoon on the 26th, a gap of 4½ miles had opened across the Morlancourt Ridge, in the triangle of ground between the Somme and the Ancre, exposing Amiens. Congreve ordered Monash to secure the triangle when he arrived at 1.00 am on 27 March. With his flanks resting on both rivers, he was to push as far east as possible, at least to an old line of trenches called the Amiens Line, which ran from Méricourt-l'Abbé on the Ancre to Sailly-le-Sec on the Somme.

The urgency of the situation demanded the most efficient battle procedure, so that orders could be distributed and administrative arrangements made in the shortest time possible. Yet the uncertainty regarding the Germans, who were 'now pushing westwards', and his own division on the move were factors militating against efficiency. Anticipating that energetic action would be required, Monash had brought with him to VII Corps Headquarters representatives from all departments of his staff and two despatch riders. Shortly after 1.00 am he dictated his orders from the instructions he had scribbled on three scraps of paper. The 11th Brigade was to occupy the line either side of the Bray–Corbie road on the Somme-Ancre triangle, moving south of the road as the 10th Brigade gradually arrived to take charge of the northern area. Wieck and Captain Pyke drove back to Doullens to give these orders to Cannan. From his own headquarters at Franvillers at dawn, Monash could 'plainly see the German cavalry operating on the high ground to the south of Morlancourt.' He felt greatly relieved when the first units of the 11th Brigade began to arrive at 8.00 am, and throughout the morning directed the occupation of the triangle by both brigades.

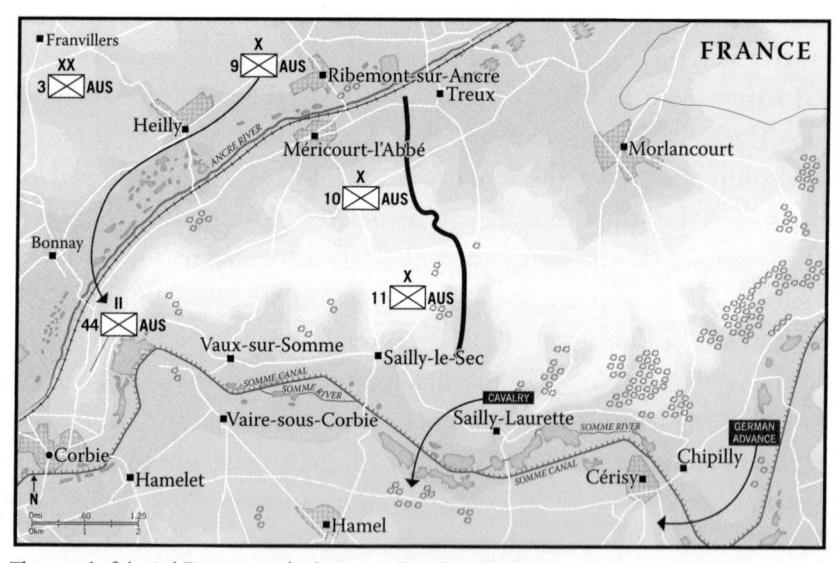

The arrival of the 3rd Division on the Somme, 26–27 March 1918

Initially in reserve, the 9th Brigade held the Amiens Line north of the Ancre at Ribemont. During the afternoon the Germans crossed the Somme at Cérisy, behind the left flank of Fifth Army, which had been exposed for three miles by Congreve's withdrawal. The right of Third Army would be turned if they advanced on the southern side of the river and then recrossed. They would then have a clear run to Amiens. Third Army's commander, General Sir Julian Byng, personally impressed on Monash the importance of preventing a crossing between Sailly and Aubigny, about five miles west. After consulting Congreve, Monash ordered the 9th Brigade to guard

CHAPTER 8

this line, while the 10th extended its left to Ribemont. Rosenthal completed the switch from north to south that night, while Monash was having his 'first good long rest'. Next day, 28 March, he reported to Birdwood: 'I now feel that the position is quite secure against all but an attack on a grand scale.'

Monash had been able to deploy the 3rd Division undisturbed, for there was practically no fighting on the 27th. His published accounts exaggerate its role in stopping the German drive on Amiens. Their advance in his sector was blunted by part of the 1st Cavalry Division supported by artillery and aircraft. None of this detracts from Monash's capable execution of his own task. Hampered by lack of information, his quick orders to McNicoll and Rosenthal ensured the safe arrival of his division at Doullens and Mondicourt, while the linking with Sinclair-MacLagan was on his initiative. For the move on 26/27 March the 'Divisional machinery ... worked like a well-oiled watch.' This was partly due to his foresight, which ensured that all branches of his staff could begin their preparations concurrently as soon as he received his instructions from Congreve. Monash's ability to visualise a plan unfolding was never more evident than in his own orders afterwards. Bean's estimate was appropriate:

> [It] shows Monash's great powers of grasp and of lucid expression at their best – the officers to whom they were read at the time recognised, with a flash of pride, 'the old man's' masterly touch. The situation that called for each phase of action was clearly explained, and the action then crisply ordered.

His seeking of White's views on the width of front a battalion should occupy was no discredit. White had constantly advised divisional commanders during the advance to the Hindenburg Line one year before when open warfare prevailed. General Sixsmith regards Monash's action as 'perfectly reasonable', because in the few days since 21 March 'the war had undergone its biggest change since trench warfare, whose principles Monash had mastered, was introduced by First Ypres in 1914.' That his division was defending the Somme-Ancre triangle less than twelve hours after its deployment began, followed by the 9th Brigade's transfer in one night from one flank to the other, were the results of Monash's 'quick, cool, successful planning'. He expressed his views in a frank letter to Jackson:

> It is a splendid illustration of the old doctrine which you and I have so often preached, that any sort of plan was better than no plan at all, and all that was wanted in this immediate neighbourhood ... was some clear definite plan communicated promptly to everybody whom it might effect and to which everybody could conform.

Monash was disturbed by the scenes he witnessed in Amiens and Doullens and by the general confusion and panic that accompanied the withdrawal. Three years of trench warfare had accustomed the British Army to fixed locations for headquarters and settled lines of communication. When the organisation was shattered, the action of units could not be coordinated and 'the recoil ... was allowed to extend over a much greater distance and to continue for longer ... than ought to have been the case.' His comments on the British Army resembled the scathing criticisms he had made at Gallipoli: 'Some of these Tommy Divisions are the absolute limit and not worth the money it costs to put them into uniform ... bad troops, bad staff, bad commanders.' Monash made no allowance for the battering these divisions had taken while trying to halt the Germans in the days before his own formation arrived on the Somme. He was more forgiving in *Australian Victories*.

While under Monash's command, the morale of the 3rd Division was at its highest before Messines and before the move south. No longer were the other divisions able to boast at the expense of the 3rd that 'they had been on the Somme'. Its performance before Amiens removed their last traces of ill-feeling. For the first time since arriving on the Western Front, Monash's men were largely free of the mud and confinement of trench warfare. There were no shell holes or craters, for the battlefield 'consisted of green fields, wheat crops ... sheep and cattle browsed unconcernedly before our trenches.' On the other side of no man's land, 1500 yards away, a series of mainly unconnected rifle pits formed the German position. Complying with Congreve's order, Monash told McNicoll and Cannan to be prepared to advance their line as far as possible on 27 March; with the cavalry screen in front of

CHAPTER 8

them, it seemed at least that the distance to the German line could be taken. When the cavalry was transferred to the southern bank of the Somme after the Germans crossed that evening, Monash postponed the operation until the morrow. The absence of detailed records complicates an assessment of his planning and conduct of what turned out to be a costly attack.

When Monash saw him early on the morning of 28 March, Cannan understood that 'the advance was intended rather as a demonstration', mainly through patrol action, to show the Germans that they could progress no further in this sector. After Monash visited McNicoll, the plan finally arranged, at about 10.30 am, was for the establishment that night of an outpost line on the spurs overlooking Treux on the Ancre and Sailly-Laurette on the Somme.[63] Shortly before noon, however, Monash was informed of Foch's anxiety 'in view of his future plans, that we should get as far in the direction of Bray as we can.' Bean, who saw Monash that day, ascertained that the Generalissimo wished to concentrate south of the Somme 'within the next few days' to restore the situation there; in the meantime, Monash was to take the hill above Morlancourt 'at once' because it overlooked his detraining point. About the same time, Congreve ordered Monash to cooperate with an immediate attack south of the river by sending patrols to occupy Sailly-Laurette. Monash responded to this flood of direction by ordering at noon an advance in two stages, each of 1000 yards, to a line well beyond that already proposed for the night operation.

According to Bean, Monash left the planning to Cannan and McNicoll, and no arrangements were made for coordination between them. Hence 'The attack ... took on an entirely different character in the two brigade sectors.' McNicoll's was the more exposed assault. Soon after it began at 5.43 pm, more than one hour late, it was stopped by heavy machine-gun and artillery fire, 500 yards from its first objective. Bean compared the advance to the 2nd Brigade's attack at Krithia, on Gallipoli, in 1915. Both were made in daylight over long distances and ground completely devoid of cover. As one of the supporting artillery brigades was under strength and the other at the limit of its range, the barrage was weak. On the Somme flank, Cannan did not receive the order for the combined operation until 3.30 pm, whereupon he asked Monash whether he could adhere to the plan to seize the Sailly-Laurette area by vigorous patrol action. Monash refused. As it was too late for Cannan to alter his first phase, patrols advancing one hour after the 10th Brigade's attack reached the spur immediately west of the village and connected with McNicoll's right. For the second phase, Cannan ordered a formal assault. In drizzle that made movement on the steep slopes difficult, the 44th Battalion was ambushed 300 yards from Sailly-Laurette. Cannan's request to renew the attack at 3.05 am on 29 March was dismissed by Monash, who had ordered his artillery forward to shell the German positions during the day. On 29–30 March the 3rd Division's line was straightened on the forward slopes of the Sailly-le-Sec-Treux spurs. At a cost of 300 casualties the first objective only had been secured. The 4th Division's concurrent destruction of a heavy German assault at Dernancourt on the Ancre was poor solace.

Lewis gunners from the 3rd Division in a reserve position that commands the Somme near Sailly-le-Sec on 29 March. Bloody fighting between the 3rd Division and the Germans advancing in the Somme-Ancre triangle occurred on 28 and 30 March on the hills to the left (AWM E04661).

Bean's criticism of Monash's attack was warranted. The original scheme was altered by conflicting requirements: the operation was enlarged, yet zero hour was brought forward, reducing the time available for preparation. These factors compelled Monash to delegate

CHAPTER 8

the planning of the attack to Cannan and McNicoll to a much greater extent than usual, resulting in the employment of tactics by each that were incompatible. The excuse that Cannan received no warning until 3.30 pm, and therefore misunderstood the intention, increases Monash's culpability rather than absolving him. He had visited his commanders during the morning before the orders from Foch and Congreve were received. Had he done so in the afternoon, Cannan would have been left in no doubt that a formal attack was intended. But Cannan grasped the tactical essentials of this operation when Monash did not. The only sensible method of advancing in daylight with little artillery support was by using strong patrols as he had suggested. Yet Monash ordered Cannan to conform with McNicoll, who used formal methods even though, having been badly wounded at Krithia, he probably knew what the outcome would be. For these reasons the argument that commanders were inexperienced in open warfare was as invalid as the plea that communications were poor. Monash did act promptly to revise his plan when the demands of Foch and Congreve were forced upon him. But thereafter his action – or inaction – was atypical. It was almost a re-enactment of the attack on Hill 971 on 8 August 1915. Tiredness may have been the cause then, though this time Monash claimed to be rested. Nonetheless, the same strictures apply.

On 30 March the circumstances were reversed, the Germans attempting a long daylight advance with little artillery support against the 11th Brigade as part of a wider offensive south of the Somme. The assault began half a mile from Cannan's outpost positions and they exacted revenge for the costly setback two days earlier. As Monash explained to Birdwood, the 11th 'swept [the] lines, wiping them out one after the other … The ground in front of us is literally covered with enemy dead.' With the exception of its 9th Brigade, this was the 3rd Division's last major engagement of the defensive battle. From 5 to 30 April the situation was quiet. Other than vigorous patrolling, offensive action was forbidden on Monash's front, where all efforts were directed towards improving the defences and minimising casualties. Heavy attacks were launched either side of the 3rd Division at Dernancourt on 5 April, which were again defeated by the 4th Division, and the previous day, at Villers-Bretonneux. Ordered to Villers-Bretonneux by GHQ on 29 March, Rosenthal's brigade 'covered itself with glory' by counter-attacking to secure the town as the Germans reached its outskirts. The 660 casualties incurred led to the disbandment of the 36th Battalion to bring its sister units up to strength after the 9th Brigade returned to the 3rd Division on 21 April. The 12th and 13th brigades, which had borne the brunt of the fighting at Dernancourt and in the Second Battle of Villers-Bretonneux on 24 April, were similarly affected. It was the harbinger of a problem that would involve Monash in serious controversy later in 1918.

April also marked the start of 'peaceful penetration', that process, favoured by the fluid conditions and the German policy of holding the line with inferior 'trench divisions', whereby patrols seized prisoners and cut off posts. The 3rd Division maintained the most constant stream of prisoners on the Australian front, striving to capture them on three days out of every five. It had also extended its line north of the Ancre, making easier coordinated action either side of the river. At the end of April, Monash 'resolved to embark upon a series of minor actions, designed not merely to capture prisoners and machine-guns, but also to hold onto the ground gained.' On the night of 30 April the 10th Brigade advanced its line 400 yards on a frontage of 800 yards, followed by the 9th penetrating 600 yards in the right brigade sector on 4 May and another 1500 yards two days later.

This was the prelude to a formal attack on 7–8 May to advance the line south of the Bray–Corbie road on the spur above Morlancourt, 1000 yards further east, which had formed part of the second objective on 28 March. It was partially successful, Rosenthal's tardy issue of orders contributing to the capture by the Germans of forty-five men from the 9th Brigade. Monash had great difficulty in persuading Hobbs, who objected to the attack because of the short time available, to swing forward the 5th Division's left to conform with Rosenthal: 'Much confusion and worry', wrote Monash who was 'very anxious during this attack'. Next day he rebuked Rosenthal and complained to White about Hobbs, probably not knowing that White agreed with

CHAPTER 8

Hobbs. Birdwood, however, had favoured the attack. On 11 May Monash handed over the sector to Smyth, and the 3rd Division moved into corps reserve. At 11.00 am on 31 May he assumed command of the Australian Corps.

A streamlined man. Monash in May 1918, a few days before taking over the Australian Corps. The portly figure he cut in the photograph in Chapter 3 is no more (AWM E02350).

The change had been heralded by Birdwood's promotion to general in October 1917, making almost certain his appointment to army command. On 13 May 1918 Haig informed him that he was to take charge of the reconstituted Fifth Army, following Gough's dismissal for the setbacks in March. Birdwood was reluctant to relinquish command of the Australian Corps, but Haig pointed out that he would thus block the appointment of an Australian officer. He felt, nevertheless, that Birdwood should retain the administrative command of the AIF, and it was this arrangement that Birdwood recommended to Pearce in nominating Monash to command the corps. Birdwood considered others. McCay had coolly asked him to give up the corps at the start of 1918 and then requested command of the 3rd Division when he refused. Birdwood said later: 'I told him I didn't want the 3rd Division ruined like he had ruined the 5th!' Hobbs could command most corps but, in Birdwood's opinion, lacked the qualities needed for the Australian Corps. This left White. Monash claimed subsequently: 'He has never been tested as a commander. As an interpreter of another man's policy he has been very brilliant indeed.' This was unfair, for White had commanded the corps during Birdwood's absences. Bean remarked that if the question had arisen a year earlier, Birdwood 'would certainly have recommended White.' He urged Haig to appoint White as the BEF's chief of staff when Kiggell was relieved at the end of 1917. But Monash had proved himself as a divisional commander and received fulsome praise for his efforts before Amiens. Congreve called him the best divisional commander he had met on the Western Front. In what was a most difficult choice, Birdwood selected Monash, taking White with him to Fifth Army as its chief of staff.

Birdwood was also fully aware of Haig's great faith in Monash. But the C-in-C also knew that White could command the corps, for his stature had increased since their first meeting at Pozières. Ironically, White's integrity worked against him. When Currie assumed command of the Canadian Corps in July 1917, Haig told White he should be commanding 1st ANZAC and was peeved by White's reply: 'God forbid! General Birdwood has a position among Australians which is far too valuable to lose.' In view of Haig's dislike of Birdwood, 'From that moment forward, Monash was Haig's man.' The C-in-C's belief hardened with the consistently favourable impression Monash made on him. When the question of Birdwood's successor arose, White's conduct was exemplary. As Monash was his senior, he could not see how Monash could be passed over without injustice. Hence he did nothing to advance his own cause, much to the chagrin of Bean and the other correspondents:

> ... it seemed that a tragic mistake was being made ... we had long believed White to be Australia's greatest soldier. We believed that Monash was by character and experience much better fitted for the administrative than for the fighting command; and that the great moral courage and singlemindedness of White, as well as his

CHAPTER 8

military knowledge, would give a much sounder basis for leadership in the field.

Bean's attitude was not moulded merely by his opinion of the two men's respective abilities. It was also shaped by his ambivalence towards Monash and his fervent belief that Monash could not stand comparison with White as a man. Aware of Haig's hint to Murdoch in September 1917 that Monash might be advanced to corps command, Bean pressed White's claims at an interview with the C-in-C the following month and wrote shortly after:

... Monash for an Australian C-in-C we cannot have. He is not the man ... The purity and absence of jealousy or political intrigue in Birdwood's administration is worth anything. There is no 'eye wash' and bluff and humbug and insincerity in it; and there is in Monash's. Besides, we do not want Australia represented by men mainly because of their ability, natural and inborn in Jews, to push themselves.

Bean and the war artist, Will Dyson, left for London on 18 May to discuss with Murdoch their view that Monash should be appointed GOC AIF because Birdwood, as commander of Fifth Army, could not discharge adequately the administration of a corps that might remain outside his formation. White would then gain the corps command. Murdoch, who had been intriguing for Birdwood's replacement by White since August 1917, readily agreed with them. Claiming that his representations were made on behalf of the AIF, particularly its generals, he cabled Hughes, then en route to the Imperial War Conference in London, to make the command changes 'strictly and expressly' temporary until his arrival. On 29 May Colonel Dodds 'positively assured' Pearce in Melbourne that the views of Bean and Murdoch did not accord with those of the senior officers in France he had consulted, and were 'entirely opposed to the feeling of the whole AIF who stoutly oppose control ... of personnel from London by officers not serving in the field.' But the damage was done, for Hughes had already acceded to Murdoch's request. Geoffrey Serle rightly calls it 'perhaps the outstanding case of sheer irresponsibility by pressmen in Australian history.'

MONASH

For the next two months Monash commanded the Australian Corps in the knowledge that outside forces were trying hard to displace him. Ironically, Monash had not worked 'underground' to secure his appointment, although he heard many rumours from December 1917 onwards that he was to receive the command.[64] His delight was manifest: 'To be the first native born Australian Corps Commander is something to have lived for, and will not be forgotten in Australian history.'[65] Among his replies to many congratulatory messages, none was more revealing than the one to his old divisional commander, Cox. The corps was at its peak, its prestige and morale higher than ever: 'It is indeed fortunate for me that I should have been called upon to take over this command at such a juncture.' Glasgow replaced Walker in the 1st Division, Rosenthal succeeded Smyth in the 2nd, and Monash handed over the 3rd to Gellibrand. Sinclair-MacLagan and Hobbs remained in command of the 4th and 5th divisions respectively. The Australian Corps had now been truly 'Australianised'.

Monash's claim to the corps rested on the success he had achieved as a divisional commander under conditions as varied as the intricately prepared Messines attack and the open warfare before Amiens, which he personally regarded as the most interesting phase of the conflict. Jackson recalled that he did 'a lot of work personally'. According to Gellibrand, Monash regarded his GSO1 as his G Clerk, and advised him to draft his own orders on taking charge of the 3rd Division. It is true that Monash supervised his subordinates very closely, but his method, *at divisional level*, certainly cannot be criticised on the grounds that it was unsuccessful. Indeed, Monash's attention to every detail ensured his familiarity with the plan as a whole, an essential precondition if he was to visualise the development of the battle in his own mind. He was also willing to discuss a plan, when, Jackson remembered, he would sometimes reply to an objection that had been raised: 'Oh! I had not thought of that; no we won't do it.' American officers attached to the 3rd Division remembered most his ability 'to say much in a few words.'

Monash never lost the confidence of his subordinates. Jackson found him a delightful man with whom to work. The comforting

CHAPTER 8

hand laid on Lieutenant George Browne's shoulder after his unit had been annihilated before Passchendaele was as reassuring as the kind word to RSM Goldstein in Monash Valley. The men's welfare remained paramount. Monash complained to Dodds when his efforts to obtain a second issue of overalls for regimental cooks, 'invariably the dirtiest men in the unit', were rebuffed by AIF Headquarters on the grounds that he was not authorised to spend his division's regimental funds on the clothing. When the Deputy Adjutant and Quartermaster General (DA&QMG), Brigadier General Robert Carruthers, issued a strongly worded order on looting, requiring officers to make a list of the civilian property they possessed, Monash objected because 'This is tantamount to saying that every officer in the AIF is a potential thief.' Rather than threaten disciplinary action, he appealed in his division to 'the feelings of humanity and sympathy of Australian troops towards the unhappy French populace.' In the mess he encouraged humour, delighting in funny stories, particularly Jewish ones. Perhaps the highest compliment to Monash as a divisional commander was

Monash (seated) with senior officers of the Australian Corps staff at Bertangles. Standing (left to right) are Brigadier Generals Foott (Chief Engineer), Carruthers (DA&QMG), Blamey (BGGS), Fraser (Brigadier General, Heavy Artillery), and Coxen (Brigadier General, Royal Artillery) (AWM E02750).

contained in a letter from Jackson shortly after he arrived in the 29th Division:

Coming here is like coming back many, many years. Reminds me of 1897 when I joined. The Rouse is sounded, one is saluted on all sides, men are regarded as machines or gun fodder ... It is a good Division, certainly a very good Division but I wish you were commanding it. The lack of attention to detail is very apparent, e.g. no fuel for the men, 4 blankets to 3 men instead of two each and a thousand and one little things that we think essential are omitted ... They are not within months of our modern ideas ... The British Army is second to none. Magnificent heroism. Magnificent discipline in these old regular battalions but the selfish inhuman cranks on the one hand and the poor doddering old men on the other who command it are calculated to bitch any show.

Chapter 9
The Best Man to Command the Corps

The gulf between corps and division was much greater than between division and brigade. Besides the five infantry divisions, the Australian Corps boasted a fixed allotment of 50 000 corps troops, comprising the 13th Australian Light Horse Regiment, the two Australian tunnelling companies, heavy and siege artillery, heavy trench mortar, signal and transport units, and a number of administrative services, which included motor ambulance convoys and twenty labour companies. The 3rd Squadron, AFC, was permanently attached for reconnaissance, contact patrolling and artillery observation. Monash allocated these units according to the operational requirements of the division or divisions they were to support. Further assistance was provided when necessary by formations drawn from army troops, among them the 5th Tank Brigade, which supported the Australian Corps in each of its set-piece battles. With a strength of 166 000 it was 'much the largest and most important' of the twenty corps in the BEF:

> My command is more than two and a half times the size of the British Army under the Duke of Wellington, or of the French Army under Napoleon Bonaparte, at the battle of Waterloo. Moreover I have in the Army Corps an artillery which is more than six times as numerous and more than a hundred times as powerful as that commanded by the Duke of Wellington.

The heavy artillery, commanded by Brigadier General Lyons Fraser, was entirely British. Carruthers, another British officer, remained as DA&QMG, although allowing an Australian, Lieutenant Colonel

George Somerville, to play a leading role in administration. Brigadier General Walter Coxen was 'one of the most able of our Australian artillery officers', but Monash feared that the command of the Australian Corps artillery might be 'just a little too big for him. He is a dour, sour, unsympathetic creature, and difficult to get on with …' He did not doubt the capacity of Blamey, a Quetta Staff College graduate who 'worked sixteen hours a day, sometimes longer, with only an occasional night off', as his chief of staff.[66] At the time of his appointment, Blamey was GSO1 of the 1st Division, having served continuously on the staff except for brief – and less than successful – periods in command of the 2nd Battalion and the 1st Brigade. Serle remarks that the extent of his contribution to Monash's success as a corps commander can never be satisfactorily determined. There is no doubt that Monash sought the advice and views of Blamey and others during the preparation of an operational plan and also used them as a sounding board for his own ideas, as he had done with Jackson in the 3rd Division. But the coming campaign would show that Monash often exercised the centralised control that had so typified his command at divisional level. Nevertheless, his eloquent post-war tribute to Blamey is reminiscent of the relationship between Plumer and Harington:

> He served me with an exemplary loyalty … Our temperaments adapted themselves to each other in a manner which was ideal. He had an extra ordinary faculty of self-effacement, posing always and conscientiously as the instrument to give effect to my policies and decisions.

The same could have been said of McGlinn or Jackson. In each of his wartime commands, Monash benefited from the services of a capable chief staff officer with whom he enjoyed amicable personal relations. Two more Australians, Brigadier General Cecil Foott and Colonel George Barber, filled the remaining principal staff appointments as Chief Engineer and Deputy Director of Medical Services.

CHAPTER 9

General Sir Henry Rawlinson. He commanded Fourth Army, of which the Australian Corps, under Monash, was the backbone during the advance in the second half of 1918. Rawlinson had a reputation for duplicity and exemplified the erratic course of the British 'learning curve'. He worked well with Monash, but disliked him as a Jew (AWM H12220).

General Sir Henry Rawlinson and Major General Archibald Montgomery were the commander and chief of staff respectively of Fourth Army, to which the Australian Corps belonged. Monash saw them almost daily, but their anti-Semitism was well concealed from him. When Rawlinson thought that the Secretary of State for India, Sir Edwin Montagu, might oppose his appointment as C-in-C India in 1920, he compared Montagu to Monash in two acrid letters to Montgomery:

> I read him as a clever, slippery, creepy crawley jew who will always back you if he thinks you are winning and have no scruples about sticking you in the back if he thinks you look like a loser ...
>
> He is clever and intelligent but his knees knock together when trouble is about. Edwin is not unlike Monash!! We know how to manage his sort.

It is one of the many ironies of the war that after his soggy performance on the Somme in 1916, Rawlinson's reputation was salvaged largely by the efforts of Monash and the Australian Corps two years later.

Monash's remarks at his first conference with divisional commanders on 6 June 1918 were based on notes that he could well have used as commander of the North Melbourne Battery or the 13th Infantry Brigade. He complained that the present training of staff officers encouraged the 'watertight compartments' he had deplored since his days in the Intelligence Corps. Henceforth their instruction must include administrative, regimental, intelligence and operational aspects, so that the tendency towards specialisation might be avoided. Each of those present offered his opinion, as well as raising for discussion other matters of concern. This interchange helped Monash to overcome a difficulty, the existence of which he had recognised at once: 'The other Divisional Commanders had hitherto been my colleagues and I was now called upon to consider their personalities and temperaments as my subordinates.' They were doing the same to him as their new commander; some had misgivings about him. The fortnightly conferences helped bring them closer together. Just as important, they were a means for the creation of 'a unity of thought and policy and a unity of tactical method throughout the whole Corps.' Through this doctrine, which he had espoused at every level of command, Monash realised the tremendous potential inherent in the grouping of all the Australian divisions under one commander.

Monash visited units from every arm and service to inculcate another familiar principle, the importance of 'high ideals, high aims and a high standard of conduct.' His addresses to them were identical, beginning with an appeal to the men's pride to uphold their unit's prestige and concluding with 'Standards and soldierly behaviour; public spirit; every man pulling his weight.' Separate remarks were directed to officers, particularly junior officers, who were 'to create and foster ... a sense of responsibility to themselves, their commanders, their comrades, their men, their country and their cause.' These visits

CHAPTER 9

assisted the transition of command. Birdwood's greatest asset had been his personality, which he impressed on the men by daily contact with them both in the trenches and at rest. Every man felt that Birdwood knew him personally. While the same could never be said of Monash, his frequent tours and inspections in the first few weeks after 31 May made him a living person who could be identified as the corps commander, rather than a name remote at some distant headquarters from which he rarely ventured.

Monash's approach reflected his carefully reasoned employment of psychology, unlike Birdwood, whose response to most command matters was, according to White, purely instinctive. When a shortage of colour patches arose because British factories were temporarily engaged in the production of more needed items, Monash complained to Dodds that the patch was a powerful factor in *esprit de corps* and the pride of the soldier in his unit, which only those who commanded Australians could appreciate. He was quite prepared to arrange for their manufacture independently of the War Office. Monash had been similarly forthright when the problem arose while he commanded the 3rd Division. His cultivation of optimism continued. He determined to feed the troops on victory by 'as far as it is humanly possible, never undertak[ing] a battle operation without an absolute guarantee of success.' The confidence developed by the men in themselves and their leaders and the contempt in which they held their opponents would compensate for their numerical inferiority and fatigue. Monash knew that the psychology of the Australian soldier was unique:

> The prestige of Australian Arms has always been my chief Battle Cry and, in order to help to achieve it, I have been at pains to see that Australian troops have received an adequate recognition of their splendid work. I have put it that they would enter upon Battle as they would enter upon a sport but no man will go on playing any game unless he can see his score placarded on the scoring board.

Monash also played to what Bean called the 'incorrigibly civilian' nature of the Australian soldier, which he knew was unique as well:

'In him there was a curious blend of a capacity for independent judgement with a readiness to submit to self-effacement in common cause', wrote Monash. 'He had the political sense highly developed, and was always a keen critic of the way in which his battalion or battery was run ... He was always mentally alert to adopt new ideas and often to invent them.' Monash's understanding of the men he led was very evident on the vexed subject of discipline. The views he had formed as commander of the 4th Brigade and the 3rd Division were crystallised in his pungent rejoinder to constant British harping on the AIF's unruliness at the expense of its performance:

> Discipline does not mean lip service, nor obsequious homage to superiors, nor servile observance of forms and customs ... In the Australian Forces no strong insistence was ever made upon the mere outward forms of discipline. The soldier was taught that personal cleanliness was necessary to ensure his health and well-being, that a soldierly bearing meant a moral and physical uplift which would help him to rise superior to his squalid environment, that punctuality meant an economy of effort, that unquestioning obedience was the only road to successful collective action. He acquired these qualities because his intelligence taught him that the reasons given him were true ones. The Australian Army is proof that individualism is the best and not the worst foundation upon which to build collective discipline.

It has to be said, though, that Monash exaggerated several claims about his methods on assuming command. Calculated to cast Birdwood in a poor light, they suggested disapproval of him on Monash's part. It was unjust for Monash to assert that he had to cultivate an 'implacable and unremitting' offensive spirit so that no opportunity would be lost of inflicting casualties on the Germans irrespective of the tiredness of his own troops. The enthusiasm in the 3rd Division on its arrival on the Somme typified the aggressive spirit that animated every Australian formation and the progressively greater examples of 'peaceful penetration' in the last months of Birdwood's command showed that it needed no cultivation by higher authority. Monash criticised Birdwood's leadership as 'hesitating and unenterprising':

> The previous operations of Australian troops were largely confined to operations definitely ordered by higher authority and there was very little initiative from the Corps authorities in propounding definite offensive plans. The result has been a very large casualty toll with very little to show for it.

This charge showed Monash at his worst. Whatever Birdwood's intellectual limitations, he was denied the opportunities afforded Monash. At no time were all five divisions grouped for operations under his command. Furthermore, neither he nor White could afford to countenance independent operations beyond raids in 1916 and 1917 in view of the terrible losses suffered by both Anzac corps in the major offensives of those years. They laboured under the same restrictions at corps level as Monash had at divisional, and only once, at Passchendaele, was he faced by difficulties of the degree that had confronted them regularly at Pozières, Mouquet Farm and Bullecourt. And as Prior and Wilson have noted, by the time Monash took charge of the Australian Corps, the BEF had grown in complexity and expertise to the point where the role of Haig and the army commanders had diminished and become less relevant. Proficiency in the technical aspects of operations had become essential and was widespread. Battles such as the Somme and Third Ypres had bred commanders at battalion, brigade, divisional and, to some extent, corps level, who were attuned to the shifting exigencies of the battlefield. Having served merely as a 'postbox' between army and division in 1914, the corps was now 'the highest level of command in the BEF concerned with the detail of operations.' Corps commanders, and sometimes divisional commanders, were central to their planning and execution. The upshot in the second half of 1918 was that the high command needed only to apply a light touch to the tiller, which potentially gave Monash freer rein than his predecessor had. Monash had proven himself technically proficient and wise to the battlefield as a divisional commander, as Rawlinson, his army commander would have been aware. To enjoy free rein, he would have to win Rawlinson's confidence as a corps commander.

Monash at Bertangles with his two ADCs, Captains Aubrey Moss (left) and Paul Simonson (right). Both were his nephews. Major Walter Berry, Camp Commandant at the headquarters, stands between them (AWM E03186).

Although contained, the stroke against the French on the Aisne on 27 May 1918 demonstrated that German offensive capacity was still considerable. As Foch and Haig realised, Ludendorff's aim was to divert Allied reserves to the French front prior to launching a final decisive blow against the BEF in Flanders. GHQ ordered frequent raids to identify units holding each sector. On 3 June, therefore, Monash sought Rawlinson's approval for an attack by the 2nd Division on that part of the Morlancourt spur overlooking Sailly-Laurette. Although Birdwood had authorised the scheme before his departure, its history began even earlier. The objective was the feature that Cannan's brigade had failed to take on 28 March and against which Rosenthal's was only partially successful on 7/8 May. Its capture would deny observation to the Germans and secure a

CHAPTER 9

better position for any future advance beyond Morlancourt. But one of the most important aims was defensive: to increase the depth of the sector held by the Australian Corps on the northern side of the Somme. Monash was acutely aware of the need to avoid casualties, but 'I am of the opinion that, in view of a certain amount of mixing up of enemy units and an exhaustion of his troops on this front, such an operation is likely to succeed with comparatively small loss to us.'

An important factor, then, was Monash's estimate, based on the results of 'peaceful penetration' in April and May, of the morale and state of the Germans opposite. The arrangements at corps level bore his stamp. The 3rd Division, on the 2nd's northern flank, was to fire a creeping barrage on its own front as a diversion. Monash also asked Lieutenant General Sir Richard Butler, formerly Haig's deputy chief of staff and now commanding III Corps further north, to do the same. Launched at dusk on 10 June, the attack was a complete success, and it was remarked that the assaulting battalions could easily have reached and captured the German gun line.

On 14 June Rawlinson discussed with Monash an attack expected on the Somme next day. It did not eventuate, prompting Rawlinson to describe the front as 'abnormally quiet'. Then two prisoners hinted at an attack on Villers-Bretonneux at the end of June. On 3 July GHQ asserted that the Germans had 'now prepared practically the whole front opposite the British Army for offensive operations ... at short notice.' Hence British commanders thought in terms of the defensive throughout June, notwithstanding GHQ's order of the 8th, issued at Foch's request, that local attacks would be required to prevent reinforcement of the imminent offensive against the French on the Matz River. As explained by Monash to his divisional commanders on 10 June, the form of the operations envisaged was either substantial raids or 'captures of territories or localities of tactical value to the enemy ... [to] injure his defensive organisation.' They were to draft proposals for at least one and preferably two of each type on their respective fronts. Clearly, these attacks could in no way be construed as heralding a major counter-offensive, but this was precisely the claim Monash would make for the operation launched from his sector.

MONASH

The key to wider action on the Australian front was the spur that left the great Santerre plateau north-east of Villers-Bretonneux and extended northwards to the Somme opposite Sailly-Laurette. Lying on the western side of the spur near its junction with the plateau were Vaire and Hamel woods, and on the eastern side Accroche and Gressaire woods. Overlooked by the hulking Wolfsberg, which crowned the spur, the village of Hamel nestled in the low ground midway between Hamel Wood and the river. After following the next spur to the west through Hill 104, the highest point of the Santerre, Sinclair-MacLagan's line reached the Somme at Bouzencourt. On 11 June he considered with Gellibrand the capture of Vaire Wood by the 4th Division, while the 3rd Division, holding the sector south of Sinclair-MacLagan's, conformed by advancing its left along the plateau.[67] Gellibrand was enthusiastic, but his colleague concluded that he would have too few men to consolidate the position gained, even though it represented only a small portion of the Hamel Spur.

Similar objections had been raised two months previously, when Rawlinson proposed the seizure of Hamel by the 5th Division as a feint to divert attention from a projected Anglo-French offensive south of Villers-Bretonneux. Monash had also urged it to protect the 3rd Division's right flank on the far side of the river. Fearing heavy casualties, Birdwood was lukewarm, but White's objections were forcible and Rawlinson eventually agreed with them. When Rawlinson pointed out that the French were making their part in the offensive conditional on the Hamel feint, White, in an outstanding example of moral courage retorted: 'If we have to carry out a perfectly valueless attack at the cost of a division which it is earnestly desirable not to waste – there seems to me something very wrong in our scheme of arrangements.'

By mid-June the situation had changed, if the objectives had not. As a result of his assaults on Morlancourt and Sailly-Laurette, Rosenthal's line north of the Somme was so far ahead of Sinclair-MacLagan's on the southern side that guns near Accroche Wood were engaging his right flank in enfilade and even in rear. So Rosenthal rejected a further advance along the Bray–Corbie road, the only

CHAPTER 9

option on his front for the offensive action that Monash had asked his divisional commanders to undertake. On the southern bank more room was needed for the defence of Villers-Bretonneux, the gateway to Amiens. Its lynch-pin was the 4th Australian Division's line on the Hill 104 spur. But no advance was possible on the southern side as long as the Hamel Spur remained in German hands. Monash conceded that its seizure was the most useful operation that could be mounted on the Australian Corps front. He knew that the opposing German divisions were mediocre. He also knew that their positions, though not well fortified in places, were on ground that favoured the defence.

Though the front lines, except on the Somme flats, were nowhere more than 400 yards apart, part of the German line ran below the brow of the Hill 104 spur to Vaire Wood and was hidden from the 4th Division's line. Pear Trench redoubt in the centre enfiladed attacks towards the Somme to its right or past Kidney Trench redoubt on its left. Vaire Wood, and conjoined Hamel Wood, were fortified. Once through these locations, the Australians faced an advance of up to 2000 yards to the Wolfsberg, from which German artillery observers, enjoying superb views, could drench them with highly accurate fire. Hamel would have to be taken on the way, which might entail costly village fighting. The line on the Santerre south of Vaire Wood comprised mainly rifle pits, but the area was devoid of cover and ironing-board flat. Australian and French attempts to take Monument and Hangard woods, on similar ground nearby had been roughly handled. Monash concluded that the likely cost of the attack, which he estimated would require at least six battalions as well as several days to redeploy the artillery, outweighed the gains. Making that prospect even grimmer, the Australian Corps was more than 8000 men under strength. Agreeing with Sinclair-MacLagan, he told Rawlinson on 13 June, 'I do not recommend that this operation be carried out at present.'

Meanwhile, the re-equipment with Mark V tanks of the 5th Tank Brigade, the armoured formation supporting Fourth Army, was completed. At 4.6 mph, the Mark V was 1 mph faster across country than the Mark IVs used at Cambrai and easier to drive, enabling it to manoeuvre and cover more ground ahead of the infantry. It was also more reliable. The Tank Corps commander, Major General Hugh Elles, and his subordinates wasted no opportunity to convince commanders of other arms that the Mark V 'would so increase the capacity of infantry and artillery that decisive defeat might be inflicted on the Germans before winter.' Among those to whom he demonstrated the new tank were Monash and Blamey.

The Hamel battlefield on the day of the attack. On the left in the middle distance are the chalk parapets of the German line, which rises towards Pear Trench. On the skyline (from the right) are Vaire, Hamel and Accroche woods. Note the two parachutes for air-dropped ammunition (AWM E03840).

It may never be known whether Rawlinson convinced Monash or vice versa that an attack on the Hamel Spur was possible immediately if tanks were employed. Monash claimed after his visit to Elles that he 'resolved to propose [the operation] conditional upon being supplied with the assistance of tanks, a small increase of my artillery and an addition to my air resources', and then mentioned the scheme verbally to Rawlinson. Conversely, Rawlinson wrote on 18 June: 'I went round the Australian Corps today, and proposed to Monash and MacLagan an attack with two battalions of tanks

CHAPTER 9

against Hamel Village and spur to improve our position north of Villers Bretonneux.' Lieutenant Colonel Fuller apparently persuaded Rawlinson to allow Mark V tanks to play a major role. Bean says that both Rawlinson and Monash conceived the idea at the same time.

What is certain is that, once it was suggested, Monash's enthusiasm for the use of tanks was boundless. The terrain was ideally suited to their employment. The Hill 104 spur, across which Sinclair-MacLagan's line ran, blocked the German view of the area immediately in rear, protecting the approach march of both infantry and tanks. With its left resting on the Somme, the combined assault would attack on a frontage that increased gradually from 6000 to 7500 yards, crossing open fields of corn crops to reach the Wolfsberg.

After discussing the operation with him on 19 June, Brigadier General Anthony Courage, commanding the 5th Tank Brigade, sent Monash his plan next day. The attack would be launched by four companies of tanks arranged in three echelons. The Advanced Section of fifteen tanks was to move as quickly as possible to the rear of the German position to demoralise its occupants, cut off their retreat and prevent their reinforcement. This action would occur ahead and independently of the twenty-one machines in the Main Body Section, which were to lead the infantry onto their objectives. The nine tanks in the last echelon, the Mopping Up Section, would be used to replace losses and subdue any remaining opposition. To escape the German barrage, the infantry would form up well in front of the tanks and follow the Main Body Section as it passed through. Aircraft were to fly over the tanks and the German lines to drown the noise of their approach and assembly. No preliminary bombardment was needed as the wire would be crushed for the infantry by the Advanced Section.

Heavily influenced by the attack at Cambrai, Courage's scheme was the embodiment of the tactical doctrine of Fuller, who would eventually become the most famous of Tank Corps officers. Other arms had to conform to the tank's 'chief power', its mobility. There would be no creeping artillery barrage, because its linear shape and slow pace imposed unacceptable restrictions on the tanks. The infantry would have to increase its own 'power of manoeuvre' by skilfully using ground while remaining in close touch with the tanks 'so that they may at once make good any opportunity the Tanks create and free the Tanks to continue their advance and so keep the battle moving forward by creating a succession of opportunities for the Infantry in rear.' Monash's thoroughness and foresight were evident in the notes of his meeting with Courage. Harassing artillery and machine-gun fire were to be 'absolutely normal and stereotyped for three nights before zero.' Plans for defensive fire once the position was captured must be ready before the battle. Machine-gun positions for the defence of the newly seized line would also have to be predetermined so that gunners could move directly to them. After Courage's explanation of the methods employed at Cambrai, Monash noted: 'Consider question of using sledges for tanks to pull up engineering stores during last advance.' Nor did Monash alter Courage's concept of the attack as 'primarily a tank operation'. As Monash explained to Rawlinson on 21 June:

> The action will be designed on lines to permit of the Tanks effecting the capture of the ground, the role of the infantry following the tanks will be:
> (i) to assist in reducing strong points and localities
> (ii) to mop up
> (iii) to consolidate the ground captured.

The infantry would also attack in three echelons. An Assaulting Wave was to escort the Main Body Section and mop up strongpoints, assisted by a few tanks. The Supporting Wave, 200 yards in rear and twice as strong, would advance past either flank of the Assaulting Wave and accompany the rest of the Main Body tanks to the objective, known as the Blue Line, to begin its consolidation. The Reserve Wave could be committed if required. Monash had already adumbrated the artillery program: 'The idea would be to simulate defensive counterpreparation while at the same time accustoming the enemy as nearly as possible to the action that will take place at zero hour …' Flavoured smoke was to be fired each morning shortly before dawn. At Courage's suggestion, a 'jumping barrage'

CHAPTER 9

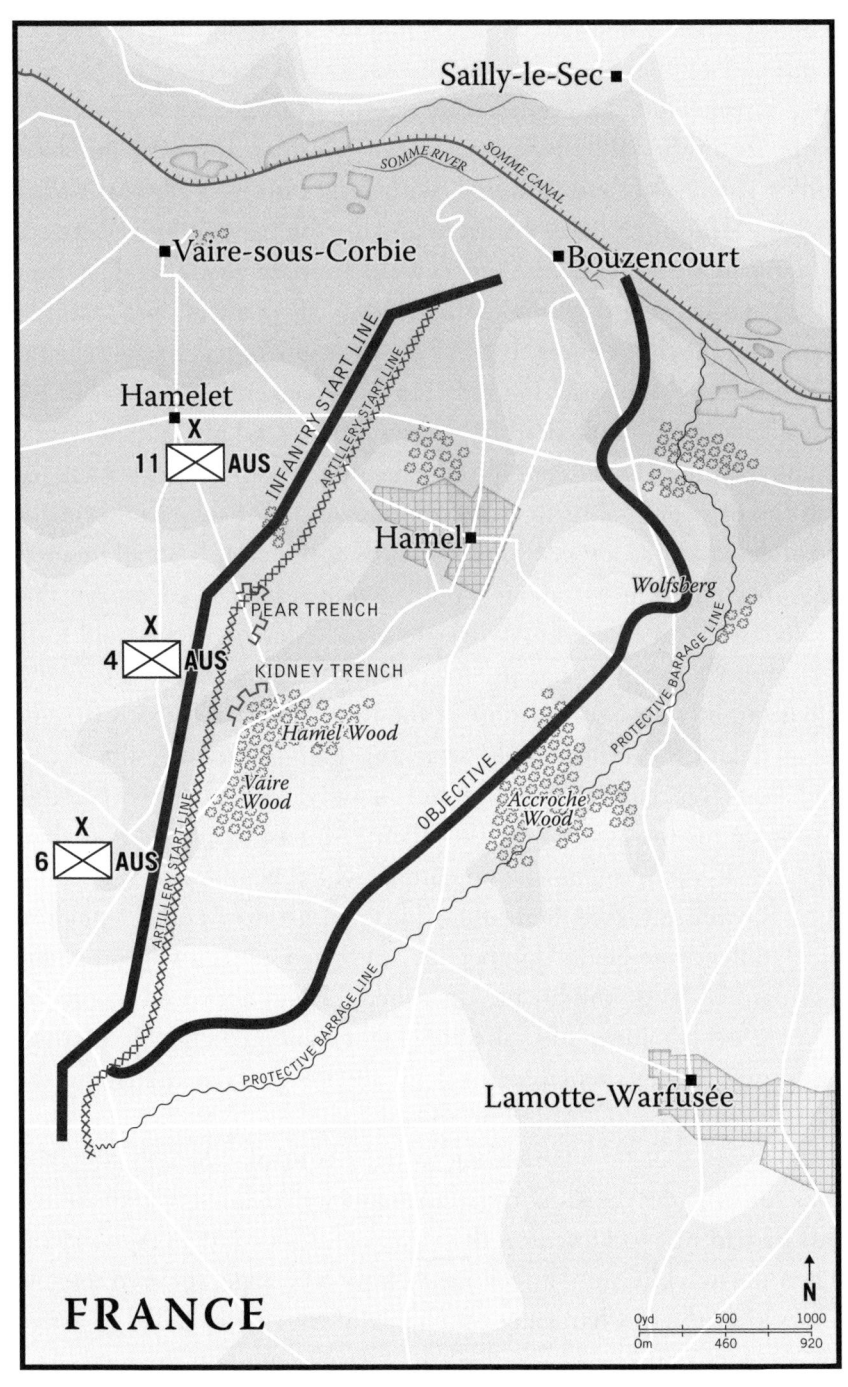

The attack on Hamel, 4 July 1918

would engage potentially troublesome positions ahead of the tanks. Courage's request for smoke on the flanks was increased by Monash to a screen along the entire corps front. But the emplacement of batteries on the Hill 104 spur to engage German anti-tank guns and tanks, if any were encountered, with direct fire was Monash's idea. Finally, 'Thorough liaison prior to and during the operation between all tank and infantry commanders would have to be a special feature.'

Monash's plan for the employment of infantry and artillery preserved the shock effect that was the basis of Courage's tank scheme. The objective was still limited, but the conventional step-by-step advance was eliminated from the method of taking it. Tanks and infantry were to reach the Blue Line as quickly as possible, leaving the capture of strongpoints to elements following. The use of tanks made possible what was, by previous standards, a ludicrously small infantry commitment. Ten battalions would assault, each on a frontage that Ludendorff had allotted to a division on 21 March. They would form a composite force so that the losses did not fall entirely on the 4th Division, in whose sector most of the Blue Line lay. The 4th Brigade from it had the central task, attacking Hamel Wood, Vaire Wood and Pear Trench, with the 2nd and 3rd divisions each contributing a brigade for the attack on either flank. Monash appointed Sinclair-MacLagan to command the operation, which would take place on 4 July. Rawlinson asked Haig for additional artillery and a squadron of Handley Page heavy bombers to attack woods and villages where German reserves might be quartered. Haig approved Monash's scheme on 25 June, but directed Lieutenant General Sir Herbert Lawrence, Kiggell's replacement as his chief of staff, to arrange for the participation of some American troops.

Showing that he was tending to tight control, Monash allocated sites for brigades' headquarters, normally a divisional responsibility. But he had not reckoned on the legacy of Bullecourt in April 1917, when the 4th Division, attacking without a barrage, suffered terrible losses after the mechanically unreliable Mark I tanks failed to arrive on one night and barely reached the German wire on the next. At a conference on 25 June, Sinclair-MacLagan and his brigadiers used

CHAPTER 9

Rosenthal's recent success north of the Somme, which was achieved by conventional methods, to defeat the views of the tank leaders. The most important of the minutes was the first: 'Decided to carry out operation under a creeping barrage.' Naturally averse to the diminution of the artillery's importance as suggested by the existing scheme, Coxen supported Sinclair-MacLagan as did Blamey, whose appreciation of both arguments concluded:

> The Artillery Barrage Method is the more certain. The Tank method would be more in the nature of an experiment ...
>
> In view of the fact that the objective is limited, that there is no difficulty as regards ammunition ... it is considered that the artillery barrage method is preferable.

Monash acquiesced. So did Rawlinson, who noted with slight concern on 26 June: 'Fixed up tanks and barrages with MacLagan. They must practise.' The number of tanks was increased to five companies – sixty tanks in all – and four supply tanks were also allotted. As the movement of the infantry close to the barrage rendered the Advanced Section of tanks redundant, they were to augment the Main Body. While the tasks of the three echelons of infantry remained the same as before, the nature of the operation had changed dramatically: '[It] ceases to be primarily a tank operation. It becomes an infantry operation in which the slight infantry power receives a considerable accretion by the addition of a large body of tanks.'

Messines, Menin Road, Polygon Wood and Broodseinde proved the efficacy of Sinclair-MacLagan's reasoning. But there were arguments at least as strong in favour of Monash's and Courage's plan. The Mark Vs were much more reliable than their predecessors – as Elles said: 'as superior to a Mark IV Tank as a 1915 motor car was superior to one of 1905' – and they would be advancing over hard ground, which presented no obstacle to them. Their shock action should offset the terrain advantages the Germans enjoyed, while the threat from anti-tank guns would be reduced greatly by smoke, by the 'jumping barrage' on likely emplacements and by direct fire batteries and aircraft waiting to engage the guns as soon as they appeared. The Germans were also weak numerically. Monash's Chief of Intelligence,

MONASH

Major Sydney Hunn, put their strength at 2790 with a further 2860 in reserve, both groups belonging to divisions of indifferent quality. Vaire Wood and Hamel Wood were strongly fortified, but elsewhere 'The trenches were shallow, silted and poorly co-ordinated for mobile defence. Wire was thin and badly placed.' For the only time in his career, Monash had been opposed by all of his subordinates, even though his arguments were no less powerful than theirs. Why did he yield? The explanation is psychological. Unless he did so, Sinclair-MacLagan and his commanders would have to execute a scheme in which neither they nor those they led had any confidence whatsoever. The optimism always emphasised by Monash, and now an exceptionally potent moral factor in view of his soldiers' ascendancy over the Germans, would be extinguished before the attack began as the spectre of Bullecourt was rekindled.

There was no more outstanding feature of the battle than Monash's wisdom in this matter. He insisted that the tanks must follow the barrage level with the infantry, despite the anxiety of the tank commanders, who claimed that shells falling even slightly short would hit their machines, which stood 8 feet 8 inches high. One tank would be hit in this way, showing that their concern was not groundless. A further tank objection was overruled when Monash directed that 'The infantry commander on the spot ... will give such orders to the Tank Section Commander as the situation demands.' All battalions spent one day at the tank training ground at Vaux-en-Amiénois, working with the tanks alongside which they would assault on 4 July. The tank crewmen took the infantry for joy rides and discussed every aspect of the operation with them. Battalion set-piece manoeuvres were repeatedly rehearsed, and trenches, strongpoints and wire entanglements constructed to show how easily the tank could crush them. As another means of developing confidence, Monash allowed brigades and battalions to plan the reduction of obstacles in their sectors. Before the 3rd Division's first major operation, at Messines, Monash had done the planning himself.

CHAPTER 9

A tank disabled by the loss of its left track during the mopping up of Hamel village. The Wolfsberg rises in the background (AWM E02864).

The artillery had to be greatly reinforced for its expanded role. Monash obtained another eleven field artillery brigades to augment the eighteen Australian ones, making a total of 326 guns or howitzers. The nine heavy artillery brigades already in the Australian Corps were joined by nine more, making 313 heavy guns available. Over 200 of them were to engage the German guns, whose locations were established by sound-ranging, flash-spotting and aerial photography, all of which had either been developed or refined in 1917. Starting 200 yards ahead of the infantry and tanks, the creeping barrage comprised three belts of fire 600 yards deep that lifted every three minutes. In order to provide the smokescreen across the entire attack frontage, one-tenth of the ammunition was smoke shell. At the end of the attack a protective barrage would continue for 38 minutes to cover the consolidation. Firepower as well as tanks were substituting for manpower. As Prior and Wilson observe, the Germans would have to 'survive in succession a bombardment from the heavy guns, then a field artillery barrage, and finally an assault delivered by tanks and infantry acting in concert.'

A combination of new and established techniques was employed in other areas. The perennial problem of prompt ammunition supply to the most advanced troops was addressed by parachute dropping from aircraft, Monash imitating the technique employed by the Germans on the Lys and the Aisne. Aerial photographs and maps were issued to every officer and NCO and notes on the enemy to every company. The use of a heavy artillery battery to fire a desultory barrage on the open expanse of the Santerre and the subsequent plotting of the shell holes was a novel way of providing the infantry with cover as they moved across it. Deception figured prominently. Diversionary operations would be launched by the 7th Brigade, extending the southern flank of the attack and, north of the Somme, by Elliott's 15th Brigade, which was to seize 1200 yards of trench overlooking the Ancre. From 26 June, 'flavoured smoke' formed part of the routine pre-dawn harassing bombardment, so that the Germans would not regard the smoke as unusual at zero hour, 3.10 am. The creeping barrage starting then would be fired along the fronts of the Australian Corps and III Corps on its left flank, while the First French Army on the right was to engage batteries in its sector. Secrecy was vital. Silent registration, made possible by enhanced survey techniques, allowed the guns to be ranged from a map rather than by firing ranging shots that betrayed their presence. Forward movement of ammunition and stores and the emplacing of guns were forbidden except by night. Next day, 'police' aircraft reported on camouflage and signs of unusual activity that might be visible to German pilots. From 27 June other aircraft flew 'noise patrols' over the German line from dusk to dawn to drown the noise of the tanks' assembly.

Because as little as possible was committed to paper in the interests of secrecy, conferences assumed a new importance. Attendances increased gradually as the development of the plan necessitated the involvement of commanders and staffs from other branches and services. Two hundred and fifty officers were present at the final meeting on 30 June, which lasted four and a half hours. Monash's agenda listed 133 separate items, from the arrangements for spare Lewis guns and water supply to the equipment of the assaulting troops and their relief after the battle. He explained to Rawlinson:

> The underlying principle of the conference was that everybody that mattered was present, and had to explain his plans and proposals;

CHAPTER 9

and that, where there was any conflict or doubt or difference of opinion, a final and unalterable decision was given, there and then, and no subsequent 'fiddling' with the plan was permitted.

Bean mentioned another result:

> The conference habit was spreading – each brigade and most battalions had similar meetings at which they worked through carefully drawn agenda in discussion with the tank, flying corps, artillery, machine gun and other officers who would be acting with them in the battle.

On 1 July, Haig called on Monash and was 'greatly impressed with his arrangements ... Monash is a most thorough and capable commander who thinks out every detail of any operation and leaves nothing to chance.' Hughes, who had finally arrived in England, decided to visit next day. Monash justifiably protested to Birdwood: 'the whole business is extremely awkward ... Mr Hughes has chosen a time which could hardly be more inconvenient.'

Much more serious was the decision of the C-in-C of the American Expeditionary Force, General John Pershing, regarding the use of his troops in the attack. Pershing's understandable aim was for the American Army to have its own sector, instead of being employed 'merely as a reserve to be sent here and there', or to strengthen depleted British and French formations. On 17 June, however, he agreed to allow two of the ten American divisions sent to the BEF for instruction, the 27th and 33rd, close to emergency defensive positions behind the Third Army and Fourth Army fronts respectively. The 65th Brigade from the 33rd Division was attached to the Australian Corps. Rawlinson hit on the idea of using troops from the 65th to swell the Australian battalions in the Hamel attack under the pretext of giving them some experience. Ten companies were eventually sent to Monash, but Pershing was not informed until 2 July. When Haig heard from Rawlinson that the American C-in-C did not want his partly trained troops to participate, he ordered their withdrawal, which occurred next morning in the case of all but the four companies originally allocated.

Prime Minister Hughes addresses the 4th Brigade before the Hamel attack. Birdwood, who accompanied Hughes on the visit, stands with his hands behind his back, while Sinclair-MacLagan (partially obscured) is on Birdwood's left (AWM E02651).

At 4.00 pm on 3 July, Monash learned with consternation from Rawlinson that these companies were to be withdrawn as well. His subsequent display of moral courage equalled White's in April. Monash told Rawlinson that it was already too late to comply, and that if the Americans did not participate, the attack would be abandoned. The decision had to be made by 6.30 pm, when the infantry began their final move to the starting line. A distraught Rawlinson claimed that he might be sent home if the attack did not proceed, whereupon Monash replied that it was more important to retain the confidence of Australians and Americans in each other than to preserve even an army commander. Rawlinson directed that unless contrary orders were received from Haig by 6.30 pm – later extended to 7.00 pm – the operation was to go ahead. With a few minutes to spare, Haig answered that the improvement of the position before Amiens was so important that it must go ahead.

Sitting by the telephone in his office at Corps Headquarters at Bertangles in the early hours of 4 July was Coxen:

> Glancing out of the window I could just discern ... the figure of a person slowly pacing up and down the gravel drive in front of the château. The figure was that of Sir John.

CHAPTER 9

Every now and again he would pause and look at his watch, awaiting zero hour.

Then came the anxious moments, five minutes, four, three, two, one to go and then the sound of the guns in the opening barrage came over the air.

Sir John stopped and looking for a moment in the direction of the battle front, his anxiety relieved, he turned and slowly ... went to his office.

Bean was on the northern heights of the Somme, looking at the Wolfsberg as dawn broke:

Almost immediately after we saw the first tank – and then three or four on either side of it on the skyline behind Hamel and crawling up the hill. Then we could make out a thick line of infantry between the various tanks – at first I thought they were stationary, but they must have been going on to their last objective.

Australians and Americans in the support line below the crest of the Wolfsberg after the attack. The assault began from the crest of the Hill 104 spur, which rises on the far side of the valley beyond Hamel. Running along its upper slope was the German line. The view beheld by German artillery observers from the Wolfsberg over the intervening ground is evident (AWM E02844A).

Australian and American dead in no man's land in front of Pear Trench, which is just out of picture to the left. Indicated by the white chalk, the German line continues across the low ground to Vaire and Hamel woods on the skyline (AWM E02620).

Ninety-three minutes after the attack had started, the length of the Blue Line had been taken. 'No battle within my previous experience, not even Messines, passed off so smoothly, so exactly to timetable, or was so free from any kind of hitch', Monash remarked. At its height he sketched the head of Hughes' chauffeur, which 'keeps my nerves cool and steady'. Some casualties were incurred when parts of the barrage fell short, while darkness and heavy fog caused the tanks to miss Pear Trench. The heaviest losses of the operation ensued from its capture by the infantry. Once it became lighter, liaison was excellent, the tanks crushing machine-gunners as soon as the infantry located them. But they fought to the last, prompting Courage to conclude in his report on the battle that without the tanks the infantry would have suffered severe casualties or been unable to progress. Every tank carried two boxes of ammunition and water for the infantry, while each carrier tank dropped 12 500 rounds of ammunition and defence stores within 500 yards of the Blue Line less than half an hour after

CHAPTER 9

its capture. At least one infantry commander thought that in this achievement, which represented the loads normally carried by 1250 men, lay the outstanding lesson of the battle. Reports on the dropping of 112 000 rounds of ammunition by aircraft were 'favourable but not enthusiastic', for many of the parachutes failed to open. The diversionary attacks were successful, the Germans bombarding the 5th Division's front on the other side of the Somme in the apparent belief that the main attack was being launched there.

GHQ published two staff sheets on the battle, which attributed the result largely to the secrecy in planning, the determination and tactical handling of platoons and to 'local and special conditions', such as the poor defences, hard ground and high morale of the Australians. Furthermore: 'The value of tanks in assisting infantry to advance was conclusively proved.' This crucial sentence describes exactly the attack on 4 July when tanks, artillery and aircraft formed part of the 'maximum array of material resources' *supporting* the infantry. Nothing like the deep armoured penetrations of Fuller's Plan 1919 or Guderian's drive across France in 1940 was intended. In this sense Smithers' estimate of Monash as a general with 'petrol in his veins' cannot be sustained, although his rider, that Monash had 'a computer in his head', is more credible. Unfortunately, the former view of Monash has gathered momentum at the hands of those unversed in the subject. One highly respected historian, for example, called him 'a pioneer of that swift, motorised warfare of which ... the Germans rather than the British became the leaders. When, in 1940, the German armoured divisions swept in a few days across [the battlefields of World War I] they were indirectly paying tribute to Monash.' Such a comparison is absurd.

Fuller asserted that the reputation of the Tank Corps was made more by Hamel than Cambrai. But Hamel was more important as a demonstration of how four independent arms could be coordinated on the battlefield. Bean called it 'a big battle on a small scale' because 'all the appurtenances of a big battle were used.' Realising its significance as a prototypical all-arms battle for the future, a later historian better described Hamel as 'a revolution, a textbook victory, a little masterpiece casting a long shadow before it.' The closeness with which the execution followed the intention supported Monash's famous description:

> A perfected modern battle plan is like nothing so much as a score for an orchestral composition, where the various arms and units are the instruments, and the tasks they perform are their respective musical phrases.

An R.E. 8 plummets earthwards while parachuting ammunition to the assault. It was either hit by an artillery shell or structurally damaged when a parachute became entangled in its wings. The wood on the skyline may be Vaire Wood (AWM E03912).

The battle cost the Australians 1200 casualties, the Americans 176. German losses amounted to over 2000 men, 3 field guns, 32 trench mortars and 177 machine-guns. Over 1600 prisoners were taken. The Germans blamed the reverse on the absence of a forward defensive system, which made tank penetration easier, and the weakening of reserves by aerial attack. But their infantry, apart from the machine-gunners, surrendered easily. Brigadier General Evan Wisdom of the 7th Brigade thought the Germans must be holding the line with their poorest troops. Still, Monash's role should not be underrated. The battle was his first big test as corps commander; its result was important for his confidence and for Rawlinson's confidence in him. On 27 June Rawlinson had described Monash as 'functioning all right', but with 'a good deal to learn'. Now he considered him 'very shrewd'. Monash had proved that he knew his business and should be left alone to carry it out. Rawlinson's role was to provide him with what he needed and

CHAPTER 9

intervene only when absolutely necessary. The success also cemented Monash's standing in the eyes of his divisional commanders.

Monash's claims for the battle, though, were overblown. It had been launched for local tactical reasons rather than from a desire to allay the 'anxiety and nervousness of the public' or to prompt commanders to 'think offensively'. Clemenceau visited Sinclair-MacLagan's headquarters on 7 July to congratulate the Australians, but this is hardly indicative of an 'electric' effect, which 'stimulated many men to the realisation that the enemy was ... not invulnerable ...' The French General Charles Mangin had probably never even heard of Monash when his Tenth Army attacked on the Matz with 144 tanks in mid-June; or on 28 June, when two of its divisions assaulted east of Villers-Cotterets; or on 3 July, when, in a diversionary attack, over 1000 prisoners were seized, 'a clear sign of faltering morale in the German Army'. Each of these attacks preceded Hamel. Haig told his wife that it was 'quite a nice success', adding that he hoped nothing would prevent his visit to England to see her on the coming weekend. The CIGS, General Sir Henry Wilson, made no mention of the battle in his diary, writing on 6 July: 'No news of importance from France.'

Georges Clemenceau, the French Prime Minister, with Sinclair-MacLagan (left) and Monash (right), during his visit to the Australians at Bussy-les-Daours on 7 July after the Hamel success. The words of Clemenceau's speech are on the Australian Corps Memorial on the Wolfsberg (AWM E02527).

Monash's view that Hamel rekindled the offensive spirit in his superiors is doubtful. Wilson's 31-page memorandum of 25 July recommended a series of attacks with limited objectives for the rest of 1918, as a prelude to the opening of the decisive offensive in the second half of 1919. Haig berated this opinion: 'Words! Words! Words! Lots of words and little else. Theoretical rubbish! Whoever drafted this stuff could never win any campaign.' Yet OAD 902, significantly titled 'Notes on the Situation which may be created in Autumn and Winter of 1918 and during 1919', contained much the same conclusions when it was published by GHQ two days later. Of the higher commanders only Foch was optimistic, confiding to Wilson on 1 July, three days before Hamel, that 'all great anxiety would be over within ten days' time.'

Foch was out by several days. On 18 July 1918, Ludendorff's last great offensive was smashed by Mangin's counter-attack towards Soissons with General Jean Degoutte's Sixth Army alongside. Over 2000 guns, 1100 aircraft and nearly 500 tanks supported the twenty-four divisions, which advanced six miles on the first day, taking 15 000 prisoners and 400 guns. Hopes of a decisive offensive against the BEF in Flanders were abandoned as the German High Command realised that Foch's regaining of the initiative signified *der Wendepunkt der Kriegslage* (literally 'the turning point of the war situation'). Ludendorff was in a state of high nervous excitement, irritable and unable to eat. It was this battle, the counter-stroke on the Marne, and not Hamel, which influenced Allied thinking in the manner described by Monash. Like the other corps commanders of the BEF, he was far removed from the strategic direction of the war, although his corps and Currie's Canadians invariably enjoyed more important roles than theirs. Monash's standing in relation to the higher commanders and strategic policy was well illustrated by the origins and conduct of the offensive before Amiens on 8 August.

On 2 April Colonel Charles Grant, a British liaison officer at Foch's headquarters, informed the War Office that the Generalissimo was considering a counter-offensive as soon as possible. Foch's Directive Générale No. 2 appeared next day. It proposed a double offensive

CHAPTER 9

against the salient created by the German stroke of 21 March, the French Second Army attacking in the Montdidier region to clear the St Just–Amiens railway and Rawlinson's Fourth Army astride the Somme to disengage Amiens itself. Both offensives were to be launched simultaneously, with General Marie-Eugène Debeney's French First Army split between them. The German Lys offensive forced a temporary postponement, but Amiens was still prominent in Foch's thinking – he described its railway junction on 27 April as 'of vital importance'. During the lull in May, Foch returned to his plans for a counter-stroke, which aimed at 'a complete transformation of the situation', according to Lieutenant General John Ducane, another British liaison officer: 'A study of the directives issued by Foch during May shows clearly that he hoped to turn the tables ... by a successful counterattack ... and that he planned to do in May what he succeeded in doing in July.' This rather dents Monash's assertion: 'There is no doubt at all that it was the success of Hamel which induced Marshal Foch to undertake a counterblow on 18 July.'

Amiens continued to feature in the instructions mentioned by Ducane. Notable among them was Directive Générale No. 3, issued on 20 May and representing a considerable expansion of the original proposals for an offensive based on Amiens. Rawlinson's would be a surprise attack launched with tanks between the Somme and the Villers-Bretonneux–Amiens railway with the Morcourt–Harbonnières ravine, five miles distant, as its objective. Foch continued: '*la surprise est un facteur d'un importance capitale.*' The operation was to be launched as soon as possible, and would be followed one or two days later by the much larger southern pincer of the French Second Army. Haig sent Rawlinson this directive on 23 May, intimating that his attacking force would comprise the Australian Corps, part of III Corps and three Canadian divisions. In order to reach the deep objectives set by Foch, leapfrogging was to be employed. When Rawlinson outlined the plan to Birdwood and White, they pointed out that guns on the northern heights of the Somme between Sailly-Laurette and the Chipilly Spur could enfilade the advance to Morcourt on the opposite side of the river. Therefore two Australian divisions should attack this area, with the remainder advancing on the left of the Canadians on the southern bank.

The German stroke on the Aisne at the end of May caused another postponement, but Rawlinson resurrected the scheme after 'peaceful penetration' and Hamel demonstrated the weakness of the German defences and the moral ascendancy gained by the Australians in Fourth Army's sector. On 13 July he requested a reinforcement of five divisions to carry out the attack. Haig agreed fully with Rawlinson's verbal explanation of the project on 16 July and received his written proposals next day. For reasons of secrecy and coordination, Rawlinson urged that the northern advance should be entirely British, with Debeney's French First Army attacking the southern flank of the Montdidier salient instead of alongside his own army. He intended Monash, with the 1st Division in reserve, and Currie to overrun the German gun line south of the Somme before reaching the final objective, known as the Blue Line. This approximated to the old Amiens Outer Defence Line between Méricourt and Harbonnières, captured by the Germans in their March offensive. Two Canadian divisions and the Cavalry Corps would then advance southwards, eventually meeting Debeney. In the meantime, Foch asked Haig to prevent the transfer of German reserves to the Marne by preparing an offensive on his front, preferably to clear the Bruay coal mines.[68] Haig clung to the Amiens operation, describing it on 17 July as 'of the greatest importance'. Foch concurred readily – it would be '*également en raison de ses résultats, de plus profitable à executer en ce moment.*' But he wanted the British and the French to attack side by side.

GHQ approved the scheme on 23 July. Next day Foch told Haig and Pershing that it was to be one of a series of blows – the French would strike again on the Marne and the Americans, now with their own sector, were to pinch out the St Mihiel salient south-east of Verdun. On 26 July Foch ordered the continuation of the Amiens attack after the first day to the line Chaulnes-Roye, a further five miles, which encompassed the confused jumble of decayed trenches and entanglements of the old Somme battlefield of 1916. On 28 July he pressed for the advancement of the operation from 10 to 8 August.

CHAPTER 9

Although Haig and Rawlinson played important roles, the driving force behind the offensive had been Foch. Ducane, who was in the best position to know, made no reference to Monash when he concluded: 'it was due to Foch's influence that the attack took the form it did in the first place and secondly, that it was energetically exploited.'

What of Monash? He was extremely keen to exploit the Hamel success, suggesting to Hobbs and Sinclair-MacLagan on the day of the battle the capture by 'peaceful penetration' of the north-eastern tip of the Hamel Spur; further advances would be contingent on a reduction of the eleven miles of front held by the Australian Corps. On 7 July, Monash suggested to Rawlinson that III Corps should take over the sector held by Elliott's brigade on his northern flank. Rawlinson approached Haig, who refused because it would necessitate an extension of Third Army's front. Haig also rejected another of Monash's proposals, the advancing of his right flank to Monument Wood, on the outskirts of Villers-Bretonneux, to flatten the salient created by the Hamel attack. 'Peaceful penetration' had already taken about one-quarter of this objective before Haig reversed his decision. By 14 July the remainder had been won, but the resistance met from stronger defences near the Mound, a hummock of spoil beside the railway east of Monument Wood, necessitated its capture in a formal attack by the 25th and 26th battalions four days later. On 15 July Rawlinson had decreed that the new line would 'represent the furthest advance to the eastward … that we are to make for the time being.'

On 17 August Monash informed Murdoch that he was responsible for the battle on the 8th. He had told Rawlinson after Hamel that he could advance 5 miles and, in reply to the army commander's question, said that a deeper penetration was possible provided he had reliable support on his right flank. He welcomed Rawlinson's suggestion of the Canadian Corps for this task. In his book, *The Australian Victories in France in 1918*, written in 1919, Monash contended that he continually impressed on Rawlinson: 'The time was … ripe for action on a scale far more decisive than had become orthodox in the British Army in the past.' The Australian Corps could undertake a prolonged offensive if its front were shortened from three to two divisions and if the Canadian Corps, *at Monash's recommendation*, advanced on its right. Writing to Bruche in October 1919, he claimed that these suggestions were made in response to Montgomery's request for specific proposals for action. In addition, Monash recalled that he insisted on the capture of the German gun line, possibly because the setting of the final objective short of it at Hamel and Morlancourt had been strongly criticised by the attacking troops.

Around 15 July Montgomery returned with Rawlinson to inform Monash that the Canadians would be sent, and to ask him how many tanks and guns he needed and how he intended to protect his flanks:

> That conversation was really the genesis of the whole plan, and Rawlinson said that he would see the Chief about the matter and would let me know if the High Command proposed to pursue the question further.

He used a historical analogy to describe his own contribution:

> It would be incorrect and unjust to attribute to James Watt or to George Stephenson the whole credit for the modern locomotive or to Galileo the whole credit for the modern science of dynamics ...
>
> In just the same way it would be wrong to attribute to me personally the whole credit for the opening of the great offensive in August 1918 ...
>
> [But] I think it would be unfair to me entirely to suppress the fact that I was the prime mover in the events from July 1st to 21st ...

By June 1928 Monash was uncertain of his role. *Australian Victories*, written without access to official records, was based on the belief that 'the initiation ... rested upon definite suggestions which I had personally made.' But a search of the available Australian and British records revealed nothing beyond Monash's proposals for the Monument Wood attack. This was not surprising, for the need for secrecy probably precluded the recording of many conversations. However, Monument Wood was the Australian Corps' main operation immediately after Hamel and, as its commander, Monash was naturally preoccupied with it. Perhaps he was thinking about a more important attack. But he could not be aware that Haig and Rawlinson were considering at the same time the wider offensive suggested by Foch, or that the use of

CHAPTER 9

the Canadians had been mooted as long ago as May, when the scheme was broached to Birdwood and White. Rawlinson's plan of 17 July was very detailed, explaining how the attack would be executed, in particular the complex manoeuvre required of Currie, and listing the number of tanks for allotment to each corps. Yet this was a bare two days after the probable date of the conversation that Monash called 'the genesis of the whole plan'.

The origin of the Amiens offensive illustrates nothing more than the normal operation of the chain of command from generalissimo downwards, with Monash's role typifying the relationship between a corps and an army commander. Rawlinson's discussions with him dwelt on the tasks and requirements of the Australian Corps in an army plan, which the army commander had prepared. As Bean finally concluded in 1935: 'we know that Monash did not devise the August offensive, though of course he was responsible for many of the details in the plan for his own Corps.' Although Rawlinson and Montgomery were 'very surprised' at Monash's public claims, White thought that his delusion was not unjustified. From lengthy post-war correspondence with Montgomery on the matter, White felt that he

> ... was practically confessing that Rawlinson encouraged Monash to believe he was conceiving it and making it clear, that at the time they were deadly anxious not to do anything which might offend the Australian Corps or antagonise Monash, or Hughes, who at that time was a cloud on the horizon, on the subject of the employment of Australian troops.

Invited to the opening of Australia House on 3 August, Monash left for leave in London on 23 July. If recalled, 'a destroyer would stand by at Dover to rush me across ... as I was not quite prepared for the alternative proposition of flying across.' Birdwood had returned to France by air after the German offensive broke on 21 March. It was symptomatic of the difference in their attitudes towards personal danger. At his conference at Flixécourt two days earlier, Rawlinson had announced that the two Dominion corps were to attack south of the Somme astride the Amiens–Nesle railway. As the line followed a south-easterly direction via Chaulnes, the Australian frontage would expand from 7200 to 9000 yards, while Currie's diminished from 4000 to 3500 yards. North of the railway was the Roman road that ran due east from Amiens through Warfusée to St Quentin. Further north still was the Somme, forming Monash's boundary with Butler's III Corps.

The river, the road and the railway were the three outstanding terrain features of Monash's sector. Between road and railway the country was flat and open and dotted with numerous woods and villages. A deep re-entrant plunged from the road at Lamotte, just east of Warfusée, to the Somme at Cérisy. Along the spur overlooking it to the west was the Green Line. On another spur to the east, which enclosed a second steep re-entrant from the road to the river at Morcourt, lay the next objective, the Red Line. Its capture would place Amiens beyond the range of the heaviest German artillery. The Blue Line was between 1000 and 1500 yards further east. Opposite Morcourt, the Somme flowed in the shape of a horseshoe around the long, finger-like Chipilly Spur. Birdwood's and White's earlier anxiety about this feature was not misplaced, for its defenders dominated both re-entrants, and could engage with artillery the Roman road and, in the summery haze beyond it, Bayonvillers and Harbonnières. The fortifications in front of the Australian Corps, though, 'would not in themselves afford much assistance to defending troops.' They were held by two divisions which had been severely handled on 4 July and a third 'moderately good but with very little initiative. It may be regarded as a good specimen of a trench division.'

Apart from his allocation of frontages to Monash and Currie at his first conference with them at Flixécourt on 21 July, Rawlinson 'imposed no limitations or conditions upon either of us as to what we should attempt to do within our own boundaries.' This freedom allowed Monash to object immediately that despite his earlier plea, the Green Line did not include the gun line in the Cérisy re-entrant, an omission that would enable the Germans to withdraw their artillery during the pause before the attack on the second objective. Rawlinson agreed to his demand to shift the Green Line to the ridge east of the re-entrant, thereby increasing the length of the initial

CHAPTER 9

advance from 2000 to 3500 yards. Later, Monash distorted the context of this alteration. He implied that Rawlinson envisaged a penetration that would not exceed two miles, whereas he, Monash, wanting to destroy the German defensive organisation along his entire front, 'prepared my plans upon the basis of a total advance, on the first day, of not less than 9000 yards.' But this was still 1000 yards short of the Morcourt re-entrant on which the Blue Line rested when the offensive was discussed *as far back as May*. Rawlinson had always intended to seize the gun line, but Monash's insistence that it must be taken in the first phase was much sounder than the army commander's plan for its capture in the second.

Monash's protest against the Somme as his northern boundary was equally well founded. He had earlier proposed either that the French should take over more of his right flank, or that III Corps should take over Elliott's line on the left, which would leave Brigadier General James Stewart's 14th Brigade as the only Australian formation north of the river. Both sides would then remain under his control. It was another example of Monash's dislike of the use of 'any bold natural or artificial feature' as a boundary: 'It creates ... a divided responsibility and necessitates between two independent commanders ... a degree of effective co-operation which can rarely be hoped for.' As things stood, the threat posed by the Chipilly Spur was a powerful argument for giving him responsibility for the northern bank. Rawlinson was unmoved, and left the difficult task of its capture to III Corps, which had not fully recovered from the mauling it had taken during Michael and in the Villers-Bretonneux battles. At Monash's suggestion, Butler's final objective was moved forward to the ridge east of Chipilly and an intermediate objective, the Brown Line was set, in case the British advance, as Monash feared, failed to reach it on the first day.

Drafted on 22 July, Monash's preliminary notes dealt with every major facet of the attack. Two divisions would advance to each of the Green and Red lines, leaving the river bends for mopping-up parties. Mobile artillery was essential, and each tank must have only one task. Roads and light railways from Villers-Bretonneux and Corbie would have to be prepared and allotted for motor traffic, mules and men. But there would be no reinforcing of the engineers with infantry, Monash's usual practice, because battalions were under strength. Though guided by previous conversations with Rawlinson and his own experience at Hamel, Monash had conceived what was essentially the corps plan of attack less than one day after the army commander explained the wider scheme. His recall to Bertangles from London on 29 July provided an even more impressive glimpse of Monash's mental prowess. Next morning he discussed with Blamey the various alternatives for movement and supply prepared by the corps staff in his absence. During the afternoon he shut himself up in his room to study the mass of detail involved. At his conference with divisional commanders next day, when they were apprised of the project for the first time, 'he was outstanding in his completeness of plan, grasp of all requirements and clarity of expression of them.'[69] Monash assured Haig, who arrived during the meeting, that he 'had all the threads of the operation in his hands.'

The most notable features were Monash's scheme for the assembly of the attacking formations and the extent of his leapfrogs. A redistribution would be necessary as the 2nd Division withdrew its 5th and 7th brigades and the 3rd Division its 9th and 11th brigades two days before the attack to concentration areas 3 to 5 miles back. Taking their place behind the line were the 4th and 5th divisions, which would assume command of the 6th and 10th brigades left to hold it. By bringing them forward, Monash shortened the approach march of the 4th and 5th divisions, which were destined for the Red and Blue lines, by almost 3 miles. According to his doctrine at Third Ypres, they would thus be 'fresh enough to resist determined counterattacks if these were launched early.' On the night before the attack, the 2nd and 3rd divisions would leapfrog through the 4th and 5th to their starting tape for the assault on the Green Line. Once this objective was taken, the second leapfrog would occur, and, on the capture of the Red Line, the reserve battalions of the brigades that had assaulted it were to carry out a third leapfrog to the Blue Line. Long before then, the 6th and 10th brigades garrisoning the original line would have passed

CHAPTER 9

into corps reserve. Monash adopted this course, 'since it includes all essentials. It gives a proper distribution of troops to objectives and ensures a minimum of fatigue to troops under ordinary conditions.'

It was also extremely complex and, as Monash acknowledged, success would rest 'upon the intelligence of the troops and the sympathetic, loyal and efficient co-operation of my own Corps Staff, and those of the Commanders acting under me.' Testing their competence was his division of the corps rear area into two zones, leaving the determination of boundaries and other coordinating details to the two divisional commanders in each. They were assisted by Monash's early allocation of existing roads for various purposes. He regarded the problem for his corps on 8 August 'as being largely one of roads'. Monash brigaded all engineers and pioneers under Foott, mainly for road-making and improvement, and allotted most of the 13th Light Horse to traffic control. The care he had lavished on the 3rd Division's approach march before Messines was repeated on a much larger scale before 8 August. After describing his plan for the assembly of the Australian Corps as 'John Monash's masterpiece', Bean added:

> ... the elaborate placing of the brigades and the timing of their starts so that each punctually took up its part in the intricate task, affords what will probably be the classical example for the launching of such operations.

Gellibrand disagreed. Believing that the divisional leapfrogs on the Red Line came too early and would break the momentum of the advance, he proposed that the first pair of divisions should freewheel along adjacent corridors until stopped, with their brigades relieving each other. He claimed that the other divisional commanders shared his view. Gellibrand confided to Bean that he 'thought Monash was probably a man with sufficiently original ideas to let them break away from the style of fighting to which they had grown accustomed – fixed objectives etc. But he was not.' Gellibrand's definition of 'original' is to be wondered at because leapfrogs in previous attacks had been executed *within* divisions, as he now advocated, but hardly ever *by* them, as Monash planned. That said, Gellibrand's method had its advantages. Momentum would not be lost through having to carry out the complex divisional reliefs and there would be two fresh divisions available for operations next day. Furthermore, the intermingling of units that might result if the Germans counter-attacked during a brigade leapfrog would be less than during a divisional one. On the other hand, the two divisions might end up carrying out a very long advance. Monash's plan, based on more centralised control, spread the advance evenly among four divisions, leaving those destined for the Blue Line in better shape to handle counter-attacks. They were more likely at the end of the advance, when fresh German formations could be arriving on the battlefield, than during the pause on the Green Line, when the Germans would still be trying regroup. Momentum overall, therefore, should be not unduly affected. True, there was no guarantee that a leapfrog would not be disrupted. But if the unexpected did arise, then the experience at Broodseinde suggested that the infantry could deal with it – and their ascendancy over the Germans now was greater than it was then. On balance, Monash's plan involved less risk.

Major General John Gellibrand (shown here as a brigadier). Tasmanian-born Gellibrand had graduated top of his class from Sandhurst in 1893, served in the Boer War and attended the Camberley Staff College before returning to Australia in 1912. Though an aggressive and able commander, his independent outlook and eccentricity often antagonised his superiors. Monash was no exception. Like Bean, Gellibrand tended to damn him with faint praise (AWM P01489_001).

CHAPTER 9

Prescribing leapfrogs by brigades at each objective within divisional corridors, the method employed by Currie was similar to Gellibrand's, and Bean described it as 'the principle normally favoured by higher commanders'. The difficult task faced by the Canadians necessitated its adoption. Their start line followed the sharp curve of the Cachy salient. Currie's southernmost division would have to attack astride the Luce, its right brigade seizing a dominant height that enfiladed his corps' advance. Hence there was the possibility of a check at the outset. This division also had to protect the exposed right flank until the French XXXI Corps, starting later, caught up with the attack. For all these reasons, the three Canadian divisions attacked abreast, on one-brigade frontages, with the fourth division in rear, unlike the two-by-two division scheme in the Australian Corps. The Canadian assault formation precluded the assembly arrangement and divisional leapfrogs used by Monash. Bean's praise of his method stands.

Besides rejecting his divisional commanders' alleged preference for corridors, Monash laid down their tactics for the attack. He broke it into three phases. Each supported by twenty-four tanks and assaulting on the right and left respectively, the 2nd and 3rd divisions were to advance under a creeping barrage at 4.20 am to the Green Line in Phase A, which Monash estimated would require 143 minutes. This was a set-piece attack, carried to the limit of field gun range and modelled on Hamel, 'the conditions of that battle being now reproduced on a much enlarged scale.' A halt of 100 minutes on the Green Line permitted the move forward of twelve artillery brigades to support the assault of the 4th and 5th divisions on the Red Line, 5000 yards away, in Phase B. The mobile use of field artillery and trench mortars in this phase was Rawlinson's suggestion, but he left the details to his corps commanders. Monash allotted one artillery brigade, together with an engineer and a machine-gun company and a field ambulance, to each infantry brigade, forming a brigade group under the infantry brigadier. This showed that control would be less centralised in Phase B, which he described as having: 'more of a character of an advance in open warfare … The place of the protective barrage will be taken by tanks and the advance will be supported by artillery.'

The surviving tanks from Phase A were to join the twenty-four tanks supporting each division during Phase B, in accordance with the principle of lightening the infantry's task as much as possible. Another example was the employment in Phase C, the exploitation to the Blue Line, of thirty-six Mark V Star tanks, a new design capable of carrying two machine-gun crews 'across a bullet swept area and placing them like a "Human Barrage" on the far side.'

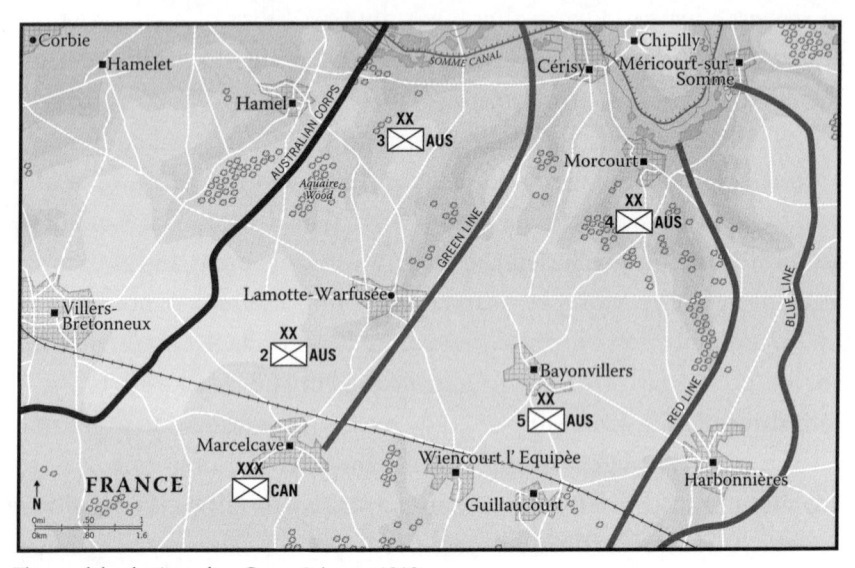

The attack by the Australian Corps, 8 August 1918

As no aspect of it was too small to escape his attention, the greatest influence on the Australian Corps scheme was Monash himself. On his appointment as corps commander, he ordered the commencement of instruction in visual signalling, thereby lessening the reliance on static communications to which he attributed the chaos in the BEF after the onset of open warfare in March. This training was intended to reduce the difficulties he expected in Phase B, when the advance of brigade and battalion headquarters precluded the use of the telephone. Four of the sixteen vehicles of the 17th Armoured Car Battalion, allotted to Monash just before the battle, would be used solely for reconnaissance as far as the old 1916 battlefield, supplying him with information on German reserves and the nature of the defences. The other twelve were to raid well beyond

CHAPTER 9

the Blue Line. Monash originally requested eighteen Whippets, light tanks armed with machine-guns, for this task, because the armoured cars were road bound. When Rawlinson refused, he ordered pioneer parties to repair the St Quentin Road as the infantry advanced along it:

> The [Pioneer] Battalion Commander pointed out that it might mean the almost total loss of the Battalion and Monash said he was prepared to face this, on account of the enormous effect that armoured cars would produce if they were able to get through soon after the attacking waves of infantry.

The staff procedures were the same as those he had instituted in the 3rd Division. Orders were conveyed in twenty-one 'Battle Instructions', which were always produced in final form by Blamey after close scrutiny by Monash. His correction of Blamey's draft 'Program of Attack' resembled his comments on pre-war promotion exam papers. Blamey stated that the 2nd and 3rd divisions must be on the start line 'by zero hour', but Monash, insisting on precision, wrote: 'one hour before zero hour'. The two corps conferences followed the same principles as the meetings before Hamel. At the second, lasting over four hours on 4 August, Monash ran through the divisional plans after prefacing his remarks with the familiar comment: 'All questions are to be raised at this table [and] while discussions on side issues may prove wearisome, all must be alert to watch for points affecting them.' No alterations to plans were permitted after this conference. He prepared a personal 'Battle Agenda' for every day between 1 and 4 August, listing all outstanding matters. Together with the conference agendas and his battle notes, they reveal an attention to detail that was not exceeded in any of Monash's other operations. One officer in each battalion was to check that the men rested on 7 August: 'no football, no wandering, but sleep.' Troops must remember to cut German telephone wires. At least one gun would have to advance almost level with the 2nd and 3rd divisions to engage immediately anti-tank guns sited near the artillery line. It was little wonder that his agenda for 3 August, besides mentioning the need for a 'Special officer for publicity', reminded Monash to 'Draft success message.'

MONASH

Monash's established principles also underpinned the minor tactical arrangements. An imaginary line between the southern end of Aquaire Wood and the junction of the Morcourt re-entrant with the St Quentin Road formed the interdivisional boundary. The flanks of each unit were to overlap to ensure contact between them, while a company of tanks was 'specially charged with the function of maintaining the attack at the junction of Divisions.' To achieve 'a dead straight barrage line', the right flank of the infantry starting tape was laid half a mile behind the existing forward trenches, from which the occupants were withdrawn shortly before zero hour. This was the simplest plan for the artillery, and it reduced the not inconsiderable probability of error, for over 600 guns were supporting the Australian Corps. Smoke was included in the barrage. Whether the dropping from aircraft of smoke bombs on troublesome positions beyond artillery range was Monash's idea is unknown. But the principle 'one Tank, one task' was attributable to him:

> ... no individual Tank was to be relied upon to serve more than one body of infantry, nor to carry out more than one phase of the battle ... in the event of any one Tank becoming disabled, its loss would impair no portion of the battle plan other than that fraction to which the Tank had been allotted.

Sinclair-MacLagan and Hobbs could advance to the Red and Blue lines assured of adequate tank support, even if all the tanks assisting the 2nd and 3rd divisions were lost in the attack on the Green Line. Instead of succeeding waves commencing their advance on the capture of the first objective, virtually the entire force – infantry, tanks and much of the artillery – would move forward at zero hour. Adopted by Rawlinson at Foch's suggestion, this procedure was copied from the method used by the Germans in March to overcome the tendency of the leading wave to outstrip those following, a problem they foresaw would arise in a deep penetration. Cambrai, 21 March 1918 and Hamel were the three battles that greatly influenced the planning of the attack on 8 August.

Measures used by Monash before Hamel to conceal the concentration of tanks and infantry were applied throughout Fourth

CHAPTER 9

Army. Both moved into position at night, 'police' aircraft checking the rear area next day for any tell-tale signs. Guns were registered from the map and not by firing a few rounds. As for the most important deceptive arrangement, Rawlinson suggested to Haig on 17 July that the release of French troops occupying the Luce sector for operations on the Marne would explain the reinforcement of his army by the 1st Australian Division. No sooner had it arrived on the Somme in April than it was rushed north to defend Hazebrouck when the Germans launched the Georgette offensive in Flanders. Monash and Currie discussed at length with Rawlinson on 21 July how best to effect the redispositions necessitated by its return and, more particularly, those of the Canadian Corps. The solution adopted was for the 4th Australian Division to take over the French line while the Canadians assembled behind them. From 6 August until it was relieved by the Canadians on the night before the attack, the entire Canadian line was held by the 13th Brigade. Meanwhile, two Canadian battalions and some signals units arrived in Plumer's area, commencing patrols and a flow of radio traffic to suggest an impending offensive there. Monash turned his visit to London to advantage by announcing before his departure that he intended to take three weeks' leave because 'no developments of any importance were to be expected.' It was perhaps fortunate that other commanders did not have so casual an attitude as Monash to the secrecy attaching to every aspect of the operation. Writing to Murdoch on 31 July, he suggested that the correspondent should arrive in France between 7 and 9 August 'but from present appearances I think it would not be convenient for you to come here later than August 8.'

The incident that most threatened surprise occurred on the northern bank of the Somme, where the 5th Division captured more of the crest overlooking Morlancourt on 29 July. While Monash was in London, Rawlinson had reversed an earlier rejection of this operation. It was a questionable decision, inviting retaliation and the possible discovery of the impending attack. III Corps had relieved the 5th Division when the riposte fell on 6 August, and 250 British prisoners were taken. Fortunately, the Germans learned nothing. Monash made 'such an outcry' that Butler was told the attack had already begun for III Corps. It was to regain immediately the ground lost. The incident reawakened Monash's fear about the inability of III Corps to capture the Chipilly Spur, and he warned Sinclair-MacLagan to be prepared to form a defensive flank from the Blue Line along the Somme to Cérisy, 'in case the *worst* should happen and the Chipilly Bend were to remain in enemy hands.' The worst seemed possible after the failure of Butler's counter-attacks on 7 August. But Monash's anxiety was not apparent to those around him, at least not to Foott, whom he discovered taking a quiet nap in anticipation of a busy night: 'after chafing me on being able to sleep on a hot afternoon, [Monash] said, "I was very glad to see you – for I knew that there was one man, at any rate, whose mind was at rest about his job of work!"'

Lieutenant Rupert Downes addresses his platoon from B Company, 29th Battalion before the advance to the Red Line at Harbonnières on 8 August. Smoke from heavy shelling obscures the background. The platoon comprises seventeen men, less than half its normal strength. This photo has become perhaps the iconic image of Australian soldiers in the First World War (AWM E02790).

CHAPTER 9

At this juncture the men were listening to a message from Monash. He appealed to every one of them to carry on to 'the utmost of his power until his goal is won, for the sake of AUSTRALIA [sic], the Empire and our cause', in this, a battle 'which will be one of the most memorable of the whole war.' Next morning, Monash was awakened shortly before 4.00 am by Major Walter Berry, a member of his staff:

> ... a few minutes after four we walked down the drive of the château. Afterwards we walked back to the château and stood there and when 4.20 arrived the boom of that barrage was just like one tremendous thump. Everything dropped at once.

The 2nd and 3rd divisions reported that their approach march and assembly were 'carried out without a hitch', but the attack began in a fog so dense that it was impossible to see more than ten feet ahead. There was only sporadic fighting as the Germans surrendered freely, often terrified by the sight of a tank looming out of the fog. By 8.43 am, the Green Line had been taken, and command of the battle front passed to Sinclair-MacLagan and Hobbs. So far, 'The advance was the most bloodless ever made by Australian infantry in a great battle.' The 4th and 5th divisions were approaching the Red Line two hours later, and at 1.15 pm Monash informed Rawlinson that the 5th Division, then on the Blue Line, had hoisted the Australian flag over Harbonnières at midday. Ahead of the 5th, the armoured cars ranged beyond the Amiens Outer Line to Vauvillers, Framerville, Proyart and Chuignolles, firing on headquarters, transport columns and billets. As Monash expected, the Germans still held Chipilly, their artillery on the spur becoming 'the chief instrument of the enemy's resistance on the Australian front.' Sinclair-MacLagan refused his flank on the river and Monash sent the corps reserve, the 1st Brigade, to reinforce him. Together with the extreme right, where the 5th Division met heavy resistance, it was the only part of the Blue Line not taken in a day in which the Australian Corps captured 7925 prisoners and 173 guns at a cost of 2000 casualties. The Canadians were equally successful, and by nightfall General Debeney's IX and XXXI Corps had joined them on the final objective.

Troops from the 5th Australian Division gathered around some field guns and a Mark V Star carrier tank in the re-entrant north of Lamotte-Warfusée on 8 August. They are waiting for the advance to the Red Line. The tank will be used in the assault on the Blue Line (AWM E03883).

As it had done on 21 March, the fog hampered the defenders much more than their opponents. After the war, Liddell Hart noted that every successful attack was launched under its cloak. Nevertheless, this offensive achieved greater surprise than any undertaken by either side. The artillery 'reached the peak of perfection'. Its counter-battery fire, to which Monash had paid particular attention, was some of the most effective of the war and killed or drove off many of the German gunners. The feebleness of the German barrage was often remarked on. Once the mist cleared, however, guns firing directly exacted a heavy toll, crippling 40 of the 142 tanks that had crossed the Australian start line. The 1st Cavalry Brigade and one company of Whippets, allotted to the Australian Corps until the Red Line was reached, achieved mixed results. Rawlinson intended them to support the two cavalry divisions, which were to advance towards Chaulnes and Roye should the chance arise. The cavalry did useful work until it was caught by German machine-guns and forced to retire to the Blue Line. Its combination with the Whippets proved a failure, as the

CHAPTER 9

Tank Corps staff had predicted. The Whippets were left behind in the early stages, but forged ahead when resistance was encountered, a 'continuous shuttle movement' ensuing. For the Australians and for Monash, these concerns were minor. Their greatest disappointment stemmed from III Corps' repulse before Chipilly Spur.

Next day the feature fell to a patrol of six Australians cooperating with British and American troops. Bill Gammage cites this exploit to support his argument, based on his distinction between the conduct of operations by generals and their execution by soldiers, that the AIF could have won its victories in 1918 without Monash. Gammage concedes that 'Of course ... soldiers need generals', but he regards the soldiers as more important by far. A counter-argument might use the successes at Messines, Hamel and now Amiens, which rested on the prior planning and preparation of generals and their training of their troops. Then, again, just as many instances existed of brave troops being wasted by faulty generalship before the battle, as evidenced by Haig before Passchendaele or Monash before Sailly-Laurette, and during the battle, as shown by Birdwood's and Godley's handling of the Sari Bair offensive in August 1915. In other words, Gammage's distinction is hollow: the planning and conduct of the battle and the fighting in the battle are complementary and equally important. It reveals a basic misunderstanding of the roles of the general and of the soldier. On 8 August 1918 the soldiers themselves were not confused. 'The sight of the various services streaming up when the mist rose never passed from the mind of the 50 000 Australians who saw it.' Sir Joseph Cook's son, a major in the 4th Division, wrote to his father: 'The organisation of the show was wonderful. Monash seems to be making good. I have seen nothing to equal it. It puts fresh heart into one to see evidence of the master hand.' Sir Joseph showed this letter to Monash who replied: '[It] is not the only evidence that has recently come to my notice that Australian soldiers now fully recognise that their many successes are due in part to the plans and dispositions and the organising ability of their commanders and staffs.'

The only major action required of Monash during the battle was the commitment of his reserve to support Sinclair-MacLagan on the

Somme flank. But the fruits of his planning were everywhere apparent. His assembly arrangements ensured that the length of the approach march for each division, and hence its freshness before the attack, were equal. Additionally, 'the troops for the critical mobile operations were already at hand, their commanders well forward where they could see their way through.' Yet Monash's concern for his men's welfare was offset by the ruthlessness of his order to the pioneers to clear the road for the armoured cars. The havoc they could and did cause justified a sacrifice that, fortunately, the pioneers were not called on to make. Underpinning the speed and ease of the exploitation to the final objective was Monash's organisation of brigade groups, which gave their commanders the resources they needed to undertake a deep penetration in open warfare without a creeping barrage. The tank casualties would have been much greater had Monash not insisted on the extension of the first objective to the German gun line. His administrative skill was as apparent as his tactical ability, and just as important. At the end of the day, even the most advanced troops received a hot meal and a drink. Montgomery ranked the supreme confidence of all troops as one of the most important contributions to the success. In the Australian Corps this feeling was engendered in no small part by the generalship of its commander.

In terms of tactical significance, 8 August was far-reaching. It demonstrated the interrelationship of aircraft for reconnaissance and ground attack; of artillery to beat down the defenders and to prevent their artillery from disrupting the infantry assault with a counter-barrage; of tanks to give close protection to the infantry and create paths through wire; and, lastly, of infantry, to knock out guns firing at tanks from close range, to close with the enemy, to mop up and to occupy the objective. Prior and Wilson aptly describe this all-arms combination, whose interdependent parts had developed a high level of expertise, as a 'weapons system'. Hamel had proven it on an experimental scale; Amiens proved it on a scale that opened the door to decisive results. Many of the great battles of World War II, such as El Alamein, were 'Amiens type battles'. The strategic effect was reflected by Ludendorff's famous comment: 'August 8th was the black

CHAPTER 9

day of the German Army in the history of this war ... [It] put the decline of [its] fighting power beyond all doubt ... The war must be ended.' It continued too, his mental decline, the symptoms of which were evident after Foch's stroke on 18 July. Even so, the Germans reacted with the trademark swiftness that flummoxed their opponents in two world wars. By early afternoon they knew the depth and width of the breach and had ordered six divisions to the area instead of the five expected by GHQ. By 9 August, Crown Prince Rupprecht's Army Group Headquarters believed its reserves were sufficient to halt the advance.

Australians surround a 28-cm railway gun, soon to be known as the Amiens gun, on 8 August after its capture by the 31st Battalion and British cavalry near Harbonnières earlier in the day. The camouflaged barrel is now displayed at the Australian War Memorial (AWM A00006).

The naming of the battle after the date on which it began hid the confusion among commanders about how best to exploit the victory. Foch's extension of the attack towards Chaulnes and Roye on 26 July was followed by a second change on 3 August, when Haig told the Generalissimo that he had instructed Rawlinson to advance on Chaulnes 'as quickly as possible' and then drive a further fifteen miles to Ham, across the Somme. On 5 August, Haig warned Rawlinson that if the operation went as planned, it would 'develop into one of considerable magnitude.' Next day, Rawlinson directed Currie to 'press on in support of the cavalry' towards Roye-Chaulnes on 9 August, while Monash, pivoting on the Somme between Méricourt and Etinehem, swung forward his right flank to conform with the Canadian advance. Why had Rawlinson acted so late? A possible answer is that he was still inclined to think of the operation as a limited offensive, even though the modifications of 26 July and 3 August had transformed it into an unlimited one. Like Monash, Rawlinson always favoured the limited attack, opposing Haig's quest for a breakthrough on the Somme in 1916 and at Third Ypres in 1917.

On 1 August Monash informed his divisional commanders: 'There is no intention of carrying the exploitation of success eastward of the Blue Line.' On 3 August: 'The Corps must be prepared as early as possible to fight a stiff defensive battle on the main line of resistance.' Monash, too, thought of the attack as limited, although he was disturbed by the conflicting impressions he received from his superiors. He pleaded with Lawrence on 5 August that if the advance was to proceed beyond the Blue Line, troops must be ready and all arrangements completed beforehand. Yet he told Bean on that day, the same day as Haig personally explained his views on the plan to him, that the objective was 'strictly limited' and that he intended 'to go only for guns and leave this junction [Chaulnes] to be dealt with by our guns. When and if we get far enough, our guns will concentrate upon it.' Reviewing the operation on 9 August, Bean wrote:

> Monash of course, as in Gallipoli, always plays for safety – he has a dread of an unfixed objective, and is the last leader in the world ever to take the responsibility of getting beyond his flanks. The capture of guns was good enough for him – he drew the line at anything more ...

The opportunity to do more on 8 August had arisen before 11.30 am, when Monash knew that the area beyond the Blue Line was empty. As no orders to continue could have reached the forward units in time, independent action by local commanders would have been necessary

CHAPTER 9

to take advantage of it. Bean asserted that it was doubtful whether the granting of such freedom was ever contemplated by Rawlinson or Monash. In Monash's case, it was not doubtful but certain, for what he had learned at Messines applied to this as it did to any other attack:

> ... in every offensive operation, large or small, a definite limit was set to the task to be performed ... under no circumstances whatever, no matter how tempting, were these limits to be exceeded ... To allow troops a free hand to exploit a local victory, by continuing their advance indefinitely, had often led to complete disorganisation and an inability to resist the shock of the enemy's inevitable reaction.

8 August was a break in, rather than a breakthrough battle. Pressure on the Germans could not be sustained long enough to prevent their recovery. As Liddell Hart says, the problem of maintaining the momentum of an advance through a defensive system that might be miles deep was solved neither by the Germans with their fluid tactics, nor by the British in the final weeks of the war. This was demonstrated by the operations during the next few days, which Bean aptly remarked 'probably furnish a classic example of how not to follow up a great attack.'

Monash prepared his preliminary orders for the continuation of the advance on 7 August. The 1st Division was to advance through the right of the 5th to a line east of Rosières, while the 5th moved its left flank forward to conform. Sinclair-MacLagan would remain on the Blue Line between the St Quentin road and the Somme. The 5th Division was to continue its drive on 10 August, but, as the corps frontage gradually widened, the 2nd would relieve it, extending the 1st Division's left flank beyond Framerville. Next day, '1 Div – if necessary, advances its line ... to include the knoll NW of Lihons', four miles from Harbonnières and overlooking Chaulnes one and a half miles to the east. As with the origins of the battle, the evolution of this scheme had followed the chain of command, Haig explaining his intention to Rawlinson about 3 August, the army commander giving his preliminary orders to Monash on the 6th, on the basis of which Monash drafted his instructions for the corps. Monash's postwar account in *Australian Victories* differed considerably from this. He claimed that on the afternoon of 8 August, Rawlinson warned him that the advance was to continue to the south-east next day:

> It was a decision which was unpalatable to me, for it condemned me to leaving the whole great bend of the Somme, on which lay Bray, Péronne and Brie, in the undisturbed possession of the enemy, whereas a vigorous advance due east ... would give without fighting, possession, or at least command, of the whole of this bend.

It is difficult to understand why Monash found this decision unpalatable on 8 August and not on the 6th or the 7th, for the importance of the Somme bend was as obvious then. Far from any record of his complaining to Rawlinson, his own plan of the 7th, in conformity with the army scheme, was intended to support the left of Currie's drive towards Chaulnes, the direction of which was south-east. In any case, an advance due east from the Australian sector would be enfiladed from the northern bank of the Somme as Sinclair-MacLagan's division already had been. Considering Monash's concern for that flank, it was strange that he should allegedly urge a plan that would continue to expose his corps to the danger. Finally, his last-minute protest hardly accorded with his emphasis on fixity of plan. The evidence suggests that Monash willingly carried out his part in a scheme than determined the action of the Australian Corps in all but its last battle.

Rawlinson did not issue his formal orders until the evening of the 8th, when the result of the French attack was known. The Australian advance would be supported by 'considerable' artillery and 'a strong body of tanks ... in order to minimise casualties.' Yet only 145 tanks remained fit for action in Fourth Army, just one more than the number allotted to the Australian Corps on the first day of the battle. At midnight, Glasgow was informed that only fourteen tanks would accompany the 1st Division, with seven available to support Hobbs. Monash added that zero was not expected before 10.00 am, but commanders would be informed as soon as it was definitely known. Rawlinson had left the setting of zero hour to the Canadians. It was an elementary blunder, for the starting time of an operation in which units other than the Canadian Corps were involved was

CHAPTER 9

his responsibility. Had Rawlinson acted, Montgomery could see no reason why the attack could not have begun at 6.00 or 7.00 am. According to Montgomery, everyone at Army Headquarters was 'so busy congratulating everyone else on their share of the victory that valuable time was lost in preparing for an advance next day.' It was the outcome of regarding the attack on 8 August as a limited operation. Just as damaging as the euphoria was a misunderstanding between Montgomery and Rawlinson. Currie's staff completed plans for the attack based on Rawlinson's assurance that a reserve division would be available. Montgomery subsequently countermanded the order, forcing the return to the line of a tired Canadian division and the preparation of fresh instructions, which were not completed until about 1.00 am. Zero hour was postponed to 11.00 am.

Wounded Australians from the 15th Brigade and wounded German prisoners shelter beside a British Whippet tank near Harbonnières on 9 August 1918. Confusion at higher headquarters delayed the 1st Division and the 15th Brigade had attacked in its place (AWM E02880).

The Australians were affected more by their own blunders than by this fumbling. Slated to attack alongside the Canadians, the 2nd and 3rd brigades from the 1st Australian Division – barely arrived from Flanders – had only just reached their staging areas up to ten miles rearwards when Monash issued his orders at midnight on 8 August.

The advance that day had moved the front line well past the intricate telephone networks that linked headquarters at all levels during the years of static warfare. While corps and divisional headquarters were still linked, despatch riders were now the main means of communication to headquarters lower down. No-one seems to have realised how long this would take on unfamiliar roads and in darkness. Brigadier Generals James Heane of the 2nd Brigade and Gordon Bennett of the 3rd, were notified about the attack around 4.00 am on 9 August and rushed by car to Glasgow's headquarters for detailed orders at 8.00 am. In turn, they had to prepare orders and issue them to the battalion commanders, who had to do likewise for the company commanders. Marrying up with the supporting tanks and establishing liaison with the Canadians were also necessary. Though both brigades had begun their long approach marches concurrently with these activities, attacking even at 11.00 am was 'an impossible task'. Why no arrangements appear to have been made to get them further forward on the evening of the 8th is puzzling as a shorter approach march would have saved time. After all, Monash had devised a complex double leapfrog arrangement to minimise the approach marches of the assault divisions in the opening attack.

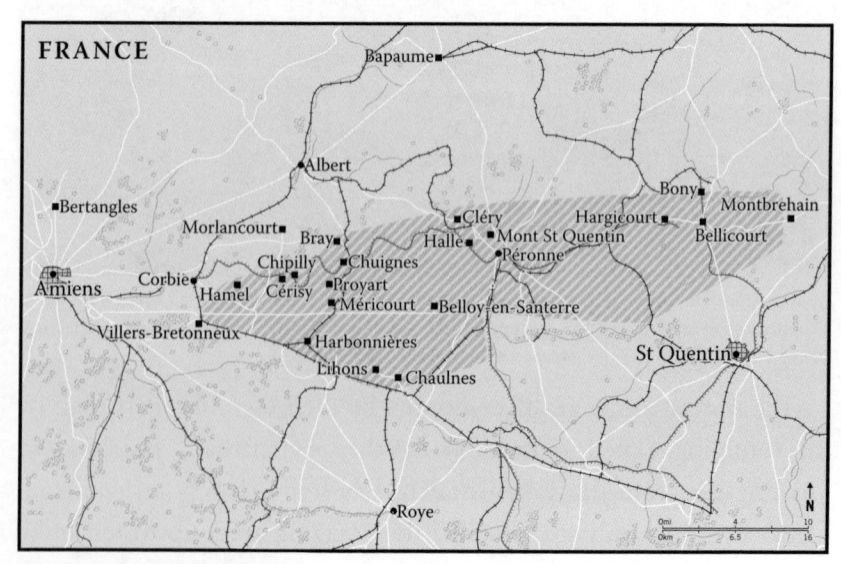

The advance astride the Somme after 8 August 1918

CHAPTER 9

Elliott's 15th Brigade advanced in place of the 1st Division, without a barrage and supported by one tank lent by the Canadians. Encountering heavy resistance, it captured Glasgow's first objective south of Vauvillers, while the village itself was taken by the 8th Brigade as planned. The 1st Division did not leapfrog the 5th until 1.30 pm and it, too, lost heavily to German machine-gun fire before reaching the foot of Lihons Hill at the edge of the French sector of the 1916 battlefield. On the left one-third of the 7th Battalion became casualties, largely because the 2nd Division failed to advance alongside, leaving that flank exposed throughout the attack. Bean blamed Monash, whom he accused of 'passing the responsibility lower down' by ordering close liaison between the attacking divisions instead of fixing a firm zero hour. As a result, Rosenthal did not assault until 4.30 pm, three hours after Glasgow.

Troops from the 1st Division in artillery formation pass through the 15th Brigade on 9 August after tanks had cleared the way. Shortly after this image was taken, two German batteries opened direct fire, destroying the tanks. As the advance continued, one of the batteries was captured (AWM E02847).

Monash was culpable, but not in the sense suggested by the Official Historian. He could not order a definite starting time; like everyone else in the Australian Corps, he had to wait for Currie's decision. He did direct, however, that once the 5th Division captured its objective, 'the 2nd ... will pass through the 5th ... and will attack the second objective ... in conjunction with [the] 1st.' Clearly, Monash expected Rosenthal and Glasgow to attack simultaneously, requiring the close liaison mentioned by Bean. The 2nd Division was still on the Green Line position of the previous day, that is, about half the distance of the 1st Division from the current starting line. Perhaps for this reason it started its preparations much later. Orders were not received by its brigades until 7.55 am, some hours after those in the 1st Division, that they must be behind the Blue Line by 11.00 am. During the morning 'Conferences of the Commanding Officers ... were held well forward on the ground.' They did not finish until 1.30 pm. As for the 'close liaison' ordered by Monash: 'There is no record of any message to or from the 1st Division or the Corps as to the 2nd Division's zero hour.' Despite visiting them in the morning, Monash, it seems, had not ensured that both commanders had the same understanding of his intentions.

There was at least one highlight for the Australians on 9 August. Advancing on the right flank next to the Canadians, the 8th Battalion captured the great German stores dump at the Rosières rail yard. It kept the Australian Corps supplied with timber, tools and barbed wire for the rest of the war (AWM E02895).

Operations on 10 and 11 August, which resulted in the capture of Lihons and nearby Rainecourt, were also characterised by hasty planning. Currie's decision to attack at 8.00 am on the 10th did not reach Glasgow until midnight on the 9th, while the barrage plan arrived too late to pass on to the assaulting companies. These were predominantly infantry attacks, similar in many respects, including the casualties incurred, to those of 1917. Lihons was a difficult objective, for the hill protecting it rose in a gentle slope on which

CHAPTER 9

there was no cover, offering exceptional fields of fire for machine-guns. Tanks were essential for its reduction, but by 11 August there were only thirty-eight available in Fourth Army. Ten of these attacked with the 1st Division; most were knocked out — another reminder of their vulnerability in open country. On 9 August five of the seven allotted to the 5th Division had been destroyed by a single anti-tank gun at Vauvillers; a field gun battery at Lihons knocked out another five assisting the 1st Division. The 2nd Division concluded that tanks should not be employed in daylight during the advance without artillery support, counter-battery fire and smoke. These conditions prevailed at Hamel and on 8 August, but were impossible to achieve on succeeding days to the extent required because of Rawlinson's failure to coordinate the attacks. Monash, like Currie, was in the dock too. In his defence, the exploitation after 8 August was Monash's first experience of a mobile battlefield as a commander at any level and involved a tempo absent from the set-pieces of which he was a master. It also came up against hardening German resistance that highlighted the weaknesses in the 'all-arms weapon system' if one or more of the components was lacking or did not function properly. Monash's initial stutters were understandable; to his credit he soon adapted. Currie quickly put these days behind him too.

Troops from the 6th Battalion rest in an old trench after losing heavily in the advance on Lihons on 10 August. All the officers in this group were casualties, leaving the staff sergeant sitting on the parapet in charge (AWM E02866).

MONASH

Real scope for Monash's generalship existed on the northern bank of the Somme, for which he had finally persuaded Rawlinson to give him responsibility on 9 August. Next morning the 13th Brigade from Sinclair-MacLagan's division took charge of the line there as far as the Bray–Corbie road and the 3rd Division relieved his two brigades south of the river. The commander of the 13th, Brigadier General Herring, who had attacked under Monash as a major at Hill 60 on Gallipoli, joined Sinclair-MacLagan, McNicoll and Gellibrand at a conference at 11.30 am on 10 August at which Monash explained his intention to seize the Etinehem Spur on the northern bank. On the southern side, the line would be advanced east of Proyart to the Méricourt bend, straightening the bulge created by the attacks of the 1st and 2nd divisions. Monash was attracted to the project 'as a species of investment', for these U-shaped spurs did not have to be taken by frontal assault, but could be sealed off at the base to prevent the escape of their garrisons. Herring had simply to advance across the Etinehem Spur and establish a line on its eastern side. On the opposite bank, McNicoll had to break through the German posts on the Amiens–St Quentin road, hurtle 1500 yards along it and then turn north for the Somme, 4500 yards distant. Although their use at night was comparatively untried, tanks were to accompany both columns, mainly for the psychological effect on the Germans, who, as in the fog on 8 August, would be able to hear but not see them. The attack was to begin at 9.30 pm that night.

Herring's assault succeeded brilliantly, the Germans evacuating Etinehem in panic. But McNicoll's advance was bombed shortly after it began, and the Germans, fully alerted, flayed the column with a welter of machine-gun and anti-tank fire, much of it from Proyart. The 37th Battalion in the lead lost a quarter of its strength and its historian's implied criticism of Monash was bitter:

> The name of the author of this extraordinary operation has not yet been divulged. The plan doubtless originated in high quarters, but subordinate commanders who disagreed with it apparently did not offer emphatic enough opposition ... the opinion of the front line soldier was that the whole enterprise was ridiculous and stupid.

CHAPTER 9

Bean partially agreed, asserting that while conditions on the northern bank may have justified the attempt there, German resistance on the southern side had increased since 9 August. But Monash thought the confusion among the Germans was widespread: 'we have only to hit him without warning and roll him up.' This estimate was not altogether implausible, for resistance had been strongest in front of Currie and the southern part of Monash's line next to his, but seemed to diminish as the line ran north to the river. Results so far showed that attacks must be launched with surprise and, because of the openness of the terrain, at night or behind smoke. Monash hoped to increase the shock effect by crashing through on a very narrow front, maintaining the momentum until the Somme was reached. He dispensed with a barrage, although the change of direction of both columns would have made the gunners' task almost impossible anyway. The operation was undoubtedly risky, but something other than the costly conventional assaults of the past two days had to be tried. Even Bean called the plan ingenious. Although their divisional commanders were present, Monash explained it directly to the brigadiers to make sure they understood. Subordinate commanders had time for reconnaissance and to issue their orders, a contrast to the disjointed attacks alongside the Canadians. In the event, misfortune had dogged the 10th Brigade. Old trenches and dumps near the road forced the six tanks to advance on it instead of along either side, curtailing their ability to manoeuvre. According to Gellibrand, McNicoll failed badly, asking for instructions instead of taking action himself, and next day he warned Monash of McNicoll's 'incapacity for any except set-pieces'. If the attack had succeeded, Monash would have been praised for his boldness. He deserved praise even in failure.

The 3rd Division completed the clearance of Proyart and the Méricourt peninsula behind it after two more days of difficult fighting. It was evident that the Germans had recovered on Fourth Army's front, as predicted by Foch when he told Haig on 2 August:

Go as far as you can on the first day, go on again on the second and again on the third, before the enemy can concentrate his reserve. After that you will certainly have to pause, but you may succeed in going so far that the enemy will have to clear out of the Amiens salient. Renew the attack as soon as you can and you may drive him over the Somme.

The opening success had exceeded Haig's wildest expectations, and on 10 August he passed on Foch's order to seize bridgeheads on the Somme on the line Noyon-Ham-Péronne. Foch was elated by the easy advance of the French First and Third armies, which he attributed to German demoralisation, when, in fact, the opposing *Eighteenth Army* and part of *Second Army* were withdrawing. Thoughts of a pause briefly vanished. Visiting Currie on the 10th, Haig's first impression was that the Generalissimo's decision to continue was correct – a message from the Cavalry Corps stated: 'enemy's opposition was diminishing'. But after speaking to Major General Tom Lambert, whose 32nd Division had recently relieved the 3rd Canadian, he was left in no doubt as to the stubborn resistance being encountered in the wilderness of wire and trenches of the old Somme battlefield. Currie began impressing on Haig and Rawlinson that his corps could do more useful work if it returned to its old stamping ground around Arras. Monash also had reservations, though the difficulties facing the Australian Corps were not so great.

Framed by the war trophies it has captured on the Morlancourt Ridge and at Hamel, Monash addresses men of the 2nd Division during a medal presentation ceremony on 13 July 1918. He often spoke to the men behind the line, but never visited them in it (AWM E02732).

CHAPTER 9

Second Lieutenant William Ruthven receives the VC from Monash during the 2nd Division's medal presentation ceremony. A Gallipoli veteran, Ruthven had revived the 22nd Battalion's stalled assault on Ville-sur-Ancre, below Morlancourt, on 19 May (AWM E02730).

Early reports on 11 August confirmed that opposition was increasing. Haig visited Monash at Bertangles to thank him for his efforts and was joined by Byng, whom he told to prepare an immediate stroke against Bapaume. Monash was frequently asked for his opinion. Learning that Haig was accompanying Monash to a conference with his divisional commanders on the outskirts of Villers-Bretonneux, Rawlinson arranged a meeting there as well. He arrived shortly after Haig, who, according to Monash, told the five Australian divisional generals: 'I have the most complete confidence in your corps commander – I want you all to know that I trust him completely.' Clemenceau and Foch joined the gathering, as well as Sir Henry Wilson, to whom Monash confided that the failure of conscription in Australia was due to Hughes' poor handling of the issue. They all sat on the grass under some trees. Tears rolling down his cheeks, Haig said in appreciation 'You do not know what the Australians and Canadians have done for the British Empire in these days.' Rawlinson made the most important announcement. Because German resistance had stiffened, Fourth Army would remain on its present line and 'devote the time to organising for a cut and dried attack which will probably be carried out on the 14 or 15 August.' The interval would allow the artillery to be brought forward and tanks to be reinforced. As Haig had told Foch in a heated argument the previous day, Byng was to take over the offensive, with Rawlinson supporting his flank between the Somme and Ancre.[70]

Although the successes of July and August established Monash's position, he commanded for much of the period in the knowledge that the conspiracy against him was continuing. On 2 June he had written to Hughes in England, informing him that Birdwood should remain as GOC AIF in spite of Murdoch's advice. Hughes could make up his mind after he had visited France and considered the views of 'those of us in the field who are really more vitally interested than anyone else.' Four days later, Murdoch tried to bribe Monash with the vision of the GOC AIF as a full general who would be 'a zealous and supreme representative of the AIF in all its battles and other interests.' He was practising the same 'subterranean methods' of which Bean had accused Monash. Their plotting was deeply hurtful. It was 'very cruel' of Murdoch to try and deprive him of his command just at the moment he attained it, Monash told Bean. The position of GOC was a poor compensation. Furthermore, Haig had said he was quite prepared to give him 'a place anywhere among his Corps Commanders' if the Australian Corps had not been vacant. Both Murdoch and Bean acknowledged that it would be very difficult to remove him, but the ideal to be aimed at was still 'Monash GOC AIF and White GOC Corps'. Hughes agreed fully that Birdwood could not remain as GOC AIF; he 'ended his career with us when he went over to the English.' Monash belatedly wrote to Pearce on 21 June, urging the retention of Birdwood, and received powerful support from Hobbs, who confided to the Defence Minister that should Monash replace Birdwood:

> ... it would mean the loss to the AIF of a Commander of very great ability and exceptional energy and experience, who enjoys absolutely the complete confidence and respect of the AIF as a fighting leader ... General Monash undoubtedly, for many reasons, is the best man to command the Corps.

CHAPTER 9

Major General Talbot Hobbs. A successful architect and devout Christian, Hobbs had been a gunner since joining the volunteers in 1883. He was a breath of fresh air for the 5th Division after McCay. A plain speaker, he backed Monash strongly when Bean and Murdoch were intriguing against him (Army Museum of WA AMWA 32297).

After speaking to the divisional commanders just before Hamel, Hughes was seriously shaken to find that only Gellibrand expressed doubts about Monash. They could not have been serious, for the Prime Minister rebuked Murdoch: 'Well, I haven't met a single one of them that thinks as you do. They all say the same thing. You tell me there are men who think the other way – where are they?' On 12 July Murdoch was on the receiving end of some forthright comments from White, who charged him with impropriety as a journalist for interfering in a Government decision made on the advice of the responsible authorities. Monash deserved his post, and Birdwood could still exercise authority as GOC while commanding Fifth Army. He, White, would accept command of the AIF only if the decision were submitted to and approved by Monash. Thereupon Murdoch dismissed White as having 'a lot of the old feeling of subservience to England ... which cannot operate in Australia as a counterforce to Bolshevism, Sinn Feinism and all present disuniting, anti-Australian sections.' On 12 August Hughes offered Birdwood the choice of remaining as GOC, provided he relinquished command of Fifth Army. Haig advised Birdwood to accept the offer, but to ask Hughes to allow the existing arrangement to continue until 30 November to avoid a change in army command at a time of major offensive operations. Hughes agreed.

King George V invests Monash with his knighthood at Bertangles (AWM E02964).

After Hamel, Monash told Murdoch that he wanted 'Fighting Honours', and would be quite content on attaining them to take over from Birdwood. By mid-August he had his 'Fighting Honours', and as if to symbolise the achievement, was knighted by the King on the steps of Bertangles. It was a most impressive occasion, with detachments of 100 men from each division lining the long drive and several hundred trophies of war, from howitzers to searchlights, framing the quadrangle of the château. Ironically, Monash made the only mistake, rising after the King had tapped him on the left shoulder instead of waiting to be tapped on the right as well. Bean supposed he was 'only half a knight'. The quest for publicity continued. Presenting medals a few weeks

CHAPTER 9

before, Monash would steer the recipient into the best position for the most flattering photograph of himself. When he took the salute, 'he kept one eye cocked on the camera; and when it was clearly preparing to open fire, he made his salute one of overpowering dignity.'

'Well done that man.' The King congratulates Monash, now wearing the ribbon of the KCB around his neck, after the investiture. Brigadier General Carruthers, DA&QMG, stands in the background between them. Captured by the Australians on 8 August, the German machine-gun on the step was among the many war trophies brought to Bertangles for the ceremony (AWM A03316).

Chapter 10
The Most Resolute Offensive

Byng's assumption of the main offensive caused the indefinite postponement of the attack that Rawlinson had foreshadowed for 15 August. On the Fourth Army front, the Somme bridges were bombarded by long-range guns and the Australian Corps resumed 'peaceful penetration' in order 'to dispose of a number of strong points, small woods and village ruins which ... were a source of annoyance to us.' The lull permitted a brief but much-needed rest. The 3rd Division was relieved on 12 August by the 17th, a British formation given to Monash after he pointed out to Rawlinson that any worthwhile break for his tired units was impossible while they had to hold a line 16 000 yards long and attack as well. The 4th and 5th divisions relieved the 1st and 17th on 16 and 18 August respectively, and another British division, the 32nd, took over from the 2nd on the 19th.[71] Every Australian division, therefore, enjoyed a respite between 12 and 23 August. The timing of reliefs demanded fine judgement by Monash. If he kept a division in the line too long, several weeks would be required to restore its vigour, leaving the corps unable to sustain the continuous offensive in which it was engaged and during which: 'I regarded it as a fundamental principle to employ whenever possible absolutely fresh and rested troops for an operation of any magnitude or importance.'

It would have been more appropriate had Monash said 'comparatively' instead of 'absolutely', for by mid-August the Australian Corps had been in action for five months without a reasonable break, and there were no 'absolutely fresh and rested troops' within its ranks. But Monash's principle was valid. The attacks at Lihons and Proyart had fallen on the 1st Division, which was the

CHAPTER 10

corps reserve on 8 August, and on the 2nd and 3rd, whose assault on the Green Line that day encountered token resistance. Because their advance was the most difficult on the 8th, the 4th and 5th divisions had only minor roles thereafter and were rested sufficiently to relieve the others for the intended attack one week later. By ensuring that hardship was shared equally, Monash forestalled any impression among the men of one division that they were being called on to do more than the others. His insistence on the responsibilities of their officers towards them was as strong as ever. Discovering a casual attitude towards the enforcement of sanitary measures to prevent disease, he published in a special order the names of thirty units, the commanders of which 'were apparently content to have their men living under filthy conditions.' Henceforth, commanders guilty of this charge would be dismissed.

Bray from the north-east. The 10th Brigade from the 3rd Division struck it from the distant high ground on the right at 1.00 am on 24 August, first enveloping it and then assaulting directly. Most of the Germans withdrew to avoid being cut off. They had used the church as a hospital. The small wooden tower carried telephone lines rearward (AWM E03116).

Byng's offensive began on 21 August. North of the Somme, III Corps, temporarily commanded by Godley in place of the ailing Butler, and the 3rd Australian Division, which had now moved alongside it on the river, were to carry forward Third Army's flank by advancing next day on the line Albert-Bray. Monash discussed the attack with Godley, but the main responsibility was left with Gellibrand who would 'concert his plan with III Corps'. The operation showcased Gellibrand's ability as a divisional commander. His sector on the high ground overlooking Bray formed a salient that protruded sharply towards the village, making the arrangement of a barrage to precede his attack almost impossible. Hence he intended to seize Happy Valley, north of Bray, for it lay ahead of the straight section of his line, from which a creeping barrage could easily be delivered. The village would then be vulnerable to encirclement, the method preferred by Gellibrand for its capture. After a partial success on the 22nd, the attack was renewed at 1.00 am on 24 August. An advance either side of Bray diverted its strong defences from the assaulting troops, who entered the village at three separate points and quickly cleared it.

Monash's attention was rivetted to the southern side of the river, where the Canadian Corps, which had been on the right of the Australians on 8 August and the days after, was moving back to Arras following Currie's representations. The 1st and 4th Canadian divisions were under Monash's command on 22 August until their departure next day, briefly expanding the Australian Corps to eight divisions. 'By the irony of events, [Monash] constantly controlled more troops and far more important operations than did ... General Birdwood, now raised to command an army.' Liddell Hart relied heavily on Monash's example to support his post-war argument against the notion 'which has become a dogma, that a commander cannot possibly handle more than three or four sub-units.' He advocated the horizontal organisation represented by the Australian Corps rather than the conventional vertical one with an army commander handling three corps commanders, who, in turn, each commanded three divisions. Liddell Hart concluded that the

CHAPTER 10

size of the corps was an important factor in Monash's success, for it endowed him with a flexibility denied his contemporaries. He was able to hold a much wider front with at least one division in reserve and one resting, allowing him to maintain the momentum of his advance for much longer than they could theirs.

As Monash noted, the offensives in the final weeks of the war, with the exception of the assault on the Hindenburg Line, did not follow an order carefully prescribed beforehand. Even Haig 'bent [his] energies … upon the problem of hitting wherever and whenever an opportunity offered.' But Monash failed to mention that a broad policy had been laid down by Foch. The Generalissimo conceived a series of deep penetrations on different parts of the front, creating salients so acute that the Germans would be forced to retire between them and thence along the front as a whole. Of course, there might be disagreement on when an offensive should be broken off, and Foch's dispute with Haig over the termination of the thrust before Amiens afforded a classic example. From his interpretation of these events in which his corps played an important part, it is clear that Monash again saw little beyond the limited horizon of a corps commander.

According to Monash, the stroke that accompanied Gellibrand's attack at Bray emerged from his belief that another blow, 'energetically exploited, could force the Germans to retire across the Somme.' Actually, it was part of Rawlinson's scheme for the cooperation of his army with Byng's, which had begun on 22 August with the assaults of III Corps and the 3rd Division. Both armies were to attack next day on a front of 33 miles, the right extremity of which was the Australian sector south of the Somme. If the operation were successful, General Sir Henry Horne's First Army would extend the breach northwards beyond the Scarpe. In the plan that Rawlinson explained to Monash on 19 August, the objectives on the northern bank were set, but he was to select those on the southern.[72]

Monash ordered the capture of all but the northern end of the Chuignes Valley, the next and the largest of the re-entrants debouching into the Somme that the corps had been crossing since

8 August. The 1st Division had the main role, seizing Chuignolles as part of an advance of some 2000 yards on a frontage of almost three miles by its 1st and 2nd brigades. On the southern flank, one brigade of the 32nd Division would advance either side of Herleville, which had proved too strong to reduce by 'peaceful penetration'. The attack was a replica of Hamel, tanks accompanying the infantry under a creeping barrage to a Green Line. All movement was to take place at night, with aircraft covering tank noise and dropping ammunition during the assault. Monash's employment of the 1st and 32nd divisions was a practical expression of the principle 'never entrust a critical operation to troops who had already been tried by previous exertion.' The 4th and 5th divisions, which were to have launched the attack on 15 August, had been in the line for several days by the 23rd. It did not matter that they had seen little action in this period; neither would be as fresh as the 1st Division, which had been relieved one week previously.

Two uncharacteristic lapses marred Monash's planning of this attack. He set the Green Line short of the old French trenches from the 1916 battlefield on the eastern slope of the valley, so that the wire protecting them would not have to be crossed under machine-gun fire. The wire, then, lay between the objective and the Germans, forming a barrier to any counter-attack. But this left the Germans with room to manoeuvre on the Foucaucourt Plateau in rear, while the 1st Division clung to the edge of the valley, the slopes of which, Brigadier General Heane of the 2nd Brigade protested, would be drenched with gas. Monash had overlooked a fundamental principle of defence, that a position must have depth. The reason is unclear. He knew that the slope on the far side of the valley, appropriately called Gibraltar, was mostly too steep for the tanks to climb. They could not be relied on to crush the wire; even so, the powerful creeping barrage would hardly leave it intact. A tenth of the barrage consisted of smoke shell to mask the advance from German frontal fire. Other smoke missions would screen it on the Somme flank. Of course there would still be risks, but the danger alluded to by Heane outweighed them.

CHAPTER 10

Major General Thomas Glasgow. Taciturn, forceful and rock steady, Queensland pastoralist Glasgow had been a light horse commander at Anzac. He performed well in France as commander of the 13th Brigade in the successful counter-attack at Villers-Bretonneux in April 1918 and as commander of the 1st Division in the attack at Chuignes in August. Though not blind to Monash's faults, he thought him highly capable (AWM A02103).

Possibly due to Heane's complaint, Monash allowed the 2nd Brigade 'to extend its hold by exploitation, if possible, after the barrage ended.' On 21 August, Monash extended the attack further, instructing the 1st Division 'to advance their observation line to a more suitable position to be determined by the Divisional Commander.' The exploitation initially confined to the 2nd Brigade was now general along Glasgow's entire frontage. Monash announced this change at his conference to explain the battle, also on 21 August, which he prefaced, as usual, with the remark: 'Settle everything finally, here and now.' But there was another, more drastic change next day. Less than twenty-four hours before the attack was to begin, Monash directed Glasgow to seize Froissy Beacon, on the Somme flank, and Garenne Wood on its southern slope. This entailed an advance across that part of the Chuignes Valley omitted from the orders he issued on 19 August.

Monash did not have to see Froissy Beacon. Its importance was obvious from the map from which he planned the operation. The steep, triangular plateau dominated the surrounding valleys and, unless it was taken as part of the main attack, Glasgow's gains further south could be threatened. With these changes, the operation took on a different character. The set-piece phase was unaltered, but there would be two exploitation phases. The 1st Brigade was to continue its attack for 1000 yards beyond the Green Line, establishing a foothold on the south-western edge of Froissy, through which the 3rd Brigade would advance to complete its capture. Monash rose at 4.00 am on 23 August to watch the commencement of the battle forty-eight minutes later. Bean described the result: 'There has never been a more completely successful fight made by one single division than that of the 1st Australian Division this day.'

Surprise was complete. As the morning was clear, the smoke barrage prevented many tank casualties and thus made an important contribution to success, for the German machine-gunners fired until they were crushed by the vehicles. The fighting for Froissy Beacon and Garenne Wood in the third phase was particularly severe, because the Germans, believing the attack had spent itself, directed strong reinforcements to both. The 3rd Brigade attacked under a creeping barrage fired by batteries rapidly pushed forward during the early phases. Glasgow had ordered the 1st Brigade to complete its exploitation across the valley, which ran south-east to Chuignes, by the time this barrage fell, thereby securing the line for the 3rd's assault. Its battalions captured Garenne Wood by encirclement and, by driving towards the Somme, threatened to envelop the Germans, who withdrew from Froissy Beacon towards Cappy. Chuignes, too, had fallen. At a cost of 1000 casualties, the 1st Division captured one quarter of the 8000 prisoners taken on 23 August by the Third and Fourth armies.

Although lauding the skill and cooperation of the regimental officers, Monash attributed much of the success to Glasgow. As a

CHAPTER 10

commander, he won through 'not so much by exceptional mental gifts, or by tactical skill of a very high order, as by his personal driving force and determination, which impressed themselves upon all his subordinates.' These qualities were tested by Monash before the battle. As a divisional commander at Messines, Passchendaele and Sailly-Laurette, Monash had been the victim of sudden alterations in plan, orders given with no time for proper distribution, and objectives to which there were strong tactical objections. No doubt the subsequent difficulties confirmed his belief in the principle of fixity of plan. Yet he forced these inconveniences on Glasgow by altering the scheme twice, the second and more important modification coming on the eve of the attack. The significance of Froissy Beacon should have been apparent to Monash when the plan was first mooted on 19 August. Its omission was an unusual error for a general who 'always understood thoroughly the ground he was to fight on.'

When Haig issued three important directives in the final week of August 1918, Monash interpreted them to suit his own view of the situation. Firstly, the C-in-C concluded on 22 August that the battles of 8 and 21 August and the attacks that followed them had further worn out the Germans and disrupted their plans. They had the means neither to launch major counter-attacks nor to resist the current advance on a very wide front. Attacks with limited objectives were now inappropriate; instead:

> ... the most resolute offensive is everywhere desirable. Risks which a month ago would have been criminal to incur ought now to be incurred as a duty ... each division should be given a distant objective which must be reached independently of its neighbour and even if one's flank is thereby exposed for the time being.

Monash received this directive next day, 23 August, when it was qualified by another instruction. Haig believed that attacks would have 'in most cases ... to deal with a system of defence organised in depth. Through such a system a sudden break can only be expected under very exceptional circumstances.'[73] Once these defences were broken, the conditions of his previous directive would apply. Commanders such as Monash should use 'their initiative and power of manoeuvre and should not be cramped by the habit of moving in continuous lines.' In accordance with this policy, the third directive required Third Army to advance on Bapaume and Fourth Army on Péronne. As resources were insufficient to press the offensive on both fronts simultaneously, Byng would continue the main thrust, with Rawlinson advancing astride the Somme to protect his right. Rawlinson's orders to Monash on 24 August were naturally based on Haig's instructions. The Germans were showing more and more signs of demoralisation, and full advantage was to be taken of moonlight to drive forward and deny them rest. North of the Somme the Australian Corps was to 'keep touch' with Godley's corps and on the southern bank 'no opportunity will be missed of making ground towards Péronne.'

The next two days were crucial. Haig pointed out to Rawlinson on 25 August the need for an equal number of divisions in support as in the line, enabling 'troops to rest and operations to be continued without intermission.' In response, Rawlinson sought reinforcement, which Haig refused because his was the subsidiary advance. Rawlinson thereupon vacillated, apparently doubting the wisdom of the 'making ground' order he had issued the previous day. This concern underlay his meeting with Monash later on the 25th, at which he warned that the presence of a new division meant that the Germans intended to reinforce their front opposite. The offensive policy had to be revised: 'the Fourth Army would now mark time and await events elsewhere.' Monash disagreed, believing that the fruits of Chuignes would be lost. Furthermore, his line was about to be shortened, the French taking charge of it as far as Lihons, which would allow the 4th Division to be rested. At his divisional commanders' conference on 26 August and in orders issued subsequently, Monash repeated verbatim Rawlinson's new directive, but circumvented his superior by adding:

> The offensive policy will be continued on the Australian Corps front by means of aggressive patrols. Close touch will be kept with the enemy in this way and advantage will be taken of any opportunity to seize the enemy's positions and to advance our line.

This was the only time that Monash broke the shackles imposed by the chain of command, and his action required moral courage. He

CHAPTER 10

may have seized on Rawlinson's instruction on 24 August to 'keep touch', but that was superseded by his order next day to 'await events elsewhere'. Monash was determined that the advantages already won must not be frittered away by allowing the Germans a respite, for then greater demands would have to be made on his own men, whose tiredness, even now, was causing serious concern. Rawlinson's diary shows that he knew what Monash was up to, so this was not a case of 'a wily corps commander outfoxing his obtuse superior'. Rather, 'Rawlinson would not impose a veto on a corps commander of proven attainments who judged that the forces at his disposal were sufficient to carry out a further operation.' The episode reflects credit on both Rawlinson and Monash. Not until 8.20 pm on 27 August did Rawlinson formally order the resumption of efforts to 'press back enemy rearguards', with the Australian Corps directing its advance on Péronne.

Monash allotted each of his divisions a lane, along which it was to move on a single brigade frontage. To maintain momentum, the leading brigade would not be relieved 'until it had reached the limits of its endurance', calculated by Monash to be at least two days. He was employing a method similar to that proposed by Gellibrand for the set-piece attack on 8 August, but it was much better suited to the rapid advance to contact that applied now. It also accorded with the trend in the BEF to decentralise control to divisions in the more fluid operational setting that often characterised the final advance. Adopting Haig's suggestion of 23 August, Monash added two field guns to each infantry battalion to deal with machine-guns and field guns left behind by the Germans to delay the advance. This was not Monash's answer to the problem, as he himself claimed. But he overrode the protests of the artillery by insisting that one fifth of the ammunition carried by each battery consist of smoke to blind the Germans. By 28 August the 3rd Division had seized Suzanne, Vaux and Curlu to face Cléry, while on the southern side the 2nd, 5th and 32nd divisions were approaching the Somme bend.

At Cléry the Somme abruptly abandons its northerly direction, making almost a right-angled turn past Péronne to follow a westerly course to the sea. The steep valleys and jutting spurs, which bedevilled the Australian advance from Sailly-le-Sec onwards, gave way to gentle slopes descending to the river a mile or so away. Its course was canalised but, extending 500 yards to the east, were marshes through which it flowed in numerous channels too deep to be waded. There were crossings at Brie and St Christ, respectively three and five miles south of Péronne, as well as the road bridge and the bridge carrying the railway to St Quentin into the town. Péronne was a formidable obstacle, with Vauban's ramparts towering some sixty feet above the Somme and its tributary, the Cologne, which between them formed a moat around it. Three hundred feet high and dominating Péronne one mile to the north was Mont St Quentin, its parched, barren slopes furrowed by the remains of old trenches and seamed by several belts of barbed-wire entanglements. Men who had served with the 2nd Brigade on Gallipoli would shudder at the resemblance to Achi Baba. Held by an excellent division, the *2nd Prussian Guards*, Mont St Quentin commanded the river and its approaches, including Cléry, lying at the foot of the long pencil-shaped Bouchavesnes Spur and connected by a footbridge to Ommiécourt on the opposite bank, and Halle, site of another crossing. Lesser divisions defended Péronne and the line from Cléry northwards along the Bouchavesnes Spur.

The Australian Corps was confronted by a position with defensive advantages at least as great as those that had defeated the 3rd Division's attack on Passchendaele on 12 October 1917. Mont St Quentin and the Bouchavesnes Spur were mutually supporting, just as the Passchendaele Ridge and the Bellevue Spur had been. As at Passchendaele, if the assault reached one feature, it would be deluged by fire from the other. Both had to be assaulted simultaneously, and both had to be taken, if Péronne were to fall. The marshy Somme was a bigger obstacle than the Ravebeek.

From the line reached on 28 August, Monash knew that the Germans would have to withdraw behind the Somme next day and, from prisoners' statements, it seemed likely that this was but a stage in a planned retirement to the Hindenburg Line. Adhering to the policy he had instituted on the 26th, he decided to follow the Germans

CHAPTER 10

across the river so that his advance would be on them even before their withdrawal from the western bank was completed. This would entail a 'bounce crossing'. The 2nd Division was to seize the high ground between Biaches and Orme de Barleux as a preliminary to securing the Halle causeway, from which it would attack the Mont. After taking Villers-Carbonnel and the Brie crossing below it, the 5th Division was to advance on the heights overlooking Le Mesnil on the eastern bank. On Hobbs's right, the 32nd Division would capture the St Christ crossing. These orders were given by Monash on the afternoon of the 28th, and it is no wonder that he did not refer to them in *Australian Victories*. The direction of the assault was due east; that is, frontally against the river line. But this was the very course that Monash deprecated: 'it would have been a costly enterprise, and fraught with every prospect of failure, should the enemy be prepared to put up any sort of fight against it.'

In fairness to Monash, he was confronted with a dilemma. Although it was the most direct attack, it was also the quickest and simplest and, if the Germans were disorganised, it might succeed. But for the past few days machine-gunners had contested his advance stoutly, necessitating at Foucaucourt, for example, a heavy bombardment before it could proceed. Monash would have to cross the river in front of them. The scheme was no more than a gamble and a desperate one at that – more so even than the jabs at Proyart and Etinehem almost three weeks previously.

The outcome went against him. As the 2nd Division crossed the slope to the river early on 29 August, artillery and machine-gun fire erupted from the eastern bank. Though the canal was reached, the marshes beyond could not be crossed. The Germans demolished the bridges, relieving many Australians who saw the torrential fire they attracted. From this time on, all crossings south of Cléry were continuously engaged. Monash now adopted the plan that he claimed was 'vaguely' forming in his mind since the day he extended his boundary north of the river: 'This was the plan of turning the line of the Somme from the north, instead of forcing it by direct assault from the west.' He should have added: 'as I had tried but failed to do.'

MONASH

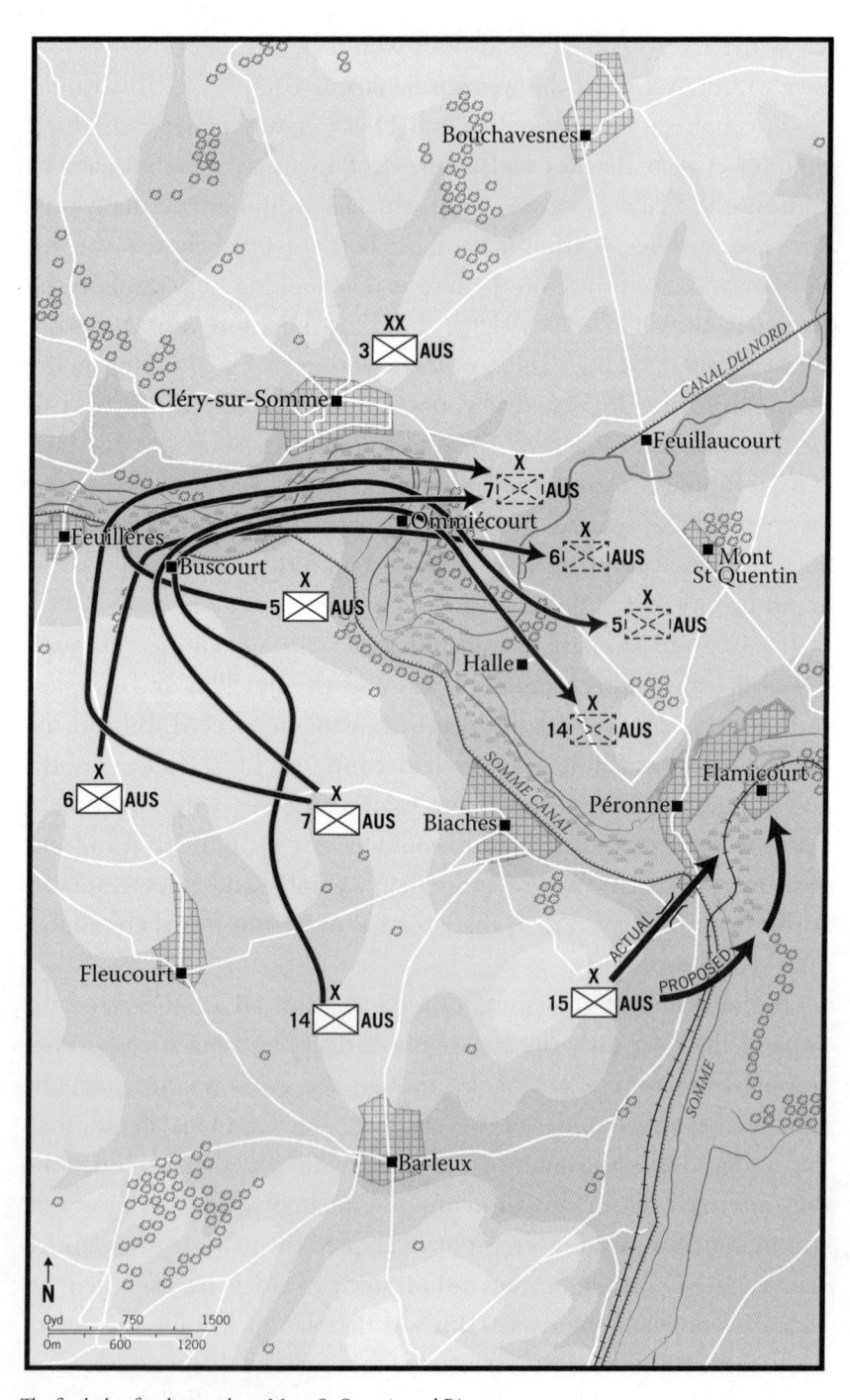

The final plan for the attack on Mont St Quentin and Péronne

CHAPTER 10

Australian engineers repairing the bridge over the Somme at Chipilly on 12 August. It was back in operation next day. Monash's insistence on rapidly restoring communications destroyed by the Germans ensured that his own advance was always well supported logistically and made possible the manoeuvre that took Mont St Quentin and Péronne (AWM E03838).

At a conference at 5.00 pm on 29 August at Hobbs's headquarters, Monash moved the frontage of the attack northwards along the river to Cléry. Each division was to side-slip to the left, the 32nd taking over the 5th's front as far as Ferme Lamire, Hobbs extending 4000 yards from there to Biaches, and Rosenthal occupying the remaining 4700 yards to Ommiécourt. The 3rd Division, which, in the original scheme had merely 'to advance in cooperation with the 3rd Corps', was now given a vital task, the seizure of Cléry and the high ground north-east of it, as well as the entire Bouchavesnes Spur. Rosenthal would cross behind Gellibrand's front line if the Halle causeway still proved impossible, and thus approach Mont St Quentin from the north-west. If unable to cross at Péronne, Hobbs was to follow Rosenthal through the 3rd Division in order to reach his new objective, the heights south of the town and the Buire Spur east of it. Conversely, if Hobbs secured the only crossing, Rosenthal would follow the 5th Division. Each was to employ a single brigade initially. The 32nd Division would cross only if resistance was light; its main task was to demonstrate along the river line, diverting attention from the northern flank. During the night, the engineers would build as many footbridges as possible for the use of the infantry at dawn on 30 August. Bridge repair generally was an important element in this plan. From the beginning of his advance, Monash had been equally concerned with the restoration of recaptured territory as with driving the Germans eastward. As soon as the infantry passed a ruined crossing, engineers began its repair, allowing him to move men, guns and supplies rapidly from one side of the river to the other. Even as he was planning the attack on Mont St Quentin, they had almost completed work on the crossing at Feuillères, about 3000 yards west of Ommiécourt.

Shortly after the battle, Monash described it as following 'a swift turning movement at night, on the lines of some of Stonewall Jackson's sudden onslaughts, but of course on a much larger scale.' Smithers goes so far as to assert that Jackson was the inspiration for the plan. Despite Monash's extensive knowledge of the American Civil War, Smithers' claim is dubious. It overlooks the frontal attack ordered in Monash's initial scheme and then neglects the nature of operations in his second plan. The 'turning movement' was contingent on both the 2nd and 5th divisions crossing the Somme near Cléry to advance through the 3rd. But this was only one possibility. If either or both of the crossings at Halle and Péronne were secured, Hobbs and Rosenthal would use them, and there would be no such movement. Bean's assessment was more realistic:

> Among the operations planned by Monash it stands out as one of movement rather than a set-piece; indeed within Australian experience of the Western Front it was the only important fight in which quick, free manoeuvre played a decisive part. It furnishes a complete answer to the comment that Monash was merely a composer of set-pieces.

CHAPTER 10

The study of Monash as a commander suggests that the provision for the 'turning movement' was predictable. In the plan for the set-piece at Passchendaele, he proposed to capture the village by an encirclement around both flanks to connect well beyond it. The operations at Etinehem and Méricourt afforded a more recent instance. Neither was a set-piece, but a hastily improvised attack, supported by tanks, to take advantage of local conditions. Both involved 'a swift turning movement at night', the audacity of which left incredulous those who had to execute them.

Seen in context, Monash's final plan for the capture of Mont St Quentin and Péronne is less surprising than first appearances suggest. Its boldness was matched by a greater appreciation of ground than his first scheme, from which the exclusion of the Bouchavesnes Spur was a weakness. Nor was the plan rigid; indeed flexibility was perhaps its outstanding feature. Divisional and brigade commanders might have to switch their formations with little warning between crossings, necessitating close liaison and a perfect understanding of one another's plan. The flawless execution of the assembly arrangements and leapfrogs on 8 August portended their abilities to do these things successfully. It was just as certain, though, that great demands would be made on already tired men. Although Rawlinson must have had some idea of the intention after Montgomery's visit to the Australian Corps on 29 August, he was not aware of the details until Monash explained them to him the following afternoon. Monash recalled that Rawlinson:

> ... was pleased to be pleasantly satirical. 'And so you think you're going to take Mont St Quentin with three battalions! What presumption! However, I don't think I ought to stop you! So, go ahead, and try! – and I wish you luck!'

'Once again', Prior and Wilson remark, 'Rawlinson had been prepared to allow his confidence in Monash's judgement and his reluctance to disrupt a winning combination to override his own misgivings.' Rawlinson was also pleased because Monash's scheme suited his wider plan for Fourth Army, which involved seizing the high ground between Buire and Nurlu, a village on the same ridge as

Mont St Quentin, but lying six miles to the north-east. In deference to Monash, the boundaries between the Australian Corps and III Corps were 'not meant to be rigidly adhered to whenever the tactical situation demands that either ... can gain ground by crossing beyond its boundary.'

The need for haste imposed severe handicaps on subordinate commanders, for it left them with progressively less time to issue orders. Rosenthal briefed his brigadiers at 7.30 pm on 29 August for the attack on Mont St Quentin at 5.00 am on the 30th. Before then, their formations had to cross the Somme. When this was impossible at Halle, he switched the 5th Brigade to Ommiécourt, but fire from the eastern outskirts of Cléry rendered the footbridge unapproachable. At 4.00 am on 30 August Rosenthal ordered the 5th Brigade to march two miles further west to the crossing that had been repaired at Feuillères. There was now no hope of launching the attack on time, for this move would take at least two hours. Then the Ommiécourt crossing was destroyed. All hinged on the seizure of Cléry and the Bouchavesnes Spur by the 3rd Division. Its leading battalion, the 38th from the 10th Brigade, had reached the outskirts of the village the evening before, dazed with exhaustion after more than seventy hours' continuous fighting. The brigade commander, McNicoll, was shocked when, at 9.00 pm, Gellibrand ordered him to attack next morning, one hour before Rosenthal's assault on Mont St Quentin was due to begin. Cooperating with the 9th Brigade, the 10th Brigade managed to clear the Germans from the heights overlooking the river bend, during which Rosenthal informed Gellibrand of the fire from the Cléry area, which had prevented his crossing. Gellibrand directed McNicoll to eliminate the nuisance, and at 11.00 am on 30 August a company from the 40th Battalion advanced just beyond the ruined village, capturing 59 prisoners, more than its own strength. While the fight progressed, the 5th Brigade crossed the river at Feuillères and secured the area east of the Ommiécourt crossing, which was quickly repaired. The attack on Mont St Quentin was postponed to 5.00 am on 31 August.

CHAPTER 10

Mont St Quentin from the point near Cléry from which the 5th Brigade launched its attack on 31 August. After capturing the summit, the attackers were forced back to Elsa Trench immediately below the trees. The 6th Brigade assaulted from there to take the summit next day (AWM E03577).

In one respect the delay was fortunate, for it permitted the move of artillery to Cléry and close to the south bank of the river, where excellent views of the battlefield could be obtained. As there was still not enough time to arrange a creeping barrage, selected localities were engaged to the limits of gun range, the bombardment lifting according to the expected rate of the infantry's advance. Alluding to the amount of artillery supporting the attack – five field brigades and four heavy brigades – Terraine asserts: 'On 31 August it was the guns that made success possible.' The weight of fire was certainly impressive, but, as General Sir Martin Farndale shrewdly notes, the use of predicted concentrations to deliver it helped to unnerve the Germans, who had grown used to the creeping barrage, and therefore aided surprise. Nothing, though, should detract from the magnificence of the infantry effort. The strength of the 5th Brigade was a pathetic 1320 all ranks or an average of 330 per battalion. As the 18th Battalion remained in reserve, fewer than 900 troops actually attacked, making as much noise as possible to convince the Germans that their numbers were greater. The defenders were overwhelmed by the speed of the assault, and almost 700 prisoners were taken as the 17th Battalion cleared Halle on the right of the attack and the 20th cleared Feuillaucourt on the Bapaume Road on the left. At 8.00 am Rosenthal informed Monash: '5 Bde report having captured Mt St Quentin from which the Australian flag now flies.'

But a salient had been formed that jutted about two miles beyond the existing line, and prompt action was needed on the flanks if the gains were to be held. Monash was not found wanting as he ordered Gellibrand at 8.35 am to capture the rest of the Bouchavesnes Spur on the left, adding: 'Casualties no longer matter.' Rosenthal was to push the 6th and 7th brigades through the 5th. On the right, Hobbs had been unable to find a crossing, which led the commander of the 15th Brigade, Elliott, temporarily to arrest his commanding officers. Monash instructed Hobbs to send his reserve brigade, the 14th, across the river at Ommiécourt, taking Rosenthal's route through Cléry to attack Péronne. As the footbridge was now under intense shellfire, the crossing was made at Buscourt, 1000 yards further west, and by 8.00 pm the 14th Brigade had assembled just east of Cléry, after taking ten hours to complete a march that in peacetime it could have accomplished in three.

Heavy counter-attacks developed against the 5th Brigade, forcing its retirement to Elsa Trench just below the summit, where it repulsed five assaults throughout the day. Feuillaucourt also had to be given up. But the 5th's precise location was obscure and heavy machine-gun fire from the newly recaptured positions prevented the advance of the 6th Brigade towards Halle, so that the 7th and the 14th brigades could not proceed much beyond Cléry. Monash's hope that the attack could be resumed that afternoon now proved illusory. The earlier success of the 5th Brigade may have made him complacent for, after issuing orders for the exploitation, he left for Corbie to discuss plans for cooperation with Godley, and then was 'busy settling down' at the new Corps Headquarters at Méricourt. No further instructions were issued until evening, when Monash discussed the next day's operations with Rosenthal, who gave his orders at 9.00 pm. The 6th Brigade was to retake the Mont and Feuillaucourt, while the 14th captured the left of

CHAPTER 10

the German line holding the 5th; that is, the slope above Péronne and the town itself. Rosenthal's conference did not end until midnight, leaving Brigadier General Stewart of the 14th Brigade less than six hours to prepare and issue his orders, for his battalion commanders to do the same, and then for the brigade to move 2500 yards in darkness across unfamiliar terrain to its start line.

A company from the 21st Battalion moves along a communication trench as the 6th Brigade renews the assault on the crest of Mont St Quentin at 1.30 pm on 1 September (AWM E03139).

The attack began at 6.00 am on 1 September and was immediately met by heavy fire that prevented the 6th Brigade advancing past Elsa Trench, which was held by the 5th. Between 1.00 and 1.30 pm, every available gun bombarded the area in front, enabling the crest to be rushed. The Prussian Guards fought to the end, but by evening the 6th Brigade, only 1334 strong at the start of the action, had established a new line 600 yards beyond the summit. Stewart also encountered strong resistance. His 53rd Battalion had to capture its start line and then, with the 54th on the right, fight through Florina and Johannes trenches, each protected by broad wire entanglements. The 53rd then struggled through Anvil Wood, north-west of Péronne, from the ramparts of which it was raked by withering fire and halted on the town's outskirts. The 54th enjoyed more success, swinging around to enter Péronne on its western side and almost reaching the town centre. Elliott then started the 15th Brigade over the river to attack Flamicourt, across the moat to the south. In the apparent belief that Mont St Quentin ahead had fallen and the northern ramparts of Péronne were secure, the 53rd was ordered to resume its advance, against the advice of regimental officers who knew the assumptions to be false. Inevitably the attack failed.

The 21st Battalion leaves Elsa Trench and heads for the hamlet atop Mont St Quentin in the 1.30 pm attack by the 6th Brigade. This assault finally took the crest (AWM E03104).

Monash was highly critical of Hobbs for his handling of the 14th Brigade since he had diverted it to Buscourt the day before:

General Hobbs is an attractive little man, and a very good commander in some ways … but he lacks the drive necessary for an operation of this sort … He had only 4,000 yards to move, and the whole morning to do it in. And yet he was not able to be in position in time to support the flank of the 5th Brigade. I don't think that should have been a very difficult operation. The troops were tired – I knew that I was asking big things of them but it was done intentionally, it was worthwhile undertaking this effort. As it was when the Germans counterattacked, the 14th Brigade was not there and the 5th Brigade was forced to come back.

CHAPTER 10

The 53rd Battalion's attack on 1 September, as seen from German machine-gun positions on the Péronne ramparts. Assaulting from the railway embankment on the left, the 53rd met heavy fire from them. As the open ground in the centre was swept by fire from Mont St Quentin, which rises on the right, and the ramparts, the 53rd had to hug the railway, only to meet heavy fire from Anvil Wood, on the outskirts of Péronne (AWM E03783).

This criticism was unjustified. It was Monash who had directed Hobbs to a bridge that proved impassable, forcing a second move to the safer crossing at Buscourt. When the 7th Brigade arrived at the same time, it gave the 14th right of way in accordance with Monash's orders at the outset of the operation. Once on the northern side, the 14th found its path blocked by the 6th Brigade, which Rosenthal had instructed to clear the pocket between Halle and Anvil Wood, supposedly secured by the 5th. As Rosenthal realised, this would have to be done *before* the exploitation ordered by Monash could proceed. The 'failure' of the 14th Brigade was attributable to circumstances beyond the control of either Hobbs or Stewart. There was more substance to Monash's and Blamey's view that Stewart should have moved his headquarters across the river. The time lost as his battalion commanders trudged back to the southern bank for their orders at 11.30 pm on 31 August forced the setting of zero hour one hour later than desired. He would also have been in closer touch with the fighting in Péronne, possibly averting the misfortune that befell the 53rd. But his error was no different to Monash's while commanding the 4th

MONASH

Brigade on 8 August 1915. Despite his criticism of their performance, the senior officers of the 5th Division were about to provide perhaps the best example of command seen in the battle so far.

Dead from the 53rd Battalion in the wire at Anvil Wood. Advancing on Péronne on 1 September, the 53rd got through the wood despite intense machine-gun fire, but was pinned down on the edge of the town. A shell bursts in the background (AWM E03149).

Concurrently with an attack towards Nurlu by the 74th Division from Godley's corps as part of the army plan, Monash instructed Hobbs to clear the rest of Péronne and take his original objectives. Hobbs issued his orders at 9.30 pm on 1 September, but Elliott, the 15th Brigade's commander, could not attend this conference. The driver sent to fetch him became lost, and Elliott, also lost, blundered into Hobbs's headquarters at 2.30 am on 2 September, by which time Stewart of the 14th Brigade was long gone. There was obviously no chance of the two brigadiers coordinating their plans, a severe handicap, because continued German resistance had already persuaded Elliott to abandon his attack on Flamicourt. His brigade would support the 14th instead. Elliott left Hobbs at 3.30 am and briefed his battalion commanders at 4.45 am for the attack starting at 6.00 am. Both Hobbs and Elliott were barely able to rest beforehand, while the 14th remained ignorant of the change in plan. Crossing on the crudely

CHAPTER 10

repaired road bridge into Péronne, the 58th Battalion, sent by Elliott to assist the 54th, was thus referred to the 56th, making the main attack in the 14th Brigade. Confusion increased when a German counter-barrage descended on the assembling 56th, whose advance was eventually halted by machine-gun fire 300 yards beyond the start line. By 10.00 am the 58th Battalion had cleared the remainder of the town, acting on the initiative of its commander. On the Mont, the 7th Brigade advanced beyond the line reached by the 6th.

A Lewis gun team from the 54th Battalion in Péronne on 2 September. They had set up the post during the attack the previous day. Much of the town has been destroyed (AWM E03183).

In 1926 White rated the capture of Mont St Quentin and Péronne as first and second, respectively, in his list of the four greatest achievements of the Australian Corps in the 1918 offensives.[74] Many in the AIF agreed. Rawlinson reportedly told Haig that the action was the finest feat of the war. As the narrative of the battle makes clear, and Monash himself openly admitted, the victory was due 'first and chiefly to the wonderful gallantry' of tired soldiers in under-strength battalions who responded to call after call. More than any other battles, Mont St Quentin and Péronne showed the quality of the instrument at Monash's disposal and how fortunate he was to command it. The contrasting results achieved by his exhausted units and the freshly arrived 74th Division, whose attack failed, make the point. The tactics were 'left largely to divisional, brigade, battalion and even platoon commanders; they were sometimes brilliant and sometimes faulty.' Monash reserved special praise for Rosenthal and Hobbs, remarking of Hobbs:

> The circumstances under which [he] was called up to intervene in the battle, at very short notice, imposed upon him, personally, difficulties of no mean order. I am prepared to admit quite frankly that the demands which I had to make upon him, his staff and his Division were severe.

It was a magnanimous, if belated, admission. Monash, too, had displayed generalship of a high order. He exerted a major influence on the battle in four ways.

Firstly, Monash never lost sight of his aim and did not hesitate to change a plan that he came to realise would not attain it. In doing so, he knew that he was creating a heavy burden for his subordinate commanders and staffs, but his knowledge of them – a quality that Bean said he lacked – made him confident they could handle it. This allowed flexibility, enabling them to take advantage of any opportunity instead of being tied to a fixed plan. Here was the greatest departure from Monash's set-pieces, which left subordinates little scope. Secondly, his policy of restoring an area as soon as it had been secured ensured the repair of the vital bridge at Feuillères. Similarly, artillery support was promptly available, because batteries had been allotted to the leading brigades. Thirdly, the battle confirmed that his misreading of ground at Chuignes was an aberration. Monash's insistence that the Bouchavesnes Spur must be taken, regardless of cost, was essential for the capture of Mont St Quentin, which in turn led to the fall of Péronne. This was also a specific example of the fourth factor, his ruthlessness. Monash drove his men relentlessly. When Hobbs urged upon him, 'with much earnestness', that the stress on his division was approaching the limits of endurance, Monash was 'compelled to harden my heart and to insist that it was imperative to recognise a great opportunity and to seize it unflinchingly.'

CHAPTER 10

Engineers from the 5th Division erecting a pontoon bridge over the Somme marshes before the assaults on Mont St Quentin and Péronne (AWM A01908).

Post-war tactical notes on the operation raised the question of whether arrangements should have been made much earlier to concentrate a strong force on the northern bank of the Somme. The point was valid, but as it involved the fixing of corps boundaries, the responsibility was Rawlinson's. Monash had frequently drawn attention to the importance of the northern bank, and it was as a result of his pleas that his authority was eventually extended to that side of the river on a one-divisional front. Could III Corps have carried out the operation, obviating the risk involved in Monash's crossing of the Somme? He 'very much doubted it.' His reservation was correct, and not just because he had 'some experience of the futility of relying too much on the sympathetic action of flank corps.' The performance of III Corps at Chipilly, its repulse at Bray and, more recently, its failure before Nurlu, supported Monash's doubt. But Monash's views were very much those of a corps commander. He made no attempt to answer the much more important question of whether the battle was at all necessary.

On 2 September the Canadian Corps, attacking as part of Horne's First Army, breached the Drocourt-Quéant Switch Line near Bullecourt, an outwork of the Hindenburg Line in front of Arras. Third Army was well to the east of Bapaume. Racked by uncertainty, Ludendorff approved a withdrawal to the main Hindenburg or Siegfried Line, which faced the southern half of Byng's front and the entire length of Rawlinson's.[75] Barrie Pitt, perhaps the only historian to downplay the Australian achievement, implies on this basis that it was largely unnecessary because the Germans would have retired irrespective of whether the Somme line was turned at Mont St Quentin or not. What Pitt overlooks is that Ludendorff had wanted to pull back to an intermediate position for the winter, while the Hindenburg Line was being completed. With the Somme line lost to the Australians on the same day as the Canadian success, he had no choice but to retire to it forthwith.

Pitt's argument also reeks of hindsight. Haig did intend to thrust south-east with the Cavalry Corps to disrupt communications behind the Germans facing Rawlinson and Byng, hoping to compel their withdrawal at least as far as the Hindenburg Line. This presumed that the Canadian attack would succeed, a result of which Haig was uncertain. As late as 31 August, he had warned Currie and Horne: 'I have no wish to attack the [Drocourt-Quéant] Line if they have any doubts about taking it.' Third and Fourth armies were 'to co-operate by vigorous action with the object of holding the enemy on their respective fronts.' Monash's attack on Mont St Quentin satisfied this requirement. It began three days earlier than the Canadian attack, a vital point, for prisoners stated that while a 'withdrawal would take place at a future date', the Somme Line 'was to be held at all costs'. If Fourth Army had waited for Horne, the Germans could have strengthened their defences on the river and the Hindenburg Line fourteen miles eastward, leaving its future progress dependent on the outcome of First Army's operation. In any case, Montgomery stated clearly that Rawlinson was determined to turn the Somme. As a subordinate commander, Monash would have been compelled to follow his orders. By anticipating them, he made easier for his corps an attack which was an essential preliminary to the resumption of the advance on Fourth Army's front.

CHAPTER 10

On 5 September the pursuit began, with the 3rd and 5th Australian divisions and the 32nd Division each advancing on a frontage occupied by a brigade group of infantry, artillery and a squadron of light horse. The Cologne and Omignon rivers ran parallel to the axis of the advance in the north and south of the corps sector, forming two valleys overlooked by rolling hills dotted with scattered woods and villages. Rawlinson set the first two bounds about three miles apart in this countryside. The third bound ran close to the old British Reserve Line and the fourth coincided with the old British Front Line, both of which the Germans had overrun in March. On 7 September the Australian Corps halted on the third bound. Haig had earlier directed Rawlinson to refrain from a vigorous pursuit, for he wanted divisions rested and communications improved before the start of a major combined offensive with the French and Americans. The pause resulted from his displeasure at Rawlinson's defiance of these instructions. But 'peaceful penetration' continued on the Australian Corps front; by 11 September the old British Reserve Line, lightly held, had been taken.

The German withdrawal had been rapid, but masterly: 'the rearguard fighting of his machine gunners was certainly a model of how such a retreat should be protected.' When the corps reached the third bound, Monash foreshadowed that the fourth, the old British Front Line, would have to be taken by a set-piece attack. On 8 September Haig asked his army commanders for proposals that would form the basis for British participation in the coming combined offensive. Both Rawlinson and Byng recommended attacking the Hindenburg Line before the defenders' morale had recovered sufficiently to make the cost prohibitive. Rawlinson pointed out that the Germans held five lines, comprising the old British Front and Outpost Lines and the more substantial Advanced, Main and Reserve trenches of the Hindenburg Line. He suggested seizing both the old British lines first, which he thought could be 'won at no great cost if they are attacked with determination on a wide front with adequate artillery support.' German morale could be gauged and excellent observation gained over the Hindenburg Line. Rawlinson recognised that a pause would be necessary before the Hindenburg Line was assaulted to rest divisions and assemble the resources needed. But a halt in front of the two old British lines would permit the Germans to reinforce them, resulting in a costly attack even before the Hindenburg system was reached. On 13 September, Haig told him to launch the attack as soon as possible.

Monash, Rawlinson and Lieutenant General Sir Walter Braithwaite, who had been Sir Ian Hamilton's chief of staff on Gallipoli and was now commanding IX Corps on Monash's right, planned the battle at Australian Corps Headquarters 'quite informally, over a cup of afternoon tea' on 13 September. At 5.20 am on the 18th, Fourth Army, supported by elements of the British Third Army and the French First Army, would attack the Old British Front (Green) and Outpost (Red) lines before exploiting to the Hindenburg Advanced or Outpost (Blue) Line. Only twenty tanks were available, of which eight were allotted to the Australian Corps, and in all but the 1st Division's sector they were not to go beyond the Green Line. As for his own plan, Monash wrote later:

> The contemplated battle presented only a few novel features. The methods of the Corps were becoming stereotyped, and by this time we all began to understand each other so well that most of what I had to say could almost be taken for granted.

Two of the ten dummy tanks built at Monash's direction and used by the Australian Corps in the attack on the Hindenburg Outpost Line (AWM C04505).

CHAPTER 10

Not surprisingly, the conference at which Monash explained his orders lasted only seventy-five minutes. The 1st Division would attack towards Hargicourt and the 4th towards Le Verguier, each on a frontage of 3500 yards. The 'few novel features' helped make up for the limitations of the army plan. Dummy tanks were constructed and placed in positions easily visible to the Germans before zero hour. The other means of compensating for the tank shortage was the addition of the 3rd and 5th divisions' machine-guns to those of the 1st and 4th, so that 250 guns delivered a barrage advancing 300 yards ahead of the infantry. The most important aspect of the plan, though, was Monash's fixing of the start line on a position that he thought would be reached by 18 September through 'peaceful penetration'. Besides reducing the infantry advance to 5000 yards, it permitted the forward move of the gun line, bringing the Hindenburg Main Line, the most obvious source of counter-attack, within range. Monash was confident about the set-piece phases of the battle, in which the old British wire would be on the wrong side of the trenches for the Germans, thereby assisting the assaults. He was less sure of the exploitation to the Blue Line, which entailed the crossing of an open valley one mile wide and seamed with uncut wire. The attack was not to be pressed if strong resistance was met there.

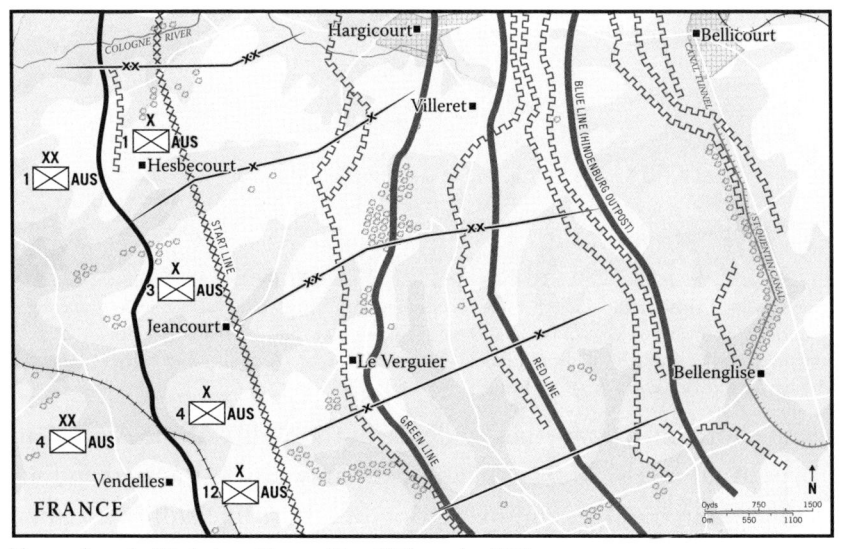

The attack on the Hindenburg Outpost Line, 18 September 1918

MONASH

Launched from the line Monash predicted his men would reach, the assault began in heavy rain and fog. The artillery barrage was 'wonderfully accurate', while a captured German battalion commander described the machine-gun barrage as 'absolutely too terrible for words'. The Red Line was secured by 10.00 am, with the only serious opposition at Le Verguier, defended by sixty machine-guns and several field guns. The 1st Division reached the Blue Line, close to the Red on its front, half an hour later, but the 4th Division, which had to advance up to 2000 yards to reach it, was stopped 500 yards short. Sinclair-MacLagan ordered a second attempt at 11.00 pm, after the two attacking battalions had rested. Artillery was brought forward during the day, so that the operation assumed the form of a set-piece. Assisted by a creeping barrage, they took the rest of the Blue Line in severe fighting. At a cost of 1260 casualties, both divisions between them captured 76 guns and 4300 prisoners.

Private James O'Hehir (right) and other soldiers from the 45th Battalion snipe at Germans scarpering up the far slope, across which runs the Hindenburg Outpost Line (Blue Line), in the attack on 18 September. By this stage, the old British Front (Green) and Outpost (Red) lines have fallen and the 45th has captured a German howitzer battery (AWM E03260).

The outcome was further evidence of the ability of the Australian Corps at all levels. Monash's use of dummy tanks, the tremendous machine-gun barrage, and his setting of a start line still in German hands to achieve a heavier artillery barrage, ensured that the

CHAPTER 10

infantry had maximum support. Bean conceded his grasp of what his command, despite its exhaustion, was capable of achieving: 'he was clearly right in his estimate that the Germans in front of us were so broken that it did not matter what trenches his infantry was in – that infantry could not stand and face our men.' Subordinate commanders performed well. Sinclair-MacLagan did not reinforce failure, but chose instead to renew the attack on a different axis and in darkness, when his men were refreshed, partly by the hot meal brought to them. These preparations reflected credit on his staff as well. Above all, there was the tactical skill of the infantry, which featured prominently in every report on the operation.

Hargicourt – a German machine-gunner who fought to the last. The massive pile of spent cartridges in the foreground attests to the fire he poured into the Australian advance (AWM E03351).

In contrast to the Australian success, III and IX Corps failed to reach the Blue Line. Further attempts by III Corps were unsuccessful and, on 20 September, Butler, who had resumed command, asked Monash to support another attempt next day. At 10.30 pm Monash warned Glasgow to provide troops for the southern 500 yards of the attack, as Butler had requested. Glasgow gave the task to the

1st Brigade, then being relieved, because it was familiar with the ground. III Corps was again repulsed, but posts were established on the objective by the Australians. The result was inconsequential, for 119 men of the 1st Battalion had mutinied, walking to the rear in protest at having to redeem their neighbour's failure once again. The incident reflected the tiredness of the men generally, a problem that in various guises, political as well as military, had weighed on Monash before this battle, the last fought by the 1st and 4th divisions. It would cause serious difficulties before the next, the attack on the Hindenburg Line.

On 4 September Monash told Bean: 'Six days rest and a bath ... restore the elasticity of a division and make it quite ready to fight again. The troops are not tired, [but] a little footsore.' Two months earlier he had refused Hobbs's request for buses to move his division forward to its assembly area for the attack on 8 August with the flippant comment that route marches were the best cure for tiredness. But Monash knew the meaning of exhaustion and what men could accomplish in spite of it. He had only to remember the demands made on the 4th Brigade between May and August 1915, compared to which the Australian Corps of 1918 was a fresh and healthy formation. Monash himself was in need of rest, requesting a few days' leave in Paris in September, which he was sure would do 'a lot of good'. In other correspondence he admitted that he felt rather tired, while his diary suggests that he was afflicted by nervous tremors.[76] Blamey noted the change in Monash's appearance and manner:

> Along with his men, he suffered severely from the strain of these last months. He became very thin, the skin hung loosely on his face. His characteristic attitude was one of deep thought. With his head carried slightly forward, he would ride in his car for long periods in silence ...

A member of Monash's staff, Sir Keith Officer, told John Terraine in 1958: 'I don't believe [Monash] thought about anything during the War except winning the War.' This is the key to an understanding of Monash's attitude in the final days. III Corps was to him evidence of the decline of the British Army, whose 'best troops have long ago

CHAPTER 10

been used up and we now have a class of men who is unintelligent, sheep-like and without initiative or individuality.' He was being overly harsh. The British Army had good divisions that fought well and even its 'average' divisions, well supported by the other elements of the 'weapon system' – especially artillery – could achieve notable results. In any case, Monash explained to brigade after brigade that they were no more overworked than their British colleagues, 'straight talking' that the men appreciated. He knew that the Germans were in a worse state, asking Bean on 21 September if he actually realised the hopelessness of their situation. Bean thought that they had about forty men per company, which Monash multiplied by the number of battalions, regiments and divisions on the Western Front. According to the calculation, German infantry strength was only 205 000. Monash doubled it for good measure, but the figure was still very small, compared to Allied strength. Having only considered the issue from the Australian viewpoint, Bean commented: 'Certainly, this is a surprising light upon the subject.' To take advantage of their demoralisation, Monash wanted to hit the Germans as hard and as often as he could, a policy with which his divisional commanders concurred. Therefore the divisions, said Monash, 'should be called upon to yield up the last particle of effort of which they were capable.' Bean agreed, concluding in the *Official History*:

> In this decisive fighting ... he was right to work his troops to the extreme limit of their endurance ... At such times victory often goes to the troops that hold out longest, withstanding strain, toil or exhaustion in perhaps unbelievable degree and for an unbelievable time.

Before 8 August Monash had been assured by Lawrence that the corps would be rested after the battle. When the promise could not be kept, he urged a shortening of the corps front to release more divisions for rest. Tactically, Monash was not averse to entering battle with inferior numbers, for mechanical resources could compensate. Even when few tanks were available: 'I welcome any pretext to take the fewest possible numbers of men into action. So long as [battalions] have 30 Lewis Guns it doesn't very much matter what else they have.' The method of attacking with troops evenly distributed along the frontage was abandoned. Units advanced directly on points of resistance, ignoring the interval between them, and in this way a battalion 300 strong could cover a frontage of one mile as frequently occurred from mid-August.

It was at this time that Monash began to appeal to the men on the grounds of prestige and to press higher commanders to give greater publicity to Australian efforts. The lack of recognition angered him. He blamed Bean when *The Times* published Rawlinson's congratulatory message to the Canadians for 8 August, but omitted his praise of the Australians. Bean's cables on Péronne were bland. Wanting the fighting described with 'a lavish hand', Monash lamented that the Australian Corps did not have an Ashmead-Bartlett. Bean and Murdoch felt he should have continued Birdwood's appeals on moral grounds. But there were frequent instances of men complaining that the British Army as a whole received credit that rightly belonged to them. Monash's representations seemed to have the desired effect, for newspapers began to give the Dominion forces a coverage that reinforced his use of the prestige of Australian arms. Impressed by the primary role of the AIF in recent offensives, the Prime Minister, too, sought greater recognition of its efforts as a means of increasing Australian influence at any peace negotiations. He arrived in the Australian sector on 12 September, at the head of the first of a number of parties of journalists and newspaper proprietors. Monash accommodated them at Amiens and not near his headquarters, where their presence would interfere with the planning of the attack on the Hindenburg Outpost Line. On the same day, Monash was ordered by Birdwood, at Hughes' direction, to send 800 original Anzacs to Australia immediately for two months' furlough.

Contrary to his claim in *Australian Victories*, Monash opposed the scheme, for most of the men would come from the 1st and 4th divisions, currently preparing for the attack. He argued that its suddenness would arouse ill-feeling, as they would be forced to leave without proper ceremony and without their kit, which could not be retrieved from the base camps in time. Monash also thought

CHAPTER 10

of himself: 'Unfortunately all this will recoil upon me, and I shall be blamed by the men as a whole for the unsatisfactory manner in which this matter has been arranged.' Birdwood insisted that Monash implement the program. He knew from personal observation that Monash was incorrect. Travelling through Bray, he found 'the lot of them there – broad smiles on the faces of everyone', and Lieutenant Colonel Stevens, described by Monash as distraught, was 'particularly happy and cheery at the prospect of getting off.'

Other commanders shared Monash's view, for 6000 men were eligible for Anzac leave. Worried that his brigade would be crippled for the next year, Elliott lamented: 'If Mr Hughes had been in the pay of the Germans, he could not have dealt us a more paralysing blow.' The Prime Minister had even spoken to the men at Bray without Monash's knowledge and asked Bean and Murdoch to publicise the arrangements lest Monash cable Australia and force their abandonment. It was only one aspect of Hughes' wider concern to preserve the corps in a war that Sir Henry Wilson predicted would last until 1920. If used at the present rate, the five divisions could not possibly be maintained until then. Hughes was adamant that 'they must be withdrawn in autumn to recuperate for the resumption of the offensive in 1919.' Wilson asked him to refer the question to Haig when he visited France. He ignored the CIGS's suggestion, telling Monash instead that the corps was to be out of the line by 15 October at the latest. Monash had independently reached the same conclusion, but when he ventured that military considerations might prevent withdrawal by the date mentioned, Hughes replied that his position as corps commander depended on it.[77]

The granting of Anzac leave did not hamper the 1st and 4th divisions in their fight for the Hindenburg Outpost Line as Monash had feared. Bean remarked: 'In the optimism of the moment all these troubles were easily shed.' But the aftermath of the battle was serious, for its cost was a key factor in forcing the disbandment of some battalions to beef up the rest. The manpower shortage had long since necessitated the reduction of British brigades from four battalions to three, but the Australian Government considered the measure particularly undesirable for the AIF, because the battalion was the focus of infantry tradition and morale. Until September, only three were broken up, all of them during the German Spring Offensive. At the end of June, however, GHQ expressed concern at the disparate strengths of Australian battalions. Only eleven of the fifty-seven were over 900 strong, seventeen were less than 800, and five fewer than 700 strong. If they were to be at a uniform strength of 900, the reduction of all brigades to three battalions must be considered. On 18 August, the Army Council ordered its implementation as soon as possible. Monash recalled the recuperative effect of a quiet winter on the health and strength of the Australian Corps after the heavy losses of Third Ypres and felt the present situation could be compared to it. He opposed any final decision until the start of the 1919 spring campaign, for 'By that time, we will be able to see how things are going.' But at Birdwood's insistence he agreed to reduce all remaining four-battalion brigades as soon as it was found to be necessary. Against this background, the withdrawal of the Anzac originals forced Monash's hand, and the 19th, 21st, 25th, 29th, 37th, 42nd, 54th and 60th battalions were selected by their divisional commanders for disbandment.

For the men in these units the blow was a shattering one. Hearing rumours of their fate, those in the 37th Battalion complained to their commanding officer, Lieutenant Colonel Story, who passed on their feelings in forthright letters to Monash, Birdwood and Hughes. When Gellibrand suspended Story for his breach of discipline, 'the last chance of a peaceful settlement disappeared.' The private soldiers of the battalion decided to obey every order on their last parade, on 21 September, except the final one to join their new battalions. McNicoll, their brigade commander, was summoned when they stood fast, and Gellibrand spoke to delegates from each company, but without result. Except for the 60th, which Elliott persuaded to disband, the other battalions affected followed the 37th's example.

Monash's response to the disbandment mutinies reflected sensitivity, balancing his strength, another essential quality that Bean thought he would lack in this situation. On 23 September, he wrote a long

CHAPTER 10

explanation to be promulgated to all ranks of why the measure was necessary and what would be done to ameliorate its effects. Wherever possible, complete companies or platoons would be transferred to the remaining battalions, and 'doubtless, also, in many cases, concessions can be made in the matter of wearing of colour patches.' Next day, he told a delegation from the 37th Battalion that he sympathised with them, indeed, their *esprit de corps* did them credit. If they persisted with their action after his frank discussion, there would be no arrests, but no reinforcements either. The unit 'simply dies with a stigma'. At the same time he persuaded Rawlinson, who secured Haig's approval, to postpone further action for fourteen days, allowing the recalcitrant battalions to participate in the coming attack on the Hindenburg Line under their own officers. This was a practical, indeed essential, step if the planning for that operation was to proceed smoothly, but it did not indicate any weakening on his part. 'I have no intention whatever', he told Dodds, 'of allowing the men in any way, to dictate to me.' He had warned them of the consequences and now the necessary protocols were set in train. They were not needed. On 12 October the 37th Battalion, reduced by its losses on the Hindenburg Line to a strength of 90 men, voluntarily passed out of existence along with the others earmarked for breaking up. Monash preferred to think of this as 'the initial stage of our demobilization.' None had resisted the step more vigorously than himself, a fact of which he was proud.

Monash was not the only commander beset by 'a sea of troubles' on the eve of Fourth Army's attack on the Hindenburg Line. Wilson warned Haig that the War Cabinet would become very anxious if it failed at a heavy cost. The C-in-C replied: 'What a wretched lot! And how well they mean to support me!! What confidence!' Planned for 29 September, the attack would be the main British stroke in the series of hammer blows to conquer territory held by the Germans since the beginning of the war, as distinct from ground they had captured in their offensives between March and July. Three major attacks were to precede it: a Franco-American one between Rheims and the Meuse on 26 September; one by the British First and Third armies near Cambrai next day, and, on 28 September, one by the British, Belgians and French in Flanders. Rawlinson allotted the principal role in the Hindenburg Line assault to the Australian Corps, and relied on its commander to shape the plan on which his army fought. Monash later called its development 'a task which proved at once the most arduous, the most responsible and the most difficult of any' that he undertook throughout the war.

Of the documents captured by the armoured cars on 8 August, the most valuable was a copy, complete with maps, of the layout of the Hindenburg Line in the area of Le Tronquoy. Though dated 4 February 1918, Fourth Army concluded that the speed of their retirement left the Germans little time to modify the scheme, so that 'a fairly accurate idea' of their dispositions and counter-attack plan was obtainable from it. Monash devoted 'hour upon hour to a concentrated study of these papers', and while they referred mainly to the sectors south of his own, the notes on Divisional Sector No. 1 contained information that was both useful and pertinent. The main feature of the Hindenburg Line there was its use of the St Quentin Canal, linking the Somme at St Quentin to the Scheldt near Vendhuille. The canal followed a deep cutting, on the eastern side of which were the defences, but at Le Tronquoy, three miles north of St Quentin and at Bellicourt, five miles further north, it ran through two tunnels above which the fortifications protruded up to 1200 yards to the west. The Bellicourt tunnel was by far the more important, beginning just south of the village with its northern exit 6000 yards away near Gouy and Le Catelet, and its course marked by the continuous bank of the original spoil, ten feet high, into which shelters had been dug. Troops were comfortably accommodated in the tunnel, immune from bombardment and able to reach the surface quickly through many concealed passages and air shafts for prompt counter-attacks. Bellicourt, above the tunnel, and Bony, 1000 yards west of it, were heavily fortified. The wire entanglements were 'enormously strong', consisting of three to five belts, each about twelve yards wide, protecting five or six trench lines studded with concrete blockhouses and with more wire in between. Three spurs rose gently to the Knoll, and Gillemont and Quennemont farms, which formed an uncaptured section of the Hindenburg

CHAPTER 10

Outpost Line about 1500 yards west of Bony. These positions were mutually supporting and the configuration of the ground on which they lay offered the same advantages to the defender as the E-shaped ridge before Passchendaele. Running through Nauroy and Le Catelet, one mile to the east of the tunnel, was the Le Catelet Line, supporting the main Hindenburg Line, and a further two miles east, the Reserve or Beaurevoir Line.

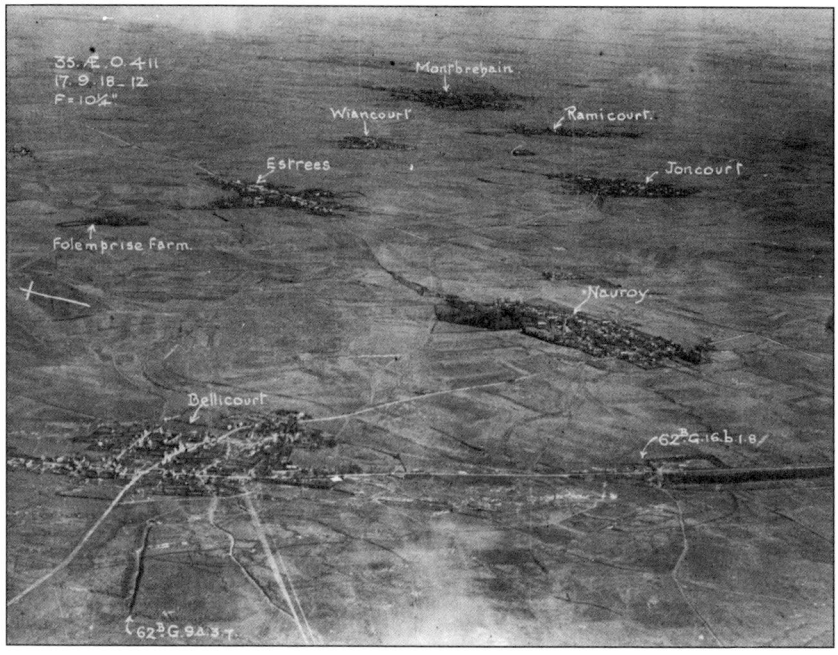

An aerial view of the ground covered by the Australian Corps in the Hindenburg Line assault. On 29 September the advance took Nauroy after crossing the canal tunnel at Bellicourt. The area to the left of Bellicourt was taken next day. Joncourt and Estrées fell on 1 October. Wiancourt, in the Beaurevoir Line, was captured on 3 October and Montbrehain on the 5th. As the crow flies, the distance is almost six miles (AWM J00123).

Bean described Monash's plan as the most elaborate of his career. It was derived largely from the complex scheme for 8 August and submitted in draft to Rawlinson on the same day as the assault on the Hindenburg Outpost Line. Monash regarded as unacceptable the casualties that would be incurred in an attack across the canal, and based his plan instead on the seizure of the 6000-yard-wide tunnel or 'bridge' over it. The first objective, denoted by the Green Line, included the Le Catelet system, and involved an advance, assisted by tanks and a creeping barrage, of 4400 yards from the start line on the Hindenburg Outpost Line. An open warfare attack on the Red Line, which encompassed the Beaurevoir system, would follow. Monash sought at least sixty tanks for the first phase, at the end of which artillery would move forward to cover the final stages of the advance to the Red Line. Thirty tanks should be available for this second phase, and no fewer than six artillery brigades to advance with the infantry. Monash envisaged zero at 6.00 am, the capture of the Green Line four hours later and, after a pause of four hours for the construction of roads for the artillery, the attack on the Red Line beginning at 2.00 pm. There was no hope of surprise, for the Germans knew after the capture of the Outpost Line that the next objective would be the main Hindenburg Line. So Monash recommended a 'systematic destructive bombardment ... lasting at least four days, not merely to destroy the defensive organisation, but also to demoralise and starve the trench garrisons.'

Rawlinson made two changes on 19 September. The assault on the Beaurevoir Line would depend on the results achieved in the initial phase of the attack, which meant that it might not be captured on the first day. 'In this modification I could readily concur', asserted Monash. Secondly, the 46th Division from IX Corps would attack directly across the canal about a mile and a half south of Bellicourt near Bellenglise, with the 32nd Division advancing through it to seize the Le Tronquoy tunnel defences once sufficient ground had been gained on the eastern side. On Monash's left flank, III Corps was to capture the high ground south-west of Vendhuille and then clear the village itself. After crossing the tunnel behind the Australian Corps, it would also advance north along the canal, paving the way for a crossing by V Corps.

Monash's dissension was vehement. It appears that two days afterwards he was still reluctant to defer to Rawlinson's views and urging him to revert to the original scheme. Explaining his development of the plan on 21 September, Monash agreed that the base of the salient formed across the tunnel *must* be widened on the first day to prevent the Germans concentrating their reserves against

CHAPTER 10

what would be a relatively small breach in the Hindenburg Line. In his plan of 18 September, he had advocated passing III and IX Corps across the tunnel for this purpose. Now he considered that the needs of his own corps would preclude their using it for at least two days. Too much time, he felt, would be lost if III and IX Corps on the flanks attempted the alternative method of forcing the canal on either side of the tunnel, which Rawlinson had just ordered the 46th Division to do. He opposed the latter course on a second ground: 'It will be cheaper to *turn* the Canal (both flanks) than to force the crossing by direct assault, and the captures will be larger.'

The St Quentin Canal, tunnel and 'bridge' on the right flank of the Australian sector before the attack. After entering the tunnel, the canal ran to the left of the road past Bellicourt (top centre). The Hindenburg Line tracked along the 'bridge' from the left of the tunnel entrance and on through the shelled area. Its barbed-wire entanglements are visible. This photograph was taken during a reconnaissance by an aircraft from No. 3 Squadron, AFC (AWM P01431.003).

Hence Monash proposed to turn right and left on the eastern bank with his corps once it had crossed the tunnel, uncovering 3000 yards on the front of IX Corps and over 5000 yards on the front of III and V Corps by 4.00 pm on 29 September. Engineers were to commence immediately the construction of bridges, to be used by the infantry and artillery of these corps at dawn on the second day. After readjusting the corps boundaries, the advance would be resumed on the third day. But this outcome still depended entirely on the establishment of a bridgehead across the tunnel at the outset. If that failed or was contained, the exploitation to facilitate the flank crossings could not occur. If the exploitation did go ahead, the outward swings would be flank on to the Germans, creating further risk. As Rawlinson realised, the chances of success were greater if the attack were launched simultaneously on a wide front, forcing the dispersion of the defenders along its length. To help achieve this, Third Army and the French First Army would attack either side of Fourth Army. Monash claimed that he agreed with Rawlinson's reasoning at the conference of 19 September. If so, then the views expressed in his plan of the 21st were puzzling.

On the other hand, the thoroughness and lucidity of Monash's scheme were outstanding, particularly in the calculation of time and space. Two artillery brigades must 'pull out of the barrage about 9 a.m. and will thus have four hours to bring up teams and waggons, limber up and march to join their [infantry] brigades on Green Line.' Monash's performance of the functions of his operations staff was reflected in this. The construction and repair of roads and traffic control were even more important than they had been on 8 August. Divisions and their supporting arms had to move rapidly from their assembly areas across a battlefield resembling in places the lunar landscape of the Somme and Ypres to reach the tunnel in the correct order, and then redeploy for the open warfare phase. Monash drafted the relevant instructions himself, ordering the preparation of four routes as near as possible to the start line. Following the infantry closely, engineers and pioneers would extend them during the attack, using road stone brought forward by trucks. Monash's intricate timetable governed the use of each road by the formation to which it had been allotted. On no account was it to use another. Tanks moving in columns alongside could compress the ground surface sufficiently for mule traffic. As usual during the attack: 'The principle of allotment is that ... all tanks will be employed on one task only.'

CHAPTER 10

Monash had already outlined many of these points to his divisional commanders at their first conference on 19 September. Other points included the need for sergeants to be capable of drafting messages in case platoon commanders became casualties, and the care of feet and boots so that troops would not suffer during the approach march. Gellibrand was particularly struck by Monash's concluding comment and remarked on it accordingly:

'… this operation is more a matter of engineering and organization than of fighting.' This last is of importance since it gives a clue to the opinion held at Corps HQ throughout the action: that the Boche defence was little more than a MG bluff.

In order to attack from a line directly opposite the tunnel, the Australian Corps side-slipped northward, taking over part of the III Corps front on 24–25 September.

Even before the Hindenburg Outpost Line attack, Rawlinson offered Monash the use of the 27th and 30th divisions of the American II Corps to replace the 1st and 4th Australian divisions for the next operation. Recalling the American efforts at Hamel, and mindful of the effect of Anzac leave, Monash 'had no reason to hesitate'. On 19 September, the corps commander, Major General George Read, was informed that his two divisions would probably participate in the attack on the Hindenburg Line. Their move into the battle area commenced four days later, a regiment from each relieving the Australians in the trenches.[78] For the first time since its arrival on the Western Front in 1916, the AIF held no part of it.

In front of the 27th Division, the British III Corps had been unable, despite repeated attempts, to capture the Hindenburg Outpost Line from which the attack on the main Hindenburg Line would begin. Monash had written of his plan of 18 September that it was 'based upon the assumption that the objective Blue Line … is in our possession all along the Army front, or can be seized in the very near future.' Haig insisted that it must be taken before the Americans entered the sector, but Butler pleaded with Rawlinson that his corps could do no more. When Rawlinson expressed dissatisfaction with Butler's performance, Haig reinforced Fourth Army with XIII Corps and approved Rawlinson's decision to allow the Americans to take over the line as planned. Because of its exhaustion, the role of III Corps in the attack was reduced. It would now advance on Monash's left only as far as the canal, whereupon XIII Corps was to mount the assault north along it. Finally, Rawlinson rejected Monash's expedient of launching the main operation from the front occupied by the 27th Division, for he feared that his complex plan might be upset. Instead, the Americans were to capture the start line in a preliminary attack on 27 September.

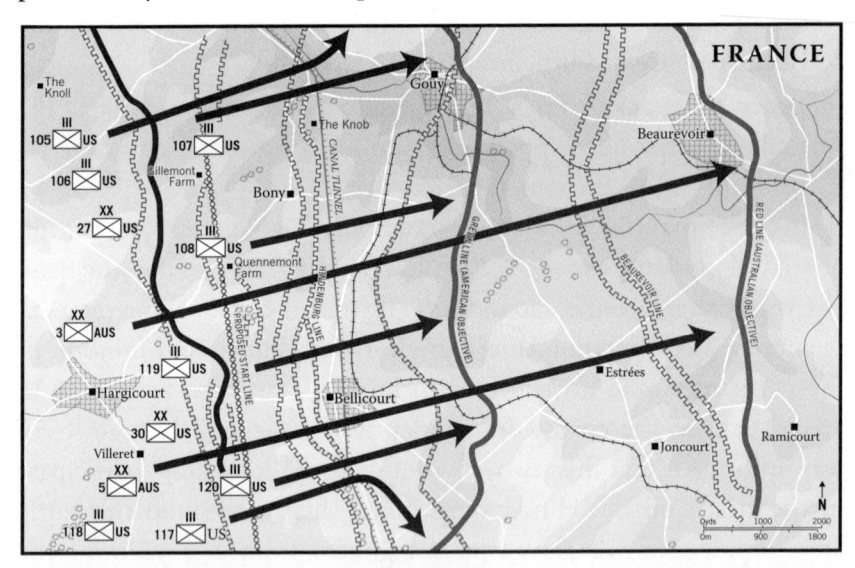

The attack on the Hindenburg Line, 29 September 1918

The Americans acted wisely from the outset. Recognising his own inexperience and that of his staff in the control of operations of such magnitude, Read placed his divisions directly under Monash. As John Eisenhower remarks, it was a courageous decision, requiring Read to swallow his pride and contravene Pershing's strict policy on the use of American formations. Monash outlined the plan to them on 23 September, explaining exactly how the 27th Division should execute its preliminary attack by allotting one battalion to each of the Knoll, Quennemont and Gillemont farms, the uncaptured positions in the Hindenburg Outpost Line. He might have been addressing his officers as commander of the 3rd Division at Lark Hill. Monash stressed

CHAPTER 10

teamwork: 'one job for each man' and 'Strict limitation to prescribed objectives.' Orders must reach the lowest leaders quickly. Troops must be fed properly and be allowed adequate sleep. Monash enjoined the importance of 'Thinking ahead – don't sit down and watch.'[79] He made a profound impression, as Major General John O'Ryan, commanding the 27th Division, remembered:

.. there was not more than five or six questions asked in all by the six officers present. But Monash's conversations and explanations were so lengthy and detailed that there did not seem to be necessity [sic] to ask many questions.[80]

Both American divisions would carry out the first phase of the main attack, each advancing with one brigade to seize the tunnel and the Green Line. The second regiments of the two brigades holding the original line were then to exploit north and south under a smoke barrage to widen the breach and assist the crossing of the flank corps. This plan was a smaller version of the one that Rawlinson had rejected on 21 September. Once the Green Line was secured, the 3rd and the 5th Australian divisions, on left and right respectively, would attack the Red Line, with the 17th Armoured Car Battalion and some Whippets raiding railway bridges beyond.

Bean later criticised Monash, who 'undoubtedly asked too much of the two fine but not fully trained American divisions.' Historians have lined up since to do the same. The Americans' task would have been daunting for well-trained and experienced troops, says one. There was the obvious strength of the tunnel defences and the problem of guarding against Germans emerging from the tunnel exits after the attack had passed them. The exploiting regiments would have to change direction to right and left – although the formations that preceded them across the tunnel could provide some protection. Monash knew all this. The American advance, he remarked, 'was a larger job than any the Australian Corps had ever undertaken.' He was also aware of the Americans' inexperience. At Hamel they had suffered disproportionately high casualties, the four participating companies losing 176 of their number. Most British and Australian commanders had formed a low opinion of the Americans' tactical ability. Elliott found one brigade losing 100 men daily because it was resupplying the forward trenches in daylight. When their folly was pointed out to them, losses dropped to about six per day. Rawlinson condemned American staff work as 'so appallingly bad'. Visiting Read's corps just before the Armistice, Maxse's staff criticised its 'indifferent training ... Officers and men don't strike one as being keen on training.' Not only Monash, but commanders senior to him must share the blame for the consequences of using them in this battle. There were extenuating circumstances, though.

Both Monash and Rawlinson were influenced by the evidence of the attack on 18 September that the Germans were badly shaken. Monash thought that they would be unable to withstand the preliminary bombardment of the main Hindenburg Line, which began on 25 September with the first British use of mustard gas. His belief had some grounds. The infantry would find much of the wire in front of the Hindenburg Line intact, but were able to penetrate it because many Germans were too numb to resist. Still, too much should not be made of Monash's estimate of the state of the enemy opposite as a mitigating factor. The fact is that once he was given II Corps, operational imperatives left him with little alternative to employing it in the first phase of the attack. As a formulaic set-piece, it was a much simpler operation than the open warfare advance without a creeping barrage to the Red Line. That phase required initiative and experience at all levels, which the Americans did not possess. Monash's critics invariably overlook – or do not appreciate – the implications of the differences between the two phases on his allotment of troops to each.

As it was, Monash did everything possible to help the Americans, forming an Australian Mission of 83 officers and 127 NCOs from the 1st and 4th divisions, all of whom were 'carefully selected in order to ensure that the best experience of the Australian Corps is made available to the Americans in France.' Sinclair-MacLagan, the Mission's commander, was attached to Read's headquarters, the two brigadiers, Brand and Mackay, and several staff officers to the two divisions and battalion commanders to brigades, while each battalion

CHAPTER 10

had four NCOs attached to advise on supply, equipment and tactics. Monash praised the efficacy of the arrangement: 'it became possible to talk to the whole American Corps in our own technical language.' He ran through the plan for cooperation between the Australians and Americans at his largest and, as it turned out, final conference of the campaign, lasting over two and a half hours, on 26 September. No alterations were permitted after the meeting. Haig arrived towards the end, and Monash 'begged me to go in and see them all ... So I went into the room and shook the senior officers by the hand and said a few words of encouragement.'

Monash needed them most. At 5.30 am next morning, the 106th Regiment, supported by twelve tanks, attacked the three spurs of the Hindenburg Outpost Line under a creeping barrage. The elaborate nature of this assault suggests that Monash no longer regarded the opposition in front of him as trifling. He wrote in his diary: 'Information comes in very slowly. Situation very obscure all day. Although they captured [sic] they mopped up *very* badly and don't hold all objectives.' The 106th had attacked with only eighteen officers in its twelve companies, whereas an Australian brigade would have employed at least forty officers. Seventeen became casualties, and as direction was lost in the heavy mist, the advance degenerated into a number of small groups moving independently of one another. At dusk it was believed that the 106th had gained most of its objectives, although pockets of Germans still remained.

During the night, patrols were unable to advance, forcing the conclusion that the main attack on 29 September would not be launched as Monash intended. Shortly after noon on the 28th, a contact aircraft reported seeing Americans on the Hindenburg Outpost Line, but most were scattered between it and the 27th's original line. This ended the discussion that had arisen on whether to start the creeping barrage next day from the original line. As O'Ryan wrote: 'To voluntarily assume the risk of destroying them ... no matter how logical it might be in the tactical sense, would be repulsive to the mass of officers and men ... and destructive of morale.' As already planned, the barrage would commence from the Hindenburg Outpost Line, still 1000 yards ahead. Some Americans were unconcerned, allegedly remarking that they were accustomed to marching quickly and would soon catch up with it.

Monash was not so confident. Rawlinson rejected his plea for one day's postponement to enable the Americans to renew the attempt, because the arrangements of the three attacking armies would have to be changed. Instead, the 27th Division would receive additional tanks for the main assault, before which it was to try to advance its line as far as possible by patrolling. At 3.00 pm Haig visited Monash, who described himself as being in 'a state of despair'. The C-in-C reassured him that 'it was not a serious matter and that he should attack tomorrow as arranged', meaning that 'the success of the operation outweighed the lives of the American infantry.' According to Bean, Haig disapproved of Monash's attitude, which implies that Monash was much more distraught than the matter-of-fact account in Haig's diary suggests. Yet it is clear that Monash was extremely anxious, and that his fears were probably not allayed by the C-in-C's soothing words. The situation was reminiscent of Passchendaele, when the 66th Division had been unable to capture the start line for the 3rd Division's attack on 12 October 1917. On that occasion there was some adjustment of the barrage, but it proved inadequate and the barrage soon outpaced the infantry. On this occasion, the Americans had to advance 1000 yards against untouched machine-guns before they even reached the barrage. Failure seemed likely and, with it, the exposure of the flank of the 30th Division attacking on the right. Bean was in the audience that evening as Monash briefed the correspondents on the attack to be launched at 6.20 am next day:

> John gave us, as usual, an absorbingly interesting account of the fight. He was very insistent on the fact that he doubted whether the Americans would succeed in carrying their objectives ... It struck all of us that John was hedging against a possible defeat in which case he would be able to throw the blame onto the Americans.

Bean was right on both counts.

CHAPTER 10

Infantry and tanks prepare to advance near Bellicourt in the assault on the Hindenburg Line on 29 September 1918 (AWM H12514).

Able to assault from the section of the Outpost Line captured by the 1st Australian Division on 18 September, the 30th Division could be supported by a creeping barrage and, with tanks crushing the wire ahead, it got to the tunnel and Bellicourt. Its advance was helped by the 46th Division from IX Corps on its right, which showed what an 'average' British division could do and crossed the canal 'on rafts, life jackets from Channel packets and anything else that would float' in one of the finest feats of the campaign. The 5th Australian Division linked up with both formations. A salient had been created, but it was exposed because the 27th Division, assaulting on the left of the 30th without a creeping barrage, had met strong resistance. Its tanks were belted. Fourteen were destroyed by direct artillery fire, for the Germans naturally concentrated their anti-tank defences at the tunnel sector, and others foundered in an old British minefield that had been forgotten. Now encountering intense machine-gun fire, the 27th Division was stalled largely on the Outpost Line. It reported heavy casualties and that groups of men had been seen hanging on in shell holes as far forward as Bony. One of the 27th's regiments, the 107th, suffered 349 men killed, the highest loss for an American unit in a single day in the war. The 3rd Australian Division was supposed to cross the Outpost Line behind the 27th at 9.00 am. Approaching the 27th's original line, it came under heavy fire from Quennemont and Gillemont farms, which precluded its further advance. Though the 3rd Division had been ordered not to become emmeshed with the Americans, the situation seemed so dangerous that local assaults were launched by the 10th and 11th brigades, one of which took Quennemont Farm. Bean commented: 'By 10 o'clock Monash's plan had gone to the winds, though he did not yet realise it.' In fact it had evaporated on the afternoon of 27 September.

Monash falsely believed that the Americans had rushed blindly on towards their objectives, disregarding his warning about the importance of careful mopping-up. He was scathing on their performance, and Bean's fear that they would provide him with a ready excuse for failure became a reality. 'Well, you see what I expected might happen has happened', Monash said. 'The Americans sold us a pup. They're simply unspeakable.' His opinion did not mellow with time, for in 1929 he ridiculed their efforts as 'a miserable fiasco'.

This convenient dismissal of the difficulties facing the 27th Division, the clear recognition of which had provoked 'a state of despair' in Monash two days previously, reflected the unreality that permeated Australian Corps Headquarters for much of 29 September. Although messages sometimes conflicted, most seemed to indicate that the attack was progressing steadily. At 9.05 am, the 3rd Division reported that the 27th was 'hung up at the outset near Quennemont Farm', but according to a report received at 10.00 am it was 'doing well', with prisoners claiming that the Hindenburg Line had been crossed. At 11.00 am the pilot of a contact aircraft stated that the Americans were all along their objective. Shortly afterwards came the first intimation of reality, as the 30th Division reported that the Germans were advancing down the canal from the north, the sector that the 27th should have taken, and were holding up the 5th Division. At 11.12 am Monash knew that the 3rd Division

CHAPTER 10

was 'dug in on west side of tunnel. Americans are held up in front of us.' Thereupon Monash claimed that he 'hastened forward with all possible speed to get into personal touch with the situation and the Divisional Commanders.' This is uncertain, for neither the Australian Corps and the 3rd Division war diaries, nor Monash's own personal diary mentions the visit. Gellibrand's contention that he merely telephoned seems more likely.

Alarmed by the lack of reliable information, Gellibrand himself had gone forward at 9.50 am, coming under machine-gun and artillery fire, which, with the reports of its survivors, convinced him that the 27th Division would be unable to capture its objective. Running the battle in his absence, Jess had reached the same conclusion by 11.40 am. Anticipating Monash's instructions, he suggested to both Cannan and McNicoll that the 9th Brigade, then the divisional reserve, 'will no doubt be ordered to go round south where the penetration is.' But these were not the orders issued by Corps Headquarters, which believed, even after Gellibrand returned, that the Americans had reached the Green Line and that all the 3rd Division had to do was mop up the intervening machine-guns to join them. When Gellibrand tried to tell him that the start line, let alone the Green Line, was still in German hands, Blamey was adamant: 'We have had the report absolutely confirmed from a number of places.' Gellibrand was to launch a frontal attack against the Hindenburg Line at 3.00 pm, without artillery support on account of the Americans in front. The 10th and 11th brigades advanced a few hundred yards and captured Gillemont Farm, but so heavy was the fire that nothing more could be attempted in daylight.

At 4.05 pm, when the failure of this pointless attack was apparent, Monash gave the order forecast by Jess during the morning. No matter what opposition remained ahead of the 3rd Division, 'the movement round the eastern side of the Hindenburg Line would cut them off.' The 9th Brigade was to attack northward from the 3rd Division's right flank, where its junction with the 5th Division formed part of the salient behind the Hindenburg Line. Alongside, the 5th's reserve formation, the 14th Brigade, would advance astride the Le Catelet Line, both formations securing the tunnel as far as its northern entrance, which included Bony. O'Ryan agreed to a barrage on those parts of the Hindenburg Line still in German hands. As heavy rain during the night prevented the 9th Brigade reaching the start line by zero hour, 6.00 am on 30 September, Cannan's brigade replaced it. In 'slow and methodical hand-to-hand fighting in a perfect tangle of trenches', wrote Monash, both brigades, assisted by a handful of tanks, cleared the remainder of the main Hindenburg system in the Australian sector. 'All done up', the 3rd and 5th divisions were relieved by the 2nd Division on 1–2 October.

Monash's close control of this second phase brought him into sharp conflict with Gellibrand. After his frustrating experience on 29 September, Gellibrand resented Monash's issuing of orders that were totally inappropriate on some occasions and emanated from a refusal to consider contrary views on others. On 30 September Monash berated him for attacking on a frontage of 4000 yards, which, he felt was much too narrow. The exchange did Monash little credit, as Gellibrand tried to explain:

GELLIBRAND: When you have a Battalion strength of 200 …

MONASH: You have a Battalion strength of more than 200. The Division has more than 2000 Infantry.

GELLIBRAND: Bayonets, sir.

MONASH: Bayonets, Lewis Guns and all the rest of it. No use estimating their strength at 200. There must be more than 200 in a Battalion.

GELLIBRAND: Deducting carrying parties and Headquarters …

MONASH: Some of the battalions are over 600 strong. I wish to know why the Division is committed on such a narrow front …

Gellibrand eventually stated that he could not advance as rapidly as Monash wanted, silencing Monash's criticism with the perhaps

CHAPTER 10

intentionally pointed remark that he had formed his conclusion after visiting the line. Nevertheless, Monash's ruthlessness, possibly born of anger, emerged as he directed Gellibrand to use his artillery freely, O'Ryan's views notwithstanding: 'There cannot be any Americans East of you. They must be either prisoners or strafed. Anyway we cannot afford to lose a battle because the Americans are supposed to be there.' Haig had said much the same three days earlier.

Ruthlessness and bullying during a battle were characteristic of Monash, but blindness to tactical realities was not. Indeed, the mixture of familiar and atypical exemplified his erratic performance in both the planning and conduct of this attack. Monash had grasped immediately that success depended on a wide initial breach of the Hindenburg Line. Yet his proposal to achieve it by flanking thrusts relied entirely on the outcome of an assault on a narrow frontage against the sector most suitable for offensive operations and defended accordingly. Reviewing the plan after the war, the Australian Army staff concluded that Rawlinson's decision to attack on a broad front increased the prospects of each of the formations involved. When the plan went awry on 29 September, even Jess, a divisional staff officer, realised that only a flanking advance behind the Germans could regain the initiative. Monash still persisted with a frontal attack when its folly was stressed by Gellibrand, who had seen for himself. Again, on 1 October, he wanted to launch a frontal assault instead of continuing the flanking drive to the north-east, which had been partially successful the previous day. This time Gellibrand's vehement opposition, expressed in 'a heart-to-heart' talk, dissuaded him. In the event, the Germans pulled out. Wanting to clear the air with Gellibrand, Monash apologised and also congratulated his division on its efforts. Nonetheless, Monash's earlier allegations with regard to battalion strengths and his attempt, from the rear, to dictate Gellibrand's frontages, were an insult to a competent divisional commander. Could it have been that these aberrations resulted from Monash's tiredness after the stress of six months of strenuous senior command with only a single break of six days before the main offensive campaign started on 8 August?

Barbed-wire entanglements protecting the Beaurevoir Line, the reserve system of the Hindenburg Line. Though poorly developed, the trenches were buttressed by numerous anti-tank gun and machine-gun posts. The wire of the main Hindenburg Line was even denser (AWM E03583).

Criticism of a different sort applied to the operations of the 2nd Division. On 3 October it was to seize the Beaurevoir Line, part of which had already been captured by IX Corps further south, and the village of Beaurevoir overlooking it almost two miles beyond. This conventional set-piece on a frontage of 5000 yards included aircraft dropping smoke bombs to blind the Germans on the heights. The Beaurevoir Line was taken, but the subsequent advance stalled on the lower slopes of the second objective. Next day the village fell to the British 25th Division, with the 2nd Division swinging its left flank forward to conform. The relief of the 2nd had already begun when Rawlinson 'desired [Monash] to retain control of the battlefront for one day longer, and avail myself of the time to make an endeavour to advance our line still further to the east.' On 5 October the 6th Brigade attacked Montbrehain, from which the British 46th Division had earlier been driven out. Monash selected the village, which was south-east of Beaurevoir, because the plateau on which it stood dominated any further advance. As only two of the 6th Brigade's battalions could be considered fresh, the 2nd Pioneer Battalion had

CHAPTER 10

to be included in the attack.[81] The supporting tanks were late, and the assault started without them. According to prisoners, it was fully expected by the Germans, who had reinforced the village with fresh troops and artillery. Despite tenacious resistance and a heavy counter-attack, Montbrehain was captured in what Bean called 'one of the most brilliant actions of Australian infantry in the First World War.'

Enemy dead in one of the trenches at Montbrehain two days after the capture of the village by the 21st and 24th battalions in October 1918 (AWM E03779).

Bean also considered the attack unnecessary, and it is difficult to disagree with his view. It cost 30 officers and 400 men, some with the Anzac chevron on their sleeves. Montbrehain could have been taken easily and with probably fewer casualties if it had been included among the objectives for a much wider operation. Although no records exist beyond Monash's account of its origins, it seems that it was devised merely to ensure that the day remaining before the completion of the 2nd Division's relief was not wasted. Admittedly, Haig was anxious for the attack, because the capture of Beaurevoir and Montbrehain removed the final obstacle to a deep cavalry exploitation of the breaching of the Hindenburg Line. Rawlinson knew this, and presumably Monash did as well. Perhaps for this reason he, Rosenthal and Blamey considered the attack worthwhile.

MONASH

After Montbrehain the 2nd Division joined the other Australian formations in a rest area by the sea near Abbeville. The Australian Corps had fought its last action of the war. Its achievements under Monash were great. At a cost of 21 243 casualties, just over a quarter of whom were killed, it took 29 144 prisoners, 338 guns and countless machine-guns and trench mortars, as well as liberating, by Monash's reckoning, 116 towns and villages in 344 square miles of territory. These figures represented about 22 per cent of the captures of the entire British Army in the last phase of the war on the Western Front.

Chapter 11

Reputations

On 21 November 1918 Monash was appointed Director-General of Repatriation and Demobilisation, beginning the work in London at the end of the month after handing over the corps to Hobbs. He persuaded Hughes that the men must not be returned to Australia by units, which the government favoured, but according to a priority determined by their length of service, a principle to which the troops themselves clung. Some 180 000 men had to be kept intelligently occupied until ships became available. Monash urged all leaders to imbue their men with a 'reconstruction morale', which would create 'a vision of the needs of Australia in the future days of peace, so that each one would be keen to reinstall himself as a useful member of his nation.' Bishop George Long's education scheme was the vehicle that gave substance to the vision, as every man awaiting repatriation could study at government expense any subject he believed might be of value to him in civil life.

Monash leads Australian troops past the saluting base in front of Buckingham Palace during the Victory March through London, 19 July 1919 (AWM D00829).

MONASH

Monash himself did not return to Australia until 26 December 1919, and he went into civilian clothes immediately. In August 1920 he accepted the chairmanship of the infant State Electricity Commission of Victoria, planning and supervising the development of the state's power scheme. The open-cut mining of brown coal at Yallourn, the construction of an enormous power station there, and the cutting of a track 120 miles long for the erection of transmission lines to Melbourne were all completed under his leadership. In 1929 Monash and Sir Harry Chauvel, the other Australian corps commander, were promoted to general. It was one of Monash's last honours. On 8 October 1931, aged 66, he died at Iona after a short illness. Attended by at least 250 000 people, his state funeral was the largest and most impressive that Australia had yet seen. It has rarely been matched since. Among the obituaries was one written by Liddell Hart for the *Telegraph* and republished in his book *Through the Fog of War*. It began:

> Sir John Monash had probably the greatest capacity for command in modern war among all who held command ... If that war had lasted another year he would almost certainly have risen from commander of the Australian Corps to command of an army; he might even have risen to be Commander-in-Chief. If capacity had been the determining factor, he would have done so.

In 1963 the well-known historian A.J.P. Taylor called Monash 'the only general of creative originality produced by the First World War'. Field Marshal Montgomery in 1968 combined the views of both Liddell Hart and Taylor:

> I would name Sir John Monash as the best general on the Western Front in Europe; he possessed real creative originality, and the war might well have been over sooner and with fewer casualties, had Haig been relieved of his command and Monash been appointed to command the British Armies in his place.

These judgements represent the conventional view of Monash the commander. To what extent are they correct?

The study of Monash's military development up to and including his command of the Australian Corps can be reduced to four

CHAPTER 11

elements. Firstly, many of his attitudes and methods did not change throughout the war. After a pre-war military career spanning thirty years, this was unsurprising. As commander of the Victorian Section of the Intelligence Corps, his efforts to ensure that officers working in one area were familiar with the duties of colleagues in another were no different to his injunction, on assuming command of the corps, against staff officers working in watertight compartments. His appreciation of the importance of staff work and his understanding of its principles found their origins in the Intelligence Corps as well. Monash's plea to the battalion commanders of the 13th Brigade in 1913 to develop a community spirit was repeated to subordinate commanders in every formation he led and formed the basis for discipline in them. The 13th Brigade's performance at Lilydale owed much to Monash's ability as a trainer. His later work with the 4th Brigade and the 3rd Division showed that it was no fluke. The same moral courage he displayed as commander of the North Melbourne Battery during the 'railway ticket affair' was shown in his confrontation with Rawlinson and GHQ over the use of the Americans before Hamel. These episodes refute the claim, quoted by Terraine, that he was GHQ's man – or for that matter, anybody else's man.

Building on this foundation was the second element, Monash's command of an infantry brigade and division. The unique circumstances of command at Anzac in 1915, where senior officers faced much the same dangers as their men, enabled him to experience the nature of war first hand. He witnessed the awful mauling of the Otago Battalion on 2 May, and at Hill 60 in August saw the effects of a last-minute change of plan that left his brigade without adequate artillery support. His laudable performance on 6/7 August showed the importance of senior commanders taking control when an operation had faltered either through enemy action or the frictions of war. Above all, he learned the limits to which men could be pushed. The sight of sick and exhausted soldiers responding to yet another call was extremely important in the context of the demands he made on the Australian Corps between August and October 1918.

MONASH

Monash's first battle as a divisional commander was the attack at Messines, and from it he adopted – not invented – a tactical approach that he applied in most of his operations on the Western Front. He regarded the limited attack as the best solution to its problems. Perhaps he followed the method too rigidly. After Morlancourt and Hamel there were numerous complaints that the objective was too shallow, that the German gun line could have been reached. This feeling had to be balanced against the knowledge that the chance of failure increased as the penetration deepened. For a general who sought to feed his troops on victory, the choice was obvious.

Concern for the welfare of the men was the principle by which the 3rd Division was commanded. But Monash was not acting merely out of humanitarian concerns; without regular relief, warm clothing and hot meals in the line whenever possible, efficiency, especially of the infantry, must decline and, with it, confidence in the leaders. This policy, too, was obvious in his command of the Australian Corps. The hot food enjoyed by the occupants of the most advanced positions reached on 8 August was as much a result of it as the refreshing water the troops of the 3rd Division found in their assembly trenches after the dreadful approach march through Ploegsteert Wood on 6–7 June 1917.

The third element was good fortune, and it was manifested in many ways other than his inheritance of the work of Birdwood and White, the creators of the Australian Corps. Before commanding a division on the Western Front, Monash had briefly experienced brigade command there. Being called on to train his division in England rather than Egypt, he had all the lessons of the Somme fighting available to him. In each of his commands, he was served by able staffs and, with few exceptions, by able leaders. The results were most apparent in the last months of 1918. Glasgow's performance at Chuignes, Gellibrand's at Bray and on the Hindenburg Line, Sinclair-MacLagan's on the Hindenburg Outpost Line, and Rosenthal's and Hobbs's efforts at Mont St Quentin and Péronne illustrated the competence of his divisional commanders. These battles demanded speedy preparation of orders and coordination with other units and

CHAPTER 11

arms, which could not have been accomplished without capable staffs at all levels. Resourceful command of brigades and battalions made possible the open warfare assaults in the second phase of many operations, as well as the advance astride the Somme between attacks. Finally, Monash and the Australian Corps were at their zenith when the Germans had reached their nadir. Glasgow considered Monash to have been especially lucky in this regard. He was also fortunate to command at a time when commanders at his level enjoyed more latitude than they had before – provided, and this was crucial, that they had demonstrated ability.

Monash's civilian training and background was the fourth element, and it runs as a leitmotif through the first three. His legal education and work in court necessitated clarity of thought and lucidity of expression. Both were evident whenever Monash chaired a conference; indeed the success of the conference method was in no small degree attributable to them. More important was his training and experience as an engineer and the 'engineering mode of thought' it fostered. Monash's mind remained open, and anything that might improve an existing technique was keenly encouraged by him. The examples ranged from the Varley smoke bomb and the use of dummy targets in no man's land to his enthusiastic adoption of the ideas of Fuller and Elles. He may have been lucky to command the Australian Corps when many significant developments occurred as the BEF's ascent of its so-called 'learning curve' gained momentum, but the onus for recognising their potential rested with him. He studied, and required all his subordinates to read, the wealth of material issuing from GHQ, so that his command was always abreast of the latest tactical techniques, whether British, French or German. Monash stated with regret that he was not strong on invention, but his relentless assimilation of the ideas of others ensured that this was not a failing. His work on bridges and buildings gave him experience of large projects. Material had to be concentrated and labour organised and directed and, if in remote areas, both had to be maintained and fed. If one part of the project was not completed on time, another could not begin and costs would increase. All of this prepared him for the problems of warfare on the Western Front.

Other important qualities resist a convenient grouping. Subordinates from RSM Goldstein to Major General Hobbs agreed how easy it was to serve under him. Even Gellibrand, perhaps his sternest critic, conceded: 'For my part it mattered not that the leopard had spots – that was natural. I could admire and follow him with comfort and pleasure despite the fact that I was well aware of his failings.' Blamey recalled that the most affectionate and cordial relationship existed between Monash and the staff. To those whose duties necessitated frequent contact with him, 'he demonstrated his great gift for extracting the best efforts they could give and for winning their personal liking as well as respect.' But the discipline in the headquarters was no different from that in the rest of the corps. Monash insisted on proper saluting, was abrupt on the telephone and yelled at his ADCs. Staff officers who saw him rarely, found Monash remote, in contrast to the affable Birdwood.

Monash could also be ruthless. As a divisional commander he had no hesitation in bringing down a barrage to retain ground won despite the possibility that his own men might be underneath it. He was willing to sacrifice entire units for a greater object, as evidenced by his remarks to the unfortunate pioneer battalion commander on 8 August and to Gellibrand regarding the capture of the Bouchavesnes Spur in the Mont St Quentin attack. His rejection of the pleas of Hobbs and others that their troops were incapable of further effort is the final disproof of Bean's assertion: 'Whether Monash possessed the ruthless will of the greatest fighting leaders may be strongly questioned.'

In view of his background, Monash's craving for recognition was understandable. Yet it is ironic that a man who had already achieved distinction, and been duly honoured, could suggest to the American corps commander whose troops he called 'unspeakable' that he might approach Pershing to obtain for himself, Monash, 'a memento and souvenir of those historic events, and I feel sure that if any recommendation from you were needed to bring this about, you would gladly do so.' Piqued at having no Belgian decoration, Monash suggested to Birdwood that a hint to the Military Secretary at GHQ 'might draw his attention to my own particular position

CHAPTER 11

in this matter.' The award of the Grand Officier de l'Ordre de la Couronne with Croix de Guerre followed. While this personal failing occasionally justified Bean's hostility towards him, it did not affect Monash's exercise of command. Bean's assistant, Arthur Bazley, knew Monash and said of him: 'He was keenly ambitious, but if, being human, he was not without the vanity of most successful men, he had the restraint and intelligence to keep that quality under control; it never trapped him into mistakes in the field.' It is an important qualification to keep in mind.

A tired man. Anzac Day 1931 and Monash leads Melbourne's Anzac Day march for the last time. He passed away six months later (National Archives A1200, L39602).

MONASH

As a counterpoint to Monash's vanity, the fellowship of the AIF profoundly moved him, and he was humbly proud to participate in it. There were many instances. At the theatre on leave, he sat next to an AIF sergeant and private and invited them to have a drink during interval, to the dismay of British officers. Through the AIF, Serle says, Monash came to appreciate the common man as he had never done before and jettisoned his pre-war belief that life was ruled by the law of the jungle. His post-war life was replete with examples. He led the Anzac Day marches in Melbourne and was the driving force behind the construction of the Shrine, its magnificent war memorial. Veterans regarded him as one of their own. 'As a soldier he's like one of ourselves, and doesn't like swank', the great Jacka remarked of Monash. At his funeral, the hundreds of tributes emphasised his personal qualities, not his achievements – 'again and again, people stressed his kindness, courtesy, considerateness and fairness.'

Monash's situation in May 1918 resembled Field Marshal Montgomery's, when Montgomery took command of the British Eighth Army in August 1942. Montgomery had served with distinction as an instructor at Camberley and Quetta, and then commanded a division in difficult circumstances in France in 1940 and an army of two corps training in England afterwards. By the time he arrived in North Africa, his ideas on fighting the Germans were highly developed. So were Monash's when he took command of the Australian Corps. He brought to it a formidable intellectual capacity, combined with lengthy civil and military experience of a kind admirably suited to its command in the second half of 1918. Contrary to Bean's claim, he did know his men and what they were capable of achieving. 'With such an army a general can work miracles', Monash often said of the AIF. His astute estimate of the Australian soldier in *Australian Victories* ranks alongside Bean's better known analysis in the *Official History*. Besides the limited attack, Monash was an enthusiastic exponent of the view that the infantry had to be supported by every conceivable contrivance. Not only would its task then become easier, but fewer men would be required to achieve it. As Gellibrand wrote: 'Monash beat all in one thing: his ability to bargain with success on the lines:

CHAPTER 11

"I'll take over another mile of front but of course I must have another three batteries, etc., etc.'" These were important elements of the operational philosophy Monash had evolved by May 1918 and, as in Montgomery's case in 1942, it served him well for the rest of the war.

Monash was not infallible. His change of plan and the hasty inclusion in it of Froissy Beacon before the Chuignes attack were lapses caused by departures from two of his strengths: fixity of plan and an ability to recognise the tactical significance of ground. His performance on the Hindenburg Line was his poorest as corps commander and rivalled that of 8 August 1915 as his worst of the war. He recognised the importance of widening the initial breach, but his method of achieving it was fraught with risks that he refused to acknowledge. The resistance at the Bellicourt tunnel showed what could have happened had the entire attack been concentrated there. When his plan had gone awry, both he and Blamey rejected the advice of Gellibrand, who was intimately aware of the situation because he had gone forward to see for himself, something Monash did only once in his career. Monash had always insisted on prompt information from subordinate commanders. His close and often bullying control of the battle depended on it, and he was lifted above the ruck of divisional and corps commanders by it. On the Hindenburg Line he disregarded it.

The Hindenburg Line showed up two more flaws in Monash as a general. Again, both were evident during his brigade and divisional commands, and it is useful to discuss them by contrasting his approach with Birdwood's. Monash did not hold back on this subject when comparing his chairmanship of the State Electricity Commission to the command of the Australian Corps:

> [Birdwood] was always 'buzzing about', looking people up, perambulating all over the place, barely ever at Headquarters and not *really* exercising any command at all … I spent as much as possible of my whole time at my Headquarters which was the legitimate locale of my duties, considering reports; planning; organizing and directing …
>
> I have brought the same conception to bear upon the discharge of my duties with the Commission, i.e. to be and stay, as far as possible,

in one place, i.e. my Headquarters office, where everybody knows where to get me, at a moment's notice, for immediate discussion or reference, and rapid decision; where I can have before me, all the time, a complete and not a partial picture of what is going on, and from which place I can, at all times, reach every possible subordinate ... with the minimum of delay.

I take leave to describe my method as scientific and efficient, and the other method, i.e. of a great sham of personal activity and of much travelling about, as dilettante and futile.

Monash's assessment of Birdwood was much closer to the truth than he knew. White could not recall Birdwood ever drafting a plan, and as for his much-vaunted visits to the men, 'he never brought back with him a reliable summary of what he had seen there ... He would say that so and so had a couple of companies overlooking such and such a post ... I would find out later that this was completely wrong.' Birdwood's habit of passing all operational matters on to White placed an extraordinary burden on the BGGS. By mid-1917 the strain was telling to such an extent that he called the corps commander 'a man of no quality ... So petty was I that even today when the chief went on leave I could not bring myself to congratulate him on his KCB ... up to now I have treated it in contemptuous silence which I could see he observed.' Gellibrand's post-war assessment of Birdwood was much more condemnatory than any of his comments on Monash.

By contrast, Monash was never among his men, at least when they were in action. He was perfectly correct not to expose himself recklessly to danger. Even so, Monash had his share of narrow escapes, particularly from chance shelling behind the line. As he said, it was 'quite futile to try and dodge [it]'. Bean observed that 'There was never any sign that he lacked physical courage; rather he was determined to avoid all except inevitable risks.' Monash himself had the last say on this controversial question after the war. As a means of maintaining morale, visits to the line were unnecessary:

> A force which finds itself well-equipped, well-fed and well-quartered, and which is able to achieve victory in battle without

CHAPTER 11

serious losses, will speedily elevate its leaders in its regard and esteem even if it has but rare personal contact with them.

The contradiction with his pre-war dictum in *100 Hints* is striking. Not once as corps commander did Monash call on a brigade headquarters during a battle. His visit to Mont St Quentin and Péronne on 6 September, four days after the fighting, was probably the closest he came to the front line. Unlike Montgomery, he never gained a personal impression of the battle by visiting the subordinate commanders fighting it. This did not matter in most of the major operations launched by the Australian Corps under his command, when his policy of remaining at his headquarters usually proved correct, as it had done when he had been a divisional commander. However, there are exceptions to every rule in warfare, which is the reason why flexibility is one of its most important principles. The Hindenburg Line was one of those exceptions. Even assuming his system of liaison officers was functioning normally, Monash did not have a 'feel' for the battle. Furthermore, all his planning was done from the map; he did not undertake a single reconnaissance as a corps commander. While his ability to translate maps into a mental picture of terrain was remarkable, it is doubtful whether the mistake at Chuignes would have occurred had Monash seen the ground. As before, Monash's method worked on most occasions, but he failed to respond in the isolated instances where a departure from custom was needed.

The second weakness also concerns Monash's style of command. His record shows that he favoured a 'top down approach ... where the initiative and planning was thought through in detail at the highest level and directed down to subordinate commanders who carried it out with little or no scope for initiative on their part.' Yet Brigadier General Foott claimed that Monash never interfered with subordinates, citing his aphorism: 'No use keeping a dog and doing your own barking.' This may have been true of quiet periods and when fluid conditions necessitated devolved decision-making, such as at Mont St Quentin and during the advances to contact between attacks. But on other occasions, Monash sometimes overreached himself by performing some of the functions that more properly belonged lower down. His plan for the movement of the guns in the second phase of the Hindenburg Line was an example. Normally, a commander would state when he wanted the guns in position, and his staff would make the necessary time and space calculations and arrangements to make sure that they were there at the appointed hour. Monash did both. The checklist he gave Jackson before Messines was another instance among many. In other words, Monash tended at times to circumscribe his dog so that its barking was indistinguishable from his own. His policy may have been justified at Gallipoli, where he had inexperienced commanders and staff officers, thus devolving much greater responsibility on himself as the brigade commander. It was less appropriate in the 3rd Division after Messines and in the Australian Corps after Hamel. Its divisional commanders and staff were all experienced, dedicated men. Perhaps Monash's style was inevitable. His pre-war career was testimony to the results gained solely by intellect and personal effort, and during the war he often exceeded his subordinates in knowledge and skill. Overall, Glasgow said, Monash had 'a genius for soldiering'. A 'hands off' approach would not have come naturally. Monash's tiredness, which so impressed Blamey towards the end of 1918, and which almost certainly affected his conduct of the attack on the Hindenburg Line, was the penalty he paid.

It is sometimes implied that any of the other Australian generals could have achieved the same results as Monash. Comparative exercises may be tempting, but they are also fruitless. None of the other generals could match Monash intellectually or in articulateness. 'Never, so far as truth was humanly attainable, did he ever half know anything', observed Frank Cutlack, who had been the 3rd Division's intelligence officer and became a war correspondent in 1918. Can it be concluded from this that if Sinclair-MacLagan commanded the corps, the attack at Hamel would have been launched without tanks? Or that if Hobbs held the position, he would not have driven the corps as Monash did, but insisted to Rawlinson that it must be relieved after Péronne? Would Rosenthal have demanded

CHAPTER 11

responsibility for both banks of the Somme and then lavished as much care on the repair of its bridges as Monash? Could any of the others have maintained morale through the gruelling advance as Monash did? These questions can never be satisfactorily resolved; and yet it is with them that any answer must lie.

Much the same applies to White. His operational planning was brilliant, as shown by the evacuation of Anzac or the assembly arrangements before Menin Road and Polygon Wood. Does this mean that he would have devised the same plan for the assembly before 8 August as Monash? Because Monash's tactical thinking on machine-guns and artillery and his administration with regard to the control of manpower were more advanced than White's, would White have made a lesser commander? Would Monash have been a better BGGS than White? After all, he discharged the functions of that post often enough. There are too many ifs and might-have-beens, making the degree of subjectivity involved too great for any judgement to be worthwhile. Both men were outstanding in their respective roles. Nothing more can be said than that.

The question of whether Monash could have replaced Haig must be treated on similar lines. Lloyd George wanted to dismiss the C-in-C for his handling of Third Ypres in 1917 and the German offensives in 1918. No worthy successor could be found except for Lieutenant General Sir Claud Jacob, whose supposed superiority was not so great as to mitigate the likely adverse political consequences of Haig's removal. But after the war, Lloyd George was informed by men whose judgement he valued that:

> ... the only soldier thrown up ... on the British side who possessed the necessary qualities for the position was a Dominion General. Competent professional soldiers whom I have consulted have all agreed that this man might and probably would have risen to the height of the occasion. But I knew nothing of this at the time.

Speculation on whether the Prime Minister was referring to Monash should have been settled by the publication of the sixth volume of his memoirs in 1936: 'Monash was ... the most resourceful general in the whole of the British Army.' But in his biography of Currie, which appeared in 1950, Hugh Urquhart recounted a conversation with Lloyd George sixteen years earlier. The former Prime Minister claimed that in the summer of 1918: 'I had not met Monash at that time and my later idea, after I had got to know Monash, was to make him chief of staff and Currie Commander-in-Chief.'

Whatever Lloyd George knew at the time, his judgement is almost valueless. Monash's reputation was, for him, a means of traducing Haig and the senior generals. Moreover, in the latter half of 1918, Haig did not need replacing, for the advance to victory had begun and was continuing largely unchecked. When Haig's dismissal had been under consideration earlier, Monash was a divisional commander, one of about sixty in the BEF. Terraine remarks correctly that Lloyd George's complaints of 'not being told' about Monash were 'quite nonsensical – there was not very much to tell.' General Sixsmith adds: 'It is questionable whether Monash would have had the authority to command men of experience and ability such as Rawlinson, Plumer and Byng.' In fact, it would have been an improbability that senior British commanders 'could have submitted to the indignity of being led by a Jewish colonial militiaman, who had never seen active service in his youth.' Nor was Monash the only general of 'creative originality' in the war. Currie, Jacob, Lord Cavan and Maxse come to mind as others. Maxse's capacity for command was certainly no less than Monash's. His methods were similar and just as successful.

Is Monash's reputation justified? Once the cobwebs of his strategic claims are cleared away and the principle established, however unpalatable it may be, that he must be judged as a corps commander and tactician, then the answer is unequivocally an affirmative. When all was said and done, Bean considered Monash 'probably the ablest and most successful British corps commander in France.' His technical mastery of all arms and tactics, particularly surprise and deception, was unsurpassed among his contemporaries. In later years he tended to deprecate the importance of this quality by claiming that a commander could rely on an expert staff in these matters. He never did. Cooperation and coordination between arms and between units in the Australian Corps was probably not exceeded anywhere in the

CHAPTER 11

BEF. Monash's employment of tanks at Hamel and his psychological approach to their use by the 4th Division, his assembly arrangements and meticulous organisation of his corps' role on 8 August, the rapid switching of brigades and steadfast maintenance of the aim at Mont St Quentin and his planning of road construction and traffic control before the Hindenburg Line were examples of his ability. Each of them contributed substantially to the outcome of the battle concerned. At the same time, he accorded equal emphasis to the administrative requirements of operations. His men 'went into action feeling, usually with justification, that, whatever might lie ahead, at least everything was right behind them.'

John Monash's achievements were not so great as to earn him a place alongside Marlborough, Napoleon or Wellington among the Great Captains, if only because he never held an independent command. Thus he never had the chance to do what Allenby did at Megiddo in 1918, or what Montgomery did at El Alamein in 1942. But by any standard Monash was a successful general and, with Currie and Maxse, a figure of major importance in World War I. It was as appropriate as it was fortunate that the Australian Corps should throw up such a man in time to command it in its last and greatest battles.

Appendix 1
The origin of the August Offensive, in particular the importance of Hill 971

Although Anzac continued to play second fiddle to Helles in June and July 1915 by holding as many Turks in place as possible, the eventual transfer there of the main effort had been considered by Hamilton even before the landing. On 20 May Birdwood promulgated extracts from a letter that showed the direction of the C-in-C's thinking: 'the maintenance of the [Anzac] position may prove to be the fulcrum for the lever which will topple over Germany and the pride of the Germans.'

Hamilton inclined to a south-easterly advance to cut off the Kilid Bahr plateau, but the plan ultimately adopted at Birdwood's instigation was for a breakout to the north of Anzac. The idea originated in discussions during Birdwood's daily visits to unit headquarters on the possibility of attacking from various sectors of the Anzac line, although he was unsure when it was first mooted or by whom.

On 13 May Birdwood outlined his thoughts in a letter to Hamilton that set out the conclusions of an appreciation prepared largely by Skeen and the ANZAC operations staff. The advantages of an advance from the northern flank far outweighed the difficulty posed by the rugged terrain:

> ... an attack, once the crest of the main Sari Bair ridge is reached, has command over successive positions down to Gaba Tepe, can be supported on the seaward side by ships' fire, and may have opportunities for spotting the enemy's guns now denied to us.

APPENDIX

And, finally, as a step to more extended operations this ridge must ultimately be secured in any case.

To secure the northern flank therefore, 971 and the whole ridge to the South should be secured, and this should be the object of any advance.

At this stage, then, Birdwood regarded Hill 971 as the critical objective, emphasising that, from the standpoint of future operations, it was 'still more important' not to stop short of it. Either simultaneously or just after the 971 attack began, a minor operation would be launched against Gaba Tepe to draw Turkish reserves from the north. With both flanks secure, the general advance beyond the main Turkish line on Gun Ridge could get under way. Of the 19 000-strong Anzac garrison, 10 300, including the 4th Brigade, were needed to hold the original line. Three thousand troops would attack Gaba Tepe, leaving Birdwood the same figure short of the 9000 he estimated as necessary for the main operation. Hence he asked for Brigadier General Cox's 29th Indian Brigade because 'The nature of the country to be operated over, indicates [it] as the most suitable reinforcement possible.' The new plan was thus meant to achieve largely the same objectives as those of the landing.

On 19 May Hamilton asked Birdwood for an official appreciation of the Anzac situation and his views 'as to the action in certain contingencies'. The Turkish attack of 19 May prevented its completion until the end of the month, and an important development occurred in the meantime. Hill 971 was dropped from the plan when reconnaissances suggested the feature was separated from the next summit, Hill Q, by a precarious razorback: 'no assault on [Hill 971] could therefore form part of an attack on the main position without being itself completely isolated.' The objectives were necessarily limited to Chunuk Bair and the twin summits of Hill Q, which offered the same advantages as 971 and views of the Narrows almost as extensive. Apart from this change, the appreciation of 30 May reflected previous thoughts on the offensive. At the same time as Gaba Tepe was attacked, three brigades, totalling 8000 men, would seize by night the crests of Battleship Hill, Chunuk Bair and Q, followed by an assault by at least one brigade along the main ridge towards Anzac, taking the Turkish positions there in rear. As it approached Russell's Top, this assault would be met by an advance from that position, while further south the whole of the 400 Plateau and Pine Ridge were to be captured.

On 25 June Hamilton sought Birdwood's opinion on the use of the three reinforcing divisions promised by Kitchener, and he replied with a third appreciation. It differed from its predecessors. Birdwood had reluctantly jettisoned the Gaba Tepe project at the insistence of Brigadier General Carruthers, then commanding the Right Section, who suggested instead an attack on Lone Pine. It dominated Gaba Tepe, and its capture was a necessary preliminary for the subsequent advance eastwards. Birdwood regarded this operation as a feint to draw Turkish reserves from the main attack launched several hours later. A second departure was the allotment of the 4th Brigade to the latter operation. Its objective was Hill 971.

The feature had thus been included, deleted and then restored to the plan. Possibly because of an 'unfortunate striving after symmetrical perfection', Birdwood and Skeen were mesmerised by it. Bean's assertion that their appreciations confirmed the importance of Chunuk Bair neglects the importance they attached to Hill 971. Except for allotting the 4th Brigade to a frontal attack on Baby 700, Godley's appreciation of 23 June was no different to theirs: 'The decisive point appears to be 971 and the ground in the vicinity'. An ANZAC appreciation of 9 July discussed methods of attacking 971 as the key to the Sari Bair crests.

Although Bean's claim that Birdwood underestimated the difficulties confronting Monash's advance to Hill 971 is undoubtedly correct, he was far more aware of them than Bean suggests. The hazards figure in every appreciation he submitted to Hamilton. Birdwood's first thoughts on 13 May pointed out that in a night advance north of Anzac, 'there is sure to be loss of cohesion and delays which will stop the whole move.' On 30 May he wrote that troops would inevitably become lost, but this 'is not a matter of consequence, as all fully know they have to press upwards, and matters will be rectified in this respect in the morning.' By 1 July he had retreated to a position on the fence:

APPENDIX

'These columns should suffice to take the ridge, but they are certain to be disorganised and weakened on arriving there.' In fact it was the hostility of the ground, far worse than that at the landing, that the attackers must regard as their 'best friends', for it prevented the establishment by the Turks of continuous trench lines, as they had done everywhere else. Birdwood confided to Kitchener: 'It will be a difficult job ... a very difficult one, but I have great hope of its success partly on account ... of its very difficulties.' Godley's attitude was even more simplistic: 'our troops managed to surmount difficult ground in the first landing and there appears to be no reason why they should not again do so.' Of the three, only Skeen, the main architect of the plan, expressed doubt that it would succeed: 'the terrain, shortage of water and artillery and the difficulty of gaining a footing on the crest would combine to produce failure.'

Appendix 2
AIF Infantry Battalions

1st Division

1st Brigade (NSW)**	2nd Brigade (Vic)**	3rd Brigade**
1st Battalion	5th Battalion	9th Battalion (Qld)
2nd Battalion	6th Battalion	10th Battalion (SA)
3rd Battalion	7th Battalion	11th Battalion (WA)
4th Battalion	8th Battalion	12th Battalion (Tas, SA, WA)

2nd Division

5th Brigade (NSW)**	6th Brigade (Vic)*	7th Brigade*
17th Battalion	21st Battalion†	25th Battalion (Qld)†
18th Battalion	22nd Battalion	26th Battalion (Qld, Tas)
19th Battalion†	23rd Battalion	27th Battalion (SA)
20th Battalion	24th Battalion	28th Battalion (WA)

3rd Division

9th Brigade (NSW)	10th Brigade	11th Brigade
33rd Battalion	37th Battalion (Vic)†	41st Battalion (Qld)
34th Battalion	38th Battalion (Vic)	42nd Battalion (Qld)†
35th Battalion	39th Battalion (Vic)	43rd Battalion (SA)
36th Battalion†	40th Battalion (Tas)	44th Battalion (WA)

4th Division

4th Brigade**±	12th Brigade	13th Brigade
13th Battalion (NSW)	45th Battalion (NSW)	49th Battalion (Qld)
14th Battalion (Vic)	46th Battalion (Vic)	50th Battalion (SA)
15th Battalion (Qld, Tas)	47th Battalion (Qld, Tas)†	51st Battalion (WA)
16th Battalion (WA, SA)	48th Battalion (WA, SA)	52nd Battalion (Tas, SA, WA)†

5th Division

8th Brigade	14th Brigade (NSW)	15th Brigade (Vic)
29th Battalion (Vic)†	53rd Battalion	57th Battalion
30th Battalion (NSW)	54th Battalion†	58th Battalion
31st Battalion (Qld, Vic)	55th Battalion	59th Battalion
32nd Battalion (SA, WA)	56th Battalion	60th Battalion

** denotes landed at Gallipoli on 25 April.
* denotes participated in Gallipoli campaign.
† denotes disbanded prior to 11 November 1918.
± denotes originally part of the NZ and A Division.

Endnotes

Chapter 1

1. The story that Monash met Ned Kelly during the bushranger's raid on Jerilderie in February 1879 is probably apocryphal. Monash liked to boast that Kelly gave him 'much sound advice', but would never say what these pearls of wisdom were. Moreover, he had left Jerilderie one year before the raid. Louis Monash and William Elliott, of course, figured prominently. In his biography of Kelly, John Molony describes the alleged meeting, but adds in a footnote that the story is based on 'oral tradition'.
2. The dux in the previous year was James Whiteside McCay, whose military career complemented Monash's until the end of World War I. The pair were also good friends.
3. According to Bean, these were capacities in which Monash had few equals in the entire BEF. (Bean, 'Monash the Soldier', *Reveille*, 31 Oct. 1931, p. 2)

Chapter 2

4. Its designation was AIC Victorian Military District (AIC Vic. MD).
5. Four engineers, an accountant, a journalist, a librarian, a survey draughtsman, a business manager, an architect, and a secretary Ports and Harbours.
6. Monash had lectured on map production at the 1909 Intelligence Course and at an Intelligence School of Instruction in January 1912, where he insisted that every AIC officer should be familiar with the theory, so as to be able to assist with the work.
7. Monash has been described as an avid student of military history. Warren Perry says he had a military work in his luggage on long journeys and that he could describe with pencil and paper how Napoleon had won at Austerlitz, how Wellington had triumphed on the Peninsula, or how Moltke had planned the operations of 1870–71. But it is difficult to find evidence of *what* Monash actually read, beyond Scott's comment that one of his favourite books was Henderson's *Stonewall Jackson and the American Civil War*.
8. Legge awarded Monash second place, as he felt his essay lacked the practical lessons illustrated by the winner he selected. Chauvel gave Monash first prize.
9. On 9 November Monash scribbled a rough note, which is preserved in his papers in the NLA, entitled 'Three Principles of Arrangements for Battle', which he carried with him at Lilydale. The principles were:
   1. When battle imminent always be ready to fight quickly on *suitable* front; this helps you decide on dispositions for approach.
   2. Envelopment is more effective than frontal attack; this helps you to select your main objective.
   3. Keep control as long as possible, i.e. don't throw in all at once; this helps you concentrate on decisive point.
10. According to Monash, Hamilton told him after the war that, as a result of this inspection, he had sent a special report to the War Office praising Monash 'and that all he need say about it was that my subsequent career had justified his prediction.'

Chapter 3

11. Bridges was then Inspector-General. White was acting CGS until Legge returned from London, where he had been Australia's representative on the Imperial General Staff.

MONASH

12 Of the 631 officers in the 1st Division, 99 were professional soldiers. For complete statistics, see Bean, *Official History*, Vol. I, p. 54.
13 Like all good generals, Monash regained his composure quickly and did not mention the incident when he presented a trophy to his assailant!
14 On Good Friday an outbreak occurred in the Haret el Wassir area, when some men warned to leave for the front decided to exact retribution for afflictions they felt were incurred at some of the brothels. After at least one house was incinerated and British military police proved ineffectual, the affair was quelled by the appearance of the Lancashire Territorials with fixed bayonets. Monash was a member of the Court of Inquiry, which examined thirty-one witnesses, 'including a number of Syrian women'. Australians and New Zealanders split the damages of £1700. See Monash's diary for 2–5 Apr 1915 for his involvement in the inquiry.
15 In the week ending 4 March 1915, Monash had only one day available to carry out battalion or lower level training.
16 It had also been practising landings at Lemnos since early March.
17 His daughter, Bertha, was nicknamed 'Bert'.

Chapter 4

18 As a result of Birdwood's message, the 29th Division was required to make another effort at Helles to relieve the situation at Anzac and attacked continuously for four days until it was 'stone cold'.
19 Monash was among the officers who were to carry out a reconnaissance aboard HMS *Queen* on 17 April, but the sortie was cancelled, possibly because of poor weather. However, his battalion commanders were taken on a reconnaissance of the peninsula before the landing. Why he did not join them is unknown.
20 Bean claims Monash landed with Pope at 6.00 pm on 25 April and took him to see Godley. This is incorrect.
21 Next day, 4th Brigade Headquarters had no knowledge of the 15th Battalion's whereabouts, other than that Jess had briefly seen Quinn near Sinclair-MacLagan's headquarters.
22 Looking back 65 years later, Captain Bertram Perry (14th Battalion) denied that the ill-feeling was caused by misdirected fire, alleging that it resulted from the prevailing confusion. He added that argument ceased after the 14th Battalion occupied Courtney's Post.
23 In the event the 29th was sent to Helles.
24 The exact relation of the 16th Battalion to the flanking New Zealanders was uncertain as late as 8 May.
25 As the author found on several occasions, even an unencumbered man, climbing at a leisurely pace in daylight, is exhausted on reaching the top.
26 Monash was also allotted half the Nelson Battalion as a reserve.
27 Robert Rhodes James quotes Jerram's remarks to depict Monash *at the end of April*, a time when the pressure on him was obviously far less than 2–3 May. For that reason, it is much more damaging than when used in its proper context. Furthermore, the words: 'He was a bewildered and tired man without an idea of what to do or how to do it', and those following, also quoted by Rhodes James, are absent from Jerram's handwritten journal.
28 Success was no more likely then, either, for Birdwood's beleaguered corps was in no condition to undertake such an operation. The Turks had expected an attack once the Anzac position was sufficiently strong, and their own assault on 1 May was made partly to forestall it.
29 The arrival of 500 reinforcements on 6–7 May marginally improved the situation.
30 As Gallipoli's terrain had been deemed unsuitable for them, the Light Horse had remained in Egypt. The heavy losses at Anzac necessitated their deployment as dismounted troops.

ENDNOTES

31 The periscope was fixed to the rifle enabling the firer to aim and shoot without raising his head above the parapet.
32 Private Albert Jacka was awarded Australia's first VC of the war for clearing the Turks out.
33 There was loud laughter whenever Godley mentioned bombs and suppressed mirth when he mentioned the 14th Battalion, 'who had held Courtney's since the Landing'.

Chapter 5

34 One veteran told the author that after two weeks on the peninsula in summer, a healthy man was 'finished'. (Interview with F. Hocking, 15 May 1980)
35 See the Appendix for the genesis of this scheme, Bean's account of which contains several errors.
36 The author retraced the route of Monash's column on 27 April 1981, Johnston's column on 26 April 1981 and both columns in April 1990. Viewing the terrain, also in April 1990, a party of battle-hardened Australian infantry commanders concluded that attempting Monash's advance by night, even on a peacetime exercise, would be foolhardy.
37 Hamilton believed, however, that Cox's judgement and experience were indispensable.
38 The time of arrival at Abdel Rahman Bair was provisionally 1.40 am 'assuming no halts or checks'.
39 Allanson was ordered forward by Cox at 6.30 am.
40 Copies of this letter were sent to Pearce and Hughes on 8 November 1915. It was also printed as a state paper for circulation to the Dardanelles Committee in London.
41 Author's emphasis.
42 Rhodes James admitted to the author on 26 March 1981 that he would introduce substantial qualification into his treatment of the Allanson-Monash episode if rewriting *Gallipoli*.
43 Godley was correct and Monash lost. The promotions were temporary and the *Gazette* proclaiming them otherwise was amended.

Chapter 6

44 Wounded while leading the 2nd Brigade in the attack at Krithia on 8 May 1915, McCay was evacuated to Egypt. He returned to Anzac before the wound had properly healed and was invalided home, arriving in November to a hero's welcome.
45 This letter was not sent, because Birdwood told Monash that McCay was about to leave Australia for Egypt. As an accurate reflection of his feelings, it is, however, invaluable. It is also certain that Monash raised the issue on McCay's arrival.
46 This system was adopted, but whether it was conceived separately by ANZAC Headquarters is unclear.

Chapter 7

47 For a telling commentary on Maxse and his 18th Division, see H. Gough, *Fifth Army*, London, 1931, pp. 147–48.
48 Monash was in error regarding Colman, whose service record shows him to have been a Roman Catholic.
49 As Monash expected, the artillery remained in England for further training.
50 For a brilliant account of what was afterwards known as 'The Big Raid', see C. H. Peters, 'Some Raiding Days', and letter, 29 February 1917, MS 1887, Mitchell Library.
51 For tactical reasons, nineteen were ultimately fired.
52 Its slaughter at the hands of von Richthofen's 'flying circus' in the Arras-Bullecourt area in April 1917 was the nadir of the RFC's fortunes in the war.

53 On 12 April 1981, the author viewed the 3rd Division's attack from the ruins of the château, which still lie on Hill 63, and from the two German pillboxes in the Uhlan system that now form part of the New Zealand Memorial, and went to all the other locations mentioned. He has visited the Messines battlefield many times since.
54 Haig thought Monash was an 'auctioneer'.
55 Attacks were still to be made in waves, but with the minimum number of platoons in each. The platoon was emphasised as a self-contained fighting unit, with distinct sections – bombing and Lewis gun, which provided the main firepower but had hitherto been temporarily attached, and two rifle sections with a number of rifle grenadiers. This structure made it a complete and independent tactical unit that was flexible enough to meet most eventualities.
56 It was to be read to each platoon. Bean says it had no recorded effect.
57 Smith was subsequently relieved.
58 Though Field Marshal Paul von Hindenburg was officially Chief of the General Staff and Ludendorff Quartermaster-General, Ludendorff provided the intellect and effectively directed the German Army.

Chapter 8

59 When it proved successful, Monash arranged a trial before senior commanders, which eventually led to the bomb's adoption by GHQ.
60 The author inspected the 3rd Division's battlefields at Broodseinde and Passchendaele on 10–11 April 1981. He has walked over them, and, indeed, the entire Ypres battlefield many times since.
61 Its career as a depot division lasted only three weeks. On 3 December 1917 it was rushed from rest at Gamaches into reserve at Péronne when the Germans successfully counter-attacked after the Cambrai stroke.
62 The Germans realised that tanks would never be able to match the speed of the infantry advance and so neglected their development.
63 But Bean says that the plan incorporated Cannan's plan for *daylight* patrols to steal the ground on his front.
64 This was Bean's allegation on 1 June. Nearly forty years later he wrote alongside this diary entry, 'I do not now believe this to be true.'
65 In fact he was not. Chauvel was the first to attain corps command, in April 1917.

Chapter 9

66 Blamey was in fact BGGS, although Monash often used him as a chief of staff and usually referred to him as such.
67 The author inspected each of Monash's battlefields on the Somme and from the river to the Hindenburg Line from 14 to 16 April 1981. He has studied them, and Montbrehain, many times since.
68 Historians, including Bean, have mistakenly regarded this as a relegation by Foch of the Amiens stroke. The Bruay attack had been included in Directive Générale No. 3 in deference to Clemenceau's continued stress on the protection of vital war industries. Foch's true attitude was revealed by his ready acquiescence in Haig's reply of the 17th. See *OH*, VI, pp. 463, 479.
69 Bean says he returned on 30 July. This is incorrect as Monash 'worked most of [that] day on forthcoming operation.' See JM, D, 30 July.
70 General Sir James Marshall-Cornwall's conclusion that Foch was correct to insist on a continuation of the Somme thrust is based not on the situation on 11 August, but on 8 August, when the Germans were in disarray. Marshall-Cornwall, *Foch as Military Commander,* London, 1972, p. 235. It is not clear whether Foch hoped the advance of his own armies would turn the flank of the Germans facing Rawlinson.

ENDNOTES

Chapter 10

71 The 32nd had replaced the 17th, which returned to Third Army to participate in its offensive of 21 August.
72 Bean implies that Rawlinson prescribed the objectives on the southern bank as well. The Fourth Army operation order proves that this is incorrect. See *OH*, VI, p. 725.
73 This shows conclusively that Haig was not expecting a breakthrough, and that the main German defence lines would be reduced only by heavy fighting. In short, it was far from an expression of imminent victory.
74 The third and fourth were Chuignes and Hamel.
75 The Siegfried Line, fifty miles long, was only one of a number of German defensive positions extending from Lille to Metz and known generally as the Hindenburg Line. As the Official Historian calls the line in front of the Australian Corps the Hindenburg Line and not the Siegfried Line, the same nomenclature will be used throughout this volume.
76 The entry for 21 December 1918 states: 'Final disappearance of tremors.'
77 After the war, Hughes criticised Monash for seeing only 'one thing – he wanted to fight on – to be in at the finish.'
78 An American infantry division consisted of two brigades, each of two regiments. In turn, each regiment comprised three battalions.
79 Monash later claimed that his exposition was 'brief and simple, but it elicited such a rain of questions' that he had to embark on a three-hour briefing, using maps, diagrams and a blackboard, 'to explain methods and reasons, mistakes and remedies, dangers and precautions, procedures and expedients.' The fact that Monash had diagrams already prepared, and that he intended to 'Take each Regiment over its task minutely' among other points on a five-page agenda, hardly suggests a brief conference.
80 Bean repeated O'Ryan's mistake in dating this conference on 25 September. That date marked the first full meeting of the Australian Corps for the operation. As Monash's diary and notes make clear, he had explained the scheme to the Americans two days before.
81 Though technical troops, all pioneers can be required to fight as infantry, but for obvious reasons the measure is adopted only as a last resort. In the advance to the Hindenburg Line pioneers were used in the infantry role because of the exhaustion and numerical weakness of the infantry battalions.

Acronyms and Abbreviations

AA	Australian Archives
AAG	Assistant Adjutant-General
AAJ	*Australian Army Journal*
ADB	*Australian Dictionary of Biography*
ADC	aide-de-camp
ADMS	Assistant Director of Medical Services
AFC	Australian Flying Corps
AIC	Australian Intelligence Corps
AIF	Australian Imperial Force
AJHS	*Journal of the Australian Jewish Historical Society*
ANZAC	Australian and New Zealand Army Corps
AV	*Australian Victories in France*
AWM	Australian War Memorial
AWRS	Australian War Records Section, AWM
BC	Bean Collection, AWM
Bde	Brigade
BEF	British Expeditionary Force
BGGS	Brigadier General, General Staff
Bn	Battalion
CB	Companion of the Order of the Bath
CGS	Chief of the General Staff
CIGS	Chief of the Imperial General Staff
C-in-C	Commander-in-Chief
Comd	Commander
CRA	Commander, Royal Artillery
CRE	Commander, Royal Engineers
CSM	Company Sergeant Major
D	Diary
DA&QMG	Deputy Adjutant and Quartermaster-General

ACRONYMS AND ABBREVIATIONS

DAG	Deputy Adjutant-General
Div	Division
DMO	Director of Military Operations
GHQ	General Headquarters
GOC	General Officer Commanding
GSO1	General Staff Officer Grade 1
GSO2	General Staff Officer Grade 2
HQ	Headquarters
IGS	Imperial General Staff
IO	Intelligence Officer
IWM	Imperial War Museum
JM	John Monash
JRAHS	*Journal of the Royal Australian Historical Society*
JRUSI	*Journal of the Royal United Services Institution*
KC	Liddell Hart Centre for Military Archives, King's College, London
KCB	Knight Commander of the Order of the Bath
KCMG	Knight Commander of the Order of St Michael and St George
LH	Light Horse
MC	Monash Collection, AWM
MEF	Mediterranean Expeditionary Force
mg(s)	machine-gun(s)
MP	Monash Papers, National Library of Australia
NAM	National Army Museum
NCO	Non-commissioned Officer
NSW	New South Wales
NZ&A	New Zealand and Australian Division
NZMR	New Zealand Mounted Rifle (Brigade)
OC	Officer Commanding
OH	*Official History of Australia in the War of 1914–1918*
OpO	Operation Order
OR	Operational Records
RFC	Royal Flying Corps
RMO	Regimental Medical Officer

RO	Routine Order
RSM	Regimental Sergeant Major
VC	Victoria Cross
VGA	Victorian Garrison Artillery
VHM	*Victorian Historical Magazine*
VM	Victoria (Vic) Monash
VMF	Victorian Military Forces
WarL	*War Letters of General Monash*, F.M. Cutlack (ed.)
YBGSC	Ypres Battle General Staff Circulars

References

Introduction

11. My introduction to C.E.W. Bean, *Official History of the War*, Vol. III: *The AIF in France in 1916*, St Lucia, 1982, contains useful material on First World War generalship. J. Monash, *The Australian Victories in France in 1918*.
12. 'collected a mythology': John Terraine to author, 16 Aug. 1979. Command functions: Van Creveld, *Command in War*, p. 6.
12–15. Early sections of the introduction are largely based on A.P. Wavell, *Generals and Generalship*, pp. 2–7. The author interviewed Maj. Gen. E.K.G. Sixsmith in Somerset, England, on 28 Mar. 1981.
15. 'The soldier and politician': B.L. Montgomery, *The Path to Leadership*, p. 22. 'Since technical proficiency': B.H. Liddell Hart, *Thoughts on War*, p. 123. 'skills and orientations': M. Janowitz, *The Professional Soldier*, p. 9. 'conventional career forms': ibid. p. 151. 'like Janowitz's great Americans': N.F. Dixon, *On the Psychology of Military Incompetence*, p. 348.
16. 'The means of transport': M. Carver (ed.), *The War Lords*, p. xi. Foch: Hackett, *The Profession of Arms*, p. 148.
17. 'The positions of his corps': C. von der Goltz, *The Nation in Arms: a treatise on modern military systems and the conduct of war*, pp. 71–72. 'But such study': Liddell Hart, *Thoughts on War*, p. 218.

Chapter 1

This chapter draws heavily on *OH*, VI, ch. 6; Gershon Bennett, 'To the Service of His Country', *Australian Jewish Herald*, 15 Oct. 1936; R. Brasch, 'Sir John Monash', *JRAHS*, 44 (1959) pp. 162–211; A.G. Serle, *John Monash: a biography*, ch. 1–7; notes by Colonel George Farlow and Matthilde (Mat) Monash, June 1933, MP.

19. The marriage also produced two younger daughters, Matthilde (Mat, 1870–1938), who remained a spinster, and Louise (Lou, 1873–1941), who married the distinguished physicist Dr Walter Rosenhain, FRS. JM's letters to Walter and Louise were addressed 'Dear Walterlou'. The headmaster's comment is in Serle, *Monash*, p. 8.
20. The contemporary was George Farlow.
21. 'embarrassingly curious': notes by J. Lewis in Serle, *Monash*, p. 59.
22. 'persons of refinement': A.J. Smithers, *Sir John Monash*, p. 19. 'a most unhappy time': JM to Walter Rosenhain, 8 Jan. 1918, MP. 'perfect confidence and trust': JM to Bertha, 24 Apr. 1915, MC.
23. R.G. Menzies, 'Sir John Monash', *AJHS*, VI (1966), pp. 81–82.
24. 'For years': Serle, *Monash*, p. 140.
25. For JM's wealth, see ibid. p. 167. 'a body of twenty': JM to Baron de Gail, 17 Oct. 1917, MP.
26. JM's comments on his world tour: *Victorian Institute of Engineers - Proceedings 1911*, pp. 28–44, and *Proceedings 1913*, pp. 11–12. *OH*, VI, p. 209. H. Essame, *The Battle for Europe*, p. 117.
27. 'engineering work': JM to E. Phillips, 12 Nov. 1918, MP. 'the man with the genius': S.H.E. Barraclough, 'Sir John Monash-Engineer', *Journal of the Institute of Engineers of Australia*, III (1931), p. 363. 'My Thoughts on the Prewar Military Career of John Monash', *JRAHS*, 67 (1981) pp. 212–26, discusses this question in some detail. 'the most highly trained mind': Blamey to *Reveille*, 12 Apr. 1937, BC.

28. 'This advantage': 'Leadership in War', JM's address to the Beefsteak Club, 30 Mar. 1926, MP. The paragraph on Currie is based on A.M. J. Hyatt, *The Military Career of Sir Arthur Currie*, pp. 6–10.

Chapter 2

31. 'Corporal Potash': Brasch in *JRAHS*, p. 174. 'call the roll': *Duties of WO and NCO, 4 Bn Vic Rifles, VMF 1886*, pp. 4–5. 'Clark, Sir William John', *ADB*, 3: 1851–1890, Melbourne, 1969, p. 423.
32. 'natural talent': Serle, *Monash*, p. 64. 'The matter': JM, D, 13 Aug. 1866. 'the utmost ... unchallengeable position': JM to VM, 15 Mar. 1918, MP.
33. 'only too glad': JM to Miller, 17 Aug. MP. 'feverishly awaiting': JM, D, 13 Aug. *The Tactical Working of Coast Artillery*, undated pamphlet, pp. 1–2, MP.
34. Exams for promotion to Major: *Standing Orders for the VMF*, section 7-2.
35. The Stanley gun is covered in correspondence between Stanley and Col. C. Dean-Pitt, June-Aug. 1889, File 1890-1294 B6, MP106/1, AA. The original address, 'Implements of War', is in MP. It was published as 'The Evolution of Modern Weapons', *JRUSI-Victoria*, III (1894), pp. 3–18.
36. 'success in a great war': 'Mechanical Science as Applied to Warfare', 5 Aug. 1892, MP. 'trivial complaints': 'Notes and Instructions for Camp', Apr. 1893, MP. 'the nature': 'Introduction to Bty Gunnery Course, 1893-94', MP. 'absolutely essential': Bty Order 97a/96, 1 Nov. 1896, MP.
37. 'His orders': Farlow's notes.
38. The railway coupon affair: JM to Farlow, 3 July 1905, MP; JM to Capt. Taylor, 3–5 July, Letter-book 2/3, Melb. Uni. 'during the whole', Hollingsworth to JM, 20 Dec. 1907, MP.
39. 'every effort': Vic. Council of Defence Report, 1896 in *Victoria- Reports of Council of Defence 1886-1900*. Vic. Council of Defence Report for 1892 shows ammunition expenditure. JM's attack on permanent officers: 'Criticisms for the Press', MP, undated and probably not sent.
40. JM's 'Military Affairs Diary 1888-1914', MP, shows that he often paraded twice or thrice weekly, in addition to annual camps and courses. The legacy left by Hutton is described in A.J. Hill, *Chauvel of the Light Horse*, p. 33.
42. The establishment of the AIC is covered by C.D. Coulthard-Clark, *The Citizen General Staff*.
43. 'by virtue': Military Order 41/08, 18 Feb. 1908. JM commented on the officers in 'Notes on Qualifications', 2 May 1908 and 'Records of Service', 7 Sept. 1909, MP. Confidential District Order (CDO) V2/09, 2 Oct. 1909, shows the allocation. Corps Order (CO) 1/08, 22 Sept. 1908, prescribed section responsibilities.
44. Examination of journals: Corps District Order 6/09, 1 Sept. 1909. Bridges' lecture, 'Intelligence in War' is in MP. AIC tasks are listed in Coulthard-Clark, *Citizen General Staff*, pp. 24–25; CDO V3/08, 2 Oct. 1908 and V4/08, 16 Nov. 1908.
45. 'inaugurated by Colonel Monash': Walters to CGS, 27 Mar. 1914, MP. JM to shire engineers, 26 July 1909, MP.
46. JM's definition of map accuracy: JM to McCay, 17 Feb. 1910, MP. JM's trans-shipment plan: JM to OC AIC NSW MD, 3 Dec. 1909, MP. The staff problem was in District Circular Memo 14/09, 4 Nov. 1909. JM's thoughts on staff work: 'Staff Duties in Operations', 18 June 1911, MP.
47. JM's comments on the staff officer: 'Practical Performance of Intelligence Duties in the Field', 26 Feb. 1912, MP.

REFERENCES

48. 'Frimley': 'Notes on Draft Exam Paper', 16 Feb 1910, MP. 'every minute detail ... belongs': JM's briefing, 11 Apr. 1911, MP. 'It is essential': CDO V2/08, 2 Oct. 1908, MP. JM's schemes for these camps are in MP. 'observation, analysis': JM to HQ 3 MD, 18 Nov. 1912, MP.
49. 'design and working': JM to McCay, 23 Apr. 1908, MP. 'A point ... at their fingertips': JM to AAG (Vic.), 4 May 1908, MP.
50. Reports on the Seymour Camp: File 1849/2/237, MP84, AA and in MP; *Argus*, 12 Feb. and *Australasian*, 19 Feb. 1910. *Course Syllabi for 1909, 1911 War Courses*, MP, contains JM's solutions and notes.
51. Liddell Hart, *Thoughts on War*, p. 223.
52. 'In common with': JM to Foster 12 Nov. 1916, MP. As corps commander, JM wrote on 14 Sept. 1918. COs 6/09, 10 June 1909 and 9/11, 23 Mar. 1911 list the problems.
53. 'mental photographs': 'Organization and Duties of the Intelligence Section of the General Staff', 19 Feb. 1912, MP. 'it should be remembered': JM to AIC officers, 7 Feb. 1912, MP. Perry's remarks are in 'The Military Life of Sir John Monash', *VHM*, XXVIII (1957) pp. 30–31. All examiners' comments are in File 1954/23/99, MP 84, AA. JM's essay was published under this title in *Commonwealth Military Journal*, Apr. 1912, pp. 269–87.
54. 'The Wilderness Essay' was analysed by Prof. Theodore Ropp, Duke University, and Dr R.C. Thompson, RMC Duntroon. 'This will impress': 'Note on Draft Exam Paper', 16 Feb. 1910, MP.
55. 'Slippery as an eel': Sellheim to JM, 8 July 1909, MP. JM replied on 28 Sept. McCay's praise was in Corps District Order 8/09, 5 Nov. 1909. CoulthardClark, *Citizen General Staff*, p. 43, contains the commandant's remarks. 'go a long way': JM to McCay, 14 June 1909, MP. 'encroaches upon': JM to McCay, 22 Nov. 1909, MP.
56. 'the actual manoeuvres': District Circular Memo 16/09, 30 Dec. 1909. JM's frustration was reflected in correspondence with McCay on 7 Feb. 1910 and 30 June 1911, MP. 'The General Staff': Kirkpatrick's 'Review of Results Obtained by AIC, 1908-10', 17 Mar. 1911, File 1902/7/66, MP84, AA. 'absolutely essential': McCay to CGS, 31 July 1912, File 1849/2/260, MP84, AA.
57. JM's despair: JM to McCay, 12 Nov., MP.
58. Bruche's recommendation is in J. Thompson, *On Lips of Living Men*, p. 135. File 311/3/126, MP84, AA, contains the confidential report.
59. JM's argument for promotion and selection: correspondence with District HQ on 18 Nov. 1912 and 25 June 1913, MP.
60. 'welded together': 'Notes for Conference with OCs', 12 Aug., MP. JM to Kruse, 5 Nov., MP. 'I don't think you realise': Wanliss to JM, 13 Sept. 1914, MP. The growing pains of the Universal Training Scheme are outlined in 'General Staff Memo on Training, 1913-14', parts 1–3, MP, and the CGS's 'Report on Progress for the Year ending 30 June 1914', File 1975/211, B197, AA.
61. 13 Bde Memo 5/13, 24 Sept. 1913, MP, asked bns to list their deficiencies. JM wrote to District HQ on 8 Oct., MP. 13 Bde training was governed by Military Order 387/13, 15 July 1913, and 'Program of Proposed Parades for 13 Bde for Quarter Ending 30 Sept. 1913', 16 July, MP. '13 Bde, Tactical Exercise, Lilydale, Dec.13-14, 1913', MP contains the problems set by JM. 'a medical question': JM to Dr H. Bryant, 14 Oct., MP.
62. JM, 'Notes for Inspection', 8 Feb. 1914, MP. 'the effect was wonderful': JM to Bruche, 26 Mar., MP.
63. 'to let all ranks': JM's lecture notes for 11 Feb., MP. R. Williams, *These are the Facts*, p. 19. The exercise is described in JM's 'Notes for Manoeuvres of 13 Bde', 31 Jan. and 'Comments', 12 Feb., MP. Hamilton to E. D. Millen, 17 Feb., Item 7/8/10b, Hamilton

MONASH

Papers, and to *Sydney Morning Herald*, 30 Nov. 1936. JM made this claim in an interview with A.F. O'Connor, 13 Feb. 1919. 'a successful term': JM to Bruche, 26 Mar., MP. Overworking troops: *Age*, 18 Feb.; *Commonwealth Parliamentary Debates*, LXXN (21 May–26 June 1914) pp. 2337–38; *Leeton Call*, 28 Feb.

64. JM's account: File A73/4/306, MP133/2, AA, and correspondence with Bruche, 26 Mar. and District HQ, 14 Apr., MP. JM expressed his hopes to Lou, 26 June 1913, and VM, 16 Mar. 1917, MP.

65. The training of JM's British contemporaries is drawn from B. Bond, *The Victorian Army and the Staff College, 1854-1914*, pp. 159–62; E.K.G. Sixsmith, *British Generalship in the Twentieth Century*, pp. 42–44; J.F.C. Fuller, *Generalship: its diseases and their cure*, p. 69; G.J. De Groot, 'Ambition, Duty and Doctrine' in Bond and Cave, *Haig*, p. 39.

66. G.F.R. Henderson, *The Science of War*, p. 3. 'I do not regard': JM to Lt E.J. Matthews, 6 Jan. 1910, MP.

67. 'constant practice': Liddell Hart, *Thoughts on War*, p. 122. 'The days passed evenly': J. Charteris, *Field Marshal Earl Haig*, p. 68. 'the smokeless': T. Pakenham, *The Boer War*, p. 574.

68. 'few had handled': Hill, *Chauvel*, p. 54.

Chapter 3

69. JM's description is based on B. Callinan, *Sir John Monash*, p. 19; F.M. Cutlack, 'General Monash: His Remarkable Record', *Sydney Morning Herald*, 27 Dec. 1918; J. Hetherington, *John Monash*, p. 12. JM's duties as Deputy Chief Censor: JM to Walter Rosenhain, 11 Aug., MP.

70. 'even if already published': 'First Draft of Censorship Regulations', 14 Aug., MP. 'These large interests': JM to Reynolds, 10 Sept., MP. Reynolds' correspondence on JM's appointment: File AIF 13/2/12, B539, AA.

71. G.F. Pearce, *Carpenter to Cabinet*, p. 125.

72. 'It may cause you': JM to Gustav Monasch, 10 Oct., MP. Gustav to JM, 16 Nov.1914 and Leo to JM, 3 Apr. 1916, MP. 'picked the eyes': *OH*, I, p. 64. Bridges and the raising of the first contingent is covered in C.E.W. Bean, *Two Men I Knew*, p. 33, and *OH*, I, ch. 3–4.

73. 'an enormous': JM to Bruche, 18 Sept., MP. JM discussed these issues with Legge on 15 and 17 Sept., MP.

74. JM's close friendship with Bruche and their annoyance with Legge is evident in correspondence Sept–Oct. 1914, MP. 'People who live': JM to Bruche, 30 Sept., MP. 'an invasion of Australia': JM to Bruche, 1 Oct., MP. JM's early expression of confidence in McGlinn: telegram to Capt. C. Jess, 24 Sept., MC.

75. 'Now I hope': JM to Jess, 24 Sept., MP. 'More will depend': 4 Bde RO 1, 17 Sept., File 707/9/(1), AWRS. 'the questionable judgement': McGlinn to JM, 22 Sept., MC. 'most vitally concerned': JM to Pethebridge, 21Sept., MP.

76. 'the slowest job ... I started ...': JM to Bruche, 1 Oct., MP. The marches are described in N.F. Wanliss, *The History of the Fourteenth Battalion AIF*, p. 4, and A. Argent, 'Quinn of Quinn's Post', *AAJ*, no. 270 (1971), p. 27. JM's scheme was dated 1 Oct. and is in MC. His request to 14 Bn: JM to Lt-Col R. E. Courtney (CO), 7 Oct., MC.

77. 'well pleased': JM to Bruche, 16 Nov., MP. 4 Bde RO 6, 17 Nov., warned COs about slovenliness. 'the dirtiest place': Nixon to his mother, 28 Nov., MS 1827, Mitchell Library. JM's ultimatum to District HQ was made on 2 Dec., MC. White's syllabus, 'Instructions for Teaching in Districts of Quotas for the Expeditionary Forces', 14 Aug., is in MC.

78. 'absolute hold ... orders given': 'Notes for CO's Conference', 28 Nov., MC. Smithers, *Sir John Monash*, p. 27. A copy of *100 Hints* is in MC.

REFERENCES

79. JM outlined the exercise in 'Notes for Brigade Tactical Exercise', Dec., MC. His criticisms are dated 15 Dec., MC. The farewell march is described in '13 Bn AIF– Brief History', File 8/10, AWM and JM, 'Notes for March of 17 December', 8 Dec., MC. 'singularly tenacious': T.A. White, *The Fighting Thirteenth*, p. 21.
80. 'looked more like veterans': Munro Ferguson to Hamilton, 25 Dec., Novar Papers. JM's complaints about arrangements for the voyage: JM to Dodds, 28 Dec., Legge, 30 Dec. and Bruche, 31 Dec., MP. See also his 'Report of SMO, 2nd Australian Convoy, Melbourne to Colombo', 13 Jan. 1915, MC.
82. 'regularly attended': 4 Bde RO 46, 27 Dec. 1914. Forsythe's praise: quoted in White, *The Fighting Thirteenth*, p. 22. The evening discussions are mentioned in JM, D, 18–19 Jan. 'the keenest interest': 'Report of SMO, 2nd Australian Convoy'. 'systematic perusal': D, 5 Jan. JM's knockdown: White, p. 22. His fear of falling overboard: D, 6 Jan. The Colombo incident: JM to Pethebridge, 15 Jan. and Malcolm to GOC Egypt, 12 Feb., MP; 'Report of SMO, 2nd Australian Convoy, Colombo-Aden', 23 Jan., MC.
83. 'revelation of Empire': JM, 29 Jan. in *War Letters of General Monash*, ed. F.M. Cutlack, p. 13.
84. Godley informed Pearce of the reception arrangements on 6 Feb., File 419/39/1, Godley-Pearce Correspondence, AWM. 'This splendid euphoria': Smithers, *Sir John Monash*, pp. 52–53. 'a fine dapper little chap': JM, 2 Feb. in *WarL*, p. 16. 'such a fine brigade': Godley to JM, 31 Jan., MP. 'what a rooting up ... right way': JM, 19 Jan. in 'War Letters of General Monash, p. 14 (this is the unedited typescript version of *War Letters*, ed. Cutlack, in MC). 'Everything is dirty': JM, 10 Feb., ibid., p. 24. The disciplinary unrest is covered in *OH*, I, pp. 128–30.
85. 'a great feather': Godley to JM, 31 Jan., MC. Coulthard-Clark criticises Bridges in *A Heritage of Spirit*, p. 135.
86. 'I was indeed frequently told ... every department': JM to Lt-Col E.W.C. Chaytor (AQMG NZ & A Div.), 30 Mar., MP.
87. Bridges' attitude on the command question: his 'Despatch 10', 6 Apr., File 112/2/489, B539, AA and an April entry in his diary. *OH*, II, pp. 394–95 covers his disdain of the Base. 'my best weapon': JM to VM, 30 May, MP. 'the efficiency and prestige': 4 Bde RO 53, 1 Feb. JM praised 4 Bde in D, 10 Feb–16 Mar. 'the best Australian brigade': Godley to JM, 18 Feb. in *WarL*, p. 19. 'tall, elegant, graceful': JM, 13 Feb. in *WarL*, p. 16. Godley's assurance on 4 Bde training: letter to Pearce, 6 Feb., Godley-Pearce Correspondence.
88. The JM–Godley exchanges on training throughout Feb.-Mar. are in MP.
89. The exercise on 19 Feb. is covered in 'NZ & A Instruction for Exercise–19 Feb.', MC and Files 519/26 and 70713, AWRS. Lt. Col. A.W. Tufnell criticised JM in his 'Comments on 4th Bde', 20 Feb., MC.
90. JM's outburst: Capt. W.A. Forsythe, D, 18 Mar., File 8/13, AWM. 'those who looked': *OH*, I, p. 137. The draft was dated 1 Mar., MC. 'The punctuality': 4 Bde RO 93, 3 Mar. 'practically nothing to do': JM, 13 Apr., 'War Letters' (typescript) p. 50. Tweedledum and Tweedledee: White to *Reveille*, 7 Apr. 1937, BC. 'I find him': Godley to Pearce, 30 Mar., Godley-Pearce Correspondence. 'an exceptionally able man', Birdwood to Munro Ferguson, 25 Feb., Novar Papers.
91. 'the great education': JM to Godley, 2 Mar., MP. Equipment and ammunition shortages: JM to Godley, 24 Feb., MP; Bridges, 'Despatch 7', 27 Feb., File A112/6/43, B539, AA. Bean commented on White and JM in D2, 20 Jan., 5 Mar; D3, 23 Apr. Pedersen, *Anzac Treasures*, p. 327. *OH*, I, p. 125.
93. Bridges' anxiety to reach Western Front: Bridges to Munro Ferguson, 31 Jan., Novar Papers.
94. The fortification exercise was outlined in 4 Bde RO 126, 27 Mar. Landing plans: Pedersen, *Anzacs*, pp. 33–36; Erickson, *Gallipoli*, pp. 111–13; *Hickey*, Gallipoli, p. 87.

96. The inadequacy of the training in Egypt for operations on the peninsula was confirmed by interviews with F.R. Hocking (6 Bde), F. Berrisford (2 Bde), 15 May 1980; H. Clive Newman (4 LH), 14 June 1980. All were Gallipoli veterans. 'romantic adventure': Carlyon, *Gallipoli*, p. 97. 'Everything points': JM, 16 Mar., 'War Letters' (typescript) p. 37. 'short notice': NZ & A Div. Special Order, 3 Apr., MC. 'beyond all praise': JM to Munro Ferguson, 5 Apr., MP. 'Now lads': 'Notes for Speeches to Men on Battalion Inspections', 9, 11 Mar., MC.

97. 'simply disembarkation practices': Roberts, *Landing at Anzac*, p. 73; 'result disastrous': JM to COs, 20 Apr., MC. 'This landing': Bean, D3, 15 Apr. 'To land': 4 Bde OpO, issued 7 p.m., 22 Apr., MC. Godley irritable and 'belated letters': JM, D, 22, 24 Apr. 'only a few years': JM to VM, 24 Apr., MP. 'Death': I. Hamilton, *Gallipoli Diary*, p. 73.

Chapter 4

98. 3 Bde in good shape: Roberts, 'The Landing at Anzac: a reassessment', *Journal of the Australian War Memorial*, No. 22, April 1993, pp. 27–29. Sinclair-MacLagan: Roberts, *Landing at Anzac*, p. 94. Moving the landing: Maj. D.J. Glasfurd to 1 Div., 6 a.m., 25 Apr., File 367/87/(1), AWRS.

99. Walker's clash with Bridges: Coulthard-Clark, *A Heritage of Spirit*, p. 160. 'trouble making up his mind': White, 'Notes on the Gallipoli Expedition', in 'Historical Notes: higher command on the landing', BC. 'alarmist and despondent tendencies': Hamilton to Lady Hamilton, 29 Apr., File 25/12/2, Hamilton Papers. 'stone cold': Dawnay to wife, 30 June, File 69/21, Dawnay Correspondence. 'Monash's Bodyguard': E.N. Wright to N. Wanliss, 10 July 1921, '14 Bn History', Source Records, AWM. 'keen expectation': JM, 25 Apr. in *WarL*, p. 33.

100. 'What did they care': Wright to Wanliss, 10 July 1921. 'never was one more glad': Bean, D5, 25 Apr. 13 Bn landing delayed: C.F. Aspinall-Oglander, *Military Operations: Gallipoli*, 2 vols, London, 1928, 1, p. 195. 14 Bn fears: Wright to Wanliss, 10 July 1921. Exaggerated losses in 15 Bn.: Sgt B.G.W. Fletcher, D, 25 Apr., 'Historical Notes: 4 Bde Landing', BC. 'dreadful night': JM, D, 25–26 Apr. Bean's erroneous claim is in *OH*, I, p. 468. 'Accidental collisions': *OH*, I, p. 506.

101. Turkish situation and losses: Aspinall-Oglander, *Military Operations*, 1, p. 271. 'distributed piecemeal': JM, D, 26 Apr. Amazement at JM's and McGlinn's move inland: Col. J.M. Beeston to JM, 7 Feb. 1917, MP. 'a hail of shrapnel': JM, D, 26 Apr. The description of Anzac and Monash Valley is based on *OH*, I, pp. 425–26, 524, 543; P.H. Liddle, *Men of Gallipoli*, pp. 98–101, and author's visits to the peninsula.

103. 'a man looking down': Lt. Col. F.S. Rosenskjar, *The Australians on Gallipoli*, p. 28, File 36714, AWRS.

104. 'the irreducible minimum': E.W. Bush, *Gallipoli*, p. 106. JM described his meeting with Bridges and Sinclair-MacLagan in an account of the landing entered by Bean in D26. Burnage's leadership: 'Recollections of Col. J.M.A. Durrant', File 8/13, '13 Bn AIF', AWM; White, *The Fighting Thirteenth*, p. 31. Disorganisation in 15 Bn: *OH*, I, pp. 468, 473–74, 484; Bean, D41, 27 Apr.; Argent, *AAJ*, p. 38.

105. Confusion surrounding Pope: 16 Bn to 1 Div., 11.15 pm, 25 Apr.; NZ & A Div. to 16 Bn, 7.20 am, 26 Apr., Files 367/87 (1) and 89 (1), AWRS. 'an almost superhuman cunning': NZ & A Div. to bdes, 7.40 pm, 26 Apr., MC.

106. 'If you get disorganised ... and so on': JM, 'Lecture 3 to Commanding Officers', 25 Oct. 1916, MC. The sector allotted to JM: ANZAC OpO 1, 27 Apr., MC. JM recalled to attend conference: D, 27 Apr.

107. The decisions reached at this important conference were summarised in ANZAC OpO 3, 27 Apr., MC. JM's annoyance: D, 27 Apr. Animosity between 14 and 15 bns: *OH*, II, p. 90. Perry to author, 29 Dec. 1980, denies any ill-feeling.

REFERENCES

108. JM's derision of Courtney: JM to VM, 4 July, 3 Dec.; to Walterlou, 25 Dec. 1915, MP. 'Yellow Streak' battalion: Stanley, *Quinn's Post*, p. 89.
109. Sinclair-MacLagan 'very done up': JM's *Account of the Landing*, Bean, D26. Irvine's death: Bean, D6, 27 Apr.; JM to VM, 18 July, MP. JM's initial orders, dated 27 Apr., are in MC. Poor communications in JM's sector: Jess to Cannan, 8 Sept. 1922, 'Historical Notes: attack at Quinn's, 9/10 May', BC. 'somewhere in this section': JM's orders, 27 Apr.
110. 'You *must* ensure': Godley to JM, 27 Apr., MC. 3 Bde ordered to retire: 1 Bde to 1 Div., 10.04 am, 27 Apr., File 367/173, AWRS.
111. Owen's anxiety: Owen to 1 Div., 6.56 pm, 27 Apr., ibid. Pope's intentions: messages to 'Reinforcements', 11.57 am; to 4 Bde, 3.10 pm, 27 Apr., MC. 'Having hard time': A. Jacka, D, 27 Apr. This entry is among extracts in '14 Bn History'. 'could do nothing ... up to now': Pope, D, 28 Apr. Records of Col. H. Pope, 'Official Historian's Notes', BC.
112. 'badly bent': Aspinall-Oglander, I, p. 295. 'the only real advantage': L.J. Bain to Wanliss, 17 Nov. 1921, '14 Bn History'.
113. '... the limit': Pope to 4 Bde, 10.00 am, 30 Apr., MC. 'We had nothing': JM, 7 June 1915, 'War Letters' (typescript) p. 77. The tactical description of the 4 Bde sector is based on *OH*, I, pp. 527, 577–78; *OH*, II, p. 48; Jess to Cannan, 8 Sept. 1922.
114. JM on battle noise: 16 May in *WarL*, p. 36. 'you can almost fancy': Lt N.T. Svenson to Bean, 24 July 1922, 'Historical Notes: attack at Quinn's 9/10 May', BC.
115. Conditions at Quinn's and Quinn's warning: Lt E.M. Little to Bean, 8 Feb. 1924, 'Historical Notes: attack at Quinn's, 9/10 May'; *OH*, II, p. 91.
116. 'an object lesson': Bean, D7, 3 May. Turkish appreciation of the importance of Monash Valley: 'Questions to and Answers by Turkish General Staff re Ops on Gallipoli', Australian Historical Mission File 11, BC. Importance recognised by JM and artillery: Bean, D7, 3 May; Maj. Gen. C. Rosenthal, D, 2 May, MS2739, Mitchell Library. 'by no means an organised command': JM to Godley, 30 Apr., MC. Birdwood's orders: Anzac Order 5, 30 Apr., 'Historical Notes: attack on Baby 700, 2/3 May', BC.
117. 4 Bde role: NZ & A Div. OpO 4, 30 Apr., MC. 'all that scrupulous care': *OH*, I, p. 597. JM's plan: 4 Bde OpO 3, 1 May, MC.
118. Walker views attack as 'hopeless': *OH*, I, p. 583. 'I take it on myself' and JM's exchange with Godley: P.F.E. Schuler, *Australia in Arms*, p. 138.
119. Pinwill's opinion: *OH*, I, p. 583. The revised plan: NZ & A OpO 5, 2 May, 'Historical Notes: attack on Baby 700'. Bean describes plan as 'simple': *OH*, I, p. 584.
120. Notification of start time; NZ & A Div. to 4 Bde, 4 pm, 2 May, 'Historical Notes: attack on Baby 700'. Enthusiasm for attack: C. Longmore, *The Old Sixteenth*, p. 46. Burnage's leadership: Account by Durrant in Bean, D128.
122. Fumbling by Johnston and Godley: H.V. Howe to R. Rhodes James, 7 Nov. 1964, Bazley Collection. 'wild with excitement': Durrant's account in Bean, D128. JM informed of failure of NZ attack and need to support 15 Bn: Durrant to 4 Bde: 11.30 pm, 2 May; 12.40 am, 3 May, MC. NZ believe 4 Bde attack successful: NZ & A Div. Report, 'Historical Notes: attack on Baby 700'. Godley reminds JM: NZ&A Div. to 4 Bde, 1.35 am, 3 May, MC.
123. 'men from the firing line': D. Jerrold, *The Royal Naval Division*, p. 121. 'a ghastly dream': Fletcher, D, 18 May, 'Historical Notes: Anzac, April-August', BC. 'It was just hell': G.T. McLintock, D, 23 Sept. 1915, MS2783, Mitchell Library. 'bloody mongrel of a general': Lewis in Shadbolt, *Voices of Gallipoli*, p. 24. Smithers, *Sir John Monash*, p. 94. 'Monash seemed to me': Bean, D7, 3 May 15.

124. Jerram's description: 'The Life of Lieutenant-Colonel Charles Frederick Jerram', Ace. No. ACQ 23/80C-ARCH 9/2/J, Royal Marines Museum, pp. 201–02. R. Rhodes James, *Gallipoli*, pp. 271–72. Birdwood does not visit head of Monash Valley until 4 May: JM, D, 4 May. 'Monash's brigade': Pugsley, *Gallipoli*, p. 185.

125. JM's views: JM, 'Report on Action of 2/3 May 1915', MP. Godley's praise: Godley to Pearce, 7 May, Godley-Pearce Correspondence. 'a short rest': Pope, D, 3 May. 'knocked out clean': Field Marshal W.R. Birdwood, *Khaki and Gown*, p. 262. Poor condition of 4 Bde: ANZAC to GHQ, 9.25 am, 3 May, File 367/52(3), AWRS; NZ & A Div. to 4 Bde, 5.10 pm, 3 May; 5.25 am, 4 May, MC.

126. JM to NZ & A Div., 3 May, MC; 7.00 am, 4 May, 'Historical Notes: landing operations–4 Bde', BC. Birdwood 'a little anxious ... produce more': ANZAC to GHQ, 1.35 pm, 4 May, File 367/52(3), AWRS. 'most awkward corner': Bean, D8, 24 May 1915.

127. Favouritism towards 14 Bn: Wanliss, *History of the Fourteenth Battalion*, pp. 34–35. Marines 'quite useless': JM, D, 8 May. Godley waving his stick and Marines as 'Royal Malingerers': Forsythe, D, 4 May. '4 Bde lads not too pleased': Maj. Gen. J. Gellibrand, D, 4 May, Folder 187/38, Gellibrand Collection. 'our boys, capably led': JM, 7 June 1915, 'War Letters' (typescript), p. 79. Opposition to 'offensive enterprise': JM, D, 9 May. The experience of the naval patrol was summarised by NZ & A Div. to ANZAC, 2.35 pm, 9 May, File 367/89(2), AWRS. The report in question was 'NZ & A Div. Report on Operations, 6 May–5 June 1915', File 367/235, AWRS.

128. Jess's recollection was quoted by Cannan in a letter to Bean, dated 6 July 1922, in 'Historical Notes: attack at Quinn's, 9/10 May'. Cannan believes his mission is reconnaissance: E.M. Little to Bean, 8 Feb. 1924. 'careless readiness': *OH*, II, p. 115.

129. Godley knew 'all along': JM, D, 10 May. JM's report on the action, undated, is in MC. Staff unimpressed: *OH*, II, p. 116. JM 'a bloody liar': Little to Bean, 8 Feb. 1924. Godley refuses request for relief: NZ & A Div. to Trotman, 7.05 am, 10 May, MC. Commanders exhausted: Pope, D, 10 May.

130. 'I am living cheek by jowl': quoted in Hill, *Chauvel*, p. 54. JM able to rest and opinion of Chauvel: D, 13, 17 May.

131. McGlinn's criticism of 4 Bde trenches: McGlinn to COs, 12 May, MC. 'deep enough for Godley': A.J. Godley, *Life of an Irish Soldier*, pp. 178–79. Supports too far back: Godley to JM, 7.55 am, 5 May, MC. Turkish mg superiority: Godley's comments on Force Order 8, 17 May, MC. Disregard of concealment: NZ & A Div. Special Order, 25 May, MC.

132. Bean criticises Quinn's: D8, 24 May. Lack of engineering materials: Hickey, *Gallipoli*, p. 89. 'The most important single factor': Rhodes James, *Gallipoli*, p. 183.

133. 'The most magnificent': C. Malthus, *Anzac: a retrospect*, p. 83. Criticism of JM for avoiding Quinn's: *OH*, VI, p. 208; Gellibrand, D, 'Narrative for May'. Liardet's comments, 16 July 1931: Item 11/1931/8, Liddell Hart Collection. Jacka's opinion of JM was expressed in correspondence with the author from B.H. Perry, 29 Nov. 1980.

134. 'Since that day': Goldstein to JM, 16 July 1916, MP. Soldiers' criticism of Bridges: Howe to Bazley, 24 Nov. 1963, Bazley Collection. 'Birdie's Bull': Rhodes James, *Gallipoli*, p. 181. 'We laugh at this shrapnel': quoted in A. Herbert, *Anzac, Mons and Kut*, p. 122.

135. Cannan's ultimatum: quoted in Little to Bean, 8 Feb. 1924. Stodart's 'fidgetyness' and Chauvel's 'interference': JM, D, 14, 16–17 May. The Turkish general attack: 'Anzac Summary of Events 12 a.m. 19 May–6 a.m. 20 May', 'Historical Notes: Anzac, April-August'; Prior, *Gallipoli*, p. 128; Sgt R.A. Hunter to Bean, 26 July 1923, 'Historical Notes: Turkish attack at Anzac', BC; '15 Bn Report on Engagement at Quinn's 18-19 May', File 367/115, AWRS.

REFERENCES

136. JM's comments: D, 19 May; 20 May, 'War Letters' (typescript), p. 65.
137. 'a young Turkish officer' and 'a sound belting': JM, 7 June, in *WarL*, p. 47. 'This incident': JM, 'Notes for Lecture 2 to COs', 25 Oct. 1916, MC. 'I cannot recall': C. Mackenzie, *Gallipoli Memories*, p. 83. JM's dugout collapses: D, 24 May.
138. The account of JM's stay aboard *Arcadian* is based on D, 26–28 May and letter, 27 May in *WarL*, p. 39.
139. 'a terrible Hades': Fletcher, D, 30 May. Narrative of the action: *OH*, II, p. 213; Account of Lt T.P. McSharry, 29 May 1915; Hill to Bean 18 Sept.; Pope to Bean, 22 Sept. 1922, 'Historical Notes: Turkish attack at Quinn's', BC.
142. 'of sallow complexion': JM to Bean, 13 Aug. 1928, 'Gallipoli Correspondence with the British Official Historian', BC. Durrant described the action in a letter to Bean, 27 Sept. 1922, 'Historical Notes: Turkish attack at Quinn's'. Birdwood's doubts about Chauvel: Birdwood to Hamilton, 14 June, File 5/10, Hamilton Papers.
143. Relief partly due to attack on Quinn's: Stanley, *Quinn's Post*, p. 82. 'dreadful scarecrows': Durrant in File 8/13, '13 Bn AIF'. Godley's address was quoted in *WarL*, p. 44. Laughter at 14 Bn: Pope, D, 2 June. One of the four finest feats: *OH*, IV, p. 488, fn. 181.
144. Bean's praise of 4 Bde: D8, 2 June. JM's praise: JM to Dr Robertson, 13 June, MP; 8 June, 'War Letters' (typescript) p. 81. Bean's article appeared in the *Age*, 8 June. JM's complaints about Bean over publicity: note, 2 June, MC; JM to VM, 31 May, MP. JM's plans for self-publicity: JM to VM, 31 May, 3 June; to Walter, 5 June, MP.
145. 'Monash is very well': Godley to Pearce, 8 July, Godley-Pearce Correspondence. 'dealt with firmly': McGlinn to COs, 6 May 1915, MC.

Chapter 5

147. JM in Reserve Gully: JM to Gibson, 18 June, MP; 18 July, in *WarL*, p. 55. 'we have been resting': Fletcher, D, 7 June. Manpower demands on 4 Bde: 4 Bde to NZ & A Div., 21 July, MC.
148. Sickness figures are from White, *The Fighting Thirteenth*, p. 44, and *OH*, II, p. 367. Ravages of dysentery: A.G. Butler, *Official History of the Australian Army Medical Services 1914-18*, 3 vols, Melbourne, 1930–43, 1, p. 248. 'Most of us': Gellibrand to Walter Gellibrand, 4 Nov. 1915, Gellibrand Collection. JM's cold: D, 26–27 July.
149. Hopelessness of medical arrangements: JM to NZ & A Div., 8, 16 June, MC. On the replacement of leaders: JM to Godley, 6 June, MC; 27 June, 2, 9 July, MP.
150. 'those promoted': Maj. J. Adams to McGlinn, 18 June, MC. 'an internal revolution': *OH*, II, pp. 427, 429. Inadequate training of reinforcements: Capt. C.E. Connelly to Capt. C.M.M. Dare (both 14 Bn), 17 June, MC; Bean, D10, 19 July.
151. Little chance of survival: C.B.B. White, 'Some Reflections on the Great War', 1 Apr. 1921, White Collection. 'you will please state': JM to Pope, 12 July, MP. JM, 'Notes for Speech to 13 Bn', 6 July, MC. 'a most thrilling day' and 'a leading part': JM, D, 19–20 June. 'advances over rough country': JM, 'Notes of Conference', 19 July, MC. 'careful and complete preparations': JM to VM, 18 July, MP.
152. Complexity of plan: Travers, *Gallipoli 1915*, p. 136.
153. 'exotic bet': Carlyon, *Gallipoli*, p. 339. 'without exception': Howe to Rhodes James, 7 Nov. 1964. Cox's original proposal: Cox to JM, 3 Aug., MC.
154. Overton's proposal is described in Maj. Gen. A.H. Russell to Bean, 14 Sept. 1922, 'Historical Notes: Battle of Sari Bair', BC.

155. 'the task of reaching Chunuk Bair ... any hope of success': Bean to Edmonds, 17 June 1931, 'Gallipoli Correspondence with British Official Historian'. Godley on use of 4th Bde: *Life of an Irish Soldier*, pp. 187–88. 'Our physical condition': Cannan to Bean, 9 Mar. 1931, 'Gallipoli Correspondence with British Official Historian'. JM says plan 'impossible': quoted in Aspinall-Oglander, *Military Operations: Gallipoli*, 2, p. 199.

157. 'any change': Butler, *Medical History*, 1, pp. 252–53. Cox's breakdown: Hamilton to Birdwood, 21 Aug., Hamilton Papers. 'he is one of those crotchetty': JM to Bertha M., 8 May 1916, MP. 'Cox hampered me greatly': JM to Bean, 4 May 1931, 'Gallipoli Correspondence with British Official Historian'.

158. Cox also constrained: Pedersen, 'I thought I could command men' in Ekins (ed.) *Ridge too far*, p. 128. JM ordered to remain in centre: loc. cit. and Aspinall-Oglander, *Military Operations: Gallipoli*, 2, p. 192. Issue of orders for assault on Hill 971: Cox's Instructions as Column Commander, 6 Aug., MC. 'it was typical': *OH*, II, p. 584. Time past a point calculation: Pedersen, 'I thought I could command men' in Ekins (ed.) *Ridge too far*, p. 129.

159. JM, 'Notes for COs' Conference', 5 Aug., MC. JM's 'Address to Officers and NCOs of the 4th Brigade', 6 Aug., is in MC.

160. 'some effort': JM, 6 Aug., 'War Letters' (typescript), p. 102. 'hell all right': Compton, D, 6 Aug., MS1243, Mitchell Library. 'summed up': Bain, D, 6 Aug., 'Historical Notes: Battle of Sari Bair'. The atmosphere before the attack was described in the following articles in *Reveille*: H.G. Loughran, '4th Brigade Inland Movement Against the Turks', 1 Aug. 1932, p. 30; F.W. Crane, 'The Concert in Anzac Reserve Gully', 1 Aug. 1933, p. 33; H.W. Murray, 'Grave and Gay', ibid. p. 13.

161. 'with great interest': notes by Lt D.R. MacDermid, 'Historical Notes: Battle of Sari Bair'. 'concertina affair': Pedersen, *Anzacs*, p. 94. 'an even pace': 'Narrative of Operations of 15th Battalion, 2135 hrs 6/7 Aug-1945 hrs 7 Aug', 'Historical Notes: Battle of Sari Bair'. 'like walking out of a warm house': JM in Bean, D14, 20 Aug. 'slower than a funeral': *OH*, II, p. 585.

162. Assembly of 6th Gurkhas: Allanson's evidence to the Dardanelles Royal Commission, File 16/1, Hamilton Papers. 'It seemed to me': Bean, D11, 6/7 Aug. 'muddled things': Maj. N.W. Thoms, c.20 Aug. in Bean, D14.

163. 'at the head of the Gap': Chaplain F.W. Wray to Bean, 31 Oct. 1922, 'Historical Notes: Battle of Sari Bair'. JM to Bean, 4 Oct. 1931 and JM in Bean, D14, 20 Aug. may be assumed as continual references. Comments by Dare and Durrant on Bean's file of correspondence with the British Official Historian corroborate JM's version.

164. 'Our line of advance': '15 Bn Narrative'.

165. 'marked difference': Pope, D, 6 Aug.; *OH*, II, p. 591. 'The sudden burst': Durrant to Bean, 17 Apr. 1931, 'Gallipoli Correspondence with British Official Historian'.

166. JM persuades Pope: JM in Bean, D14, 20 Aug. Allanson D (AWM), 6/7 Aug. Extracts from this typed diary are held as 'Diary of Major Allanson, 6-10 Aug 15', in 'Historical Notes: Battle of Sari Bair'. It is more detailed than the printed version, 50 copies of which were produced for private circulation by Allanson. A copy of the latter, referred to as D(NAM), is held in the National Army Museum, London. 'what upset me most': quoted by Rhodes James, *Gallipoli*, p. 272. Allanson keen to leave: Allanson to J. North, 8 June 1936, Item 1/3/38, North Papers. 'with one armed Gurkha': JM to Bean, 4 May 1931.

168. Criticism of JM: White to Bean, 27 Feb. 1931, 'Gallipoli Correspondence with British Official Historian'; Murdoch to Fisher, 23 Sept., Pearce Collection; North to Allanson, 12 Dec. 1935, Item l/3126, North Papers. 'looking rather worried': Bain, D, 7 Aug.

REFERENCES

169. 'poor old things ... sleepy old John Monash': Bean, D10, 30 Aug. The first discussion was on 29 Aug. 'hopelessly stopped': Allanson, D(NAM), 6 Aug. Allanson 'excitable and unreliable': Godley to Birdwood, 14, 27 Feb. 1917, Birdwood Collection. 'a fine soldier': quoted in Rhodes James to North, 28 Feb. 1964, Item 1/3/402, North Papers. Dislike of Australians: Allanson to North, 18 Dec. 1935; North to Bean, 9 June 1936, Items I/3/28, 76, North Papers. Account written several years after war: author's interview with R. Rhodes James, 26 Mar. 1981.
170. Smithers, *Sir John Monash*, p. 119. Hill expressed his view to the author on 23 Mar. 1980. Howe gave his in his letter to Rhodes James, 7 Nov. 1964. The veteran was F. Hocking. Bean's criticism of JM: D11, 8/9 Aug.; *OH*, II, p. 589.
171. 'I gave Bean': JM to VM, 30 June, MP. 'Bean to tea': JM, D, 20 Aug. 106–07. Disorganisation of 4 Bde: see messages sent by each bn between 4.45 pm and 5.45 pm, 7 Aug. in MC.
172. 'General Monash': Dare to Bean, 3 Mar. 1931, 'Gallipoli Correspondence with British Official Historian'. Rhodes James's view: *Gallipoli*, p. 272. 'always very proud': Bean, *Sydney Sun*, 11 Oct. 1931.
173. 'It was horrible': Bain, D, 7 Aug. 'I feel confident': Godley to JM, 8.35 pm, 7 Aug., MC.
175. 'an attack with such troops': JM in Bean, D14, 20 Aug. JM places Pope in command: JM to Bean, 4 May 1931.
177. Medical arrangements for 8 Aug. attack: Butler, *Medical History*, 1, p. 301. 'there was opened upon it' and 'the last controlled movement': *OH*, II, pp. 656, 658. 'seemed to wilt': Dare to Bean, 3 Mar. 1931. Rankine 'quite useless': Loughran, D, 8 Aug., 'Historical Notes: Battle of Sari Bair'.
178. Pope recommends withdrawal: Pope to JM, 7.05 am, 8 Aug., 'Historical Notes: Battle of Sari Bair'. JM's alternatives: Bean, D14, 20 Aug. 'utterly broken': *OH*, II, pp. 660–61. 'There seemed no defined system': undated notes by C. Smith in 'Historical Notes: Battle of Sari Bair'. Dare refuses to withdraw: Dare to Pope, 7.10 am, 8 Aug., 'Historical Notes: Battle of Sari Bair'. 'a bloody rumour': Loughran, D, 8 Aug. 'a mournful procession': notes by C. Smith.
179. 'very worn and depressed': Pope to wife, 2 Sept., 'Historical Notes: Battle of Sari Bair'. JM against attack: letter, 16 Aug. in *WarL*, p. 63.
180. JM's fatigue: D, 8 Aug. Importance of Chunuk Bair: Pugsley, *Anzac Experience*, p. 114. 'The real cause': JM, 5 Sept., 'War Letters' (typescript), p. 108.
181. Criticism of Birdwood and Godley: Allanson to North, 12 Aug. 1934, Item l/3/15, North Papers; J. North, *Gallipoli: the fading vision*, pp. 228–31.
182. Godley's outburst quoted in North to Bean, 30 June 1936, Item I/3/77, North Papers. Cox's praise of 4 Bde front: Memo 1774/M, 10 Aug., MC. 'The boys': Crooks, D, 10 Aug., MS838, Mitchell Library. Appeal for return of detachments: JM to Godley, 13 Aug., MC.
183. Maintaining morale: JM, D, 10 Aug.; Longmore, *The Old Sixteenth*, p. 79. JM urges occupation of Hill 60: Bean, D10, 29 Aug. JM discusses 4 Bde role in combined advance: JM to Cox, 7.05 pm, 7.30 pm, 14 Aug., MC.
184. JM's orders: OpO 10, 21 Aug., MC.
185. 'sheer force of will': Dare to Bean, 16 July; Durrant to Bean, 21 July 1931, 'Gallipoli Correspondence with British Official Historian'. No signals officers: Crawley, *Climax at Gallipoli*, p. 63. 'a certain part of the Hill': Ford to Bean, 13 Aug. 1931, ibid. 'somewhat curtailed': 'Report on Operations, 11-31 Aug. 1915, NZ & A Div. War Diary'. JM informed at 1.15 pm: Cox to Commanders, 1.15 pm, 21 Aug., MC.

186. 'just sufficient': Loughran, D, 24 Aug. 'such devices': Durrant to Bean, 21 July 1931. JM eschews changes to orders: 'Lecture 2 to 3 Div. Officers', 25 Oct. 1916, MP.
187. JM's exchange with Godley is in correspondence 22–24 Aug., MC. Bean's criticism: D15, 21 Aug. Deplorable condition of 4 Bde: Butler, *Medical History*, 1, p. 320. 'the fittest and best': JM to Russell, 25 Aug., MP. Action taken: Loughran, D, 26 Aug.; JM to NZ & A Div., 26 Aug., MP.
188. 'a much more difficult job': Cox to wife, 29 Aug., File 12/11/302, Personal Records, AWM. Turks reorient defences: Steel and Hart, *Defeat at Gallipoli*, p. 298. Orders for the attack: Russell's OpO 5, 27 Aug.; Adams's OpO 1, undated, MC.
189. More stretcher-bearers: 13 Bn RMO to McGlinn, 27 Aug., MC. Withering fire against 4 Bde: Loughran, D, 28 Aug.; Bean, D10, 28 Aug.; A.N. Brierley, '2nd Hill 60: Intense Fire', *Reveille*,1 Aug. 1932, p. 44. JM's disgust: D, 27 Aug. The JM-Cox exchange, 28 Aug., is in MP. JM complains: D, 3 Sept. Commanders exhausted: Adams to JM, 28 Aug., MC; JM to Godley, 28 Aug., MP; letter, 5 Sept. in *WarL*, p. 67.
190. 'extreme worry': JM, D, 28 Aug. 14 Bn strength: Wanliss, *History of the Fourteenth Battalion*, p. 75. Argument over assistance to 161 Bde: Godley to JM, 29, 30 Aug., MC. JM, 'Draft Instructions for Cannan', 30 Aug., MC. JM's exchange with Cannan, 4–5 Sept. and 'toughest and fiercest': JM to Wallaby Walking Club, 23 Sept., are in MP.
191. 'Lost count': Jacka, D, Aug. period.
192. 'a decent sleep': JM, D, 13–14 Sept. 'They told us': JM, 30ct. in *WarL*, p. 74. JM and 4 Bde on Lemnos: letter 20 Sept. in *WarL*, p. 69.
193. 'NZ & A Div. Memorandum on Training while at Camp Mudros', 11 Sept., MC.
194. 'so much restored': Godley to Pearce, 7 Nov., Godley-Pearce Correspondence. 4 Bde under strength: JM to Godley, 27 Sept., MC. 2 Div. untrained: Birdwood to Munro Ferguson, 16 Sept., Birdwood Collection. 'a far worse enemy': JM to Steward (Governor-General's Secretary), 12 Nov., MC. Routine at Anzac: JM to COs, 14, 18 Nov., MC.
195. JM addressed by Kitchener and learns of withdrawal: letters, 13 Nov., 12 Dec. in *WarL*, pp. 85, 92. 'a gradual reduction': Army Corps Order 21, 14 Dec., 'Historical Notes: Evacuation of Anzac', BC. 'All this means': JM, 18 Dec. in *WarL*, pp. 98–99. Dare's skit: 'The Final Handicap', 16 Dec., MC.
196. JM forgets portfolio: D, 19 Dec. JM's thoughts on campaign: *Argus*, 13 Jan. 1920. Advice to nephews: JM to 2 Bde, 11 Nov.; to VM, 25 Nov., MP. 'he is very unpopular': Moss to JM, 9 Dec., MP. JM seeks recognition: JM to Moss, 1 Dec.; to VM 14 Aug., 5 Sept., 19 Oct., 10 Nov., MP.
197. The campaign against Legge: Bean, D9, 8, 23-24 Jun.; JM to VM, 30 June; to Chauvel 14 June, MP; Chauvel to JM, 14 June, MP. JM's fight for seniority: Legge to JM, 12 July, MP; JM to NZ & A Div., 4, 15 Nov.; to Pearce, 18 Nov., MC.
198. Birdwood on JM: Birdwood to Munro Ferguson, 26 Nov., Birdwood Collection.
199. Birdwood mildly anti-Semitic: Serle, *John Monash*, p. 254. 'the Dug Out King': quoted in North to Bean, 30 June 1936. 'Heavens–What does he think': quoted in Bean, Dl13, 30 May 1918. 'If one stops': JM, 10 Oct. 1915, 'War Letters' (typescript), p. 126.

Chapter 6

201. 'all bluff': JM, 27 Jan., 'War Letters' (typescript), p. 168. 'a beautiful little town': JM to VM, 15 Jan. VM's illness: JM to Walterlou, 19 Jan.; to White, 28 Jan.; to Gibson, 18 Feb., MP.
202. 'Most certainly': JM to VM, 2 July 1915, MP. Salary inadequate: JM to NZ & A Div., 20 Feb., MP. 'all the absurd slobber' and comments on Godley and Russell: JM to VM, 15 Jan. 'Heaven help us': Godley in Bean, D47, 19 June.

REFERENCES

203. 'I am getting busy': JM to Bella Card, 27 Jan., MP.
204. 'an opportunity': JM, 'Notes for COs' Meeting', 23 Dec. 1915, MC. JM's dissatisfaction with guard and saluting: 4 Bde ROs 378, 23 Jan.; 379, 24 Jan., File 707/9(4), AWRS. JM's address: 'Notes for Lecture to Officers', 11 Jan., MC. 4 Bde training: 'Training Order 2', 8 Jan., File 943119, AWRS; JM, 'Notes for Lecture to Officers', 14 Jan.; 'Instruction for Tactical Exercise on 31 Jan.', MC.
205. 'very successful': JM, D, 31 Jan. Div. exercise: JM, D, 8, 11, 17 Feb. 'The proceedings': JM to McCay, 11 Feb., MP. JM's suggestion on training: JM to Russell, 13 Jan., MP. 'Russell has given me': JM to Walterlou, 19 Jan., MP.
206. 'characteristic example': JM to Russell, 23 Jan., MC. JM dissatisfied with 4 Bde: JM to COs, 16 Feb., MC. Birdwood on 4 Bde: Birdwood to Murray, 25 Feb., Item 1132/13/3f, Robertson Papers.
207. 'a distinct eye to his future': Murray to Robertson, 23, 26 Mar., Items 1132/15,16a, Robertson Papers. 'an officer of high attainment': Pearce to Birdwood, 4 Feb., Birdwood Collection. 'Monash I regard': Birdwood to Munro Ferguson, 11 Feb., ibid.
208. JM's German origins: Gellibrand's comments on *AV*, Gellibrand Collection; Bean, D8, 2 June 1915; JM to Oscar Behrend, 18 Feb., MP. 'I do not consider': Birdwood to Munro Ferguson, 11 Feb. Chauvel and 3 Div.: Birdwood to Pearce, 24 Mar., Birdwood Collection. JM indifferent: JM to VM, 22 Apr., MP. 'At any rate': JM, 5 Mar. in *WarL*, pp. 107–18. Godley's plan: JM, D, 22 Jan.
209. Moss's confidences: Moss to JM, 23 Jan., 4 Feb., MC. 'there will be': JM to McCay, 11 Feb., MP. 'Do all you can': JM to VM, 15 Jan., MP. Formation of new divs: C.E.W. Bean, *Anzac to Amiens*, p. 189; *Two Men I Knew*, p. 126.
210. 'He is far and away': JM to VM, 22 Apr., MP. 'a seething mass': E.J. Rule, *Jacka's Mob*, pp. 34–35.
211. JM's suggestion on colour patches: JM to White, 17 Feb., MP. JM on army and 4 Bde: JM to VM 22 Apr.; letter, 5 Mar. in *WarL*, p. 107: JM to McGlinn, 20 May, MP.
212. JM believes AIF destined for Western Front: JM to Bertha, 22 Jan., MP. Murray-Robertson correspondence: letters 1 Mar., 5 Apr., Items 1133/13/I, 1132/19, Robertson Papers. JM's 'Report on March to Serapeum', to 4 Div., 4 Apr., is in MC.
213. 'boozers mostly': Durrant in File 8/13, '13 Bn AIF', AWM. JM cursed: Rule, *Jacka's Mob*, p. 36. Assessments of the march are from *OH*, III, p. 291; White, *The Fighting Thirteenth*, p. 59. 'we have not yet': Pope to JM, 11 May, MP.
214. Prince of Wales's visit: JM to VM, 22 Apr., MP. Anzac Day: JM, 26 Apr. in *WarL*, pp. 112–13. 'twenty mortal hours': JM, 15 Apr. in *WarL*, p. 111. JM struck; Serle, *John Monash*, p. 262. 'by no means ... Camel Corps exclusively': JM, 12 May, 'War Letters' (typescript), p. 185.
215. '"eno' to wish"': Cox to JM, 11 Apr., MP. 'I make a great impression': JM, D, 29 Apr. JM's address, sent to Cox on 16 May, is in MP. 'a sound and healthy public opinion': JM to Cox, 22 May, MC.
215–17. 'If one man shirks': JM, 'Address to 15 Bn', 21 May, MC.
217. JM on Cox: 8 May, 'War Letters' (typescript), p. 183. Cox on JM: quoted in Durrant to *Reveille*, 16 Apr. 1937, BC. JM recommended to command 3 Div.: Cox to Birdwood, 3 May; Godley to Birdwood, 20 May, 1 June; Birdwood to Munro Ferguson, 6 June, Birdwood Collection; Godley to Pearce, 31 May, Godley-Pearce Correspondence.
218. The move north: Wanliss, *History of the Fourteenth Battalion*, p. 104. Cox 'very pleased': JM, D, 10 June. 'Imagine the change': JM to Walterlou, 11 June, MP.
219. 'all ranks': Cox to JM, 30 June, MP. 4 Bde's entry into line: JM to Bernard, 20, 24 June; to Dare, 22 June; to Cox, 23 June, MP.

220. 'It hasn't taken us many hours': JM, 20 June, 'War Letters' (typescript), p. 195. Legge's remark: 2 Bde to Bns, 17 May, File 213/1, AWRS. 'night raids on dormitories': D. Winter, *Death's Men*, p. 93. JM's planning for raid: JM to 2 Div., 22 June; to Russell, 25 June; to Cox, 1 July; 4 Bde Opo 14, 30 June, MC.
221. 'orders and arrangements': 2 NZ Inf. Bde, 'Report on Raid 16 June 1916', MC. Results of raid: JM's report, 3 July, MC. 'the nursery': Bean, *Anzac to Amiens*, p. 215. 'my appointment': JM, D, 24 June.
222. Starts to worry: JM to Walterlou, 8 July, MP. 'Coming now to look at it': JM to VM, 18 July, MP.

Chapter 7

223. 'a training': *OH*, III, p. 176. Lessons imperfectly applied: Sheffield, *Forgotten Victory*, pp. 174, 181.
224. 18 Div. attack on Thiepval: Maxse, 'Conference Agenda', 21 Sept. 1916; 'Report to 2 Corps', 14 Jan. 1917, Items 17, 29, Maxse Papers. 'as if glued to the barrage': V.W. Germains, *The Kitchener Armies*, p. 279. 'enforced the issue': Charteris, *Field Marshal Earl Haig*, p. 204.
225. 'close supervision': P. Simkins, 'Haig and his army commanders' in Bond and Cave (eds.), *Haig: a reappraisal 70 years on*, p. 94. McCay at Fromelles: Pedersen, *Fromelles*, p. 43. 'impossible frontal assaults': 2 Army to 1 ANZAC, 22 June, File 75/8, AWRS. 'inability': Sheffield, *Somme*, p. 161. 'bite and hold': Prior and Wilson, *Command on the Western Front*, p. 395; Philpott, *Bloody Victory*, p. 360. 'bumpy continuum': Stevenson, *To Win the Battle*, p. 215. 'type of mind': JM, 'Leadership in War'.
226. 'No continuity of policy': Jackson to JM, 6 Feb. 1918, MP. Terraine's claim: *The Smoke and the Fire*, pp. 114–18. JM describes 3 Div.: letter, 18 July, in *WarL*, p. 125. 'the nearest point': Terraine, *The Smoke and the Fire*, p. 114.
227. JM's staff 'a very fine one': letter, 18 July in *WarL*, p. 125. Jackson's transfer and 2 Div staff: *OH*, III, p. 604; Sheffield, *Command and Morale*, p. 65. Praise of Jackson: JM to 1 ANZAC, 25 Oct., MP; Rosenthal, D, 3 Dec. 1917. Praise of Grimwade: JM to VM, 26 Oct., MP.
228. 'Quite a record': JM to VM, 11 Aug., MP. 'pleased to do anything': JM to White, 31 July, MP. 'an active mind': JM to Foster, 7 May 1917, MP. 'I have nothing' and 'quite a tremendous person': letters, 22 July, 16 Sept., 'War Letters' (typescript), pp. 207, 220. 'such an effective slap': McGlinn to VM, 27 Aug., MP.
229. McCay's warning: McCay to JM, 18 May, MP. JM unconcerned: JM to Birdwood, 10 July, MP. 'I am bound to say': JM to Locke, 28 Aug., MP. 'encouraged by the nature': *OH*, IV, p. 562. 'some division': JM, 22 July, 'War Letters' (typescript), p. 207. JM's principles: 'Notes for First Conference', 26 July, MC.
230. 'Instead of an isolated instructor': JM to Locke, 28 Aug. 'simultaneous progressive stages': JM, 'Report on the Training of Infantry and Pioneer Units', 24 Aug., MP. 'This Division': Howard to Sir John French, 'Report on 3rd Division', 27 Aug., MC. Artillery training: Serle, *John Monash*, pp. 275–76. 'engineer platoon': D.A. Whitehead, 'Papers Re 9 Inf Bde', MS3059/1, Mitchell Library. Bustard trench system: JM to Durrant, 2 Oct., MP.
231. JM informed on Somme fighting: Birdwood to JM, 20 Aug.; JM to K. Murdoch, 12 Oct., MP. Bustard exercise: JM, 6 Nov. in *WarL*, p. 143; Bruche in Thompson, *On Lips of Living Men*, pp.135–36.
232. 'these big men': Walter Rosenhain to VM, 29 Nov., MP. 'a tremendous Napoleon': Birdwood to Munro Ferguson, 20 Oct., Birdwood Collection. 'It is high time': 3 Div. Circular G26/338, 14 Nov., MC. 'the necessity': JM to Brig. Gen. King-King, 19 Aug., MP. JM's three lectures to commanders are in MC.

REFERENCES

233. 'a curious paralysis': JM, 'Notes for Lecture on Court Martial', 24 Sept., MC.
234. 'take the backbone': quoted in Jackson to Liddell Hart, 4 Oct. 1935, Item I/516/Ib, Liddell Hart Papers. White's view: White to Bazley, 7 Apr. 1937, BC. Participation in Lord Mayor's Procession: JM to AIF Admin. HQ, 26 Oct., MP. The Royal Review: JM, 'Notes for the King's Inspection-Orders and Agenda', 23 Sept., MC; letter, 30 Sept., in *WarL*, p. 133.
235. 'They tell us': JM to White, 31 July, MP. 'It might foreshadow': JM, D, 11 Aug. 'Poor Monash': Birdwood to Munro Ferguson, 5 Sept., Birdwood Collection.
236. 'little short of a scandal': JM to White, 22 Aug., MP. Further 5000 possibly required: JM to Col T. Griffiths (AAG), 10 Sept., MP. Haig's remark: quoted in Birdwood to JM, 4 Oct., MP. JM's principle: JM to White, 16 Sept., MP. White apologises: White to JM, 20 Sept., MP. 'the 3rd Division': White to JM, 26 Aug., MP.
236–37. JM on conscription: JM to Agnes Murphy, 5 May 1917, MP.
237. As already arranged': *OH*, III, p. 893. 'the right kind of human material': JM, interviewed by H.K. Ellison, June 1919, MP. 'an extremely severe strain': W. Rosenhain to VM, 29 Nov., MP.
238. 'down on the Somme': V. Brahms, *The Spirit of the Forty Second*, pp. 15–16. JM's order on wearing hat brims down: JM to L.H. Chomley (*British Australasian*), 19 Aug. 16; to Lt. Col. Lamb (CO, 3 Div. Training Bn) 27 May 1917, MP. 'the granting of a few awards': JM to Cannan, 13 Jan. 1917, MP.
239. Refusal to establish pickets in Nieppe: JM to brigs., 20 Dec. 1916, MP. 3 Div. crime rate lowest: JM to Dr J.W. Springthorpe 13 Jan. 1918, MP. 'Scarcely a day': JM to Birdwood, 12 Dec., MP. 'To put it plainly': JM to Godley, 25 Jan. 1917, MP. 'not before impressing': White to JM, 16 Jan., MP.
240. 1757 detached: JM, 'Minute on Manpower Saving', 23 Feb., MC. JM and shell-shock: JM to 2 ANZAC, 30 Jan., MP. 'a very bad record': JM to 9 and 10 Bdes, 4 Dec. 1916, MP. Praise of JM: Birdwood to Pearce, 24 Dec., Birdwood Collection. 'I think': JM to McCay, 15 Apr. 1917, MP. JM on Training Group: JM to McCay, 20 June; to Dodds, 22 July, MP.
241. 'considerable importance': JM to O'Donnell, 15 Apr., MP.
242. 3 Div. sickness: JM to Donnelly, 20 Jan., MP. 'under cover': 3 Div. Instruction, 11 Jan., MC. 'I attach': JM to Cannan, 2 May, MP. JM on div. command: letters, 21 Dec. 1916, 'War Letters' (typescript), p. 251; 11 Jan. 1917, in *WarL*, pp. 154–63.
243. JM on Haig: letter, 21 Dec., in *WarL*, p. 151. 'any great human sympathies': Birdwood to Munro Ferguson, 4 July 1916, Birdwood Collection. 'never more brilliantly displayed': *OH*, VI, p. 185. Haig's views on Australians and JM: Terraine, *Douglas Haig: The educated soldier*, pp. 214–17. Concern caused by VM: JM to VM, 5 Feb., 16 Mar., MP.
244. 'I am heartily sick': JM to Gibson, 29 Apr., MP. 'gaining credit': 3 Div. Circular 24A, 11 Jan., MC. 3 Div. most experienced raiders: *OH*, IV, p. 565. 'stepping stones': JM to 2 ANZAC, 26 Dec., MP. 'the most important': *OH*, IV, p. 567.
245. 'success was undoubted': N.G. McNicol, *The Thirty-Seventh*, p. 56. JM's planning: JM, 'Preliminary Notes for Minor Enterprise to be Carried out by 10 Bde', 17 Jan., MC. Flavoured smoke: Jackson to Liddell Hart, 4 Oct. 1935. 'The whole system': JM to White, 27 Feb., MP. Raiding casualties: JM to Foster, 7 May, MP. Raids 'invaluable': JM, 'Leadership in War'.
246. 'As a morale raiser': 'Notes on Certain Lessons of the Great War', 6 Apr. 1933, WO File 33/1305, PRO. Lt. Col. A.A. Argent interviewed Cannan on 9 Aug. 1972 and sent his notes to the author on 19 Nov. 1980. 'no Divisional Commander': Jackson to Liddell Hart, 4 Oct. 1935.
247. 'Harington's doctrine': JM to Plumer, 8 Feb., MP. Plumer and Australians: Powell, *Plumer*,

p. 151. 'private soldier': Passingham, *Pillars of Fire*, p. 24. Haig's attitude to Plumer: Harington to Edmonds, 21 Nov. 1934, Item II/l/63A, Edmonds Papers; Edmonds' talk with Liddell Hart, 10 Jan. 1935, Item II/1935/58, Liddell Hart Papers.

248. Haig proposes Messines as a diversion for Somme: R. Blake, *The Private Papers of Douglas Haig, 1916-1919*, p. 125. JM informed: 'Notes from Corps Commander's Conference', 29 Nov., MC. 'bringing up to date': C. Falls, *The Great War*, p. 281. Artillery resources: Farndale, *Western Front*, pp. 184–85; Terraine, *Western Front*, p. 230. Plumer's conception of the barrage: OAD 458 to 2 Army, 24 May, Haig, D, Ace. 3155, Papers of Field Marshal Sir Douglas Haig. Haig inserted important documents at the end of the appropriate daily entry in his diary. The OAD series were directives on operational matters, including future intentions. They were possibly the most crucial documents issued by GHQ.

250. Importance of Black Line: 2 Army to corps, *GSOS*, 15 May; G695, 18 May, 'Second Army War Diary', PRO. 'just as far as': B. H. Liddell Hart, *History of the First World War*, p. 393. 'a fairly heavy': *OH*, IV, p. 576. Messines church painted by Hitler: R. Coombs, *Before Endeavours Fade*, p. 57.

251. 'the right hand man': Jackson to Liddell Hart, 4 Oct.1935.

252. 'renovated and made anew': JM, 'First Notes of Magnum Opus', 27 Mar., MC. 'purposely did not aim': JM to Harington, 16 Apr., MP.

253. 'bombing blocks ... this battalion' and 'of the *very highest importance*': 3 Div., 'Magnum Opus-Provisional Divisional and Barrage Plan', 15 Apr., MC.

255. Alteration to Black Line: JM, 'Notes from Corps Commander's Conference', 9 May, MC; '2 Anzac Provisional Plan of Attack', 16 May, OR. JM decides against use of 11 Bde: 'Notes for Brigadiers' Conference', 12 May, MC. JM changes Div. plan: 'Summary of Div. Conference of 13 May', MC.

257. 'the plan set out': Jobson to JM, 7 May, MC. Godley's plan for Green Line: '2 Anzac Provisional Plan of Attack', 16 May. JM refuses to submit final schemes: JM to Godley, 21 May, MP.

258. 'I have reason': JM to McNicoll, 27 May, MP. 'part of the Operation Order': 3 Div., 'Preliminary Instructions', 6 May, OR. 'I never saw': Harington to Edmonds, 27 Jan. 1932, 'Official Historian's Correspondence: Western Front', BC. Jackson's praise: Jackson to Liddell Hart, 4 Oct 1935. 'Everything is being done': JM, 1 June, 'War Letters' (typescript), p. 302.

259. 2 ANZAC maps incorrect. JM to Brig. Gen. C.W. Gwynn (Chief of Staff, 2 ANZAC), 2 Apr., MP. 'a comprehensive picture': McNicol, *The Thirty-Seventh*, p. 89. Approach routes: 9 Bde, 'Instruction No. 3', c.15 May, MC. JM insists on telephone: 3 Div. to NZ Div. 30 May, OR.

260. Plumer's visits: JM, D, 29 Mar.-7 June. Vimy attack JM, 15 May, in *WarL*, p. 176. Bombardment program, *OH*, IV, p. 578. 'the true role': *AV*, p. 96.

261. Distribution of artillery and selection of HQ: 3 Div. to 2 ANZAC, 20, 21 May; 2 ANZAC to 3 Div., 3 May, OR. JM seeks tanks: JM to Jackson, 25 May, OR. Specialist engineering knowledge: JM to Harington, 10 May; to Godley, 11 June, MP. 'better to grasp': JM to McNicoll, 25 May, OR. JM rigorously questions COs: Jackson to Liddell Hart, 4 Oct. 1935.

262. 'all men': 9 Bde, 'Instruction No. 6', 29 May, MC. 'I have seen': Durrant to *Reveille*, 16 Apr. 1937, BC. 'nothing to chance': JM to Grimwade, 9 Dec. 1916, MP. 'a heavy conference': JM, D, 29 Apr. 'The ADMS': Butler, *Official Medical History*, 2, pp. 164–65.

263. 'This was a new experience': G. Drake-Brockman, *The Turning Wheel*, p. 117. 'in my opinion': Haig, D, 24 May. Smithers, *Sir John Monash*, p. 243. Currie on Vimy: quoted in Harington to JM, 17 Apr., MP.

REFERENCES

264. 'The work': notes by Lt. Col. Murray (GSO1 Training 2 ANZAC) 8Apr., MC. JM's exercise: JM to bdes, 14 Apr., MC. 'sending a stream': 3 Div. MO Circular 30, 22 May, MC. 'on every occasion': JM to brigs, 13 May, MP. 'striking a heavy blow': JM to bdes, 3 June, MC. Bean's claim: *OH*, IV, fn 65, p. 579. 'to say the least': *OH*, IV, p. 571. JM unable to sleep: D, 6 June.
265. 3 Div. approach march: JM to 2 ANZAC, 'Narrative of Operations', 26 June, MC. 'Throughout the night': *OH*, IV, p. 591.
266. 'Zero hour arrives': E. Simonson to W. Rosenhain, 7 June, MC. 'machine like precision': '2nd Anzac War Diary', 7 June. 'left brigade': 3 Div. G14 to 2 ANZAC, 5.02 am, 7 June, OR. 'the particular care': *OH*, IV, p. 607. 'at the Bustard': Morshead to Jobson, 7 June, Morshead Collection. Story takes 37 Bn: JM's interview with Smith, 21 June, MC. 37 Bn casualties and postponement: Cutlack, 'Narrative of Operations', 16 June, MC. Cutlack was 3 Div.'s IO. 'extremely fragmentary': '2nd Anzac War Diary', 7 June.
267. JM's order: JM to brigs., 2.46 pm, 7 June, OR.
268. McNicoll's signal: 10 Bde to 3 Div., 8.45 pm, 7 June, OR. 'this system': *OH*, IV, p. 645.
269. JM accuses Smith: JM's interview, 21 June. JM's report: JM to Godley, 9.12 pm, 7 June, OR. JM's orders for 44 Bn's attack: JM to McNicoll, 9.50 pm, 12.10 am; to Gwynn, 12.20 pm, 7–8 June, OR. 44 Bn attack: 3 Div. to 2 ANZAC, 4.20 am, 8 June, OR; Cutlack's 'Narrative'; 'Proceedings of Conference held by Godley', 5 June, OR; '2nd Anzac War Diary', 8 June; JM to McNicoll, 3.12 pm, 8 June, OR. Bean's claim: *OH*, IV, p. 649.
271. 'lacked as yet': *OH*, IV, pp. 656–57. 'If there is one characteristic': Carver, *The War Lords*, p. xi.
272. Cannan's criticism: quoted in Gellibrand's comments on AV. McNicoll least manageable: JM to VM, 15 Jan., MP. Holmes visits bns: *OH*, IV, p. 654. JM's plan for 10 June: JM to 2 ANZAC, 7 June, MC. 'ought to provide': JM to Jobson, 10 June, OR.
273. Losses: '3 Div. Casualty Statement', 7-13 June, MC. Comments on Messines: A.J.P. Taylor, *The First World War*, p. 190; Edmonds to Bean, 3 July 1918, 'Official Historian's Correspondence: Western Front'; OAD 291/27, 'Proceedings of Army Commanders' Conference', 14 June, Haig, D; C. Harington, *Plumer of Messines*, pp. 94–95; '2 Army Intelligence Summary', 1–11 June, MC. 'foredoomed': Prior and Wilson, *Passchendaele*, p. 65. E. Ludendorff, *My War Memories, 1914-18*, 2 vols, 2, p. 429.
274. 'The attack': JM, 19 May, 'War Letters' (typescript), p. 299. 'I am the greatest possible believer': JM to W. Rosenhain, 14 June, MP. 3 Div. captures: JM to 2 ANZAC, 26 June. A liquid sector: JM to Walterlou, 24 June, MP. 'no commander': A.W. Bazley, 'Sir John Monash', *Reveille*,1 May 1937, p. 3. 3 Div. has half average sick rate: JM to Godley, 12 Apr. 1917, MP. 'any lack': JM to Springthorpe, 13 Jan. 1918, MP.
275. JM and honours list: JM to Godley; Godley to JM, 22 June; White to JM, 30 June, MP.

Chapter 8

276. Genesis of Passchendaele: Liddell Hart, 'The Genesis of Passchendaele', c.1934, Item II/1934/61, Liddell Hart Papers; E.K.G. Sixsmith, *Douglas Haig*, p. 132; OAD 434, Haig, D, 7 May 1917. Tactical conduct: W.R. Robertson, *Soldiers and Statesmen*, 2 vols, 2, p. 235; Prior and Wilson, *Passchendaele*, p. 53, 198; J.F.C. Fuller, *The Conduct of War 1789-1961*, p. 171; J.E. Edmonds, *Military Operations: France and Belgium 1917*, 5 vols, 2, p. 127; A. Farrar-Hockley, *Goughie*, p. 217; H. Gough, *The Fifth Army*, pp. 197–98; Simkins, 'Herbert Plumer' in Becket and Corvi (eds.), *Haig's Generals*, p. 154; *OH*, IV, p. 698.
278–79. German defensive system: 'Experience of the German 1st Army in the Somme Battle'; 'Principles of Command in the Defensive Battle in Position Warfare', GHQ translations, 3 May 1917, 21 Sept. 1918, White Collection.

279. 'the enemy': Haig, D, 10 May. GHQ seeks advice: GHQ Memo OB/2089, 7 Aug., 'Second Army War Diary'. JM's views: 3 Div. to 2 ANZAC, 8 Aug., MC.
280. 2 ANZAC to launch minor operations: 2 ANZAC SG440 to divs, 5 July, OR.
281. 3 Div. Scheme; Jackson to 2 ANZAC, 4 July; JM, 'Notes Regarding the Task of 3 Div. During Contemplated Operations', 15 July, OR. JM suggests start well before 31 July: 3 Div. to 2 ANZAC, 11 July, OR.
282. Varley bomb: JM, 'Notes for Demonstration', 21 Aug., MC. JM's use of smoke: Elliott to Bean, 10 June 1929, Elliott Collection. 'long and important conference': JM, D, 24 July. Machine-gun barrage: 'Account of Operations by 42 and 43 Bns', 31 July, MC.
283. 'did good work': JM, 3 Aug., in *WarL*, p. 185. 'into which I have tried': JM to Jackson, 15 July, OR. 'acrimony': JM to Dodds, 2 Aug., MP. Commanders' responsibilities: JM, 'Notes for divisional Conference', 8 Aug.; 'Comments', 17 Aug., MC.
284. 'Every detail': Haig, D, 22 Sept. JM and Haig: JM, 6 Aug., 24 Sept., in *WarL*, pp. 186, 193–94; Terraine, interview with author, London, 19 Mar. 1981; Haig, D, 9 June.
285. 'after much trouble': JM to Dodds, 14, 26 Aug., MP. Dismissal of Jobson: JM to Jobson, 8 Feb., MP; Bean D93, undated note; *OH*, V, pp. 299–300; Jackson to JM, 17 Mar., MP.; JM, 'Notes on Jobson', 31 July; ADMS to JM, 27 Jul.; JM to Jobson, 30 July, MC; JM to VM, 1 Sept., MP.
287. Rosenthal: Bean, D7, 5 May 15; Drake-Brockman, *The Turning Wheel*, p. 117; *OH*, V, p. 301. 'Mutual confidence': C. Rosenthal, 'A Great Soldier and a Great Scholar', *Reveille*, 31 Oct.1931, p. 4. JM designs baths: JM to Birdwood, 9 Jan., MP. 'A Corner of Blighty': Butler to JM, 20 Apr. 1918, MP. Goldstein's complaint: Dodds to JM,13 Feb.1918, MP. Upjohn's grievance: Upjohn to JM, 9 Feb. 1918, MP.
288. 'protective patrols': 3 Div. to 2 ANZAC, 11 Sept., MC. 'present conditions': JM to Jackson, 19 Aug., MC. 'I personally attach': JM to Jackson, 12 Aug., File 947/37, AWRS. 'all the drive': JM, 'Notes for Divisional Conference', 10 Aug., MC.
289. 'Concerted attack: McNicol, *The Thirty-Seventh*, p. 119. 3 Div. to join Ypres offensive: JM, 'Notes from Corps Conference', 5 Sept., MC. 'part and parcel': Gough, *The Fifth Army*, p. 195. 'difficult to understand': Terraine, *Douglas Haig*, pp. 338–39. 'fatal moments': Lloyd, *Passchendaele*, p. 79.
290. Gough's observation: quoted in Macdonald, *They Called it Passchendaele*, p. 160. 'The battlefield': *OH*, IV, p. 721. 'If all goes well': JM, 1 Sept., 'War letters' (typescript), p. 329.
292. 'on average': 2 Army Intelligence, 'Weather of September and October', 1 Sept. OR. 3 Div. plan: JM, 'Notes for Brigadiers' Conference', 17 Sept., MC. 'not yet possible': 3 Div. to brigs, 19 Sept., File 947/37, AWRS.
293. JM proposes boundary, JM to 2 ANZAC, 21 Sept., MP. 'Each front line platoon': 3 Div. to brigs, 19 Sept.
294. 'The 3rd beside the 2nd': Bean, D65, 28 Sept. JM informed of new plan: '3 Div. War Diary', 23 Sept. 'cold and dark': JM, 1 Oct., in *WarL*, p. 195.
295. JM's plan for Broodseinde: JM to 2 ANZAC, 26 Sept., MC.
296. 'in all probability': JM to McNicoll, 28 Sept., MP. Changes of plan: 'Ypres Battle General Staff Circulars' (YBGSC) 8, 30 Sept.; 10, 1 Oct., MC.
297. 'Very busy': JM, D, 3 Oct. JM's revised plan: YBGSC 5, 29 Sept., MC. Flank parties and an 'ample supply of runners': YBGSCs 14, 17, 2 Oct., MC.
298. Lack of aerial photographs: JM to 2 ANZAC, 26 Sept., MC. JM's decision on assembly: 3 Div. Circular G45/236, 25 Sept., OR; Jackson, 'Notes on Visit to the Forward Area', 24 Sept., MC; YBGSC 7, 30 Sept., MC.

REFERENCES

299. Use of smoke and infantry as engineers: YBGSC 17, 2 0ct.; 3 Div. Circular SG386/4, 25 Sept., OR. 'its systems of supply': *OH*, IV, p. 835. White's hardest task: White to Bean, 17 June 1932, White Collection. 'The Battalions to move': YBGSC 7, 30 Sept.
300. 'the probability': JM to 2 ANZAC, 1 Oct., MP. 'The losses incurred': 'German Records Relative to Australian Operations on the Western Front', collected by J.J. Herbertson, Class. 111.05, AWM. Plumer's HQ forecasts counter-attack: 2 Army, 'The Enemy's Probable Intentions for Counterattack East of Ypres', 1 Oct., OR. 'whatever happens': JM to brigs, 3 Oct., MP.
302. 3 Div. attack: 'Narrative of 3 Div. Units in Battle of 4 Oct. 1917', 9 Oct., MC; *OH*, IV, p. 866; '3 Div. War Diary', 4 Oct.
303. 'Everything going well': JM to Godley, 10.40 am, 4 Oct., OR. 'Artillery observers ... your best': JM to McNicoll, 11.08 am, 4 Oct., OR. 'I think': JM to Godley, 10.40 am, 4 Oct. Godley urges exploitation: Godley, *Irish Soldier*, p. 224. 'It all depends': JM to Godley, 11.46 am, 4 Oct., OR.
304. 'Think it over': JM to brigs, noon, 4 Oct., OR. 'one day': Jackson to Liddell Hart, 4 Oct. 1935. 'no way responsible': Butler, *Official Medical History*, 2, p. 231.
305. Bean's concession: *OH*, IV, p. 840. 'the way': quoted in 3 Div. to units, 5 Oct., OR. 'Great happenings': JM, 7 Oct., in *WarL*, p. 198. JM 'entirely shared': Terraine, *The Smoke and the Fire*, p. 196. 'Now we have them': quoted in Harington to Edmonds, 12 Dec. 1932, 'Official Historian's Correspondence: Western Front'. 'feeble and wild': Terraine, *Douglas Haig*, p. 369. 7 Oct conference: Edmonds, *Military Operations: France and Belgium 1917*, 2, p. 325; Prior and Wilson, *Passchendaele*, pp. 160–61.
306. 'I suspect': Bean, D90, undated. Charteris says no hope: J. Charteris, *At GHQ*, p. 259. 'a travelling planet': Bean, D90, 10 Oct. 1917.
307. Godley's warning: JM, 'Notes from Corps Conference', 7 Oct., MC. 'Things now rushed': JM, 'Notes for Brigadiers' Conference', 7 Oct., MC. 'almost totally neglected': JM to 2 ANZAC, 1 Nov., MP. German defences: 'Report on Enemy Opposite 2 Anzac front, 28 Sep.-16 Oct.', MC.
308. 'Quite impassable': '2 Army Intelligence Summary 811, 7 Oct.', OR.
309. 'strongly held': '3 Div. Narrative of Operations-12/10/17', 1 Nov., MC. 'I have introduced': JM, 18 Oct., in *WarL*, p. 203. JM's chief fear: JM to Harington, 14 Oct., MP.
310. 'practically the same': *OH*, IV, p. 907. 'Appears': Rosenthal, D, 9-10 Oct. 'there was no-one': McNicoll to JM, 4.40 pm, 10 Oct., MC. 'a twenty four hour postponement': JM, 15 Oct., in *WarL*, pp. 199–200. 'If Generals Monash and Godley': *OH*, IV, pp. 907–08.
311. Birdwood and Haig and 'the enemy': Haig, D, 10, 23 Oct. 'sacred duty': Macdonald, *Passchendaele*, p. 56. Harper, *Dark Journey*, p. 103. 'Things are bloody': Morshead to White (9 Bde), 12 Oct., Morshead Collection. 'a few pebbles': Pedersen, *Anzacs*, p. 264. 'The massing of machine guns': '2 Army Intelligence Summary 817', 13 Oct., OR. 'gluey mud': JM to 2 ANZAC, 14 Oct., MP. 'although the SOS line': Bean, D90, 14 Oct.
312. These messages, exchanged between JM, Godley and 9, 10, 11 Bdes between 10.50 am and 2.11 pm, are in OR.
313. Losses: 'Div. Casualty Statistics', 28 Mar. 1918, MC. Sixsmith's comment: letter to author, 16 Aug. 1979.
314. Currie 'continuously forward': A.M.J. Hyatt, 'Sir Arthur Currie at Passchendaele', *Stand-To*, IX (Jan.-Feb. 1965), p. 18. 'senior officers': JM, 'Notes for Brigadiers' Conference', 26 Oct., MC. 'Our men': JM, 18 Oct., in *WarL*, p. 202. Prior and Wilson, *Passchendaele*, p. 200. de Lisle's assessment: quoted in Winter, *Death's Men*, p. 212.
315. 3 Div. under strength: JM to Gwynn, 29 Oct., MP. 'Old Monash': Bean, D92, 2 Nov.

315–16. 'so at last ... about the waist and neck': JM to VM, 14 Nov., MP.
316. 'more than earned': JM to VM, 18 Oct., MP. 'The University is pretty sure': JM to VM, 15 Mar. 1918, MP.
317. 'safe defence': JM, 'Notes for Brigadiers' Conference', 10 Nov., File 213/1(4), AWRS. 'the pressing outstanding question': 3 Div. to units, 2 Nov., MC. 'a short heart to heart talk': JM, 'Notes for Speech to Junior Officers', 18 Jan., MC. 'which is the more desirable ... into their hands': JM, 'Minutes of Ravelsberg Conference with COs', 26 Feb., MC.
318. 'we must be': JM, 'Notes for Brigadiers' Conference', 2 Nov., MC. 3 Div. raids: JM to Aust. Corps, 1 Dec., MC; to White, 1 Dec., MP; Bean, D99, 12 Feb.
319. 'securing the moral effect': JM, 'Plan for the Capture of Warneton', 22 Feb., MC. JM differs with White on mgs: 3 Div. Circular GSA, 17 Feb., MC; White to JM, 18 Jan., MP; 18 Feb., MC. JM critical of artillery policy: JM to Aust. Corps, 19 Feb., MP; White to JM, 5 Dec. 1917, MC. JM, D, 10 Jan.
320. The March offensive: C. Barnett, 'Offensive 1918', in N. Frankland and C. Dowling, *Decisive Battles of the Twentieth Century*, pp. 71–72; T. Ropp, *War in the Modern World*, p. 247; Essame, *The Battle for Europe*, p. 34. 'British Army': Holmes, *Western Front*, p. 193.
321. 'the German would find our front': Haig, D, 2 Mar. See also Field Marshal Sir Henry Wilson (CIGS), D, Microfilm, IWM, 30 Jan., 18 Mar. Gough and GHQ complacency: Harris, *Douglas Haig*, p. 449. Confidence at GHQ: Stevenson, *Backs to the Wall*, p. 53. 'three days: De Groot, *Douglas Haig*, pp. 374–75. JM, 'Ravelsberg Conference', 26 Feb.
322. 'Strengthen our forward dispositions': JM, 'Notes from Corps Conference', 19 Feb., MC. 'much upset': Haig, D, 23 Mar. somewhat haggard': G. Blaxland, *Amiens 1918*, p. 80. Initial moves of 3 Div.: Jess, Wieck to JM, 24–25 Mar., MC.
323. 'responded capably': AV, p. 22. 3 Div. allotted to VII Corps: '3 Div War Diary', 7.25 pm, 26 Mar. 'tactical situation': *OH*, V, p. 271. JM's orders are in MC.
324. 'plainly see the German cavalry': JM, 2 Apr., in *WarL*, p. 228.
325. 'first good long rest': JM, D, 27 Mar. 'I now feel': JM to Birdwood, 28 Mar., MP. 'Divisional machinery' and 'It is a splendid illustration': JM to Jackson, 29 Mar., MP. 'Monash's great powers': *OH*, V, p. 177. JM seeks White's views: Bean, *Two Men I Knew*, p. 162. 'perfectly reasonable': Sixsmith, interview with author, 28 Mar., 1981.
326. 'quick, cool, successful planning': C.E.W. Bean, 'Monash the Soldier', *Reveille*, 31 Oct. 1931, p. 2. 'the recoil', *AV*, p. 23. 'Some of these Tommy Divisions': JM, 4 Apr., 'War Letters' (typescript), p. 394. Battering of British divisions: Simkins, *Somme to Victory*, pp. 129–30,138–39. 3 Div. morale: Capt. C.H. Peters, letter, 15 Apr., MS1887, Mitchell Library. Ill-feeling removed: W.D. Joynt, *Saving the Channel Ports 1918*, p. 113. 'consisted of green fields': Brahms, *The Spirit of the Forty Second*, p. 65.
327. 'the advance': *OH*, V, p. 212. Final plan: '3 Div. War Diary', 10 am, 28 Mar.; *OH*, V, p. 212. 'in view of his future plans' and 'within the next few days': Bean, D103, 29 Mar. The Sailly-Laurette attack and Bean's criticism are in *OH*, V, pp. 215–26.
329. 'swept the lines': JM to Birdwood, 30 Mar., MC.
330. 'covered itself with glory': Rosenthal to JM, 5 Apr., MP. Peaceful Penetration: *OH*, VI, p. 45. 'resolved to embark': *AV*, p. 37. 'Much confusion and worry': JM, D, 7 May.
332. 'I told him': quoted in JM to VM, 12 Jan., MP. Birdwood on Hobbs and White: quoted in Bean, *Two Men I Knew*, pp. 160, 169; *OH*, VI, p. 190. 'He has never been tested': JM, interview with A.F. O'Connor, 13 Feb. 1919. Congreve on JM: quoted in *OH*, VI, p. 190. 'God forbid!': quoted in Bean, D90, 12 Oct. 1917. 'From that moment forward': J. Terraine, 'Monash: Australian Commander', *History Today*, XVI (Jan. 1966), p. 18. 'it seemed': Bean, *Two Men I Knew*, p. 171.

REFERENCES

333. 'Monash for an Australian C-in-C': Bean, D91, 18 Oct. 17. 'strictly and expressly': Murdoch to Hughes, 20 May, Hughes Papers, Series 23, MS1538, National Library. 'entirely opposed': Dodds to Pearce, 29 May, Pearce Collection. 'perhaps the outstanding case': Serle, *John Monash*, p. 328.
334. 'the first native born': JM, 14 May, 'War Letters' (typescript), p. 404. 'It is indeed fortunate': JM to Cox, 14 June, MP. Bean's remark and marginal addition are in D111, 1 June. Open warfare most interesting phase: JM's *Personal Records*, AWRS Details, MC. 'a lot of work personally' and 'Oh! I had not thought of that': Jackson to Liddell Hart, 4 Oct. 1935. JM's views on GSO1: Gellibrand's comments on *AV*. 'to say much': Hersey to Peck, 19 July 1917, MP.
335. G.S. Browne in Thompson, *On Lips of Living Men*, p. 137. 'invariably the dirtiest men': JM to Dodds, 8 Apr., MC. 'This is tantamount': JM to Carruthers, 12 May, MC. 'the feelings of humanity': 3 Div. Order, 11 May, MC.
336. 'Coming here': Jackson to JM, 23 June, MP.

Chapter 9

337. 'My command': JM, 31 May, in *WarL*, p. 245.
338. 'one of the most able': JM to VM, 16 Mar., MP. Blamey: J. Hetherington, *Blamey, Controversial Soldier*, p. 45; *AV*, p. 296; Serle, *John Monash*, p. 381.
339. 'I read him ... manage his sort': Rawlinson to Montgomery, 8 May, 9 Sept. 1920, Montgomery-Massingberd Papers.
340. JM, 'Notes for First Corps Conference', 6 June, MC. 'The other Divisional Commanders': *AV*, p. 40. Div commanders' misgivings: Stevenson, *War with Germany*, p. 175. 'a unity of thought': JM, 'History and Constitution of the Australian Army Corps', 3 Oct., MC. These notes were prepared for Dr J.W. Springthorpe and used by him for his articles on the Corps, entitled 'The Spearhead', which appeared in the *Age* in 1919. 'high ideals': JM, 'Personal Notes', 4 Oct., MC. JM's addresses: 'Notes for Visits to 5-6 Bdes', 22-23 June; '11 Bde', 9 July, MC.
341. White on Birdwood: quoted in Bean, D113, 30 May. JM and colour patches: JM to AIF Admin. HQ, 17 July, MP. 'as far as it is humanly possible ... on the scoring board': JM, 'Personal Notes'. 'incorrigibly civilian': *OH*, VI, p. 5.
342. JM on Australian soldier: *AV*, pp. 263–65.
343. 'The previous operations': JM, 'Personal Notes'. BEF and its command: Prior and Wilson, *Command on the Western Front*, pp. 305, 343; G.D. Sheffield, 'The performance of British troops in 1918' in Dennis and Grey (eds.), *1918. Defining Victory*, p. 93; Simpson, *Directing Operations*, p. 226.
345. 'I am of the opinion': JM to 4 Army, 3 June, OR. JM seeks assistance from Butler: Aust. Corps Order 111, 6 June, MC. Remarks on gun line: F.M. Cutlack, *The Australians: their final campaign 1918*, p. 205. 'abnormally quiet': Rawlinson, D, 14, 22 June, Item 5201/33/28, Rawlinson Collection, NAM. 'now prepared': GHQ OAD 880, 3 July, Montgomery-Massingberd Papers. 'captures of territories': Aust. Corps S/4612 to GOCs, 20 June, OR.
346. 'If we have to carry out': Bean, D113, 30 May.
347. Hamel battlefield: Pedersen, *Hamel*, pp. 22–23. Aust Corps 8000 under strength: Prior and Wilson, *Command on the Western Front*, p. 296. 'I do not recommend': JM to 4 Army, 13 June, OR.
348. 'would so increase the capacity': Elles to GHQ, 'Defensive and Offensive Use of Tanks', 3 Jan., OR. Decision to use tanks: *AV*, p. 44; Rawlinson quoted in F. Maurice, *The Life of General Lord Rawlinson of Trent*, p. 221; A.J. Trythall, *Boney Fuller*, p. 65; Bean, *Anzac to Amiens*, pp. 459–60.

349. Courage's plan: Courage to JM, 20 June, OR.
350. 'any opportunity the Tanks create': Tank Corps HQ, 'Characteristics and Tactics of the Mark V, Mark V Star and Medium A Tanks', 27 June, Blamey Papers. 'Consider question': JM, 'Preliminary Notes re Hamel', 19 June, MC. 'The action' and 'Thorough liaison': JM to 4 Army, S/4671, 21 June, OR. 'The idea': JM, Notes on S/4671, 21 June, OR.
352. Battalion frontages: C.R.M. Cruttwell, *A History of the Great War*, p. 532. Haig approves: Haig, D, 25 June.
353. 'Decided to carry out operation': 'Notes for 4 Div. conference', 25 June, MC. 'The Artillery Barrage Method': Blamey, 'Pros and Cons of Tank Method', c.25 June, OR. 'Fixed up tanks': Rawlinson, D, 26 June. 'It ceases': JM to 4 Army, 26 June, OR. 'as superior': Elles to GHQ, 3 Jan., OR.
354. Hunn's estimate: 'Forecast of Available Enemy Infantry', 22 June, OR. 'The trenches': R. A. Beaumont, 'Hamel 1918: a study in military-political interaction', *Military Affairs*, XXXL (Spring 1967), p. 11. JM overrules tank commanders: *AV*, pp. 49–50; Aust. Corps S/4730 to units, 1 July, MC.
355. Artillery plan: Pedersen, *Hamel*, pp. 51–53; Prior and Wilson, *Command on the Western Front*, p. 298.
356. Imitation of German ammo dropping: 5 Div. Int. Summary, 19 June, Blamey Papers. Conference on 30 June: JM, Rawlinson, D, 30 June; JM, 'Agenda for Conference on 30 June', MC; JM to Rawlinson, 5 July, MP; *OH*, VI, pp. 268–69.
357. Haig 'greatly impressed': Haig, D, 1 July. 'the whole business': JM to Birdwood, 29 June, MP. 'merely as a reserve': J.J. Pershing, *My Experiences in the World War*, p. 272.
358. Decision on employment of Americans: *AV*, pp. 53–54; Bean, D116, 3 July. 'Glancing out of the window': Coxen to *Reveille*, 12 Apr. 1937, BC.
359. 'the first tank': Bean, D116, 4 Jul.
360. Tactical analysis of Hamel: *AV*, p. 56; JM, 4 July, in *WarL*, p. 250; Courage to 4 Army, 13 July, OR; *OH*, VI, p. 305.
361. GHQ staff sheets: SS218, 'Notes Compiled by GS Fourth Army on the Operation of the Australian Corps Against Hamel on 4 July'; 'GHQ Notes on Recent Fighting', No. 19, 5 Aug., MC. Smithers' estimate: *Sir John Monash*, p. 291. The historian was Geoffrey Blainey in *Sydney Morning Herald*, 5 May 1973. J.F.C. Fuller, *Memoirs of an Unconventional Soldier*, pp. 287–90. 'all the appurtenances': Bean, 'Narrative of 1918', MC.
362. 'little masterpiece', Terraine, *To Win a War*, p. 85. 'A perfected modern battle plan': *AV*, p. 56. German explanation: Herbertson, 'German Records', p. 195. Wisdom's view: quoted in *OH*, VI, p. 327. Rawlinson on JM: Rawlinson to Birdwood, 27 June, Birdwood Collection; D, 6 July.
363. Div commanders: Stevenson, *War with Germany*, p. 176. Reasons for the battle and Clemenceau's visit: Cutlack, *The Australians*, p. 213; *AV*, pp. 44, 64. 'a clear sign': Terraine, *To Win a War*, p. 85. 'quite a nice success': Haig to Lady H., 4 July, Haig Papers. 'No news': Wilson, D, 6 July.
364. Wilson's memorandum: 'British Military Policy 1918-19', 25 July, Haig, D. Haig's comments quoted in Terraine, *Douglas Haig*, p. 461. GHQ OAD 902, 27 July, 4 Army Records, Rawlinson Collection. 'all great anxiety': quoted in C.E. Callwell, *Field Marshal Sir Henry Wilson*, 2 Vols, 2, p. 112. Ludendorff's state: Wolfgang Foerster, *Ludendorff– der Feldherr Ludendorff im Unglück*, Wiesbaden, 1952 (BII, Lud. 3, Bundesarchiv-Militiirarchiv, Freiburg), p. 18. Foch considering counter-offensive: Grant to DMO, War Office, 2 Apr., File WO 158/84, PRO. Foch's plan: 'Directive Générale No. 2', 3 Apr., File WO 158/28, PRO.

REFERENCES

365. 'of vital importance': 'Record of Abbeville Conference', 27 Apr., ibid. 'A study of the directives': J.P. Ducane, *Marshal Foch* (1920), p. 36. This private publication, held by the IWM, recounts Lt. Gen. J.P. Ducane's experience as GHQ Liaison Officer to Foch. It is one of the most important documents on the origins of the Amiens offensive. 'There is no doubt': JM, 8 Nov., in *WarL*, p. 275. 'la surprise': Foch, 'Directive Générale No. 3', 20 May, Haig, D. Rawlinson's scheme: Rawlinson to GHQ, 17 July, MC.
366. 'of the greatest importance': A. Duff Cooper, *Haig*, 2 vols, 2, p. 330. 'également en raison': Foch to Haig, 20 July, File WO 158/28, PRO.
367. 'it was due': Ducane, *Marshal Foch*, p. 62. JM keen to exploit Hamel: JM to Hobbs and Sinclair-MacLagan, 4 July, MC. JM wants front shortened: JM to 4 Army, 7 July, OR. 'the furthest advance': JM, 'Notes for Army Commander's Conference', 15 July, MP. The JM-Murdoch conversation was quoted by Bean in D116, 11 Aug. 'The time was ripe': *AV*, p. 69.
368. 'That conversation': JM to Bruche, 10 Oct. 1919, MP. 'the initiation': JM to Treloar (Director AWM), 16 June 1928, File 12/3/71, AWM. Search reveals nothing: Treloar to Bean, 12 July 1928, ibid.
369. 'we know that Monash': Bean to White, 30 June 1935, White Collection. 'was practically confessing': White to Bean, 27 June 1935, ibid. 'a destroyer would stand by': JM, 2 Aug., in *WarL*, p. 253.
370. Strength of German defences: 'Aust. Corps Intelligence Report 106/1004', 1 Aug., MC. 'imposed no limitations': JM to Bruche, 10 Oct.
371. 'prepared my plans': *AV*, p. 84. 'a divided responsibility': *AV*, p. 74. JM, 'Preliminary Notes for Battle of Amiens', 22 July, MC.
372. 'he was outstanding': Blamey to *Reveille*, 12 Apr. 1937, BC. 'all the threads': Haig, D, 31 July. Assembly of divs: JM, 'Allotment of Infantry to Objectives', c. 23 July, MC.
373. 'the intelligence of the troops': *AV*, p. 95. 'largely one of roads': *OH*, VI, p. 503. 'the elaborate placing': Bean in *Reveille*, 31 Oct. 1931, p. 2. Gellibrand's disagreement: Sadler, *Paladin*, p. 170; Gellibrand's comments on *AV*; Bean, D116, 12 Aug.; *OH*, VI, p. 491.
375. Currie's plan: G.W.L. Nicholson, *Canadian Expeditionary Force 1914-1919*, p. 397. JM's tactics: *AV*, p. 84; 'Allotment of Infantry to Objectives'; Characteristics of the Mark V and Mark V Star Tanks', 27 Jan. 1918, Blamey Papers. The date of this latter paper disposes of Smithers' claim (*Sir John Monash*, pp. 228–29) that JM was the first to advocate the use of Mark V Stars as carriers of machine-gun teams. This was one of their intended roles all along.
376. Signalling training: Aust. Corps to divs., 8 July, OR.
377. 'The Battalion Commander pointed out': Jackson to Liddell Hart, 4 Oct. 1935. 'zero hour': Battle Instruction (BI) 7, Draft, 2 Aug., MC. 'All questions': JM, 'Notes for Final Corps Conference', 4 Aug., MC. 'no football': JM, 'Battle Notes', 3 Aug., MC. 'Draft success message': JM, 'Personal Battle Agenda', 3 Aug., MC.
378. 'specially charged': Smithers, *Sir John Monash*, p. 227. 'no individual Tank': *AV*, p. 107.
379. Redispositions discussed: JM to Bruche, 10 Oct. 1919. 'no developments': JM, 'The Decisive Battle', in *Argus*, 4 Aug. 1928. 'from present appearances': JM to Murdoch, 27 July, MP.
380. 'such an outcry': Bean, D116, 7 Aug. 'in case the worst should happen': JM to Sinclair-MacLagan, 6 Aug., MP. 'After chafing me': Foott to *Reveille*, 3 Apr. 1937, BC.
381. 'to the utmost of his power': JM's draft, 7 Aug., MC. 'a few minutes after four': W. Berry in Thompson, *On Lips of Living Men*, p. 142. Narrative of the battle: 2 Div. 4.54 am; 3 Div. 5.02 am to Aust. Corps, 8 Aug., OR; *OH*, VI, pp. 544, 571; JM to 4 Army, 1.15 pm, 8 Aug., MC; 'Report on the Operations of the Australian Corps, Phase A, 8 Aug.', 26 Oct., MC.
382. Cloak of fog: Liddell Hart, *Thoughts on War*, p. 284. Artillery: Farndale, *Western Front*, p. 288; Pedersen, *Anzacs*, pp. 375–76. Tank losses: 5 Tank Bde, 'Report on Operations, 8 Aug.', File 925/1, AWRS.

383. 'a continuous shuttle movement': J.F.C. Fuller, *The Decisive Battles of the Western World*, 3 vols, 3, p. 290. W. Gammage, 'Sir John Monash: A Historical View', *Historical Studies*, XVI (1974), p. 116. 'The sight of the various services': *OH*, VI, p. 605. 'the organisation': G.S. Cook to Sir J. Cook, 14 Aug., MC. 'It is not the only evidence': JM to Sir J. Cook, 2 Sept., MC.

384. 'the troops': Sixsmith, *British Generalship*, p. 142. Montgomery's view: A.A. Montgomery, *The Story of the Fourth Army*, p. 30; Prior and Wilson, *Command on the Western Front*, p. 309. 'Amiens type battles': Sixsmith, interview with author, 28 Mar. 1981. 'the black day': Ludendorff, *My War Memories*, 2, pp. 679, 684.

385. German response: GHQ, 'Possible Reinforcement of Somme-Montdidier Front', 6 Aug., MC. Herbertson, 'German Records', p. 206. 'as quickly as possible': Haig, D., 3 Aug.

386. 'considerable magnitude': GHQ OAD 900/13, 5 Aug., File 112/2, Dill Papers. Field Marshal Sir J.G. Dill was then Deputy Chief of the Operations Staff. 'press on': 4 Army 20(G) to corps commanders, 6 Aug., OR. 'There is no intention': JM to GOCs, 1 Aug., MC. 'The Corps': BI 12, 3 Aug., MC. JM pleads with Lawrence and 'to go only for guns': Bean, D116, 6 Aug. 'Monash of course': ibid., 9 Aug.

387. Bean's assertion: *OH*, VI, p. 604. 'in every offensive operation': JM, 'Leadership in War'. Problem of maintaining momentum: B.H. Liddell Hart, *The Liddell Hart Memoirs*, 2 vols, 1, p. 43. 'classic example': *OH*, VI, p. 684. '1 Div - if necessary': JM, 'After Battle of 8 Aug.', 7 Aug., MC.

388. 'It was a decision': *AV*, p. 134. Availability of tanks: BI 1, Series B, 8 Aug., MC.

389. 'so busy congratulating': A. A. Montgomery, '8 August 1918', *Royal Artillery Journal* (reprint), LVI (1929), p. 7. The misunderstanding is described in Nicholson, *Canadian Expeditionary Force*, p. 410.

390. Communications problems: Pedersen, 'Maintaining the advance' in Ekins (ed.), *1918*, p. 137. 'impossible task', Stevenson, *To Win the Battle*, p. 199. Edgar, *Glasgow*, p. 232.

391–92. Attack on 9 Aug: *OH*, VI, pp. 618–19, 636. Attack by 2 Div.: BI 2, Series B, 8 Aug., MC; *OH*, VI, p. 637; 2 Div., 'Report on Operations of 9 Aug. 1918', Blamey Collection.

393. Tank losses: 5 Tank Bde, 'Report on Operations of 9 Aug.', File 925/1, AWRS; *OH*, VI, p. 683.

394. 'a species of investment': *AV*, p. 138. The orders for this attack are contained in BI 3, Series B, 10 Aug., MC. 'The name of the author': McNicol, *The Thirty-Seventh*, p. 222.

395. JM's opinion: quoted in *OH*, VI, p. 685. Plan ingenious: loc. cit. McNicoll's 'incapacity': Gellibrand, D, 9-10 Aug. 'Go as far as you can': Ducane, *Marshal Foch*, p. 61.

396. Haig leans towards halting 4 Army: Haig, D, 8, 10-11 Aug.

397. 'I have most complete confidence': quoted in Bean, D116, 11 Aug. JM criticises Hughes: quoted in Wilson, D, 11 Aug. 'You do not know': Hetherington, *Blamey*, p. 47. 'devote the time': 4 Army, 'Notes of Army Conference', 11 Aug., OR.

398–99. The conspiracy against JM: JM to Hughes, 2 June; to Pearce, 21 June; Murdoch to JM, 6 June; Hobbs to Pearce, 27 June, MC; Bean, D114, 10, 12 June; D115, 16 June; D116, 2 July; *Two Men I Knew*, p. 173; Murdoch to Bean, 12 July, Murdoch Papers.

400. JM wants 'Fighting Honours': quoted in Bean, D116, 7 July. Knighting of JM: JM, 14 Aug., in *WarL*, pp. 259–60; Bean, D116, 21 July, 12 Aug.

Chapter 10

402. The lull and relief of Aust. divs: *AV*, pp. 142–45.

403. 'apparently content': Special Order, 20 Aug., MC.

404. 3 Div. attack on Bray: *OH*, VI, p. 725. 'By the irony of events': *OH*, VI, p. 733. 'which has become a dogma': Liddell Hart to Brig Gen. Dorman-Smith, 26 Nov. 1942, Item I/242/47, Liddell Hart Collection.

REFERENCES

405. 'bent his energies': *AV*, p. 153. 'energetically exploited': *AV*, p. 149. The Fourth Army Order is 4 Army 20/9(G) to corps, 19 Aug., OR. Plan for Chuignes: BI2, Series C, 19 Aug., MC.
406. 'never to entrust': JM, 'Leadership in War'.
407. JM's expansion of the attack: *OH*, VI, p. 735; BIs 3, 21 Aug.; 7, 22 Aug., Series C, MC; JM, 'Notes for Conference', 21 Aug., MC.
408. Narrative of the battle: JM, D, 23 Aug.; Bean, 'Narrative of Aust. Corps Operations to September 1918', MC; *Anzac to Amiens*, p. 477; 5 Tank Bde, 'Report on Operations of 23 Aug. 1918', File 925/1, AWRS; 'Report on Operations of the Australian Corps, Phase C, 15 Aug.-4 Sept. 1918', MC.
409. 'exceptional mental gifts': *AV*, p. 159. 'always understood thoroughly': W.M. Hughes, in Thompson, *On Lips of Living Men*, p. 140. The three directives were: GHQ OADs 911, 22 Aug., MC; 912, 23 Aug., File V2/2, Dill Papers; 907113, 24 Aug., 4 Army Papers, Rawlinson Collection, IWM.
410. 'no opportunity': 4 Army G38 to corps, 24 Aug., Montgomery-Massingberd Papers. 'troops to rest': Haig, D, 25 Aug. 'The Fourth Army': *AV*, pp. 166–67. 'The offensive policy': BI 10, Series C, 26 Aug., MC.
411. 'wily corps commander ... further operation': Prior and Wilson, *Command on the Western Front*, pp. 341–42. 'press back enemy rearguards': 4 Army G100 to corps, 27 Aug., Montgomery-Massingberd Papers. 'the limits of its endurance': *AV*, p. 167. Haig's suggestion is in Haig, D, 23 Aug. Decentralisation to divs: Simpson, *Directing Operations*, pp. 162–65, 226.
412. German withdrawal likely: *OH*, VI, pp. 780–81.
413–15. JM's orders for crossing the Somme: BI 12, Series C, 28 Aug., MC. 'A costly enterprise' and 'this was the plan': *AV*, p. 176. The new plan: BI 13, Series C, 29 Aug.; JM, 'Notes for Conference', 29 Aug., MC.
416. Importance of rebuilding crossings: *AV*, pp. 165–66. Comments on the battle: JM, 8 Sept., in *WarL*, p. 266; Smithers, *Sir John Monash*, pp. 247–48; *OH*, VI, p. 873.
417. 'And so you think': *AV*, p. 181. 'Once again': Prior and Wilson, *Command on the Western Front*, p. 342.
418. 'not meant to be rigidly adhered to': 4 Army 20/15(G) to corps, 30 Aug., OR. Rosenthal's orders: 2 Div., 'Report on Operations 26/27 Aug.-4/5 Sept. 1918', 20 Sept., Blamey Collection. 40 Bn clears Cléry: *OH*, VI, pp. 801–02.
419. 'On 31 August': Terraine, *To Win a War*, p.129. Germans unnerved: Farndale, *Western Front*, p. 295. 5 Bde strength: 2 Div., 'Report on Operations'.
420. '5 Bde report': 2 Div. to Aust. Corps, 8 am, 31 Aug., '2 Div. War Diary'. 'Casualties': quoted in *OH*, VI, p. 822. Elliott arrests COs: Bean, D116, 30 Aug. 14 Bde crosses: *AV*, p. 188. 'busy settling down': JM, D, 31 Aug.
423–23. Criticism of Hobbs and Stewart: quoted in Bean, D116, 1 Sept.
424. Clearance of Péronne: 5 Div., 'Report on Operations 31 Aug.-2 Sept. 1918', 19 Sept., File 75/38, AWRS.
425. White on Mont St Quentin: White to Chauvel, 7 Aug. 1926, White Collection. AIF view: *OH*, VI, p. 873. Rawlinson's view: Serle, *Monash*, p. 356. The remainder of this paragraph is based on *AV*, pp. 177, 193; *OH*, VI, p. 873.
426. 'to harden my heart': *AV*, p. 194.
427. The tactical notes are in *The Operations of the Australian Corps in France, 1 July–8 Oct. 1918*, p. 31 (AWM). This pamphlet was published by the Aust. Army in 1923 as a summary of the campaign and its lessons. 'some experience': *AV*, p. 176.

MONASH

428. Ludendorff uncertain and approves withdrawal: *My War Memories*, 2, pp. 695–96; Foerster, *Ludendorff im Unglück*, p. 55. Aust. effort a waste: B. Pitt, *1918 The Last Act*, pp. 217–19. 'I have no wish': Haig, D, 31 Aug. 'vigorous action': GHQ OAD 907/16, 29 Aug., 4 Army Records, Rawlinson Collection. Prisoners' statements: quoted in 2 Div. to Aust. Corps, 1 Sept., MC. Rawlinson determined to turn Somme: Montgomery, *The Story of the Fourth Army*, p. 97.
429. Haig slows 4 Army: GHQ OAD 915, 3 Sept., File I/2/2, Dill Papers. Haig displeased: Haig, D, 6 Sept. 'the rearguard fighting': Cutlack, *The Australians*, p. 301. JM forecasts set piece: JM, 'Notes for Advance to the Hindenburg Line', 7 Sept., MC. 'at no great cost': Rawlinson to GHQ, 11 Sept., Montgomery-Massingberd Papers.
430–31. Planning the attack: *AV*, pp. 221–24; *OH*, VI, p. 890; 4 Army 20/18(G), 19(G), 13-14 Sept., OR; JM, 'Notes for Conference', 13, 16 Sept., MC.
432. Narrative of the battle: 'Aust. Corps, Fourth Army War Diaries', 18 Sept.; 'Report on Operations of the Australian Corps, Phase D, 4-20 Sept. 1918', MC; *AV*, p. 223; Bean, *Anzac to Amiens*, p. 486.
433. 'he was clearly right': Bean, D116, 18 Sept.
434–45. JM's exhaustion: Bean, D116, 4 Sept.; Lt. Gen. J.J. Hobbs, D, 1 Aug., notes lent to author by A.J. Hill. JM to Rawlinson, 7 Sept.; to Dodds, 2 Oct., MP; Blamey in *Reveille*, 31 Oct. 1931, p. 10. JM on tiredness of the Aust. Corps: Terraine, *The Smoke and the Fire*, p. 201; JM, 11 Sept., 'War Letters' (typescript), p. 456; *AV*, p. 202; *OH*, VI, pp. 487–88, 940; Bean, D116, 6 Aug., 4, 8, 21 Sept. British Army: Sheffield, *Command and Morale*, p. 134; and *Forgotten Victory*, p. 251.
436. 'a lavish hand': Bean, D116, 21 Aug., 4 Sept. Ordered to grant furlough: Birdwood to JM, 12 Sept., MP.
437. Anzac leave: JM to Birdwood, 15 Sept.; Birdwood's reply, 16 Sept., MP; Elliott to wife, 23 Sept., Elliott Collection; Bean, D116, 17 Sept.; *OH*, VI, p. 879; Hughes in *Daily Guardian*, 9 June 1930.
438–39. The disbandment mutinies: *OH*, VI, p. 896; Lawrence to Birdwood, 22 June, File 721175, AWRS; JM to Dodds, 7 Sept., 26 Sept., MP; McNicol, *The Thirty-seventh*, pp. 248, 258; Bean, D117, 27 Sept.; JM to GOCs, 23 Sept., MC; JM, 'Meeting with 37 Bn Representatives', 24 Sept., MC; JM to Murdoch, 15 Apr. 1919, Murdoch Papers.
439. Wilson's warning: quoted in Haig, D, 1 Sept. 'What a wretched lot!': Haig to Wilson, 1 Sept., File 7B, Wilson Correspondence, IWM.
440. 'a task': *AV*, p. 242. 'a fairly accurate idea': 4 Army to Corps, 7 Sept., Blamey Papers. The description of the Hindenburg Line is based largely on GHQ, 'Tactical Appreciation of the Various Sectors of the Hindenburg Line-Div. Sector No. 1', 8 Sept., MC.
441. Bean on JM's plan: *Anzac to Amiens*, p. 489. The plan is reproduced in full in *AV*, pp. 236–40.
442. 'In this modification': *AV*, p. 241. Rawlinson's alterations: *OH*, VI, p. 948.
443. 'It will be cheaper': JM, 'Plan for Beaurevoir Offensive', 21 Sept., MC.
444. JM claims agreement with Rawlinson: *AV*, p. 241. 'pull out of the barrage': JM, 'Plan for Beaurevoir Offensive'. Control of movement: JM, 'Organization of Roads and Traffic and Troop Movement', 25 Sept., MC. 'The principle of allotment': BI 10, Series E, 25 Sept., MC.
445. JM's notes for this conference are in MC. 'this operation': Gellibrand, 'The Action of the 3rd Australian Division at Bony 29 Sept–1 Oct. 1918', Gellibrand Collection. 'no reason to hesitate': *AV*, pp. 235–36. 'based upon the assumption': quoted in *AV*, pp. 236–37. Haig-Butler exchange: *OH*, VI, p. 951; Haig, D, 22 Sept.
446. Eisenhower's remark: M.A. Yockelson, *Borrowed soldiers*, p. xii.

REFERENCES

447. 'one job for each man': JM, 'Notes for Conference (American)', 22 Sept. JM on conference: *AV*, p. 248. 'there was not': J.F. O'Ryan, *The Story of the 27th Division*, p. 254. Bean's criticism is in *Reveille*, 31 Oct. 1931, p. 2. Other historians: e.g. Sadler, *The Paladin*, p. 175. 'a larger job': Bean, D117, 27 Sept. American casualties at Hamel: Bean, *Anzac to Amiens*, p. 462.
448. Poor training of Americans: Elliott to wife, 28 Aug., Elliott Collection; Rawlinson to Wilson, 23 Aug., Rawlinson Collection, NAM; Brig. Gen. W. J. Duggan, 'Notes on Visit to 2nd American Corps 6-9 Nov. 1918', Maxse Papers. Success of mustard gas: 4 Army, 'Notes of Fourth Army's Attack on the Hindenburg Line', 29 Sept., OR. Australian Mission: Aust. Corps GS Circular 37, 20 Sept., MC; *AV*, p. 244.
449. Haig's arrival: Haig, D, 26 Sept. American attack unsuccessful: JM, D, 27 Sept; *OH*, VI, p. 983; 'Operation Report of the 27th Division AEF, 23 Sept.-21 Oct. 1918', OR; O'Ryan, *The Story of the 27th Division*, p. 300; G.A.B. Dewar and J.H. Boraston, *Sir Douglas Haig's Command*, I, p. 326.
450. JM's anxiety: Haig, D, 28 Sept. 'success of the operation': Sheffield, *The chief*, pp. 322–23; *OH*, VI, p. 956. 'John gave us': Bean, D117, 28 Sept.
451. Tank losses: 5 Tank Bde, 'Report on Operations 29 Sept.–5 Oct. 1918', OR. 46 Div. crossing: Smithers, *Sir John Monash*, p. 268.
452. 'By 10 o'clock': *OH*, VI, p. 995. 'Well you see': quoted in Bean, D117, 30 Sept. 'a miserable fiasco': JM to Bean, 15 Nov. 1929, File 106.1, AWM. Conflicting reports to Aust. Corps: from 3 Div., 9.05 am, 29 Sept., OR; 30 Div., 10 am, MC; pilot quoted in *OH*, VI, p. 976.
453. 'dug in on west side ... hastened forward': *AV*, p. 261. Gellibrand says JM merely telephoned: comments on *AV*. Gellibrand goes forward: 'The Action of the 3rd Australian Division at Bony'. 'will no doubt': Jess to Cannan, 11.40 am; to McNicoll, 11.50 am, 29 Sept., OR. Blamey adamant: Blamey to Gellibrand, 1.10 pm, 29 Sept., OR. 'The movement round': JM to Jess, 4.05 pm, 29 Sept., Gellibrand Collection.
454. 'slow and methodical': *AV*, p. 267. 'All done up': Sig. C.J. Britton, D, 1 Oct., MS1396, Mitchell Library. JM-Gellibrand exchange: telephone conversation, 5.15 pm, Gellibrand Collection.
455. JM's performance: *The Operations of the Australian Corps in France*, p. 43; Bean, D117, 30 Sept.; Gellibrand quoted in Serle, *John Monash*, p. 367. JM's apology and congratulations: Sadler, *Paladin*, p. 180.
456. The narrative of the Montbrehain attack is drawn from *AV*, p. 278; 2 Div., 'Report on Operations 3-5 Oct. 1918', Blamey Collection; *OH*, VI, p. 1043.
458. The achievements of the Aust. Corps are listed in *AV*, pp. 284–86.

Chapter 11

459. 'a vision of the needs of Australia': *OH*, VI, p. 1057.
460. JM's funeral: Serle, *John Monash*, pp. 526–27. Opinions of JM: B.H. Liddell Hart, *Through the Fog of War*, p. 149; Taylor, *The First World War*, p. 232; B.L.M. Montgomery, *A History of Warfare*, p. 494.
463. Glasgow on JM: Edgar, *Sir William Glasgow*, p. 219. JM not strong on invention: quoted in *OH*, VI, p. 207.
464. 'For my part': Gellibrand, comments on *AV*. The most affectionate: Blamey in *Reveille*, 31 Oct. 1931, p. 10. Corps HQ and JM: Serle, *John Monash*, pp. 330, 381. 'Whether Monash possessed the ruthless will': *OH*, VI, p. 1092. JM seeks honours: JM to Birdwood, 2 Oct.; to Read, 24 Dec. 1918, MP.
465. 'He was keenly ambitious': Bazley in *Reveille*, 1 May 1937, p. 15.

466. JM and AIF: This para based on Serle, *John Monash*, pp. 391, 467, 525. 'with such an army': Serle, *John Monash*, p. 396. 'Monash beat all': Gellibrand, comments on *AV*.
467. 'Birdwood was always buzzing about': JM to F. Swinburne (SEC), 20 July 1925, MP.
468. Criticism of Birdwood: White, quoted in Bean, D113, 30 May; White to Gellibrand, 8 June 1917, Gellibrand Collection; Gellibrand, 'Touching Birdwood', c.11 Nov. 1918, ibid. 'quite futile': JM to Walter Rosenhain, 20 June 1916, MP. 'There was never any sign': *OH*, VI, p. 208. 'a force which finds itself': JM, 'Leadership in War'.
469. 'top down approach': Pugsley, *Anzac Experience*, p. 212. 'No use keeping a dog', Foott to *Reveille*, 3 Apr. 1937, BC.
470. Glasgow on JM: Edgar, *Sir William Glasgow*, p. 219. Others could have achieved same results: Gammage in *Historical Studies*, p. 114. 'Never': Cutlack: *WarL*.
471–72. JM and Haig: D. Lloyd George, *War Memoirs of David Lloyd George*, 6 vols, 4, pp. 2267–68; 6, p. 3424; H.M. Urquhart, *Arthur Currie*, p. 227; Terraine in *History Today*, p. 14; Sixsmith to author, 16 Aug. 1979. 'could have submitted': Serle, *John Monash*, p. 378.
472. Bean on JM: Serle, *John Monash*, p. 398. JM made the claim on technical mastery in 'Leadership in War'.
473. 'went into action': *OH*, VI, p. 1092.

Appendix 1

474. Hamilton's views were promulgated as a Special Army Corps Order, 20 May. Copy in MC. Birdwood unsure who mooted northern breakout: Birdwood to Bean, 21 Aug. 1922, 'Historical Notes: Battle of Sari Bair'. 'an attack, once the crest': 'Notes on the Situation Immediately Confronting Anzac', File 367/150, AWRS. This important document merits closer examination. Bean was unsure of its date, writing across the head 'about June 1915', and did not use it in the *Official History*. He also omits Birdwood's letter to Hamilton of 13 May, mentioned by Aspinall-Oglander, whose contents are identical to the letter above. Hence it is probable that this document is the appreciation on which that letter was based. The emphasis on Hill 971, the three-pronged attack on that feature, Gaba Tepe and Gun Ridge, and the limitation of Birdwood's request for reinforcements to the Indian Brigade, date it about mid-May and certainly not June.
475. 'action in certain contingencies: Hamilton to Birdwood, 17 May, File 5/10, Hamilton Papers. 'no assault on it': Birdwood to Hamilton, 30 May, Birdwood Collection.
476. 'unfortunate striving': North, *Gallipoli*, p. 223. Bean's assertion: *OH*, II, p. 456. 'The decisive point': Godley, 'Plan of Attack on Ridge 971', c. 23 June, File 367/235, AWRS. The late ANZAC appreciation: 'Summary of Situation at Anzac', 9 July, is in File 367/53(6), AWRS. Birdwood aware of the hazards: 'Notes on the Situation Immediately Confronting Anzac'; Birdwood to Hamilton, 30 May; Birdwood, 'Proposals for Using Reinforcements', 1 July, 'Historical Notes: Battle of Sari Bair'; Birdwood to Kitchener, 9 July, Birdwood Collection.
477. Godley's attitude: Godley, 'Plan of Attack on Ridge 971'. Skeen's pessimism is quoted in Walker to Bean, 23 Sept. 1923, 'Historical Notes: Battle of Sari Bair'.

A note on sources

Much of the vast literature on World War I has been written in the shadow of the official histories, British and Australian. Although the work of Brigadier General Sir James Edmonds was always controversial, it is an enduring tribute to the quality of Charles Bean's volumes that the arguments and conclusions of their author have only recently begun to be challenged – and to a limited extent even then. New evidence has made some of his judgements, such as on Monash, questionable. Bean's view of the history's purpose as an inspirational tool for a young nation, as well as a memorial to the men who made it, has become a subject of debate. His assessments of the other AIF commanders, whom he knew personally, were written when most were alive. They now co-exist with more detailed studies completed without that constraint.

But Bean's narrative of what happened on the ground is still considered sound, and so forms the basis of a wealth of other writing. Perhaps unsurprisingly then, many of the secondary sources consulted contained little that Bean – or Edmonds – had not said before. Only the more useful publications have been included in the bibliography.

The distinction between official and other sources also presents difficulty. No complete set of OADs is held in a single location either in Australia or Britain, while many operational reports of Australian formations in 1917–18 could not be found in the AWRS or Operational Records files. Often, however, they were located within individual collections. Most of the important OADs are distributed among the papers of Haig, Rawlinson, Montgomery and Dill. Similarly, the report of the 3rd Division's attack on the Hindenburg Line and Gellibrand's telephone exchanges with Monash and Blamey are part of the Gellibrand Collection. The Monash Collection contains all the 3rd Division's orders up to 31 May 1918 and the Battle Instructions for the Australian Corps thereafter. Translations of German documents are in the White Papers. Many official documents were used in this work, but lack of space precluded listing each of them in the bibliography under the collection in which it is held. As long as the approximate date of the document is known, referencing information on it can be found in the endnotes for the operation or period concerned.

Nevertheless, some significant gaps remain. Mystery surrounds many aspects of the origins of the 4th Brigade's attack on Hill 971 on 8 August 1915 and the 2nd Division's assault on Montbrehain on 5 October 1918. Suspicions that Monash may have destroyed his own records on these operations because they reflected poorly on him have to be considered against the lack of pertinent material in the official sources. Of the records of all the Australian generals, though, Monash's are easily the most voluminous and the best. Only one of his divisional commanders, Gellibrand, left a substantial collection. Two of them, Glasgow and Sinclair-MacLagan, left nothing at all.

Select Bibliography

This bibliography has been arranged under the following headings:
I. The Monash Papers
II. Official Sources
   A. Manuscript
   B. Printed
III. Other Sources
   A. Manuscript
   B. Official Histories
   C. Unpublished Theses
   D. Newspapers
   E. Books &c. by Monash
   F. Books &c. on Monash
   G. Books and articles
   H. Correspondence and Interviews
   I. Battlefield Inspections

I. THE MONASH PAPERS

AUSTRALIA

NATIONAL LIBRARY OF AUSTRALIA, CANBERRA

The author was generously allowed limited access to Monash's vast personal collection, then held at Monash University, Melbourne, by Dr Geoffrey Serle at the same time as Dr Serle was writing the authoritative biography. The collection has since been returned to the National Library as MS1884. Sixteen boxes were consulted. They contained the following:

Pre-war Military Papers

Correspondence with McCay and HQ 3MD on AIC or 13 Bde matters.

Instructions, problems and answers for exercises and courses attended by Monash as a student and instructor.

MONASH

Lectures by Monash on various military subjects, such as reconnaissance, staff duties and administration.

Orders, memos, memoranda and instructions for the NM Battery, AIC and 13 Bde.

Records of the Victorian Section of the Intelligence Corps, including the Corps Diary.

Umpire's reports by Monash on manoeuvres conducted at Easter Camps, 1908–13.

Monash's 'Military Affairs Diary, 1884–1914', listing all militia parades attended by Monash in the period and the pay he received for them. Also contains personal particulars of members of the NM Battery.

Pre-war lectures and manuscripts on non-military subjects (*see* Books and Articles by Monash).

Biographical sketches by Mathilde (Mat) Monash and Colonel George Farlow.

Wartime Military Papers

Outletters

> Two correspondence books for the period 28 May–7 November 1915, containing letters to Godley, Cox, Russell, Chauvel, Legge, Burnage, Cannan and Pope; reports on actions 2/3, 9/10 May.
>
> Sixteen private and official letter-books for the period 28 May 1915–7 November 1918, mainly containing letters to Vic and Gibson, but some to Godley, McCay, McGlinn, Russell and other commanders.
>
> Monash to HQ 3MD, Legge, Bruche and McGlinn on the raising of 4 Bde and its departure for Egypt.
>
> Monash to Jobson, Rosenthal, McNicoll, Cannan and many British and Australian senior officers, including Plumer, Rawlinson, Harington, Montgomery, Birdwood, Godley and White, on matters relating to the Western Front.

SELECT BIBLIOGRAPHY

Inletters

Mostly military, 1916–18, including letters from Cannan, Pope, Courtney, Burnage, Rankin, Dare, Durrant, Godley, Birdwood, White, Chauvel, Cox, McNicoll, Rosenthal, Glasgow, Sinclair-MacLagan, Gellibrand, Hobbs, Dodds and Harington.

Personal Diaries for 1915, 1916, 1917 and 1918.

Press Cuttings 1914–18.

Post-war Papers

Articles and lectures on military and engineering subjects, interviews *(see* Books and Articles by Monash).

AUSTRALIAN WAR MEMORIAL, CANBERRA

Sixteen boxes of Wartime Military Papers, held as 3DRL 2316 and consisting of:

Monash's confidential correspondence with Hughes, Pearce, Munro Ferguson and Murdoch.

Many letters to and from the Australian and British commanders listed above.

Personal particulars completed by Monash for the AWRS.

Typescript of 'War Letters of General Monash' (the unedited typescript, later published as *War Letters of General Monash*, ed. F.M. Cutlack).

Notes for lectures to the 3rd Division.

Agenda and some minutes for conferences of the 3rd Division and Australian Corps. The Ravelsberg conference is the most complete.

Battle messages and signals to and from Headquarters 4th Brigade, 3rd Division and Australian Corps.

Operational and administrative appreciations and plans for the 3rd Division and Australian Corps.

Operation orders for the 4th Brigade, 3rd Division and Australian Corps.

Operational Reports and Narratives for the 4th Brigade, 3rd Division and Australian Corps.

Miscellaneous material on the Australian Corps prepared by Monash for Dr John Springthorpe, including a general narrative of operations by Bean.

OLD SCOTCH COLLEGIANS ASSOCIATION, MELBOURNE

Monash's academic record at Scotch College, 1877–81.

ARCHIVES OF THE STATE ELECTRICITY COMMISSION OF VICTORIA, MELBOURNE

Monash's letter to George Swinburne, dated 20 July 1925, on the command of the Australian Corps.

UNIVERSITY OF MELBOURNE

Letter-book of pre-war military correspondence.

Monash's academic record at Melbourne University, 1882–1921.

II. OFFICIAL SOURCES

A. Manuscript

AUSTRALIA

AUSTRALIAN WAR MEMORIAL, CANBERRA

Australian War Records Section Files

Following the example of the Canadian Expeditionary Force, the AWRS was established in 1917, under Major John Treloar, as part of the AIF. Its branches in England, France, Egypt and Palestine collected unit war records, maps and newspapers, as well as directing the work of official war artists and photographers. The collection ranges from unit routine orders and administrative instructions to records of AIF conferences; operational orders and reports, especially those pertaining to Gallipoli; tactical doctrine for the period 1916-18; some intelligence reports and reports on the employment of weapons. The following files were consulted:

File 41/1:   Armistice of 24 May 1915 – various reports.

SELECT BIBLIOGRAPHY

File 75/8:	France, employment of artillery and the general scheme of artillery working and organization.
File 75/38:	5 Div. Reports on Operations, Sept.-Oct. 1918.
File 213/1:	*Conferences:* GS 2 and 4 Armies, 1916-18. GS 1 and 2 Anzac, 1916-18. GS 3 Div. 1917-18. GS 1-5 divs 1917-18.
File 243/14:	Defence Schemes, Aust. Corps, 1918.
File 367/4:	Copies of records compiled by Lt. Col. F.S. Rosenskjar – 'Anzac–Landing of Covering Force April 1915'.
File 367/37 (1) to (8)	4 Bde Signals and Reports, Gallipoli, Aug.-Dec. 1915.
File 367/44:	Anzac GS, Messages and Signals, May-Dec. 1915.
File 367/52:	Gallipoli Phase 1. Signals and Instructions, Anzac GS, Mar.-July 1915.
File 367/53 (6):	Anzac–Signals and Instructions, Feb.-July 1915.
File 367/86:	Gallipoli Phase 1. NZ & A Div. and 4 Bde, Signals, Reports and Casualties.
File 367/87 (1):	Gallipoli Phase 1. GS 1 Div., Action Signals 24-30 Apr. 1915.
File 367/89 (1) and (2)	Gallipoli Phase 1. NZ & A Div. GS, Apr.-Aug. 1915.
File 367/104:	Gallipoli Phase 1. NZ & A Div., Miscellaneous, May-July 1915.
File 367/115:	Gallipoli Phase 1. 13, 14, 15, 16 bns, Apr.-July 1915.
File 367/150:	Notes dealing with the situation confronting Anzac, June 1915.
File 367/173:	Gallipoli, Daily Reports, NZ & A Div.
File 367/224:	Messages and Signals, 1 Div., NZ & A Div., 29 Apr. 1915.

File 367/235: Report on operations against Sari Bair, 6-10 Aug. 1915, of forces under the command of Maj. Gen. Godley.

File 519/26: 4 Bde operations on Suez, Feb. 1915.

File 707/3: Routine Orders, NZ & A Div., Dec. 1914-Feb. 1916.

File 707/9 (1) to (7): Routine Orders for 4 Bde and 13, 14, 15, 16 bns, Oct. 1914-Dec. 1916.

File 721/75: Reorganization of Infantry Brigades on a Three Battalion Basis, 1918.

File 925/1: 5 Tank Brigade Orders, Instructions and Reports on Operations with the Aust. Corps, Aug. 1918.

File 941/2: Training, Infantry, Egypt, 1914-16.

File 943/19: Special Training Order by Brig. Gen. Monash, Ismailia, 1916.

File 947/34: Training, France, Infantry: 3 Div. HQ, 1916.

File 947/37: Training, France, Infantry: 3 Div. HQ, 1917.

Operational Records Files

Not completely opened until the end of 1980, these files were among the principal source materials for the four volumes of the *Official History* covering AIF operations on the Western Front. Bean and the AWM staff divided the AIF's time in France and Belgium into twelve periods, giving each a date and title. All material relating to a particular period was then arranged into a number of sub-periods, breaking down this vast collection into a number of smaller, more manageable segments. The following files were consulted:

Box 191, Item 3: 2 ANZAC GS, 1-19 May 1917.
Item 7: 2 ANZAC GS, 30 June-30 July 1917.
Item 28: 3 Div. GS, 1-19 May 1917.
Item 29: 3 Div. GS, 20 May-6 June 1917.

Box 209, Item 7: 2 Army Intelligence, 1-10 Oct. 1917.
Item 8: 2 Army Intelligence, 11-23 Oct. 1917.

SELECT BIBLIOGRAPHY

Box 250, Item 2: 3 Div. GS, 5-23 Sept. 1917.
    Item 3: 3 Div. GS, 24-30 Sept. 1917.
    Item 4: 3 Div. GS, 1-10 Oct. 1917.
    Item 5: 3 Div. GS, 11-23 Oct. 1917.
Box 345, Item 15: GHQ BEF, 22 May-1June 1917.
Box 350, Item 6: 4 Army Intelligence, 16-18 June 1918.
Box 358, Item 16: Tank Corps HQ, 16-28 June 1918.
    Item 17: Tank Corps HQ, 29 June-12 July 1918.
Box 360, Item 3: Aust. Corps GS, 8-20 Apr. 1918.
Box 361, Item 1: Aust. Corps GS, 2-15 June 1918.
    Item 2: Aust. Corps GS, 16-28 June 1918.
    Item 3: Aust. Corps, 29 June-12 July 1918.
Box 408, Item 4: 4 Div. GS, 16-28 June 1918.
    Item 5: 4 Div. GS, 29 June-12 July 1918.
Box 472, Item 2: 4 Army GS, 5-12 Aug. 1918.
    Item 4: 4 Army GS and Intelligence, 13-21 Aug. 1918.
Box 473, Item 1: 4 Army GS, 27 Aug.-5 Sept. 1918.
    Item 4: 4 Army GS, 11-24 Sept. 1918.
Box 474, Item 1: 4 Army GS, 25 Sept.-2 Oct. 1918.
Box 481, Item 3: Tank Corps HQ, 25 Sept.-2 Oct. 1918.
    Item 8: Tank Corps HQ–Proposals for the Offensive Use of Tanks 1918, based on the Cambrai Experience.
Box 487, Item 2: 27 Div. AEF, Aug.-Oct. 1918.
Box 488, Item 2: Aust. Corps GS, 5-12 Aug. 1918.
Box 489, Item 1: Aust. Corps GS, 27 Aug.-5 Sept. 1918.

War diaries of Australian formations and units that served under Monash, 1914-18. The worth of diaries varied considerably. Some contained no more than a daily entry of one line, while others, especially those of the 15th Battalion, 10th Brigade, 2nd, 3rd and NZ & A divisions, 2nd ANZAC and the Australian Corps, were rich sources.

MONASH

Final Report of the Dardanelles Royal Commission, 1917.

Operations of the Australian Corps in France, 1 July-5 Oct. 1918, published by the Australian Army Staff, 1923.

German Records Relative to Australian Operations on the Western Front (Class No. 111.05), compiled by Captain J.J. Herbertson.

File 106.1: Correspondence and Miscellaneous Matters relating to the *Official History.*

File 12/3/71: Enquiry from Monash concerning a letter signed by him, suggesting a large-scale attack and outlining the plan. Date of letter 4-30 July 1918.

AUSTRALIAN ARCHIVES, MELBOURNE

Defence Correspondence Files, Multiple Number Series with A, B, D, or E Prefix 1913-17, A2023 (ex MP133/2):

    File A73/4/306:   13 Infantry Brigade Camp, Press Reports.

Defence Correspondence Files, Multiple Number Series 1906-17, A289 (ex MP84/1):

File 311/3/126:	Abolition of HQ AIC. Disposition of Monash, Semmens and Holdsworth.
File 1849/2/24:	Major Monash to transfer to AIC.
File 1849/2/237:	Employment of AIC officers at camps of training.
File 1849/2/260:	OC Int. Corps (McCay) granted leave.
File 1862/7/213:	Foster's Schools and Courses, Oct.-Dec. 1911.
File 1902/7/66:	Review of results obtained by the AIC, 1908-10.
File 1954/23/99:	Gold Medal Essay, 1912. Essays and Judges' Criticisms.

Defence Correspondence Files, Annual Single Number Series 1901-06, B168:

    File 06/3198:   Major J. Monash. 'C.A.F.O.' Decoration, 1906.

Defence Secret and Confidential Correspondence Files, Multiple

SELECT BIBLIOGRAPHY

Number Series 1906-36, B197:

    File 1975/2/11:   Progress reports by the CGS, 1913-14.

Defence Correspondence Files, Multiple Number Series with AIF Prefix 1914-17, B539:

    File 13/2/12:   Colonel Monash Appointed to the Command of the 4th Brigade.

    File 112/2/441:   Despatches from Bridges and AIF Base Egypt, 1915-16.

    File 112/2/489:   Despatch 10 from Bridges, dated 6 Apr. 1915.

    File A112/6/43:   Despatches from Bridges and AIF HQ 1914-16; letters on various subjects by Mc.Anderson and Sellheim.

    File 264/1/164:   Training and Equipment of 41 and 42 bns, March 1916.

    File 264/1/181:   Training and Equipment of 43 Bn, April 1916.

Victorian Department of Defence Correspondence Files, Annual Single Number Series 1879-1901, MP106:

    File 1890-1294 B6: Victorian Department of Defence Correspondence, 1879-1900.

GREAT BRITAIN

THE NATIONAL ARCHIVES, LONDON

CAB 23/1:   War Cabinet Paper 40, Requirements for Home Defence, 22 Jan. 1917.

WO 33/1305:   Notes on Certain Lessons of the Great War, 6 Apr. 1933.

WO 95/275:   War Diary, Second Army.

WO 158/28:   Foch-Haig Correspondence, 23 Mar.-31 May 1918.

WO 158/84:   Correspondence between Colonel C.J.C. Grant and the Director of Military Operations at the War Office.

ROYAL MARINES MUSEUM, SOUTHEND

ACQ B/1/185-ARCH 11/13/24(A): War Diary, Royal Marine Brigade, Dardanelles, 1915-16.

WEST GERMANY BUNDESARCHIV—MILITÄRARCHIV, FREIBURG

File PH 3/61: Ludendorffs Strategie vom April bis Oktober 1918 (Potsdam, Herbst, 1944, fur den Präsident der Kriegsgeschichtlichen Forschungsamtanstalt des Heeres). Possibly prepared by the German Army Staff, because it was facing in autumn 1944 a situation similar to Ludendorff's in the latter half of 1918.

File PH 51/45: Heeresgruppe Rupprecht: Westoperationen 1918.

B. Printed

Commonwealth Parliamentary Debates, LXXIV, 21 May-26 June 1914.

Commonwealth Gazettes: 71: 12 Dec. 1903.
15: 28 Mar. 1908.
45: 21 June 1913.
74: 19 Sept. 1914.

Official Yearbook of the Commonwealth of Australia, vol. 1, Melbourne, 1908.

Victorian Government Gazettes: 120: 18 Oct. 1895.
99: 25 Sept. 1896.
42: 9 Apr. 1897.

Victoria–Reports of the Council of Defence 1886-1900, Bound volume, Class. No. 301.012, AWM.

III. OTHER SOURCES

A. Manuscript

AUSTRALIA

AUSTRALIAN WAR MEMORIAL, CANBERRA

Bazley, A. Papers including correspondence with H. V. Howe on Gallipoli (3DRL 3520).

SELECT BIBLIOGRAPHY

Bean, C.E.W. (AWM 38). Diaries and notebooks containing material on Monash at Gallipoli and the Western Front. The following were used: Diaries 1, 2, 3, 5, 6, 7, 8, 9, 10, 11, 14, 15, 26, 28, 41, 43, 65, 90, 91, 92, 93, 99, 103, 116, 117, 128, 146. Notebook 276, 'Appreciation of Individual Soldiers', contains correspondence used in the Official History and for the compilation of Reveille articles on Monash and other Australian commanders.

Historical Notes, Gallipoli. These files are the equivalent of the Operational Records files for the Gallipoli Campaign. They consist of correspondence with soldier and general alike on aspects of operations at Anzac and Helles. The following files were consulted:

    Gallipoli

    Higher Command on the Landing

    1st Division Orders for Anzac Landing

    4th Brigade Landing

    Landing Operations, 4th Brigade

    Anzac: Apr.-Aug.

    Attack on Baby 700, 2/3 May

    Attack at Quinn's Post, 9/10 May

    Turkish Attack at Anzac, 19 May

    Turkish Attack at Quinn's Post, 29 May

    Battle of Sari Bair

    Suvla

    Evacuation of Anzac

Australian Historical Mission File 11: Questions to and Answers by Turkish General Staff re Operations on Gallipoli.

Official Historian's Notes: Records of Colonel H. Pope (includes Pope's Diary).

Gallipoli Correspondence with the British Official Historian.

MONASH

Western Front Correspondence with the British Official Historian.

Birdwood, Field Marshal Lord. Collection, 1914-19 (3DRL 3376).

Blamey, Field Marshal Sir Thomas. Papers 1914-18, including Divisional Operations Reports, 1918 (3DRL 6643).

Cox, General Sir H.V. Papers and Diary, 1915-17 (1DRL 0221).

Elliott, Major General H.E. Papers (2DRL 0513).

Godley, General Sir A.J. Correspondence, 1914-17 (3DRL 2233).

Morshead, Lieutenant General Sir L.J. Papers 1916-18 (3DRL 2632).

Pearce, Sir George. Papers relating to war of 1914-18 (3DRL 2222).

Gellibrand, Major General Sir J. Papers including diary 1914-18 and 3 Div. Operational Reports and Battle Messages, 1918 (3DRL 1473 and 6541).

White, General Sir Brudenell. Papers including GHQ translations of captured German documents (3DRL 6549).

Source notes for battalion histories.

File 8/10: 13 Bn AIF–A Brief History.

File 8/13: File entitled 14 Bn History.

MITCHELL LIBRARY, SYDNEY

Britton, Sig. C.J. Diary, 1918.

Compton, Sig. A.R. Diary, 1915.

Crooks, Lt T.R. Diary, 1915.

McLintock, Pte G.T. Diary, 1915.

Marks, Colonel D. Diary, 1914-15.

Nixon, Pte Rupert. Correspondence, 1914-15.

Peters, Captain C.H. Letters 1917-18 and account of 'The Big Raid'.

Rosenthal, Major General Sir Charles. Diary, 1914-19.

SELECT BIBLIOGRAPHY

Whitehead, D.A. Papers re 9 Inf. Bde.

NATIONAL LIBRARY OF AUSTRALIA, CANBERRA

Hughes, W.M. Papers (MS 1538, Series 23).

Murdoch, Sir Keith. Papers (MS 2383).

Novar, Viscount. Papers of Sir Ronald Munro Ferguson, 1914-18 (MS 696).

GREAT BRITAIN

IMPERIAL WAR MUSEUM, LONDON

Ataturk, 'Memoirs of the Anafartalar Battles'.

Birdwood, Field Marshal Lord. Correspondence with Col. D. Rintoul.

Bridges, Major General Sir William. Diary, 1914-15.

Dawnay, Major General G.P. Papers.

Ducane, General Sir J.P. 'Marshal Foch' (1920).

McGrigor, Captain A.M. Diary, 1915-18.

Maxse, General Sir Ivor. Papers, 1916-18, including operational and training reports as GOC 18 Div and as IG Training.

Rawlinson, Field Marshal Lord. Fourth Army Collection.

Wilson, Field Marshal Sir Henry. Papers and Diary, 1917-18.

LIDDELL HART CENTRE FOR MILITARY ARCHIVES, KING'S COLLEGE, UNIVERSITY OF LONDON

Dill, Field Marshal Sir J.G. Papers 1917-18.

Edmonds, Brigadier General Sir J. E. Papers.

Hamilton, General Sir Ian. Diary and Papers, 1914-17, including evidence to the Dardanelles Commission.

Kiggell, Lieutenant General Sir L.E. Papers.

Liddell Hart, Captain Sir B.H. Papers including records of interview with commanders, senior staff officers and politicians, book reviews and thoughts on the 'Great War'. Jackson's letter of 4 October 1935 is in this collection.

Montgomery, Field Marshal Sir A.A. (Montgomery-Massingberd). Papers.

North, J. Papers including correspondence with Allanson and Rhodes James.

Robertson, Field Marshal Sir W. Papers, 1916-18.

NATIONAL ARMY MUSEUM, LONDON

Allanson, Colonel C. J. L. *Diary 1915* (printed).

Rawlinson, Field Marshal Lord. Papers 1914-18 and Diary 1918.

ROYAL MARINES MUSEUM, SOUTHEND

Acc. ACQ 23/80C-ARCH 9/2/J: 'The Life of Lieutenant-Colonel Charles Frederick Jerram' (handwritten journal).

NATIONAL LIBRARY OF SCOTLAND, EDINBURGH

Haig, Field Marshal Earl. Papers and Diary, 1916-18.

WEST GERMANY

BUNDESARCHIV–MILITARARCHIV, FREIBURG

Foerster, Wolfgang, *Ludendorff-der Feldherr Ludendorff im Unglück. Eine Studie über seine seelische Haltung in der Endphase des ersten Weltkrieges.* Wiesbaden, 1952 (BII, Lud. 3).

OTHERS

Hobbs, Lt. Gen. Sir Talbot. Diary, 1918 (Held by Mr J. Hunn, Perth, WA).

B. Official Histories

AUSTRALIA

Bean, C.E.W. (ed.). *Official History of Australia in the War of 1914-1918,* 12 vols, Sydney, 1921-42.

—. vol. I, *The Story of Anzac,* 1921.

SELECT BIBLIOGRAPHY

—. vol. II, *The Story of Anzac*, 1937.

—. vol. III, *The AIF in France*, 1937.

—. vol. IV, *The AIF in France*, 1933.

—. vol. V, *The AIF in France During the Main German Offensive, 1918,* 1937.

—. vol. VI, *The AIF in France During the Allied Offensive, 1918,* 1942.

Butler, A.G. *Official History of the Australian Army Medical Services 1914-18*, 3 vols, Melbourne, 1930-43.

—. vol. I, *Gallipoli, Palestine and New Guinea*, 1930.

—. vol. II, *The Western Front,* 1940.

UNITED KINGDOM

Aspinall-Oglander, Brig. Gen. C.F. *Military Operations: Gallipoli.* 2 vols, London, 1929, 1932.

Edmonds, Brig. Gen. J.E. (ed.). *Military Operations: France and Belgium 1917,* 5 vols, London, 1940-48.

—. vol. 2, *Messines and 3rd Ypres (Passchendaele),* 1948.

CANADA

Nicholson, G.W.L. *Canadian Expeditionary Force 1914-1919.* Ottawa, 1962.

GERMANY

Der Weltkrieg 1914 bis 1918: Vierzehnter Band – Westfront im Jahre 1918. London, 1944.

C. Unpublished Theses

Hyatt, A.M.J. The Military Career of Sir Arthur Currie. Ph.D., Duke University, 1965.

Millar, T.B. History of the Defence Forces of Port Phillip and the Colony of Victoria 1836-1900. M.A., University of Melbourne, 1957.

D. Newspapers

These were invaluable in the pre-war period, when they contained many articles on Victorian and then Australian defence and commentaries on Annual Camps of Continuous Training. Some interesting material on the war was found in post-war issues, but the restrictions imposed by wartime censorship rendered newspapers of limited use during the war itself. The newspapers used most frequently were the *Age, Argus, Australasian, Sydney Morning Herald* and *Sydney Sun*.

E. Books, Articles and Addresses by Monash

BOOKS

The Australian Victories in France in 1918, London, 1920.

War Letters of General Monash, ed. F.M. Cutlack, Sydney, 1934.

ARTICLES AND ADDRESSES–MILITARY

'Implements of War', address, 1892.

'Mechanical Science as Applied to Warfare', address, 1892.

'Modern Artillery', address, 1893 and 1895.

'Military Explosives', address, 1894.

'The Evolution of Modern Weapons', address, 1894.

'The Evolution of Modern Weapons', *Journal of the United Service Institute of Victoria,* III (1894) pp. 3-18.

'Lessons of the Wilderness Campaign', *Commonwealth Military Journal,* Apr. 1912, pp. 269-87.

100 Hints for Company Officers, Melbourne 1914.

'Leadership in War', address, 30 March 1926.

'The Decisive Battle–ten years ago', *Argus,* 4 August 1928.

ARTICLES AND ADDRESSES–NON-MILITARY

'Heat', c. 1892.

SELECT BIBLIOGRAPHY

'Victorian Coal and Coal Mining', July 1895.

'The Rise of Mohammedanism', July 1889.

'The Superintendence of Contracts', address, 1890.

'Some Impressions of Travel', *Victorian Institute of Engineers–Proceedings 1911,* XII (1912) pp. 28-49.

'Notes on Some Recent Structures in Reinforced Concrete', *Victorian Institute of Engineers–Proceedings 1912,* XIII (1913) pp. 145-52.

'Presidential Address to the Victorian Institute of Engineers, 5 March 1913', *Victorian Institute of Engineers – Proceedings 1913,* XIV (1914) pp. 11-24.

F. Books and Articles on Monash

Anonymous, 'Monash', *Constructional Review,* L (1977) pp. 20-3.

Barraclough, S.G.E. 'Sir John Monash–Engineer', *Journal of the Institute of Engineers of Australia,* III (1931) pp. 363-4.

Bazley, A.W. 'Sir John Monash', *Reveille,* 10 May 1937, pp. 2-3, 15.

Bean, C.E.W. 'Monash The Soldier', *Reveille* (Monash Memorial Issue), 31 Oct. 1931, pp. 2-3.

—. 'The Battle of August 8', *Sydney Sun,* 8 Oct. 1931.

Bennett, G. 'To the Service of His Country' (First Monash Oration), *Australian Jewish Herald,* 15 Oct. 1936.

Blamey, T.A. 'Disliked Show–Sir John Monash's Simple Tastes', *Reveille* (Monash Memorial Issue), 31 Oct. 1931, pp. 10, 27.

Brasch, Rabbi Dr R. 'Sir John Monash', *JRAHS,* 44 (1959) pp. 162-211.

Callinan, B. *Sir John Monash* (Daniel Mannix Memorial Lecture, 17 June 1980), Melbourne, 1981.

Cutlack, F.M. 'General Monash: his remarkable record', *Sydney Morning Herald,* 27 Dec. 1918.

Eggleston, Sir Frederick. 'Confidential Notes on Victorian Politics–Sir John Monash', MS2, ANU.

Gammage, W. 'Sir John Monash: a military view', *Historical Studies*, XVI (1974), pp. 112-18.

Gordon, M. 'The Centenary of the Birth of Sir John Monash', *AJHS*, VI (1966), pp. 69-80.

Hetherington, J. *John Monash*. London, 1962.

Menzies, Sir Robert. 'Sir John Monash' (Address at Monash Centenary Memorial Service, 11 Apr. 1965), *AJHS*, VI (1966) pp. 81-4.

Northwood, V. *Monash*. Melbourne, 1961.

Pedersen, P.A. 'Some Thoughts on the Prewar Military Career of Sir John Monash', *JRAHS*, 67 (1981) pp. 212-26.

Perry, E.W.O. 'General Sir John Monash–A Glimpse of his Career and Methods of Command', *AAJ*, no. 296 (1974) pp. 22-39.

—. 'The Military Life of Sir John Monash', *VHM*, XXVIII (1957) pp. 25-42.

Rosenthal, Maj. Gen. C. 'A Great Soldier and a Great Scholar', *Reveille* (Monash Memorial Issue), 31 Oct. 1931, p. 4.

Smithers, A.J. *Sir John Monash*. London, 1973.

Terraine, J. 'Monash: Australian Commander', *History Today*, XVI (Jan. 1966) pp. 12-20.

Thompson, J. *On Lips of Living Men*. Melbourne, 1962.

G. Books and Articles

Argent, A. 'Quinn of Quinn's Post', *AAJ*, no. 270 (1971) pp. 22-51.

Bean, C.E.W. *Anzac to Amiens*. 5th ed., Canberra, 1968.

—. *Gallipoli Mission*. Canberra, 1948.

—. *Two Men I Knew: William Bridges and Brudenell White*. Sydney, 1957.

SELECT BIBLIOGRAPHY

Beaumont, R.A. 'Hamel 1918: a study in military-political interaction', *Military Affairs,* XXXI (Spring 1967) pp. 10-16.

Beeston, J.L. *Five Months at Anzac.* Sydney, 1916.

Bidwell, Brig. S. *Gunners at War.* London, 1970.

Birdwood, Field Marshal W. R. *Khaki and Gown.* London, 1941.

Blake, R. *The Private Papers of Douglas Haig, 1914-1919.* London, 1952.

Blaxland, G. *Amiens 1918.* London, 1981.

Bond, B. *The Victorian Army and the Staff College, 1854-1914.* London, 1972.

Bond, B. and Cave, N. (eds.), *Haig. A Reappraisal 70 Years On.* Barnsley, 1999.

Brahms, V. *The Spirit of the Forty Second.* Brisbane, 1938.

Brierley, A.N. '2nd Hill 60: intense fire', *Reveille,* 1 Aug. 1932, p. 44.

Bush, E.W. *Gallipoli.* London, 1975.

Callwell, Maj. Gen. (Sir) C.E. *Field Marshal Sir Henry Wilson. His Life and Diaries.* vol. 2, London, 1927.

Carlyon, L. *Gallipoli.* Sydney, 2001.

Carver, Field Marshal (Sir) Michael (ed.). *The War Lords.* London, 1976.

Cassar, G.H. *Kitchener: architect of victory.* London, 1977.

Charteris, Brig. Gen. J. *At GHQ.* London, 1931.

—. *Field Marshal Earl Haig.* London, 1929.

Coombs, R. *Before Endeavours Fade.* London, 1976.

Cooper, A. Duff. *Haig.* vol. 2, London, 1935.

Coulthard-Clark, C.D. *A Heritage of Spirit.* Melbourne, 1979.

—. *The Citizen General Staff.* Canberra, 1976.

Crane, F.W. 'The Concert in Anzac Reserve Gully', *Reveille,* 1 Aug. 1933, p. 33.

Crawley, R. *Climax at Gallipoli*. Oklahoma, 2014.

Cruttwell, C.R.M. *A History of the Great War*. Oxford, 1964.

Cutlack, F.M. *The Australians: their final campaign 1918*. London, 1918.

Dewar, G.A.B. and Boraston, J.H. *Sir Douglas Haig's Command*. vol. 2, London, 1923.

Dixon, N.F. *On the Psychology of Military Incompetence*. London, 1976.

Drake-Brockman, G. *The Turning Wheel*. Perth, 1960.

Edgar, P. *Sir William Glasgow*. Newport, 2011.

Ellis, J. *Eye Deep in Hell*. Glasgow, 1977.

Erickson, E. *Gallipoli. Command under Fire*. Oxford, 2015.

Essame, H. *The Battle for Europe 1918*. London, 1972.

Falls, C. *The Great War*. New York, 1961.

Farndale, Gen. Sir M.F. *History of the Royal Regiment of Artillery. The Western Front 1914-18*. London, 1986.

Farrar-Hockley, Gen. Sir A. *Goughie: the life of Sir Hubert Gough*. London, 1975.

Frankland, N. and Dowling, C. (eds). *Decisive Battles of the Twentieth Century*. Melbourne, 1976.

Fuller, Maj. Gen. J.F.C. *Generalship: its diseases and their cure*. London, 1933.

—. *Memoirs of an Unconventional Soldier*. London, 1936.

—. *The Conduct of War 1789-1961*. London, 1977.

—. *The Decisive Battles of the Western World*. vol. 3, London, 1963.

Gammage, W. *The Broken Years*. Ringwood, 1975.

Germains, V.W. *The Kitchener Armies*. London, 1930.

Godley, A.J. *Life of an Irish Soldier*. London, 1939.

Goltz, C. von der. *The Nation in Arms: a treatise on modern military systems and the conduct of war*. London, 1913.

SELECT BIBLIOGRAPHY

Gooch, J. 'The Creation of the British General Staff 1904-1914', *RUSI,* LXVI (1971) pp. 50-3.

Gough, Gen. (Sir) H. *The Fifth Army.* London, 1931.

Hackett, Gen. (Sir), *The Profession of Arms.* London, 1983.

Harris, J.P. *Douglas Haig and the First World War.* Cambridge, 2008.

Hamilton, I. *Gallipoli Diary.* abridged ed., London, 1930.

Harington, Gen. C. *Plumer of Messines.* London, 1935.

Harper, G. *Dark Journey.* Auckland, 2007.

Henderson, G.F.R. *The Science of War.* London, 1933.

Herbert, A. *Anzac, Mons and Kut.* London, 1919.

Herring, Brig. Gen. S.C. E. 'Three Waves Dash for Hill 60', *Reveille,* 1 Aug. 1932, p. 54.

Hetherington, J. *Blamey, Controversial Soldier: a biography of Field Marshal Sir Thomas Blamey, GBE, KCB, CMG, DSO, ED.* Canberra, 1973.

Hickey, M. *Gallipoli.* London, 1998.

Hill, A.J. *Chauvel of the Light Horse: a biography of General Sir Harry Chauvel.* Melbourne, 1978.

Holmes, R. *The Western Front.* London, 1999.

Hyatt, A.M.J. 'Sir Arthur Currie at Passchendaele', *Stand-To,* IX Jan.-Feb. 1965, pp. 16-20.

James, R.R. *Gallipoli.* London, 1965.

Janowitz, M. *The Professional Soldier.* London, 1970.

Jerrold, D. *The Royal Naval Division.* London, 1923.

Joynt, W.D. *Saving the Channel Ports 1918.* Melbourne, 1975.

Liddell Hart, B.H. *History of the First World War.* London, 1970.

—. *The Liddell Hart Memoirs.* vol. 1, New York, 1965.

—. *The Tanks*. vol. 1, London, 1959.

—. *Thoughts on War*. London, 1946.

—. *Through the Fog of War*. London, 1930.

Liddle, P.H. *Men of Gallipoli*. London, 1976.

Lloyd, A. *The War in the Trenches*. London, 1976.

Lloyd, N. *Passchendaele. A New History*. London, 2017.

Lloyd George, D. *War Memoirs of David Lloyd George*. vol. 4, London, 1933-36.

Longmore, C. *The Old Sixteenth*. Perth, 1929.

Ludendorff, Gen. E. *My War Memories, 1914-18*. 2 vols, London, 1919.

Macdonald, A. *Passchendaele. The Anatomy of a Tragedy*. Auckland, 2013.

MacDonald, L. *They Called it Passchendaele*. London, 1919.

McNicol, N.G. *The Thirty-Seventh: history of the Thirty-Seventh Battalion, A.I.F.* Melbourne, 1936.

Mackenzie, C. *Gallipoli Memories*. London, 1929.

Malthus, C. *Anzac: a retrospect*. Christchurch, 1965.

Marshall-Cornwall, J. *Foch as Military Commander*. London, 1972.

—. *Haig as Military Commander*. London, 1976.

Maurice, F. *The Life of General Lord Rawlinson of Trent*. London, 1928.

Meaney, N. *The Search for Security in the Pacific, 1901-1914*. Sydney, 1970.

Middlebrook, M. *The Kaiser's Battle*. London, 1978.

Molony, J. *I am Ned Kelly*. Ringwood, 1980.

Montgomery, Maj. Gen. (Sir) A.A. '8 August 1918', *Royal Artillery Journal* (reprint), LVI (1929) pp. 1-19.

—. *The Story of the Fourth Army in the Battle of the Hundred Days*. London, 1931.

SELECT BIBLIOGRAPHY

Montgomery, Field Marshal (Viscount). *A History of Warfare*. London, 1968.

—. *The Path to Leadership*. London, 1976.

Moore, W. *See How They Ran*. London, 1970.

Moorehead, A. *Gallipoli*. Melbourne, 1978.

Murray, Lt. Col. H.W. 'Grave and Gay: VC's reflections', *Reveille*, 1 Aug. 1933, p. 13.

North, J. *Gallipoli: the fading vision*. London, 1936.

O'Ryan, Maj. Gen. J. F. *The Story of the 27th Division*. New York, 1921.

Pakenham, T. *The Boer War*. London, 1979.

Passingham, I. *Pillars of Fire. The Battle of Messines Ridge June 1917*. Stroud, 2004.

Pearce, G.F. *Carpenter to Cabinet*. London, 1951.

Powell, A. *Plumer. The Soldier's General*. London, 1990.

Pedersen, P.A. '"I thought I could command men." Monash and the assault on Hill 971' in Ekins, A. (ed.). *A Ridge too far*. Auckland, 2013.

—. *Anzac Treasures. The Gallipoli Collection of the Australian War Memorial*. Sydney, 2014.

—. *Fromelles*. Barnsley, 2004.

—. *Hamel*. Barnsley, 2003.

—. 'Maintaining the Advance' in Ekins, A (ed.), *1918. Year of Victory*. Auckland, 2010.

—. *The Anzacs. Gallipoli to the Western Front*. Melbourne and Sydney, 2007.

Perry, E.W.O. 'Major-General M. F. Downes, CMG', *VHM* (reprint), XLI (1970) pp. 425-70.

—. 'Major-General Sir Charles Rosenthal', *VHM* (reprint), XL (1969) pp. 101-60.

Pershing, Gen. J.J. *My Experiences in the World War.* London, 1931.

Philpott, W. *Bloody Victory.* London, 2009.

Pitt, B. *1918 The Last Act.* London, 1962.

Prior, R. *Gallipoli. The End of the Myth.* Sydney, 2009.

Prior, R. and Wilson, T. *Command on the Western Front.* Oxford, 1992.

—. *Passchendaele. The Untold Story.* Melbourne, 2002.

Pugsley, C. *The Anzac Experience.* Auckland, 2004.

Roberts, C. *The Landing at Anzac 1915.* Sydney, 2015.

—. 'The Landing at Anzac: a reassessment', *Journal of the Australian War Memorial*, No. 22, April 1993, pp. 25-34.

Robertson, W.R. *Soldiers and Statesmen.* 2 vols, London, 1926.

Robson, K.F. *The First AIF.* Melbourne, 1970.

Ropp, T. *War in the Modern World.* London, 1959.

Roskill, S.W. *Hankey, Man of Secrets.* vol. 1, London, 1970.

Rule, E.J. *Jacka's Mob.* Sydney, 1933.

Sadler, P. *The Paladin. A Life of Major General Sir John Gellibrand.* South Melbourne, 2000.

Schuler, P.F.E. *Australia in Arms.* London, 1916.

Serle, G. *John Monash: a biography.* Melbourne, 1982.

Serle, G. and Nairn, B. (eds). *Australian Dictionary of Biography, 1851-1890.* vols 3-6, Melbourne, 1969-76.

Shadbolt, M. *Voices of Gallipoli.* Auckland, 1988.

Sheffield, G. *Command and Morale. The British Army on the Western Front 1914-1918.* Barnsley, 2014.

—. *Forgotten Victory. The First World War: Myths and realities.* London, 2002.

—. *The Somme.* London, 2003.

SELECT BIBLIOGRAPHY

Simkins, P. *From the Somme to Victory. The British Army's Experience on the Western Front 1916-1918.* Barnsley, 2014.

—. 'Herbert Plumer' in Beckett, I.F.W and Corvi, S.J. *Haig's Generals.* Barnsley, 2006.

Sixsmith, Maj. Gen. E.K.G. *Douglas Haig.* London, 1976.

—. *British Generalship in the Twentieth Century.* London, 1970.

Stanley, P. *Quinn's Post.* Crows Nest, 2005.

Steel, N. and Hart, P. *Defeat at Gallipoli.* London, 1994.

Stevenson, D. *With our Backs to the Wall. Victory and Defeat in 1918.* London, 2011.

Stevenson, R. *Centenary History of Australia and the Great War. 3. The War with Germany,* Melbourne, 2015.

—. *To Win the Battle. The First Australian Division in the Great War 1914-1918.* Port Melbourne, 2013.

Taylor, A.J.P. *The First World War.* Ringwood, 1972.

Terraine, J. 'A Matter of Principle', *JRUSI,* LXXXII (June 1967) pp. 64-6.

—. *Douglas Haig: the educated soldier.* London, 1963.

—. *The Road to Passchendaele.* London, 1977.

—. *The Smoke and the Fire.* London, 1980.

—. *The Western Front.* London, 1970.

—. *To Win a War: 1918, the year of victory.* London, 1979.

Tilney, Lt. Col. L.E. 'Night March: 4 Bde Steadiness', *Reveille,* 1 Aug. 1932, p. 47.

Travers, T. *Gallipoli 1915.* Stroud, 2002.

Trythall, A.J. *Boney Fuller.* London, 1977.

Urquhart, H.M. *Arthur Currie.* Toronto, 1950.

Vazenry, G.R. *Military Forces of Victoria 1854-1967.* Melbourne, 1970.

Waite, F. *The New Zealanders at Gallipoli.* Auckland, 1921.

Wanliss, N.F. *The History of the Fourteenth Battalion AIF.* Melbourne, 1929.

Wavell, Field Marshal (Lord) A.P. *Generals and Generalship.* London, 1941.

White, T.A. *The Fighting Thirteenth.* Sydney, 1924.

Williams, Air Marshal R. *These are the Facts.* Melbourne, 1977.

William-Ellis, C. *The Tank Corps.* London, 1918.

Winter, D. *Death's Men.* London, 1978.

Woollcombe, R. *The First Tank Battle: Cambrai 1917.* London, 1967.

Yockelson, M.A. *Borrowed soldiers. American soldiers under British command.* 1918. Oklahoma, 2008.

H. Correspondence and Interviews

I did not always agree with the interpretations and conclusions of military historians with whom I discussed various aspects of the subject. Nevertheless, they often raised points that I had not considered or, on other occasions, gave me a different perspective on matters that I had dismissed as unimportant.

CORRESPONDENCE

Argent, Lt. Col. A.A. 16 and 23 June 1980, 19 Nov. 1980, 29 Jan. 1981.

Bond, B. 9 Oct. 1979.

Hyatt, A.M. J. 5 Jan. 1981.

Montgomery-Massingberd, J. 19 Mar. 1981.

O'Neill, R. J. 15 Oct. 1979.

Perry, B.H. (4 Bde), 29 Nov. 1980, 29 Dec. 1980.

Sixsmith, Maj. Gen. E.K.G. 16 Aug. 1979, 16 June and 19 July 1980.

SELECT BIBLIOGRAPHY

Terraine, J. 16 Aug. 1979.

INTERVIEWS

Berrisford, F. (2 Bde). Melbourne, 15 May 1980.

Carrington, Prof. C.E. London, 27 Mar. 1981.

Hocking, F.R. (6 Bde). Melbourne, 15 May 1980.

James, R.R. MP, House of Commons. London, 26 Mar. and 7 Apr.1981.

Newman, H.C. (3 LH). Canberra, 14 June 1980.

Ropp, Prof. T. (Duke University). Canberra, July 1980.

Terraine, J. London, 19 Mar. and 8 Apr. 1981.

Thompson, Dr R.C. Faculty of Military Studies, University of New South Wales at Duntroon, July 1980.

Sixsmith, Maj. Gen. E.K.G. Somerset, 28-29 Mar. 1981.

Smithers, A.J. Ickham, Kent, 22 Mar. and 5 Apr. 1981.

My discussions with Mr A.J. Hill, Mr E.W.O. Perry, Dr Geoffrey Serle and Mr Denis Winter (London) were so numerous as to make impractical a listing of each of them. In the same vein, I have discussed Monash with countless historians and on countless occasions since this book was written.

I. Battlefield Inspections

My itinerary was as follows:

10-12 Apr. 1981: Broodseinde, Passchendaele, Messines.

14-16 Apr. 1981: Retracing the Somme advance of the Australian Corps from Sailly-Laurette to the Hindenburg Line.

24-28 Apr. 1981: Gallipoli.

Besides being the most interesting phase of my research, these inspections were among the most valuable. The observation and fields of fire enjoyed by the Germans, the difficulty of keeping direction in the attack, the problem of knowing when the objective had been reached in featureless terrain and a score of other details can never be conveyed adequately by a map. In other words, an examination of the battlefield brought an operation to life and contributed to an assessment of Monash as a commander by making obvious many of the advantages or disadvantages that faced him. I have also analysed Monash's operations – and the Australian operations in which he was not involved – on numerous visits to Gallipoli and the Western Front since 1981.

Index

3rd Division 52, 106, 208, 228–9, 235, 275, 331–2, 372, 462
    Amiens 372, 375, 394
    Australian Corps, transfer to 315
    commanders *227*, 228, 334
    discipline 229, 238–9, 284–5, 342
    Flanders offensive 1917 283, 292–9, 302, 307, 311–14
    France, move to 237–8
    Hamel 352
    Hindenburg Line, advance towards 429, 431, 447, 452–3
    Messines, at 250, 255, 260, 264–6, 272–4
    Monash, appointment of 217–18, 221–2
    Mont St Quentin, advance towards 418
    morale 326
    nicknames 238
    Péronne, advance towards 411, 415
    raids 244–6, 264, 318–19
    Somme 1918 323–5, *324*, 330, 395, 402–5
    structure 226
    training 223, 229–34, 237, 240–1, 283–4, 288–9, 462
3rd Divisional Training Group 240
4th Brigade 70, 73, 144, *173*, 209
    AIF reorganisation, impact of 210–11
    ANZACs 80
    August offensives (Gallipoli) 152–5, 157, 159, 161–2, 168–71, 178–9, 182–9, 475
    command structure 73–6, 86
    Egypt, in 83–7, 89–91, *89*, 93–4, 209, *210*
    Gallipoli 95, 96, 99, 101, 104, 106, 110, 112–13, 116–26, 131, 143–4, *160*, 187, 191
    Hamel 352
    Ismailia 201
    Lemnos, on 191–4, *191*
    life at Gallipoli 147–8
    loss of experienced officers and NCOs 149–51, 189–90
    reinforcements 150–1, 155
    Suez, march to 213
    training 76–9, 82, 87, *89*, 93–4, 150–1, 193–4, 204–5, 217, 219
    transportation to Egypt 80–4
    Western Front 218–21, 223, 227
5-inch breechloading gun 35

100 Hints for Company Officers 78, 215, 232, 293, 469
400 Plateau 98, 105, 116, 118, 137, 476

A

'A Corner of Blighty in Paris' 287
Abbeville 458
Abdel Rahman Bair 153, *154*, 155, 157–8, 164–6, 172, 175, 177
Abraham Heights 295, 302
Accroche Wood 346
Achi Baba 94, 99, 112, 126, 412
Adams, Lieutenant Colonel John 188, 189
administration 13, 15, 26, 34, 46–7, 65–6, 145, 192, 206, 332
    staff work, importance of 46, 51–2, 189, 247, 299
    Western Front, on 219–20, 242
Aerodrome camp 84
Aghyl Dere 152–5, 157, 162–4, 166, *167*, 168, 175, 177, 182, 190
aircraft 16, 220, 231, 325, 337
    Amiens, at 384
    Hamel, at 355–6, *362*
    Handley Page heavy bombers 352
    Messines, at 249, 266
    'noise patrols' 356, 406
    Passchendaele, at 283
Aisne River 344, 356, 366
Alai Tepe 307
Albert 320
Albert-Bray line 404
Albrecht Line 278, 289–90
Alexandra, Queen 235
Alexandria 83–4
Allanson, Major Cecil 162, 166–70, 172, 180
Allenby, Field Marshal Edmund 29, 65, 473
Alma pillbox 295
American Forces 439, 445–50, 455
    II Corps 445, 448
    27th Division 357, 445–7, 449–53
    30th Division 445, 450, 451
    33rd Division 357
    65th Brigade 357
    106th Regiment 449
    Hamel 352, 357, 362
Amiens 320, 323, 325, 326, 332, 334, 347, 358, 436

MONASH

Amiens gun *385*
Amiens Line 323, 324
Amiens–Nesle railway 369
Amiens offensive (August 1918) 365–6, 369–79, 383
    Blue Line 1918 370, 371, 372, 374, 376, 378, 380, 382, 386–7, 392
    Brown Line 1918 371
    commencement of assault 381–3
    Green Line 1918 370, 371, 372, 374, 378, 381, 392, 403
    Monash's plan 372–9, 384
    Red Line 1918 370, 371, 372, 378, 382
    tactical significance 384–7
    zero hour 388–91
Ancre River 323, 324, 327, 328, 330, 398
Anderson, J.T. Noble 23
Anderson Street bridge 23, *24*
Anglo-Russian crisis (1878) 30
anti-Semitism 91, 199, 284, 333, 339, 472
Anvil Wood 421, 423, *424*
Anzac Cove 97, 99
Anzac Day 214, *465*, 466
Anzac tradition 196
Aquaire Wood 378
Aragon 192
Arcadian 138, 284
Armentières 218, 223, 241–2
Armin, General Sixt von 300
Armistice 223
Arras 263, 320, 396, 404, 428
artillery 16, 93–4, 260–1, 411
    Amiens 375, 378, 388
    Boer War 40
    coastal 33–4
    counter-bombardment 248, 382, 425
    creeping barrages 223, 248, 257, 273, 345, 349, 353, 356, 375, 406, 419, 432, 449, 451
    Gallipoli 135, 185–6
    German 220, *251*, 320–1
    Hamel, at 350, 353, 355
    heavy 337–8, 355
    Hindenburg Line, advance towards 432, 442, 444
    jumping barrages 350
    Messines, at 248–9
    Monash lectures on 35–6
    Mont St Quentin, advance towards 419, 426
    Passchendaele, at 290, 310
    silent registration (ranging) 356
    training 229–30
    Western Front 227, 244
Asma Dere 153–4, 157, 166, 175, 177

Aubigny 324
Augustus Wood 303, 311
Australia Valley 164, 166, *167*
Australian Army
    13th Infantry Brigade 59–64, 68, 73, 77–8, 79, 340
    commanders 27–8 *see also* commanders
Australian Corps 319, 334, 337, 396, 402–3, 412, 418, 425
    establishment 315
    formation and units 337–8
    Hindenburg Line, advance towards 429–30, 442, 445, 458
    Monash in command 331–4, 461, 469
    recognition for 436
Australian Flying Corps (AFC) 316
    3rd Squadron 337
Australian Imperial Force (AIF) 72, 315, 466, 478
    1st Battalion 434
    1st Brigade 72, 95, 97, 161, 197, 381, 406, 408
    1st Division 72, 80, 84, 98, 101, 105, 112, 117, 145, 197–8, 223, 298, 334, 402–3, 406–7, 448
        Amiens 366, 379, 387, 389–9, 391–2, *391*
        Hindenburg Line, advance towards 431, 432, 434, 437, 445
    2nd Brigade 72, 100, 126, 327, 389, 390, 406–7
    2nd Division 80, 189, 197, 207, 218, 221, 295, 299, 301, 334, 344, 352, *396–7*, 402–3
        Amiens 372, 375, 387, 391–3
        Hindenburg Line, advance towards 454, 456–8
        Péronne, advance towards 411, 413
    3rd Battalion 109, 111
    3rd Brigade 72, 95, 98, 100, 110, 389, 390, 408
    3rd Division *see* 3rd Division
    4th Brigade *see* 4th Brigade
    4th Division 207–8, 212, 218, 255, 257, 266, 268–9, 309, 315, 318, 322, 330, 334, 347, 402–3, 448
        Amiens 372, 379, 381
        Hamel 352–3
        Hindenburg Line, advance towards 431, 432, 434, 437, 445
    5th Brigade 207, 218, 219, 372
        Mont St Quentin 418–21, 423
    5th Division 207–8, 212, 225, 292, 322, 330, 332, 334, 346, 361, *382*, 402–3
        Amiens 372, 379, 381, 387, 391, 393
        Hindenburg Line, advance towards 429, 431, 447, 451, 452–4

INDEX

Péronne/Mont St Quentin, advance towards 411, 413, 415, 424
6th Battalion *393*
6th Brigade 220, 372, 420–1, 423, 425, 456
7th Battalion 391
7th Brigade 218, 356, 362, 372, 420, 423, 425
8th Brigade 209, 212, 391
9th Brigade 226, 227, 228, 230, 282, 285, 287, 319, 330, 372, 453
   Flanders offensive 1917 292, 309, 313
   Messines 252, 255, 256, 261, 264
   Somme 1918 323–6, 329, 330, 418
10th Battalion 109, 285
10th Brigade 226, 228, 231, 244–5, 372, 452
   Flanders offensive 1917 292, 299, 309, 311–13
   Messines 252, 255, 264, 272
   Somme 1918 324–5, 328, 330, 395, 418
11th Battalion 109, 285
11th Brigade 226, 228, 282, 316, 372, 452
   Flanders offensive 1917 292, 294, 299, 302
   Messines 255, 269
   Somme 1918 323, 324, 329
12th Battalion 109
12th Brigade 210, 226, 330
13th Battalion 149, 210
   August offensives (Gallipoli) 158, 161, 163, 168, 171, 184–5, 188–9
   landing and early days at Gallipoli 75, 77, 100, 104, 107, 109, 113, 117, 119–20, 122–3, 126, 129, 135, 139, 141, 143
13th Brigade 330, 379, 394
14th Battalion 150, 190, 210
   August offensives (Gallipoli) 158, 164, 168, 171, 175, 177–9, 184, 188, 189
   landing and early days at Gallipoli 76, 77, 99, 100, 104, 106–10, 117, 126–7, 135
   Western Front 219, 220
14th Brigade 213, 371, 420–5, 454
15th Brigade 356, *389*, 391, 420, 422, 424
15th Battalion 210
   August offensive 161, 164–6, 171, 175, 177–9, 184, 188
   landing and early days at Gallipoli 75, 76, 100, 104, 106, 107, 109, 113, 117, 119, 124, 126, 128–9, 135, 139, 141
16th Battalion 151, *191*, 210, 212
   August offensives (Gallipoli) 164–6, 171, 175, 177–8
   landing and early days at Gallipoli 75, 100, 107, 109, 111, 113, 119–20, 122–3, 126, 128–9, 135, 139

17th Battalion 189, 420
18th Battalion 419
19th Battalion 438
20th Battalion 220, 420
21st Battalion *421*, *422*, 438
25th Battalion 367, 438
26th Battalion 367
29th Battalion 438
32nd Division 402, 406, 411, 413, 415–16, 429
33rd Battalion 253, 255, 266
34th Battalion 255, 285
35th Battalion 255
36th Battalion 255, 313, 330
37th Battalion 238, 245, 256, 257, 266–9, *270*, 281, 394, 438–9
38th Battalion 256, 309, 311, 418
39th Battalion 254, 256, 318
40th Battalion 254, 256, 267, 298, 302, 418
41st Battalion 264, 301–2, 313
42nd Battalion 282, 438
43rd Battalion 256, 282
44th Battalion 269–71, 328
45th Battalion 210, 266, *432*
46th Battalion 210
47th Battalion 210, 266, 267–9
48th Battalion 210, 269–70
53rd Battalion 421–3, *423*, *424*
54th Battalion 421–2, 425, *425*, 438
56th Battalion 425
58th Battalion 425
60th Battalion 438
Australian Corps *see* Australian Corps
Australian and New Zealand Army Corps *see* Australian and New Zealand Army Corps (ANZAC)
Australian Light Horse *see* Australian Light Horse
'civilian' soldiers 341–2
commanders 197–8
demobilization 11, 439, 459
education and retraining 459
embarkation 80
leave, issue of (1918) 436–8
mutiny following disbandment order 438–9
reorganisation 206–11, 438–9
repatriation *see* repatriation
transportation to Egypt 80–4
welfare of soldiers 233, 238, 274, 287, 317, 335, 341–2, 354, 384, 402, 426, 434, 436–7, 461–2
Australian Intelligence Corps (AIC) 42–5, 48–57, *51*, 68, 89, 461

547

MONASH

Australian Intermediate Base 87
Australian Light Horse
   1st Light Horse Brigade 72, 80, 129
   1st Light Horse Regiment 129
   2nd Light Horse Brigade 70, 81
   2nd Light Horse Regiment 129
   3rd Light Horse Brigade 152
   13th Light Horse Regiment 337, 373
Australian Mission 448
Australian and New Zealand Army Corps (ANZAC) 80
   1st ANZAC 206, 212, 220, 223, 292, 293, 302, 307
   2nd ANZAC 207, 212, 238, 243, 250–1, 255, 258–9, 266, 280–1, 292, 293, 303, 307
   NZ and A Division *see* NZ and A Division

B

Baby 700 98, 101, 103, 110, 113, 116–17, 137, 253, 476
   August offensives (Gallipoli) 152
   May assault on 117–25, *121*, 146
Bailleul 218, 222
Bain, Company Sergeant Major Les 160, 168, 170
Bapaume 397, 410, 428
Barber, Colonel George 338
Basseux 323
Battleship Hill 119, 152, 475
Bauchop's Hill 152, 161, 162, 165, 190
Bayonvillers 370
Bazley, Arthur 274, 465
Bean, C.E. 72, *93*, 97, 264, 435, 437, 457
   Gallipoli 100, 107, 116, 132, 137, 143, 153, 162
   Hamel, at 359
   'internal revolution' amongst soldiers 150
   Monash, on 11–12, 26, 90, 123–4, 169, 170–1, 172, 187, 271, 325, 328, 332–3, 373, 386–7, 433, 450, 472
   Monash, relationship with 91, 144–5, 171, 333, 398, 436
Beaurevoir 456–7
Beaurevoir Line 441–2, 456–7, *456*
Beersheba 201
Beeston, Colonel John 187
Bellenglise 442
Bellevue-Meetcheele Spur 307, 309, 311
Bellevue Spur 303, 412
Bellicourt 440, 442, 451
   tunnel 440–1, 467
Bennett, Brigadier General Henry Gordon 390
Bernard, Lieutenant Colonel Denis 219
Berry, Major Walter *344*, 381

Bertangles 358, 372, 397, *400*, *401*
Bethleem Farm 251, 255, 261
Biaches 413, 415
Birdwood, Lieutenant General Sir William 80, 84, *85*, 87, 99, 169, 191, 194, 202, 222, 245, 274, 292, 322, 346, 357, 369
   AIF, administrative control over 206–7, 209–10, 212, 217–18, 227, 235–6, 315, 331–2, 398–400
   Anzac leave issue 436–8
   August offensives (Gallipoli) 152, 155, 181, 182
   commanders, appointment of AIF 196–8
   conscription referendum 237
   Dardanelles Army, command of 195
   Fifth Army, command of 331–3, 399–400
   Flanders offensive 1917 296–7
   Gallipoli 94–5, 106, 110, 116, 118–19, 124–6, 131, 132, 134, 137, 142, 474–7
   Haig and 243
   leadership style 202, 341, 342–3, 464, 467–8
   Monash, impressions of 90, 145, 198–9, 207–8, 218, 240, 274, 284–5, 311, 331–3
   Morcourt, advance to 365–6
'bite and hold' tactics 225, 249–50, 273–4, 276, 290
Blamey, Field Marshal Sir Thomas 27, 91, 123, 197, *335*, 338, 353, 372, 423, 434, 453, 457, 464, 470
Blaringhem 322
Blauwepoortbeek 274
Bléquin 283, 316
Bloody Angle 103, 114, 119–20
Boer War *see* South African War (Boer War)
Bois Grenier 218–19, 227, 231, 239
boldness 14
bombs 132, 193
Bony 440–1, 452
Bordeaux pillbox 295, 302
Bouchavesnes Spur 412, 415, 417, 418, 420, 426, 464
Braithwaite, Lieutenant General Sir Walter 103–4, 430
Brand, Brigadier General Charles 222, 231, 448
Brandhoek 305
Bray 327, 388, *403*, 404–5, 427, 437, 462
Bray–Corbie road 394
Bremen Redoubt 302
Bridges, Major General William 41–2, *41*, 44, 46, 56, 59, 69, 84–5, 91, 93, 146, 197, 274
   AIF, appointment to 72–4
   Bean, relationship with 91
   death 109, 134

INDEX

Gallipoli 95, 98, 99, 101, 104, 109, 118–19, 134, 143–4
  Monash, relationship with 86–7, 208
Bridoux salient 220
Brie 388, 412, 413
Brierley, Lieutenant Alan 189
British Army
  III Corps 345, 365, 367, 370, 371, 379–80, 383, 404, 405, 415, 418, 427
    Hindenburg Line, advance towards 433–4, 443, 445
  V Corps 293, 442, 443
  VII Corps 323
  IX Corps 152, 180, 183–5, 430, 433, 442–3, 451, 456, 430
    Flanders offensive 1917 293
    Hindenburg Line, advance towards 433, 442, 443, 451, 456
    Messines 250, 257
  X Corps 250, 257, 322–3
    Flanders offensive 1917 293
  XIII Corps 445–6
  1st Cavalry Division 325
  5th Tank Brigade 337, 347, 349
  6th King's Own Royal Lancasters 175
  10th Hampshires 185, 187
  14th Sikhs 166, 178
  17th Division 402
  18th Division 224
  25th Division 250, 281, 456
  29th Brigade 184
  29th Division 94, 112, 226
  29th Indian Brigade 110, 152, 184, 475
  32nd Division 442
  40th Brigade 161, 183
  46th Division 442, 443, 451, 456
  49th Division 307
  57th Division 261
  66th Division 307, 309–10, 450
  74th Division 424, 426
  87th Brigade 226, 316
  161st Brigade 190
  Chatham Battalion 112, 122
  commanders 11
  criticism of 180–1, 326, 336, 434–5
  Deal Battalion 112
  Fifth Army 276, 281, 290, 320, 321, 324, 331–3
  First Army 405, 427, 439
  Fourth Army 11, 225, 278, 339, 347, 365–6, 379, 388, 393, 395, 397, 402, 408, 410, 417, 428, 439, 444, 445
  Portsmouth Battalion 112, 122–3
  Reserve Army 224
  Royal Marine Light Infantry Brigade 112, 123, 124, 127, 129
  Royal Naval Division 94, 112
  Second Army 218, 238, 247–8, 283, 296, 300
  Tank Corps *see* Tank Corps
  Third Army 320, 323, 324, 367, 404, 408, 410, 428, 430, 439, 444
British Expeditionary Force (BEF) 65, 206, 212, 241, 248, 276, 315, 337, 343, 364, 472–3
  decentralising control 411
  'learning curve' 224–5, 339, 463
British Front Line (old) 429
British Reserve Line 429
Broadmeadows Camp 76, 77, 79
Broodseinde 292, 293, 295, 300, *301*, 304, 309, 353, 374
  assessment of Monash's performance 304, 307
Browne, Lieutenant George 335
Bruay coal mines 366
Bruche, Lieutenant Colonel Julius 58, 64, 74, 231, 368
Brune Gaye 259
Buire Spur 416, 417
Bulair 94
Bulford Review 234–5
Bullecourt 314, 343, 352, 354, 427
Burnage, Lieutenant Colonel Granville *83*, 104, 120, 123, 139, 141, 149
Buscourt 423
Bustard 230, 231
Butler, Lieutenant General Sir Richard 284, 345, 370, 371, 380, 404
  Hindenburg Line, advance towards 433, 445
Byng, General Sir Julian 324, 397–8, 402, 404–5, 410, 472
  Hindenburg Line, advance towards 428, 429

C

Cachy Salient 375
Cairo 83, 84–5
Camberley 28, 64–6, 72
Cambrai 314, 321, 322, 348, 349–50, 361, 439
Camiers 288, 319
Campbell, Colonel G.R. 70
Canadian Forces 28, 260, 263, 315, 332, 365–9, 395, 404, 427–8
  Amiens 375, 379, 381, 386, 388–91
Cannan, Lieutenant Colonel James 104, 128–9, 135, 139, 190–1, 238, 246, 281, 285
  August offensives (Gallipoli) 151, 154, 159, 164–5, 172, 177–8

549

MONASH

Flanders offensive 1917 282, 296, 302
   Messines 256, 271, 272
   Somme 1918 324, 326–9
   Western Front 228, 242, 344, 453–4
Cape Helles 94, 98, 112, 126, 151, 157, 474
Cappy 408
Carlyon, Les 153
Carruthers, Brigadier General Robert 335, *335*, 337, 476
Carver, Field Marshal Lord M. 16, 271
casualties 199–200, 343, *360*, 408, *424*, *457*, 458
   American forces 447–8, 449, 451–2
   Amiens 391
   August offensives (Gallipoli) 167, 182, 185, 187, 189, 191
   Broodseinde 302, 313
   burial of dead 137, *138*
   evacuation of 100, 149, 178–9, 187–8, 206, 274, 304–5, 309
   Flanders offensive 314, 315
   friendly fire 107, 180
   Gallipoli 100, 105, 108, 113, 125, 128
   Hamel 360, 362, 447
   Hindenburg Line, Allied advance towards 432, *433*
   illness and disease 148, 187–8, 242, 285
   maladministration of returning soldiers 149, 236
   Messines 267, 273, 313
   Monash on 233, 240, 345, 420, 441, 464
   Montbrehain 457
   officers 109, 149
   Passchendaele 311–12, *312*, 313
   postwar revulsion regarding 11
   raids 245
   Somme 1918 328, 330, 394
   Turkish 101, 135
   Western Front 220, 245–6
Casula 229
cavalry 30, 34–5, 54, 305, 325–7, 366, 382–3, 386, 428, 457
   German 324
Cavan, General (Lord) 263, 472
censorship 69–70
Cérisy 324, 370, 380
Chailak Dere 161
Chamchik Punar 157, 167
Charteris, Brigadier General John 224, 305, 306
Château de las Hutte 250
Château La Motte 243
Chaulnes 369, 382, 385, 387–8
Chaulnes-Roye Line 366, 385–6

Chauvel, General Sir Henry 'Harry' 41, 53, 68, 197–8, 203, 207, 460
   character 142, 146
   Gallipoli 129–30, *130*, 135, 139–42
   Monash, relationship with 130–1
   Mounted Division, control over 207, 208, 217
Chemin des Dames 263, 276
Cheshire Ridge 190, 194
The Chessboard 113, 115, 119–20, 122–3, 125
Chipilly Spur 365, 370–1, 380, 381, 383, 427
Chuignes 405, 408, 426, 462, 467, 469
Chuignolles 381, 406
Chunuk Bair 94, 95, 116, 119, 475, 476
   August offensives 152, 153, 155, 167, 175, 180, 181
Clemenceau, Georges 363, *363*, 397
Cléry 411–13, 415, 418–20
Close, Colonel C.F. 45
Colman, Lieutenant Arthur 227–8
Cologne River 412, 429
Colombo 82–3, 84
commanders 27–8, 134, *227*, 462–3
   adapt and change, ability to 225–6
   Australian Corps 337–8
   battlefield communications 16–17, 271–2
   casualties 109, 149
   chain of command 36, 288–9
   criticisms of 11, 133–4, 169, 170, 181, 225–6, 283
   disorganisation (Western Front) 219–20, 239–40
   headquarters, remaining in 271–2, 275, 310–11, 453, 467–9
   horizontal organisation 404
   liaison officers, use of 246–7, 298, 448–9
   Monash on 78–9, 219, 426
   selection of 75–6, 197, 219, 227–8
   staff officers 47
   successful, qualities of 12–17, 26, 29, 51–2
   training 65, 214–15, 232–4, 240–1, 247, 317–18, 340
communications 259, 288
   'Army Centre' 247
   Broodseinde 297, 299, 303
   commanders, between 262–2
   conferences 263, 356–7, 377, 463
   despatch riders 390
   Flanders offensive 312
   importance of good 17, 90, 124, 233, 262–3
   issues 16, 89, 105, 107, 120, 123, 185, 303, 312–13, 452–3
   Messines, confusion at 268–72

INDEX

'percolation of orders' 262
visual signalling 376
Western Front raids, on 221
Compton, Sergeant Albert 160
Congreve, Lieutenant General Sir Walter 323–7, 329, 332
conscription referendum 236–7, 318, 397
consolidation 225
Cook, Sir Joseph 383
Corbett, Staff Sergeant Major 129
Corbie 371, 420
courage 79
   moral 13, 26, 124, 145, 246, 346, 358, 410
   physical 13, 246, 258, 369, 467
Courage, Brigadier General Anthony 349–52, 360
Courtney, Lieutenant Colonel Richard 107–8, 133
Courtney's Post 103, *103*, 104, 107, *108*, 113–14, 116–17, 126, 135, 137
Cox, Brigadier General Vaughn 215, 217, 218, 353
   AIF reorganisation 207–9, 214
   Gallipoli 152–4, 157–9, 163, 166–9, 172, 175, 178, 180–4, 188, 189, 475
   Monash, relationship with 217, 222, 334
Coxen, Brigadier General Walter *335*, 338, 358
creative imagination 17, 51–2, 78, 246, 298, 304, 334, 460, 469, 472
Crest Farm 313
Crest Farm Spur 307
Croisilles 320
Crooks, Lieutenant Tom 182
Curlu 411
Currie, Lieutenant General Sir Arthur 28–9, *29*, 67, 244, 263, 314, 332, 370, 404, 428, 472, 473
   Amiens offensive 1918 365–6, 369, 375, 386, 388, 391, 392
Cutlack, Frank 470

D

Damakjelik Bair 152, 153, 182
Daniel, Brigadier-General 190–1
Dardanelles Army 195, 206
Dardanelles Royal Commission 153, 169
Dardanelles Straits 94
Dare, Major Charles 177, 179, 185, 189, 195, 219
Daring and Dash crossings 297
Davidson Major General John 278
Dead Man's Ridge 111, 113–15
Dean-Pitt, Colonel 39
Debeney, General Marie-Eugène 366, 381
defence in depth (elastic defence)
   Allies 316–17, 322
   German 278–80, 288, 307, 409

Degoutte, General Jean 364
delegation of authority 12, 27
demobilization 11, 439, 459
Department of Defence (Victoria) 30
   cost cutting 38–9, 56
Dernancourt 328, 329–30
Desmond Trench 296
determination 14
diet 147, 182
discipline 78–9, 84–5, 145, 194, 203–4, 206, 215, 217, 342, 464
   3rd Division 229, 238–9, 283–4, 342
   Australian training camps 229
   courts martial 233–4
   laxity, Monash's crusade against 242, 403
   loss of experienced officers and NCOs 150–1
   march to Suez 213
   Monash on 342
   reorganisation post battle, and 106, 110
disease *see* illness and disease
Dixmude 276
Dochy Farm 295
Dodds, Lieutenant Colonel Thomas 80, 86, 287, 333, 335, 341, 439
Doullens 322–3, 325, 326
   Conference 322
Douve (stream) 251, 256, 267, 274
   footbridges *254*
Downes, Lieutenant Rupert *380*
Drake-Brockman, Major Geoffrey 262–3
Drionville 284
Drocourt-Quéant Switch Line 427–8
Ducane, Lieutenant General John 365, 367
Durrant, Captain James 122, 142, 151, 189, 213, 262
dysentery 148, 190, 192
Dyson, Will 333

E

Edmonds, Brigadier General Sir James 305
Egypt 83–7, 89–91, *89*, 93–4, 96, 155, 192, 212, 223, 230, 234, 462
   Turkish threat 201
Eisenhower, John 446
El Alamein 384, 473
Elles, Major General Hugh 348, 353, 463
Elliott, Brigadier General Harold 'Pompey' 282, 356, 367, 371, 391, 437, 438
   Péronne/Mont St Quentin 420, 422, 424–5
Elliott, William 19–20
Elsa Trench 420, 421, 422
engineers 230, *427*

551

bridge construction and repairs *415*, 416, 426, *427*, 443, 463
road construction and repairs 373, 377, 444
Enoggera 76
Erquinghem 218, 219
Essame, Major General Hubert 26–7
Étaples 241
Etinehem 386, 394, 413, 417
Ewing, Thomas 42

F
Factory Farm 272
Farlow, Colonel George 21, 31, 33, 37, 48
Farmar, Colonel Harold *227*, 252
Farndale, General Sir Martin 419
Ferguson, Sir Ronald Munro 80
Ferme Lamire 415
Ferry Post 201
Feuillaucourt 420
Feuillères 416, 418, 426
Fisherman's Hut 94, 97, 102
Flamicourt 422, 424
Flandern 1 Line 279, 295, 302, 307
Flandern 2 Line 279
Flandern 3 Line 279
Flanders 238, *291*
Flanders offensive 1917 276–8, *277*, 289–90
  Blue Line 296–7, 302–3, 307, 308–9, 311, 313
  Green Line 309
  impact of 314–15
  Monash's plan 295–8, 308, 310–11
  preparations 278, 282–3
  Red Line 296, 297, 308–9, 311–13
Fletcher, Lieutenant Basil 123
flexibility 17, 27, 89, 405, 417, 469
flies 147
Flixécourt 369, 370
Florina Trench 421
Foch, Marshal F. 16, 322, 327, 329, 344, 345, 364–7, 378, 385, 395–6, 405
  Directive Générale No. 3 365–6
  Villers-Bretonneux conference 397–8
Foott, Brigadier General Cecil *335*, 338, 373, 469
Ford, Lieutenant Hubert 185
foresight 27
Forsythe, Captain William 82, 104
Foster, Colonel Hubert 50, 52, 59
Foucaucourt Plateau 406, 413
Framerville 381, 387
Franvillers 323, 324
Fraser, Brigadier General Lyons *335*, 337
French, Field Marshal Sir John 234, 247–8

French Army 212, 306, 320, 439
  9th Corps 381
  31st Corps 375, 381
  First Army 356, 365–6, 396, 430, 444
  Gallipoli, at 94
  mutiny 276
  Second Army 365
  Sixth Army 364
  Tenth Army 363
  Third Army 396
Frévent 322
Frezenberg 295
Froissy Beacon 407–9, 467
Fromelles 225, 235
frontal assaults 17, 63, 205, 225, 255, 313, 394, 413, 416, 453, 455, 476
Fuller, Lieutenant Colonel J.F.C. 290, 349, 361, 463
Fyansford bridge *25*

G
Gaba Tepe 94, 97, 98, 137, 474–5, 476
Gallipoli 94, 96, 474–7
  August offensive 152–67, *156*, 171
  evacuation of wounded 100
  failure, reasons for 96, 98
  landings 96–7, 98, 100
  life at 147–8, 160–1
  map *92*, *102*
  May armistice 137, *138*
  Monash at 96–7, 99–102, 106–14, 116–20, 122–96, *148*
    assessment of performance 172, 179–80, 186, 199–200
    No. 3 Section 126–30, 134–5
  original plan of attack 94–5
  reconnaissance 152, 154–5
  stalemate 194
  terrain 96, 103–4, 153–5, *154*, 168, 169, 177
  Turkish mining operations 127–9, 139
  withdrawal from 195, 206
Gammage, Bill 383
Garenne Wood 408
gas 16, 230, 245, 448
  Messines, at 248, 251, 265
  smoke, use of 245
gas respirators 220
Gellibrand, Major General Sir John 28, 91, 127, 133, 148, 208, 334, 346, *374*, 394–5, 399, 411, 445
  Bray 404–5, 462
  Hindenburg Line, advance towards 453–5, 462
  leapfrogging, on 373–4

INDEX

Monash, on 464, 466–7
Mont St Quentin/Péronne, advance towards 415, 418, 420
mutiny of 37th Battalion 438
General Officer Commanding (GOC) 40–1
George V, King 234–5, 400, *400*, *401*
Georgette offensive 379
German Army 220, 347, 364, 387, 395, 435
   2nd Prussian Guards 412
   1918 offensive 314 *see also* Operation Michael
   'black day' 384–5
   counter-attacks 257, 273, 279–80, 282–3, 288, 300–2, 420
   defence in depth 278–80, 288, 307, 409
   Fourth Army 300
   morale 345, 410, 419, 429, 435
   storm troops 320
German Officers' Trench 115
Germans
   internment in Australia 69
Gheluvelt 248
Gheluvelt Plateau 279, 289–90, 292
Gibraltar 406
Gibson, John 25, 28, 201, 243–4
Gillemont Farm 440, 446, 452, 453
Gillison, Chaplain Andrew 160
Glasfurd, Brigadier General Duncan 91, 210, 213
Glasgow, Major General Sir Thomas 28, 334, 388, 390, 391–2, *407*, 407–9, 462, 470
   Hindenburg Line, advance towards 433
Godley, Major General Alexander 80, 84–7, *88*, 90, 101, 169, 194, 196, 198, 202, 207, 230, 404, 420
   2nd ANZAC 207, 238, 255
   August offensives (Gallipoli) 152–5, 157, 162, 181–2, 184, 187, 188
   character and leadership style 202–3
   Flanders offensive 1917 280, 292–3, 303–4, 313
   Gallipoli 96, 97, 99, 100, 101, 106, 110, 116–19, 122–31, *130*, 134–5, 137, 140, 142–3, 149, 151, 189–90, 195, 476, 477
   Messines 250, 255, 257, 260–1, 266, 269, 271–2, 274
   Monash, relationship with 87–8, 126, 145, 150, 190–1, 203, 217, 222, 303, 311, 315
   reorganisation of Allied forces 206
Goldstein, Lieutenant 133, 287, 335, 464
Goldstein, Major Jacob 33
Goltz, Field Marshal Baron von der 16
good fortune 14, 462–3
Gordon, Brigadier General Joseph
Gough, General Sir Hubert 29, 65, 224, 276, 278
   criticism of 11

Flanders offensive 1917 280, 282, 283, 289, 293, 305
   German 1918 offensive 320–1
Gouy 440
Grant, Colonel Charles 364
Gravenstafel Spur 295–8, 302, 307, 309
Gressaire Wood 346
Grey Farm 251
Griffiths, Major Tom 198
Grimwade, Brigadier General Harold 227, 262, 320
Groot, Gerard de 321
Gurkhas 157, 162, 164, 166, 171, 180
Gwynn, Brigadier General Charles 269

H

Haig, Field Marshal Sir Douglas 29, 65, 67, *211*, 212, 244, 279, 284, 343, 344, 364, 400, 405, 425
   American forces at Hamel 357–8
   Amiens offensive 1918 367, 368, 385–6
   August 1918 directives 409–10
   Birdwood and 243, 315
   criticism of 11, 13, 14, 224–5, 243
   Flanders offensive 276–8, *277*, 289–90, 305–6, 311, 386
   George V, and 234–5
   German 1918 offensive 321–2
   Hindenburg Line, advance towards 429–30, 445, 449, 450, 455
   Messines 247, 250, 255, 273, 274
   Monash, and 243, 263, 284–5, 311, 331–3, 357, 397, 471–2
   Morcourt, advance to 366
   organisation of infantry battalions 240
   Plumer, and 247
   Somme offensive 220, 235–6, 386, 395–6
   Villers-Bretonneux conference 397–8
Halle 412, 415, 416, 418, 420, 423
Ham 385
Hamel 346, *348*, 349, *351*, 361–4, 383, 470
   Blue Line 352, 360
   commencement of assault 359–60
   diversionary operations 356, 361
   Monash's plan for 349, 352–9, 372, 378–9, 462, 473
   textbook victory, as 361–2
Hamel Spur 346–7, 348, 367
Hamel Wood 346, 347, 354
Hamilton, General Sir Ian 61, *62*, 63, 80, 195, 197, 284, 430
   Gallipoli 94–5, 97, 99, 112, 126, 138–9, 142, 181, 474, 476

553

Hanebeek Valley 295, 297
Hangard Wood 347
Happy Valley 404
Harbonnières 366, 370, 381, 387
Hargicourt 431
Harington, Major General Charles 247, 258, 273, 293, 305, 338
Harper, Glyn 311
Hazebrouck 379
Heane, Brigadier General James 390, 406–7
Heliopolis 84, *86*, *89*
Henderson, Lieutenant Colonel George 52
Herbert, Aubrey 134
Herleville 406
Herring, Brigadier General Sydney
    Gallipoli 104, 141, 151, 184, 187, 195
    Western Front 394
Hill 60 (Gallipoli) 171, 173, 183–9, *183*, 190, 394, 461
Hill 63 (Flanders) 250, 251
Hill 100 (Gallipoli) 184
Hill 104 (France) 346–7, 349, 352
Hill 971 (Gallipoli) 14, 94, 95, 116, 152, 153, 157–9, 166, 171
    August assault on 173–8, *176*, 329, 474–7
Hill Q (Gallipoli) 94, 152, 157, 164, 175, 180, 181, 475
Hill, A.J. 170
Hill, Captain John 140–1
Hindenburg Line 325, 428, 448
    Allied advance towards 429–33, *432*, 439–55, *441*, *451*
        Blue Line 430, 431, 432
        Green Line 430
        Monash's plan 441–5, 467, 469–70
        Red Line 430, 432
    assault on 405
    German withdrawal towards 412, 428–30, 440
Hindenburg Main Line 431
Hindenburg Outpost Line 429, 430, *431*, 437, 440–54, *446*, 462
    American troops 445–53
    Green Line 441, 444, 447, 453
    Red Line 442
Hitler, Corporal Adolf 250
Hobbs, Lieutenant General Talbot 28, 198, 298, 330–1, 332, 334, 367, 398, *399*, 464, 470
    Amiens 378, 381, 388
    Monash's assessment of 422–3, 426
    Péronne/Mont St Quentin 413, 415–16, 420, 422–3, 424, 462
Hollingsworth, Staff Sergeant A. 38

Holmes, Brigadier General William 203, 207, 219, 269, 272, 283
Horne, General Sir Henry 405, 427–8
Houplines 244–5
Howard, Major General Sir Francis 230
Howe, Lieutenant Hedley 153, 170
Howse, Surgeon General Neville 238
Hughes, W.M. 15, 209, 236–7, 333, 369, 397, 398–400
    demobilization of AIF 459
    visit to Western Front 357, *358*, 436–7
Hunn, Major Sydney 354
Huns' Walk 267, 270
Hunter-Weston, Major General Sir Aylmer 94, 98, 151
Hutton, Major General Sir Edward 40
Hyde Park Corner 250

I

illness and disease 285
    Gallipoli 136, 147–8, 182, 187–8
    Western Front 242
Imbros 151
Imperial General Staff 45, 57
Imperial War Conference 333
information *see* communications; intelligence (military)
intelligence (military) 42–5, 168, 224–5, 241, 288, 340
    collection of information 44–5, 271
    importance of 233, 440
    topography 44, 45–6
Inventions Board 26
Iona 25, 460
Irvine, Major Frank 109
Irving, Brigadier General Godfrey 203, 213
Ismailia 201, 205
Israel pillbox 295, 302

J

Jacka, Captain Albert 111, 133, *136*, 191, 466
Jackson, Brigadier General George 225–7, *227*, 234, 246, 260, 281, 289, 293, 304, 316, 326
    Broodseinde 298–9
    Messines 255, 258, 262, 470
    Monash, relationship with 334–5, 336, 338
    Passchendaele 310
Jacob, Lieutenant General Sir Claud 471, 472
Japan 30
Jerilderie 19–20
Jerram, Major Charles 124

INDEX

Jess, Captain Carl 74, *81*, 119, 128, 134, 316, 322, 453, 455
Jobson, Brigadier General Alexander 228
    Messines 253, 255, 257, 272
    removal from command 285–7
Johannes Trench 421
Johnston, Brigadier General Francis 95, 122, 124
    August offensives (Gallipoli) 152, 154, 167, 175
Judah pillbox 295, 302

K

Kaiajik Dere 157, 177–8, 182–4, *183*, 186–7, 190
Keiberg 292
Kidney Trench 347
Kiggell, Lieutenant General Sir Launcelot 284, 332, 352
Kilid Bahr plateau 94, 95, 474
Kirke Committee 246
Kirkpatrick, Major General George 56, 197
Kitchener, Lord 49, 56, 59, 195, 201, 476, 477
The Knoll 440, 446
Koja Chemen Tepe 94
Krithia 112, 228, 327
Kruse, Major J.A.R. 60
Kum Kale 94

L

La Douve Farm 251, *267*, 272
La Fère 320
La Grange, Baroness 243
La Houssoie 220
La Petite Douve Farm 251, 254
La Potterie Farm 251, 272–3
La Rolanderie Farm 221
Lamb, Lieutenant Colonel Malcolm 240
Lambert, Major General Tom 396
Lamotte 370
Lancashire Landing 151
Lark Hill 229, 230, 235, 258
Lawrence, Major General Sir Herbert 207, 352, 435
Le Catelet 440, 441
Le Mesnil 413
Le Tronquoy 440, 442
Le Verguier 431, 432
Legge, Colonel James 53, 70, *71*, 80, 86, 149, 197–8, 203, 208, 220, 227
    4th Brigade, establishment of 73–5
Lemnos 96, 97, 99, 191–4
Lewis, Private Henry 123
Lewis guns 231, 279, 319, *425*, 435
Liardet, Lieutenant Colonel Claude 133–4

Liddell Hart, B.H. 14, 15, 17, 51, 66, 133, 382, 387, 404, 460
Lihons 392–3, 402, 410
Lihons Hill 391
Lille 280
Lilydale camp 61–3, 79, 139, 205, 461
limited objectives 273–4, 276, 290, 304, 352, 386, 462
Linton, Colonel Richard 70
Lisle, Lieutenant General Sir Beauvoir de 314
Lloyd George, David 314, 471–2
Locke, Lieutenant William *173*, 175
Lone Pine 151, 152, 161, 168, 476
Long, Bishop George 459
Lord Mayor of London's Procession 234
Loughran, Captain Henry 170, 178, 187
Luce River 375
Ludendorff, General Erich 273, 278, 300, 307, 344, 352, 364, 385
    'black day' 384–5
    Hindenburg Line, withdrawal to 428
Lumbres 283
Luther, Captain John 178
Lys River 238, 241, 280, 316, 356, 365

M

McCay, Colonel James 42, *42*, 44, 52, 55–6, 59, 72, 146, 196, 197–8, 202, 205, 222, 240
    AIF reorganisation 207, 208, 209, 331
    Fromelles 225
    Gallipoli 95, 98, 107
    training scheme 228–9
McGlinn, Lieutenant Colonel John 74, 75, 90, 91, 133, 197, 228, 338
    Gallipoli 101, 131, 163, *173*, 189
McGregor, Captain Roy 137
McGregor, Captain Stanley 188
machine guns 16, 67, 135, 145, 319–20
    German 221, 248, 278, 307, 413, *433*
    Hindenburg Line, Allied advance towards 431, 432
    long range 248
    massed 288
    Turkish skill 131
Mackay, Brigadier 448
Mackenzie, Lieutenant Compton 137
MacLagan's Ridge 101
MacLaurin, Colonel Henry 72, 103, 107–9
MacLaurin's Hill 100, 101, 104
McLintock, Private George 123
McNicoll, Brigadier General Walter 228, 283, 285

Flanders offensive 1917 296, 302, 303, 309, 310, 312–13
Messines 253, 255–7, 258, 261, 268–72
mutiny of 37th Battalion 438
raids, Western Front 245
Somme 1918 325, 326–9, 394–5, 418, 453
McSharry, Lieutenant Terence 140
Mal Tepe 94–6
Malcolm, Brigadier General Henry 83
Malone, Lieutenant Colonel William 132
Mangin, General Charles 363, 364
manpower shortage 235–6, 321, 437–8
Mansbridge, Lieutenant Colonel William 269–70, 272, 275
map-making 45–6, 158, 298
  errors 89, 175
Marks, Lieutenant Douglas 173
Marne River 364, 366, 379
Marseilles 218
Matz River 345
Maxse, Major General Ivor 224, 232, 247, 263, 322, 448, 472, 473
medical personnel 137, 163, 177, 179, 187, 238
  Broodseinde 304–5
  stretcher bearers 252, 309
Mediterranean Expeditionary Force (MEF) 94, 96, 195, 206
Melba, Dame Nellie 24
Melbourne Harbour Trust 23
Mena Camp 84, 91, 223
Menin 279
Menin Gate 294
Menin Road 290, 293, 296, 299, 353, 471
Menzies, R.G. 23
Mercer, Brigadier General David 112
Méricourt 366, 386, 394, 395, 417, 420
Méricourt-l'Abbé 323
Merris 218
Messines 247, *249*, 250, *268*, *270*, 276, 334, 353, 383
  aircraft, use of 249, 266
  approach routes 265–6
  artillery barrage 265, 268
  Black Line 250, 252, 255–8, *256*, 266, 268–9, 312
  commencement of assault 266
  communication issues 268–72
  German counter-attacks 257, 267, 273
  Green Line 250, 255–8, 267–9, 271, 312
  large terrain models of battlefield *259*
  mines *see* mines
  plan for assault 248–50, 252–63, 272, 275, 462

Messines-Wytschaete Ridge 247–8
Meuse River 439
militarism 15–16
Military Handbook of Australia 44
military technology 35–6, 67
  independent arms, coordination of 361–2, 393, 472–3
  innovations 225–6, 282, 355–6, 463
militia 64
  Permanent and Citizen Forces 40, 59
  Victorian 30–8
Millen, Edward 70
Miller, Joe 33
mines 231
  destruction caused by *265*
  Messines 248, 264, 273
  Minenwerfer Fuzes 245
Mitchell, David 24, 25
Moascar 201, 206, 213
Molenaarelsthoek 292
momentum 254, 373–4, 387, 395–6, 405, 411
Monasch, Gustav 72
Monasch, Leo 72
Monash, Bertha 22, *81*
Monash, Bertha (nee Manasse) 19–20
Monash, Hannah Victoria (Vic) (nee Moss) 22, *81*, 144, 209
  illness 201–2, 243
  letters from Monash 151, 196, 222, 242, 243–4
Monash, Lieutenant General Sir John 11, 66, *81*, *83*, *193*, 207, *210*, *227*, *335*, *363*, *396*, *465*
  3rd Division *see* 3rd Division
  4th Brigade *see* 4th Brigade
  13th Infantry Brigade 59–64, 68, 73, 77–8, 79, 340
  age 14
  AIF, appointment to 70–2
  attention to detail 12, 48, 145, 158, 172, 179, 195, 234, 257, 258, 262, 275, 334, 373, 444–5, 473
  Australian Corps, command of 331
  Australian Intelligence Corps (AIC) 42–5, 48–57, *51*, 68, 461
  The Australian Victories in France in 1918 11, 367, 368, 387, 413, 436, 466
  awards and recognition 196, 316, 400, 460, 464–5
  Bean, relationship with 91, 144–5, 171, 436
  birth 19
  'breakdown' 166, 168–70
  Bridges, relationship with 86–7, 208
  cartography 45–6

INDEX

character 129, 146, 335–6
Chauvel, relationship with 130–1
civil training and experience 12, 15, 21–5, 27–9, 35, 47, 65–7, 205, 220, 232, 258, 261, 463
commander, as 13–15, 231–2, 287, 293, 335–6, 340–1, 404–5, 416–17, 433, 434–5, 455, 460–73
    weaknesses/lapses 179, 406, 467–70
conspiracy against 333, 398–9
Cox, relationship with 217, 222
criticism of 13, 79, 133, 168
death 460
decision making 12, 17–18, 250, 470
depression 24, 84
Deputy Chief Censor 69–70
Director-General of Repatriation and Demobilisation 459
disenchantment with the war 202
education 19–21, 29, 50–1, 66
employment, post-war 460
engineering 21–6, *25*, 463
financial concerns 243–4
Flanders offensive 1917, planning for 279–81, 288
Gallipoli *see* Gallipoli
German language 24, 44
German origins 207–8
Godley, relationship with 87–8, 126, 150, 190–1, 203, 217, 222, 303, 315
Gold Medal Essay Competition 53–4
Grand Officier de l'Ordre de la Couronne with Croix de Guerre 465
Haig, and 243, 263, 284–5, 331–3, 357, 471–2
Hamilton, relationship with 139, 284
health concerns 82, 190, 192
Jackson, relationship with 334–5, 336, 338
kindness and generosity 466
Knight Commander of the Bath (KCB) 316, 400, *400*, *401*
leadership and man-management 22, 36–8, 48–9, 52, 54–5, 59–60, 63–4, 76–7, 159, 170, 182, 199, 215, 217, 229–30, 239–41, 335–6, 340–1, 411, 438–9, 454–5, 464–6
lecturing 35–6, 82, 204–5, 215, 217, 231–2, 258
Lemnos, on 192
letters home 151, 196, 222, 242, 243–4
literary aspirations 20
London, in 379
marriage 22

Messines *see* Messines
militia, career in 30–68, *31*, *34*
mythology surrounding 12
North Melbourne Battery 32–8, 43, 48, 54, 340, 461
obituaries 460
organisational ability 20–1
physical appearance 69, 90, 138, 234, 316, *331*, 434
promotion, competition for 197–8, 208–9, 222, 331–4
publicity/self-advertising 144, 168, 196, 209, 238, 275, 316, 363, 367–8, 377, 400–1, 436, 464–5
Rawlinson, relationship with 339, 343–5, 362–3, 397, 411, 417–18
Rosenthal, relationship with 287
Russell, relationship with 203, 205–6
ruthlessness 18, 199, 384, 426, 455, 464
state funeral 460
University (D) Company 30–2, *31*
Victorian Garrison Artillery (VGA) 32–40, 58
Victory March *459*
war, on 244
War Letters 169
welfare of soldiers, concern for 233, 238, 274, 287, 317, 335, 341–2, 354, 384, 402, 426, 434, 461–2
White, and 234, 319–20, 325, 471
'Wilderness Essay' 53–4
Monash, Louis 19–20
Monash, Mathilde (Mat) 20
Monash & Anderson 23, 24
Monash Valley 102–3, *103*, 104, 110, 113–16, *114*, *115*, 119–20, 124, 133–5, 142–3, 196
Mondicourt 322, 323, 325
Monier Pipe Company 23–4
Monro, General Sir Charles 195, 206
Mont St Quentin 412, *414*, 415–25, *419*, 462, 469
    assessment of Monash's plan/role 417–18, 426–7, 473
    tactical significance 428
Montagu, Sir Edwin 339
Montbrehain 456–8, *457*
Montdidier 365, 366
Montgomery, Major General Archibald 15, 339, 368, 384, 389, 417, 428, 460, 466–7, 469, 473
Montigny 323
Monument Wood 347, 367, 368
Moore, Lieutenant Colonel Athelstan 120, 122
mopping-up operations 279, 281, 309
    tanks 349, 350

moral courage 13, 26, 124, 145, 246, 346, 358, 410
Morcourt 365–6, 370–1, 378
Morcourt–Harbonnières ravine 365
Morlancourt 330, 344–5, 346, 368, 379, 462
Morlancourt Ridge 323, 324, 327
Morlancourt Spur 344
Morshead, Lieutenant Colonel Leslie 266, 311
Mortar Ridge 116–17, 119
Moss, Captain Aubrey 196, 209, 228, *344*
motor vehicles 16
  casualty evacuation 309
  intelligence gathering on 45
  reconnaissance, for 376
Mount Sorrel 249
Mouquet Farm 343
Mudros Harbour 96
Murdoch, Keith 168, 236, 333, 398–9, 436, 437
Murray, General Sir Archibald 206–7, 212

N
The Narrows 94, 181
Nauroy 441
Naval and Military Club 40
The Nek 103, 113, 119–20, 125, 152, 155, 167, 168
New Zealand Army 84, 181
  Auckland Battalion 100
  Canterbury Battalion 122
  Flanders offensive 1917 281, 292, 307, 309, 311
  Gallipoli 95, 97, 100, 101, 107, 111, 119–26, 143, 180, 185
  Messines 250, 251, 261
  Nelson Battalion 112, 122–3
  NZ Mounted Rifles (NZMR) Brigade 80, 152, 154–5, 165, 184
  Otago Battalion 101, 110, 111, 119–23, 461
  Wellington Battalion 101, 132–3
  Western Front, on 221
NZ and A Division 203
  Egypt 80, 85, 89, 91, 201
  Gallipoli 95–6, 105, 107, 116, 118–19, 131, 142, 152, 162, 195, 198
Newlands, Staff Clerk 55
Nielles-les-Bléquin 322
Nieppe 239
Nivelle, General Robert 276
no-man's land *360*
  patrolling 318
North, John 170
North Melbourne Battery 32–8, 43, 48, 54, 340, 461

No. 1 Outpost (Anzac) 182
No. 2 Outpost (Anzac) 162, 181
No. 3 Outpost (Anzac) 152, 161
Nurlu 417, 424, 427

O
O'Donnell, Major Francis 241
Officer, Sir Keith 434
officers *see* commanders
O'Hehir, Private James *432*
Oise River 320
Old British Main (Green) Line 430
Omignon River 429
Ommiécourt 412, 415, 416, 418, 420
Oosttaverne Line (Green Line) 249, 250, 251, 255, 256, 257, 266, *268*, 272–3
Operation Michael 320–2
operations 46–7, 199
  diversionary 356, 361
optimism 233, 341
orders 377, 454
  promulgation of 232, 447, 462–3
  understanding of 232–3
Orme de Barleux 413
O'Ryan, Major General John 447, 449, 455
Ostend 276
outflanking movement 152–3
Overton, Major Percy 152–4, 157, 162–4, 172, 175, 179
Owen, Lieutenant Colonel Robert 111

P
Parnell, J.W. 31
Passchendaele 248, 275, 295, *306*, *308*, 311–14, 335, 383, 412, 417, 441, 450 *see also* Flanders offensive 1917
  November assault 314
  repulse *313*
Passchendaele-Staden-Clercken Ridge 276
patience 26
patrolling no-man's land 318
peaceful penetration 330, 342, 345, 366, 367, 402, 429, 431
Pear Trench 347, 352
Pearce, George Foster 70–1, 75, 87, 145, 197, 198, 202, 207–8, 275, 333, 398
Peck, Lieutenant Colonel John 270–1, 272
Péronne 388, 410–11, *414*, 415–16, 421–5, *425*, 462, 469
  assessment of Monash's plan/role 417–18, 426–7
Pershing, General John 357, 366, 446, 464

INDEX

Pétain, General Philippe 260, 322
Pethebridge, Samuel 75
Pilckem Ridge 289
pillboxes, German *265*, 267, 278, 295, 440
'pinching out' 249–50, 366
Pine Ridge 476
Pinwill, Major William 119, 162
Pitt, Barry 428
planning and preparation 224, 263, 275, 279–80, 288
    changes to plans, impact of 406–9, 426, 461
    conferences 263, 356–7, 377, 415
    importance of 17, 26, 65–6, 145, 189, 199, 258, 307, 326, 362, 383, 467–8
    raids (Western Front) 220
    secrecy, importance of 356–7
    unity of action 255, 340
platoon doctrine 263–4, 293
Ploegsteert Wood 250, 251, 259, 264–5, 316, 462
Plugge's Plateau 101, 106
Plumer, General Sir Herbert 218, 247, 263, 278, 279, 285, 338, 379, 472
    Flanders offensive 1917 280, 290, 293, 296, 303–4, 305
    Haig, and 247
    Messines 247–50, 257, 260, 268, 273
Poelcappelle 279, 306, 308
politics 14–15, 32
Polygon Wood 279, 290, 292, 296–7, 298, 300, 353, 471
Pont de Nieppe 264
Pope, Lieutenant Colonel Harold 151, 183, 189–90, 213
    August offensives (Gallipoli) 154, 159, 165, 172, 175, 178–80
    landing and early days at Gallipoli 100, 105, 110–13, 123, 129, 138, 139–41, 151, 154
Pope's Hill 111–14, 116, 122, 126–8, 135, 137, 139, 167
Port Phillip Bay 33
Pozières 227, 231, 260, 343
preparation *see* planning and preparation
Prince of Wales, visit of 213–14
Prior, Robin 314, 343, 355, 384, 417
prisoners of war
    Allied 330, 379
    German 245, 274, 330, 345, 362, 364, 381, 408, 418, 419, 432, 458
    Turkish 141–2
'protective patrols' 288
Proyart 381, 394, 395, 402, 413
psychology 318, 341, 354, 473

Pugsley, Chris 124
punctuality 26, 90, 342
Pyke, Captain Clarence 227, 324

Q
Quelmes 264
Quennemont Farm 440, 446, 452
Quetta 72, 338
Quinn, Major Hugh 104, 115–16, *140*, 141
Quinn's Post 103, *103*, 104, 107, 110, 113–16, 119–20, 126–8, 132–7, *133*, 139–42, *141*, 167

R
radio 16
raiding 244–6, 264, 318–19, 344
Rainecourt 392
Rankine, Colonel Robert 158, 177, 189
Ravebeek 308, 412
Ravelsberg 275, 321
Rawlinson, General Sir Henry 29, 339–40, *339*, 356, 370–1, 378, 394, 402, 405, 427, 470, 472
    American forces at Hamel 357–8
    Amiens offensive 1918 367–9, 375, 379, 381–2, 385–9
    criticism of 11, 225, 340
    German withdrawal to Hindenburg Line 428
    Hamel assault 346, 348–50, 353
    Hindenburg Line, advance towards 429–30, 440, 442–6, 450, 455–7
    Monash, relationship with 339, 343–5, 362–3, 397, 411, 417–18
    Morcourt, advance to 365–6
    Péronne/Mont St Quentin 410–11, 425
    Villers-Bretonneux conference 397–8
Read, Major General George 445, 446, 448
Reid, Lieutenant 43
reinforced concrete 24–5, 27
Reinforced Concrete and Monier Pipe Construction Company 25
reorganisation, importance of 106, 110, 145
repatriation 11
reserve companies 255
Reserve Line *see* Beaurevoir Line
Reserve Gully 13, 101, 143, 147–51, *148*, 155, 157, *160*, 182
Rest Gully 101
Reynolds, Major Edgar 70
Rhiems 439
Rhodes James, Robert 166, 169–70, 172
Rhododendron Ridge 152, 155, 167, 182
Ribemont 324–5
rifles 67

559

Lee Enfield 150
  periscope 132, 193
Riga 321
roads, construction and repairs 373, 377, 444
Roberts, Brigadier Chris 98
Robertson, Field Marshal Sir William 66, 207, 212
Romarin 264
Rosenhain, Walter 237–8
Rosenthal, Brigadier General Sir Charles 28, 227, *286*, 287, 323, 334, 344, 391, 457, 470
  Monash, relationship with 287
  Passchendaele 309–10
  Péronne/Mont St Quentin 415–16, 418, 420–1, 423, 426
  Somme 1918 325, 330, 346
Rosières 387
  rail yard *392*
Royal Flying Corps (RFC)
  Messines, at 249
Royal Review (Bulford Field) 234–5
Roye 382, 385
Rule, Lieutenant Edgar 213
Rupprecht, Crown Prince 385
Russell, Brigadier General Andrew 203–6, *203*, 230
  Gallipoli 154–5, 161, 183–5, 187, 188, 189, 195, 196
  Messines 257
  Western Front 221, 292, 300
Russell's Top 103, 104, 105, 107, 110–13, 116, 117, 122, 476
Russian Army 306
Ruthven, Second Lieutenant William *397*
Ryrie, Colonel Granville 81

S

Sailly-Laurette 327–8, 344, 346, 365, 383
Sailly-le-Sec 323, 324, *328*, 412
Sailly-le-Sec-Treux spurs 328
St Christ 412, 413
St Just–Amiens railway 365
St Mihiel salient 366
St Quentin 370, 387, 412
  Canal 440, *443*
  road repairs 377, 444
St Yves 249
Salisbury Plain 234, 237
Salonika Force 195
Sanders, Marshal Otto Liman von 132
Santerre plateau 346–7, 356
Sari Bair Range 14, 94, 96, 98, 152, 177, 181, 383, 474, 476
Sarpi Camp 191–4

Scarpe 405
Scheldt River 440
Schnitzel Farm 251, 253, 266
Second Ridge 98, 103, 105
secrecy 356–7
Seeangchoon 96, 97, 99
  hospital ship, as 100
Seine pillbox 295
Sellheim, Lieutenant Colonel Victor 54, 55
Semmens, Major James 43, 57
Septième Barn 261
Serapeum 201, 212–14, 229
Serle, Geoffrey 333, 338, 466
set piece manoeuvres 354, 375, 393, 408, 411, 416–17, 426, 429, 431–2, 438, 456
Sheffield, Garry 225
shell-shock 240
Shrapnel Gully 101, 102, 105, 106, 110, 122
Simonson, Lieutenant Eric 196, 227, 316
Simonson, Paul 316, *344*
Sinai 84
Sinclair-MacLagan, Major General Ewen 27, 72, *95*, 203, 394, 448, 470
  Amiens 378, 380, 381, 383, 387, 388
  Gallipoli 95, 98, 99, 100, 101, 109, 111, 146, 394
  Hamel 352, 353
  Hindenburg Outpost Line, advance towards 432, 433, 462
  Western Front 283, 318, 323, 325, 334, 346, 348, *363*, 367
Sixsmith, Major General Eric 14, 313, 325, 472
Skeen, Lieutenant Colonel Andrew 155, 195, 474, 476, 477
Slim, Field Marshal Lord 169
Smith, Charles 144
Smith, Lieutenant Colonel Walter 266, 269
Smithers, A.J. 78, 84, 123, 170, 263, 361, 416
smoke 282, 297, 299, 304, 352, 355, 356, 378, 406, 408, 411, 463
  'flavoured' 245, 350, 356
Smyth, Major General Nevill 293, 331, 334
snipers 109, 111–12, 134, 184, *432*
Soissons 364
soldier spirit 62, 78
Somerville, Lieutenant Colonel George 338
Somme 218, 320, 323, 346, 366, 370, 388, 398
  Allied advance (August 1918) *390*
  'bounce crossing' 413
  bridge repairs *415*, 416, 426
  Somme offensive 220, 223, 225, 235, 263, 310–11

INDEX

South African War (Boer War) 40, 66, 93
the Sphinx 102, *143*, 299
Springfield pillbox 295, 297, 302
Staden 248
staff work, importance of 46, 51–2, 189, 247, 299
Stanley, Captain John 35, 59
State Electricity Commission of Victoria 460, 467
Steele's Post 103, 104, 109, 116, 135
Steenwerck 243, 252
Steignast Farm 251, 267, 281
Stevens, Lieutenant Colonel 437
Stevenson, David 321
Stewart, Brigadier General James 371, 421, 423, 424
Stodart, Lieutenant Colonel Robert 135
Stokes mortars 214, 220, 260, 279, 302
Stopford, Lieutenant General Sir Fred 152, 180
Stormy Trench 260
Story, Lieutenant Colonel Charles 266, 268, 438
stragglers 110
strategy and tactics 13, 50–3, 231
    'bite and hold' 225, 249–50, 273–4, 276, 290
    'bounce crossing' 413
    defence in depth (elastic defence) 278–80, 288, 307, 316–17, 322, 409
    limited objectives 273–4, 276, 290, 304, 352, 386, 462
    Monash's lectures 232–3
    mopping-up 279, 281, 309, 349, 350
    peaceful penetration 330, 342, 345, 366, 367, 402, 429, 431
    'pinching out' 249–50, 366
    'protective patrols' 288
    set piece manoeuvres 354, 375, 393, 408, 411, 416–17, 426, 429, 431–2, 438, 456
    'turning movement' 416–17, 443
Suez Canal 83, 201, 214
    march to 212–13
supply and logistics 16, 44, 54, 235, 372, 462
    13th Infantry Brigade 60, 63–4
    ammunition, parachute drops 355–6, 361
    Egypt, in 91, 214
    equipment shortages 60, 91, 192, 228, 235, 237
    Gallipoli 113, 117, 145, 147, 182–3
    life in the trenches (Gallipoli) 147–8
    Messines 252–253
    mismanagement by GHQ 192
    staff work, importance of 46–7, 51–2, 299
    tanks carrying ammunition and water 360–1
    understanding 13
    Victorian Garrison Artillery 39–40

Suvla 152, 153, 181
Suvla Plain 154, 173, *174*
Suzanne 411

T

Table Top 152
Tactical Exercises Without Troops 61, 288
Tank Corps 348
tanks 16, 249, 261, 314, 337, 348–54, *355*, 394, 406, 435, *451*
    Amiens, at 375–7, 378, 388, 392
    dummy *430*, 431
    Hamel, at 359–60, 361, 473
    Hindenburg Line, advance towards 430, 444, 449, 450, 457
    Mark *I* 352
    Mark IV 249, 348, 353
    Mark V 347–9, 353
    Monash, and 348–50
    training with 354
    Whippets 377, 382–3, 389, 447
Taylor, A.J.P. 273, 460
Taylor's Gap 162–4, 172
Tel-el-Kebir 201, 207, 209, *210*
Temperley, Major General Arthur 181
Terraine, John 284, 289, 305, 419, 434, 461, 472
Thiepval 224
tidiness 26, 342
Tidworth Training Centre 235
Tilney, Major Les 123, 149, 151, 154, 158, 163–5, 175
topography
    collection of information 44, 45–6
    understanding 13
training 65, 106, 223
    3rd Division 223, 229–34, 237, 240–1, 283–4, 288–9
    AIC 44, 54
    AIF 73–4, 76–9, 82, 87, 89–91, *89*, 93–4, 193–4, 204–5, 235–6, 462
    American troops 448
    Australian Army 60–3, 79
    Lilydale camp 61–3, 79, 205
    militia 36–7, 40
    officers 214–15, 232–4, 240–1, 247, 340
    platoon doctrine 264
    reinforcements 150–1
    signals 204
    tanks, with 354
    Western Front raids 221
Transylvania 218
trench foot 240

trench warfare 16, 67, 193, 223, 325–6
    Gallipoli *108*, 114–15, 131–3, 185–6
    life in the trenches
        Gallipoli 147–8, 194
        Western Front 242
    training 214, 230–1
Treux 327
troop movement 448
    concealing 282, 378–9
    leapfrogging 252, 289, 295, 297, 302, 308–9, 372–5, 391, 417
    problems with 299–300, 390
    timing of reliefs 402–3, 406, 411, 434–7
Trotman, Brigadier General Charles 112, 125, 126–7, 129–30
Tulloch, Major General Sir Alexander 35, 39
Turkish Army 84, 89
    August offensives (Gallipoli) 153, 162–4, 167, 180, 185–6
    Gallipoli, at 94, 98, 100–1, 105, 112, 125, 127–9, 135
    May armistice 137, *138*
    mining operations 127–9, 139

U
Uhlan trench system 251
Ulcer trench system 251
Ulster Reserve 266
Ulysses 80–3, *83*
Uncanny Trench 255
United Services Institution of Victoria 40
unity of thought and policy 255, 340
Universal Training Scheme 49, 59–61
University Club 25
Upjohn, Sergeant Herbert 287

V
Vaire Wood 346, 347, 352, 354
Varley, Lieutenant Ambrose 282
Vauban 412
Vauvillers 381, 391, 393
Vaux 411
Vaux-en-Amiénois 354
Vendhuille 442
Verdun 212, 276, 306, 366
Very lights 221
Victorian Garrison Artillery (VGA) 32–40, *34*, 58
Victorian Institute of Engineers 25–6
Victorian Military Forces 30–8
Victorian Rifles
    University (D) Company 30, *31*
Victory March *459*

Villers-Bretonneux 330, 345–7, 349, 367, 371
    conference 397
Villers-Bretonneux–Amiens railway 365
Villers-Cotterets 363
Villiers-Stuart, Major Charles 105
Vimy Ridge 260, 263, 273
Volunteer Force 30

W
Walden Point 162
Walker, Brigadier General Harold 99, 106, 109, 111–12, 118–19, 145, 151, 172, 197, 298, 334
Walker's Ridge 102, 107, 122, 143, 154
Wallaby Club 26
Walters, Lieutenant 43, 45
Wanliss, Lieutenant Colonel David 60
Warfusée 370
Warneton 280, 319
Warneton Line 249, 251, 281–3
Wavell, General Archibald
    qualities of a good general 12–15
welfare of soldiers 233, 238, 274, 287, 317, 335, 341–2, 354, 384, 402, 426, 434, 461–2
    leave for original Anzacs 436–8
Western Front 212
    conditions 16–17, 223, 241–2, *241*, 290, 304–5, *308*, 314, 317, 382
    map *216*
    'nursery' sector 220–1
    raids 220–1
White, General Cyril Brudenell 41, 47, 57–8, *58*, 72, 77, 207, 228, 236, 239, 243, 245, 292, 330–1, 343, 346, 358, 369, 468
    AIF reorganisation 210–11, 315, 398
    Bean, relationship with 91
    commander, as 332–3, 471
    Flanders offensive 1917 296
    Gallipoli 105, 131, 137, 151, 195, 199
    Monash, and 234, 319–20, 325, 471
    Morcourt, advance to 365–6
    Murdoch, and 399–400
Wieck, Major George 322, 324
Wilhelm Line 279, 290, 292
Williams, Air Marshal Sir Richard 63
Williamson, Lieutenant Lofty *210*
Wilson, General Sir Henry 363–4, 397, 437, 439
Wilson, Trevor 314, 343, 355, 384, 417
Windmill Cabaret Spur 295, *301*, 302
Windmill Ridge 281, 285
wire 221, 281, 406, 440, *456*
    exit gaps 230
    tanks and 349

INDEX

wire-cutting bombardments 248, 264
Wisdom, Brigadier General Evan 362
Wolfsberg 346, 347, 349, *355*, 359, *359*
Wray, Chaplain Frederick 170
Wytschaete 248, 250

Y

Ypres 276
    Ramparts 294–5, *294*, 304
    Third Battle *see* Passchendaele
Ypres–Roulers railway 276, 293–4, *312*
Ypres salient 248
    defence of 247, 276

Z

Zonnebeke 279, 292, 294–5, 296, 302